have only gained their distinct character over time. It is impossible to talk about Edmonton and not mention West Edmonton Mall, the world's largest shopping and amusement complex.

But for most visitors to Alberta, the great outdoors, not the big cities or the fast bucks, is the main draw. The mountain playgrounds of Banff and Jasper National Parks show off the Canadian Rockies at their best, with pristine glaciers, rushing rivers, and snowcapped peaks reflected in hundreds of high-country lakes. But there are lesser-known gems to explore as well — the wilderness of Waterton Lakes National Park, the ancient landscape of Writing-On-Stone Provincial Park, and the recreational opportunities of Kananaskis Country. Some of the best scenery can be appreciated from roads such as the mountainous Icefields Parkway, but to really get to know the province, visitors need to leave their vehicles behind and plan on hiking, biking, horseback riding, canoeing, or cross-country skiing. Those who like to add a little sport to their recreation time are drawn to Alberta by world-class golf, fish-filled lakes and streams, and powder-packed alpine resorts.

prairie wheat field

© ANDREW HEMPSTEAD

Alberta's abundance and variety of wildlife will amaze you. The province's parks, and much of the rest of the province, are home to moose, elk, bighorn sheep, wolves, bears, and an amazing array of birds; approximately 340 species of birds migrate through or nest in Alberta. And ancient wildlife thrived here, too; one of the world's greatest concentrations of dinosaur bones continues to be unearthed in the Red Deer River Valley outside Drumheller. "Dinosaur Valley," as it's called, attracts tourist tyros and professional paleontologists alike to learn more about earth's once-dominant former tenants.

Throughout the province, outdoor adventures, wide-open spaces, and accessible wilderness beckon, and big-city culture awaits when you come down from the hills. So whether your interests lean toward high peaks or high tea, you're sure to find plenty to suit you in Alberta.

Moraine Lake

Contents

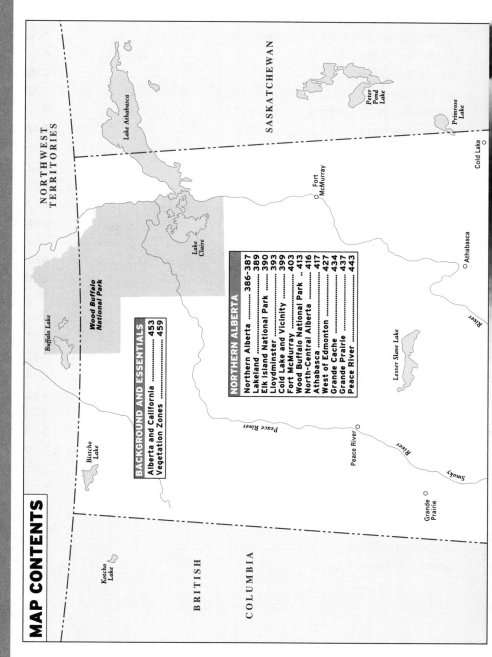

MAP CONTENTS

NORTHWEST TERRITORIES

SASKATCHEWAN

BRITISH

COLUMBIA

Kotcho Lake

Bistcho Lake

Buffalo Lake

Wood Buffalo National Park

Lake Athabasca

Lake Claire

Peace River

Smoky River

River

Grande Prairie

Peace River

Lesser Slave Lake

Athabasca

Fort McMurray

Cold Lake

Peter Pond Lake

Primrose Lake

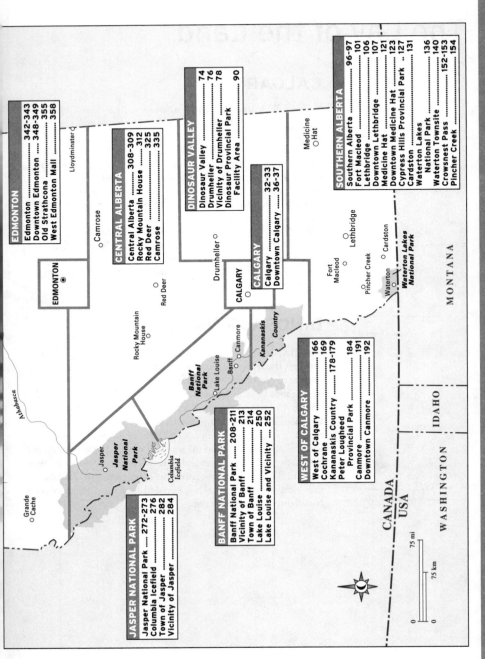

The Lay of the Land

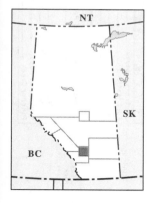

CALGARY

Ya-Hoo! Welcome to Cowtown, where a little over 100 years ago a North West Mounted Police detachment set up camp and today you'll find a world center for the oil-and-gas industry, with ultra-modern skyscrapers going up faster than any town planner ever imagined. While oil drives the economy, it's a different type of energy you find during the second week of July, when the Calgary Stampede transforms the city into party central, Western-style. But even if the rodeo isn't your thing, Calgary offers many reasons to visit—get high at the Calgary Tower, take in local history at the Glenbow Museum and Fort Calgary Historic Park, relive the glories of 1988 at Canada Olympic Park. Children aren't forgotten either; especially for the younger generation is the Creative Kids Museum, while Calgary Zoo is one of the country's finest.

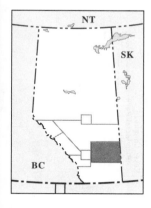

DINOSAUR VALLEY

East of Calgary, the Red Deer River has carved a deep chasm through the otherwise featureless prairies. In doing so, it has unearthed one of the world's most extensive dinosaur fossil beds, a place that UNESCO has declared a World Heritage Site, and one that is remarkably accessible. The region's main town is Drumheller, home to Royal Tyrrell Museum, which should ideally be your first stop (unless you have children who spy the world's largest dinosaur on the way into town). The surrounding landscape, known as "badlands," is where the dinosaur bones are found. The main concentration is protected by Dinosaur Provincial Park, where taking a guided tour provides a perfect complement to the museum.

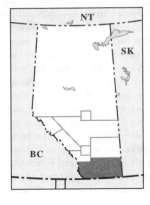

SOUTHERN ALBERTA

Encompassing a wide swathe of the province south from Calgary, this region has a little of everything but is compact enough to be a destination in itself. In the west is Waterton Lakes National Park, a speck on the map compared to its famous neighbors to the north but laced with walking trails and blessed with dozens of scenic highlights. The difference between the scenery immediately east of Waterton and further north is that the transition to plains is dramatic—just an hour's drive from the park you are surrounded by prairie and attractions like the Remington Carriage Museum and the intriguing history of Head-Smashed-In Buffalo Jump. The southeastern region of Alberta may look relatively empty on a map—and it is—but there are some delightful natural features for those with the time to search them out, including Writing-On-Stone Provincial Park and Red Rock Coulee.

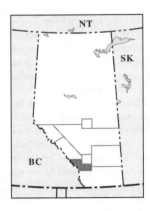

WEST OF CALGARY

Before rushing west from Calgary to Banff along the Trasn-Canada Highway, consider detouring through some of Canada's finest ranching land and exploring a region of the Canadian Rockies that is in many ways as scenic as famous Banff and Jasper, but a lot less crowded and commercialized. The best way to appreciate the rolling ranchland is on horseback, but there are also specific attractions like Bar U Ranch and the annual races at Millarville that bring the Old West to life. All roads west lead to the mountains, which are protected here by Kananaskis Country, which is a series of interconnected parks. The provincial government has spent millions of dollars creating something for everyone, from fish-stocked lakes, to 1,300 kilometers (800 mi) of hiking trails, to challenging golf courses, to a ski resort that hosted the 1988 Winter Olympic Games. The catch? There isn't one—even entry is free. North of here is Canmore, which is transforming itself from a coal-mining town to a hotbed of recreational pursuits with an Aspen-esque property market.

BANFF NATIONAL PARK

Banff. The crown jewel in Canada's national park system and home to the world's most photographed lakes. But what is this park that was originally established as a tourist attraction really like? Lake Louise, Moraine Lake, and the Icefields Parkway are just some of the park's awe-inspiring highlights, while the town of Banff is the commercial hub. Visiting each of these spots is definitely part of the Banff experience, but the park extends well beyond the reach of the regular tour-bus crowd. Biking along the shoreline of Lake Minnewanka, exploring Larch Valley when fall colors are at their height, canoeing across Bow Lake, and hiking in to backcountry Skoki Lodge may not be as well known, but each activity allows a glimpse of the park you won't see in the tourist brochures. The grandeur of accommodations such as the Fairmont Banff Springs and Fairmont Chateau Lake Louise never fails to impress. Or go low budget in one of the hostels or spend the night under the stars in one of the many campgrounds.

JASPER NATIONAL PARK

Beyond a simple sign at Sunwapta Pass that lets you know you've left Banff National Park and entered Jasper is a natural attraction that will leave you breathless—Columbia Icefield, the largest and most accessible glacier field in the Canadian Rockies. Those not content with just looking can jump aboard a big-wheeled Ice Explorer and get up close and personal with the ancient ice flow. Continuing north, the Icefields Parkway eventually reaches the town of Jasper, a smaller, quieter version of Banff that offers a good range of accommodations and other services. Take a walk down Maligne Canyon, a boat tour on Maligne Lake, and hike the trails below Mount Edith Cavell and you'll be following in the footsteps of millions before you. Walk the hallowed fairways of Jasper Park Lodge Golf Course and you'll have a different story to tell back at the country club. The many summer-only bungalow camps scattered around town are an authentic way to enjoy an overnight stay.

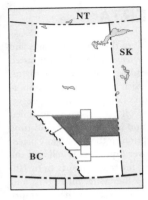

CENTRAL ALBERTA

Highway 2 may provide the quickest route between Calgary and Edmonton, but tempting detours beckon east and west. On the mountain-side of the highway, rolling foothills are dotted with farming communities including picturesque Markerville and sites of historical importance such as Rocky Mountain House National Historic Site, where a major trading post helped open up the west. You can continue into the mountains proper, or veer east, back out onto the prairies. Plot your course carefully and hit highlights such as the Lacombe Corn Maze and Reynolds-Alberta Museum with little extra driving. Or don't drive at all and jump aboard a steam train with Alberta Prairie Railway Excursions.

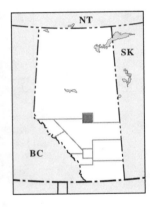

EDMONTON

The provincial capital lies near the geographical center of Alberta, with the downtown core rising from the north-side North Saskatchewan River. The attractions are spread throughout city limits, making an excuse to leave the confines of downtown. Best known is West Edmonton Mall, the world's largest shopping and entertainment complex. But beyond experiencing the glitz of the mall, you should take in the displays of the Royal Alberta Museum, step back in time at Fort Edmonton Park, and wander the restored streets of Old Strathcona. But visiting the capital isn't just about ticking off the main attractions. The city has a wonderful urban park system, with much of the riverfront land protected in its natural state. It's also a place to play world-class golf at reasonable rates, soak up the atmosphere of summer festivals, and indulge in a little culture before heading back out in the countryside.

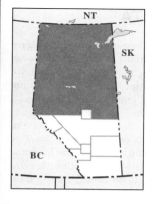

NORTHERN ALBERTA

Northern Alberta encompasses half of the entire province, and a trip there is as much adventure as vacation. It's a forested landscape, punctuated by roads leading to small service towns, historic trading posts, lakes filled with fish, and—most importantly for many people—the world's largest known oil reserve. Fort McMurray, the center of the oil action, has quadrupled its population in the last decade, and is unique for its old-time boom mentality, but it's the exception to the rule. Most places in the north have changed little over time. Locals will lead the way to their favorite fishing holes, fur trading posts from 100 years ago sit in stark testimony to Alberta's recent history, and the forests are filled with campgrounds that beckon with empty sites—even on the busiest summer weekend.

Planning Your Trip

Planning a trip can be overwhelming, but don't let it be. The first thing you should do is forget about any preconceived notions you have about travel to Canada—or more precisely Alberta—and instead focus on the experience. Of course you'll want to glimpse the famous lakes, watch the action of a rodeo, and step back in time through the dinosaur-filled badlands, but try to plan your trip around simply being in Alberta. Think less about specific "sights" and open yourself to discovery.

Start by trying to identify the type of activities you're interested in, which parks you just can't miss, which towns sound interesting, and how much money you want to spend. Once you have put together an outline of your trip, book lodging—as far in advance as possible, especially if you want to include the famous mountain resorts in your itinerary.

Even though the main attractions of Alberta are within a few hours' drive of Calgary, the province is vast. Driving your own vehicle (or a rental car) is a practical way to travel, and it'll give you the flexibility to stay at lodgings out of the main tourist towns. With direct flights from throughout North America and beyond, reaching Alberta is easy, and once you've arrived you should plan on renting a vehicle.

WHEN TO GO

Alberta's biggest influx of visitors is during summer, when the focus is on everything outdoors—camping, fishing, golfing, hiking, swimming, canoeing, and more specific pursuits, like bird-watching. In winter, the focus is on the Canadian Rockies, where skiers and snowboarders from around the world descend on major resorts.

Summer (late June–early September) is definitely high season, especially the school holiday period of July through August. Simply said, the weather is unbeatable. The season is dominated by long, warm—and sometimes hot—days, everything is open, and there's plenty to do and see. Crowds, high prices (especially in the Canadian Rockies), and difficulty securing reservations are the downside of summer travel. Obviously these factors aren't a consideration if money is no object or if you plan on camping.

Late spring and early fall are excellent times to visit Alberta for two reasons: You'll avoid the crowds and you'll save money. **Spring** (mid-April–late June) is notable for long days of sunlight (in late June it stays light until after 10 P.M., or until 11 P.M. in the far north) and a sense of optimism for the upcoming warm months. Golf courses begin opening in early May, it's warm enough to camp out, and the famously photogenic lakes become ice-free in June. **Fall** (mid-September–November) can be delightful, especially September, with lingering warm temperatures and a noticeable decrease in crowds immediately after the long weekend at the beginning of the month. While fall colors in general lack the intensity of those in the eastern provinces and New England, larch turn a brilliant yellow throughout high alpine areas in late September, as do aspen throughout the foothills.

Local ski resorts beginning opening for the **winter** season (December–mid-April) in late November. The best snow conditions are January–February, although for enthusiasts looking for a combination of good snow and warmer weather, March is an excellent time of year to visit. Winter officially ends before mid-April, but some ski resorts stay open well into May, and it's not until this time of year that the ground begins to warm.

WHAT TO TAKE

Start by packing everything you think you'll need. Then put half of it back in your closet.

The airlines have generous baggage limits and you can always upgrade to a larger rental car, but that's not the point—you just never need as much as you think you do.

When planning your trip to Alberta, prepare for the outdoors. At the top of your must-bring list should be walking or hiking boots. If you buy a pair especially for the trip, make sure you wear them once or twice before leaving home—just to make sure they are comfortable. In summer, temperatures rarely drop below freezing, so you don't need a down jacket or winter boots. But you should be geared up for a variety of weather conditions, especially at the change of seasons. Do this by preparing to dress in layers, including at least one pair of fleece pants and a heavy long-sleeved top. For dining out, casual dress is accepted at all but the most upscale city restaurants, where a tie and jacket are required. Summer does get hot. Bring sunglasses and a wide-brimmed hat to provide protection from the strong sunlight. Finally, bug spray is a summer necessity, but you can pick up the brands that are most effective once you arrive.

Wintertime in Alberta brings very different advice. Thanks to modern technology, you can purchase clothing that allows you to be warm and comfortable no matter how cold the temperature gets. Again, dress in layers, starting with long thermal underwear. The best type of outer layer is breathable, wind-resistant pants and a jacket. Warm boots with new liners, lined mittens, and a wool hat are a must. If you're traveling from warmer climes, purchase all the winter necessities in the gateway cities of Calgary or Vancouver. You can also buy clothing in Banff, Canmore, and Jasper, but it's generally more expensive.

Electrical appliances from the United States work in Canada, but those from other parts of the world require a current converter (transformer) to bring the voltage down. Many travel-size shavers, hair dryers, and irons have built-in converters.

Choosing a suitcase or backpack is also important. Think about the type of traveling you'll be doing before making a final decision. A midsize suitcase with wheels is best for carting through airports and lugging around hotels. Fold-over bags are good for keeping formal clothing wrinkle-free, but unless you're in town on business or attending a snazzy function, you probably won't require much in the way of dressy clothing. Besides, this type of suitcase is a bother to pack and unpack.

Airlines allow at least one piece of carry-on luggage per person, which must be small enough to fit in the overhead compartments. (Most luggage stores have guidelines to help you choose the right size.) All valuables, medications, smaller breakable items, and vital documents (driver's license, credit card, passport, a printout of your reservations, etc.) should be packed in your carry-on, along with a sweater, bottled water, and reading materials. Even if you're traveling by bus, train, or your own vehicle, it's a good idea to keep all these things in an easy-to-reach carry-on-style bag. The most convenient carry-on bags are small backpacks, which can double as daypacks for sightseeing or hiking.

Explore Alberta

THE BEST OF ALBERTA

Many visitors to Alberta will concentrate their time in the mountains. While we've made arrangements for the more adventurous souls among you in *A Mountain Adventure,* this one-week itinerary stretches itself beyond the famous national parks to include the two main cities and other highlights along the way. Starting and ending from Calgary, it covers around 1,300 kilometers (800 miles) sans detours.

For those of you fortunate enough to have more than a week to visit, we've included a number of options for extending the itinerary to take in even more of Alberta's highlights.

Day 1

Drive east from Calgary into Dinosaur Valley and **Dinosaur Provincial Park.** Continue the theme with a visit to the **Royal Tyrrell Museum.** Stay overnight in Drumheller or begin driving north and stay overnight in Red Deer.

Day 2

Continue north to Edmonton, where the highlights include the **Royal Alberta Museum, Muttart Conservatory,** and **Fort Edmonton Park.** These can be seen in a long day, but you'll also want to take a break from the official attractions to include a shopping trip to **West Edmonton Mall.**

Day 3

Drive to Jasper, visit the enchanting **Maligne Canyon,** and take a boat tour on super-scenic **Maligne Lake.** If you have some extra time, spend a few hours driving the **Mount Edith Cavell** road. Spend the night at a cabin accommodation south of town.

Day 4

Rise early to drive the Icefields Parkway to Lake Louise, where you will be staying overnight. The trip is less than 300 kilometers (186 miles), but there are so many highlights en route (the **Columbia Icefield, Bow Lake,** and **Peyto Lake** are simply the best of the best stops).

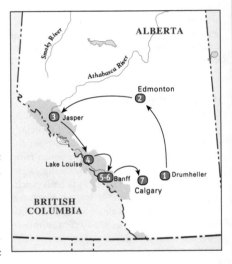

Day 5

The best time to see **Lake Louise** in all her glory is early in the morning, which allows plenty of time for the walk to **Lake Agnes** for an early lunch. From Lake Louise, it's a short drive to **Moraine Lake,** where you take to the water in a rented canoe. Drive to Banff via the Bow Valley Parkway (the trail through Johnston Canyon makes a good excuse to stop along the way), and check into your hotel for the next two nights.

Day 6

The town of Banff is certainly in a picturesque location, but I encourage you to leave the paved sidewalk beyond and explore natural attractions like Lake Minnewanka or hike to the top of Tunnel Mountain. On the afternoon of Day 6, relax with a round of golf at the Banff Springs Golf Course or soak up the luxury of the Willow Stream Spa at the **Fairmont Banff Springs.**

Day 7

Leaving the mountains behind and heading back to Calgary, make time to take in the Olympic legacy that is **Canada Olympic Park** before heading out to the airport. If your flight doesn't leave until later in the day, also plan stops at **Calgary Tower** and the **Glenbow Museum.** If you have another day in Calgary, visit **Fort Calgary Historic Park** as well.

If You Have More Time

Two Days in Southern Alberta: Taking in the sights of Southern Alberta is especially convenient for those driving north from the United States. Otherwise, drive south from Calgary into southern Alberta, taking Highway 22 to get a taste of Alberta's famous ranching country. Stop at **Bar U Ranch National Historic Site** to get a closer look at the Western lifestyle and then at **Head-Smashed-In Buffalo Jump** to learn about native plains culture. Continue on to your lodgings at **Waterton Lakes National Park.**

The next day, explore the park, where you may see deer, elk, and bears on a morning drive along the **Akamina Parkway.** Enjoy lunch with a view at the Prince of Wales Hotel and then head east to Cardston and the impressive carriage collection at **Remington Carriage Museum.**

Kananaskis Country: Now that you've seen the famous national parks of the Canadian Rockies, do you want to spend time where the locals go? If so, head into Kananaskis Country from Banff or Calgary. The drive over Highwood Pass and the hike to **Rawson Lake** are a good combination for a day trip that will get you back in time for a dish of delicious Alberta beef.

Explore Central Alberta: There's plenty to explore between the province's two major cities. Heading north from Calgary toward Edmonton, make sure to stop in **Markerville,** a delightful place for breakfast or lunch, and then lose the kids for an hour at the **Lacombe Corn Maze.** Arrive in Stettler for a steam-train ride through the plains with **Alberta Prairie Railway Excursions.** Afterwards, you should have just enough time to continue on to Edmonton and check in for the night.

Edmonton Excursions: Take a morning or afternoon flight to Fort McMurray, where you have made hotel reservations far in advance. Yes, it's a long way to travel for a **Syncrude/Suncor Plant Tour,** but you'll get to experience a modern-day boom, one centered on the world's largest known reserve of oil.

Return to Edmonton the following day on an afternoon flight, then take a short drive east to **Elk Island National Park.** Dusk is an excellent time for viewing the abundant big game, including moose and bison.

A MOUNTAIN ADVENTURE

The vast majority of international visitors to Alberta head straight to the mountains, as we do for this travel strategy. But instead of staying at a Best Western and eating at McDonalds, this itinerary encourages you to sleep, eat, and explore away from the crowds. I've included accommodation recommendations in keeping with this theme, but you're more than welcome to pitch a tent to save a few bucks.

Day 1
Fly into Calgary, pick up a rental car and head for Banff National Park and the delightful Baker Creek Chalets for a two-night stay. Dinner at the restaurant here will leave you raving.

Day 2
The hike to **Bourgeau Lake** is a full-day excursion limited to the adventurous—like yourself.

Day 3
Rise early and be one of the first to watch the first rays of light hit **Lake Louise,** then drive over to equally scenic **Moraine Lake.** As the first tour buses start to arrive, leave the lake behind by hiking into **Larch Valley.**

Summer traffic along the Icefields Parkway is usually heavy, but it's one of the world's most scenic drives and you won't want to miss this route. Most highway travelers stop quickly at the main lookout points, snapping a few clichéd pictures along the way, and continue to their chain hotel in Jasper. But looking to avoid the masses, you break the journey with an overnight stay at Num-ti-Jah Lodge, overlooking **Bow Lake.**

Day 4
Peyto Lake is at its picture-postcard best early in the morning. Take the short trail up Bow Summit for a different perspective. As you continue north, the **Columbia Icefield** comes into view after about one hour of driving. Sure, take a Snocoach tour, but also take time to explore the wasteland left behind by the receding glacier and hike to **Wilcox Pass** for a sweeping view of the valley. Check into Tekarra Lodge for two nights.

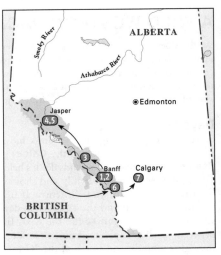

Day 5
Park at the lower end of **Maligne Canyon** for a short walk, then continue to **Maligne Lake.** Join the boat tour that takes you to a part of the lake that is otherwise inaccessible, or set aside a few of hours for a hike in the **Opal Hills.** The afternoon is spent in the **Cavell Meadows** below the imposing face of **Mount Edith Cavell.**

Day 6
Head back south along the Icefields Parkway, making a detour at Saskatchewan River Crossing to **Nordegg,** a historic coal-mining town that, though still in the mountains, has a much quieter setting than Banff or Jasper. The tepees of Sundance Lodges in Kananaskis Country are where you rest your head tonight.

Day 7

Calgary is just an hour's drive from Kananaskis Country, so with an afternoon flight, or one that leaves the next morning, you have plenty of time to visit delightful **Rawson Lake** and take the scenic drive over **Highwood Pass.**

A WILD WESTERN VACATION

While Alberta prides itself on its Western heritage, it is the mountains that draw the masses. Hence this itinerary that swerves from the ordinary to give you a taste of how to plan a Western-themed adventure—and yes, you *do* get to visit Banff as well. Although rental cars weren't a transportation option for the first cowboys that arrived in Alberta, unless you have a horse and a lot of time, you'll need one for this itinerary.

Days 1-2

Start your trip in Calgary. You don't have to plan your vacation around the **Calgary Stampede,** but many thousands do. It's held during the second week of July and should fill a full two days of your itinerary. If it's Stampede Week, attend the **rodeo** one day and the **chuck wagon races** the next. In between, you'll have plenty of time to soak up the sights, sounds, and smells of the "Greatest Outdoor Show on Earth" as well as the opportunity to join the line-up for a beer at famously Western **Ranchman's.**

With rodeos held every summer weekend somewhere in Alberta, there are plenty of options other times of the year (go to www.rodeocanada.com to see them all). These include Ponoka the week before the Stampede and Medicine Hat a couple of weeks later.

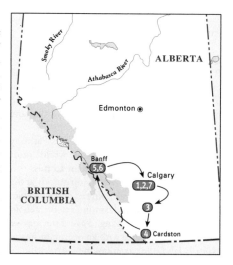

Day 3

Drive out to Cochrane, site of the first major ranch in western Canada (a suitably Western statue marks the site) and then saddle up for a horseback ride at Griffin Valley Ranch, the only place in the province that allows unguided riding. Drive south to **Bar U Ranch National Historic Site,** which re-creates a century-old ranch. Then head to Fort Macleod, where you will stay for the night.

Day 4

Before the arrival of Europeans, the natives called the foothills home, hunting bison at **Head-Smashed-In Buffalo Jump.** In the afternoon, visit the **Remington Carriage Museum,** which relives the era of horse-drawn travel. Spend the night at the Great Canadian Barn Dance Campground (cabins supplied) in Hill Spring, where a local family cooks up a storm and then leads the way in a barn dance.

Day 5

Drive back north through Kananaskis Country to Banff, from which Warner Guiding and Outfitting leads overnight pack trips to a remote backcountry cabin.

Day 6

Upon your return to Banff, and after two days in the saddle, you'll probably find the atmosphere at Wild Bill's a little corny, but hey, the beer's cold and the Alberta beef cooked to perfection.

Day 7

Return to Calgary for your flight home.

THE CALL OF THE NORTH

Northern Alberta is so vast and so remote that it deserves its own itinerary. I'm not suggesting that if this is your first trip to the province you miss out on the action of the Calgary Stampede or the beauty of the Canadian Rockies, but instead this is an ideal itinerary for those visiting Alberta for the second or third time, or for Edmonton locals who are looking for an alternative to vacationing at a central Alberta lake resort. In this 10-day strategy I assume you are camping, but there are enough motels en route to ensure everyone gets to enjoy this part of the province.

Day 1

Head east from Edmonton to begin a counterclockwise loop of northern Alberta. If you're from out of province, make a stop at the **Royal Alberta Museum** before leaving city limits to learn about the wildlife you may see out on the road (and the wildlife you don't want to run into). Speaking of wildlife, a day spent in **Elk Island National Park** is almost guaranteed to include sightings of bison, elk, and moose. As dawn and dusk are prime wildlife-viewing times, plan on an overnight at the park campground.

Day 2

As you continue toward Smoky Lake (or detouring to Vegreville if you need a photo of the world's largest Easter egg), today's highlight is **Métis Crossing,** an outdoor museum celebrating the culture of the Métis people. Drive north to Fort McMurray (book your campsite in advance if possible or camp out of town at Gregoire Lake Provincial Park).

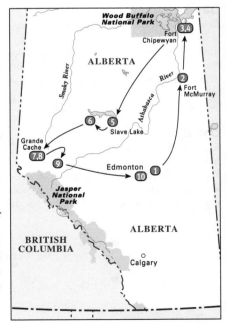

Day 3

Taking a **Syncrude/Suncor Plant Tour** is not in keeping with the theme of this nature-related itinerary, but seeing the development of the world's largest known oil reserve is eye-opening. Besides, you can leave memories of the heavy haulers behind by spending the afternoon visiting the local bison enclosure or taking a kayaking trip along the river. Pack light for an afternoon flight to Fort Chipewyan and check into the Fort Chipewyan Lodge.

Day 4

Today is spent exploring **Wood Buffalo National Park.** Employ the services of a local boat operator to motor into this vast wilderness accessible from Fort Chipewyan by water only. You'll see plenty of birds and maybe wildlife including bears, bison, and wolves from the safety of a boat.

Day 5

Return to Fort McMurray and begin the longest day of driving on this itinerary (around 480 km/300 mi) to **Lesser Slave Lake Provincial Park** via the historic river port of Athabasca. While sunset in this park is an absolute delight, early arrivals can go hiking, swimming, or do absolutely nothing at all.

Day 6

After a buffet breakfast at the Hearthstone Grill in Slave Lake, head to Spruce Point Park. Lesser Slave Lake is renowned by anglers, especially along the shallow southern shore, and this resort caters to those looking to hook the big one. In addition to camping facilities, it offers boat and tackle rentals, as well as guided trips.

Day 7

Continuing west through north-central Alberta, bird-watchers will want to spend time with their binoculars in the bird hides around McLennan, self-proclaimed bird capital of Canada. Soak up the lifestyle of early white settlers at **Historic Dunvegan,** which is also a good lunch stop. Spend the night at Grande Cache, enjoying an evening round of golf for a fraction of the cost of other mountain courses.

Day 8

Today is spent on horseback traversing the mountainous terrain of Willmore Wilderness Park. Local outfitters supply the horse, you are simply along for the ride.

Day 9

Departing Grande Cache early, you will have the better part of the day to enjoy **William A. Switzer Provincial Park,** which is also your overnight stop. Fishing, canoeing, or hiking—the choice is yours.

Day 10

Rejoining the Yellowhead Highway at Hinton you'll immediately notice the increased traffic, but don't sweat it—while your fellow travelers are bemoaning the crowds of the Canadian Rockies, you'll have 10 memorable days of solitude behind you. Break up the four-hour drive back to the capital with a detour through Sundance Provincial Park or beach time at Wabamun Lake.

WINTER FUN

December through April sees Alberta blanketed in snow. If you travel in winter, the focus of your vacation will be very different than a summer trip. Instead of hiking and canoeing and barbecuing, you'll be skiing and snowshoeing, then retreating to relax around a roaring fire each evening. Naturally, this itinerary centers on the famous Canadian Rockies. But if you want to experience Alberta beyond the mountains and have an extra day, the Royal Tyrrell Museum is an interesting add-on from Calgary. Or if the backcountry ski trip is a little beyond your fitness level, spend the two extra days at West Edmonton Mall.

Day 1

Arrive in Calgary and make your way to the city's Four Points by Sheraton. Skiing is only a small component of visiting **Canada Olympic Park,** across the road from this hotel. Most days you can watch training sessions at the massive ski jumps or down the luge track, while taking to the slopes yourself where Olympians competed in slalom events in the 1988 Olympic Winter Games.

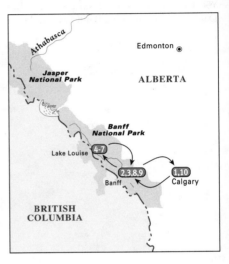

Day 2

Head west to Banff and spend the rest of the day skiing or snowboarding at **Mount Norquay,** where runs vary from an easy magic carpet to heart-thumping moguls, all within sight of town.

Day 3

Pack your overnight bag for **Sunshine Village.** High above the treeline and accessible only by gondola, here you get to take advantage of the only on-hill accommodations in the mountain parks (the oversized outdoor hot tub is a bonus).

Day 4

Take advantage of spending an extra day at Sunshine Village (it's included in your accommodations) and then catch the shuttle bus to **Lake Louise** and your accommodation at the famous Fairmont Chateau Lake Louise. Join in the postcard view by trying ice-skating in front of the chateau on the rink on the lake, which is lit well into the night.

Day 5

One day skiing or boarding at Lake Louise will only allow a taste of the terrain at Canada's second-largest alpine resort, but be sure to at least ride the main chairlift, which lifts high above the treeline to allow magnificent views in all directions. Spend a relaxing night in Lake Louise.

Day 6

Nestled in a snow-filled valley far from any road is **Skoki Lodge,** accessible only on cross-country skis. It takes fit skiers around three hours, and up to five for those not used to this form of recreation. But either way, upon arrival your friendly hosts will greet you with hot chocolate.

Day 7

Spend the day skiing around Skoki Valley, returning to the lodge for a second night.

Day 8

Return to Banff and soothe those aching limbs by taking a soak at the **Upper Hot Springs.**

Day 9

Yes, I know, you want to ski every day. But Day 9 is about exploring Banff beyond the resorts. In the morning join a guided "ice walk" through the frozen waterfalls of **Johnston Canyon.** Wander the streets of Banff, visiting the **Whyte Museum of the Canadian Rockies** and learning about the feats of local skiers at the Hall of Fame in Cascade Plaza. Catch up on souvenir shopping. In the evening, go for a sleigh ride along the **Bow River.**

Day 10

Return to Calgary for onward flights.

CALGARY

Calgary's nickname, Cowtown, is cherished by the city's 1,000,000 residents, who prefer that romantic vision of their beloved home to the city's more modern identity as a world energy and financial center. The city's rapid growth, from a North West Mounted Police (NWMP) post to a large and vibrant metropolis in little more than 100 years, can be credited largely to the effects of resource development, particularly oil and natural gas.

Once run by gentlemen who had made their fortunes in ranching, Calgary is still an important cattle market. But the oil-and-gas bonanzas of the 1940s, 1950s, and 1970s changed everything. The resources discovered throughout western Canada brought enormous wealth and growth to the city, turning it into the headquarters for a burgeoning energy in-

dustry. With the price of oil predicted to hit $100 a barrel in the near future, Calgary is in the middle of another boom. With the city's rapid growth comes all the problems plaguing major cities around the world, with one major exception—the distinct lack of manufacturing and industrial sites means there is little pollution.

Downtown is a massive cluster of modern steel-and-glass skyscrapers, the legacy of an explosion of wealth in the 1970s, with cranes once again making their appearance as new commercial projects totaling over $1 billion are currently under construction. Set in this futuristic mirage on the prairie are banks, insurance companies, investment companies, and the head offices of hundreds of oil companies. But not forgetting its roots, each

© ANDREW HEMPSTEAD

HIGHLIGHTS

◖ Calgary Tower: It's not the city's tallest building, but from the observation deck you get a wonderful idea of Cowtown's layout, making this a great first stop on your sightseeing itinerary (page 35).

◖ Creative Kids Museum: If it's indoor weather (or even if it's not), this bright, modern museum is the place to spend time with younger children (page 39).

◖ Glenbow Museum: One of Canada's finest private museums, the Glenbow is renowned for its coverage of native history, and the new *Mavericks* display will entrance even non-museum types (page 39).

◖ Fort Calgary Historic Park: The site of Calgary's original riverside settlement has risen from the past to provide an insight into the hardships of the city's earliest residents (page 40).

◖ Canada Olympic Park: Follow in the footsteps of Eddie the Eagle and the Jamaican bobsled team at the site of the 1988 Olympic Winter Games (page 41).

◖ Calgary Zoo: Yes, you'll see all the usual suspects (hippos, kangaroos, gorillas), but also a wide range of Canadian mammals – including some you don't want to meet in the wild (page 43).

◖ Calgary Stampede: Few cities in the world are associated as closely with a festival as Calgary is with the Stampede, a 10-day, early-July celebration of everything cowboy (page 52).

LOOK FOR ◖ TO FIND RECOMMENDED SIGHTS, ACTIVITIES, DINING, AND LODGING.

July the city sets aside all the material success it's achieved as a boomtown to put on the greatest outdoor show on earth—the Calgary Stampede, a Western extravaganza second to none.

PLANNING YOUR TIME

For the vast majority of visitors arriving by air, Calgary International Airport is their first stop in Alberta, and it's straight off to the mountain national parks of Banff and Jasper. But even with a week in Alberta, it's worth scheduling a day in Calgary—maybe to settle in upon arrival, or to relax the day before flying out. Two major attractions within walking distance of downtown hotels are the **Calgary Tower** and the **Glenbow Museum,** both easily visited in a casual morning. With children in tow, replace the tower with the fun of the **Creative Kids Museum.** After lunch at a steakhouse such as Hy's, you can learn about the city's earliest history at **Fort Calgary Historic Park** and then cross the river to see some of Canada's iconic wildlife

at the **Calgary Zoo.** Sports fans won't want to miss **Canada Olympic Park,** either on your second day in the city or on the way to or from the mountains.

Attending the **Calgary Stampede** is a vacation in itself for tens of thousands of visitors each year, but you will want to plan ahead by making accommodation reservations and getting tickets well in advance. Even if you're not a rodeo fan, if your itinerary has you in Calgary in early July, plan to visit the Stampede grounds for the day (no advance tickets required), just to say you've experienced the "Greatest Outdoor Show on Earth."

HISTORY

In addition to being one of Canada's largest cities, Calgary is also one of the youngest; at 140 years old, it has a heritage rather than a history. Native Blackfoot people moved through the area approximately 2,000 years ago, but they had no particular interest in the direct vicinity of what is now Calgary. Approximately 300 years ago, Sarcee and Stoney natives moved down from the north and commenced continual warring between tribes. White settlers first arrived in the late 1700s. David Thompson wintered in the area, then the Palliser Expedition passed by on its way west to the Rockies. But it wasn't until the late 1860s that any real activity started. Buffalo had disappeared from the American plains, and as hunters moved north, so did the whiskey traders, bringing with them all the problems associated with this illegal trade.

Fort Calgary

The NWMP established a post at Fort Macleod soon after they came west to quell the whiskey trade. In 1875, a second fort was established on a terrace at the confluence of the Bow and Elbow Rivers. Inspector J. F. Macleod, who took over command of the fort in 1876, coined the name Calgary. It comes from Calgary Bay, a remote village on the Isle of Mull in Scotland said to translate from Gaelic as "garden on the cove."

The Coming of the Railway

For many years, the Canadian Pacific Railway had planned to build a northern route across the continent through Edmonton and Yellowhead Pass. But eventually the powers in the east changed their minds and decided on a southern route through Kicking Horse Pass. This meant that the line passed right through Fort Calgary. In 1883, a station was built on an alluvial plain between the Bow and Elbow Rivers. A townsite was laid out around it, settlers streamed in for free land, and nine years after the railway arrived, Calgary acquired city status—something that had taken its northern rival, Edmonton, more than 100 years to obtain.

In 1886, a major fire destroyed most of the town's buildings. City planners decreed that all new structures were to be built of sandstone, which gave the fledgling town a more permanent look. The many sandstone buildings still standing today—the Palliser Hotel, the Hudson's Bay Company store, and the courthouse, for example—are a legacy of this early bylaw.

Ranching

An open grazing policy, initiated by the Dominion Government, encouraged ranchers in the United States to drive their cattle from overgrazed lands to the fertile plains around Calgary. Slowly, a ranching industry and local beef market developed. The first large ranch was established west of Calgary, and soon many NWMP retirees, English aristocrats, and wealthy American citizens had invested in nearby land. Calgary's first millionaire was Pat Burns, who developed a meatpacking empire that still thrives today. Linked to international markets by rail and sea, Calgary's fortunes continued to rise with those of the ranching industry, receiving only a minor setback in 1905 when Edmonton was declared the provincial capital. During the first 10 years of the 20th century, the city's population increased 1,000 percent, and rail lines were built in all directions, radiating from the city like enormous spokes. Immigration slowed, and the economy spiraled downward as the effects of World War I were felt.

CALGARY

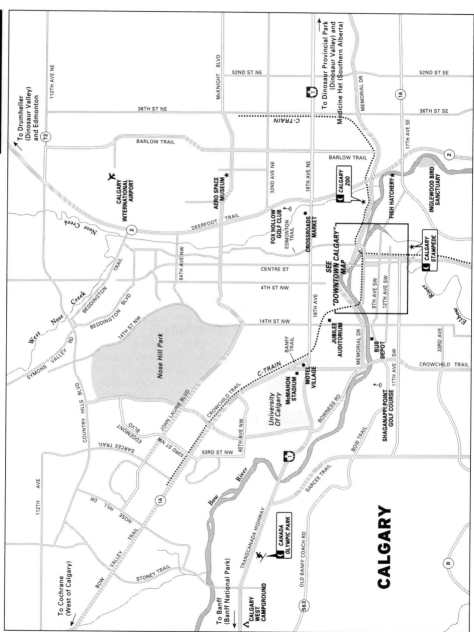

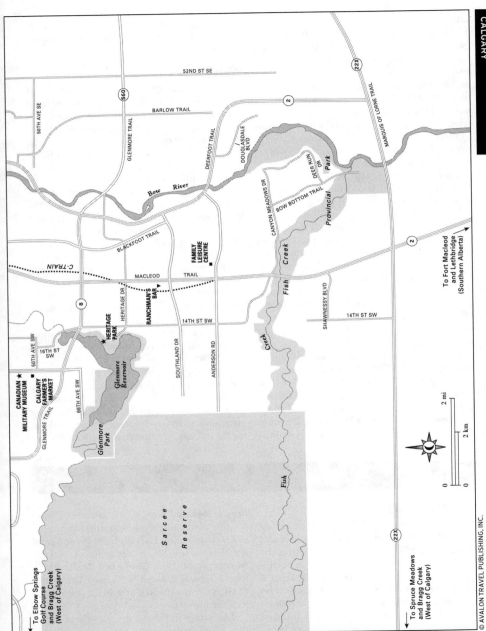

52ND ST SE

560

50TH AVE SE

BARLOW TRAIL

GLENMORE TRAIL

2

DEERFOOT TRAIL

DOUGLASDALE BLVD

MARQUIS OF LORNE TRAIL

22X

DEER RUN DR

Park

CANYON MEADOWS DR

BOW BOTTOM TRAIL

Provincial

Bow River

Fish Creek

BLACKFOOT TRAIL

FAMILY LEISURE CENTRE

C-TRAIN

MACLEOD TRAIL

HERITAGE DR

RANCHMAN'S BAR

14TH ST SW

8

★ HERITAGE PARK

SOUTHLAND DR

ANDERSON RD

Creek

SHAWNESSY BLVD

14TH ST SW

2

To Fort Macleod and Lethbridge (Southern Alberta)

50TH AVE SW

16TH ST SW

66TH AVE SW

★ CANADIAN MILITARY MUSEUM

■ CALGARY FARMER'S MARKET

GLENMORE TRAIL

Glenmore Park

Glenmore Reservoir

S a r c e e   R e s e r v e

Fish

To Elbow Springs Golf Course and Bragg Creek (West of Calgary)

To Spruce Meadows and Bragg Creek (West of Calgary)

22X

0   2 mi

0   2 km

Oil

The discovery of oil at Turner Valley in Calgary's backyard in 1914 signaled the start of an industry that was the making of modern Calgary. The opening of an oil refinery in 1923 and further major discoveries nearby transformed a medium-sized cowtown into a world leader in the petroleum and natural-gas industries. At its peak, the city was the headquarters of more than 400 related companies. Calgary became Canada's fastest-growing city, doubling its population between 1950 and 1975. During the worldwide energy crisis of the 1970s, oil prices soared. Although most of the oil was extracted from farther afield, the city boomed as a world energy and financial center. Construction in the city center during this period was never-ending, as many corporations from around the world moved their headquarters to Alberta. During this period, Calgary had Canada's highest per capita disposable income and was home to more Americans than any other Canadian city. Much of the wealth obtained from oil and gas was channeled back into the city, not just for office towers but also for sporting facilities, cultural centers, and parks for citizens and visitors alike to enjoy. During the early 1980s, the province was hit by a prolonged downturn in the oil market. But good fortune prevailed when the International Olympic Committee announced that Calgary had been awarded the **1988 Winter Olympic Games.** Life was injected into the economi-

cally ravaged city, construction started anew, and the high-spirited Calgarians were smiling once again.

Today and the Future

Calgary is currently the fastest-growing city in Canada. The population has increased by more than 25 percent since 1996, with current estimates having the city grow another 25 percent to 1.25 million people in the next decade. Even with $4 billion currently slated for new infrastructure, the city is struggling to address the needs of this expansion, which includes new schools, hospitals, and a ring road planned to eventually encircle the entire city. Much of the land in and around downtown has been rezoned for multifamily dwellings, with the area south of downtown seeing massive redevelopment and controversial plans in place for the East Village project immediately east of downtown. City limits continue to expand at a phenomenal rate—especially in the northwest, north, and south—with new suburbs, housing estates, and commercial centers extending as far as the eye can see. But Calgary is still a small town at heart, enjoying tremendous civic and public support. Many of the city's self-made millionaires bequeath their money to the city, and residents in their thousands are always willing to volunteer their time at events such as the Calgary Stampede. This civic pride makes the city a great place to live and an enjoyable destination for the millions of tourists who visit each year.

Sights

ORIENTATION

The TransCanada Highway (Highway 1) passes through the city north of downtown and is known as **16th Avenue North** within the city limits. Highway 2, Alberta's major north–south highway, becomes **Deerfoot Trail** as it passes through the city. Many major arteries are known as **trails,** named for their historical significance, not, as some suggest, for their condition. The main route south from down-

town is **Macleod Trail,** a 12-kilometer (7.5-mi) strip of malls, motels, restaurants, and retail stores. If you enter Calgary from the west and are heading south, a handy bypass to take is **Sarcee Trail,** then **Glenmore Trail,** which joins Highway 2 south of the city. **Crowchild Trail** starts downtown and heads northwest past the university to Cochrane.

The street-numbering system is divided into four quadrants. At first it can be more

confusing than the well-meaning city planner intended, but after initial disorientation, the system soon proves its usefulness. Basically, the four quadrants are geographically named—northwest, northeast, southwest, and southeast. Each street address has a corresponding abbreviation tacked onto it (NW, NE, SW, and SE). The north–south division is the Bow River. The east–west division is at Macleod Trail, and north of the downtown at Centre Street. Streets run north to south and avenues from east to west. Both streets and avenues are numbered progressively from the quadrant divisions (e.g., an address on 58th Avenue SE is on the 58th street south of the Bow River, is east of Macleod Trail, and is on a street that runs east to west). Things don't get any easier in the many new subdivisions that dominate the outer flanks of the city. Many street names are *very* similar to one another, so check whether you want, for example, Mackenzie Lake Bay, Mackenzie Lake Place, Mackenzie Lake Road, or Mackenzie Lake Avenue. Fill the gas tank, pack a hearty lunch, and good luck!

DOWNTOWN

The downtown core is a mass of modern steel-and-glass high-tech high-rises built during the oil boom of the 1970s and early 1980s. Calgary's skyline was transformed during this period, and many historic buildings were knocked down to make way for a wave of development that slowed considerably during the 1990s. The last few years have seen a subtle change in direction, with developers incorporating historic buildings in new projects, especially along Stephen Avenue Walk. The best way to get around is on foot or on the C-train, which is free along 7th Avenue.

Crisscrossing downtown is the Plus 15 walkway system, a series of interconnecting, enclosed sidewalks elevated at least 4.5 meters (15 feet—hence the name) above road level. In total, 47 bridges and 12 kilometers (7.5 mi) of public walkway link downtown stores, four large malls, hotels, food courts, and office buildings to give pedestrians protection from the elements. All walkways are well marked and wheelchair accessible. The following sights can be visited separately or seen on a walking tour (in the order presented).

Stephen Avenue Walk

The traditional center of the city is 8th Avenue, between 1st Street SE and 3rd Street SW—a traffic-free zone known as Stephen Avenue Walk. This bustling, tree-lined pedestrian mall has fountains, benches, cafés, restaurants, and souvenir shops. In summer, the mall is full with shoppers and tourists, and at lunchtime, thousands of office workers descend from the buildings above. Many of Calgary's earliest sandstone buildings still stand along the mall on the block between 1st and 2nd Streets SW. On the corner of 1st Street SW is the **Alberta Hotel,** one of the city's most popular meeting places until Prohibition in 1916.

◖ Calgary Tower

Ninth Avenue, south of the mall, has banks, some of Calgary's best hotels, parking stations, the Telus Convention Centre, the Glenbow Museum (see *Museums* in this chapter), and one of the city's most famous landmarks, the Calgary Tower (at the corner of Centre St., 403/266-7171, daily 7 A.M.–10:30 P.M.). Built in 1968 (and known then as the Husky Tower), this 190-meter (620-ft) tower dominated the skyline until 1985, when the nearby Petro-Canada towers went up. Although it's now only Calgary's fourth-tallest building, the ride to the top is a worthwhile introduction to the city. The Observation Terrace affords a bird's-eye view of the Canadian Rockies and the ski-jump towers at Canada Olympic Park to the west; the Olympic Saddledome (in Stampede Park) to the south; and the city below, literally—a glass floor allows visitors to stand right over the top of Ninth Avenue. The nonreflective window glass is perfect for photography, binoculars are available for guest use, and audiovisual terminals describe the sights below. The tower also houses two restaurants, a snack bar, and a gift shop. The one-minute elevator ride to the top costs adult $13, senior and child $10.

CALGARY

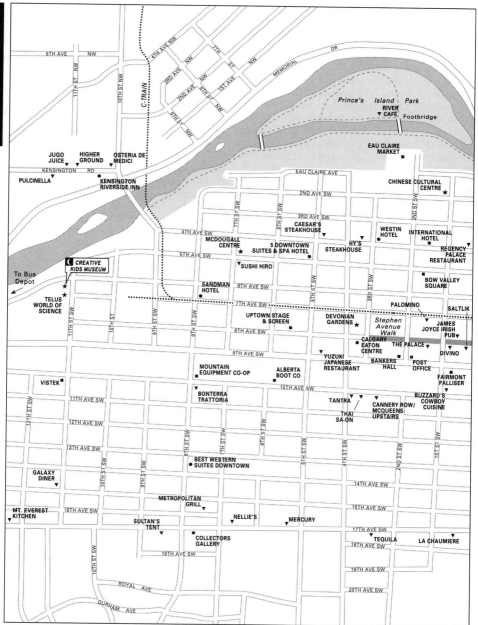

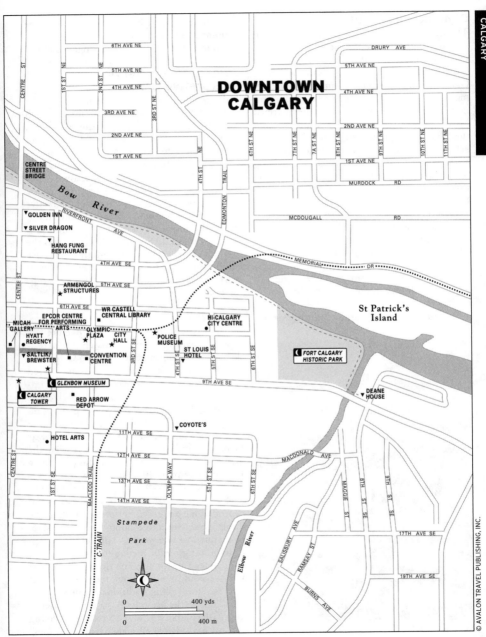

DOWNTOWN CALGARY

© AVALON TRAVEL PUBLISHING, INC.

Olympic Plaza and Vicinity

This downtown park at the east end of Stephen Avenue Walk (on the corner of 2nd St. SE), which is filled with office workers each lunch hour, was used during the 1988 Winter Olympic Games for the nightly medal-presentation ceremonies. Plaques here commemorate medal winners, and the bricks on the ground are inscribed by members of the public who helped sponsor the Olympics by "purchasing" individual bricks before the Games. In summer, outdoor concerts are held here, and in winter, the shallow wading pool freezes over and is used as an ice-skating rink. Across 2nd Street SE from the plaza is **City Hall,** built in 1911. It still houses some city offices, although most have moved next door to the modern **Civic Complex.**

Back across 2nd Street SE is the **Epcor Centre for Performing Arts,** incorporating two of Calgary's historic sandstone buildings. The complex houses three theaters and the 2,000-seat **Jack Singer Concert Hall,** home to the city's orchestra.

In front of the Education Building on 1st Street SE (between 5th and 6th Avenues) are the **Armengol Structures**—expressionless, raceless, humanlike forms with outstretched arms.

Calgary Police Service Interpretive Centre

This small museum lies a couple of blocks east of Olympic Plaza (2nd Floor, 316 7th Ave. SE, 403/268-4566, July–Aug. Mon.–Fri. 9:30 A.M.–4 P.M., Sat. noon–4 P.M., the rest of the year Mon. 9:30 A.M.–4 P.M., Wed. noon–4 P.M., adult $2). Interesting displays include memorabilia from all of western Canada's police services, mock-ups of famous crime scenes, a modern police car, and a variety of interactive activities such as taking a Breathalyzer test. But there's also a series of more gloomy exhibits including Dead End Street, which re-creates the life of a homeless person, and an interactive exhibit on domestic abuse. Not exactly what you're on vacation to experience, but interesting nonetheless.

Chinatown

At the east end of town on 3rd Avenue is a small Chinatown of approximately 2,000 residents. Chinese immigrants came to Calgary in the 1880s to work on the railroads and stayed to establish food markets, restaurants, and import stores. Chinatown has seen its share of prejudice, from marauding whites gaining revenge for an outbreak of smallpox to bungling city bureaucrats who demanded that the streets be narrow and signs be in Chinese to give the area an authentic look. The **Calgary Chinese Cultural Centre** (197 1st St. SW, 403/262-5071, daily 9 A.M.– 9 P.M.) is one of the largest such centers in Canada. It's topped by a grand central dome patterned in the same style as the Temple of Heaven in Beijing. The centerpiece of its intricate tile work is a glistening golden dragon hanging 20 meters (66 ft) above the floor. Head up to the 3rd floor for the best views, passing a mural along the way. At street level is a store selling traditional Chinese medicines and on the lower level is a small museum and gallery (daily 11 A.M.–5 P.M.) displaying the cultural history of Calgarians of Chinese

© ANDREW HEMPSTEAD

Olympic Plaza

descent. One of the museum's most intriguing pieces is the world's oldest known seismograph, which dates to A.D. 132.

West on First Avenue

Eau Claire Market at the north end of 3rd Street SW is a colorful indoor market filled with stalls selling fresh fruit from British Columbia, seafood from the Pacific, Alberta beef, bakery items, and exotic imports. Under the same roof are specialty shops, an IMAX and regular theaters, and nine restaurants.

The northern limit of downtown is along the Bow River, where picturesque **Prince's Island Park** is linked to the mainland by a bridge at the end of 3rd Street SW. Jogging paths, tables, and grassy areas are scattered among the trees on this manmade island. To the east is **Centre Street Bridge,** guarded on either side by large (restored) stone lions. For a good view of the city, cross the bridge and follow the trail along the cliff to the west.

McDougall Centre

From the north end of town, walk south along Barclay Mall (3rd St. SW), then west on 5th Avenue (or take the Plus 15 walkway system from the Canterra Tower) to 7th Street and the McDougall Centre (455 6th St. SW, 403/297-8687, Mon.–Fri. 8:30 A.M.–4:30 P.M.), a Renaissance Revival building that is the southern headquarters for the government of Alberta. It was declared a historic site in 1982.

Telus World of Science

This complex (701 11th St. SW, 403/268-8300, www.calgaryscience.ca, summer daily 9:30 A.M.–5 P.M., the rest of the year Tues.–Sun. 10 A.M.–5 P.M., adult $15, senior $12, child $10, includes admission to the Creative Kids Museum) is a little farther out (you could either walk the five blocks west from 6th Street or jump aboard the C-train that runs along 7th Avenue SW and walk the last block). The center's main attractions are kid-oriented, but that's not a bad thing. It's a wonderful facility chockablock with hands-on science exhibits. WOWtown is especially for the under-seven crowd—there's a working crane model, playground and maze, microscopes, optical illusions, and even a "quiet room." In the **Discovery Dome,** dynamic audiovisuals are projected onto a massive concave screen.

◖ Creative Kids Museum

Connected to the science center (admission fees cover both facilities) is another child-friendly attraction, the Creative Kids Museum (701 11th St. SW, 403/268-8302, www.creativekidsmuseum.com, summer daily 9:30 A.M.–5 P.M., the rest of the year Tues.–Sun. 10 A.M.–5 P.M., adult $15, senior $12, child $10), which opened in late 2006. It's sensory overload in rooms such as Scribble Dee Dee, where young ones hone their painting skills; Sound and Music, with the opportunity to make music; Mindscapes, comprising models of Alberta landscapes that are fully climbable; and Perception, a series of interactive games.

Devonian Gardens

The C-train will whisk you from the Telus World of Science back into the heart of the city to Devonian Gardens. A glass-enclosed elevator rises to the 4th floor of Toronto Dominion Square (8th Ave. and 3rd St. SW, 403/221-4274, daily 9 A.M.–9 P.M., free), where a one-hectare (2.5-acre) indoor garden features 16,000 subtropical plants and 4,000 local plants—138 species in all. Within the gardens are waterfalls, fountains, pools, and bridges. Lunchtime entertainers and art exhibits can often be enjoyed in this serene environment.

MUSEUMS
◖ Glenbow Museum

Adjacent to Stephen Avenue Walk, this excellent museum (130 9th Ave. SE, 403/268-4100, daily 9 A.M.–5 P.M., Thursday until 9 P.M., adult $12, senior $9, child $8) chronicles the entire history of western Canada through three floors of informative exhibits and well-displayed artifacts. The museum's permanent collections of contemporary and Inuit art, as well as special exhibitions from national and international collections, are on the 2nd floor.

The 3rd-floor "Niitsitapiisinni: Our Way of Life" gallery is the best part of the museum. Developed under the watchful eye of Blackfoot elders, it details the stories and traditions of native peoples through interpretive panels and displays of ceremonial artifacts, jewelry, and a full-size tepee. The 3rd floor also presents "Mavericks: An Incorrigible History of Alberta," telling the story of prominent Albertans from various eras in local history—the fur trade, the North West Mounted Police, pioneering settlers, ranching, and the oil industry. On the 4th floor is a display titled "Warriors: A Global Journey Through Five Centuries," as well as a large collection of rocks and gems (including a meteorite). The Glenbow's renowned library and archives are open Tuesday–Friday 10 A.M.–5 P.M.

Aerospace Museum

This museum (beside McKnight Blvd. at 4629 McCall Way NE, 403/250-3752, daily 10 A.M.–5 P.M., adult $6, senior $3.50, child $2) traces the history of aviation in Canada through a large collection of aircraft scattered around the grounds, including a restored Sopwith triplane from World War I. Inside the main building is the *Silver Dart,* Canada's first airplane; one of North America's largest collections of aircraft engines; uniforms; photographs dating back to the flight of one of Calgary's first airplanes, the *West Wind,* in 1914; and a gift store packed with flight-related literature.

Nickle Arts Museum

This museum on the University of Calgary campus (off 32nd Ave. NW at 2500 University Dr., 403/220-7234, Mon.–Fri. 10 A.M.–5 P.M., adult $5, child $2) displays western Canadian art and a collection of coins from the Ancient World. Throughout the year, more than 20 exhibitions of contemporary and historical art are displayed in one of three galleries.

Canadian Military Museum

Combining former naval and regiments museums, as well as new galleries devoted to the Canadian Air Force, the Canadian Military Museum (4520 Crowchild Trail SW, 403/974-2850, July to mid-Sept. daily 9:30 A.M.–4 P.M., the rest of the year Mon.–Thurs. 9:30 A.M.–9 P.M., Fri.–Sun. 9:30 A.M.–4 P.M., adult $8, senior $5, child $3) opened in 2007 as Canada's largest military museum. Highlights include the history of four regiments—Lord Strathcona's Horse Regiment, Princess Patricia's Canadian Light Infantry, the King's Own Calgary Regiment, and the Calgary Highlanders—and the importance of Canada's navy, which was the Allies' third-largest navy in 1945. On display are three fighter aircraft that flew from the decks of aircraft carriers, as well as uniforms, models, flags, photographs, and a memorial to those who lost their lives in the Korean War.

HISTORIC PARKS
◖ Fort Calgary Historic Park

In 1875, with the onset of a harsh winter, the newly arrived NWMP built Fort Calgary at the confluence of the Bow and Elbow Rivers in less than six weeks. The original fort was replaced by a more permanent brick building in 1914, but this was later demolished and, by the 1970s, the area was an industrial wasteland. After much work, the 16-hectare (40-acre) site has been transformed into a two-part historic park (750 9th Ave. SE, 403/290-1875, May–early Oct. daily 9 A.M.–5 P.M., adult $10, senior $9, child $6). Most of the focus is on the interpretive center, housing a replica of 1888 barracks, complete with volunteer RCMP veterans on hand to answer questions. Inside, the lives of Canada's famous "Mounties," the legacy of natives, hardy pioneers, and the wild frontier they tamed are all brought to life through convincingly costumed interpreters. Various shops and businesses from Calgary's earliest days, including an entire 1930s streetscape, are inside. Beside the barracks is an exact replica of the original fort, built using tools and techniques that are more than 100 years old. History comes alive through a variety of activities and programs, including carpenters at work, a room especially for kids that is filled with games of a bygone era, a museum shop styled on an old Hudson's Bay Company store, and a canteen

© ANDREW HEMPSTEAD

Fort Calgary

selling meals that I imagine are more appealing than those the original officers enjoyed. Tours of the fort (included in general admission) leave at regular intervals through the day from the main lobby of the barracks. To get to Fort Calgary, either walk along the river from downtown or hop aboard bus #1 (Forest Lawn) or #14 (East Calgary) from 7th Avenue.

Across the Elbow River from the interpretive center stands **Hunt House,** the oldest structure on its original site in Calgary. The house was built in 1876 for a Hudson's Bay Company employee. On the same side of the Elbow River as Hunt House is the larger **Deane House,** with sweeping river views. Built in 1906 for a commanding officer of the NWMP, this is one of the oldest restored homes in the city.

Heritage Park

This 27-hectare (66-acre) park (1900 Heritage Dr. SW, 403/268-8500, mid-May–Aug. daily 9 A.M.–5 P.M., Sept.–early Oct. Sat.–Sun. only 9 A.M.–5 P.M., adult $14, senior $12, child $9, an extra $9 per person for a ride pass) is on a peninsula jutting into Glenbow Reservoir southwest of downtown. More than 100 buildings and exhibits help re-create an early-20th-century pioneer village. Many of the buildings have been moved to the park from their original locations. Highlights include a Hudson's Bay Company fort, a two-story outhouse, a working blacksmith's shop, an 1896 church, a tepee, and an old schoolhouse with original desks. A boardwalk links stores crammed with antiques, and horse-drawn buggies carry passengers along the streets. You can also ride in authentic passenger cars pulled by a steam locomotive or enjoy a cruise in a paddlewheeler on the reservoir. A traditional bakery sells cakes and pastries, and full meals are served in the Wainwright Hotel. To get there from downtown, take the C-train to Heritage Station and transfer to bus #502 (weekends only).

◖ CANADA OLYMPIC PARK

The 1988 Winter Olympic Games are remembered for many things, but particularly a bobsled team from Jamaica, the antics

The ski jumps at Canada Olympic Park are a city landmark.

of English plumber/ski-jumper "Eddie the Eagle," and most of all for their success. This 95-hectare (235-acre) park (403/247-5452, www.coda.ab.ca) on the south side of the TransCanada Highway on the western outskirts of the city is the legacy Calgarians get to enjoy year-round. It was developed especially for the Paralympics and the ski-jumping, luge, bobsled, and freestyle skiing events of the games. Now the park offers activities year-round, including tours of the facilities, luge rides, summer ski-jumping, and sports training camps. In winter, the beginner/intermediate runs are filled with locals who are able to hit the snow as early as November with the help of a complex snowmaking system. Many ski-jumping, bobsled, and luge events of national and international standard are held here throughout winter.

Olympic Hall of Fame

This is North America's largest museum (summer daily 9 A.M.–5 P.M., the rest of the year daily 9 A.M.–4 P.M., adult $6, child $4.50) devoted to the Olympic Games. Three floors catalog the entire history of the Winter Olympic Games through more than 1,500 exhibits, interactive video displays, costumes and memorabilia, an athletes timeline, a bobsled and ski-jump simulator, and highlights from the last five Winter Olympic Games held at Albertville (France), Lillehammer (Norway), Nagano (Japan), Salt Lake City (United States), and Turin (Italy) including costumes worn by Jamie Sale and David Pelletier during their infamous silver-then-gold-medal-winning final skate.

Ski-Jumping, Luge, and Bobsled Facilities

Visible from throughout the city are the 70- and 90-meter ski-jump towers, synonymous with the Winter Olympic Games. These two jumps are still used for national and international competitions and training. A glass-enclosed elevator rises to the observation level. The jump complex has three additional jumps of 15, 30, and 50 meters, which are used for junior competitions and training. All but the

Canada Olympic Park provides good family skiing and snowboarding.

© ANDREW HEMPSTEAD

90-meter jump have plastic-surfaced landing strips and are used during summer.

At the western end of the park are the luge and bobsled tracks. A complex refrigeration system keeps the tracks usable even on relatively hot days (up to 28°C/80°F). At the bottom of the hill is the Ice House, home to the National Sliding Centre, the world's only year-round facility where athletes can practice their dynamic starts for luge, bobsled, and skeleton. You can, too—it costs just $6 per "start" (July–Aug. daily noon–4 P.M.).

Tours

To get the most out of a visit, plan on joining a Behind the Scenes Walking Tour, departing the main reception July–August daily at 1 P.M. These two-hour tours cover all the highlights, including a trip to the observation deck of the 90-meter ski-jump tower, a visit to the luge and bobsled tracks, a movie showing highlights from the 1988 Winter Olympic Games, and Hall of Fame admission. The cost is $25 per

person. The alternative is an Olympic Odyssey Audio Tour, which covers the same areas, but instead of a guide, you walk around with a hands-free headset. This tour costs adult $15, family $45 and is offered in summer daily 9 A.M.–5 P.M., the rest of the year daily 9 A.M.–4 P.M. Once the official tour is done, head back over to the Ice House to try your hand at the luge (see above), rent a mountain bike ($30 for two hours) and ride the trails ($19 includes unlimited chairlift rides), or just relax on the sun-drenched deck with lunch from the Paskapoo Lounge.

Food

At the top of the hill, the former start-house for the luge is now the **Naturbahn Teahouse** (403/247-5452, summer Mon.–Fri. 10 A.M.–5 P.M.). The teahouse is also open year-round for Sunday brunch (11 A.M.–4 P.M.), good value at adult $18, senior $17, child $10.

OTHER PARKS
◖ Calgary Zoo

The Calgary Zoo (1300 Zoo Rd. NE, 403/232-9300, year-round daily 9 A.M.–5 P.M., adult $16, senior $14, child $8) is one of Canada's finest zoos. It was established in 1920 near the heart of downtown on St. Georges Island and has become noted for its realistic simulation of animal habitats. Unique viewing areas have been designed to allow visitors the best look at the zoo's 1,000-plus animals. For example, in Destination Africa, giraffes tower over a huge glass-walled pool that provides a home to two hippos, with sunken stadium seating allowing visitors a fish-eye view of hippos' often-relaxing day. The second "ecosystem" of Destination Africa is a massive building that re-creates a rainforest, with gorillas and monkeys absolutely everywhere. Other highlights include a section on Australia's nocturnal animals (lights are turned on at night, reversing night and day and allowing visitors to watch nocturnal animals during their active periods), exotic mammals such as lions and tigers, and conservatories filled with tropical flowers, butterflies, and birds. One of the largest display

areas is Canadian Wilds, devoted to the mammals you may or may not see on your travels through Alberta. In the Prehistoric Park section, the world of dinosaurs is brought to life with 27 full-size replicas set amid plantlife and rock formations supposedly similar to those found in Alberta in prehistoric times, but looking more like badlands. Nature Tales is a daily interpretive program that takes in everything from trained elephants strutting their stuff to grizzly-bear feeding. The zoo offers eight food outlets and a variety of picnic areas and playgrounds. The main parking lot is off Memorial Drive east of downtown, or jump aboard the 202 Whitehorn C-train running east along 7th Avenue.

Stampede Park

Best known for hosting the Calgary Exhibition and Stampede, these grounds south of downtown (at 17th Ave. and 2nd St. SE) are used for many activities and events year-round. In the center of the park is the saddle-shaped 18,800-seat **Saddledome,** which boasts the world's largest cable-suspended roof and is one of Calgary's most distinctive structures. It was used for hockey and figure-skating events during the 1988 Winter Olympic Games and is now home to the NHL Calgary Flames. "The Dome" is constantly in use for concerts, trade shows, and entertainment events. The **Grain Academy** on the Plus 15 level of the **Roundup Centre** (403/263-4594, Apr.–Sept. Mon.–Fri. 10 A.M.–4 P.M., Sat. noon–4 P.M., free) is a museum cataloging the history of cereal-based agriculture in the province through working models and hands-on displays. Take the C-train from downtown to Victoria Park/Stampede or Stampede/Erlton.

Sam Livingston Fish Hatchery

Pearce Estate Park, a pleasant spot for a picnic, is home to this hatchery (403/297-6561, summer Mon.–Fri. 10 A.M.–4 P.M., Sat.–Sun. 1–5 P.M., the rest of the year weekdays only, free). The facility produces approximately 2.5 million trout per year, which are used to stock 300 lakes and rivers throughout the province.

A self-guided tour (grab a brochure at the main office) leads through the hatchery, from the incubation room to holding tanks and an area containing various displays and a theater. To reach the park and hatchery, take 17th Avenue east from the city and turn north onto 17th Street SE.

Inglewood Bird Sanctuary

More than 250 species of birds have been noted in this 32-hectare (79-acre) park on the bank of the Bow River, east of downtown. The land was originally owned by a member of the NWMP and was established as a park in 1929. Walking trails are open year-round, but before heading out it's worth dropping by the interpretive center (403/221-4500, May–Sept. daily 10 A.M.–5 P.M., Oct.–Apr. Tues.–Sun. 10 A.M.–4 P.M., donation) to learn more about the urban ecosystem and to pick up a bird list. To get there, take 9th Avenue SE to Sanctuary Road and follow the signs to a parking area on the south bank of the river.

Nose Hill Park

This oasis of prairie surrounded by residential development lies northwest of downtown. The land was bought up in the late 1960s and remains in a totally natural state. The park has no formed pathways or planted gardens, just 1,127 hectares of fescue grasslands bisected by wooded coulees and rough trails, much like natives would have encountered thousands of years ago. To get to the park, take 14th Street NW north out of downtown; this street forms the park's eastern boundary, and John Laurie Boulevard runs along its southern boundary.

Fish Creek Provincial Park

At the southern edge of the city, this 1,170-hectare (2,900-acre) park is one of the largest urban parks in North America. Many prehistoric sites have been discovered on its grounds, including campsites and buffalo jumps. In more recent times, the Calgary–Fort Benton Trail passed through the park. The site—much of which was once owned by Patrick Burns, the meat magnate—was officially declared a park

MIDNAPORE

The last rest stop for early travelers along the Macleod Trail, linking Fort Macleod to Fort Calgary, was just south of Fish Creek. A trading post and crude cabins constituted the town. The post office opened and was manned by a postmaster with dubious reading skills. One of the first parcels he received was addressed to Midnapore, India, and had been misdirected through him. Fear of losing his job kept him from asking too many questions, and as the community had no official name he directed that all mail to this post be addressed to Midnapore. The name stuck, and a suburb of Calgary came to have the same name as an Indian city on the opposite side of the world.

in 1975. Three geographical regions meet in the area, giving the park a diversity of habitat. Stands of aspen and spruce predominate, but a mixed-grass prairie, as well as balsam, poplar, and willow, can be found along the floodplains at the east end of the park. The ground is colorfully carpeted with 364 recorded species of wildflowers, and wildlife is abundant. Mule deer and ground squirrels are common, and white-tailed deer, coyotes, beavers, and the occasional moose are also present. An interpretive trail begins south of Bow Valley Ranch and leads through a grove of balsam and poplar to a shallow, conglomerate cave. An information display is located on the west side of Macleod Trail overlooking the site of Alberta's first woolen mill. The easiest access to the heart of the park is to turn east on Canyon Meadows Drive from Macleod Trail, then south on Bow River Bottom Trail.

Recreation

The **City of Calgary** (403/268-2489, www .calgary.ca) operates a wide variety of recreational facilities, including swimming pools and golf courses, throughout the city. They also run a variety of excursions, such as canoeing and horseback riding, as well as inexpensive courses ranging from fly-tying to rock-climbing.

WALKING AND BIKING

A good way to get a feel for the city is by walking or biking along the 210 kilometers (130 mi) of paved trails within the city limits. The trail system is concentrated along the Bow River as it winds through the city; other options are limited. Along the riverbank, the trail passes through numerous parks and older neighborhoods to various sights such as Fort Calgary and Inglewood Bird Sanctuary. From Fort Calgary, a trail passes under 9th Avenue SE and follows the Elbow River, crossing it several times before ending at Glenmore Reservoir and Heritage Park. Ask at tourist information centers for a map detailing all trails.

The ski slopes at **Canada Olympic Park** (west of downtown along the TransCanada Hwy., 403/247-5452) are the perfect place to hone your downhill mountain-bike skills. Full-suspension-bike rental is $30 for two hours or $50 for a full day, while a day pass for the chairlift is $19.

SWIMMING AND FITNESS CENTERS

The **City of Calgary** (403/268-2489) operates eight outdoor pools (open June through early Sept.) and 12 indoor pools (open year-round). Facilities at each vary. Admission at indoor pools includes the use of the sauna, hot tub, and exercise room. Admission to all pools is adult $5.50–9.50, around half price for seniors and kids.

The **YMCA** (101 3rd St. SW, 403/269-6701, Mon.–Fri. 5:30 A.M.–10 P.M., Sat.–Sun. 7 A.M.– 7 P.M., $8.50) is a modern fitness center beside Eau Claire Market at the north end of downtown. All facilities are first-class, including an

Olympic-size pool, a weight room, an exercise room, a jogging track, squash courts, a hot tub, and a sauna.

The large **Family Leisure Centre** (11150 Bonaventure Dr. SE, 403/278-7542, daily 9 A.M.–9 P.M.) has a lot more to offer than just swimming. Entry of adult $9, child $5 includes use of regular pools as well as a giant indoor water slide, a wave pool, and even a skating rink.

GOLF

More than 40 public, semiprivate, and private golf courses are located in and around the city limits. Many courses begin opening in April for a season that lasts up to seven months. The City of Calgary operates a few public courses, including **Shaganappi Point** (1200 26th St. SW, 403/974-1810, $38), a short 27-hole layout with panoramic views over the Bow River to downtown.

The following are a few of my other favorites that, while farther out, are well worth the drive. **Springbank Links** (125 Hackamore Trail NW, Springbank, 403/202-2000, $68) offers nine holes of true target golf and nine holes of links-style play with knee-high rough. **Elbow Springs Golf Club** (southwest of the city along Highway 8, 403/246-2800, $74) is flatter and a relatively easy 27-hole layout, but still challenging from the back markers. One unique feature is the ponds stocked with *huge* rainbow trout. **Heritage Pointe Golf and Country Club** (south of downtown on Dunmore Rd., 403/256-2002, $110 includes a power cart) is generally regarded as one of Canada's best courses that allows public play. It features three distinct sets of nine holes. An hour's drive east of downtown, **Speargrass** (Hwy. 24, 403/901-1134, $69 includes power cart) is defined by fescue-framed fairways and the Bow River, which flows along one side of the course. Finally there's **Fox Hollow Golf Club** (at the corner of Deerfoot Trail and 32nd Ave. NE, 403/277-4653, $38), a public course notable for the fact that it opens whenever the weather allows year-round.

TOURS

Brewster (403/221-8242, www.brewster.ca) runs a Calgary City Sights tour lasting four hours. Included on the itinerary are downtown, various historic buildings, Canada Olympic Park, and Fort Calgary. The tours run June through early October and cost adult $48, child $24. Pickups are at most major hotels. Brewster also runs day tours departing Calgary daily to Banff, Lake Louise, and the Columbia Icefield. The latter is a grueling 15-hour trip that departs at 6 A.M. Brewster's downtown office is located on Stephen Avenue Walk at the corner of Centre Street.

AMUSEMENT PARKS

Calaway Park (10 km/6.2 mi west of city limits along the TransCanada Hwy., 403/240-3822, May–June Sat.–Sun. 10 A.M.–8 P.M., July–Aug. daily 10 A.M.–8 P.M., Sept.–mid-Oct. Sat.–Sun. 11 A.M.–6 P.M.) is western Canada's largest outdoor amusement park, with 27 rides including a double-loop roller coaster. Other attractions include an enormous maze, Western-themed mini-golf, a zoo for the kids, a trout-fishing pond, live entertainment in the Western-style "Showtime Theatre," and many eateries. Admission including most rides is $25 for those aged 7–49, $19 for those aged 3–6 and 50 and over.

WINTER RECREATION

When Calgarians talk about going skiing or snowboarding for the day, they are usually referring to the five world-class winter resorts in the Rockies, a one- to two-hour drive to the west. The city's only downhill facilities are at **Canada Olympic Park** (403/247-5452), which has three chairlifts and a T-bar serving a vertical rise of 150 meters (500 ft). Although the slopes aren't extensive, on the plus side are a long season (mid-Nov. to late March), night skiing (weeknights until 9 P.M.), extensive lodge facilities including rentals, and excellent teaching staff. Lift tickets can be purchased on an hourly basis ($24 for four hours) or for a full day ($32). Seniors pay just $16 for a full day on the slopes.

SPRUCE MEADOWS

It is somewhat ironic that a city known around the world for its rodeo is also home to the world's premier show-jumping facility, **Spruce Meadows** (Spruce Meadows Way, 403/974-4200, www.sprucemeadows.com). Ever-encroaching residential developments do nothing to take away from the wonderfully refined atmosphere within the white picket fence that surrounds the sprawling 120-hectare (300-acre) site. The facility comprises six grassed outdoor rings, two indoor arenas, seven stables holding 700 horse stalls, 90 full-time employees (and many thousands of volunteers), and its own television station that broadcasts to 90 countries.

© ANDREW HEMPSTEAD

Spruce Meadows hosts a packed schedule of tournaments that attract the world's best riders and up to 50,000 spectators a day. The four big tournaments are the **National,** the first week of June; **Canada One,** the last week of June; the **North American,** the first week of July; and the **Masters,** the first week of September. The Masters is the world's richest show-jumping tournament, with one million dollars up for grabs on the Sunday afternoon ride-off.

In Europe, the world of show-jumping can be very hoity-toity. At Spruce Meadows, the atmosphere couldn't be more different, which makes it a wonderful place to spend a day – even for non-horse lovers. The pomp and ceremony associated with the sport is present – it's just not obvious to the casual observer. Instead, visitors spread out picnic lunches on grassy embankments, wander through the stables, and watch the superstars of the sport up close and personal. During the major tournaments, browsing through the on-site agricultural fair, arts and crafts booths, and a large marketplace pro-

moting Alberta attractions will round out a busy day of following the competitions from ring to ring.

General admission is a bargain at just adult $5, senior and child free. Except on the busiest of days, this will get you a prime viewing position at any of the rings. The exception is tournament weekends, when covered reserved seating ($25-30) is the best way to watch the action. To get to Spruce Meadows on tournament weekends, take C-train south to Fish Creek-Lacombe Station, from which bus transfers to the grounds are free. By car, take Macleod Trail south to Highway 22X and turn right toward the mountains along Spruce Meadows Way.

SPECTATOR SPORTS
Hockey

There's no better way to spend a winter's night in Calgary than by attending a home game of the **Calgary Flames** (403/777-2177, www.calgary flames.com), the city's National Hockey League franchise. On these nights, the Saddledome in Stampede Park fills with 20,000 hockey fans who follow every game with a passion. No matter whether the team is winning or losing, the atmosphere is electric. After a prolonged slump (they last won the Stanley Cup in 1989), they reached the finals in the 2003–04 season and are now one of the most competitive NHL franchises. The regular season runs October–April, and games are usually held in the early evening (7 P.M. weeknights, 8 P.M. Sat., 6 P.M. Sun.). Tickets start at $35 for nosebleed seats, but if you want to be rink-side, expect to pay up to $180.

Football

The **Stampeders** (403/289-0205, www.stam peders.com) are Calgary's franchise in the Canadian Football League (CFL), an organization similar to the U.S. NFL. Although the team's popularity fluctuates with its performance, crowd levels remain high through even the longest losing streaks. Near the end of the season, weather can be a deciding factor in both the games' results and attendance. At kick-off in the Stampeders' final game of 1993, the temperature was -20°C and -33°C with the windchill, but more than 20,000 Calgarians braved the weather to attend. The season runs July–November. Home games are played at the 35,500-seat **McMahon Stadium** (1817 Crowchild Trail NW). From downtown, take the C-train to Banff Trail Station. Tickets range $27–88.

Motor Racing

Race City Motorsport Park (68th St. SE and 114th Ave., 403/272-7223, www.racecity.com) has three world-class tracks and is the premier motorsport facility in western Canada. It hosts national stock-car, motorcycle, and drag-racing events throughout summer on Saturday at 7 P.M. and Sunday at 1 P.M. Prices vary according to event but generally run $10–21.

Arts, Entertainment, and Shopping

Calgary Straight (www.calgarystraight.com) and *ffwd* (www.ffwdweekly.com) are free weekly magazines available throughout the city. They list theater events, cinema screenings, and art displays, and keep everyone abreast of the local music scene. Tickets to major concerts, performances, and sporting events are available in advance from **Ticketmaster** (403/777-0000, www.ticketmaster.ca).

THE ARTS
Art Galleries

It may put a dent in Calgary's cowtown image, but the city does have a remarkable number of galleries displaying and selling work by Albertan and Canadian artisans. Unfortunately, they are not concentrated in any one area, and most require some effort to find. Renowned for its authentic native art, **Micah Gallery** is the exception. It's right downtown on Stephen Avenue Walk (110 8th Ave. SW, 403/245-1340). Across the river from downtown, Kensington Road is dotted with galleries. Most affordable is **Galleria Arts & Crafts** (1141 Kensington Rd., 270-3612), with two stories of shelf space stocked with paintings, etchings, metal sculptures, jewelry, and wood carvings. Another cluster of galleries lies along 17th Avenue SW. Here, **Collectors Gallery** (829 17th Ave. SW, 403/245-8300) sells the work of prominent 19th- and 20th-century Canadian artists.

Theater

Calgary's Western image belies a cultural diversity that goes further than being able to get a few foreign beers at the local saloon. In fact, the city

has 10 professional theater companies, an opera, an orchestra, and a ballet troupe. The main season for performances is September–May.

Alberta Theatre Projects (403/294-7475, www.atplive.com) is a well-established company based in the downtown Epcor Centre for Performing Arts (220 9th Ave. SE). Usual performances are of contemporary material. Expect to pay under $20 for matinees and up to $66 for the very best evening seats. Also based at the Epcor Centre for Performing Arts is **Theatre Calgary** (403/294-7440, www.theatrecalgary.com). **Lunchbox Theatre** (2nd Level, Bow Valley Square, 205 5th Ave. SW, 403/265-4292, www.lunchboxtheatre.com) runs especially for the lunchtime crowd from September to early May. Adults pay $16, seniors $13 for usually comedic content. For adult-oriented experimental productions, consider a performance by **One Yellow Rabbit** (Epcor Centre for Performing Arts, 403/264-3224, www.oyr.org).

Theatersports is a concept of improvisation-comedy theater that developed at the University of Calgary in the 1970s. The original performances led to the formation of the **Loose Moose Theatre Company** (403/265-5682, www.loosemoose.com), which today offers this lighthearted form of entertainment Friday and Saturday nights upstairs in the Crossroads Market (1235 26th Ave., SE).

Music and Dance

Calgary Opera (403/262-7286, www.calgaryopera.com) performs at the Jubilee Auditorium (1415 14th Ave. NW) October–April. Tickets range $22–88. The 2,000-seat Jack Singer Concert Hall at the Epcor Centre for Performing Arts is home to the **Calgary Philharmonic Orchestra** (403/571-0270, www.cpo-live.com), one of Canada's top orchestras. **Alberta Ballet** (403/245-4222, www.albertaballet.com) performs at locations throughout the city.

Cinemas

Most major shopping malls—including Eau Claire Market, closest to downtown—have a **Cineplex** cinema. For information, call the 24-hour film line (403/263-3166) or check the website (www.cineplex.com). **Uptown Stage & Screen** (612 8th Ave. SW, 403/265-0120) is a restored downtown theater that has a reputation for alternative, art, and foreign films. Over the Bow River from downtown, the 1935 **Plaza Theatre** (1133 Kensington Rd. NW, Kensington, 403/283-3636) shows everything from mainstream to Hindi.

NIGHTLIFE
Boot-Scootin' Bars

With a nickname like Cowtown it's not surprising that some of Calgary's hottest nightspots play country music. **Ranchman's** (9615 Macleod Trail SW, 403/253-1100) is *the* place to check out first, especially during Stampede Week. Some of country's hottest stars have played this authentic honky-tonk. Food is served at a bar out front all day, then at 7 P.M. the large dance hall opens with a band keeping the crowd boot-scootin' most nights. The hall is a museum of rodeo memorabilia and photographs, with a chuck wagon hanging from the ceiling. In the vicinity, **Outlaws** (7400 Macleod Trail SW, 403/255-4646) is as much rock as country. On the south side of the railway tracks from downtown, the peanut shells have been swept off the floor at the old Dusty's saloon, which has been reincarnated as hip **Coyote's** (1088 Olympic Way SE, 403/770-2200). The crowd is urban-slick, but when country music plays, the fancy-dancing crowd seems to know every word.

Other Bars and Nightspots

The aforementioned bars are open for lunch and offer a quiet atmosphere through the afternoon. Other options for a quiet drink include lounge bars in major downtown hotels. Of these, the **Sandstone Lounge** (Hyatt Regency, 700 Centre St., 403/717-1234) stands out for its central location (off Stephen Avenue Walk), classy surroundings, and extensive drink selection. **Raw Bar** (Hotel Arts, 119 12th Ave. SW, 403/266-4611, daily 11 A.M.–9 P.M.) is as exotic as it gets in Calgary—a cabana-like setting around an outdoor pool. Back on

Stephen Avenue Walk, in an old bank building, **James Joyce Irish Pub** (114 8th Ave. SW, 403/262-0708) has Guinness on tap and a menu of traditional British dishes. Nearby is **Ceilis** (803 8th Ave. SW, 403/265-1200), an Irish pub with over 60 beers on tap. Also downtown, **The Garage** (in Eau Claire Market, 403/262-6762) attracts a lively crowd for its pool tables and afternoon happy hour.

Calgary's infamous Electric Avenue, once the prime destination for partiers, has been relegated to history. A new concentration of clubs and pubs has sprung up farther east around 12th Avenue and Centre Street. But the late-night set is a flighty bunch, and an often unpleasant streetside atmosphere at closing time brings me to recommend avoiding this area late at night. If you're looking to dance the night away (without doing it in a line), there's a number of non-country alternatives. Downtown in a grandly restored theater, **The Palace** (218 8th Ave. SW, 403/263-9980) has a large dance floor and big-time lighting and sound systems. **Mercury** (550 17th Ave. SW, 403/229-0222) attracts a young, hip crowd for its cocktail-bar ambience—the perfect pre-nightclub hangout. For many Mercury patrons, the next stop is **Tequila** (219 17th Ave. SW, 403/209-2215), where a DJ spins house and hip-hop for a young party crowd. Also within walking distance is the **Metropolitan Grill** (880 16th Ave. SW, 403/802-2393), where the over-25 crowd gravitates to the outdoor patio on warm summer nights. Glitzy **Tantra** (355 10th Ave. SW, 403/264-0202) attracts the beautiful, high-end crowd, but remains welcoming.

One of Calgary's most infamous nightspots is the **Back Alley** (4630 Macleod Trail SW, 403/287-2500), which is far from refined but probably deserves a mention because it's outlasted the other flashes in the pan.

Jazz and Blues
The days of Buddy Guy and Junior Wells taking to the stage of the venerable King Edward Hotel are just a memory, but a couple of modern venues attract jazz and blues enthusiasts. One of the most popular jazz clubs in town

is **Beat Niq** (at the lower level of 811 1st St., 403/263-1650), a New York–style jazz club that welcomes everyone. It's open Tuesday–Saturday from 8:30 P.M. and the cover charge is $10–15. **Red Onion Bar & Grill** (12100 Macleod Trail, 403/225-0332) is a modern venue with live blues or jazz most nights, and a pleasant deck that catches the afternoon sun.

SHOPPING
Plazas and Malls
The largest shopping center downtown is **Calgary Eaton Centre,** on Stephen Avenue Walk at 4th Street SW. This center is linked to other plazas by the Plus 15 Walkway System. Other downtown shopping complexes are **Eau Claire Market,** at the entrance to Prince's Island Park, where the emphasis is on fresh foods and trendy boutiques; **TD Square,** at 7th Avenue and 2nd Street SW; and **The Bay,** part of Alberta's history with its link to the Hudson's Bay Company. **Uptown 17** is a strip of more than 400 retail shops, restaurants, and galleries along 17th Avenue SW. **Kensington,** across the Bow River from downtown, is an eclectic mix of specialty shops.

Markets
Ensconced in a massive hangar at a former military barracks is **Calgary Farmers' Market** (Crowchild Trail between 33rd and 50th Ave. SW, 403/244-4548, Fri.–Sat. 9 A.M.–5 P.M., Sun. 9 A.M.–4 P.M.). Here you'll find rows and rows of local produce as well as prepared foods like the well-researched Simple Simon Pies.

Crossroads Market (1235 16th Ave. SE, 403/291-5208, Fri.–Sun. 9 A.M.–5 P.M.) also has produce, but is better known for its arts and crafts.

Camping Gear and Western Wear
Mountain Equipment Co-op (830 10th Ave. SW, 403/269-2420) is Calgary's largest camping store. This massive outlet boasts an extensive range of high-quality clothing, climbing and mountaineering equipment (including a climbing wall), tents, sleeping bags, kayaks and canoes, books and maps, and other accessories.

The store is a cooperative owned by its members, similar to the American REI stores, except that to purchase anything you must be a member (a once-only $5 charge). To order a copy of the co-op's mail-order catalog, call 800/663-2667. Across the road, a similar supply of equipment is offered at **Coast Mountain Sports** (817 10th Ave. SW, 403/264-2444). The selection may be smaller than at MEC, but many name-brand items are perpetually sale priced.

Alberta Boot Co. (614 10th Ave. SW, 403/263-4605), within walking distance of downtown, is Alberta's only Western-boot manufacturer. This outlet shop has thousands of pairs for sale in all shapes and sizes, all made from leather. Boots start at $250 and go all the way up to $1,700 for alligator hide. You'll find **Lammle's Western Wear** outlets in all the major malls and at Calgary International Airport. Another popular Western outfitter is **Riley & McCormick** on Stephen Avenue Walk (220 8th Ave. SW, 403/262-1556) and at the airport.

Bookstores
McNally Robinson (120 Stephen Ave. Walk, 403/538-1797 or 866/798-1797, www.mcnally robinson.com, Mon.–Thurs. 9 A.M.–9 P.M., Fri.–Sat. 9 A.M.–10 P.M., Sun. 11 A.M.–5 P.M.) is western Canada's leading independent bookseller. The Calgary store takes up both stories of a heritage building overlooking downtown's busiest pedestrian thoroughfare and comes complete with a full-service restaurant. Set around a central atrium is a large collection of books sensibly cataloged in easy-to-find sections. One of the largest areas is devoted to Canada and another to children's literature.

For topographic, city, and wall maps, as well as travel guides and atlases, **Map Town** (400 5th Ave. SW, 403/266-2241 or 877/921-6277, www.maptown.com, Mon.–Fri. 9 A.M.–6 P.M., Sat. 10 A.M.– 5 P.M.) should have what you're looking for. Tech-savvy travelers will be impressed by the selection of GPS units and related software, as well as the scanning service, which allows you to have topo maps sent directly to your email inbox.

The suburb of Kensington, immediately northwest of downtown, has a variety of new bookstores, including **Pages** (1135 Kensington Rd. NW, 403/283-6655, Mon.–Sat. 10 A.M.– 5:30 P.M., Thurs.–Fri. until 9 P.M., and Sun. noon–5 P.M.), which offers a thoughtful selection of Canadian fiction and nonfiction titles.

Indigo Books & Music has 15 stores across Calgary, including **Chapters** megastores in Chinook Centre (6455 Macleod Trail, 403/212-0090) and another farther south (9631 Macleod Trail, 403/212-1442), and an **Indigo** store in Signal Hill Centre (Sarcee Trail SW, 403/246-2221). The company also operates stores in major malls and Calgary International Airport under the Coles name.

Used Books
Fair's Fair (1609 14th St. SW, 403/245-2778, daily from 10 A.M.) is the biggest of Calgary's secondhand and collector bookstores. Surprise, surprise, it's remarkably well organized, with a solid collection of well-labeled Canadiana filling more than one room. Fair's Fair has another large outlet in Inglewood (907 9th Ave. SE, 403/237-8156). On the north side of downtown, **Annie's Book Company** (912 16th Ave. NW, 403/282-1330) is a real gem. Hard-to-find used books are the specialty, but Annie's also stocks a selection of new books by Calgary authors and serves up delicious coffee, tea, and sweet treats.

Festivals and Events

Spring

In conjunction with the **Roughstock** agricultural fair, Calgary's rodeo season kicks off with **Rodeo Royal** (403/261-0101) at the Saddledome on the third weekend of March. **Calgary International Children's Festival** (403/294-7414, www.calgarychildfest.org) is the third week of May. Events include theater, puppetry, and performances by musicians from around the world. It's held in the Epcor Centre for Performing Arts and Olympic Plaza. Olympic Plaza and Prince's Island Park come alive with the sights, sounds, and tastes of the Caribbean in mid-June for **Carifest** (www.carifestcalgary.ca).

Summer

Few cities in the world are associated as closely with an event as Calgary is with the **Calgary Stampede.** For details of the "Greatest Outdoor Show on Earth," held each summer in July, see *Calgary Stampede* later in this section.

Canada Day is celebrated on July 1 in Prince's Island Park, Fort Calgary, the zoo, and Heritage Park. The **Calgary Folk Music Festival** (403/233-0904, www.calgaryfolk fest.com), during the last weekend of July, is an indoor and outdoor extravaganza of Canadian and international performers that centers on Prince's Island Park. The second week of August, and also at this downtown riverfront park is **Afrikadey!** (403/234-9110, www.afrika dey.com), with performances and workshops by African-influenced musicians and artists and screenings of African-themed films.

Fall

In October, **hockey** and **skiing and snowboarding** fever hits the city as the **NHL Calgary Flames** start their season and the first snow flies. Late September through early October sees screenings of movies during the **Calgary International Film Festival** (403/283-1490, www.calgaryfilm.com) at the historic Uptown Stage & Screen and Plaza theaters. This is followed by **Wordfest** (403/294-7492, www.word fest.com), where authors talk about their books, workshops are given, and many readings take place at venues throughout the city and in Banff. As Halloween approaches a good place for kids is Calgary Zoo (403/232-9300), where there are **Boo at the Zoo** celebrations after dark throughout the last week of October.

Winter

Calgary has joined other major Canadian cities by celebrating New Year's Eve with a **First Night** festival. Although severely curtailed by the weather, Calgarians enjoy the winter with the opening of the theater, ballet, and opera seasons. National and international ski-jumping, luge, and bobsledding events are held at **Canada Olympic Park** November–March.

◖ CALGARY STAMPEDE

Every July, the city's perennial rough-and-ready Cowtown image is thrust to the forefront when a fever known as Stampede hits town. For 10 days, Calgarians let their hair down—business leaders don Stetsons, bankers wear boots, half the town walks around in too-tight denim outfits, and the rate of serious crime drops. Nine months later, maternity hospitals report a rise in business. For most Calgarians, it is known simply as The Week (always capitalized). The Stampede is many things to many people but is certainly not for the cynic. It is a celebration of the city's past—of endless sunny days when life was broncos, bulls, and steers, of cowboys riding through the streets, and saloons on every corner. But it is not just about the past. It's the Cowtown image Calgarians cherish and the frontier image that visitors expect. On downtown streets, everyone is your neighbor. Flapjacks and bacon are served free of charge around the city; normally staid citizens shout "Ya-HOO!" for no particular reason; Indians ride up and down the streets on horseback; and there's drinking and dancing until dawn every night.

The epicenter of the action is **Stampede Park,** immediately south of the city center,

60,000 people lined the streets for the parade, and 40,000 attended each day of rodeo events. This turnout was amazing, considering that barely more than 65,000 people lived in Calgary at the time. The highlight of the event was on the final day when Tom Three Persons, a little-known Blood Indian rider from southern Alberta, rode the legendary bronc Cyclone for eight seconds to collect the world-championship saddle and $1,000.

The following year, Weadick took the show to Winnipeg, then World War I intervened, and not until 1919 was the Calgary show revived with Weadick at the helm. In the era of popular Hollywood westerns, Weadick convinced moviemakers down south that the event was worthy of screening. In 1925, *Calgary Stampede* was released, putting the city on the map. As it turned out, the inaugural show wasn't the first and last, but rather the beginning of an annual extravaganza that is billed, and rightly so, as "The Greatest Outdoor Show on Earth."

Be prepared for big crowds every day of the Stampede.

where more than 100,000 people converge each day. The nucleus of the Stampede, the park hosts the world's richest outdoor rodeo and the just-as-spectacular chuck wagon races, where professional cowboys from all over the planet compete to share $1.6 million over 10 days. But Stampede Park offers a lot more than a show of cowboy skills. The gigantic midway takes at least a day to get around: a staggering number of attractions, displays, and free entertainment cost only the price of gate admission; and a glittering grandstand show, complete with fireworks, ends each day's shenanigans.

History

Early in the 20th century, Guy Weadick, an American cowpoke, got the idea that people would pay to see traditional cowboy skills combined with vaudeville showmanship. In 1912, with the backing of local businessmen, Weadick put on a show billed as "The Last and Best Great Western Frontier Days," the name a reference to the fact that many Albertans thought the local cattle industry was near its end. An estimated

Stampede Parade

Although Stampede Park opens on Thursday evening for **Sneak-a-Peek** (an event that alone attracts approximately 40,000 eager patrons), Stampede Week officially begins Friday morning with a spectacular parade through the streets of downtown Calgary. The approximately 150 parade participants include close to 4,000 people and 700 horses, and the procession takes two hours to pass any one point. It features an amazing array of floats, each cheered by the 250,000 people who line the streets up to 10 deep. The loudest "Ya-HOOs" are usually reserved for Alberta's oldest residents, Stampede royalty, and members of Calgary's professional sports teams, but this is the Stampede, so even politicians and street sweepers elicit enthusiastic cheers.

The parade proceeds west along 6th Avenue from 2nd Street SE, then south on 10th Street SW and east on 9th Avenue. Starting time is 9 A.M., but crowds start gathering at 6 A.M. and you'll be lucky to get a front-row spot much after 7 A.M.

RODEO EVENTS

For those watching for the first time, a rodeo can look like organized confusion. Although staying on the animals isn't as easy as professional cowboys make it look, learning the rules is, and it will make the events more enjoyable. The rodeo is made up of six traditional events, three of which are judged on points and three of which are timed.

BAREBACK RIDING

In this event, the rider doesn't use a saddle or reins. He is cinched to a handhold and a leather pad attached to the horse's back. The idea is to stay on the wildly bucking horse for eight seconds. As the cowboy leaves the chute, he must keep both spurs above the horse's shoulders until the horse's front hooves hit the ground. Riders are judged on style and rhythm, which is achieved by spurring effectively and remaining in control. The cowboy is disqualified if he doesn't last eight seconds, if he loses a stirrup, or if he touches the animal with his hand. Scores are given out of 100, with a maximum of 50 points allotted for the horse's power and bucking pattern, and a maximum of 50 awarded to the rider for his control and spurring action. Scores above 85 are usually good enough to win.

SADDLE BRONC RIDING

This event differs from bareback riding in that the horse is saddled and the rider, rather than being cinched to the animal, hangs onto a rein attached to the halter. Again, both

spurs must be above the horse's shoulders until after the first jump. Bronc riding is one of the classic rodeo events, and when performed properly, is a joy to watch. Riders are judged by spurring action and are disqualified for falling before eight seconds have elapsed. The highest score ever achieved in this event was a 95 by Australian Glenn O'Neill at the Innisfail Rodeo in 1996.

bareback riding

© ANDREW HEMPSTEAD

Rodeo

The pinnacle of any cowboy's career is walking away with the $100,000 winner's check on the last day of competition in the Calgary Stampede. For the first eight days, 20 of the world's best cowboys and cowgirls compete in two pools for the right to ride on the final Sunday. Saturday is a wildcard event. On each of the 10 days, the rodeo goes at 1:30 P.M. Although Stampede Week is about a lot more than the rodeo, everyone loves to watch this event. Cowboys compete in bronc riding, bareback riding, bull riding, calf roping, and steer wrestling, and cowgirls compete in barrel racing. Bull fighting and nonstop chatter from hilarious rodeo clowns all keep the action going between the more traditional rodeo events.

Chuck Wagon Races

The **Rangeland Derby** chuck wagon races feature nine heats each evening starting at 8 P.M. At the end of the week, the top four drivers from the preliminary rounds compete in a $100,000 dash-for-the-cash final. Chuck

BULL RIDING

Traditionally the last event in a rodeo, bull riding is considered to be the most exciting eight seconds in sports. The cowboy must hang onto a 1,800-pound bull for the required eight seconds with as much control as possible. No spurring is required (for obvious reasons), although if he gets the chance to do so, it earns the cowboy extra points. Disqualification occurs if the cowboy's loose hand touches either himself or the animal, or if he doesn't last eight seconds, which is the case more often than not. Like in bareback riding, the cowboy has one hand cinched to the animal in a handhold of braided rope. Riders are tied so tightly to the animal that if they are bucked off on the side away from their riding hand, they often become "hung up" and are dragged around like a rag doll until rescued by a rodeo clown. Scores are given out of 100; because of the difficulty of bull riding, just staying on for eight seconds ensures a good ride, but look for a score of around 85 to win.

CALF ROPING

This timed event has its roots in the Old West, when calves had to be roped and tied down to receive a brand or medical treatment. The calf is released from a chute and followed closely by a mounted cowboy. The cowboy must lasso the calf, dismount, race to the animal, and tie a "pigging string" around any three of its legs. The cowboy then throws his hands into the air to signal the end of his run. After remounting his horse, the cowboy rides forward, slackening the rope. He's disqualified if the calf's legs don't remain tied for six seconds. The fastest time wins, with a 10-second penalty for breaking the gate. Any time under eight seconds is good.

STEER WRESTLING

Also known as "bull-dogging," this timed event is for the big boys. The steer, which may weigh up to five times as much as the cowboy, jumps out of the chute, followed closely by a "hazer" (mounted cowboy) who rides alongside, jumps off his horse at full speed, and slides onto the steer's back, attempting to get hold of its horns. The cowboy slows down by digging his feet into the ground, using a twisting motion to throw the steer to the ground. The fastest time wins. Look for a winning score under four seconds (the world record is 2.2 seconds).

BARREL RACING

This is the only rodeo event for women. Riders must guide their horses around three barrels, set in a cloverleaf pattern, before making a hat-flying dash to the finish line. To do this requires great skill and an excellent relationship between the cowgirl and her horse. The fastest time wins, and there's a five-second penalty for knocking down a barrel. An average winning time is around 15 seconds.

---

wagon racing is an exciting sport any time, but at the Stampede the pressure is intense as drivers push themselves to stay in the running. The grandstand in the infield makes steering the chuck wagons through an initial figure eight difficult, heightening the action before they burst onto the track for what is known as the Half Mile of Hell to the finish line. The first team across the finish line does not always win the race; drivers must avoid 34 penalties, ranging from 1 to 10 seconds, which are added to their overall time.

Other Highlights

The cavernous **Roundup Centre** holds various commercial exhibits and demonstrations (plenty of free samples), Kitchen Theatre showcasing Calgary's culinary scene, and a Western Showcase of art and photography. At the front of the Roundup Centre is **Stampede Corral,** where you might find dog shows, the Calgary Stampede Show Band, or a talent show for seniors. A **midway** takes center stage on the western edge of the park with the thrills and spills of rides such as the

Steer wrestling is for the big boys.

reverse bungee drawing as many spectators as paying customers.

Agricultural displays are situated in the center of Stampede Park. **Centennial Fair** is an outdoor stage with children's attractions such as duck races and magicians. In the **Agricultural Building** livestock is displayed, and the World Blacksmith's Competition and horse shows take place next door in the **John Deere Show Ring.**

At the far end of Stampede Park, across the Elbow River, is **Indian Village.** Here, members of the five nations who signed Treaty Seven 100 years ago—the Blackfoot, Blood, Piegan, Sarcee, and Stoney—set up camp for the duration of the Stampede. Each tepee has its own colorful design. Behind the village is a stage where native dance competitions are held.

Once you've paid gate admission, all entertainment (except the rodeo and chuck wagon races) is free. Well-known Canadian performers appear at the outdoor **Coca-Cola Stage** from 11 A.M. to midnight. **Nashville North** is

an indoor venue with a bar, live country acts, and a dance floor; open until 2 A.M.

Tickets

Advance tickets for the afternoon rodeos and evening chuck wagon races/grandstand shows go on sale the year before the event (usually sometime in September), with the best seats selling out well in advance. The grandstand is divided into sections, each with a different price tag. The best views are from the "A" section, closest to the infield yet high enough not to miss all the action. To either side are the "B" and "C" sections, also with good views. Above the main level is the Clubhouse level, divided into another four sections all enclosed by glass and air-conditioned. These seats might not have the atmosphere of the lower or higher levels, but they are protected from the elements and patrons have access to a bar, full-service restaurant, and lounge area. Ticket prices for the first eight days of rodeo competition range $28–60 ($48 for section A). The evening chuck wagon races/grandstand shows

CALGARY

The Indian Village showcases native traditions.

run $35–75 ($64 for section A). Tickets for the final two days of competition are an extra $3–5. Tickets to both the rodeos and chuck wagon races/grandstand shows include admission to Stampede Park ($12). Order tickets by phone (403/269-9822 or 800/661-1767) or online (www.calgarystampede.com).

If you didn't purchase your tickets in advance, you'll need to pay the $12 **general admission** at the gate. Then, once on the grounds, you can purchase "rush seating" tickets for the afternoon's rodeo (adult $12, child $6) or the chuck wagon race/grandstand show (adult $15, child $8) 90 minutes prior to show

time from the booths in front of the grandstand. You'll only have access to either an area of the infield with poor views or seats well away from the action.

Information
Check either of Calgary's daily newspapers for a pull-out section with results of the previous day's competition and a schedule of events on the grounds and around town. At Stampede Park, a schedule and maps are available at distinctive **Howdy Folk Chuckwagons** topped with cowboy hats and staffed by friendly volunteers.

Future dates for the Calgary Stampede include July 6–15, 2007; July 4–13, 2008; and July 3–12, 2009.

Contact the Calgary Stampede office at 403/261-0101 or 800/661-1260, www.calgary stampede.com.

Getting There and Parking
The C-train runs at least every 10 minutes eastbound along 7th Avenue downtown to one of two Stampede stations ($2.25 one-way). Many hotels and campgrounds run shuttle services to downtown for the Friday parade and then to Stampede Park for the rest of the week; expect to pay $15 round-trip per person.

If you decide to drive, parking close to the grounds is possible, but the roads can be chaotic. Many local residents turn their gardens into parking lots—most stand out on the road waving at you as if to say that their month's rent depends on the $15–20 parking fee. The official parking lots throughout the area immediately north of Stampede Park usually charge $15 per day in the morning, rising as high as $25 in the afternoon, depending on how busy they are.

Accommodations and Camping

Accommodations in Calgary vary from campgrounds, a hostel, and budget motels to a broad selection of high-quality hotels catering to top-end travelers and business conventions. Most downtown hotels offer drastically reduced rates on weekends—Friday and Saturday nights might be half the regular room rate. During Stampede Week, prices are higher than the rest of the year and accommodations are booked months in advance. Rates quoted below are for a double room in summer, but outside of Stampede week.

The bed-and-breakfast scene in Calgary is alive and well. Most are located off the main tourist routes. The **Bed & Breakfast Association of Calgary** (www.bbcalgary.com) represents around 40 of these homes offering rooms to visitors. The association doesn't offer a reservation service, but is simply a grouping of properties that meet certain standards.

DOWNTOWN
Under $50
Part of the worldwide Hostelling International organization, **HI-Calgary City Centre** (520 7th Avenue SE, 403/670-7580 or 888/762-4122, www.hihostels.ca) is an excellent choice for budget travelers, both for its convenient location and wide variety of facilities. It has 110 beds, most in eight-bed dormitories, but there is one private room. Other amenities include a fully equipped kitchen, laundry facilities, a large common room, Internet kiosks, bike rental, an outdoor barbecue, a game room, a snack bar, lockers, and free parking. Members of Hostelling International pay $22 for a dorm bed ($27 for nonmembers) or $60 s or d ($68 for nonmembers) in the private room. It's one block east of the City Hall C-train station and the Airport Shuttle Express stops out front ($18 one-way).

$50-100
The most central bed-and-breakfast is **Inglewood B&B** (1006 8th Ave. SE, 403/262-6570, www.inglewoodbedandbreakfast.com),

named for the historic neighborhood in which it lies. Its location is excellent—close to the river and Stampede Park, as well as a 10-minute stroll from downtown. The three rooms within this modern Victorian-style home, each with private bathrooms, range $85–135 s or d, depending on the room configuration. Rates include a cooked breakfast of your own choosing.

Least expensive of Calgary's downtown hotels is the 1912 **Regis Plaza Hotel** (124 7th Ave. SE, 403/262-4641, www.regisplaza hotel.com, $69–98 s or d). It is one of the few old hotels that has survived Calgary's ongoing construction boom. Of the 100 rooms, only 30 have ensuites—the rest share bathroom facilities—but all have televisions and a zippy 1970s decor.

Although the Regis Plaza is the only downtown hotel that quotes rates under $100, it's possible to get a room for around that amount at a more expensive property by planning a weekend stay or finding a special on the hotel's website.

$100-150
Across the railway tracks from downtown, the **Best Western Suites Downtown** (1330 8th St. SW, 403/268-6900 or 800/981-2555, www.bestwestern.com) features more than 120 self-contained units, each with contemporary styling, a kitchen, and air-conditioning. Rates for a standard suite start at $125 s or d, but an upgrade to a king bed and jetted tub is usually only around $20 extra.

$150-200
◖ **Hotel Arts** (119 12th Ave. SW, 403/266-4611 or 800/661-9378, www.hotelarts.com) is a newish 12-story, 188-room accommodation on the south side of the railway tracks, within easy walking distance of Stampede Park. The rooms are contemporary-slick, with 42-inch LCD flat-screen TVs, cordless phones, high-speed Internet access, luxurious bathrooms, and plush beds with goose-down du-

vets. Downstairs is a fitness room, an outdoor heated pool surrounded by a beautiful patio, a restaurant, and a lounge. Summer rates are $159 s or d, but rooms go for around $100 with 21-day advance purchase—an excellent deal.

A few blocks west of the downtown shopping district, but linked by the C-train, you'll find the 301-room **Sandman Hotel** (888 7th Ave. SW, 403/237-8626 or 800/726-3626, www.sandmanhotels.com, $169 s or d). This full-service property features an indoor pool, a family-style restaurant, and large, attractive rooms. Pay under $130 through the website.

Least expensive of the hotels right downtown is the **(5 Downtown Suites & Spa** (618 5th Ave. SW, 403/451-5551 or 888/561-7666, www.5calgary.com). Although the 300 rooms are unremarkable, bonuses include full kitchens, free hot breakfast buffet, free weekend parking, a free business center, spa services, five-cents-per minute calls anywhere in North America, and an outdoor pool. Rack rates are $180–230, but check the website to save at least $60 in any number of ways.

$200-250

The **International Hotel of Calgary** (220 4th Ave. SW, 403/265-9600 or 800/661-8627, www.internationalhotel.ca) features 250 one- and two-bedroom suites, an indoor pool, a fitness room, and a restaurant. Regular rates are $229–269, with seniors enjoying a solid discount.

Over $250

When I spend the night in Calgary on business I try to stay somewhere different every time (in the name of research). But when it's a special occasion, it's difficult to beat the **(Kensington Riverside Inn** (1126 Memorial Dr. NW, Kensington, 403/228-4442 or 877/313-3733, www.kensingtonriversideinn.com, $269–369 s or d), surprisingly the city's only boutique hotel. Why? From the moment I'm tempted by a homemade cookie from the jar at the reception to the moment I slide between the Egyptian cotton sheets that top out ultra-comfortable mattresses, the inn has a captivating atmosphere that is

© ANDREW HEMPSTEAD

Kensington Riverside Inn

unlike any other city accommodation. Each of the 19 guest rooms has a slightly different feel (from bold contemporary to warmly inviting) and layout (some have a private balcony, others have a gas fireplace or jetted tub), but it's in-room niceties such as heated towel racks or a quiet hour spent in the central living room with evening hors d'oeuvres that make the inn super special. A coffee tray and morning paper left by your door, followed by a gourmet breakfast served in the downstairs dining room, are included in the rates. The inn is across the Bow River from downtown in Kensington, one of Calgary's hippest neighborhoods.

One block north from the Calgary Tower is the **Hyatt Regency Calgary** (700 Centre St., 403/717-1234 or 800/233-1234, www.hyatt.com). Incorporating a historic building along Stephen Avenue Walk in its construction, this 21-story hotel features an indoor swimming pool, a refined lounge, and a renowned restaurant specializing in Canadian cuisine. The hotel's Stillwater Spa is the premier spa facility in Calgary—spend any time here and you'll forget you're in a city hotel. The up-to-date guest rooms won't take your breath away, but they have a wide range of amenities and luxurious bathrooms; from $270 s or d weeknights and $160 weekends. Parking is an additional $16.

In the heart of the shopping district, the **Westin Hotel** (320 4th Ave. SW, 403/266-1611 or 800/937-8461, www.westin.com) has a wide range of facilities, including a rooftop indoor swimming pool, a café, the renowned Owl's Nest Restaurant, a lounge, and more than 500 rooms. Standard rooms are $250 s or d, and more spacious "Tower" suites start at $280.

Easily Calgary's best-known hotel, the gracious **Fairmont Palliser** (133 9th Ave. SE, 403/263-0520 or 800/257-7544, www.fairmont.com, from $320 s or d) was built in 1914 by the Canadian Pacific Railway for the same clientele as the company's famous properties in Banff and Jasper. The rooms may seem smallish by modern standards, and the hotel lacks certain recreational facilities, but the elegance and character of the grande dame of Calgary accommodations are priceless. The cavernous lobby has original marble columns and staircases, a magnificent chandelier, and solid-brass doors that open onto busy 9th Avenue. As you'd expect, staying at the Palliser isn't cheap, but it's a luxurious way to enjoy the city.

MACLEOD TRAIL

A string of hotels along Macleod Trail south of downtown picks up highway traffic as it enters the city. Most midpriced chains are represented, with the following just a sampling.

$100-150

Most of the chain motels along Macleod Trail fall into this price category. Book in advance or online to pick up rates around $100 a night.

Southernmost of the motels on Macleod Trail is the 34-room **Stetson Village Inn** (10002 Macleod Trail SW, 403/271-3210 or 888/322-3210, www.stetsoninn.ca, $111 s or d), an older-style place tucked between shopping malls. Local calls are free and the adjoining restaurant and lounge open nightly. The rates could be lower (and they are in winter—$60 s or d), but it's a prime spot for getting out of the city to begin your exploration of Southern Alberta.

The **Best Western Calgary Centre Inn** (3630 Macleod Trail SW, 403/287-3900 or 877/287-3900, www.bwcalgarycentre.com, $130 s or d) may be close to the geographical center of the city, but it's not downtown as the name suggests. Each of the rooms is decorated in a bright and breezy color scheme, and comes stocked with amenities such as a hair dryer and coffeemaker. On the premises are an indoor pool and a fitness center. Rates include continental breakfast.

A few blocks farther south, with a C-train station on its back doorstep, stands **Holiday Inn Macleod Trail** (4206 Macleod Trail SW, 403/287-2700 or 800/661-1889, www.holidayinn.com, $149 s or d). Facilities here include a large indoor pool, a restaurant, and a lounge.

MOTEL VILLAGE

Motel Village is Calgary's main concentration of moderately priced motels. The "village" is

not an official designation, just a dozen motels bunched together on a single block bordered by 16th Avenue NW, Crowchild Trail, and Banff Trail. From the adjacent Banff Trail station, downtown is a short, safe ride away on the C-train.

$100-150

The **(Comfort Inn** (2369 Banff Trail NW, 403/289-2581 or 800/228-5150, www.comfort inncalgary.com) combines a wide range of amenities with reasonable rates to be my pick of Motel Village accommodations. All rooms have a simple yet snazzy contemporary look, along with high-speed Internet, a coffeemaker, a hair dryer, and an ironing facility, and there will be a national paper delivered to your door each morning. Other features include an indoor pool and waterslide complex. Rates starting at $109 s or d include a light breakfast (or upgrade to a King Suite for $189).

The **Quality Inn University** (2359 Banff Trail NW, 403/289-1973 or 800/661-4667, www.qualityinnuofc.com, $119 s or d) is not closer to the university than other motels are, but is a good solid choice for comfortable accommodations. Rooms are set around a fancy atrium that has an indoor pool at its epicenter. The Executive Suite ($209) is massive. The on-site lounge and restaurant offer a typical hotel environment.

Best Western Village Park Inn (1804 Crowchild Trail NW, 403/289-0241 or 800/774-7716, www.villageparkinn.com, $145 s or d) features 159 spacious rooms well-equipped for business and leisure travelers, and a huge atrium containing a lounge with an adjoining restaurant (6:30 A.M.–11 P.M.) and a swimming pool. It also has a Discount Car Rental desk—rent from here to avoid the extra airport charges.

In the same price range as those above is **Econo Lodge–Motel Village** (2440 16th Ave. NW, 403/289-2561 or 800/917-7779, www.econolodgecalgary.com, $105–135 s or d), which offers well-equipped rooms and a fitness room, and the **Holiday Inn Express** (2227 Banff Trail NW, 403/289-6600,

www.holidayinn.com, $140 s or d), which has a small outdoor pool.

WEST OF DOWNTOWN

Known as 16th Avenue NW within city limits, a string of inexpensive motels lines the Trans-Canada Highway heading west from the city toward the Canadian Rockies, but none are particularly good value.

$100-150

Tucked away on the forested Paskapoo Slopes, beside Canada Olympic Park, **(Ripley Ridge Retreat** (430 85th St. SW, 403/288-3415 or 877/344-3400, www.ripleyridge.com, $115–225 s or d) offers guests the choice of accommodations in two rustic cabins—one with a full kitchen, the other with a woodstove and loft—or in spacious, comfortable units such as the Vista Suite, which features panoramic city views from a private sitting room. The on-site Nature's Essence Spa is a big draw for many visitors, who stay as part of spa package, such as a two-night deal for $340 per person.

Directly opposite Canada Olympic Park is the **Four Points by Sheraton Calgary West** (8220 Bow Ridge Crescent NW, 403/288-4441 or 877/288-4441, www.fourpointscalgarywest.com, $139 s, $149 d), a real standout for motel accommodations on this side of the city. The 150 rooms are big and bright and each has a balcony (ask for one with a view of Canada Olympic Park). Along with city-hotel luxuries like high-speed Internet and room service, other amenities include an indoor pool and water slide, a fitness center, the Mountain Oasis Retreat spa facility, and a restaurant (breakfast under $10) and lounge. Check the hotel website for rates well under $100 and for suites for less than the rack rate. Some packages include airport shuttles—perfect if you're renting from Hertz, which has a desk in the lobby.

$150-200

Across the road from the Sheraton is **Sandman Hotel & Suites** (125 Bow Ridge Crescent NW, 403/288-6033 or 800/726-3626, www.sandman hotels.com, $185 s or d), which opened in

2006. It features spacious modern rooms, an indoor pool, a fitness room, and a 24-hour Denny's restaurant.

NORTHEAST (AIRPORT)

Many hotels lie in the northeast section of the city at varying distances from Calgary International Airport. All of those detailed below have airport shuttles, and most can be contacted directly by courtesy phone from the airport. If you're reading this book, chances are you're flying into Calgary. If not, and you're planning on flying out of Calgary, it's worth knowing that these same hotels will let you leave a vehicle with them free of charge until your return *and* use their shuttle service simply for staying overnight.

$50-100

Check hotel websites listed below for rooms around the $100 mark, or take the easy way out and book your stay at the no-frills **Pointe Inn** (1808 19th St. NE, 403/291-4681 or 800/661-8164, www.pointeinn.com, $85 s, $95 d). Facilities include a launderette, a café, a restaurant, and a lounge. Request a nonsmoking room.

$100-150

Holiday Inn Calgary Airport (1250 McKinnon Dr. NE, 403/230-1999 or 800/465-4329, www.holidayinn.com, $149–169 s or d) is a little farther from the airport than the other choices, but since there's a free shuttle that is of little consequence. The rooms are exactly what you expect from Holiday Inn, the restaurant has surprisingly good city views, and the indoor pool is the perfect place to refresh yourself after a long flight.

Similarly priced is the **Radisson Hotel Calgary Airport** (2120 16th Ave. NE, 403/291-4666 or 800/333-3333, www.radisson.com), which features 185 comfortable rooms, a large lobby filled with greenery and comfortable seating, an indoor pool, a fitness center, spa services, and a Western-style saloon. Standard rooms are $145, or upgrade to Business Class for $165 and enjoy better views, an evening turndown service, and breakfast.

Over $150

Delta Calgary Airport Hotel (403/291-2600 or 877/814-7706, www.deltahotels.com, $219 s or d) is the only accommodation right at the airport. The main terminal is linked to the hotel lobby by a walkway that leads into an expansive atrium and restaurant. The medium-sized rooms come with luxuries like down duvets and plush bathrobes, each has a writing desk, and most importantly, they are well sound-proofed. Half are sold as Premier Rooms, which are the same size as regular rooms but come with upgraded furnishings for a few bucks extra. Hotel amenities include two restaurants, a lounge, an indoor pool, and a business center. Delta properties across Canada fill the upper niche of the travel market, but they also offer some great bargains—this property is no different, so check the website before being perturbed by the price tag.

Not right at the airport but of a similarly high standard is the **Sheraton Cavalier** (2620 32nd Ave. NE, 403/291-0107 or 800/325-3535, www.sheratoncavalier.com). This full-service hostelry boasts a variety of dining options, a lounge, a fitness room, Calgary's largest indoor waterpark (complete with a wading pool), and a business center. The 306 rooms are modern, spacious, and equipped with high-speed Internet that runs through the television. Rack rates are $269 s or d, but use the hotel website to find rooms for a little more than half that price.

CAMPING

No camping is available within the Calgary city limits, although campgrounds can be found along all major routes into the city. Shuttle buses run to and from campgrounds into Stampede Park during the Calgary Stampede. Reservations are necessary during Stampede week.

West

The only Calgary campground with an outdoor swimming pool is **Calgary West Campground** (221 101st St. SW, 403/288-0411 or 888/562-0842, www.cmy.ab.ca, mid-Apr.–mid-Oct.), on a north-facing hill a short way west of Canada Olympic Park. In addition

to the pool, modern facilities include showers, a laundry room, a game room, and a grocery store. Around 320 sites are laid out on terraces, so no one misses out on the views. Unserviced sites are $27, hookups $32–39.

Calaway Park (10 km/6.2 mi west of city limits, 403/249-7372, www.calawaypark.com, mid-May–Aug.) is farther out along the Trans-Canada Highway. It offers a large, open camping area. Trees are scarce, but on clear days the view of the Canadian Rockies is spectacular. The toilets, showers, and laundry room are in a trailer but are of reasonable standard. Tent sites $22, powered sites $27, and full hookups $33. The adjoining overflow area (no services, $22) is used during Stampede Week by campers who should have made reservations, but didn't. As a bonus, all guests receive discounted admission to Calaway Park.

North

Whispering Spruce Campground (403/226-0097, www.whisperingspruce.com, Apr.–Oct., tent sites $19, hookups $23–26) is on the west side of Highway 2, 10 kilometers (6.2 mi) north of the airport. Facilities include showers, a small grocery store, laundry, a game room, and horseshoe pits.

East

Mountainview Farm Campground, three kilometers (1.9 mi) east of the city limits on the TransCanada Highway (403/293-6640, www.calgarycamping.com, tent sites $24, hookups $28–33) doesn't have a view of the mountains, but it does have a small petting farm, mini-golf, and hay rides. The sites are very close together. Facilities include showers, a grocery store, and a laundry room.

South

South of Calgary on the Highwood River is **Nature's Hideaway Family Campground** (RR1, DeWinton, 403/938-8185, www.natures hideaway.com, mid-Apr.–Oct., unserviced sites $25, hookups $30–40). Although farther out than all of the others, it is in a densely wooded floodplain where birds are abundant and deer and coyotes are seen often. The facilities are a little tired, but on the plus side, there's no end of things to do—swimming, fishing, trail rides, and weekend dances. On-site is a grocery store and free firewood. To get there, head south on Highway 2, then take Highway 552 east for 12 kilometers (7.5 mi), then go north for one kilometer (0.6 mi), then east for two kilometers (1.2 mi) more.

Food

Calgary may lack the cultural trappings that Alberta's capital, Edmonton, boasts, but it gives that city a run for its money in the restaurant department. Southwest of downtown, along 17th Avenue and 4th Street, a once-quieter part of the city has been transformed into a focal point for Calgary's restaurant scene, with cuisine to suit all tastes. Familiar North American fast-food restaurants line Macleod Trail south of the city center.

DOWNTOWN

All of the major high-rise buildings have plazas with inexpensive food courts, coffeehouses, and cappuccino bars—the perfect places for people-watching. Local suits all have their own favorite haunts, but only two places really stand out to me as trying that little bit harder to be different and to please at the same time. Both are owned by the same company, Sunterra, which started out as a family farm before moving into processing then retail. **Sunterra Village Marché** (Plus 15 Level, TransCanada Tower, 450 1st St. SW, 403/262-8240, Mon.–Fri. 6 A.M.–8 P.M.) is set up to represent a French streetscape, complete with a patisserie, carvery, salad counter, deli, wine bar, and juice joint. Meals can be packaged to go, but plan on "eating in" at a wide variety of seating styles, including outdoors. **Sunterra Marché**

CALGARY CUISINE

Calgary has grown up (and out) so much in the last decade that defining the local cuisine is almost impossible. Steakhouses such as **Hy's** and **Caesar's** were long the mainstay, and happily they still thrive. In the last decade they've been joined by dozens of top-class restaurants that specialize in giving Canadian produce a modern makeover, with **Thomsons, Divino, Catch,** and **Saltlik** leading the way. A few old diners survive; those such as the **Galaxy,** off trendy 17th Avenue SW, and **Peter's Drive-In,** along the TransCanada Highway, have been amazingly popular for over three decades. But in both cases, you could be eating anywhere in North America. **Buzzard's** is what everyone wants to think Calgary used to be like, but it is about as authentic as downtown bankers wearing blue jeans for Stampede. While you can't go wrong eating at any of these places, two other restaurants stand out for top-notch food and a distinctive I-must-be-in-Calgary ambience.

Built in 1906 for the superintendent of Fort Calgary, **Deane House** (806 9th Ave., 403/269-7747, Mon.-Fri. 11 A.M.-3 P.M., Sat.-Sun. 10 A.M.-3 P.M.) is a casual dining room surrounded by carefully tended gardens that re-create those laid out 100 years ago. The menu offers a wide choice of simple, healthy lunchtime fare, mostly under $12 (olive-crusted salmon is the exception), making it the perfect place to head after spending the morning at adjacent Fort Calgary.

In the far south of the city, **The Ranche** (off Bow Bottom Trail SE, 403/225-3939, Mon.-Fri. 11:30 A.M.-9 P.M., Sat. 5-10 P.M., Sun. 10:30 A.M.-9 P.M.) is a beautifully restored Victorian mansion that was the headquarters of the Bow Valley Ranch in the late 1880s. While the surroundings are old-style stately, the food is anything but, with elk, buffalo, and beef (from the owner's ranch) combined with organic vegetables and local ingredients to create an imaginative menu that is among the best in the city. Expect to pay $15-24 for a lunch entrée or $26-32 at dinner. For Sunday brunch, the eggs Benedict with Canadian back bacon ($12) is an easy choice.

© ANDREW HEMPSTEAD

Deane House

(Plus 15 Level, Bankers Hall, 855 2nd St. SW, 403/269-3610, Mon.–Fri. 6:30 A.M.–6:30 P.M., Sat. 9:30 A.M.–5:30 P.M.) has a much smaller selection, but the same high quality of gourmet-to-go lunches.

Eau Claire Market and Vicinity

At the entrance to Prince's Island Park, this expansive indoor market has a large food court and several restaurants. In the food court, you'll find a great seafood outlet, a bakery, Asian-food places such as the Thai **Touch of Ginger** (403/234-8550), and a **Ben & Jerry's** (403/266-1779) ice cream outlet. **Cajun Charlie's** (403/233-8101, $9–20), opposite the food court, is a striking orange-and-black eatery serving Louisiana bayou dishes.

Outside the market's western entrance is **Joey Tomato's** (200 Barclay Pde. SW, 403/263-6336, daily from 11 A.M.), a trendy

© ANDREW HEMPSTEAD

1886 Buffalo Café, beside Eau Claire Market

bistro-style restaurant serving moderately priced Italian favorites. Last time I visited, the pork ribs were as juicy as they come. This place is a big hit with the lunchtime and after-work crowd, especially the large outdoor section on summer afternoons.

Across from Joey Tomato's you'll find (**1886 Buffalo Café** (187 Barclay Pde. SW, 403/269-9255, Mon.–Fri. 6 A.M.–3 P.M., weekends 7 A.M.–3 P.M.). Named for the year it was built, it's at least 100 years older than other buildings in the neighborhood. This restaurant oozes an authentic Old Calgary ambience. Inexpensive breakfasts attracts the most interesting group of diners, but the place is busy all day. Portions are generous, coffee refills are free, and when you've finished your meal, ask to see the museum downstairs.

Steak

When (**Hy's Steakhouse** (316 4th Ave. SW, 403/263-2222, Mon.–Fri. 11:30 A.M.–2:30 P.M. and Mon.–Sat. 5–11 P.M.) opened in 1956, it was an innovation. Up until that time, all the

city's best restaurants were in hotels. Not only was Hy's expensive, it specialized in Alberta beef, something that was not regarded as "top end" food 50 years ago. Not much has changed over the years at Hy's, but no one seems to mind. It's the perfect place to dig into perfectly prepared steaks ($30–44) or sample smaller portions at lunch (mostly under $20) in the atmosphere of a refined gentleman's club.

Caesar's Steak House (512 4th Ave. SW, 403/264-1222, Mon.–Fri. 11 A.M.–midnight, Sat. 4:30 P.M.–midnight) hasn't been around for as long as Hy's, but 30 years is still a long time in the restaurant business. The elegant room is decorated in a Roman-style setting with dark woods, leather seating, and dim lighting—just what you expect from a steakhouse. Although the menu includes ribs and seafood, it's juicy prime cuts of Alberta beef ($25–40) that this place is known for.

Striving hard to be the flashiest steakhouse in town, **Saltlik** (101 Stephen Ave. Walk, 403/537-1160, daily for lunch and dinner) stretches the rules when it comes to tradition—

it's big, bold, and brassy, the exact opposite to Caesar's and Hy's.

You don't need to spend a fortune to dig into a juicy steak at **Buzzard's Cowboy Cuisine** (140 10th Ave., 403/264-6959, daily 11 A.M.–11 P.M.), easily found by its barn-board porch and the broken-down wagon out front. Choices range from steak burgers for under $10 to charbroiled buffalo for $24, and it wouldn't be a complete meal at Buzzard's without sharing a platter of prairie oysters ($8) to start.

Seafood

Yes, Calgary is a long way from the ocean, but it nonetheless has a few excellent seafood restaurants. Across the railway tracks from downtown are two of the best: **Cannery Row** (317 10th Ave. SW, 403/269-8889) and, directly upstairs, **McQueens Upstairs** (403/269-4722). Cannery Row is a casual affair, with an open kitchen, an oyster bar, and the ambience of a San Francisco seafood restaurant. Dishes such as grilled swordfish, jambalaya, and blackened snapper are mostly under $20. The menu at McQueens Upstairs is more sophisticated and varied. Dinner entrées start at $21 and rise to over $40 for fresh lobster. Both restaurants are open Monday–Friday for lunch and daily for dinner, and have weekend evening entertainment (blues or jazz at McQueens).

Within the Hyatt Regency building, the sophisticated ambience of **Catch** (100 Stephen Ave. Walk, 403/206-0000, Mon.–Fri. 11:30 A.M.–1:30 P.M., Mon.–Sat. 5:30–9:30 P.M.) is as big an attraction as the menu of seasonal seafood that is flown in daily from both of Canada's coasts. The main level is an oyster bar, where you can sample a variety of shucked oysters with an extensive choice of drinks, while more formal dining is upstairs in the main room. Here, mains range $32–35.

Canadian

Thomsons (Hyatt Regency, 700 Centre St. SE, 403/537-4449, daily 6:30 A.M.–1:30 P.M. and 5–9:30 P.M.) is in a historic sandstone building cleverly integrated with a modern hotel, but it's not aimed at the hotel crowd. First off,

the buffet breakfast ($16) is as good as it gets, with omelets made to order and real maple syrup to douse your pancakes. The rest of the day, the menu is dominated by Canadian game and seafood. Maybe start with PEI mussels in a cider broth, then choose from something as simple as a caribou burger ($15) or splurge on the bison rib eye with cherry chutney ($32). Just make sure to leave room for the smoothest crème brûlée ($7) in the city.

Walk north from Eau Claire Market to reach the ◖ **River Café** (Prince's Island Park, 403/261-7670, Mon.–Fri. 11 A.M.–11 P.M., Sat. and Sun. 11 A.M.–10 P.M.), a cozy, rustic dining room that will surprise you with some of Calgary's finest cooking. More of a restaurant than a café, it features extensive use of produce and ingredients sourced from across Canada. Standouts include buffalo, Alberta beef, and salmon dishes, with the latter often incorporating maple syrup. Lunch mains range $16–26 (including a delicious salmon eggs benedict) while dinner mains are $23–45.

Had a bad experience dining in a revolving restaurant? Haven't we all. Hopefully your meal at the **Panorama Dining Room** (101 9th Ave. SW, 403/508-5822, Mon.–Sat. 7–10:30 A.M. and 11 A.M.–2:30 P.M., Sunday brunch 9:30 A.M.–1:30 P.M., and daily 5–9:30 P.M.) atop the Calgary Tower will be memorable for more than the view. A full rotation takes one hour. Breakfast is an especially good value—choose from a menu of dishes less than $12, which includes tea or coffee, juices, and a small selection of fruit. The rest of the day, the menu features healthy, modern cooking that uses lots of Canadian produce. Expect to pay around $13–21 for lunch and $17–38 for a main course at dinner.

Divino Wine & Cheese Bistro (113 Stephen Ave. Walk SW, 403/410-5555, Mon.–Fri. 11 A.M.–11 P.M., Sat.–Sun. 5–11 P.M.) has a sleek, contemporary European feel that somehow doesn't look out of place surrounded by the exposed sandstone walls of the historic Wine & Spirits Building. Lunchtime options include a healthy grilled ahi tuna salad ($16) with mains ranging from $24 to $36 for the elk rib eye roast.

Smokehouse

In a city that has traditionally loved its beef, it should be no surprise that a Southern-style smokehouse is popular. One block off Stephen Avenue Walk, **Palomino** (109 7th Ave. SW, 403/532-1911, weekdays for lunch and daily for dinner, no reservations) fits the bill. The biggest change to a building that once held a furniture shop is a massive smoker capable of holding 300 kilograms (750 pounds) of meat at any one time. Forget about that diet and tuck into pork ribs ($17–21), massive beef bones ($21), a "Fat Ass Platter" for four ($60), and, as the menu suggests, buy a round of drinks for the kitchen ($20).

Asian

Chinatown, along 2nd and 3rd Avenues east of Centre Street, naturally has the best assortment of Chinese restaurants. **Hang Fung Restaurant** (119 3rd Ave. SE, 403/269-4646, daily for lunch and dinner), tucked behind a Chinese grocery store of the same name, doesn't try to be anything it's not. Chinese locals come here for simple inexpensive meals, mostly under $10. Just as inexpensive is **Golden Inn Restaurant** (107 2nd Ave. SE, 403/269-2211), which is popular with the local Chinese as well as with professionals, and late-shift workers appreciate its long hours (open until 4 A.M.). The menu features mostly Cantonese-style deep-fried food. For a Chinese buffet, head to **Regency Palace Restaurant** (328 Centre St. SE, 403/777-2288), a cavernous establishment seating approximately 600 people. Open for lunch Monday–Friday and daily for dinner. The **Emperor Seafood Restaurant** (403/265-4738), in the Chinese Cultural Centre, also offers a lunchtime buffet.

Yuzuki Japanese Restaurant (510 9th Ave. SW, 403/261-7701, weekdays for lunch, daily for dinner) is a good downtown eatery where the most expensive lunch item is the assorted sushi for $14, which comes with miso soup. More upscale is **Sushi Hiro** (727 5th Ave. SW, 403/233-0605, closed Sunday). Sushi choices change regularly but generally include red salmon, yellowtail, sea urchin, and salmon roe. The tempu-

ras ($14–16) are also excellent. If you sit at the oak-and-green-marble sushi counter, you'll be able to ask the chef what's best.

Tucked away a few doors down from the seafood combo of Cannery Row and McQueens Upstairs is **◖ Thai Sa-On** (351 10th Ave. SW, 403/264-3526, dinner nightly), a small space that's big on the tastes of Thailand. The menu offers a great variety of red and green curries, but I tried the red snapper—medium spiced, baked, and served whole—and couldn't have been happier. The prices? For downtown dining, the food is ridiculously inexpensive, with the snapper costing $20.

KENSINGTON

Across the Bow River from downtown lies the trendy suburb of Kensington, which is home to several coffeehouses and restaurants. One of the nicest cafés is **Higher Ground** (1126 Kensington Rd. NW, 403/270-3780, Mon.–Fri. 7 A.M.–11 P.M., weekends from 8 P.M.), a specialty coffee shop with a few windowfront tables and wireless Internet. Head to **Jugo Juice** (1154 Kensington Crescent NW, 403/270-0120) and enjoy freshly squeezed juices and a great variety of healthy smoothies outside along a narrow sidewalk.

The casual, two-story **◖ Pulcinella** (1147 Kensington Crescent NW, 403/283-1166, Mon.–Sat. 11:30 A.M.–2:30 P.M. and 5–11 P.M., Sun. 4–10 P.M.) has the most traditional pizza you will find in Canada, right down to an oven constructed of stone imported from the slopes of Mount Vesuvius. Pizzas (around $18–24 for two people) have perfectly formed crusts and chunky ingredients, many of which have been imported from the mother country.

A few blocks toward the city, Kensington's busiest intersection offers a bunch of eateries, including another Italian restaurant, **Osteria de Medici** (201 10th St. NW, 403/283-5553, Mon.–Sat. 11:30 A.M.–11 P.M., Sun. 5–10 P.M.). Although still traditional, the atmosphere is more refined and the menu more adventurous than Pulcinella, but service is friendly and prices not as high as they could be (dinner mains $15–28).

UPTOWN 17TH AVENUE

The area immediately south of downtown offers a diverse choice of dining options. The major concentrations of restaurants are along 17th Avenue SW as well as south for a couple of blocks along 4th Street.

Breakfast

C Nellie's (738 17th Avenue SW, 403/244-4616, daily 8 A.M.–3 P.M.), in the heart of Calgary's trendiest dining strip, is a pleasant surprise. It's a small, outwardly low-key place with a big reputation (so much so that it's now one of five Nellie's restaurants in the city). Service is fast and efficient and, most importantly, the food's great. Breakfasts claim the spotlight—if you're hungry, don't bother with the menu, just order the Belly Buster ($9).

The **Galaxy Diner** (1413 11th St. SW, 403/228-0001, Mon.–Fri. 7 A.M.–3 P.M., Sat.–Sun. 8 A.M.–8 P.M.) is an original 1950s diner where cooked breakfasts start at $7, including bottomless coffee and a second serving of hash browns.

Canadian

Formerly a brewpub, **Wildwood Grill** (2417 4th St., 402/228-0100, daily for lunch and dinner) has evolved into a respected restaurant serving up a wide selection of Canadian cuisine in a modern mountain setting. Think pheasant spring rolls or buffalo pate (both $10) as starters and bison short ribs braised in juniper-berry sauce ($25) for a main. In the adjacent pub, bring back childhood memories with a meatloaf ($13) that substitutes veal for beef.

European

Few restaurants in the city are as popular as **Chianti** (1438 17th Ave. SW, 403/229-1600, daily for lunch and dinner until midnight). More than 20 well-prepared pasta dishes are featured on the menu, and all of the pasta is made daily on the premises. Among many specialties are an antipasto platter ($14.50 for two) and Frutti Di Mare, a spicy seafood combination served on a bed of pasta; at $17, it's the most expensive entrée. All regular pasta entrées are less than $12. The restaurant is dark and noisy in typical Italian style. The owner often sings with an accordionist on weekends.

Closer to downtown, **Bonterra Trattoria** (1016 8th St. SW, 403/262-8480, Mon.–Fri. 11:30 A.M.–2:30 P.M., daily 5–10 P.M.) has a stylish dining room with a vaulted ceiling and lots of exposed woodwork. Tables out on the Mediterranean-style patio are in great demand through summer. The menu is modern Italian, with pastas from $15 and the seafood cannelloni a worthwhile splurge at $26. The nationalistic wine list has only a few bottles under $30, but all are available by the glass.

La Chaumiere (139 17th Ave. SW, 403/228-5690, Mon.–Fri. noon–2:30 P.M. and Mon.–Sat. from 5:45 P.M., dinner reservations required) occupies an elaborate space east of the main restaurant strip. Generally regarded as one of North America's premier French restaurants, diners here enjoy combinations like lobster bisque ($8) and roasted rack of Alberta lamb ($32). The formal service is meticulous.

Asian and African

A longtime favorite with locals and budget-conscious travelers in the know, **Restaurant Indonesia** (1604 14th St. SW, 403/244-0645, daily for lunch and dinner) is a busy, inexpensive eatery at the west end of 17th Avenue. Indonesian food is very similar to Chinese, although the sauces prepared here are usually richer and spicier, and vegetarian choices are more varied. Expect to pay under $60 for three courses for two.

Moving up in price and spice is **C Mt. Everest Kitchen** (1448 17th Ave. SW, 403/806-2337, daily for lunch and dinner), which blends traditional Nepalese cuisine with that of the surrounding Indian and Chinese cultures. Lunch is served buffet style ($14); most dinners come out of the clay oven and can be spiced to order. The mixed grill of meats ($22) is a good way to sample the highlights.

When you enter **Sultan's Tent** (909 17th Ave. SW, 403/244-2333, daily for lunch and dinner), a server appears with a silver kettle and

basin filled with orange blossom–scented water with which to wash your hands. It's all part of Moroccan custom and part of the fun. The restaurant features swinging lanterns, richly colored tapestries hanging from the walls, piped-in Arabic music, and, most important, delicious Moroccan delicacies. Try Guelli's Sultan Feast ($29.50), a six-course dinner.

Information and Services

Information Centers
Tourism Calgary (403/263-8510 or 800/661-1678, www.tourismcalgary.com) promotes the city to the world. The organization also operates two Visitor Service Centres. The one that greets visitors arriving by air is across from Carousel 4 at **Calgary International Airport** (year-round, daily 6 A.M.–11 P.M.). The other is right downtown, at the base of the **Calgary Tower** (101 9th Ave. SW, daily in summer 8 A.M.–8 P.M., the rest of the year Mon.–Fri. 8:30 A.M.–4:30 P.M.).

Libraries
The Calgary Public Library Board's 18 branch libraries are scattered throughout the city. The largest is **W. R. Castell Central Library** (616 Macleod Trail SE, 403/260-2600, www.calgary-publiclibrary.com, Mon.–Thurs. 10 A.M.–9 P.M., Fri.–Sat. 10 A.M.–5 P.M., Sun. 1:30–5 P.M.). Four floors of books, magazines, and newspapers from around the world are enough to keep most people busy on a rainy afternoon.

Post and Internet
The downtown post office is at 207 9th Avenue SW. All city libraries provide free Internet access, while all downtown hotels have either a business center with Internet access or in-room modems. Wireless Internet is becoming common in hotels as well as many cafés. Alternatively, head to **Hard Disk Cafe** (638 11th Ave. SW, 403/261-5686, daily 7 A.M.–7 P.M.) for some online surfing.

Banks
Calforex, in the Lancaster Building (304 8th Ave. SW, 403/290-0330), exchanges foreign currency and lets you wire international payments. **American Express Travel Service** (421 7th Ave. SW, 403/261-5982) offers all of the same currency services with the advantages of also being a travel agency. Most major banks carry U.S. currency and can handle basic foreign-exchange transactions.

Photography
I've been trusting my photographic needs to **Vistek** (1231 10th Ave. SW, 403/244-0333 or 800/561-0333, Mon.–Fri. 8:30 A.M.–6 P.M., Sat. 9:30 A.M.–5 P.M.) for many years. Turnaround time on print film is one hour; on slide film it's overnight. They also have knowledgeable service and sales divisions, with the latter up to speed on the latest digital and video technology.

Laundry
Handy self-service launderettes are **14th Street Coin Laundry** (1211 14th St. SW, 403/541-1636, daily 7 A.M.–11 P.M.), which has washers big enough to handle sleeping bags and blankets, and **Heritage Hill Coin Laundry** (156-8228 MacLeod Trail SE, 403/258-3946).

Emergency Services
For medical emergencies, call 911 or contact **Foothills Hospital** (1403 29th Ave. NW, 403/670-1110) or **Rockyview General Hospital** (7007 14th St. SW, 403/943-3000). Opened in late 2006 across 16th Avenue from Foothills Hospital, the **Alberta Children's Hospital** (2888 Shaganappi Trail NW, 403/955-7211) is difficult to miss with its colorfully modern exterior. For the **Calgary Police,** call 911 in an emergency or 403/266-1234 for non-urgent matters.

Getting There and Around

GETTING THERE
Air
Calgary International Airport (airport code YYC; www.calgaryairport.com) is within the city limits northeast of downtown. It is served by more than a dozen scheduled airlines and used by seven million passengers each year (Canada's fourth-busiest airport). Arrivals is on the lower level, where passengers are greeted by White Hat volunteers who are dressed in traditional Western attire and answer visitors' questions about the airport, transportation, and the city. Across from the baggage carousels is an information desk (daily 6 A.M.–11 P.M.) and a bank of interactive computer terminals linked to hotels and other tourist services. The desks for all major rental-car outlets are across the road.

A cab to downtown runs approximately $35, or take the **Airport Shuttle Express** (403/509-4799, www.airportshuttleexpress.com) to major downtown hotels for $18 per person one-way. This service runs daily 5:30 A.M.–1 A.M.

For details of airlines flying into Calgary, see the *Getting There* section of the *Essentials* chapter or click through the links on the airport website.

Bus
The **Greyhound** bus depot (850 16th St. SW, 403/265-9111 or 800/661-8747, www.greyhound.ca) is two blocks away from the C-train stop ($2 into town), or you can cross the overhead pedestrian bridge at the terminal's southern entrance and catch a transit bus. To walk the entire distance to town would take 20 minutes. A cab from the bus depot to downtown runs $9, to HI–Calgary City Centre $10. The depot is cavernous. It has a restaurant, a Royal Bank cash machine, information boards, and lockers large enough to hold backpacks ($2). Greyhound buses connect Calgary daily with Edmonton (3.5 hours), Banff (two hours), Vancouver (15 hours), and all other points within the prov-

ince. No seat reservations are taken. Just turn up, buy your ticket, and hop aboard. If you buy your ticket seven days in advance, discounts apply. If you plan to travel extensively by bus, the Discovery Pass is a good deal.

From their offices near the Calgary Tower, **Red Arrow** (205 9th Ave. SE, 403/531-0350, www.redarrow.pwt.ca) shuttles passengers between Calgary and downtown Edmonton, with some services continuing to Fort McMurray in northern Alberta.

GETTING AROUND
Bus
Calgary Transit (403/262-1000, www.calgarytransit.com) goes just about everywhere in town by combining two light-rail lines with extensive bus routes. Buses are adult $2.25, child $1.50—deposit the exact change in the box beside the driver and request a transfer (valid for 90 minutes). A day pass, which is valid for unlimited bus and rail travel, is adult $5.60, child $3.60. The best place for information and schedules is the **Calgary Transit Customer Service Centre** (244 7th Ave. SW, Mon.–Fri. 8:30 A.M.–5 P.M.).

C-Train
C-train, the light-rail transit (LRT) system, has two lines that total 40 kilometers (25 mi) of track and 36 stations. Both converge on 7th Avenue, running parallel for the entire distance through downtown. From here, the 202 (also known as Whitehorn) runs past the zoo and the Max Bell Theatre to suburban McKnight-Westwinds. The other line (201) starts in the northwest at Crowchild station (northwest of Dalhousie), with stops at the university and Banff Trail (Motel Village). On the south side of the city, stations include two for Stampede Park and a bunch along Macleod Trail before ending in the far south of the city at Somerset-Bridlewood. C-train travel is free along 7th Avenue and $2.25 to all other destinations.

Passengers with Disabilities

All C-trains and stations are wheelchair accessible. Low-floor buses are employed on many bus routes; call ahead for a schedule. **Calgary Handi-bus** (403/537-7770, www.calgaryhandibus.com) provides wheelchair-accessible transportation throughout the city. A book of eight tickets is $12, but visitors receive free service for a limited length of time.

Taxi

The flag charge for a cab in Calgary is $2.75, and it's $1.45 for every kilometer. Taxi companies include **Advance** (403/777-1111), **Associated Cabs** (403/299-1111), **Checker Cabs** (403/299-9999), **Red Top** (403/974-4444), and **Yellow Cab** (403/974-1111).

Car Rental

If you're planning on starting your Alberta travels from Calgary and need a rental car, make reservations as far in advance as possible to secure the best rates. Rentals beginning from the airport incur additional charges, so consider renting from downtown or one of the many hotels that have representatives based in their lobbies.

Rental agencies and their local numbers include: **Avis** (403/269-6166), **Budget** (403/226-1550), **Discount** (403/299-1224), **Dollar** (403/221-1888), **Economy** (403/291-1640), **Enterprise** (403/263-1273), **Hertz** (403/221-1300), **National** (403/221-1690), **Rent-a-Wreck** (403/287-1444), and **Thrifty** (403/262-4400).

DINOSAUR VALLEY

East of Calgary, the Red Deer River has carved a deep valley through the otherwise featureless prairie, and in doing so has unearthed one of the world's most significant paleontological resources. But we should start at the beginning. As tremendous pressures deep below the Earth's surface forced the Rocky Mountains skyward 100 million years ago, a vast amount of water and sand, silt, and clay flowed eastward, piling up layer upon layer. Around 75 million years ago, the land east of what is now Calgary was a lush, almost tropical wetland that supported many kinds of animals. Many died in floods and were buried in the sediment. Jumping forward to 15,000 years ago, the end of the last ice age began, and with it the process of erosion. The layers of sediment were relatively non-resistant to water and wind erosion,

and over time a stark yet fascinating moonlike landscape known as the badlands formed. Remember those entombed creatures? Their preservation and subsequent forces of erosion have combined to create some of the world's richest dinosaur fossil beds. Hundreds of specimens from the Cretaceous period—displayed in museums throughout the world—have been unearthed along a 120-kilometer (75-mi) stretch of the river valley.

For generations, natives had regarded the ancient bones as belonging to giant buffalo. During early geographical surveys of southern Alberta by George Mercer Dawson, the first official dinosaur discovery was recorded. In 1884, one of Dawson's assistants, Joseph Burr Tyrrell, collected and sent bone specimens to Ottawa for scientific investigation. Their iden-

© ANDREW HEMPSTEAD

HIGHLIGHTS

◖ **Royal Tyrrell Museum:** The world's biggest museum devoted entirely to paleontology is the place to learn about the importance of Alberta's dinosaur-rich badlands (page 75).

◖ **World's Largest Dinosaur:** This one is especially for children – climb the stairs within this fiberglass monument and you'll soon emerge in the open mouth of a ferocious dinosaur (page 77).

◖ **Wayne:** With just a few dozen residents, this tiny town is a shadow of its former self, but the Western-style saloon still pours cold beer and the surrounding badlands make for a stunning backdrop (page 80).

◖ **Brooks Aqueduct:** This historic engineering marvel stands in mute testimony to man's ingenuity at irrigating the parched prairies (page 87).

◖ **Interpretive Tours at Dinosaur Provincial Park:** You can head out to explore the park yourself, but to really make the most of a visit, plan on joining a guided hike or bus tour into fossil fields otherwise off limits to the general public (page 91).

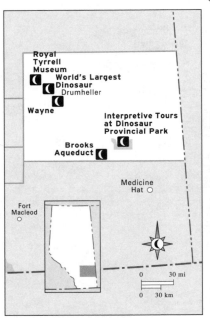

LOOK FOR ◖ TO FIND RECOMMENDED SIGHTS, ACTIVITIES, DINING, AND LODGING.

tification initiated the first real dinosaur rush. For the first century of digging, all of the dinosaur bones uncovered were transported to museums around the world for further study. A little over 100 years after Tyrrell's discovery, a magnificent museum bearing his name opened in the valley's main town, Drumheller. With more than 50 full-size dinosaurs exhibited, it is the world's largest dinosaur museum. Out in the field, Dinosaur Provincial Park is the mother lode for paleontologists. This UNESCO World Heritage Site includes a "graveyard" of more than 300 dinosaurs of 35 species, many of which have been found nowhere else in the world. As a comparison, Utah's Dinosaur Natural Monument has yielded just 12 species. The valley has more than just dinosaur skeletons, though; paleontologists have unearthed skin impressions, eggshells, dung, and footprints, as well as fossilized insects, fish, amphibians, crocodiles, and reptiles.

PLANNING YOUR TIME

Before charging out into the badlands, it is important to understand that the two major destinations, the town of Drumheller and Dinosaur Provincial Park, are not close to each other (even many Albertans assume they are), even though they are inextricably linked by dinosaurs. It is possible to visit each separately on a day trip from Calgary, but to visit both destinations in

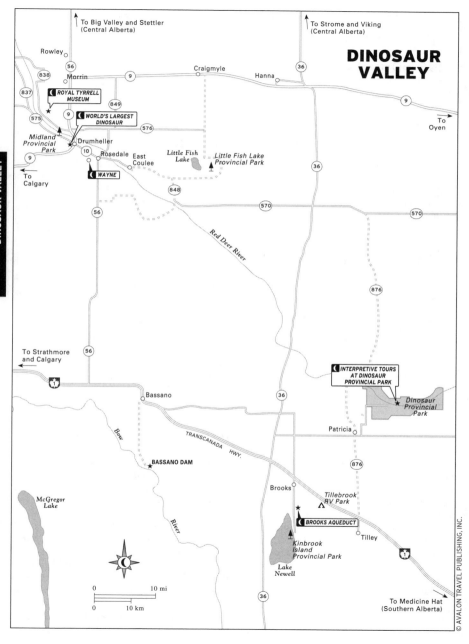

one day is a little much. Therefore, I'd recommend two day trips from Calgary, or a two-day excursion with an overnight along the way. With two days dedicated to dinosaurs, an itinerary might look something like this. Visit Drumheller's **Royal Tyrell Museum,** climb to the top of the **World's Largest Dinosaur,** and then spend the afternoon exploring the river valley, making your way to places like the ghost town of **Wayne.** The following day will be dedicated to exploring the region where many of the dinosaurs have been unearthed, a two-hour drive from either Drumheller or Calgary. Joining an **interpretive tour at Dinosaur Provincial Park** is the best way to learn more about the ancient creatures, but you should ensure a spot by making reservations well in advance. On the way back to Calgary, make the short detour to **Brooks Aqueduct.**

While campers heading to Dinosaur Valley are spoilt for choice, those looking for indoor accommodations should be aware that choices throughout the region are limited, so plan accordingly.

DINOSAUR VALLEY

Drumheller and Vicinity

Drumheller is one of Alberta's major tourist destinations. More than half a million people flock to this desolate part of Canada for one reason: dinosaurs. The city (pop. 6,600) is set in a spectacular lunarlike landscape in the Red Deer River Valley 138 kilometers (86 mi) northeast of Calgary. Ancient glacial meltwaters gouged a deep valley into the surrounding rolling prairie, and wind and water have continued the erosion process ever since. The city's proximity to some of the world's premier dinosaur fossil beds has made it a mecca for paleontologists. Scientists from around the globe come to Drumheller and its environs to learn more about the prehistoric animals that roamed the earth millions of years ago. For tourists, the Royal Tyrrell Museum is definitely the highlight of a visit to Drumheller, but there are many other diversions along the valley. Downtown itself is a little rough around the edges, but has been bought to life in recent years with the addition of dinosaur sculptures and murals.

History

For all the dinosaurs' popularity, coal, not dinosaurs, was the catalyst for the area's first settlement. Coal deposits had been found in the area by early explorers, but the first mine didn't open until 1911. By 1913, when the rail link was completed with Calgary, over 100 mines were in operation. Coal dominated the economy until after World War II, when diesel replaced steam and demand for coal dwindled. Today, the town is an agricultural and oil center, with 3,000 oil wells perforating the farmland within a close radius of town.

◖ ROYAL TYRRELL MUSEUM

So many of the world's great museums are simply showcases for natural history, yet nestled in the badlands six kilometers (3.7 mi) northwest of Drumheller, the Royal Tyrrell Museum (North Dinosaur Trail, 403/823-7707 or 888/440-4240, www.tyrrellmuseum.com, mid-May–Aug. daily 9 A.M.–9 P.M., Sept.–mid-Oct. daily 10 A.M.–5 P.M., the rest of the year Tues.–Sun. 10 A.M.–5 P.M., adult $15, senior $12, youth $9, under six free), the world's largest museum devoted entirely to paleontology, is a lot more. It integrates display areas with fieldwork done literally on the doorstep (it lies close by that first "official" discovery), with specimens transported to the museum for research and cataloging. Even for those visitors with little or no interest in dinosaurs, it's easy to spend half a day in the massive complex. The museum holds more than 80,000 specimens, including 50 full-size dinosaur skeletons, the world's largest such display.

The adventure starts as soon as you enter the facility, with a group of life-sized

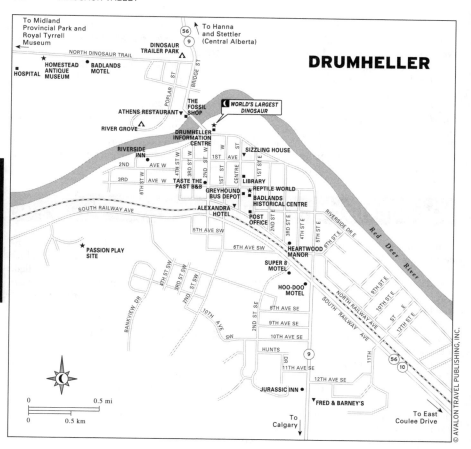

To Midland
Provincial Park and
Royal Tyrrell
Museum

To Hanna
and Stettler
(Central Alberta)

NORTH DINOSAUR TRAIL

DINOSAUR
TRAILER PARK

DRUMHELLER

HOSPITAL

HOMESTEAD
ANTIQUE
MUSEUM

BADLANDS
MOTEL

THE
FOSSIL
SHOP

WORLD'S LARGEST
DINOSAUR

ATHENS RESTAURANT

RIVER GROVE

DRUMHELLER
INFORMATION
CENTRE

RIVERSIDE
INN

SIZZLING HOUSE

2ND AVE W

1ST AVE

3RD AVE W

TASTE THE
PAST B&B

LIBRARY

REPTILE WORLD

GREYHOUND
BUS DEPOT

BADLANDS
HISTORICAL CENTRE

ALEXANDRA
HOTEL

POST
OFFICE

5TH AVE SW

SOUTH RAILWAY AVE

6TH AVE SW

HEARTWOOD
MANOR

PASSION PLAY
SITE

SUPER 8
MOTEL

HOO-DOO
MOTEL

Red Deer River

NORTH RAILWAY AVE

SOUTH RAILWAY AVE

RIVERSIDE DR E

8TH AVE SE

9TH AVE SE

10TH AVE SE

HUNTS

11TH AVE SE

12TH AVE SE

JURASSIC INN

FRED & BARNEY'S

To
Calgary

To East
Coulee Drive

0   0.5 mi

0   0.5 km

© AVALON TRAVEL PUBLISHING, INC.

Albertosaurus dinosaurs in a Cretaceous setting to welcome you. Beyond the lobby is a massive slowly revolving model of the earth set against a starry night—a perfect introduction to this planet's place in the universe. Beyond the globe, a "timeline" of exhibits covers 3.8 billion years of life on this planet, beginning with early life forms and the development of Charles Darwin's theory of evolution. Before the age of the dinosaurs, the Precambrian and Paleozoic eras saw life on Earth develop at an amazing rate. These periods are cataloged through numerous displays, such as the one of British Columbia's Burgess Shale, where circumstances allowed the fossilization of a community of soft-bodied marine creatures 530 million years ago. But the museum's showpiece is Dinosaur Hall, a vast open area where reconstructed skeletons and full-size replicas of dinosaurs are backed by realistic dioramas of their habitat. Another feature is the two-story paleoconservatory, featuring more than 100 species of plants, many of which flourished during the period when dinosaurs roamed the earth. Nearing the end of the tour, the various theories for the cause of the dinosaurs' extinction approximately 64 million years ago are presented.

DINOSAUR VALLEY

at the Royal Tyrrell Museum

The coming of the ice ages is described in detail, and humanity's appearance on Earth is put into perspective.

The museum is also a major research center; a large window into the main preparation laboratory allows you to view the delicate work of technicians as they clear the rock away from newly unearthed bones.

Interpretive Program

The badlands surrounding the complex can be explored along two short trails, but to get the most out of the experience, plan on joining a **Dinosite!** guided hike. These depart up to five times daily, last 90 minutes, and cost adult $12, child $8.

At the time of publication, the museum's popular Day Digs were suspended (excavation of the dig site was completed in 2006), but check the museum website for updates. Children continue to be catered for with a number of fossil-oriented excursions, including the three-night **Badlands Science Camp,** to which parents are also invited. The program lasts three nights (adult $225, child $190) and includes meals and tepee accommodations.

◖ WORLD'S LARGEST DINOSAUR

Start your downtown Drumheller touring by making your way to the visitors center, at the north end of 2nd Street W and signposted along all approaches. It's impossible to miss—out front is the world's largest dinosaur (403/823-8100, daily 9 A.M.–6 P.M., adult $2, children under five free). An actual *Tyrannosaurus rex* would have been intimidating enough towering over its fellow creatures millions of years ago. But this one is even bigger—at 26 meters (85 ft) high, it is four times as big as the real thing. A flight of stairs leads up to a viewpoint in its open mouth.

OTHER DOWNTOWN SIGHTS

The **Badlands Historical Centre** (335 1st St. E, 403/823-2593, May–Sept. daily 10 A.M.–6 P.M., July–Aug. until 9 P.M., adult $4) is a small museum with an interesting display

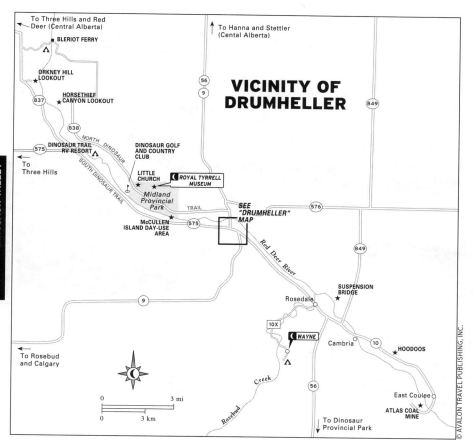

of privately owned and donated prehistoric pieces, most of which have been collected from the Red Deer River Valley. Exhibits include interpretive boards explaining the geography of the ancient inland sea, the process of coal formation, and the fossilization process. Items of particular interest are the mounted 10-meter-long (33-ft-long) skeleton of an edmontosaurus and the skull of a pachyrhinosaurus (the first of its species found), and a 10,000-year-old bison skeleton.

On the same block as the historical center, the country's largest collection of reptiles is housed at **Reptile World** (95 3rd Ave. E,

403/823-8623, summer daily 9 A.M.–10 P.M., in spring and fall until 6 P.M., adult $6.50, senior and child $4.50), where you can view and handle these much-maligned creatures.

It's easy to spend hours in the many shops that sell fossils, but the best in town is **The Fossil Shop** (61 Bridge St., 403/823-6774, daily in summer). Pieces start at $10 for chunks of unidentifiable dinosaur bones and go to thousands of dollars for magnificent ammonites from the United States. The owner is a knowledgeable local man who has spent his life collecting fossils from around the world.

Beyond the Fossil Shop is the **Homestead**

Antique Museum (two km/1.2 mi west of downtown, 403/823-2600, July–Aug. daily 9 A.M.–8 P.M., May–June and Sept.–Oct. daily 10 A.M.–5 P.M., $3), featuring mostly pioneer artifacts housed in a Quonset hut. The collection includes Indian relics, pioneer clothing, mining equipment, musical instruments, a two-headed calf, and re-creations of an early beauty parlor and barbershop. Outside is an array of farm machinery, automobiles, and a buffalo rubbing stone.

MIDLAND PROVINCIAL PARK

This 595-hectare (1,470-acre) park covers the lower part of Fox Creek Coulee on the northern bank of the Red Deer River. **McMullen Island,** created by an old river meander, is a secluded day-use area shaded by willows and cottonwoods. Pathways lead along the riverbank, and barbecues and a generous supply of wood are available. On the badlands side of the highway, the origins of the park become apparent. The only remaining building from extensive coal-mining operations is the mine office, from where the last miner's paycheck was handed out in 1959. Trails lead from this one-room building to slag heaps and foundations, the only remains of the actual mines. Many visitors to the park are not even aware that they're in it. The Royal Tyrrell Museum (see entry earlier in this chapter), from where rangers conduct short hikes during summer, is at the western end of the park.

LITTLE FISH LAKE PROVINCIAL PARK

Undulating hills of northern fescue grassland and the clear waters of Little Fish Lake provide the backdrop for this small park located 45 kilometers (28 mi) east of Drumheller via East Coulee. (For sights along the way, see *East Coulee Drive* in the following *Scenic Drives* section.) The park is also accessible off Highway 9, 40 kilometers (25 mi) south from Craigmyle. Both access roads are gravel. The nearby **Hand Hills** were used by both Cree and Blackfoot as a viewpoint. Many indications of the area's prehistory—mainly tepee

rings and campsites—have been found at the southeast end of the lake. The beach and cool water of the lake attract people from Drumheller, so the park can get busy on weekends. The lake is also popular with vacationing waterfowl en route to their summer arctic homes or returning in the fall. The primitive campground has pit toilets, a kitchen shelter, and firewood. Sites are $13.

SCENIC DRIVES
Dinosaur Trail

This 56-kilometer (35-mi) circular route to the west of Drumheller starts and ends in town and passes many worthwhile stops, including two spectacular viewpoints. After passing the access road to Royal Tyrrell Museum, the first point of interest is the **Little Church,** often described as being able to seat thousands—but only six at a time. The road then climbs steeply out of the valley onto the prairie benchland. Take the first access road on the left—it doubles back to **Horsethief Canyon Lookout,** where you can catch spectacular views of the badlands and the multicolored walls of the canyons. Slip, slide, or somersault down the embankment here into the mysterious lunar-like landscape, and it's easy to imagine why early explorers were so intrigued by the valley and how easy it was for thieves to hide stolen horses along the coulees in the early 1900s.

The halfway point of the trail is the crossing of the Red Deer River on the eight-vehicle **Bleriot Ferry,** one of the few remaining cable ferries in Alberta. It operates April–November daily 8 A.M.–10:40 P.M. Upstream from the ferry, a major dinosaur discovery was made in 1923 when the fossilized bones of a duck-billed edmontosaurus were unearthed. The road continues along the top of the valley to **Orkney Hill Lookout** for more panoramic views across the badlands and the lush valley floor. A "buffalo jump," where Indians once stampeded great herds of bison off the edge of the cliff, was located nearby, but centuries of erosion have changed the clay and sandstone landscape so dramatically that the actual position of the jump is now impossible to define.

East Coulee Drive

This 25-kilometer (15.5-mi) road, southeast from Drumheller, passes three historic coal-mining communities in an area dotted with mine shafts and abandoned buildings. The first town along this route is **Rosedale**. The community began on the opposite side of the Red Deer River around the Star Mine, but after the combined car and rail bridge was washed out, the town was moved to its present site. For many years, the mine still operated, with workers crossing the river on a suspension bridge to get to work. The bridge was built in 1931 but was later replaced by a cable-trolley system. Today, the original bridge has been upgraded and is safe for those who want to venture across it.

From Rosedale, Highway 10 continues southeast, crossing the Red Deer River at the abandoned mining town of Cambria and passing **hoodoos** to the left. These strangely shaped rock formations along the river valley have been carved by eons of wind and rain.

Hoodoos are a highlight along East Coulee Drive.

The harder rock on top is more resistant to erosion than the rock beneath it, resulting in the odd, mushroom-shaped pillars.

East Coulee once had a population of 3,000, but now it's under 500. Mining has taken place here since 1924, but building a rail line from Drumheller proved expensive. Eventually, part of the riverbank was blasted into the river, and the spur was completed in 1928. Full-time production at the main Atlas Mine ended in 1955, but the mine operated intermittently until the 1970s. Now protected as a National Historic Site, the **Atlas Coal Mine** (403/823-2220, mid-May–June daily 9:30 A.M.–5:30 P.M., July–Aug. daily 9:30 A.M.–8:30 P.M., Sept. daily 10 A.M.–5 P.M., adult $6, under six free) is through town and over the river. A wooden ore-sorting tipple—the last one standing in Canada—towers above the mine buildings. It's a great place to just walk around, or you can take the guided tour to learn more about the mining process. Back in town is **East Coulee School Museum** (403/822-3970, daily 9 A.M.–6 P.M., closed weekends Sept.–May), featuring a restored schoolroom, a coal-mining room, an art gallery, and a tearoom.

◖ Wayne

A worthwhile detour from East Coulee Drive is to Wayne, an almost–ghost town tucked up a valley alongside Rosebud Creek. It is nine kilometers (5.6 mi) south along Highway 10X, which spurs away from the river just south of Rosedale and crosses the creek 11 times. In its heyday early in the 20th century, Wayne had 1,500 residents, most of whom worked in the Rosedeer Mine. It was never known as a law-abiding town. During Alberta's Prohibition days, many moonshiners operated in the surrounding hills, safe from the nearest Royal Canadian Mounted Police (RCMP) patrol in Drumheller. By the time the mine closed in 1962, the population had dipped to 250 and then as low as 15 in the early 1990s, but now the population stands at approximately 30. Many old buildings remain, making it a popular setting for film crews. The oldest operating business in the sleepy hamlet is the 1913

A VILLAGE WITH A ROSY FUTURE

The past few decades have seen dozens of villages disappear from the prairies, as grain elevators get torn down, businesses close, and populations relocate to larger centers. But instead of withering up and dying, the small hamlet of **Rosebud,** 35 kilometers (22 mi) southwest of Drumheller and 100 kilometers (62 mi) northeast of Calgary, has seen a renaissance of sorts. This reversal in fortune can be attributed to the residents, the driving force behind what began as a small theater school and has grown to become a renowned college offering three-year fine-art-degree courses. Along the way, bed-and-breakfasts have opened, arty shops have sprung up around town, and many homes have been given new life.

Students in residence showcase their performance skills at the **Rosebud Theatre** (403/677-2001 or 800/267-7553, www.rosebud theatre.com), along the main street. The fun actually starts across the road from the theater in the restored Mercantile Building, where the actors and actresses serve up a buffet meal. Then everyone heads over to the 220-seat theater for a lively production, always lighthearted and often with a rural theme. Popular with day-trippers from Calgary, the daytime show (Wed.–Sun.) begins with lunch at 11 A.M., followed by the performance at 1:30 P.M. ($44). In the evening (Thurs.–Sat.), plan on being seated by 6 P.M. for dinner, with the show starting at 8:30 P.M. ($49).

Rosebud Country Inn (403/677-2211 or 866/677-2211, www.rosebudcountryinn.com, $120–150 s or d) is a stylish accommodation with 12 guest rooms. Some are on the small side, but all are charmingly decorated, with the central feature being a sleigh bed. Also on the plus side is air-conditioning and a long wraparound deck with river views. Rooms have private bathrooms and televisions, but no phones, and one is wheelchair accessible. Keep an eye on the goings-on in the village from the sunny veranda. Breakfast, presented buffet style, is included in the rates.

Rosedeer Hotel (403/823-9189) and its **Last Chance Saloon,** where the walls are lined with memorabilia from the town's glory days. It opens daily at noon, just in time for a lunchtime buffalo burger. The hotel's back porch overlooking the creek is a great place to sip on a beer and wallow in nostalgia, but unfortunately you won't be able to stay the night.

RECREATION AND ENTERTAINMENT

Drumheller's popularity as a tourist destination is relatively recent, and unfortunately this is reflected in facilities tailored almost exclusively to the needs of local residents. There's a bright spot for golfers, though. **Dinosaur Golf and Country Club** (403/823-5622, mid-Apr.–Sept.) is undoubtedly one of the most interesting in the province, with the back nine holes of lush fairways and greens winding through arid badlands, on high ridges, and through narrow coulees. It is located past the Royal Tyrrell Mu-

seum; greens fees are $49 (Mon.–Thurs. seniors pay $33) and a power cart with GPS is $32. The course has rentals, a range, and a restaurant.

Canadian Badlands Passion Play

This Canadian version of the theatrical production of the life of Jesus Christ tells the story of his birth, his death, and his resurrection. The three-hour production is an enormous affair, with a cast of hundreds in a natural amphitheater with bench seating for 2,500 set among the badlands. It takes place six times during the month of July. Tickets are $25 adult, $12.50 child. To get to the site, take South Dinosaur Trail west from downtown and follow the signs south on 17th Street (403/823-2001, www.canadianpassionplay.com).

Nightlife

Drumheller has always been a hard-drinking coal-mining town, and the after-dark scene reflects this tradition. Apart from the quiet lounge

in the Drumheller Inn, there is nowhere respectable to go. The **Alexandra Hotel** (30 Railway Ave. W, 403/823-2642) is a lively rock 'n' roll bar where bands play most nights; there's a cover charge Friday and Saturday. Go anywhere else and, if you're not careful, you'll finish up with more broken bones than an albertosaurus.

ACCOMMODATIONS AND CAMPING

Outside of the cities and the Canadian Rockies, Drumheller is the province's next-largest tourist center, attracting more than half a million visitors annually. Yet fewer than 450 hotel beds are available in town. Therefore, it is *imperative* you make reservations as far in advance as possible, especially through summer. If you do manage to get a room, you'll probably be paying more than you want. Options out of town include staying at the Rosebud Country Inn (see sidebar "A Village with a Rosy Future") or the Best Western property in Hanna (see the following section). The same applies if you're camping—make reservations or plan on staying at an out-of-town facility.

$50-100

Right on the town's main thoroughfare, **Taste the Past B&B** (281 2nd St. W, 403/823-5889, $85 s, $95–100 s or d) occupies the 100-year-old home of a coal baron. Guests choose between three simple rooms, but no one chooses to miss the full-cooked breakfast served in the sunny dining room. Period furnishings decorate public areas, including the living room, which is laid out around a fireplace. Outside, the well-tended garden is dotted with fossils.

Compared to other places in town, the rooms at **Badlands Motel** (toward the museum at 801 N. Dinosaur Trail, 403/823-5155, $70 s, $80 d, $90 kitchenette) are a steal. Decor is a little plain, but rooms are spacious and air-conditioned. Part of the complex is a pancake house that is busy from 6 A.M. when the doors first open for breakfast.

Similarly priced is the **Hoo-doo Motel** (corner of Highways 9 and 56, 403/823-5662, $95 s or d).

$100-150

Within walking distance of downtown is **Heartwood Manor** (320 N. Railway Ave., 403/823-6495 or 888/823-6495, www.innsat heartwood.com, $110–250 s or d), a classic country inn that looks a little out of place surrounded by older homes. You can splurge on the Main Turret room with a carriage bed, a fireplace, a jetted tub, and separate sitting area. Or choose one of six other rooms, all with a cozy Victorian feel thanks to antiques and plush duvets. All rooms have ensuites, but only some have televisions and phones. Rates include breakfast, served bedside if requested.

Two newer motels provide clean and comfortable accommodations, and each has an indoor pool. They are somewhat overpriced, but you really don't have much of a choice. The **Super 8 Motel** (680 2nd St., 403/823-8887 or 888/823-8882, www.super8.com, $149 s or d) is situated at Drumheller's busiest intersection. The 70 rooms are each equipped with a small fridge and a microwave. Rates include a light breakfast and use of the indoor pool and waterslide. Farther up the hill (back toward Calgary), as the highway enters the river valley, **Best Western Jurassic Inn** (1103 Hwy. 9, 403/823-7700 or 888/823-3466, www.best western.com, $139 s or d) offers similar facilities as well as a fitness room, a lounge, and one of Drumheller's better restaurants.

Camping

There are plenty of choices here, but reservations should still be made as far in advance as possible.

A personal favorite is **Dinosaur Trail RV Resort** (11 km/7 mi along North Dinosaur Trail, 403/823-9333, www.dinosaur trailrv.com, May–Sept.), an oasis of green between the river and the badlands five kilometers (3.1 mi) beyond the Tyrrell Museum. After a day exploring the region, back at the campground there's the option of casting a line from the riverbank for goldeye, floating downriver in a canoe (staff provide the upstream drop-off), cooling off in the outdoor pool, or exploring the adjacent badlands on

© ANDREW HEMPSTEAD

Heartwood Manor

foot. Other facilities include horseshoe pits, a playground, a grocery store, and a laundry. A number of serviced sites are laid out along the river, but most are dotted around the immaculately manicured grounds, shaded by rows of mature trees. Sites range from $26 for tents to $37 for a full hookup.

Back toward Drumheller, **River Grove Campground** (25 Poplar St., 403/823-6655, May–Sept., tent sites $25, hookups $29–36) is in a well-treed spot beside the Red Deer River and also offers welcome relief from the heat of the badlands. Serviced sites are semiprivate; tenters have more options and are able to disappear among the trees. The campground offers a nice stretch of sandy beach (by Albertan standards), mini-golf, and an arcade, and town is just a short stroll away. In the same vicinity, **Dinosaur Trailer Park** (corner of Highway 9 and North Dinosaur Trail, 403/823-3291, Apr.–Oct.) is also within walking distance of town. Find a spot among the permanent residents for $20–28.

At the end of the Dinosaur Trail is **Bleriot**

Ferry Provincial Recreation Area ($15) with 35 sites, plenty of free firewood, a kitchen shelter, and a small beach on the river.

Rosedale, east of Drumheller, has a small, free campground with pit toilets and a kitchen. It's at the back of town along the road to Wayne. Continuing up this road, **Wayne** has a small camping area ($9) with pit toilets and picnic tables over the green bridge.

FOOD

Like the accommodation scene, finding a restaurant in Drumheller is easy enough; finding a place you'll leave saying "that was a good meal" is a different matter.

At the Badlands Motel, out toward the museum, **Whif's Flapjack House** (801 N. Dinosaur Trail, 403/823-7595, 6 a.m.–3 p.m.) serves up a continuous flow of pancakes ($5–8) from when the doors first open each morning. It's your regular small-town burger joint the rest of the day.

All dishes at the **C Athens Restaurant** (71 Bridge St. N, 403/823-9400, 11 a.m.–10 p.m.)

are made from scratch, and everything is excellent. Appetizers are $4–8; try the lemon soup or large Greek salad. Greek entrées start at $12. The house specialty is Kleftiko, juicy spring lamb baked with herbs and spices; have it with the Greek salad for the full effect, or try the generous portion of moussaka. The small dining room is lively and informal, an abundance of greenery hangs from the ceiling, and later in the evening the chef can often be seen chatting with satisfied patrons. At the Best Western Jurassic Inn, **Stavros Family Restaurant** (1103 Highway 9, 403/823-7700, daily for breakfast, lunch, and dinner) has a clean, cool, and comfortable setting. The menu mixes European staples with familiar North American dishes, all for well under $20 per main.

Downtown, small-town **Sizzling House** (160 Centre St., 403/823-8098, daily for lunch and dinner), a popular and inexpensive eatery (everything except the seafood is under $10), dishes up mostly Szechuan and Beijing cuisine but also some Thai dishes. Finally, Drumheller is probably the only place in the world where you can find a Chinese restaurant called **Fred & Barney's** (1222 Hwy. 9 S, 403/823-3803, daily for lunch and dinner).

INFORMATION AND SERVICES

Drumheller Information Centre is in the local chamber of commerce building beside the Red Deer River at the corner of Riverside Drive and 2nd Street W (403/823-8100 or 866/823-3100, www.traveldrumheller.com, daily 9 A.M.–6 P.M., until 9 P.M. Fri. and Sat. during summer). You can't miss it—look for the seven-story *Tyrannosaurus rex* in front.

Drumheller Public Library (224 Centre St., 403/823-5382, Tues.–Thurs. 11 A.M.–8 P.M., Fri.–Sat. 11 A.M.–5 P.M., Sun. 1–5 P.M.) has public Internet access.

The post office is at 96 Railway Avenue E. You can wash your dusty clothes at the launderette in the Esso gas station on Highway 9 on the south side of town. It's open until 8 P.M. **Drumheller Hospital** (403/823-6500) is across the river from downtown at 351 9th Street NW.

It's impossible to miss Drumheller Information Centre – the world's largest dinosaur towers high above.

© ANDREW HEMPSTEAD

GETTING THERE AND AROUND

Greyhound (308 Centre St., 403/823-7566 or 800/661-8747, www.greyhound.ca) has frequent service between Calgary and Drumheller.

The town has no transit system, nor is there a shuttle out to the museum. For a cab, call **Roy's Taxi** (403/823-8883) or **Jack's Taxi** (403/823-2220).

HIGHWAY 9 EAST
Hanna
Hanna, 80 kilometers (50 mi) northeast of Drumheller along Highway 9, is a bustling prairie town of 2,500. Giant replicas of the Canada gray goose grace the entrances to town, but these birds are only part-time residents, resting in surrounding fields on migration routes. Hanna's best-known former residents are the members of the band Nickelback, who spent their younger years honing their now-distinctive grunge-rock sound on stage at Hanna's National Hotel.

Hanna, a onetime divisional point along the Canadian National Railway, is home to the country's only functioning turntable, where trains were turned around, and an adjacent roundhouse, where steam locomotives were sent for repair. Both structures have been saved from demolition and are slated for a long-term restoration project. **Hanna Museum** (east end of 4th Ave., 403/854-4244, June–Aug. daily 10 A.M.–6 P.M., $2) is a re-creation of a 19th-century village with a church, railway station, jail cell, steam engine, hospital, and schoolhouse.

Much of the bucking stock that throws the cowboys and woos the crowds at the Calgary Exhibition and Stampede is bred and raised through the "Born to Buck" program at **Stampede Ranch,** 50 kilometers (31 mi) south of Hanna along Highway 36. The 8,815-hectare (21,780-acre) spread is home to around 400 horses and 60 bulls. The ranch welcomes visitors by prior appointment only (403/566-3909), but don't let anyone talk you into going on a trail ride.

The **Hanna Inn** (113 Palliser Trail, 403/854-2400 or 888/854-2401, www.bestwestern.com) is a modern Best Western property where rack rates are $109 s or d. Each semispacious room comes with a fridge, microwave, coffeemaker, hair dryer, and large television. There's even room service, something not usually associated with small-town prairie motels. Off the lobby is an indoor pool and a fitness center. The inn's restaurant is popular with locals, serving steaks, seafood, and pasta until midnight. Back downtown, in an old butcher's shop, is **Food for Thought** (403/854-3850), a hopping deli serving delicious sandwiches.

Campers have a few choices. Beside the museum are some hookups (May–Sept., $15); three kilometers (1.9 mi) west of town is **Fox Lake Campground** (403/854-4433, May–Sept., $10–18) with swimming and free firewood; and 25 kilometers (15 mi) south is **Prairie Oasis Park** (403/779-2155, May–Oct., $10 unserviced, $15 powered), which has a good beach and swimming.

Hanna Tourist Booth (202 1st St, 403/854-4494, www.hanna.ca, mid-May–June daily

4–8 P.M., July and Aug. daily noon–8 P.M.) is in a train caboose along the highway beside Petro-Canada.

Oyen

From Hanna, Highway 9 continues east through many small communities to a short spur leading into Oyen, just west of the Saskatchewan border. At the north end of Main Street is a replica of a pronghorn antelope. Their numbers were decreasing until three national parks were created to protect them.

DINOSAUR VALLEY

PRONGHORN

These agile and graceful animals (often mistakenly called antelope) that roam Alberta's shortgrass prairie have made a remarkable comeback after being hunted to near extinction in the first quarter of the 20th century. They are easily recognized by their dark muzzles, tan bodies, and large white patches on the rump, cheeks, neck, and belly. Both sexes grow hollow, pronged horns that are shed annually.

Pronghorns have adapted well to life on the plains and are endowed with incredible attributes vital to their survival. Able to sustain speeds up to 80 kph (50 mph) over long distances, they are one of the fastest mammals in the New World. An oversized windpipe helps them to dissipate heat quickly as they breathe, allowing for large extended outbursts of energy. Telescopic eyesight enables them to detect movement over 1.5 kilometers (0.9 mi) away. When a member of the herd senses danger, hairs on its white rump will stand erect, silently alerting comrades to the threat.

The pronghorn's diet consists primarily of sagebrush, but they'll eat weeds and sometimes grass as well. They obtain sufficient moisture from these plants to allow them to survive hot, dry summers without much to drink. And as a safeguard against the long and severe prairie winters, these amazing creatures have developed hollow body hairs to insulate them from the cold.

When their numbers rebounded, the parks were abolished, and today many thousand live on the prairies. **Oyen Crossroads Museum** (312 1st Ave. E, 403/664-2330, July–Aug. daily 9 A.M.–5 P.M.) has many artifacts relating to the history of the area.

The **campground** in town is opposite the golf course; $10 for powered sites. At the junction of Highways 9 and 41 is a **Travel Alberta Information Centre** (403/664-2486, mid-May–June daily 9 A.M.–6 P.M., July–Aug. daily 9 A.M.–6 P.M.), handy for those entering the province here (this highway is the most direct route between Calgary and Saskatoon).

HIGHWAY 56 NORTH

As Highway 56 passes out of the Red Deer River Valley on the north side of Drumheller, it climbs onto the prairie benchland and heads due north for 100 kilometers (62 mi) to Stettler. Along the route, the towns of Rowley and Big Valley are worth investigating, and **Morrin,** just off the highway, 22 kilometers (14 mi) north of Drumheller, has an interesting sod house, similar to those that many of Alberta's earliest pioneers lived in.

Rowley

The first time I visited Rowley was late one evening. The streets were empty (as they are most of the time), and yet within a few minutes I was in the community hall having coffee and apple pie with members of the town's rapidly shrinking population. It's just that sort of town. Like other prairie towns, many of its residents have moved to larger centers and the town looks much as it did in the 1940s, but residents of Rowley have made good from bad. They actively promote the town and its empty buildings as a site for TV commercials and movies. Most of the shopfronts along the main street are locked, but someone is usually around to unlock them. In the back of the old café, you can watch videos of clips filmed in town. A small museum is near the rail line.

Big Valley

Located just west of Highway 56, Big Valley is a quiet town of 300 with a restored railway station. Through town to the west, the Red Deer River has carved a canyon 120 meters (400 ft) into the surrounding prairie.

Calgary to Dinosaur Provincial Park

STRATHMORE AND VICINITY

From Calgary, the TransCanada Highway parallels the Bow River (although it's never in sight) 100 kilometers (62 mi) to Bassano. The only town along the way is Strathmore, home to the large **Calgary Stockyards** (west side of town, 403/240-7694). Livestock auctions take place throughout summer and fall; if you're interested in attending, check www.calgary stockyards.com for a schedule. The year's biggest event is **Strathmore Heritage Days** (403/934-5811, www.strathmorerodeo.com), hosted at the agricultural grounds on the first weekend of August. Events include one of Canada's largest rodeos (daily at 1 P.M.), a stop on the World Professional Chuckwagon Association circuit (nightly at 6:30 P.M.), a midway,

and country music performers. These traditional rodeo goings-on are often overshadowed by the Saturday-night Running of the Bulls, where local adrenaline junkies pay $100 to get chased around the main rodeo ring by about 30 bloodthirsty bulls. It's actually a lot tamer than the Pamplona version, and a little different in that participants must be sober.

Wyndham-Carseland Provincial Park

Visit this 178-hectare (440-acre) park for the fishing and bird-watching. Rainbow and brown trout, up to 60 centimeters (24 inches) long, are caught in the Bow River where it flows through the park; the best fishing is in the deeper main channel. Also within the park

is a large population of white pelicans, as well as prairie falcons, Canada geese, kingfishers, and great blue herons. A 200-site campground is spread out along the river, and all sites are $20. The park is about 30 kilometers (19 mi) south of Strathmore via Highway 24 or 817.

BASSANO

Bassano is on the TransCanada Highway midway between Calgary and Medicine Hat. It's a thriving agricultural town of 1,200 people.

Bassano Dam

The biggest local attraction is this dam, nine kilometers (5.6 mi) south of Highway 1. To get there, follow the signs through town, along the rail line, and through the fields (if you cross a single-lane bridge, you're on the right road). The dam combines a 2.3-kilometer (1.4-mi) earthen embankment with a spillway at a sharp bend in the Bow River. Water is diverted from behind the spillway into a 4,500-kilometer (2,800-mi) system of gravity-fed canals supplying water to the 100,000-hectare (250,000-acre) **Eastern Irrigation District**, land that would otherwise be agriculturally worthless. Built by the Canadian Pacific Railway between 1910 and 1914, the dam was known as the most important structure of its type in the world because of its great length and unique foundations.

BROOKS

Brooks (pop. 10,000) is in the heart of Alberta's extensive irrigated farmlands, 160 kilometers (100 mi) east of Calgary along the TransCanada Highway. The town began as a railway stop in the 1880s, thriving when the Canadian Pacific Railway completed the irrigation system centered on Bassano Dam. Today, the oil-and-gas industry is important to the local economy, but it's Canada's largest meatpacking plant, on the west side of town, that gets most of the attention. The facility employs around 2,500 people, most of them immigrants from places like Sudan. This gives Brooks an interesting small-town ethnic diversity unlike anywhere else in Canada. For visitors, Brooks offers all tourist services and

is a good base for exploring Dinosaur Provincial Park (covered later in this chapter).

◖ Brooks Aqueduct

Brooks Aqueduct, seven kilometers (4.3 mi) southeast of town, was a vital link within the Eastern Irrigation District until decommissioned in the 1970s. It carried water across a shallow valley to dry prairie on the other side, opening up a massive chunk of otherwise unproductive land to farming. At the time of its completion in 1914, the 3.2-kilometer (two-mi) aqueduct was the longest concrete structure of its type in the world and had been designed and built using unique engineering principles. Although now replaced by an earth-filled canal, the impressive structure has been preserved as a National Historic Site and now serves as a monument to those who developed the region. Admission to the small interpretive center (403/362-4451, mid-May–Aug., daily 10 A.M.–6 P.M.) is free.

Brooks & District Museum

Brooks & District Museum (Sutherland Dr., 403/362-5073, Tues.–Fri. 10 A.M.–6 P.M., Sat.–Sun. noon–5 P.M., donation) catalogs the area's past from the era of dinosaurs to the heady days of a short-lived oil boom. Many restored buildings dot the grounds, including a log cabin built as an outpost for the North West Mounted Police (NWMP) in 1912, and the entrance is guarded by a five-meter-high replica of a hadrosaur. To reach the museum from Highway 1, take the eastern access road into Brooks.

Alberta Crop Diversification Centre

Curious gardeners won't want to miss the Alberta Crop Diversification Centre (two km/1.2 mi east of town, 403/362-3391), where research is done on greenhouse crops, various fruits, ornamental flowers, vegetables, oil seeds, and weed control. The grounds are an oasis of flowerbeds and experimental plots. Most of the outdoor beds are accessible for visitors on a self-guided walk, or join the tours that leave

DINOSAUR VALLEY

June–August Monday–Friday at 10:15 A.M. and 2 P.M.

Kinbrook Island Provincial Park

Part of this 48-hectare (120-acre) park 13 kilometers (eight mi) south of Brooks is an island in **Lake Newell**, the largest manmade body of water in Canada. Although the lake was developed as a constant source of water for Eastern Irrigation District farmland, it's swimming, fishing, and boating that draws the summertime crowds. The lake is home to northern pike, walleye, and whitefish, the latter two of which have been stocked in years gone by. The large expanses of freshwater attract many species of gulls, pelicans, and cormorants, which nest on the islands. The campground has showers, laundry, firewood, and picnic shelters, and a concession with bike rentals operates during summer. Unserviced sites are $20, powered sites $25; reservations are taken at 403/362-2962.

Accommodations and Camping

Vacant motel rooms can be difficult to find in Brooks because it's the last major stop along the TransCanada Highway before Calgary. The best of a bunch of cheapies along 2nd Street W (off the westernmost access to town) is **Tel-Star Motor Inn** (813 2nd St. W, 403/362-3466 or 800/260-6211, $66 s, $68 d). Each air-conditioned room has a microwave and fridge. As usual, the **Super 8 Motel** (Cassils Rd., 403/362-8000 or 800/800-8000, www.super8.com, $89 s, $95 d) is a good mid-priced choice. At the eastern access to town, this location features 61 air-conditioned rooms, each with a microwave. A continental breakfast is included in the rates. All 100 rooms at the **Heritage Inn** (1303 2nd St. W, 403/362-6666 or 888/888-4374, www.heritageinn.net, $85–95 s or d) are fairly spacious with comfortable

beds. Each also has a writing desk and coffeemaker. Other amenities include an indoor pool, a coffee shop, and a restaurant.

Kiwanis Campground (Cassils Rd. by eastern access, $10–14) has a few pull-though powered sites and a handy highway location, but better options exist out of town. Halfway between Brooks and Tilley is **Tillebrook Provincial Park** (403/362-4525, mid-Apr.–Oct., tents $20, hookups $23), one of several campgrounds built along the TransCanada Highway during that road's construction. Tillebrook is an excellent base for exploring Dinosaur Provincial Park and Lake Newell and is one of the province's best-developed parks. It has powered sites, enclosed kitchen shelters with gas stoves, showers, a launderette, and a trail to the aqueduct.

Food

Downtown, **Koffee Bean Kafe** (403 2nd Ave. W, 403/362-6467) is a reliable spot for coffee. Sandwiches are made to order and the cakes looked tempting when I stopped by. For something a little more substantial, try **Egan's** (119 15th Ave. W, 403/501-5656, daily for lunch and dinner), a kid-friendly Irish pub.

Information

Coming from the west, take the second Brooks exit from the TransCanada Highway to reach **Brooks Information Centre** (Cassils Rd., 403/362-6881, www.brooks.ca, Wed.–Sun. 11 A.M.–6 P.M.).

East to Medicine Hat

Continuing southeast from Brooks on the TransCanada Highway, it's approximately 100 kilometers (62 mi) across the prairies to Medicine Hat. For more information on Medicine Hat, see the *Southern Alberta* chapter.

Dinosaur Provincial Park

Badlands stretch along many river valleys throughout the North American plains, and some of the most spectacular sights are in 7,330-hectare (18,000-acre) Dinosaur Provincial Park, 200 kilometers (124 mi) east of Calgary. But the park is best known for being one of the most important dinosaur fossil beds in the world. Thirty-five species of dinosaurs— from every known family of the Cretaceous period—have been unearthed here, along with the skeletal remains of crocodiles, turtles, fish, lizards, frogs, and flying reptiles. Not only is the diversity of specimens great, but so is the sheer volume; more than 300 museum-quality specimens have been removed and are exhibited in museums around the world.

Originally established in 1955 to protect the fossil bone beds, the park's environment is extremely complex and is unique within the surrounding prairie ecosystem. Stands of cottonwoods, a variety of animal life, and, most important, the extensive bone beds, were instrumental in UNESCO's designation of the park as a World Heritage Site in 1979. In 1985, the opening of the Royal Tyrrell Museum, 100 kilometers (62 mi) upstream in Drumheller, meant that bones that had previously been shipped to museums throughout the world for scientific analysis and display could now remain within the province. The Royal Tyrrell Museum operates a field station in the park, where many of the bones are cataloged and stored. The displays, films, and interpretive programs offered at the center will best prepare you to begin your visit to the park.

Prehistory

Seventy-five million years ago, during Cretaceous times, the area was a low-lying marsh at the mouth of a river flowing into the Bearpaw Sea. The Bearpaw was the last in a succession of vast seas that covered the interior plains for 30 million years. Swamp grasses and reeds grew in the wetlands, whereas on higher ground, giant redwoods and palms towered over a dense forest. Dinosaurs flourished in this subtropical environment.

Over millions of years, great quantities of silt and mud were flushed downriver, building up a delta at the edge of the sea. In time, this delta hardened, and the countless layers formed sedimentary rock. Soon after, great pressures beneath the earth's surface pushed the crust upward, forming a jagged mountain range that we know today as the Rocky Mountains. This event dramatically changed the climate of the plains region from tropical to temperate, probably killing off the dinosaurs approximately 64 million years ago. From then until one million years ago, the climate changed many times until the first of many sheets of ice covered the plains. As the final sheet receded, approximately 15,000 years ago, millions of liters of sediment-laden meltwater scoured the relatively soft bedrock into an area we know as the badlands. The erosion process continues to this day, no longer by the action of glacial meltwater but rather by rain and wind. The carving action has created a dramatic landscape of hoodoos, pinnacles, mesas, and gorges in the sandstone here, which is 100 times softer than that of the Rockies. The hills are tiered with layers of rock in browns, reds, grays, and whites. Many are rounded, some are steep, others are ruddy and cracked, but they all have one thing in common—they are laden with dinosaur bones. As the Red Deer River curves through the park, it cuts deeply into the ancient river delta, exposing the layers of sedimentary rock and revealing the once-buried fossil treasures.

Fieldwork in the Park

Each summer, paleontologists from around the world converge on the park for an intense period of digging that starts in late June and lasts for approximately 10 weeks. The earliest dinosaur hunters simply excavated whole or partial skeletons for museum display. Although

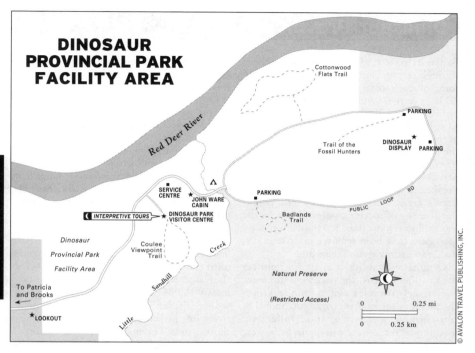

DINOSAUR VALLEY

the basic excavation methods haven't changed, the types of excavation have. "Bonebeds" of up to one hectare are painstakingly excavated over multiple summers. Access to much of the park is restricted in order to protect the fossil beds. Digging takes place within the restricted areas. Work is often continued from the previous season, or commences on new sites, but there's never a lack of bones. New finds are often discovered with little digging, having been exposed by wind and rain since the previous season.

Excavating the bones is an extremely tedious procedure; therefore, only a few sites are worked on at a time, with preference given to particularly important finds such as a new species. Getting the bones out of the ground is only the beginning of a long process that culminates with their scientific analysis and display by experts at museums around the world.

EXPLORING THE PARK

Much of the park is protected as a natural preserve and is off-limits to unguided visitors because excavations are taking place. The natural preserve protects the bone beds and the valley's fragile environment. It also keeps visitors from becoming disoriented in the uniform landscape and ending up spending the night among the bobcats and rattlesnakes. The area is well-marked and should not be entered except on a guided tour. One other important rule: *Surface-collecting and digging for bones anywhere within the park is prohibited.*

Dinosaur Park Visitor Centre

Your first stop should be the Dinosaur Park Visitor Centre (403/378-4342, late May to Aug. daily 8:30 A.M.–9 P.M., Sept. 9 A.M.–4:30 P.M., the rest of the year weekdays 9 A.M.–4 P.M., adult $3, senior $2.50, child $2), which is a field station associated with the Royal Tyr-

rell Museum. It offers many interesting displays that provide an overview of the park, its natural history, and the dinosaurs contained within. Complete dinosaur skeletons, a reconstructed 1914 paleontologist field camp, and a dinosaur documentary are highlights.

(Interpretive Tours

To make the most of your time in the park, you will want to join one of the park's daily tours. Not only do the guides provide an insight into the area, but some of the tours concentrate on the natural preserve where unguided public access is not allowed. The tours are *very* popular, and this is reflected in the procedure for purchasing tickets. Advance tickets (adult $8, child $4.50) go on sale May 1 and must be picked up 30 minutes before the departure time. To reserve a seat, call 403/378-4344, May–August Monday–Friday 9 A.M.–4 P.M. A small percentage of places on each tour are sold the day of as Rush tickets (adult $6.50, child $4.50); be

at the visitor center when it opens at 8:30 A.M. to ensure that you get a ticket. Finally, if seats become available through no-shows, you may be able to snag a seat at the last minute. An overview of the tours follows, or check www .dinosaurpark.ca for a schedule.

The **Badlands Bus Tour** takes you on a two-hour ride around the public loop road with an interpretive guide who will point out the park's landforms and talk about its prehistoric inhabitants. The **Centrosaurus Bone Bed Hike** takes visitors on a 2.5-hour guided hike into a restricted area where more than 300 centrosaurus skeletons have been identified. The **Camel's End Coulee Hike** is an easy 2.5-kilometer (1.5-mi) guided walk to discover the unique flora and fauna of the badlands. Best suited for families with younger children is the **Fossil Safari Hike** to a dig site. Finally, the **Prep Lab Talk** is a 40-minute behind-the-scenes look at the visitor center. This is the only tour that doesn't require reservations.

Documentaries are shown at the visitor center in the evenings, and special events are often staged somewhere in the park. The entire interpretive program operates June–August, with certain tours offered in late May and September.

On Your Own

You may explore the area bounded by the public loop road and take three short interpretive trails on your own. The **loop road** passes through part of the area where bones were removed during the Great Canadian Dinosaur Rush. By staying within its limits, hikers are prevented from becoming lost, although the classic badlands terrain is still littered with fragments of bones, and the area is large enough to make you feel "lost in time." It's a fantastic place to explore. Of special interest are two dinosaur dig sites excavated earlier in the 20th century, one of which contains a still-intact skeleton of a duck-billed hadrosaur.

The **Badlands Trail** is a 1.3-kilometer (0.8-mi) loop that starts just east of the campground and passes into the restricted area. The **Coulee Viewpoint Trail,** which begins

© ROYAL TYRRELL MUSEUM OF PALAEONTOLOGY

The Royal Tyrrell Museum is a world leader in dinosaur research, with much of the fieldwork taking place in Dinosaur Provincial Park.

DINOSAUR VALLEY

behind the Field Station, climbs steadily for 500 meters (1,650 ft) to a high ridge above Little Sandhill Creek. This one-kilometer (0.6-mi) trail takes 20 minutes. It's easy to ignore the nearby floodplains, but the large stands of cottonwoods you'll see were a contributing factor to the park being designated as a UNESCO World Heritage Site. The **Cottonwood Flats Trail** starts 1.4 kilometers (0.9 mi) along the loop road, leading through the trees and into old river channels that lend themselves to good bird-watching. Allow 30 minutes round-trip.

The 1902 log cabin of black cowboy John Ware has been moved to the park and restored, and it is now open to the public. Many regard Ware—originally a southern slave who came north on an 1882 cattle drive—as the greatest horseman ever to ride in the Canadian West.

ACCOMMODATIONS AND CAMPING

The park's campground is nestled below the badlands beside Little Sandhill Creek. It has 128 sites on two loops, pit toilets, a kitchen shelter, and a few powered sites. Unserviced sites cost $20, powered sites $23. In summer, the campground fills up by early afternoon, so plan ahead by reserving a site (403/378-3700).

Aside from the regular motels in Brooks, old-time accommodations are provided at the **Patricia Hotel** (16 km/10 mi southwest from the park, 403/378-4647). Known for its Western atmosphere, the hotel has basic rooms with shared and private baths from $40 s, $45 d. In the downstairs bar, many of the cattle brands on the walls date back more than 50 years. Choose from buffalo burgers or steaks at the nightly cook-your-own barbecue.

INFORMATION AND SERVICES

The only commercial facility within the park is the **Dinosaur Service Centre** (403/378-3777, late May–Aug. daily 10 A.M.–6 P.M.), where you can purchase hot snacks and cold drinks. Within the center are laundry facilities and coin showers, both of which are open 24 hours. No groceries are available in the park.

For information, contact Dinosaur Provincial Park at 403/378-4342, www.cd.gov.ab.ca/parks/dinosaur.

SOUTHERN ALBERTA

Southern Alberta is bordered to the east by Saskatchewan, to the south by Montana in the United States, and to the west by British Columbia. The Alberta–British Columbia border is along the Continental Divide, where the Canadian Rockies rise dramatically from the prairies and are visible from up to 200 kilometers (124 mi) away. From high in these mountains, the Oldman, Crowsnest, Waterton, St. Mary, and Belly Rivers flow east through the rolling foothills and across the shortgrass prairies into the South Saskatchewan River, which eventually drains into Hudson Bay. Among southern Alberta's rivers, only the Milk River is not part of this system; from its headwaters in northern Montana, the river flows north and east across southern Alberta before reentering the United States west of Wild Horse. From there, it joins the Missouri/Mississippi River System, eventually draining into the Gulf of Mexico. All of these rivers have carved deep gorges into the prairies, providing havens for many species of wildlife, including pronghorn, deer, foxes, coyotes, and bobcats.

For many people, a trip to southern Alberta starts in Calgary, from where they take Highway 2 south through Fort Macleod to Alberta's third-largest city, Lethbridge, a farming and ranching center 216 kilometers (134 mi) southeast of Calgary. Lethbridge offers many interesting things to see, including Fort Whoop-Up, a reconstruction of a notorious post where whiskey and guns were once traded with natives for buffalo hides.

East of Lethbridge, in an area declared "unsuitable for agriculture" by early explorer John Palliser, the city of Medicine Hat has grown up

HIGHLIGHTS

◖ Head-Smashed-In Buffalo Jump: The name may be the first thing to get your attention, but it is the ingenuity of generations of natives who used this ancient site that will amaze you (page 103).

◖ Sir Alexander Galt Museum: This fine museum covers the entire human history of southern Alberta, with sweeping valley views a bonus (page 107).

◖ Writing-on-Stone Provincial Park: One of North America's largest concentrations of native rock art is the highlight of this remote prairie park. Set on the Milk River, it also offers great canoeing (page 115).

◖ Red Rock Coulee: Hidden on a windswept ridge far from any highway, the photogenic vehicle-sized concretions that make up this badlands geological gem will amaze you (page 119).

◖ Remington Carriage Museum: With over 200 beautifully restored carriages on display, this museum will have you yearning for the romanticism of the world before automobiles (page 130).

◖ Akamina Parkway: You'll want to take both scenic drives in Waterton Lakes National Park, but this one gets the nod as a must-see attraction. Why? At the end of the road you can rent a canoe and paddle out onto magnificent Cameron Lake (page 141).

◖ Crypt Lake: This hike is undoubtedly the most spectacular in Waterton Lakes National Park, but it is also challenging, with one section requiring passage through a natural tunnel (page 144).

◖ Frank Slide: It is impossible not to be awed by the scope of the rock slide that devastated the town of Frank in 1913 (page 159).

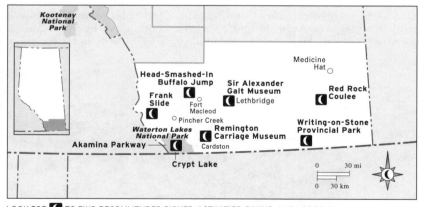

LOOK FOR **◖** TO FIND RECOMMENDED SIGHTS, ACTIVITIES, DINING, AND LODGING.

SOUTHERN ALBERTA

on top of vast reserves of natural gas. As you travel south from Medicine Hat, the Cypress Hills soon come into view, rising 500 meters (1,640 ft) above the prairies. The tree-covered plateau provides a refuge for many species of mammals, and mountain plants flourish here, far from the Rockies.

Southern Alberta reveals plentiful evidence of its history and prehistory. Thousands of years of wind and water erosion have uncovered the world's best-preserved dinosaur eggs near Milk River and have carved mysterious-looking sandstone hoodoos farther downstream at Writing-on-Stone Provincial Park—named for the abundant rock carvings and paintings created there by ancient artists. Head-Smashed-In Buffalo Jump, west of Fort Macleod, was used for at least 5,700 years by native peoples to drive massive herds of buffalo to their deaths.

The breathtaking mountainscapes of Waterton Lakes National Park are comparable to those of Banff and Jasper National Parks, Waterton's two northern neighbors. The route to the park is scenic because the transition from prairie to mountain peaks is abrupt. Most activities in the park center around the park's namesake, but the park also offers some of the best wildlife-viewing opportunities in the province. One of the highlights of a visit to Waterton is an international cruise across the border to Goat Haunt, Montana.

The Municipality of Crowsnest Pass comprises several small communities that extend from the ranching center of Pincher Creek west to the British Columbia border. They were established to serve the pass's coal-mining industry, but after a series of disasters—some mining-related, some not—the mines closed. Today the towns are only shadows of their former selves, and the entire corridor has been declared an ecomuseum. Here you can walk through the foundations of once-thriving communities, tour an underground mine, or climb infamous Turtle Mountain.

PLANNING YOUR TIME

The way you approach your time in southern Alberta starts with the direction of travel.

From Calgary, if your vacation is all about the south, it is a 600-kilometer (373-mi) loop on the three major highways (Hwys. 2, 3, and 1) to hit the major cities of Lethbridge and Medicine Hat. Most of the highlights are away from the main routes, however, so you would be more likely to cover 1,000 kilometers (621 mi), for which three or fours days is a good amount of time to allow. Alternatively, if you are approaching from the United States, after crossing the border from Montana you could easily spend three days winding your way north to Calgary and Banff. Regardless, even if you're zooming north in a single day you won't want to miss the native history associated with **Head-Smashed-In Buffalo Jump.** Spread out over two days, plan on adding **Sir Alexander Galt Museum** in Lethbridge and the **Remington Carriage Museum** in Cardston to your itinerary. **Writing-On-Stone Provincial Park** is fairly remote, unless you're coming north through Great Falls (Montana), from where it's only a short detour. Accommodations are nonexistent in and around the park, but the drive is worthwhile for the high concentration of native rock art. The path from this park to Medicine Hat is a network of rural roads through the driest portion of the province. You'll see numerous abandoned towns, irrigation reservoirs, and natural features such as **Red Rock Coulee.**

Simply because of its out-of-the-way location, you'll want to spend at least one day in Waterton Lakes National Park, exploring the two main roads, including the **Akamina Parkway** to Cameron Lake. This still allows time to walk some shorter trails. If you're a keen hiker, schedule a hike to magnificent **Crypt Lake.** The highway through the Crowsnest Pass makes a loop through the Canadian Rockies possible, or opens up an entire new vacation in the Kootenays region of British Columbia. Either way, you drive through the Crowsnest Pass, a low-key yet scenic area rich in coal-mining history, but also with its share of misery, which is most apparent at the **Frank Slide,** where a slab of Turtle Mountain destroyed a town in 1913.

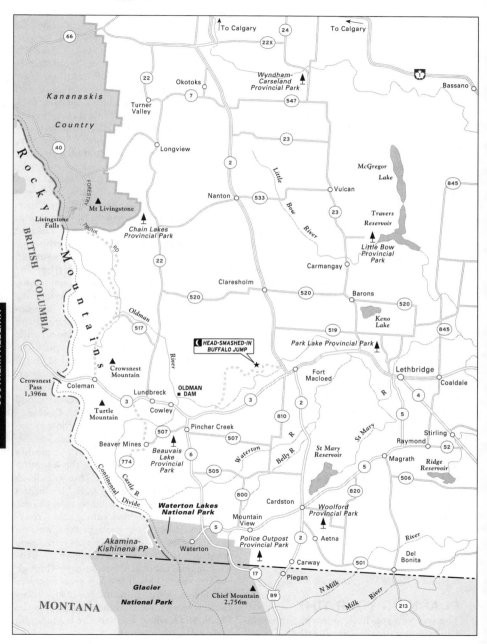

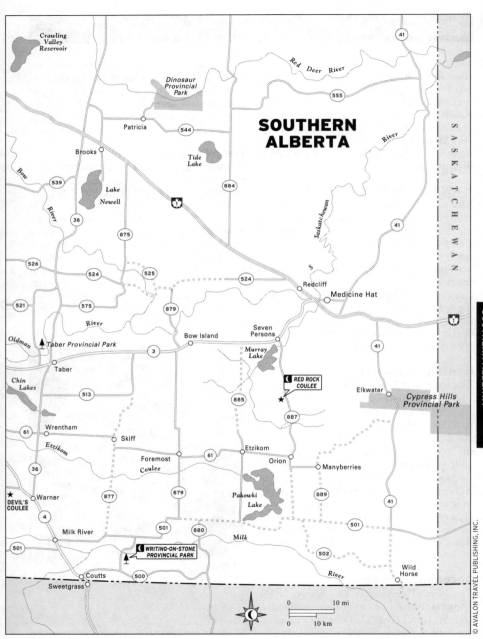

SOUTHERN ALBERTA

Crawling
Valley
Reservoir

Dinosaur
Provincial
Park

Red Deer River

41

555

SOUTHERN
ALBERTA

Patricia

544

River

Brooks

Tide
Lake

884

S
A
S
K
A
T
C
H
E
W
A
N

Bow

539

Lake
Newell

River

1

41

36

875

Saskatchewan

526

524

525

524

Redcliff

521

575

879

Medicine Hat

River

Bow Island

Seven
Persons

S

Oldman

Taber Provincial Park

3

Murray
Lake

RED ROCK
COULEE

41

Taber

Chin
Lakes

513

885

Elkwater

Cypress Hills
Provincial Park

887

61

Wrentham

Skiff

Etzikom

Etzikom

Orion

Manyberries

36

Foremost

61

889

41

Coulee

DEVIL'S
COULEE

Warner

877

879

Pakowki
Lake

4

Milk River

501

880

Milk

501

502

Wild
Horse

WRITING-ON-STONE
PROVINCIAL PARK

Coutts

500

River

Sweetgrass

0   10 mi

0   10 km

Calgary to Lethbridge

The trip between Calgary and Lethbridge takes about two hours nonstop, but there are many tempting detours in between, including the ranching country southwest of Calgary (see *Ranchlands* in the *West of Calgary* chapter), the Porcupine Hills west of Claresholm, historic Fort Macleod, and Head-Smashed-In Buffalo Jump, one of the best-preserved sites of its type in North America.

NANTON AND VICINITY

This town of 2,000 people, 70 kilometers (43 mi) south of Calgary, is a stop along busy Highway 2 and a supply center for nearby ranches. The highway divides on its way through town, with downtown businesses sandwiched between the two lanes. The air museum is accessed heading south while one of the province's only concentration of antiques shops lines the northbound lanes. Also northbound is an early-20th-century schoolhouse that functions as the local **information center** (403/646-5933, July–Aug. daily 9 A.M.–5 P.M.).

Nanton Lancaster Society Air Museum

This museum (Hwy. 2 southbound, 403/646-2270, May–Oct. daily 9 A.M.–5 P.M., Nov.–Apr. Sat.–Sun. 10 A.M.–4 P.M.) provides a home for one of the few Lancaster bombers still in existence. The Lancaster is a Canadian-built four-engined heavy bomber that played a major role in World War II air offensives on Nazi Germany. On the guided tour, you can sit in the plane's cockpit and look through the sight of the machine gun. A replica of another classic—a Vickers Viking biplane—sits outside. Other displays focus on Canada's role in World War II.

Accommodations

The best place to stay in Nanton is the **Ranchland Inn** (on Hwy. 2 northbound at 18th St., 403/646-2933, $65 s, $75 d), offering 26 basic but comfortable rooms. Across the railway tracks east of downtown along 18th Street is **Nanton Campground** (mid-May–Oct., $12), right beside the local 18-hole golf course. Scattered among a grove of trees, the sites have picnic tables, and campers have the use of a covered cooking shelter and showers.

Willow Creek Provincial Park and Vicinity

South of Nanton, along the eastern edge of the Porcupine Hills and 14 kilometers (8.7 mi) west of the traffic roar on Highway 2, is Willow Creek Provincial Park. Willow Creek is a quiet stream that meanders through a forested valley, with generations of native tribes having camped in the area (near the park entrance are tepee rings well-hidden in the grass). But in 2005 floodwater poured through the park, destroying infrastructure that took until early 2007 to repair. Up on the benchland is a campground (403/549-2162, May–mid-Oct., $20)

Nanton's antiques shops are well worth a stop.

with limited facilities. To reach the park, head west from Highway 2 at Stavely.

Farther downstream on Willow Creek lies another historical site. **The Leavings** was a stopover on the Macleod Trail, aptly named to remind travelers they were leaving the last supply of water before Calgary. Later used as a North West Mounted Police (NWMP) post, the site was abandoned when the railway was laid farther to the east. Many sandstone foundations remain, as well as some log cabins and a sandstone barn with tree-trunk floorboards. By road the site is seven kilometers (4.3 mi) west of Highway 2 near Pultenay.

CLARESHOLM

When the Calgary and Edmonton Railway Line extended south from Calgary in 1891, a new town emerged at its southern terminus. As boomtown storefronts sprang up along the rail line and large landholdings were bought nearby, the town quickly gained a reputation as the hub of a leading grain-producing area and has prospered ever since.

Most people stop at Claresholm (pop. 3,600), 100 kilometers (62 mi) south of Calgary, just long enough to fill up with gas, grab a burger, and stretch their legs. But it's worth more than a quick stop—allow at least enough time to pop into the museum and then do a lap of the downtown core and its many historic buildings (those facing Highway 2 are the oldest).

Sights

The **Claresholm Museum** (5126 Railway Ave., 403/625-3131, mid-May–Aug. daily 9:30 A.M.– 5:30 P.M., donation), in the sandstone Canadian Pacific Railway (CPR) station, holds an array of historical displays, including a dental clinic and a rail ticket office. A brochure entitled *A Walking Tour of Claresholm,* available from the museum, details the town's historic buildings and sites. The Claresholm **tourist information center** is also inside the museum.

The **Appaloosa Horse Club of Canada** has a small display at its Canadian headquarters (4189 3rd St. E, 403/625-3326, year-round Mon.–Fri. 8:30 A.M.–4:30 P.M.). One of only two such displays in the world, the centerpiece in the false-fronted building is a native saddle dating to 1810.

Accommodations and Camping

Motels and fast-food restaurants line Highway 2. The nicest rooms (by far) are at the ◖ **Bluebird Motel** (403/625-3395 or 800/661-4891, www.bluebirdmotel.ab.ca, $69–86 s or d) at the north end of town. All rooms are air-conditioned and feature coffeemakers and large TVs, most also have refrigerators, and the more expensive ones have cooking facilities.

Centennial Park (4th St. W, north off Hwy. 520, 403/625-2751) is in a residential area close to the golf course. It offers powered sites, showers, and kitchen shelters; unserviced sites $13, hookups $17–20.

Porcupine Hills

The Porcupine Hills, west of Claresholm on Highway 520, rest between the mountains and the plains, yet rise higher than the foothills to the west and support vegetation from four climatic zones: grassland, parkland, subalpine forest, and montane. They are bordered to the east by Highway 2, to the west by Highway 22, and extend south to Head-Smashed-In Buffalo Jump and north past Nanton. The Blackfoot call the area *Ky-es-kaghp-ogh-suy-is* (porcupine tails), describing how the forested ridges looked to natives. The heavily wooded Porcupine Hills are home to a variety of wildlife, including white-tailed and mule deer, elk, moose, coyote, lynx, beaver, pheasant, and wild turkey.

From Claresholm, Highway 520 climbs slowly west for 32 kilometers (20 mi), passes through Burke Creek Ranch (one of Alberta's oldest ranches—look for classic buildings scattered by the creek), and continues into the **Rocky Mountain Forest Reserve.** It eventually crests a hill, affording breathtaking views of the Canadian Rockies before dropping to Highway 22. At this hillcrest, **Skyline Road** branches off to the south into the Porcupine Hills, where rewarding hiking trails and sweeping views await explorers. Roads through this area can take you all the way to Cowley.

SOUTHERN ALBERTA

HIGHWAY 23 SOUTH

An eastern alternative to four-lane Highway 2 between Calgary and Lethbridge is Highway 23. From High River, it runs east past Frank Lake; after 35 kilometers (22 mi) it turns south, skirting the western edge of the prairies. Along the way you'll pass the wheat-farming towns of Vulcan, Champion, Carmangay, and Barons. Highway 23 ends on Highway 3, 17 kilometers (10.5 mi) west of Lethbridge.

Vulcan

Halfway between Calgary and Lethbridge on Highway 23 lies Vulcan (pop. 1,600), named after the Greek god who lived on Mount Olympus—the townsite sits on a not-so-Olympian rise above the surrounding prairie. Vulcan is also known as the "Wheat Capital of Canada" and has 12 grain elevators capable of holding more than two million bushels of grain total. The town also plays on its name, hosting "conventions" and operating the distinctive **Vulcan Tourism and Trek Station** (115 Centre St. E, 403/485-2944, May–Sept. Mon.–Sat. 9 A.M.–6 P.M., Sun. noon–6 P.M.) as an information center. Inside is a wealth of movie-related memorabilia while out front is a replica of the USS *Enterprise,* with a description in both English and Klingon.

Little Bow Provincial Park

On the banks of Travers Reservoir east of Champion is Little Bow Provincial Park, an extremely popular place for fishing, swimming, and boating, especially on summer weekends. Heavy irrigation creates the park's green lawns and lush vegetation—a welcome sight after driving through parched and scorched prairies. Some of the province's largest pike live in the reservoir, a feature that attracts anglers year-round. Canoe rentals are available from a lakeside concession. The large campground (403/897-3937, May–early Oct., $20) has a beach, kitchen shelter, showers, and firewood.

On the access road to the park, 1.6 kilometers (one mi) from Highway 23, a stone cairn marks the site of Cleverville, a once-busy town forced to move when bypassed by

the CPR. The new town, now at the junction of Highway 23 and the park access road, was named Champion and today serves as a center for nearby wheat farms. The **Champion Inn** (403/897-3055) offers basic but clean rooms with shared bathrooms for $45 s or d, $50 with private bathroom. Downstairs is a restaurant (daily 7 A.M.–10 P.M.) and a bar.

Tepee Rings in a Field

In an unimposing grassy field between Highway 23 and Little Bow River just north of Carmangay are nine circles of stone, mute testimony to the prehistoric people who roamed the plains of North America. Dated at 300 to 1,700 years old, the stones, known as tepee rings, were used to hold down the edges of natives' conical, bison-hide-covered tents. The lack of other artifacts, such as tools and bones, leads archaeologists to believe that this particular site was used for only a short time. A well-worn path leads from interpretive boards to a ring that has been partially disturbed; better rings lay to the left of the path.

FORT MACLEOD

Southern Alberta's oldest permanent settlement is Fort Macleod (pop. 3,200), 172 kilometers (107 mi) south of Calgary and 44 kilometers (27 mi) west of Lethbridge and just east of the junction of Highways 2 and 3. While nearby Head-Smashed-In Buffalo Jump gets all the attention, the downtown core of Fort Macleod is one of western Canada's finest remaining examples of an early-1900s streetscape.

History

In 1873, the West was in turmoil. Relations between American whiskey traders and natives had reached an all-time low, and intertribal wars were resulting in murder and massacre. That's when politicians in eastern Canada decided to curb the unbecoming behavior. A paramilitary mounted police force, led by Colonel James F. Macleod, was sent west with orders to close down Fort Whoop-Up, a notorious whiskey-trading post located where the city of Lethbridge now stands. After finding it

empty, they decided to push farther west and build their own fort. The site chosen was an island in the Oldman River, one kilometer (0.6 mi) east of the present town of Fort Macleod. These early Mounties constructed the fort for the same reason as the whiskey traders—to prevent attacks by natives. But although the whiskey traders were encouraging natives to visit and trade their precious pelts, the police force was trying to drive the traders out of the region. These first troops of the NWMP eventually put an end to the illicit whiskey trade,

and with the help of Métis scout Jerry Potts—who ironically didn't mind a drop of the hard stuff himself—they managed to restore peace between the warring tribes. Potts stayed at Fort Macleod until he died and is buried in the local cemetery. The original fort had continual flooding problems. It was relocated to higher ground in the 1880s, and the town of Fort Macleod gradually grew up around it.

Historic Downtown

In 1906, a fire destroyed most of the wooden

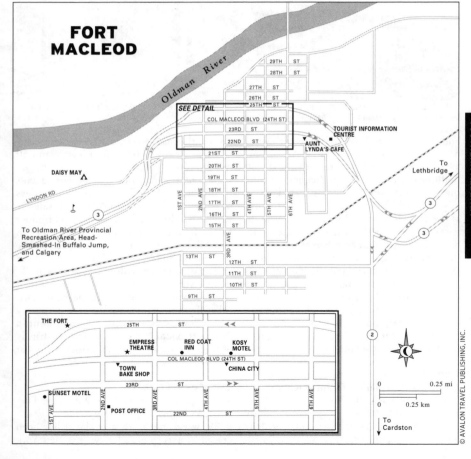

SOUTHERN ALBERTA

© ANDREW HEMPSTEAD

Col. Macleod Boulevard, Fort Macleod's main street, is protected as a provincial historic area for its many 100-year-old buildings.

buildings, so a bylaw was passed requiring any new structures to be built of brick or stone. The legacy of this bylaw remains in the 30 buildings of historical significance forming the downtown core, which has been declared a "provincial historic area." Many buildings along Col. Macleod Boulevard (the main street) function as they did during the town's boom years: the **Queen's Hotel** has rooms, the **Empress Theatre** is the oldest operating theater in the province, and the town office is contained in the only remaining courthouse that dates from Alberta's days as part of the North-West Territories. Throughout summer, guided walking tours of town leave regularly from the fort. Or you can get the walking-tour brochure and do it at your own pace.

The Fort

The original fort on the Oldman River would have looked much like the replica fort (219 25th St., 403/553-4703, July–Aug. daily 9 A.M.–6 P.M., the first two weeks of Sept. daily 9 A.M.–5 P.M., adult $8, senior $7, child $4.50)

just off the main street, a crude structure approximately 40 meters (130 ft) wide and 50 meters (160 ft) long lined with buildings facing a central courtyard. The museum details the history of the NWMP and the early days of settlement in southern Alberta. Inside are various buildings reflecting aspects of frontier life, including a chapel, a blacksmith shop, an NWMP building, a law office, a tepee, and the Centennial Building, which is devoted to history of the Plains tribes. Two corner blockhouses with panoramic views of the Oldman River were used as lookouts. In the main arena, riders dress in period costume and perform a scaled-down version of the famous **Mounted Police Musical Ride**—a spectacular display of precision riding—July and August daily at 10 A.M., 11:30 A.M., 2 P.M., and 3:30 P.M.

Empress Theatre

The stage of the venerable 1912 Empress Theatre (235 Main St., 403/553-4404 or 800/540-9229, www.empresstheatre.ab.ca) has been graced by acts from as far away as New York

and Australia. Through its long history it has hosted vaudeville shows, opera and theater performances, political rallies, and film screenings—changing uses with the changing times. Extra care has been taken to return it to its former glory, down to restoring existing floorboards and reupholstering the original seats. Now once again it provides a venue for live shows and musical theater, with room for over 350 patrons, 100 of which get to sit on the balcony. Through the months of summer, three or four different productions are performed by the Great West Theatre. Most shows are less than $10. In July and August free walking tours depart the lobby daily at 12:15 P.M., 2:45 P.M., and 4:15 P.M.; reservations are not necessary.

Accommodations

Motel rooms fill up fast every afternoon in summer, so book ahead or check in early. All of the motels offer air-conditioned rooms—a definite plus to combat the summer heat. Rates fluctuate with the season; expect to pay 20–30 percent less outside of summer.

At the **Kosy Motel** (433 24th St., 403/553-3115, $60 s, $70 d), the 12 rooms are clean and comfortable and each has a small fridge. Barbecues are also supplied. At the west entrance to town is the **Sunset Motel** (104 Highway 3 W, 403/553-4448 or 888/554-2784, $58 s, $64 d), where each of the 22 rooms has a small fridge. Coffee and toast are available in the morning. One step up is the **Red Coat Inn** (359 24th St., 403/553-4434 or 800/423-4434, www.redcoat inn.com, $70 s, $75 d, $100 kitchenette), offering air-conditioned rooms and an indoor pool.

Daisy May Campground (249 Lyndon Rd., 403/553-2455, May–Sept.) is beside the oldest golf course west of Winnipeg and is within walking distance of downtown. It provides showers, a camp kitchen, a heated pool, laundry facilities, and a game room. Tent sites cost $20, hookups $22–27.

Food

At the east end of the main street, **Aunty Lynda's Cafe** (2323 7th Ave., 403/553-2655, Mon.–Sat. 8 A.M.–9 P.M.) offers welcoming

home-style cooking, including breakfasts well under $10. **China City** (404 24th St., 403/553-4066, Mon.–Sat. 6 A.M.–midnight, Sun. 6 A.M.–10 P.M.) is your typical all-day, small-town diner, and the locals never want it any other way. Big breakfasts are $6 and lunch and dinner items range $6.50–16, with, as the name suggests, many Chinese choices.

Information and Services

The tourist information center (east end of town on Hwy. 3, 403/553-4955, www.fort macleod.com) is open mid-May to August daily 9 A.M.–5 P.M. The Fort gift shop has a large selection of local history and Canadiana books. The library (264 Col. Macleod Blvd., 403/553-3880) is open Monday–Saturday 1–5 P.M. Behind the Sunset Motel is **Laundrette Kome Kleen** (daily 8 A.M.–10 P.M.).

Greyhound (2302 2nd Ave., 403/553-3383, www.greyhound.ca) leaves five times daily for Calgary and twice daily for Lethbridge.

◖ HEAD-SMASHED-IN BUFFALO JUMP

Archaeologists have discovered dozens of buffalo jumps across the North American plains. The largest, oldest, and best preserved is Head-Smashed-In, which is located along a weathered sandstone cliff in the Porcupine Hills 19 kilometers (12 mi) northwest of Fort Macleod. At the base is a vast graveyard with thousands of years' worth of bones from butchered bison piled 10 meters (33 ft) high. The jump represents an exceptionally sophisticated and ingenious hunting technique used by Plains natives at least 5,700 years ago—possibly up to 10,000 years ago—to cunningly outwit thousands of bison, once the largest mammal on the plains.

At the time white settlers arrived on the prairies, more than 60 million American bison (also known as buffalo) roamed the plains. The people of the plains depended almost entirely on these prehistoric-looking beasts for their survival. They ate the meat fresh or dried it for pemmican; made tepees, clothing, and moccasins from the hides; and fashioned tools and

decorations from the horns. Several methods were used to kill the bison, but by far the most successful method was to drive entire herds over a cliff face. The topography of this region was ideal for such a jump. To the west is a large basin of approximately 40 square kilometers (15 square miles) where bison grazed. They were herded from the basin east along carefully constructed stone cairns (known as drive lines) that led to a precipice where the stampeding bison, with no chance of stopping, plunged to their deaths. Nearby was a campsite where they butchered and processed the meat.

The site has been well preserved. Although a small section of the hill has been excavated, most of it appears today the same as it has for thousands of years. The relative height of the cliff, however, drastically decreased with the buildup of bones. Along with the bones are countless numbers of artifacts such as stone points, knives, and scrapers used to skin the fallen beasts. Metal arrowheads found in the top layer of bones indicate that the jump was used up until the coming of whites in the late 1700s. In recognizing the site's cultural and historical importance, UNESCO declared the jump a World Heritage Site in 1981.

Allow at least two hours at the Head-Smashed-In Interpretive Centre.

How the Jump Got Its Name

The name Head-Smashed-In has no connection to the condition of the bison's heads after tumbling over the cliff. It came from a Blackfoot legend: About 150 years ago, a young hunter wanted to watch the buffalo as they were driven over the steep cliff. He stood under a ledge watching as the stampeding beasts fell in front of him, but the hunt was better than usual, and as the animals piled up, he became wedged between the animals and the cliff. Later his people found him, his skull crushed under the weight of the buffalo—hence the name, Head-Smashed-In.

Interpretive Centre

As you approach the jump site along Spring Point Road, the Head-Smashed-In Interpretive Centre (403/553-2731, www.head-smashed-in.com, summer daily 9 A.M.–6 P.M., the rest of the year daily 10 A.M.–5 P.M., adult $9, senior $8, child $5) doesn't become visible until you've parked your car and actually arrived at the entrance. The center—disguised in the natural topography of the landscape—is set into a cliff, part of which had to be blasted away to build it. A series of ramps and elevators marks the beginning of your tour as you rise to the roof from where a trail leads along the clifftop to the jump site. It isn't hard to imagine the sounds and spectacle of thousands of bison stampeding over the rise to the north and tumbling to their deaths below. To the east is the **Calderwood Buffalo Jump,** which can be seen farther along the cliff face.

Back inside you walk down floor by floor, passing displays and films explaining in an interesting and informative way the traditional way of life that existed on the prairies for nearly 10,000 years, as well as the sudden changes that took place when the first white men arrived. The lowest level describes the archaeological methods used to excavate the site and

how the ancient cultures of the various Plains peoples are unraveled from the evidence found. A 10-minute movie, *In Search of the Buffalo,* cataloging the hunt, is shown every half hour on Level Four.

Outside the center is another trail that leads along the base of the cliff for a different perspective. Here a large aluminum building covers a recent dig site; the ground is littered with shattered bones. The center also has a gift shop and café selling, of all things, buffalo burgers. Through July and August, dancing and drumming demonstrations take place Wednesday afternoon.

Lethbridge

An urban oasis on the prairies, this city of rich ethnic origins has come a long way since the 1860s when Fort Whoop-Up, the most notorious whiskey-trading fort in the West, was the main reason folks came to town. Today, Lethbridge is an important commercial center serving the surrounding ranch and farm country. With a population of 70,000, it is Alberta's third-largest city, and on any given day the downtown streets are busy with a colorful array of ranchers, cowboys, Hutterites, natives, and suited professionals. The city is also a transportation hub, with Highways 3, 4, and 5 converging here. Calgary is 216 kilometers (134 mi) to the north, Medicine Hat 168 kilometers (104 mi) to the east, Waterton Lakes National Park 130 kilometers (81 mi) to the west, and the U.S. border 105 kilometers (65 mi) to the south.

In the last 30 years, Lethbridge has blossomed in a controlled way. Many of the city's sites of historical importance have been preserved, or in the case of Fort Whoop-Up, reconstructed. The Sir Alexander Galt Museum is already one of the best museums in the province and is still expanding, and the Nikka Yuko Japanese Garden is symbolic of the culture from which many of the city's residents descended.

History

This area was the territory of various tribes of the powerful Blackfoot Confederacy. They sheltered themselves from the extreme winters at a site in the Oldman River Valley known to them as *Sik-ooh-kotoks* (black rocks). The first white traders to the area arrived in the 1850s. Soon after came the whiskey traders who had been forced north by the U.S. Army. Fort Whoop-Up, built on the east bank of the Oldman River, became the most notorious of approximately 50 whiskey posts in southern Alberta.

The arrival of whiskey on the plains coincided with a smallpox epidemic and the dislocation of the Cree, who had been forced by the arrival of European settlers into the territory of the Blackfoot, their traditional enemies. These factors combined to create a setting for the last great intertribal battle to be fought in North America.

At dawn on October 25, 1870, a party of approximately 800 Cree warriors attacked a band of Blood Blackfoot camping on the west bank of the Oldman River. Unknown to the Cree, a large party of Peigan Blackfoot was camped nearby. Alerted by scouts, the Peigan crossed the river and joined the fray, forcing the Cree back into what is now known as Indian Battle Park. More than 300 Cree and approximately 50 Blackfoot were killed.

By 1880, the whiskey forts had been closed down by the NWMP, and the last of the natives had been resettled in reserves.

In the 1880s an English entrepreneur named Elliot Galt heard of a small coal-mining operation beside the Oldman River and with the help of his father, Sir Alexander Galt, financed a large-scale drift mine in the east bank of the river, where the Coalbanks Interpretive Site now sits. At first the Galts used sternwheel river steamers to transport the coal to Medicine Hat, but on many occasions the current was

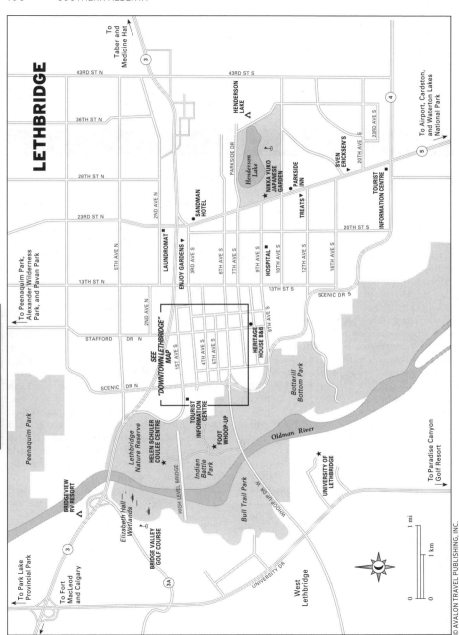

LETHBRIDGE

SEE "DOWNTOWN LETHBRIDGE" MAP

To Taber and Medicine Hat

43RD ST N

43RD ST S

To Airport, Cardston, and Waterton Lakes National Park

HENDERSON LAKE

36TH ST N

23RD AVE S

20TH AVE S

PARKSIDE DR

Henderson Lake

SVEN ERICKSEN'S

28TH ST N

2ND AVE N

NIKKA YUKO JAPANESE GARDEN

PARKSIDE INN

TOURIST INFORMATION CENTRE

SANDMAN HOTEL

TREATS

23RD ST N

20TH ST S

5TH AVE N

LAUNDROMAT

3RD AVE S

6TH AVE S

7TH AVE S

9TH AVE S

HOSPITAL

10TH AVE S

12TH AVE S

16TH AVE S

ENJOY GARDENS

13TH ST N

13TH ST S

SCENIC DR S

2ND AVE N

9TH AVE S

STAFFORD DR N

4TH AVE S

5TH AVE S

HERITAGE HOUSE B&B

Botterill Bottom Park

1ST AVE S

SCENIC DR N

To Peenaquim Park, Alexander Wilderness Park, and Pavan Park

TOURIST INFORMATION CENTRE

FORT WHOOP-UP

Oldman River

Lethbridge Nature Reserve

HELEN SCHULER COULEE CENTRE

Indian Battle Park

Peenaquim Park

To Paradise Canyon Golf Resort

BRIDGEVIEW RV RESORT

HIGH LEVEL BRIDGE

Bull Trail Park

UNIVERSITY OF LETHBRIDGE

WHOOP-UP DR W

To Park Lake Provincial Park

To Fort MacLeod and Calgary

Elizabeth Hall Wetlands

BRIDGE VALLEY GOLF COURSE

UNIVERSITY DR

West Lethbridge

0   1 mi

0   1 km

so strong that the steamers required as much coal for the return trip as they were capable of hauling on the way out. So, after two years, a narrow-gauge railway was constructed to haul the coal. This advance shifted the community's focus away from the river's edge and up onto the prairie, where the town that took root came to be named Lethbridge. William Lethbridge was an Englishman who never set foot in Alberta, but since he was a friend of Galt and a major financier in the Galts' coal mine, the town was named for him.

In 1909, the High Level Bridge—at that time the highest and longest structure of its type in the world—was constructed over the river valley, completing a more permanent link to Fort Macleod and Calgary. The last of the mines closed in 1942, and by 1960 the first of

what is now a string of urban parks along the valley was established.

SIGHTS

Downtown Lethbridge is relatively compact and parking is easy to come by. It's possible to walk from here to the sights and parks along the valley bottom, but then you're left with an uphill trek back to your vehicle.

◖ Sir Alexander Galt Museum

Considered one of the best small-city museums in the country, this facility (5th Ave. S off Scenic Dr., 403/320-3898, mid-May–mid-Sept. daily 10 A.M.–6 P.M., mid-Sept.–mid-May daily 10 A.M.–4:30 P.M., adult $5, senior $4, child $3) is in a former hospital that has a glass-walled addition built in 2006 especially

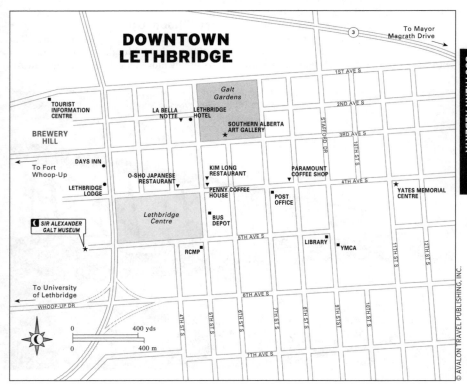

to house the magnificent Discovery Hall. Here, there are a wealth of interactive displays that tell the story of southern Alberta's natural and human history in such an interesting way you won't realize you're actually learning something. The west-facing window provides a view across the valley—in effect a panorama of the city's past. From this vantage point, you can see the site of the last major intertribal battle in North America, old coal mines, Fort Whoop-Up, and the High Level Bridge. Other galleries contain exhibits explaining the history of the coal mines, the introduction of irrigation, the area's immigrants, and the city since World War II. Two additional galleries have rotating art exhibits of local interest.

Southern Alberta Art Gallery

The downtown Southern Alberta Art Gallery (601 3rd Ave. S, 403/327-8770, Tues.–Sat. 10 A.M.–5 P.M., Sun. 1–5 P.M., donation) has contemporary and historical exhibitions that change throughout the year. The gallery is within **Galt Gardens,** a well-tended park with lots of nice big trees that provide a shaded spot for lunching locals.

High Level Bridge

High Level Bridge spans 1.6 kilometers (one mi) and towers 100 meters (330 ft) above the Oldman River Valley; it was once the longest and highest trestle-construction bridge in the world. It was built by the CPR for $1.3 million in 1909, replacing 22 wooden bridges and drastically reducing the length of the line between Lethbridge and Fort Macleod. More than 12,000 tons of steel, 17,000 cubic yards of concrete, and 7,600 gallons of paint were used in its construction. Of the many views of the bridge available along the valley, none is better than standing directly underneath it (walk down from the tourist information center on Brewery Hill).

Fort Whoop-Up

After the U.S. Army put a stop to the illicit whiskey trade in Montana, these traders of sorts simply moved north into what is now Al-

© ANDREW HEMPSTEAD

High Level Bridge

berta. In December 1869, John Healy and Alfred Hamilton came north from Fort Benton, Montana, and established a fort on the Oldman River that soon became the most notorious whiskey-trading post in the West. The story goes that its name was coined by someone who had returned to Fort Benton and, when asked how things were going at Hamilton's Fort, replied, "Oh, they're still whoopin' it up." Trading was simple: Natives pushed buffalo hides through a small opening in the fort wall; in return they were handed a tin cup of whiskey (which was often watered down). The success of the trade led to the formation of the NWMP, who rode west with orders to close down all whiskey-trading forts and end the lawless industry. The Mounties were preceded by word of their approach, and the fort was empty by the time they arrived in 1874.

The replica Fort Whoop-Up (Indian Battle Park, 403/329-0444, mid-May–early Sept. daily 9 A.M.–5 P.M., spring and fall Wed.–Sat. 1–4 P.M., adult $7, senior $6, child $5) looks much as it would have in 1869 (except for the soda machine). Costumed staff relive the days when "firewater" was traded for hides and pelts in the Trade Room, a vegetable garden is planted each spring, and visitors are free to climb the corner bastion which was once used as a lookout. A cannon used to defend the fort is on display, an audiovisual presentation is shown, and the Whoop-Up flag—now the official flag of Lethbridge—flies high above. To get there from the city center, turn west onto 3rd Avenue S and follow it down into the coulee.

Lethbridge Nature Reserve and Helen Schuler Coulee Centre

Lethbridge is unique in that it's built on the prairie benchlands and not beside the river that flows so close to town. The largely undisturbed Oldman River Valley has been developed into reserves and parks. One of these, the Lethbridge Nature Reserve, is an 82-hectare (202-acre) area of floodplain and coulees. It's home to the great horned owl—Alberta's provincial bird—porcupines, white-tailed deer, and prairie rattlesnakes. It's also home to

the Helen Schuler Coulee Centre (403/320-3064, June–Aug. Sun.–Thurs. 10 A.M.–8 P.M., Fri.–Sat. 10 A.M.–6 P.M., the rest of the year Tues.–Sun. 1–4 P.M., free), offering interpretive displays focusing on the entire urban park system. The center is the best place to start exploring the valley. From here, three short trails lead around the floodplain and through stands of cottonwood trees. To get there from downtown, head west on 3rd Avenue S, take a right just before Fort Whoop-Up, and pass under the High Level Bridge.

Other Valley Parks

The most historically important urban park in Lethbridge is 102-hectare (252-acre) **Indian Battle Park.** It is named after the last great battle fought between the Cree and the Blackfoot, which took place on the west side of the river in 1870. Within the park, beside Fort Whoop-Up, is a "medicine stone" that the Blackfoot believed had sacred significance—for many years they left offerings around it. Also in the park, the **Coalbanks Interpretive Site** is at the original mine entrance between Fort Whoop-Up and the Helen Schuler Coulee Centre. Coalbanks, founded in 1874, was the original settlement in the valley. Indian Battle Park extends from the Oldman River to behind the buildings on Scenic Drive. Many viewpoints can be found along the top of the coulee, which is accessible by timber steps leading up from the floodplain.

Botterill Bottom Park, adjacent to Indian Battle Park, houses underground utility lines and cannot be developed. Across the Oldman River is **Bull Trail Park,** an undeveloped area that extends south to the university. To the north is **Elizabeth Hall Wetlands,** a 15-hectare (37-acre) reserve of floodplain habitat that encompasses an oxbow pond. North of the Lethbridge Nature Reserve is **Peenaquim Park,** 97 hectares (240 acres) of floodplain that was formerly a stockyard. Access to **Alexander Wilderness Park** is from Stafford Drive N. This road descends into a coulee, and three short trails radiate out along the floodplain to viewpoints of the Oldman River.

SOUTHERN ALBERTA

Nikka Yuko Japanese Garden

This garden (Henderson Lake Park, Mayor Magrath Dr., 403/328-3511, mid-May–mid-Oct. daily 9 A.M.–5 P.M., July–Aug. until 8 P.M., adult $7, senior $5, child $4) was established in 1967 by the City of Lethbridge and its Japanese residents as a monument "to the contribution made to Canadian culture by Canadians of Japanese origin." It has been designed as a place to relax and contemplate, with no bright flowers, only green shrubs and gardens of rock and sand. The buildings and bridges were built in Japan under the supervision of a renowned Japanese architect. The main pavilion is of traditional design, housing a *tokonoma,* or tea-ceremony room. Japanese women in traditional dress lead visitors through the gardens and explain the philosophy behind different aspects of the design. A short trail leads around the main body of water to the bell tower, whose gentle "gong" signifies good things happening in both countries simultaneously. A special presentation is made Sunday at 1:30 P.M., which may be anything

© ANDREW HEMPSTEAD

Nikka Yuko Japanese Garden

from a bonsai-pruning demonstration to a traditional Japanese sword fight.

RECREATION

Activities in **Henderson Lake Park** on Mayor Magrath Drive center around a 20-hectare (50-acre) lake. The park features an outdoor swimming pool (403/320-3054), tennis courts, lots of day-use areas, and a paved trail that encircles the entire lake. **Henderson Lake Golf Club** (403/329-6767, $35) is also within the park, and a couple of the holes run close to the water. The city's best public golfing is at **Paradise Canyon Golf Resort** (403/381-4653 or 877/707-4653), constructed on a reclaimed floodplain along the Oldman River. Most holes are wide open, with river and valley views. Water isn't the only hazard here—last time I played we were forced to wait as a female moose and her calf ambled across the fairway. Greens fee is $50, or purchase a stay-and-play package for $120 per person. Even if you're not a golfer, the clubhouse has a wonderful restaurant and lounge with lots of outdoor seating. To get to Paradise Canyon, follow University Drive south beyond the university.

A popular out-of-town recreation spot is **Park Lake Provincial Park,** 17 kilometers (10.5 mi) north of Lethbridge on Highway 25 then five kilometers (3.1 mi) northwest along SH101. This once-arid prairie region has been transformed by irrigation. In summer, the lake is a good spot for swimming, windsurfing, fishing, and boating (boat rentals available), and a sandy beach is shaded by poplars.

ENTERTAINMENT AND EVENTS

Lethbridge's bar scene is not particularly attractive to travelers, but there is one exception, the **Cotton Blossom Lounge.** Surrounded by greenery in the wonderfully humid atrium of the Lethbridge Lodge Hotel (320 Scenic Dr. S, 403/328-1123), it is open Monday–Saturday at 11 A.M. and Sunday at 5 P.M. with complimentary hors d'oeuvres served Monday–Thursday at 4:30 P.M. and live entertainment (usually piano) Monday–Saturday from 4:30 P.M.

Theater and Music

The Sterndale Bennett Theatre in the Yates Memorial Centre (1002 4th Ave. S) is home to the **New West Theatre** (403/329-7328, www.newwesttheatre.com), an amateur company whose popular October–March productions sell out most nights. **Lethbridge Symphony Orchestra** (403/328-6808, www.lethbridgesymphony.org) also has its office in Yates Centre but performs at locations throughout the city during an October–May season. Tickets cost $20–28.

Nightlife

The city's biggest nightclub is **Studio 54** in the Lethbridge Hotel (202 5th St. S, 403/328-6099), with shooter and beer bars, pool tables, and a decent-sized dance floor. The nightly Power Hour (8–9 P.M.) of discounted draft is almost as popular as Tight-Ass Tuesday, which has nothing to do with Wrangler jeans and everything to do with attracting hordes of university students for $6.25 jugs of draft.

Festivals and Events

For a city of its size, Lethbridge offers surprisingly few festivals. The year's biggest event, **Whoop-Up Days,** is held at Exhibition Park (403/328-4491, www.exhibitionpark.ca) and at other locations in the city throughout the third week of August. The celebration features pancake breakfasts, a parade, a midway, a casino, a trade show, and grandstand events such as a rodeo. Nightly concerts and cabarets end each day's excitement.

ACCOMMODATIONS AND CAMPING
$50-100

Heritage House B&B (1115 8th Ave. S, 403/328-3824) is an excellent alternative to the motels. The 1937 home is considered one of the finest examples of International Art Deco design in the province. Its two guest rooms are spacious and tastefully decorated, a hearty breakfast is served downstairs in the dining room, and town is only a short walk along the tree-lined streets of Lethbridge's most sought-after suburb. The bathroom is shared, but for $60 s, $80 d, that is of little consequence.

Out on Mayor Magrath Drive is a string of motels that fall into this price range. One of these, the **Parkside Inn** (1009 Mayor Magrath Dr., 403/328-2366 or 800/240-1471), is your run-of-the-mill motel with a restaurant and a country nightclub on the premises. Rooms are air-conditioned and go for $55 s, $65 d, on the low side for Lethbridge, but about what they're worth all the same.

The downtown **Days Inn** (100 3rd Ave. S, 403/327-6000 or 800/661-8085, from $94 s or d) offers full-on consistency and plenty of amenities at a reasonable price. Rates include continental breakfast, in-room coffee, in-room high-speed Internet, a daily paper, and use of an indoor pool and exercise room.

Over $100

Inside the nine-story **Sandman Hotel Lethbridge** (421 Mayor Magrath Dr. S, 403/328-1111 or 800/726-3626, www.sandmanhotels.com) all 139 rooms are tastefully decorated and

Heritage House B&B

© ANDREW HEMPSTEAD

Lethbridge is blessed with an accessible urban park system that protects much of the river valley.

air-conditioned. Also in the hotel are an indoor pool, a business center, and a 24-hour restaurant. Standard rooms are $109, or upgrade to a king suite for $129.

Lethbridge Lodge (320 Scenic Dr. S, 403/328-1123 or 800/661-1232, www.lethbridge lodge.com) is a modern, full-service hotel with a prime downtown location. The 191 big, bright rooms come in five configurations, including Courtyard Suites with a separate bedroom and living area overlooking an enclosed tropical atrium. Amenities include a restaurant, a lounge, and an indoor pool. Rack rate is $159 s or d, but check the website for rates discounted to around $120.

Camping

Henderson Lake Campground (7th Ave. S in Henderson Lake Park, 403/328-5452, tent sites $21, hookups $27–31) has showers, a laundry room, groceries, firewood, and fire rings. The serviced section is little more than a paved parking lot, but tenters and those with small vans

enjoy the privacy afforded by trees at the back of the campground. **Bridgeview RV Resort** (910 4th Ave. S, 403/381-2357, tents $24, hookups $34–36) on the west bank of the Oldman River has similar facilities to Henderson Lake Campground, as well as an outdoor heated pool and a restaurant (but the nearby highway can be noisy). Another alternative is **Park Lake Provincial Park** (403/382-4097, May–early Oct., unserviced sites $15, powered sites $20), 17 kilometers (10.5 mi) north of town on Highway 25 then five kilometers (3.1 mi) northwest along SH101. No reservations taken.

FOOD
Downtown

Lethbridge has some fine coffee shops; the pick of the bunch is **Penny Coffee House** (331 5th St. S, 403/320-5282, Mon.–Fri. 7:30 A.M.–10 P.M., Sat. 7:30 A.M.–5:30 P.M., Sun. 10 A.M.–5 P.M.), where coffee is under $2, refills are free, and a nice, thick, healthy sandwich with soup is $6.50. You'll find a

very different atmosphere at the **Paramount Coffee Shop** (342 8th St. S, 403/327-5476, Mon.–Fri. 5:30 A.M.–4:30 P.M.), which is one of those classic hole-in-the-wall diners with a single laminated counter and a menu that hasn't changed since the 1950s.

Good, inexpensive Vietnamese food is dished up at **Kim Long Restaurant** (329 5th St. S, 403/380-3866, Sun.–Thurs. 10 A.M.– 10 P.M., Fri.–Sat. until midnight). Most dishes are less than $10. If the menu looks Greek to you, ask to see the family photo album with color photographs of each dish. One block west, **O-Sho Japanese Restaurant** (311 4th St. S, 403/327-8382, Mon.–Fri. 11:30 A.M.– 2:30 P.M. and Mon.–Sat. 4:30–10 P.M.) serves authentic Japanese cuisine; you can sit at standard tables or dine in traditional style on mats in partitioned lounges. Lunch is $5–9.50, dinner $8.50–16.

Bontanica (Lethbridge Lodge, 320 Scenic Dr. S, 403/328-1123, daily 7 A.M.–10 P.M.) is a cool, clean space with lots of healthy choices. The breakfast is especially good and prices all day are surprisingly inexpensive (a dinner buffet Sun.–Tues. is $13 and Thurs.-night ribs are $16). Off the hotel lobby is a coffee bar.

You'll find the city's best dining ambience at **La Bella Notte** (401 2nd Ave. S, 403/331-3319, daily from 11:30 A.M. for lunch and dinner). Originally a firehall, the building has been extensively renovated, including a tiled floor, restored spiral staircase leading to an upstairs lounge, and an earthy heritage color scheme. The menu features lots of Canadian ingredients, with many dishes prepared using traditional Italian techniques. Mains ranging $14–38 include oven-roasted quail with a peach and Champagne glaze and citrus and chili-crusted wild boar tenderloin.

Mayor Magrath Drive

As well as having the bulk of Lethbridge's accommodations, this road has many fast-food and family restaurants. **Treats Eatery** (1104 Mayor Magrath Dr. S, 403/380-4880, Mon.–Sat. 11 A.M.–10 P.M., Sun. 4–10 P.M.) is a Western-style family-dining restaurant. It

has an enormous gold-rimmed wagon wheel hanging from the ceiling—ask to sit away from it if you like. The menu is straightforward, basically burgers and beef, but is well priced, with steaks $18–24. It's impossible to miss **Sven Ericksen's Family Restaurant** (1715 Mayor Magrath Dr. S, 403/328-7756, Mon.–Fri. 11 A.M.–10 P.M., Sat.–Sun. 11 A.M.– 11 P.M., $14–33), a hulking redbrick building with white columns along the front. The menu here is heavy on seafood, which seems odd for a place so far from the ocean, but enough beef and chicken dishes are offered for fishophobes to get by.

INFORMATION AND SERVICES

Lethbridge has two information centers. The biggest is the **Mayor Magrath Tourist Information Centre** (2805 Scenic Dr., 403/320-1222, summer daily 9 A.M.–8 P.M., the rest of the year daily 9 A.M.–5 P.M.) on the south side of the city where Mayor Magrath Drive and Scenic Drive meet. The second, **Brewery Gardens Tourist Information Centre** (403/320-1223, mid-May to Sept. daily 9 A.M.–8 P.M., Sept.– Oct. Tues.–Sat. 9 A.M.–5 P.M.), is on the western edge of downtown. If you're traveling in from the west (Fort Macleod), take the 1st Avenue S exit as Highway 3 climbs from the Oldman River Valley; it's straight after the High Level Bridge on the right. The **Chinook Country Tourist Association** (403/329-6777 or 800/661-1222, www.chinookcountry.com) operates both centers.

Lethbridge Public Library (810 5th Ave. S, 403/380-7310, Mon.–Thurs. 9:30 A.M.– 9 P.M., Fri.–Sat. 9:30 A.M.–5:30 P.M., Sun. 1:30–5:30 P.M.) is an excellent facility with a wide range of literature.

The post office (704 4th Ave. S) is in a historic stone building. Make a rainy day of it at **Family Coin Laundry** (128 Mayor Magrath Dr. N, daily 7:30 A.M.–8:30 P.M.), one block north of the highway, where there's a lounge, a TV, and free coffee. Contact **Lethbridge Regional Hospital** (9th Ave. and 18th St. S, 403/382-6111) or the **RCMP** (403/329-5010) for emergency services or police assistance.

SOUTHERN ALBERTA

GETTING THERE AND AROUND

Lethbridge Airport is eight kilometers (five mi) south of town on Highway 5. It is served by **Air Canada** connectors (888/247-2262) from Calgary four to seven times daily. Major motels and car rental companies have courtesy phones at the airport. A cab to downtown is approximately $20.

Buses leave twice daily from the **Greyhound** bus depot (411 5th St. S, 403/327-1551 or 800/661-8747, www.greyhound.ca) for Fort Macleod, four times daily for Calgary, and twice daily to Medicine Hat and to the U.S.

border at Coutts, where connections to Great Falls and Helena (Montana) can be made.

Lethbridge Transit (403/320-3885) buses run daily, with limited service on Sunday. The main routes radiate from Lethbridge Centre on 4th Avenue S out to the university, Henderson Lake Park, and south along Mayor Magrath Drive. The adult fare is $2. The various car-rental agencies are **Budget** (403/328-6555), **Enterprise** (403/328-3517), **Hertz** (403/382-3470), and **National** (403/380-3070). For a taxi, call **Fifth Avenue Cabs** (403/381-1111), **Lethbridge Cabs** (403/327-4005), or **Royal Taxi** (403/328-5333).

East of Lethbridge

THE MILK RIVER

The Milk River is unique among western Canada's river systems. All of the others eventually drain into either the Pacific Ocean, the Arctic Ocean, or Hudson Bay, but the Milk River flows south to the Missouri River, eventually draining into the Gulf of Mexico. The area itself is historically unique for western Canada because it has been under the jurisdiction of seven different governments and countries, as well as the Hudson's Bay Company. During the 1700s, France claimed all the lands of the Mississippi, so a small part of Alberta was under French rule. Later, the same area was part of the Spanish empire, and it has also, at one time or another, fallen under the rule of the Hudson's Bay Company, the British, and the Americans. It finally became part of the province of Alberta in 1905.

Devil's Coulee

On May 14, 1987, Wendy Slobada, an amateur paleontologist, was exploring the coulees near her family's ranch outside of Milk River when she discovered some fossilized eggshells. The find sent waves of excitement around the scientific world, and the site became known as **Devil's Coulee Dinosaur Egg Site,** one of the most exciting fossil discoveries ever made.

What she had found were clutches of eggs that had been laid by hadrosaurs approximately 75 million years ago. Each prehistoric egg was about 20 centimeters (eight inches) long and contained the perfectly formed bones of embryonic dinosaurs. No other find in the entire world has taught scientists more about this part of the dinosaur's life cycle.

Devil's Coulee Dinosaur Heritage Museum (403/642-2118, www.devilscoulee.com, June–Aug. daily 9 A.M.–5 P.M.) is in the village of Warner, on Highway 4, 66 kilometers (41 mi) southeast of Lethbridge and 20 kilometers (12 mi) northwest of the small town of Milk River. It is only a small facility, but a display reconstructs the site. Tours to the site of the find leave from the museum weekends in June and daily July–August at 10 A.M. and 1 P.M. Tour cost is $18 per person and advance reservations are required.

The Town of Milk River

The town of Milk River (pop. 800) sits on the northern bank of its namesake, 86 kilometers (53 mi) southeast of Lethbridge. It's a terribly uninspiring place, existing only to serve highway travelers. One redeeming feature is the **Delicia Bakery** (113 Main St., 403/647-3990), which lives up to its name. The best nearby camping is in Writing-on-Stone Provincial Park, 43 ki-

lometers (27 mi) west, although **Under 8 Flags Campground** (south side of town, year-round, tents $12, hookups $15–20) has a few sites beside the highway. Firewood is free and campers enjoy a discount at the adjacent golf course.

Highway 15 through Montana crosses into Alberta 40 kilometers (25 mi) south of Milk River at the **Coutts-Sweetgrass** border crossing. This is the main route into Alberta from the United States and the crossing is open 24 hours a day year-round. A **Travel Alberta Information Centre** (403/647-3938, mid-May–Aug. daily 8 A.M.–7 P.M., Sept.–mid-Oct. daily 9 A.M.–5 P.M.) greets travelers about 35 kilometers (22 mi) after crossing the border. It provides copious information and an interpretive center highlighting aspects of tourism within the province.

◖ WRITING-ON-STONE PROVINCIAL PARK

This park, off Highway 501 43 kilometers (27 mi) east of the town of Milk River, has the largest concentrations of petroglyphs (rock carvings) and pictographs (rock paintings) found in North America. But that's only one of the reasons to venture out into this remote part of the province: A warm river for swimming, great canoeing, intriguing rock formations, and abundant wildlife round out one of Alberta's premier nonmountain parks.

The park protects a stretch of the Milk River that has cut a deep valley into the rolling shortgrass prairie. Soft sandstone and shale cliffs are capped with harder, iron-rich sediments. Years of wind and water erosion have carved out the softer, lower rock, leaving mushroom-shaped pinnacles and columns called **hoodoos.** Several plant and animal species here are found nowhere else in Alberta. Look for pronghorn on the grassland, bobcats and mule deer in the coulees, and yellow-bellied marmots sunning themselves on sandstone outcrops. Don't look *too* hard for rattlesnakes, though, which are usually found in shady spots among the cliffs.

SOUTHERN ALBERTA

© ANDREW HEMPSTEAD

hoodoos above the campground at Writing-on-Stone Provincial Park

The Meaning of It All

Writing-on-Stone was a place of great spiritual importance to generations of natives, a place for contact with the supernatural. They attempted to interpret previous carvings and paintings, added their own artwork to the rock, and left gifts of tobacco and beads as a way of communicating with the spirits of the dead. Much of the cliff art remains visible today, providing clues to the region's early inhabitants.

Artifacts excavated from below the cliffs suggest that the area had been inhabited for at least 3,000 years, but any rock art of that age would have been destroyed by erosion long ago. Dating the remaining petroglyphs and pictographs is difficult. They aren't covered in the layers of sediment usually used to date sites, nor can radiocarbon dating be applied because that technique requires wood or bone to test. The only way of dating the rock art is to estimate its age based on recognizable artistic styles or the depiction of certain historic events (such as the arrival of the white man). Of the carvings visible today, the earliest are thought to be the work of the Shoshoni, created approximately 700 years ago. Their work is characterized by warriors on foot carrying ornately decorated shields, while isolated images of elk, bears, and rattlesnakes appear as simple stylized outlines. During the 1730s, the Shoshoni were driven into the mountains by the Blackfoot, who had acquired horses and guns before other native bands. The valley's strange rock formations led the Blackfoot to believe that the area was a magical place—a place to be respected and feared—and that existing carvings were created by the spirits. The Blackfoot added their own artistry to the rocks, and many of the Blackfoot carvings are panels that tell a story. A striking change of lifestyle was documented on the rock faces, corresponding to the arrival of guns and horses to the Plains tribes. Mounted warriors armed with rifles dominate later artworks, the most famous being a battle scene containing more than 250 characters.

Into the 20th Century

An NWMP post was established at Writing-on-Stone in 1889 to stop the whiskey trade and curb fighting among natives. The Mounties passed time by using the petroglyphs for target practice and carving their names into a cliff that has become known as Signature Rock. The original NWMP post buildings were washed away by floodwaters, replaced, then destroyed by fire in 1918. In 1957, the area was officially designated a provincial park.

Access to much of the park is restricted to prevent further damage to the carvings. A reconstructed NWMP post sits within this area at the mouth of **Police Coulee.** The best way to get a feel for the park and its history is by participating in the interpretive program; details are posted on notice boards throughout the park. The **Hoodoo Interpretive Trail** is a two-kilometer (1.2-mi) hike along the cliffs, with numbered posts that correspond to a trail brochure available from the information center. Along the way are some examples of petroglyphs and pictographs (including the famous battle scene) that have been ravaged by time and vandals.

Camping and Information

The park has an excellent campground (unserviced sites $20, powered sites $25) nestled below the hoodoos in a stand of cottonwood trees. Adjacent is a beach and canoe rentals and an interpretive program is operated in conjunction with park staff. Although the campground is open year-round, firewood ($8 per bundle) and facilities such as showers are only available May–early September.

For more information on the park, call 403/647-2364.

THE DRY BELT

The drive described in this section, traveling east along Highway 61 deep into the southeastern corner of Alberta, may sound rather unappealing, but it is in fact a fascinating journey that will open your eyes to the hardships faced by those who earn a living from the land. I travel this route for every edition of this book—not because there's ever much to update, but because in some uncomplicated way, it's one of my favorite places in all of Alberta.

The Land, the History

Not a tree in sight—just rolling shortgrass prairie, occasionally dissected by dried-up streams and eroded gullies. This is the sight that first greeted settlers to the area, and even with the help of complex irrigation systems, the land looks similar today. The far southeastern corner of Alberta has never been heavily populated, but not for a lack of trying. Before it was linked to the outside world by rail, settlers entered the area. Small villages emerged, but as was often the case, the CPR decided to bypass many of these fledgling settlements and create its own towns. Population bases moved, and towns slipped into oblivion.

Highway 61 passes through this dry, unforgiving part of the province, past the towns of Wrentham and Skiff, with their boarded-up buildings and grim futures, to the town of Foremost and on through other small communities whose future hangs in the balance. The highway finally peters out at Manyberries, whose lone hotel, as a final insult, I found for sale on eBay.

Foremost

In 1915, the CPR built a rail line east from Stirling through to Saskatchewan with great hopes of the area becoming heavily settled. But they hadn't counted on years of heavy drought, dust storms, and outbreaks of influenza that severely affected the populations of towns in the area. One of the few surviving towns was Foremost, whose population of 500 has remained relatively stable through trying times. Irrigation has played a major role in Foremost's longevity. The interpretive center at **Forty Mile Coulee Reservoir,** 23 kilometers (14 mi) north of town, explains the importance of irrigation to these farming communities. Nearby is a viewpoint and day-use area.

On the west side of town is a 24-site **campground** (Apr.–Oct., tents $8, hookups $18–22) with showers, power, and a covered cooking shelter.

Etzikom

Once a thriving center with many businesses

GOING, GOING, GONE

The Canadian Pacific Railroad built towns approximately every 16 kilometers (10 mi) along its lines, its strategy being that farmers would have access to a grain elevator within a day's haul of their farms, yet the towns would be far enough apart to survive independently.

Between Foremost and Etzikom, though, the town of **Nemiscam** hasn't survived. The once-busy streets are lined with boarded-up businesses. Hardy prairie grasses have pushed through concrete sidewalks. A rusty swing in the playground squeaks as an endless wind blows. All that remains of Nemiscam Golf & Country Club are bright-blue hole markers. And at the top of town is a home that was obviously the grandest in Nemiscam, but like so many others, it has long been abandoned. A few families still call the hamlet home, sending their children to school in Foremost and heading off to Medicine Hat for their shopping needs. Somehow, through it all, an air of prairie dignity remains along the empty streets of Nemiscam.

© ANDREW HEMPSTEAD

and two hotels, Etzikom is now home to fewer than 100 people. The only museum along Highway 61 is **Etzikom Museum** (403/666-3737, summer Mon.–Sat. 10 A.M.–5 P.M., Sun. noon–6 P.M., adult $4, senior $3.50), at the east end of town in the now-empty school. Indoor displays let you relive the past—the railway, influenza, droughts, and the tenacity of its people—but it's an outdoor display of wind power in Canada that will catch your eye. More than a dozen windmills dot the old school yard, including a clunky European-style one and another that once stood on Martha's Vineyard.

Continuing East

The farmland east of Etzikom is particularly poor. The railway town of **Pakowki** slipped into oblivion long ago, its early residents preferring to do business in **Orion,** the next town to the east. Orion itself was originally a thriving prairie town, but a terrible drought throughout much of the 1920s forced most farmers into bankruptcy. To the south of Orion on Highway 887 are the **Manyberries Sandhills,** a prairie phenomenon well worth the detour, especially in the berry-picking season. From Orion, Highway 887 heads north to Seven Persons and Medicine Hat. Highway 61 jogs south and east from Orion to the small town of **Manyberries,** which once had a population of 500, two grain elevators, and an annual rodeo. From this point, Highway 889 heads northeast to Cypress Hills Provincial Park or south then east to Saskatchewan; either way it's gravel.

HIGHWAY 3 EAST FROM LETHBRIDGE
Coaldale

The first town east of Lethbridge on Highway 3 is Coaldale, with a population of 7,200. The area was first settled in 1889 by Mennonites, and when the CPR built a rail line between Lethbridge and Medicine Hat in 1926, the company encouraged more Mennonite families to farm in the region. With their long agricultural traditions and doctrines of simple living, Mennonites were always welcome additions to prairie communities such as Coaldale. Today this rural community and its Mennonite population continue to prosper, mostly because of their proximity to Lethbridge.

The main reason to leave the highway here is to visit the **Alberta Birds of Prey Centre** (north of Hwy. 3 at 20th St., then left on 16th Ave., 403/345-4262, mid-May–mid-Sept. daily 9:30 A.M.–5 P.M., adult $8, senior $7, child $5). The aim of this off-the-beaten-path center is to ensure the survival of birds of prey such as hawks, falcons, eagles, burrowing owls, and great horned owls, Alberta's provincial bird. Many of the birds are brought to the center injured or as young chicks. They are nurtured at the center until they are strong enough to be released back into the wild. The Natural History Centre features the works of various wildlife artists and has displays cataloging human fascination with birds of prey through thousands of years. Integrated with this main building is an aviary where you can view birds that are recovering from injury and tame birds fly free (well, kind of, anyway). Entry includes an invitation to watch daily "flying programs" (10 A.M. and 12:30, 2, and 3:30 P.M.) and the opportunity to be photographed with a falcon.

Accommodations are at **Coaldale Motor Inn** (913 19th Ave., 403/345-2555, $60 s or d), which offers 16 air-conditioned rooms, a restaurant, and a lounge bar.

Taber

Taber, 51 kilometers (32 mi) east of Lethbridge, is most famous for its deliciously sweet corn. It's also a base for the food-processing industry and a service center for the oil-and-gas industry. The name Taber was taken from "tabernacle," reflecting the religious influence of the early Mormon settlers. Local Blackfoot called the settlement *Itah Soyop* (Where We Eat From). Apparently, they mistook the name Taber for table, or so the story goes.

Taber corn, as it is called, can be bought throughout western Canada and is the cornerstone of the town's economy. Long hot days of sunshine and cool nights bring out a sweetness that is not found in regular corn. August and early September is the best time to look

for corn vendors along the road. Or find corn and other fresh local produce each Thursday at the farmers market in the Taber Agriplex. On the last weekend of August, when the corn has ripened, the town's **Cornfest** celebration takes place, with a pancake breakfast, a midway, hot-air-balloon flights, a classic-car show, and, of course, plenty of corn to taste.

On the eastern outskirts of town is the **Taber Sugar Beet Factory,** which processes more than 500,000 tons of sugar beets annually. During peak periods, enormous piles of beets sit beside the highway waiting to be processed into icing sugar, granulated sugar, and various powdered sugars. The factory does not offer tours, and judging by the smell *outside* the factory, this is a good thing.

Overnight options are the **Taber Motel** (403/223-4411 or 877/232-2022, $50 s, $60 d) or the much larger **Heritage Inn** (403/223-4424 or 888/888-4374, www.heritageinn.net, $76 s, $84 d), with a restaurant and lounge. Both are along the highway.

On the north side of Taber's only traffic light (look for the giant corn husks) is the Taber Community Centre, home to a small museum and an **information center** (403/223-2265, www.taberchamber.com, summer Mon.–Fri. 9 A.M.–7 P.M., Sat.–Sun. 10 A.M.–6 P.M., the rest of the year Mon.–Fri. 9 A.M.–4 P.M.).

Bow Island

This small town 58 kilometers (36 mi) east of Taber isn't on an island and isn't even near water. It's named for an island north of town on Grassy Lake, which isn't really a lake but part of the Bow River. (Go figure.) Vast reserves of natural gas in the area around Bow Island were first tapped in 1909 by a discovery well named Old Glory, which soon developed into Alberta's first commercial gas field. The reserve of gas declined by the 1920s, and Bow Island's role in the industry changed; it became the first major gas-storage field in Canada. Today its storage reservoirs help meet southern Alberta's peak winter demand. Agriculture now plays an important role in the town's economy, as evidenced by large grain elevators and an alfalfa dehydrating and cubing plant two kilometers (1.2 mi) west of town.

◖ Red Rock Coulee

South of Seven Persons, the last community on Highway 3 before Medicine Hat, is a small area of badlands on a gentle rise in the surrounding plains. The bedrock here is relatively close to the surface, and wind and water erosion have cut through the topsoil to expose it. In some places, the erosion has extended into the bedrock itself, revealing varicolored strata laid down millions of years ago. This strange landscape is dotted with red boulder-shaped concretions measuring up to 2.5 meters (eight ft) across. These intriguing rock formations formed under the surface of a prehistoric sea, when sand, calcite, and iron oxide collected on a nucleus of shells, bones, and corals. They became part of the bedrock as layers of sediment were laid down, but as erosion took its course, the surrounding bedrock disappeared and the concretions emerged. The formations here are believed to be the largest of their type in the world. To get there, follow Highway 887 south from Seven Persons for 23 kilometers (14 mi). Where the road curves sharply to the east (left), continue straight ahead uphill on an unsealed road and park at the lone picnic table. The boulders are laid out below and to the south.

SOUTHERN ALBERTA

Medicine Hat and Vicinity

The prosperous industrial city of Medicine Hat (pop. 56,000) is in the southeastern corner of the province, 168 kilometers (104 mi) east of Lethbridge and 40 kilometers (25 mi) west of the Saskatchewan border. Known as "The Hat" to locals, the city straddles the South Saskatchewan River along which many areas are protected as parkland. The city also holds interesting attractions such as the remains of Canada's once-thriving pottery industry and an archaeological site regarded as one of the most extensive and richest finds from the late prehistoric time period of native history. Travelers keeping an eye on their spending will also appreciate Medicine Hat—it is home to Alberta's cheapest motels and consistently has Canada's cheapest gas prices.

History

Medicine Hat was built on some of western Canada's most extensive natural-gas fields. The gas was discovered by accident in 1883 by a CPR crew drilling for water. At first, nobody was particularly excited, except for the workers who got to heat their isolated homes. But eventually the word got out about the size of the reserves beneath the town, leading English writer Rudyard Kipling to describe Medicine Hat as "a city with all hell for a basement." It wasn't long before industries developed around the gas fields; oil-and-gas extraction operations, petrochemical plants, mills, farms, and fertilizer factories today generate $1.5 billion annually. New housing estates, modern shopping centers, an award-winning city hall, and a downtown arts complex are testimony to the success of these local industries. As an added bonus, a river that flows beneath the city gives Medicine Hat an unlimited supply of water for its industries.

The Name Medicine Hat

For centuries before white settlers came to the area, the Cree and the Blackfoot had battled each other over the right to claim this land as their own. Many tales recording these battles describe how the name Medicine Hat evolved. One of the most popular legends tells the story of the Cree chief who led his people to the cliffs above the South Saskatchewan River. Here, the Great Serpent told him that he must sacrifice his wife to the river in exchange for a *saamis* (medicine hat). This would give him magical powers and allow him to defeat the Blackfoot when they attacked later that night. Another story tells of how the Blackfoot were forced into the waters of the South Saskatchewan River by the Cree, who then fired an arrow into the heart of the Blackfoot medicine man. As he slowly sank below the water's surface, his hat was swept away into the hands of the Cree. The Blackfoot saw this as a terrible omen and retreated.

SIGHTS AND RECREATION
Saamis Tepee

It makes sense that you stay on the TransCanada Highway (approaching from either direction) and take the signposted exit (South Ridge Drive) to the Saamis Tepee—it's the location of Medicine Hat's main information center. Besides, standing more than 20 stories high beside the TransCanada Highway, with a base diameter of 50 meters (160 ft) and made entirely of steel (it weighs 1,000 tons), this is one sight you don't need detailed directions to find. Originally erected during the 1988 Calgary Winter Olympics to commemorate the cultural roles played by natives in the history of North America, it has since been moved to its present site. It overlooks Seven Persons Creek Coulee, an archaeological site used in late prehistoric times as a native camp where buffalo were dried and processed. A self-guided interpretive trail, beginning at the tepee, leads to a bluff and into the valley where the camp was located. Native American ceremonial events are sometimes held here. The site is open year-round, but during the summer months free tours are offered, and a small interpretive center (403/527-0073, Wed.–Sun. 9 A.M.–5 P.M.) sells native arts and crafts.

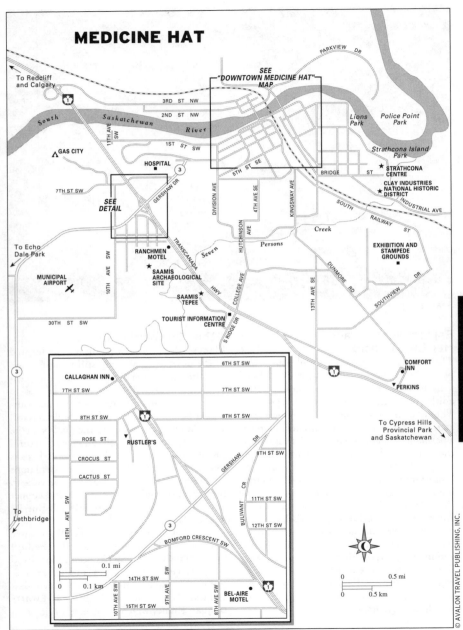

MEDICINE HAT

Saamis Tepee

Esplanade Arts and Heritage Centre

This modern, architecturally pleasing complex (401 1st St. SE, 403/502-8580, Mon.–Fri. 10 A.M.–5 P.M., Sat.–Sun. noon–5 P.M., adult $4, child $3, free for everyone on Thurs.) combines a museum, art gallery, theater, and archives. The museum portion holds a permanent collection of exhibits explaining the history of the natives that once inhabited the plains, the growth of the city, and the important role played by ranching and farming in southeastern Alberta, the NWMP, and the arrival of the railway. Local, provincial, and nationally acclaimed artists have their work displayed in the art gallery, although the center is best known for hosting national and international exhibitions. The Discovery Centre is a unique concept that brings facets of the museum, gallery, and theater into a learning environment for children; call for a schedule of events.

Other Downtown Sights

Many early-20th-century buildings located in the downtown area are still in active use, including private homes, churches, and businesses. The availability of local clay led to thriving brick-manufacturing plants here during the late 1800s; many original buildings still stand in mute testimony to the quality of the bricks. Because of the abundance of natural gas in the area, city officials in the early days found it cheaper to leave the city's gas lamps on 24 hours a day rather than pay someone to turn them on and off. More than 200 copper replicas now line the streets, still burning 24 hours a day.

Near City Hall on 1st Street SE are three fine examples of the area's brickwork. The 1919 **Provincial Courthouse** has been restored and features an elaborately carved entrance, an interior marble-walled stairway, and a leaded-glass archway. Across the road is the 1887 **Ewart-Duggan Home,** which is the oldest brick resi-

dence still standing in Alberta and is topped by its original cedar shingles. On the corner of 4th Avenue is the **Kerr-Wallace Home,** the oldest of many early prestigious homes along 1st Street toward the TransCanada Highway (Highway 1).

Among other historical landmarks are the 1913 **St. Patrick's Church** (across the river from downtown on 2nd St.), said to be one of the finest examples of Gothic Revival architecture in North America; the **CPR station** (east of downtown), built shortly after the railway came to town in 1883; and the 1905 **Canadian Bank of Commerce** (corner of 6th Ave. and 2nd St.), a classic example of early bank architecture. These buildings and others are listed in the *Historic Walking Tour* brochure available from the tourist information center.

Another notable piece of architecture from a much later era is the **Medicine Hat City Hall,** which won the Canadian Architectural Award in 1986. Located on the banks of the South Saskatchewan River, it's open to the public on weekdays and contains many fine pieces of art.

Clay Industries National Historic District

Nearby clay deposits led to a large pottery and brick industry that thrived from the late 1880s to World War II. The clay was mass-produced into high-quality china at various factories on the north side of the railway line east of downtown. It is this area that is now protected as a historic district. For the first 50 years of the last century, **Medalta** was a household name in Canada. Their china, popular in homes and used exclusively by CPR-owned hotels, is now prized by collectors. The buildings, which have been declared a National Historical Site, were

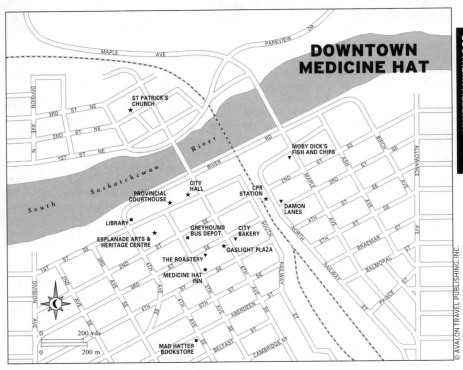

© ANDREW HEMPSTEAD

The kilns at Medalta Potteries once produced some of Canada's finest china.

closed in 1954, and fire, wind, and rain have taken their toll. The site (713 Medalta Ave. SE, 403/526-2777, mid-May–early Sept. daily 9:30 A.M.–5 P.M., the rest of the year Tues.–Sat. 9:30 A.M.–noon and 1–4:30 P.M., adult $8, senior and child $6) has been partly restored, displaying the history of the clay and pottery industries in Medicine Hat, and has some fine examples of the now highly prized Medalta pieces. The original kilns are open for inspection and there is a gift shop filled with pottery. Admission includes a walking tour. Across the road is the **Hycroft** factory, renowned for its 1950s and 1960s commemorative plates. Medalta and Hycroft were once bitter rivals, with Hycroft winning out in the end (if that's what you can call toilet bowl production), remaining open until 1989.

City Parks

Medicine Hat's urban park system covers more than 400 hectares (990 acres) of open space and natural environment linked by 50 kilometers (31 mi) of multiuse trails developed for walking, biking, and cross-country skiing.

Close to downtown, **Strathcona Island Park,** on the banks of the South Saskatchewan River, is a heavily wooded area linked to the city center by a riverside trail that leads through **Lions Park.** From Lions Park, there's a viewpoint of the steep cliffs formed by the undercutting power of the river at a shallow point. The park is at the north end of 5th Street SE.

On the north side of the river, opposite Strathcona Island Park, is **Police Point Park** (turn off Parkview Dr. just past the golf club), which has seven kilometers (4.3 mi) of hiking trails that wind through stands of 200-year-old cottonwood trees and provide opportunities for spotting resident white-tailed deer, foxes, and beavers. An **interpretive center** (403/529-6225, June–Aug. Tues.–Sun. 9 A.M.–5 P.M.) outlines the area's natural and human history through exhibits and films.

West of the airport on Holsam Road is **Echo Dale Park,** where the locals head on hot weekends to sunbake on the sandy beach and swim, fish, and boat in the manmade lake. Within the park is 100-year-old **Echo Dale Farm**

(403/527-7344, summer daily 9 A.M.–9 P.M.), where a garden reflects the crops of early settlers. There's a variety of farm animals, and a corn roast wraps up the summer season on the last Sunday of August.

Redcliff

Northwest of Medicine Hat, across the South Saskatchewan River, is Redcliff, the "Greenhouse Capital of the Prairies." Many small towns associate themselves with grand monikers, but in this case, Redcliff's claim can't be disputed. Over 200,000 square meters (2.15 million square ft) of greenhouses fill the town. Along the north side of the highway are large concentrations, but on the south side dozens of sprawling greenhouses intermingle with residential blocks. They are filled with brilliantly colored flowers and various vegetables such as cucumbers (18 million grown annually) and tomatoes (10 million grown annually). Some are open to the public for vegetable sales—just cruise the streets and look for the signs.

Medicine Hat Exhibition and Stampede

An annual extravaganza since 1887, this event has grown to become Alberta's second-richest rodeo (behind the Calgary Stampede), guaranteeing knuckle-clenching, bronc-riding, foot-stompin' fun during the last week of July. Various events are held throughout the city, culminating with the weekend rodeo and chuck wagon races. The stampede also features many exhibitors displaying their wares, as well as a midway, a Pioneer Village, a trade show, and lots of free entertainment. A top country act is featured on Saturday night. For more information, contact the stampede office (403/527-1234, www.mhstampede.com).

ACCOMMODATIONS AND CAMPING
Under $50

Medicine Hat is one of the only places in Alberta with motels offering rooms for less than $50. Most of the cheapies are bunched together along the downtown side of the TransCanada Highway around Gershaw Drive. The best value is the **Bel-Aire Motel** (633 14th St. SW, 403/527-4421, $40 s, $44 d). The 12 rooms are cooled by noisy air-conditioners and each has a small fridge. Rooms at the others aren't as nice (obviously, this is relative) as at the Bel Aire, but they're as cheap as you'll find on your travels. Try the **Ranchmen Motel** (1617 Bomford Cres., 403/527-2263, $45 s, $57 d), with a tired looking mini-golf course.

$50-100

Rising from an area of strip malls beside the TransCanada Highway, the **Ⓒ Comfort Inn** (2317 TransCanada Hwy., 403/504-1700 or 800/228-5150, www.choicehotels.com) is easily recognized by its modern lines and burgundy-and-yellow color scheme. The sharp design is carried through into the 100 guest rooms, each of which comes loaded with amenities. Other features are an indoor pool, a business center, high-speed Internet throughout, and a fitness room. Local calls and a big continental breakfast are included in the rates of $90 s or d (reduced to $70 outside of summer), making it an excellent choice for a mid-priced stay in Medicine Hat.

A good value up on the highway is the **Callaghan Inn** (954 7th St. SW, 403/527-8844 or 800/661-4440, www.callaghaninn.ca, $74 s, $92 d), with an indoor pool, a fitness room, and a restaurant.

The **Medicine Hat Inn** (530 4th St. SE, 403/526-1313 or 800/730-3887, $62 s, $72 d) is the only accommodation downtown. I doubt whether the rooms have been renovated since the first edition of this book (1992), and this is reflected in the low rates for a central location.

Camping

Gas City Campground (580 1st St. SE, 403/528-8158, May–Oct., unserviced sites $17, hookups $26–33) is on the edge of town, has nearly 100 sites, and is far enough away from the highway to be relatively quiet. From the back of the campground, a trail heads along the river and into town. At night, this is a good spot to view the illumination of Medicine Hat's industrial core. Good hot showers,

laundry facilities, groceries, and full hookups make this the place to try first. To get there, turn off the highway at 7th Street SW and follow the signs down 11th Avenue.

FOOD

The Roastery (513 3rd St. SE, 403/529-2344, Mon.–Fri. 7 A.M.–5:30 P.M., Sat. 8 A.M.–5:30 P.M., Sun. 10 A.M.–5 P.M.) is a funky little space with a few tables out front. Coffee is just $1.50. In Gaslight Plaza, **Café Mundo** (579 3rd St. SE, 403/528-2808, Mon.–Fri. 7:30 A.M.–5:30 P.M.) is in a pleasant setting away from the busy street front. The filled bagels (from $3) are good value.

In a converted 1912 residence, **Damon Lanes** (730 3rd St. SE, 403/529-2224, Tues.–Sat. 11 A.M.–4 P.M.) offers a wide range of teas to complement light lunches. On the same side of the railway tracks, **Moby Dick's Fish and Chips** (140 Maple Ave. SE, 403/526-1807, Mon.–Sat. 11 A.M.–9 P.M., Sun. 3–8 P.M.) is a delightful variety of English dishes. Fish in batter is from $3 per piece, fries $2. Also on the menu are other seafood specialties (from $14), traditional pub grub (from $6), and nine different meat pies (from $7).

If you're staying in one of the cheap highway motels, money is obviously important to you. If that's the case, you'll want to head to ◖ **Rustler's** (901 8th St. SW, 403/526-8004, daily 6 A.M.–11 P.M.) for a meal. It's one of the city's oldest eating establishments and because of its history (see the menu for the amusing tale), a real Wild West atmosphere prevails. Seating is out back in the tavern or in a restaurant section, where a glass tabletop reveals a poker game complete with gun and blood-stained playing cards. The place is popular all day, but breakfast is especially crowded. Large portions of eggs, bacon, and hash browns begin at $5, omelets at $5.50. For the rest of the day, it's hard to beat the beef. Last time through I enjoyed the Alberta rib eye with roast potatoes and vegetables ($12–18 depending on the cut). The vegetables were ordinary, but the steak was exactly as I ordered it.

Southeast along the highway near the Com-fort Inn is **Perkins** (2301 TransCanada Hwy., 403/527-9311, daily for breakfast, lunch, and dinner). This bright and cheery family restaurant is part of a big U.S. chain, but there are only a few north of the border. The menu is huge, with all breakfasts and lunches well under $10. Service is fast, friendly, and efficient.

INFORMATION

To get to the tourist information center (8 Gehring Rd. SE, 403/527-6422 or 800/481-2822, www.tourismmedicinehat.com, mid-June–August daily 8 A.M.–7 P.M., the rest of the year Mon.–Fri. 9 A.M.–5 P.M., Sat. 10 A.M.–3 P.M.), take the Southridge Drive exit from the TransCanada Highway just east of the big tepee. A good city website is www.city.medicine-hat.ab.ca.

Up the hill from downtown, **Mad Hatter Bookstore** (399 Aberdeen St. SE, 403/526-8563, Mon.–Fri. 9:30 A.M.–5:30 P.M., Sat. 9 A.M.–5 P.M.) has thousands of used books in relatively well-organized categories. The large **Medicine Hat Public Library** (414 1st St. SE, 403/502-8527, Mon.–Thurs. 10 A.M.–9 P.M., Fri.–Sat. 10 A.M.–5:30 P.M., Sun. 1–5:30 P.M.) overlooks the river and has a free paperback exchange.

GETTING THERE AND AROUND

Medicine Hat Municipal Airport is five kilometers (3.1 mi) west of downtown on Highway 3 toward Lethbridge. Within the airport is a small café and courtesy phones for Avis and National rental cars. **Air Canada** (888/247-2262) flies daily between Medicine Hat and Calgary. No city bus serves the airport. Cabs meet all flights; expect to pay approximately $8 to get downtown.

The **Greyhound** bus depot (557 2nd St. SE, 403/527-4418, www.greyhound.ca, 5 A.M.–11 P.M.) is in a convenient downtown location. Inside the terminal are coin lockers and a popular café. Buses run twice daily to and from Calgary with a change in Fort Macleod. Buses also go east to Regina and Winnipeg four times daily.

Medicine Hat Transit (403/529-8214) buses run from downtown throughout the suburbs daily except Sunday. One-way fare anywhere on the route is $2. For a cab, call **Deluxe Central Taxi** (403/526-3333).

CYPRESS HILLS PROVINCIAL PARK

Covering an area of 200 square kilometers (77 square mi), Cypress Hills is the fourth-largest provincial park in Alberta. It occupies only a small section of an upland plateau that extends well into Saskatchewan, with the entire area protected as **Cypress Hills Interprovincial Park.** The hills rise as much as 500 meters (1,640 ft) above the surrounding grasslands, and, at their greatest elevation (1,466 m/4,800 ft, the same as the town of Banff), they are the

highest point between the Canadian Rockies and Labrador. A forested oasis in the middle of the prairies, the park is thickly covered in lodgepole pine with stands of white spruce, poplar, and aspen. The French word for lodgepole pine is *cyprés,* which led to the hills being named Les Montagnes de Cyprés, and in turn Cypress Hills, when in fact cypress trees have never grown in the park. Fall and spring are particularly pleasant times of year to visit the park—crowds are nonexistent and wildlife is more visible—but bring a jacket.

The park is 70 kilometers (43 mi) southeast of Medicine Hat along Highway 41. It offers good hiking, fishing, or just plain relaxing, and is popular as a place to escape the high summer temperatures of the prairies. The only commercial facilities within the park are in the townsite

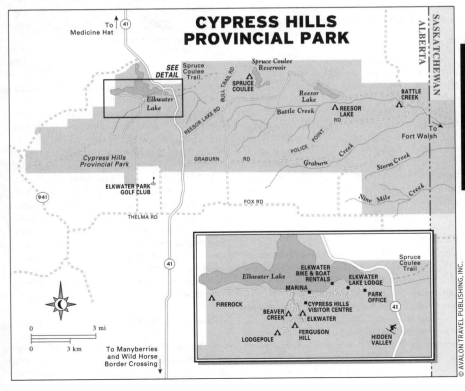

of **Elkwater,** which sits in a natural amphitheater overlooking **Elkwater Lake.** The facilities are limited (no bank, one restaurant, one motel, one gas station), so come prepared.

The Land

The hills are capped with a conglomerate composed of rounded pebbles carried east from the Rockies by a broad stream approximately 40 million years ago. When the massive sheets of ice moved slowly southward during the ice age, they thinned and split at the 1,400-meter (4,600-ft) level of the plateau. The top 100 meters (330 ft) remained unglaciated, forming a *nunatak* (an island of land surrounded by ice) of approximately 150 square kilometers (58 square mi). When the climate warmed and the sheet of ice slowly receded, its meltwaters rushed around and through the hills, slashing into the plateau and forming the narrow canyons and coulees that are visible today.

Flora

The park supports more than 400 recorded plant species in four ecological zones: prairie, parkland, foothills, and boreal forest. The best way to view the flora of the park is on foot; many trails pass through two or three zones in the space of an hour's walking. Sixteen species of orchids are found in the park—some are very common, whereas others, such as the sparrow's egg lady's slipper, are exceedingly rare. The book *A Guide to the Orchids of Cypress Hills,* by Robert M. Fisher, will tell you all you want to know. The visitors center has a copy of the book you can look at.

Fauna

The unique environment of the hills provides a favorable habitat for 37 species of mammals, 400 species of birds, and a few turtles. Big game was once common throughout the hills, but in 1926 the last remaining large mammal—a wolf—was shot. Soon thereafter, elk were reintroduced to the park and now number more than 200. Moose, never before present in the park, were introduced in the 1950s and now number about 60. Other large mammals

© ANDREW HEMPSTEAD

Foxes are common throughout the Cypress Hills.

present in the park are mule deer, white-tailed deer, coyotes, and beavers.

Many bird species here are more typically found in the Canadian Rockies foothills, 250 kilometers (150 mi) to the west. About 90 species are transient, coming to the hills only to nest. Other species spend the entire year in the park. This is the only spot in the province with recordings of the common poorwill, which is rarely seen but occasionally heard. Wild turkeys were introduced in the 1930s, and their descendants can be heard warbling in certain parts of the park. Elkwater Lake and Spruce Coulee Reservoir are good spots for waterbird-watching. Cormorants and trumpeter swans are common. A bird checklist is available at the visitors center.

Cultural History

To the native bands of Cree, Blackfoot, and Assiniboine, this area was known as "Thunder Breeding Hills," a mysterious place that was home to plains grizzly bears, cougars,

wolves, and kit foxes—all long since extinct in the area. These people followed the wandering herds of bison and had little need to visit the hills except to pick berries and collect various plants for medicinal and ceremonial uses. Little evidence of this early culture remains, although one archaeological site dating from 5000 B.C. has been studied. After the Cypress Hills Massacre, when 20 innocent Assiniboine were killed, the NWMP sent approximately 300 men to Fort Walsh (on the Saskatchewan side of the hills). The fort is now a National Historical Site.

Exploring the Park

Various roads link the townsite of Elkwater to lakes and viewpoints within the park. Because of glacial sediment called *loess,* the paved roads at higher elevations are terribly potholed. Unpaved roads are even worse and can become impassable after heavy rain. To access the center of the park, take Reesor Lake Road east from Highway 41, passing a herd of cattle and a viewpoint with spectacular vistas of the transition from grassland to boreal forest. The road then descends steeply to **Reesor Lake,** which has a campground, a picnic area, a short hiking trail to a viewpoint, and excellent fishing for rainbow trout. Bull Trail Road off Reesor Lake Road leads to **Spruce Coulee** and a reservoir stocked with eastern brook and rainbow trout. Unmarked gravel roads crisscross the park and head into Saskatchewan. Hiking within the park is limited. Most of the trails are easy to moderate, following the shores of Elkwater Lake (wheelchair accessible) and climbing out of the townsite into open fields and mixed forests. **Spruce Coulee Trail** (eight km/five mi) is the longest hike. It starts behind the rodeo grounds and leads through woodland and past a few beaver ponds before reaching Spruce Coulee.

Just east of the marina, **Elkwater Boat & Bike Rentals** (403/893-3835) rents mountain bikes ($5 per hour, $25 per day), canoes ($8 per hour, $40 per day), motorboats ($16 per hour), and Jet Skis ($55 per hour). Golfers have been walking the rolling fairways of **Elkwater Park**

Golf Club (403/893-2167, $23, or $60 for five days) since 1937.

Winter Recreation

Although summer is the park's busiest time of year, many people are attracted by the range of winter activities possible. **Hidden Valley** (403/893-3961) is a decent-sized alpine resort (by prairie standards) with a vertical drop of 176 meters (580 ft) and two lifts and two rope tows that access a few beginner and intermediate runs, and a small snowboarding park. A full day skiing or boarding costs $32. The hill is three kilometers (1.9 mi) south of Elkwater. Equipment rentals are available at the hill.

The park also offers 25 kilometers (15.5 mi) of cross-country ski trails for all levels of expertise, ice fishing on the lakes, toboggan hills, and winter camping for the brave.

Accommodations and Food

The old Green Tree Motel has been replaced by the stellar **⊂ Elkwater Lake Lodge** (401 4th St., 403/893-3811 or 888/893-3811, www.elkwaterlakelodge.com), and a good thing too. The new version features spacious air-conditioned, kitchen-equipped standard rooms ($105 s or d, or $115 with a deck), fireplace rooms ($120–130 s or d), condos with one to three bedrooms (from $115 s or d), and rustic cabins with kitchens ($125 s or d). But my favorite are the Alpine Cabins ($160 s or d), with vaulted ceilings, full kitchens, and patios with outdoor fireplaces. Other amenities include an indoor saltwater pool, a hot tub, a library filled with local literature, and landscaped gardens that include an outdoor rock fireplace. Also on site is **Buglers,** an inviting restaurant open daily for breakfast, lunch, and dinner. The dinner menu covers all bases, with mains ranging $18–28 and delicious cheesecake for $6.

Camping

Within the park are more than 500 campsites in 12 campgrounds. The main camping season is mid-May to mid-September although some campgrounds remain open year-round with limited facilities. Closest to Elkwater

are **Beaver Creek Campground** ($30) with full hookups and **Elkwater Campground** ($20–30) with unserviced sites and hookups. Both have showers. Through Elkwater Campground and up the hill is **Ferguson Hill Campground** ($20) and then **Lodgepole Campground** ($20). **Firerock Campground** (unserviced sites $20, powered $25) on Elkwater Lake is particularly nice. It is linked to town by the Shoreline Trail. **Reesor Lake Campground** ($20, no showers or hookups) at the eastern end of the park is much quieter—listen for bugling elk in the fall. An eight-kilometer (five-mi) hike from the rodeo grounds follows an abandoned road to **Spruce Coulee** (or you can drive), where you'll find 10 walk-in tent sites ($15) and good fishing in the reservoir. Reservations for some campgrounds are taken (call 403/893-3835 or 403/893-3782 Mon.–Fri. only).

Information and Services

The large **Cypress Hills Visitor Centre** (403/893-3833, mid-May–Aug. daily 9 A.M.–5 P.M.) overlooks Elkwater Lake, a short walk from the townsite campgrounds. Audiovisual programs explain the natural history and archaeological and historical resources of the park, and a nightly interpretive program operates during July and August. For information in the off-season, try the park office (403/893-3777, Mon.–Fri. 8:15 A.M.–4:30 P.M.). The website www.cypresshills.com is a good source of general park information.

Cardston and Vicinity

Cardston is a town of 3,500 at the base of the foothills 76 kilometers (47 mi) southwest of Lethbridge and 35 kilometers (22 mi) north of the U.S. border. Its rich heritage and a fine carriage museum make it an interesting stop in itself, as well as a good base for exploring Waterton Lakes National Park (a half-hour drive to the west). The town was founded in 1887 by Charles Ora Card of the Church of Jesus Christ of Latter-day Saints (better known as the Mormon Church) after leading 11 families north from Utah in covered wagons. Card chose a spot to settle on Lee Creek and soon established a townsite, including a main street more than 30 meters (100 ft) wide, resembling those in Salt Lake City. These settlers developed Alberta's first irrigation system, which has grown to become the lifeblood of southern Alberta's economic base.

SIGHTS
◖ Remington Carriage Museum
This world-class museum (623 Main St., 403/653-5139, mid-May–mid-Sept. daily 9 A.M.–6 P.M., the rest of the year daily 10 A.M.–5 P.M., adult $8, senior $7, child $4)

focusing on the era of horse-drawn transportation holds North America's largest collection of carriages, buggies, and wagons—around 225 at last count. The main exhibit galleries tell the story of the horse-and-buggy era through a life-sized early-20th-century townscape. You can transport yourself through time by watching blacksmiths at work in the carriage factory, listening to deals being made at the carriage dealer, or wandering over to the racetrack, where the rich liked to be seen on their elegant carriages. Throughout summer, rides are offered on restored and replica carriages (adult $4, child $2.50) and there's a full schedule of events in the arena, including the mid-August World Championship Miniature Chuckwagon Races. The center also has a theater, restaurant, and a gift shop.

Alberta Temple
While living in simple log cabins, the early Mormon pioneers started planning the construction of the first Mormon temple built outside of the United States. The Cardston Alberta Temple of the Church of Jesus Christ of Latter Day Saints, to give its full name, is a

grandly symmetrical marble and granite structure that is visible from just about everywhere in town. Only members of the Mormon faith in good standing may enter the temple itself, but a visitors center (348 3rd St. W, 403/653-1696, May–Sept. daily 9 A.M.–9 P.M., free) beside the main entrance is open to the public. It depicts the story of the decade-long construction process, with photographs of the stone being hauled in from British Columbia and the massive derrick used to move the blocks into place. It's a friendly little room staffed by church members who are genuinely interested in talking to visitors about their temple.

Card Pioneer Home

When Charles Ora Card first arrived in 1887, he built a small log cabin on what would become Cardston's main drag. Today his humble home stands in its original location (337 Main St., July–Aug. Mon.–Sat. 1:30 A.M.–5 P.M., donation). It was the center of the community for many years. Town meetings were held inside, and travelers rested there before a hotel was built in 1894.

Courthouse Museum

This small, solid courthouse (3rd Ave. just off Main St., 403/653-4322, June–Aug. Mon.–Sat.

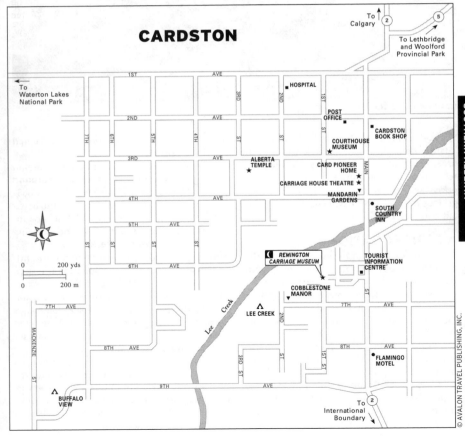

SOUTHERN ALBERTA

© AVALON TRAVEL PUBLISHING, INC.

© ANDREW HEMPSTEAD

Cardston Courthouse Museum

9 A.M.–12:30 P.M.) was built in 1907 from locally quarried sandstone and was used longer than any other courthouse in the province before being refurnished as a museum. Exhibits include a pioneer home, artifacts from early settlers, and a geology display. In the basement are the original jail cells with graffiti-covered walls.

ACCOMMODATIONS

The choices are simple here—good-value motel rooms or camping downtown or in one of the nearby provincial parks. Least expensive of Cardston's motels is the **Flamingo Motel,** two blocks up the hill from the Remington Carriage Museum (848 Main St., 403/653-3952 or 888/806-6835, $65 s, $75 d). The 38 rooms each have a fridge and microwave while other amenities include a small outdoor pool, barbecue area, and coin laundry. **South Country Inn** (404 Main St., 403/653-8000 or 888/653-2615, www.south countryinn.ca, $81 s, $94 d) is the newer of the town's three motels, is closer to down-

town, and has an indoor pool and attached family restaurant.

Within walking distance of the Remington Carriage Museum is **Lee Creek Campground** (at the end of 7th Ave. W, off Main St., 403/653-3734, May–Sept., unserviced sites $15, full hookups $20), an excellent facility with full hookups and showers. Farther out you'll find camping at **Woolford Provincial Park** (403/382-4097, May–Sept., $13), although facilities are limited to picnic tables, firewood, and pit toilets. Sites are $13 per night. To reach the park, travel three kilometers (1.9 mi) northeast of Cardston on Highway 3, then southeast for 13 kilometers (eight mi) along a gravel road. The campground is small, and facilities are limited to picnic tables, firewood, and pit toilets. Sites are $13 per night. Also east of town, Highway 505 west from Spring Coulee quickly leads to the signs for the two campgrounds within **St. Mary's Reservoir Provincial Recreation Area** (mid-May–Oct., $10), also with limited facilities, but with beautiful sandy beaches and warm water.

FAMILY CAMPING FUN

Rather than just a place to bed down for the night, the **Great Canadian Barn Dance Campground** (Wynder Rd., Hill Spring, 403/626-3407 or 866/626-3407, www.greatcanadianbarndance.com, May–Oct.) is a vacation destination for hundreds of Albertan families each weekend. As the name suggests, the action at this converted farm property with distant mountain views revolves around a barn dance, held in an authentic barn. A casual roast beef dinner is included in the admission of adult $22.50, child $16. Although the facility is busiest on weekends, you can camp through the week, with activities such as swimming and canoeing to keep the young ones happy. Full hookups start at $25, with sites closest to the lake going for $30. Unserviced sites are $20. The facility is roughly halfway between Cardston and Pincher Creek; to get there from the former, head 15 kilometers (nine miles) north on Highway 2 then 26 kilometers (16 miles) west on Highway 505 to Wynder Road. The distances from Pincher Creek – south on Highway 6, and then east on Highway 505 – are similar.

© ANDREW HEMPSTEAD

FOOD AND ENTERTAINMENT

Cobblestone Manor (173 7th Ave. W, 403/653-2701, Mon.–Sat. for breakfast, lunch, and dinner) is a unique place to indulge in some fine food. The original log structure dates to 1889, two years after the first Mormons arrived. In 1913, an eccentric gentleman from Belgium bought the home and added more rooms, using cobblestones for building blocks. The interior wall panels and ceilings are inlaid with thousands of pieces of hardwood, and the stained-glass bookshelves, Tiffany lights, and antique furniture add to the Old World ambience. The food is traditional European, with mains starting from $18.

In the Remington Carriage Museum, the **Carriage House Restaurant** (623 Main St., 403/653-5139, summer daily 9 A.M.–5 P.M., Thurs.–Sat. until 9 P.M.) is a good place for a meal after touring the museum, or return

in the evening for a roast-beef buffet ($16 per person). Along the main street, you'll find the usual array of small-town restaurants, including **Mandarin Gardens** (365 Main St., 403/653-1288, daily 11 A.M.–8:30 P.M.), which is surprisingly busy with the locals.

Carriage House Theatre (353 Main St., 403/653-1000) has a summer program of live theater productions, including musicals, comedy, and special events with a local theme. The performances are held July–August Tuesday–Saturday nights at 7:30 P.M. and cost around $15.

INFORMATION

The tourist information center (621 Main St., 403/653-3787, mid-May–Aug. daily 8 A.M.–8 P.M.) is in a big open-plan building at the entrance to the carriage museum. **Cardston Book Shop** (226 Main St., 403/653-4222, Mon.–Sat. 9 A.M.–6 P.M.) has an interesting selection of religious books and texts, as well as a small selection of general Canadiana.

SOUTH FROM CARDSTON

South of Cardston is the Old Mormon Trail that settlers from Utah used on their way north. The town of **Aetna,** just off Highway 2, was once a thriving Mormon community with a cheese factory, a school, and a store. A worthwhile stop in Aetna is **Jensen's Trading Post,** a general store with an interesting collection of antiques.

If you're heading east from here, this is the beginning of the true prairie, and it's hard not to keep glancing in the rearview mirror for glimpses of the mountains you're leaving behind. From Aetna, Highway 501 skirts the International Boundary, passing the ruins of a community once known as Whiskey Gap. It crosses Highway 62 north of the Del Bonita port of entry (June 1–Sept. 15 daily 9 A.M.–9 P.M., the rest of the year daily 9 A.M.–6 P.M.) and continues east to Milk River through arid grassland not suitable for cultivation (see *The Milk River* earlier in this chapter). Along much of the way the Sweetgrass Hills in Montana are visible rising high above the prairies south of Writing-on-Stone Provincial Park.

Beyond the turnoff to Aetna, Highway 2 continues to the International Boundary. **Police Outpost Provincial Park,** on a small lake beside the International Boundary, is accessible along a 23-kilometer (14-mi) gravel road 10 kilometers (6.2 mi) south of Cardston. The police outpost that gave the lake and park their name was set up in 1891 to control smuggling of whiskey north across the border, but the remote location led to its closure soon after. From the park, spectacular **Chief Mountain** can be seen to the southwest. Most of the park is grassland interspersed with isolated stands of aspen and wetlands, where birdlife is prolific. Fishing in Outpost Lake is good for rainbow trout. The park's campground has pit toilets and picnic tables; sites are $17.

The highway crosses into Montana at the Carway-Piegan port of entry (year-round daily 7 A.M.–11 P.M.).

Waterton Lakes National Park

Everybody traveling to this rugged 526-square-kilometer (203-square-mile) park does so by choice. It's not on the way to anywhere else or on a major highway, but rather is tucked away in the extreme southwestern corner of Alberta. The park is bounded to the north and east by the rolling prairies covering southern Alberta; to the south by the U.S. border and Glacier National Park in Montana; and to the west by the Continental Divide, which forms the Alberta–British Columbia border. The natural mountain splendor, a chain of deep glacial lakes, large and diverse populations of wildlife, an unbelievable variety of day hikes, and a changing face each season make this park a gem that shouldn't be missed.

The route to Waterton is almost as scenic as the park itself. From whichever direction you arrive, the transition from prairie to mountains is abrupt, almost devoid of the foothills that characterize other areas along the eastern slopes of the Canadian Rockies. From the park gate, two roads penetrate the mountains to the west. One ends at a large glaciated lake, the other at a spectacular canyon.

Note: Most park businesses are closed for the winter, including all but a couple of accommodations. The main access road is plowed regularly, and the Akamina Parkway is cleared to allow access to cross-country ski trails.

Park Entry

All visitors to Waterton Lakes are required to stop at the park entrance and buy a permit. Park entry for one day is adult $8, senior $6, child $4, to a maximum of $18 per vehicle.

THE LAND
Geology

Major upheavals under the earth's surface that occurred approximately 85 million years ago forced huge plates of rock upward and began folding them over each other. One major sheet, known as the Lewis Overthrust, forms the backbone of Waterton's topography as we see it today. It slid up and over much-younger bedrock along a 300-kilometer (186-mi) length extending north to the Bow Valley. Approximately 45 million years ago, this powerful uplift ceased, and the forces of erosion took over. About 1.9 million years ago, glaciers from the sheet of ice that once covered most of Alberta crept through the mountains. As these thick sheets of ice advanced and retreated with climatic changes, they gouged out valleys such as the classically U-shaped **Waterton Valley.** The three Waterton Lakes are depressions left at the base of the steep-sided mountains after the ice had completely retreated 11,000 years ago. The deepest lake is 150 meters (500 ft). **Cameron Lake,** at the end of the Akamina Parkway, was formed when a moraine—the pile of rock that accumulates at the foot of a retreating glacier—dammed Cameron Creek. From the lake, Cameron Creek flows through a glaciated valley before dropping into the much deeper Waterton Valley at **Cameron Falls,** behind the town of Waterton. The town itself sits on an alluvial fan composed of silt and gravel picked up by mountain streams and deposited in Upper Waterton Lake.

Climate

Climate plays an active role in the park's natural landscape. This corner of the province tends to receive more rain, snow, and wind—much more wind—than other parts of Alberta. These factors, combined with the park's varied topography, create an environment where approximately 900 species of plants have been recorded—more than half the known species in Alberta. Wind is the most powerful presence in the park. Prevailing winds from the south and west bring Pacific weather over the divide, creating a climate similar to that experienced farther west. These warm fronts endow the region with **chinooks,** dry winds that can raise temperatures in the park by up to 40°C in 24 hours. One of the nicest aspects of the park is that it can be enjoyed in all seasons. Summer

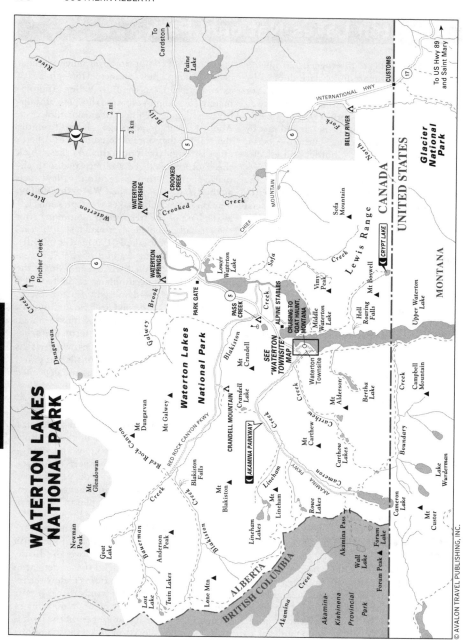

WATERTON LAKES NATIONAL PARK

SOUTHERN ALBERTA

© AVALON TRAVEL PUBLISHING, INC.

for the sunny windless days, fall for the wildlife-viewing, winter for the solitude, and spring for the long days of sunlight as the park seems to be waking up from its winter slumber. Be aware, however, that many of the park's best sights and hiking trails lie at high elevations; some areas may be snowed in until mid-June.

Flora

Botanists have recorded 1,200 species of plants growing within the park's several different vegetation zones. In the park's northeastern corner, near the park gate, a region of prairies is covered in semiarid vegetation such as fescue grass. As Highway 5 enters the park it passes **Maskinonge Lake,** a wetlands area of marshy ponds where aquatic plants flourish. Parkland habitat dominated by aspen is found along the north side of Blakiston Valley and near Belly River Campground, whereas montane forest covers most mountain valleys and lower slopes. This latter zone is dominated by a high canopy of lodgepole pine and Douglas fir, shading a forest floor covered with wildflowers and berries. An easily accessible section of this habitat is along the lower half of Bertha Lake Trail; an interpretive brochure is available at the Waterton Visitor Centre.

Above the montane forest is the subalpine zone, which rises as far as the timberline. These distinct forests of larch, fir, Engelmann spruce, and whitebark pine can be seen along the Carthew Lakes Trail. On the west-facing slopes of Cameron Lakes are mature groves of subalpine trees up to 400 years old—this oldest growth in the park has managed to escape fire over the centuries. Blanketing the open mountain slopes in this zone is bear grass, which grows up to one meter in height and is topped by a bright blossom often likened to a lighted torch. Above the treeline is the alpine zone where harsh winds and short summer seasons make trees a rarity. Only lichens and alpine wildflowers flourish at these high altitudes. Crypt Lake is a good place for viewing this zone.

Fauna

Two major flyways pass the park, and from September to November many thousands of waterfowl stop on Maskinonge and Lower Waterton Lakes. On a power pole beside the entrance to the park is an active osprey nest—ask staff to point it out for you.

Wildlife-viewing in the park requires patience and a little know-how, but the rewards are ample, as good as anywhere in Canada. Elk inhabit the park year-round. A large herd gathers by Entrance Road in late fall, wintering on the lowlands. By early fall many mule deer are wandering around town. Bighorn sheep are often seen on the north side of Blakiston Valley or on the slopes above the Waterton Visitor Centre; occasionally they end up in town. White-tailed deer are best viewed along Red Rock Canyon Parkway. The park has a small population of moose occasionally seen in low-lying wetlands. Mountain goats rarely leave the high peaks of the backcountry, but from Goat, Crypt, or Bertha Lakes you might catch a glimpse of one perched on a cliff high above you.

The most common predators in the park are the coyotes that spend their summer days chasing ground squirrels around the prairie and parkland areas. For its size, Waterton has a healthy population of cougars, but these shy, solitary animals are rarely seen. Approximately 50 black bears live in the park. They spend most of the summer in the heavily forested montane regions. During August and September, scan the slopes of Blakiston Valley, where they can often be seen feasting on Saskatoon berries before going into winter hibernation. Much larger than black bears are the grizzlies, which roam the entire backcountry but are rarely encountered.

Golden-mantled ground squirrels live on the Bear's Hump and around Cameron Falls. Columbian ground squirrels are just about everywhere. Chipmunks scamper about on Bertha Lake Trail. The best times for viewing beavers are dawn and dusk along the Belly River. Muskrats can be seen on the edges of Maskinonge Lake eating bulrushes. Mink also live in the lake but are seen only by those with patience.

© ANDREW HEMPSTEAD

Bighorn sheep are commonly spotted around the edge of Waterton townsite.

HISTORY

Evidence found within the park suggests that the Kootenai (also spelled Kootenay) people who lived west of the park made trips across the Continental Divide approximately 8,400 years ago to hunt bison on the plains and fish in the lakes. They camped in the valleys during winter, sheltering from the harsh weather. But by approximately 1,500 years ago, they were spending more time in the West and crossing the mountains only a few times a year to hunt bison. By the 1700s, the Blackfoot—with the help of horses—had expanded their territory from the Battle River throughout southwestern Alberta. They patrolled the mountains on horseback, making it difficult for the Kootenai hunting parties to cross, but their dominance was short-lived. With the arrival of guns and the encroaching homesteads of early settlers, Blackfoot tribes retreated to the east, leaving the Waterton Lakes Valley uninhabited.

"Kootenai" Brown

John George Brown was born in England in the 1840s and reputedly educated at Oxford Uni-

versity. He joined the army and went to India, later continuing to San Francisco. Then, like thousands of others, he headed for the Cariboo goldfields of British Columbia, quickly spending any of the gold he found. After a while he moved on, heading east into Waterton Valley, where his party was attacked by Blackfoot. He was shot in the back with an arrow and pulled it out himself. Brown acquired his nickname through his close association with the Kootenai people, hunting buffalo and wolves with them until they had all but disappeared.

Even though Brown had been toughened by the times, he was a conservationist at heart. After marrying in 1869, he built a cabin by the Waterton Lakes and became the valley's first permanent resident. Soon he started promoting the beauty of the area to the people of Fort Macleod. One of his friends, local rancher F. W. Godsal, began lobbying the federal government to establish a reserve. In 1895 an area was set aside as a Forest Reserve, with Brown as its first warden. In 1911 the area was declared a national park and Brown, age 71, was appointed its superintendent. He continued to push for an

expansion of park boundaries until his final retirement at age 75. He died a few years later. His grave along the main access road to the townsite is a fitting resting place for one of Alberta's most celebrated mountain men.

Oil City

Kootenai Brown was the first person to notice beads of oil floating on Cameron Creek. He and a business partner siphoned it from the water's surface, bottled it, and sold it in Fort Macleod and Cardston. This created much interest among the oil-starved entrepreneurs of Alberta, who formed the Rocky Mountain Development Co. to do some exploratory drilling. At this stage, the park was still a Forest Reserve; the trees were protected, but prospecting and mining were still allowed. A rough road was constructed through the Cameron Creek Valley, and in September 1901 the company struck oil at a depth of 311 meters (1,020 ft). It was the first producing oil well in western Canada and only the second in the country. In the resulting euphoria, a townsite named Oil City was cleared and surveyed, a bunkhouse and dining hall were constructed, and the foundations for a hotel were laid, but the boom was short-lived. Drilling rigs kept breaking down, and the flow of oil soon slowed to a trickle. A monument along the Akamina Parkway stands at the site of the well, and a little farther up the road at a roadside marker a trail leads through thick undergrowth to the townsite. All that remain are the ill-fated hotel foundations and some depressions in the ground.

Waterton-Glacier International Peace Park

Shortly after Montana's Glacier National Park was created in 1910, the Canadian government set aside an area of land in the Waterton Valley as Waterton Lakes Dominion Park (later to be renamed a national park). Many people followed the footsteps of Kootenai Brown, and a small town named Waterton Lakes grew up on the Cameron Creek Delta. The town had no rail link, so unlike Banff and Jasper—its famous mountain neighbors to the north—it

didn't draw large crowds of tourists. Nevertheless, it soon became a popular summer retreat with a hotel, a restaurant, and a dance hall. The Great Northern Railway decided to operate a bus service from its Montana rail line to Jasper, with a stop at Waterton Lakes. This led to the construction of the **Prince of Wales Hotel** and summer boat cruises back across the U.S. border and into Glacier National Park. This brought the two parks closer together, and in 1932 Waterton–Glacier International Peace Park was established, the first of its kind in the world. The parks are administered separately but cooperate in preserving this pristine mountain wilderness through combined wildlife management, interpretive programs, and search-and-rescue operations. Peace Park celebrations take place each year, and the **Peace Park Pavilion** by the lake is dedicated to this unique bond. In 1979, UNESCO declared the park a **Biosphere Reserve**, only the second such reserve in Canada. The park gained further recognition in 1995, when, along with Glacier National Park, it was declared a **World Heritage Site** by UNESCO.

WATERTON TOWNSITE

Make your first stop the **Waterton Visitor Centre** (403/859-5133; June–Aug. daily 9 A.M.–8 P.M., May and early Sept. daily 9 A.M.–5 P.M., closed the rest of the year), on the slight rise before the road descends to the townsite.

Waterton Heritage Centre

The park's only official manmade "sight" is the Waterton Heritage Centre (117 Waterton Ave., 403/859-2624; May–Sept. daily 10 A.M.–5 P.M., July and Aug. daily until 8 P.M.). This small museum contains exhibits telling the story of the park's natural and human history, including a section of aspen in which a trapper carved his initials over 100 years ago. It also holds a selection of paintings and woodcarvings created by local artists as well as a selection of local interest books. The heritage center is operated by the Waterton Natural History Association, which runs a variety of educational programs.

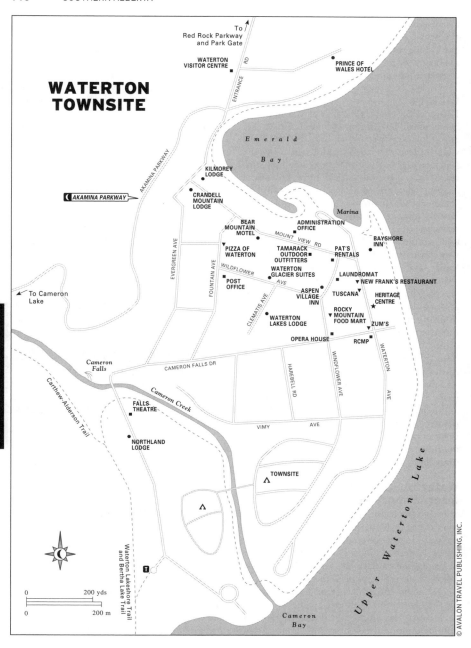

WATERTON TOWNSITE

To Red Rock Parkway and Park Gate

WATERTON VISITOR CENTRE

PRINCE OF WALES HOTEL

ENTRANCE RD

AKAMINA PARKWAY

Emerald Bay

KILMOREY LODGE

◀ AKAMINA PARKWAY ▶

CRANDELL MOUNTAIN LODGE

Marina

BEAR MOUNTAIN MOTEL

ADMINISTRATION OFFICE

MOUNT VIEW RD

BAYSHORE INN

EVERGREEN AVE

PIZZA OF WATERTON

TAMARACK OUTDOOR OUTFITTERS

PAT'S RENTALS

WILDFLOWER AVE

FOUNTAIN AVE

WATERTON GLACIER SUITES

LAUNDROMAT

POST OFFICE

NEW FRANK'S RESTAURANT

To Cameron Lake

ASPEN VILLAGE INN

TUSCANA

HERITAGE CENTRE

CLEMATIS AVE

WATERTON LAKES LODGE

ROCKY MOUNTAIN FOOD MART

ZUM'S

OPERA HOUSE

RCMP

WATERTON AVE

Cameron Falls

CAMERON FALLS DR

HAREBELL RD

WINDFLOWER AVE

AVE

Carthew-Alderson Trail

Cameron Creek

FALLS THEATRE

VIMY AVE

NORTHLAND LODGE

TOWNSITE
Λ

Λ

Waterton Lakeshore Trail and Bertha Lake Trail

T

Upper Waterton Lake

0   200 yds
0   200 m

Cameron Bay

From the heritage center, wander south along the lakeshore to a large picnic area and the trailhead for the Waterton Lakeshore Trail (see *Hiking*) or north to the **International Peace Park Pavilion** and stunning views across Emerald Bay to the Prince of Wales Hotel.

SCENIC DRIVES
Akamina Parkway
This road starts in the townsite and switchbacks up into the Cameron Creek Valley, making an elevation gain of 400 meters (1,310 ft) before ending after 16 kilometers (10 mi) at Cameron Lake. The viewpoint one kilometer (0.6 mi) from the junction of the park road is on a tight curve, so park off the road. From this lookout, views extend over the townsite and the **Bear's Hump,** which was originally part of a high ridge that extended across the lake to Vimy Peak (glacial action ultimately wore down the rest of the ridge). This section of the road is also a good place to view bighorn sheep. Between here and Cameron Lake there

are several picnic areas and stops of interest, including the site of Alberta's first producing oil well and, a little farther along the road, the site of **Oil City,** the town that never was.

Cameron Lake, at the end of the road, is a 2.5-kilometer-long (1.5-mile-long) subalpine lake that reaches depths of more than 40 meters (130 ft). It lies in a large cirque carved out about 11,000 years ago by a receding glacier. Mount Custer at the southern end of the lake is in Montana. Waterton has no glaciers, but Herbst Glacier on Mount Custer can be seen from here. To the west (right) of Custer is **Forum Peak** (2,225 m/7,300 ft), whose summit cairn marks the boundaries of Alberta, Montana, and British Columbia.

Beside the lakeshore are enclosed information boards and a concession stand (June–Aug. daily 7:30 A.M.–7:30 P.M.) selling light snacks and renting kayaks ($20 s, $25 d per hour) as well as canoes, rowboats, and paddleboats (all $25 for the first hour, $20 for additional hours). A narrow trail leads along the lake's

© ANDREW HEMPSTEAD

Travelers along the Akamina Parkway are rewarded with magnificent views across Cameron Lake from the end of the road.

SOUTHERN ALBERTA

west shoreline, ending after 1.5 kilometers (0.9 mi) at a viewing platform surrounded by cow parsnip; allow 30 minutes each way. Take notice of bear warnings for this trail, as it ends in prime grizzly habitat.

Red Rock Canyon Parkway

The best roadside wildlife-viewing within the park is along this 13-kilometer (eight-mile) road that starts near the golf course and finishes at **Red Rock Canyon.** The transition between rolling prairies and mountains takes place abruptly as you travel up the Blakiston Valley. Black bears (and very occasionally grizzly bears) can be seen feeding on saskatoon berries along the open slopes to the north. **Mount Blakiston** (2,920 m/9,580 ft), the park's highest summit, is visible from a viewpoint three kilometers (1.9 mi) along the road. The road passes interpretive signs, picnic areas, and Crandell Mountain Campground. At the end of the road is Red Rock Canyon, a water-carved gorge where the bedrock, known as argillite, contains a high concentration of iron. The iron oxidizes and turns red when exposed to air—literally going rusty. A short interpretive trail leads along the canyon.

Chief Mountain International Highway

This 25-kilometer (15.5-mi) highway, part of Highway 6, borders the eastern boundaries of the park and joins it to Glacier National Park in Montana. It starts east of the park gate at **Maskinonge Lake** and climbs for seven kilometers (4.3 mi) to a viewpoint where many jagged peaks and the entrance to Waterton Valley can be seen. The road then rounds Sofa Mountain, which still bears the scars from a wildfire that swept up its lower slopes in 1998. To the south, the distinctive peak is Chief Mountain, which has been separated from the main mountain range by erosion. The road then passes the Belly River Campground, and climbs to the border crossing of **Chief Mountain.** Hours of operation at this port of entry are: mid-May to the end of May daily 9 A.M.–6 P.M., June to early September daily

Maskinonge Lake

© ANDREW HEMPSTEAD

7 A.M.–10 P.M., early September to the end of the month daily 9 A.M.–6 P.M. When the post is closed, you must use the Carway-Piegan port of entry (year-round daily 7 A.M.–11 P.M.). It's on Alberta Highway 2 south of Cardston (or on Montana Highway 89 north of St. Mary, depending on your direction of travel).

HIKING

Although the park is relatively small, its trail system is extensive; 224 kilometers (140 mi) of well-maintained trails lead to alpine lakes and lofty summits affording spectacular views. One of the most appealing aspects of hiking in Waterton is that with higher trailheads than other parks in the Canadian Rockies, the tree line is reached quickly. Most of the lakes can be reached in a few hours. Once you've finished hiking the trails in Waterton, you can cross the international border and start on the 1,200 kilometers (746 mi) of trails in Glacier National Park.

The eight hikes detailed comprise only a small cross-section of Waterton's extensive trail system.

Bertha Lake

Most of the hikes climb to alpine lakes or viewpoints. Government topographic maps (one map covers the entire park) are available at the heritage center, but the best map for hikers is the Gem Trek version ($9), also widely available.

Bear's Hump

- Length: 1.2 kilometers/.7 mile (40 minutes) one-way

- Elevation gain: 225 meters/740 feet

- Rating: moderate

- Trailhead: Waterton Visitor Centre

This is one of the most popular short hikes in the park; although steep, it affords panoramic views of the Waterton Valley. From the back of the visitor center parking lot, the trail switchbacks up the northern flanks of the Bear's Hump, finishing at a rocky ledge high above town. From this vantage point the sweeping view extends north and east across the prairies and south along Upper Waterton Lake to Glacier National Park.

Bertha Lake

- Length: 5.8 kilometers/3.6 miles (two hours) one-way

- Elevation gain: 460 meters/1,510 feet

- Rating: Moderate

- Trailhead: South side of the townsite along Evergreen Avenue

Bertha Lake is a popular destination with day hikers and campers alike. For the first 1.5 kilometers (0.9 mi), moderate elevation gain is made to a lookout point and the junction of the Waterton Lakeshore Trail. Then the trail branches right and levels off for just over one kilometer (0.6 mi) to **Lower Bertha Falls.** While many casual hikers turn around at this point, you should plan on continuing to the final destination. It's uphill all the way as the trail crosses an old avalanche slope before switchbacking up through a subalpine forest to its maximum elevation on a ridge above the hanging valley in which Bertha Lake lies. Filtered views of **Upper Bertha Falls** provide

an excuse for a break along the way. From the trail's high point, it's a short walk down to the lakeshore, from where you can continue along either shoreline, or just relax under the trees with a picnic lunch. The lake itself is beautiful, both for its dark turquoise coloring and backdrop of mountain peaks.

Waterton Lakeshore

- Length: 14 kilometers/8.7 miles (four hours) one-way

- Elevation gain: minimal

- Rating: Moderate

- Trailhead: South side of the townsite along Evergreen Avenue

This trail follows the heavily forested western shores of Upper Waterton Lake across the international boundary to **Goat Haunt, Montana,** linking up with more than 1,200 kilometers (746 mi) of trails in Glacier National Park. Many hikers take the Waterton Cruise Company's **MV International** (403/859-2362, June–Sept. only, $18) one way and hike the other. Starting from town, the first 1.5 kilometers (0.9 mi) climbs steadily to a lookout point high above the lake, and then branches left off the Bertha Lake Trail, descending to Bertha Bay. The boat dock at Boundary Bay, six kilometers (3.7 mi) from town, is a good place for lunch. Hikers heading south and planning to camp in Glacier National Park must register at the Waterton Visitor Centre.

◖ Crypt Lake

- Length: 8.7 kilometers/5.4 miles (3–4 hours) one-way

- Elevation gain: 680 meters/2,230 feet

- Rating: Moderate/difficult

- Trailhead: Crypt Landing; access is by boat. The **Crypt Lake Shuttle** (403/859-2362, June–Sept., $16 round-trip) leaves the marina daily at 9 and 10 A.M. for Crypt Landing; return trips depart at 4 and 5:30 P.M.

This is one of the most spectacular day hikes in Canada. Access to the trailhead on the eastern side of Upper Waterton Lake is by boat. The trail switchbacks for 2.5 kilometers (1.6 mi) past a series of waterfalls and continues steeply up to a small green lake before reaching a campground. The final ascent to Crypt Lake from the campground causes the most problems, especially for those who suffer from claustrophobia or acrophobia. A ladder on the cliff face leads into a natural tunnel that you must crawl through on your hands and knees. The next part of the trail is along a narrow precipice with a cable for support. The lake at the end of the trail, nestled in a hanging valley, is no disappointment. Its dark green waters are rarely free of floating ice, and the steep walls of the cirque rise more than 500 meters (1,640 feet) above the lake on three sides. The international boundary is at the southern end of the lake. A good way to avoid the crowds on this trail is to camp at the dock and set out before the first boat arrives in the morning.

Crandell Lake

- Length: 2.4 kilometers/1.5 miles (40 minutes) one-way

- Elevation gain: 120 meters/395 feet

- Rating: Easy

- Trailhead: Crandell Campground, Red Rock Canyon Parkway

This easy hike to a subalpine lake is popular with campers staying at Crandell Campground. Alternatively, the trailhead can be reached by noncampers along the Canyon Church Camp access road.

The lake can also be accessed from a trailhead seven kilometers (4.3 mi) west of town along the Akamina Parkway. This trail is shorter (0.8 km/.5 mi) and follows a wagon road that was cut through the valley to Oil City.

Carthew-Alderson

- Length: 20 kilometers/12.4 miles (6–7 hours) one-way

- Elevation gain: 650 meters/2,130 feet

- Rating: Moderate/difficult
- Trailhead: End of Akamina Parkway, 16 kilometers (10 mi) from Waterton townsite

This hike linking the end of the Akamina Parkway to Waterton townsite can be completed in one long day or done with an overnight stop at Alderson Lake, 13 kilometers (eight mi) from the trailhead. The trail leads through most of the climatic zones of the park and offers some of the best scenery to be had on any one hike. Transportation to the trailhead can be arranged through **Tamarack Outdoor Outfitters** (Mount View Rd., 403/859-2378, $12 one-way), which operates a hiker shuttle service to this and other trailheads in the park. From the Cameron Lake parking lot, the trail climbs four kilometers (2.5 mi) to **Summit Lake**, a worthy destination in itself. The trail then forks to the left and climbs steeply to Carthew Ridge. After rising above the tree line and crossing a scree slope, the trail reaches its highest elevation of 2,310 meters (7,580 ft) at **Carthew Summit**. The views from here are spectacular, even more so if you scramble up to one of Mount Carthew's lower peaks. To the north is a hint of prairie, to the southeast the magnificent bowl-shaped cirque around Cameron Lake. To the south, the Carthew Lakes lie directly below, while glaciated peaks in Montana line the horizon. From this summit, the trail descends steeply to the Carthew Lakes, reenters the subalpine forest, and emerges at **Alderson Lake,** which is nestled under the headwalls of Mount Alderson. The trail then descends through the Carthew Creek Valley and finishes at Cameron Falls in the townsite.

OTHER RECREATION
Cruising to Goat Haunt, Montana
This is the most popular organized activity in Waterton. From the marina in downtown Waterton townsite, **Waterton Inter-Nation Shoreline Cruise Company** (403/859-2362) runs scheduled cruises across the international boundary to Goat Haunt, Montana, at the southern end of Upper Waterton Lake. The 45-minute trip along the lakeshore passes spectacular mountain scenery and usually wildlife. A half-hour stopover is made at Goat Haunt, which lies in a remote part of Glacier National Park and consists of little more than a dock and interpretive displays. You can return on the same boat or go hiking and return later in the day. If you are planning an overnight hike from here, you are required to register at the Waterton Visitor Centre before heading out on the lake. Another popular option is to take an early boat trip and walk back to town on the **Waterton Lakeshore Trail,** which takes about four hours. Departures are twice daily May–June and September to early October and four times daily in July and August (first departure at 9 A.M.). Remember, you are crossing into another country on this cruise, so correct documentation is required, including for U.S. citizens. Early and late in the season, the border crossing is closed, and therefore the cruise doesn't include a landing. Tickets cost $32 round-trip, $18 one-way (children are half price), and you'll need to book ahead in summer. The same company operates a regular shuttle service to the Crypt Lake trailhead for $16 round-trip.

Fishing
Fishing in the lakes is average, with most anglers chasing brook and rainbow trout, pike, and whitefish. A national-park fishing license is required and can be obtained from the Waterton Visitor Centre or any of the administration offices. The license costs $10 for seven days or $35 for an annual permit.

Diving
On any given summer day, scuba divers can be seen slipping into the frigid waters of Emerald Bay. A steamer was scuttled in the bay in 1918. It had been used to haul logs and as a tearoom but now sits on the lake's floor, attracting divers who find it a novelty to explore a sunken ship so far from the ocean. No equipment rental is available in the park. The closest is at **Anderson Aquatics** in Lethbridge (314 11th St. S, 403/328-5040), where you can also get your tanks filled. Full gear rental from Anderson is

$50 per day, $75 for the weekend, including air fills. Through this shop, certification courses and field trips to Waterton Lakes are organized throughout the summer. Stop in on your way to the park for a rundown on all the dives, or ask at the Waterton Visitor Centre.

Golf

The rolling fairways and spectacular mountain backdrop of **Waterton Lakes Golf Course** (403/859-2114) can distract even the keenest golfer's attention. The 18-hole course, designed by Stanley Thompson and dating to 1929, is not particularly long (6,103 yards) or difficult, but the surrounding mountains and unhurried pace of play make for a pleasant environment. The course is four kilometers (2.5 mi) north of the townsite on the main access road and is open June to early October. A round of golf costs $38. Club rentals are $8, and a power cart is an additional $28 per round. At the end of your round, plan on relaxing at the clubhouse over a light meal and cold drink.

Horseback Riding

Just off the main park access road before town is **Alpine Stables** (403/859-2462), which offers hour-long trail rides (starting on the hour 9 A.M.–5 P.M.) for $25. Two-hour rides cost $42 and pass through prime wildlife-viewing habitat. The three-hour ride, costing $58, takes in the bison paddock, while eight hours in the saddle opens up possibilities such as a climb to the summit of Vimy Peak for $119. These longer rides leave on demand, so call ahead to make a reservation.

When the Sun Goes Down

Roasting marshmallows at your campsite, sitting around a roaring fire at your lodge, listening to a park's interpretive program, or going for a moonlit walk along the lakeshore—these are the best ways to spend your evenings, and they can all be yours at no charge.

Interpretive programs typically begin in late June and run through to the first weekend of September. The subject matter changes from year to year, but you can rely on interesting,

interactive topics that mix learning with fun. Presentations at the **Falls Theatre** (in town, across the road from Cameron Falls) and at Crandell Theatre (Crandell Campground) usually begin nightly at 8 P.M., with guest speakers appearing at the Falls Theatre Saturday night. Ask at the Waterton Visitor Centre (403/859-5133) for a printed schedule.

Waterton's few bars and lounges are all affiliated with lodgings. One of the nicest is the **Rams Head Lounge** in the Kilmorey Lodge (117 Evergreen Ave., 403/859-2334), which has a rustic mountain ambience centered around a wood-burning fireplace. On sunny afternoons and warmer nights, there is no finer place to spend an hour or two than this lounge's lakefront deck. **Wolf's Den Lounge** (Waterton Lakes Lodge, corner of Windflower Ave. and Cameron Falls Rd., 403/859-2151) is more modern and has big-screen TVs and bands on high-season weekends. Being the biggest and most central bar in town, the **Thirsty Bear Saloon** (Bayshore Inn, Waterton Ave., 403/859-2211, daily 11 A.M.–2 A.M.) gets crowded with young seasonal workers. It pours happy hour daily 3–6 P.M., and a band plays two or three nights a week. In the Prince of Wales Hotel, the staid **Windsor Lounge** (403/859-2231) has panoramic views across the lake and live entertainment most summer nights.

Waterton Lakes Opera House (309 Windflower Ave., 403/859-2466) shows movies daily at 7:30 and 9:30 P.M.

ACCOMMODATIONS AND CAMPING

Waterton has a limited number of accommodations. Most start opening in May and by mid-October are closed, with only the hostel, Kilmorey Lodge, Crandell Mountain Lodge, and Waterton Glacier Suites open year-round. All accommodations are within the townsite, so walking to the marina and shops isn't a problem.

Finding a room on short notice shouldn't be too difficult in May, June, and September, but for July and August reserve as far in advance as possible.

Under $50

HI-Waterton Alpine Centre (101 Clematis Dr., 403/859-2150 or 888/985-6343, www.watertonlakeslodge.com) is in a wing of Waterton Lakes Lodge, one of the village's premier accommodations. Just 21 beds are spread through six rooms, with a maximum of four beds in any one room. Amenities include a small lounge area, shared kitchen, and washrooms. Hostel guests also enjoy discounted admission to the Waterton Health Club ($3 instead of $6), which is part of the lodge complex and right next door to the hostel section. Dorm beds are $31 for members of Hostelling International, $35 for nonmembers—a great deal for those travelers who are willing to share living facilities. Family rooms are $93 and $105. Check-in is after 4 P.M.

$50-100

One block from the main street, the **Bear Mountain Motel** (208 Mount View Rd., 403/859-2366, www.bearmountainmotel.com, mid-May–Sept.) is an older park-at-your-door 34-unit motel with basic furnishings and no phones. Standard rooms are $80 s, $85 d, with some kitchenettes from $95.

Also in this price bracket is **Northland Lodge** (Evergreen Ave., 403/859-2353, www.northlandlodgecanada.com, mid-May–mid-Oct.), a rambling old home backing onto wilderness but just a short walk from both Cameron Falls and the main street. It features nine guest rooms, a lounge with a TV and fireplace, and a deck. The two rooms that share a bathroom are $85 s or d, while those with private bath are $99–179 s or d; rates include tea, coffee, and muffins in the morning.

$100-150

Kilmorey Lodge (117 Evergreen Ave., 403/859-2334 or 888/859-8669, www.kilmorey lodge.com), a historic 1920s inn on the shores of Emerald Bay, provides an excellent value for the money. Victorian furnishings, lots of exposed timber, squeaking floorboards, and historic photographs add to the charm. From the lobby a narrow stairway leads up to 23 rooms tucked under the eaves, many of which

have spectacular lake views. Each is furnished with antiques, and the beds have down comforters to ensure a good night's sleep. Downstairs is one of the town's finest restaurants and the library, where guests congregate around a roaring log fire to chat about their adventures. Outside is a gazebo for enjoying a quiet drink on those warm summer nights. Standard rooms during summer start at $130 s or d, rising to $260 for the spacious Deluxe King. Some rooms have lake views, but book in advance for these. Inexpensive packages are offered in winter.

Across the road from the Kilmorey Lodge is **Crandell Mountain Lodge** (Mount View Rd., 403/859-2288 or 866/859-2288, www.crandellmountainlodge.com), a centrally located country-style inn. Each of the 17 rooms has a private bath and is beautifully finished with country-style furnishings (no phones). Two rooms are wheelchair accessible. The smallest rooms are $129 s or d, most—with a choice of fireplace or kitchenette—are $159, and the largest suites are $199. Rates are reduced around 30 percent between mid-September and May.

Well suited for families, **Aspen Village Inn** (111 Windflower Ave., 403/859-2255 or 888/859-8669, www.aspenvillageinn.com, May–mid-Oct.) has super-spacious rooms, a playground, and a picnic area. Grownups aren't forgotten—the outdoor hot tub is the perfect place to soak weary bones. Accommodations are in two wings and multi-room cottages. The latter range from one bedroom, no kitchen ($159 s or d) to three bedrooms and a kitchen ($198). Lodge rooms range $139–245 s or d, with, for example, a two-bedroom kitchen-equipped unit going for $210.

At the **Bayshore Inn** (Waterton Ave., 403/859-2211 or 888/527-9555, www.bayshore inn.com, mid-Apr.–mid-Oct.; $144–154 s or d) you're paying for a prime waterfront location rather than a memorable room. On-site amenities include a hot tub, restaurant, café, and pub. In spring, the Bayshore offers excellent meal-inclusive packages for the same price as their summertime room-only rates.

$150-200

Waterton Glacier Suites (Windflower Ave., 403/859-2004 or 866/621-3330, www.waterton suites.com) is open year-round and provides excellent value. Each of the 26 units features stylish modern decor that hints at Western, is air-conditioned, and offers a fridge and microwave. Two-bedroom suites are $169 s or d, units with a jetted tub and fireplace are $225, and spacious loft units are $259. Off-season rates range $135–175.

Over $200

Modern **Waterton Lakes Lodge** (corner of Windflower Ave. and Cameron Falls Rd., 403/859-2151 or 866/985-6343, www.waterton lakeslodge.com, April–Oct.) is on a 1.5-hectare (3.7-acre) site in the heart of town. All 80 rooms are large and modern, and each has mountain-themed decor and mountain views. In-room amenities include air-conditioning, a TV/VCR combination, Internet access, and a coffeemaker. The complex also holds the Waterton Health Club (free entry for guests), a tiered restaurant, a small café, and a lounge with big-screen TVs. Lodge rooms are $205 s, $215 d, while those with kitchenettes are $265 s, $285 d. Check the website for steeply discounted off-season rates.

Waterton's best-known landmark is the **Prince of Wales Hotel** (403/236-3400 or 406/892-2525, www.glacierparkinc.com, mid-May–mid-Sept.), a seven-story gabled structure built in 1927 on a hill overlooking Upper Waterton Lake. It was another grand mountain resort financed by the railway except, unlike those in Banff and Jasper, it had no rail link and has always been U.S.-owned. It was built as part of a chain of first-class hotels in Glacier National Park and is still owned by the company that controls those south of the border. Early guests were transported to the hotel by bus from the Great Northern Railway in Montana. After extensive restoration inside and out, the hotel has been returned to its former splendor, best appreciated by standing in the lobby area and gazing out across the lake and up into the exposed timberframe ceiling. Off

Prince of Wales Hotel

© ANDREW HEMPSTEAD

the lobby you'll find a restaurant, lounge, and gift shop. Rates for the smallest (and they're small) Value Rooms are $265–275 s or d, depending on the view. Standard rooms start at $290, rising to $345 for those with a lake view. The opulence and history of this hotel are unequaled in Waterton, but don't expect the facilities of a similarly priced city hostelry: rooms have no television, and Value Rooms on the upper floors have no elevator access.

Park Campgrounds

The park's three campgrounds hold a total of 391 campsites. The most popular camping spot—thanks to a central location and top-notch amenities—is the **Townsite Campground** (mid-Apr.–mid-Oct.), within walking distance of the lake, trailheads, restaurants, and shops. Many of its more than 238 sites have power, water, and sewer hookups. The campground also offers showers and kitchen shelters. Walk-in tent sites are $23, unserviced sites $26, hookups $34. Reservations are taken for a percentage of sites through the

Parks Canada Campground Reservation Service (877/737-3783, www.pccamping.ca). The remaining sites—available on a first-come, first-served basis—fill up by early afternoon most summer days.

The 129 sites at **Crandell Campground** (mid-May–early Sept.), 10 kilometers (6.2 mi) from the townsite on Red Rock Canyon Parkway, are sprinkled through a lightly forested area of the valley bottom. Fees are $21 per site per night. This campground has flush toilets and kitchen shelters but no hookups. Pleasant Crandell Lake is an easy 2.4-kilometer (1.5-mi) walk from the southwest corner of the campground.

Belly River Campground (mid-May–early Sept.), 26 kilometers (16 mi) from the townsite along Chief Mountain International Highway, is the smallest (24 sites) and most primitive of the park's developed campgrounds. The campground is located beside a shallow, slow-moving body of water. Facilities are limited to pit toilets, a kitchen shelter, and drinking water; sites are $15 per night.

Commercial Campgrounds

You're a little way from the action at the commercial campgrounds outside the park, but the wider range of facilities (especially if you have a young family) and the peace of mind in being able to reserve a site with hookups make them a viable alternative. **Waterton Springs Campground** (three km/1.9 mi north of the park gate on Hwy. 6, 403/859-2247 or 866/859-2247, www.watertonspringscamping.com, late May–Sept.) centers around a large building holding modern bathrooms, a lounge, a general store, and a laundry room. Also on site are a playground and a fishing pond stocked with rainbow trout. Tent sites are $17; trailers and RVs pay $21–28.

On Highway 5, six kilometers (3.7 mi) east of the park gate, is **Crooked Creek Campground** (403/653-1100, mid-May–Sept.), operated by the not-for-profit Waterton Natural History Association. The sites are close together, so it's best suited to RVs, but the price is right—$20 for full hookups. Back along the road a little is the turn for **Waterton Riverside Campground**

(403/653-2888, mid-May–Sept.), with a mix of tent sites ($19) and powered sites ($22).

FOOD

When it's time to eat, the park offers everything from meals to fit the most austere budget to fine dining. Unless you're planning a meal at the Prince of Wales, the dress code in park restaurants is casual.

If you plan on cooking your own food, stock up before you get to the park. Groceries are available at the **Rocky Mountain Food Mart** (Windflower Ave., daily 8 A.M.–10 P.M.), while **Tamarack Outdoor Outfitters** (Mount View Rd.) has light snacks and lunches for hikers and picnickers.

Waterton has a smattering of coffee shops and small cafés. **Waterton Bagel & Coffee Co.** (in the theater building on the corner of Windflower Ave. and Cameron Falls Dr., 403/859-2211, daily 7 A.M.–9:30 P.M.) brews up the best coffee in town.

Pizza of Waterton (103 Fountain Ave., 403/859-2660, daily midday–midnight) dishes up the best—okay, the only—pizza in town. It's actually pretty good, piled high with toppings of your choice. A 12-inch (good for two) costs $21, beer is $4, and there's a choice of wines for under $20 per bottle. Eat inside or out, or take your order back to your campsite.

One of the park's most popular restaurants is the **Lamp Post Dining Room** (Kilmorey Lodge, 403/859-2334, daily 7:30 A.M.–10 P.M.). It has all the charm of the Prince of Wales Hotel but with a more casual atmosphere and reasonable prices to match. The game-oriented menu offers mouthwatering mains ranging from curried couscous ($19) to roasted Cornish game hen topped with an almond cranberry sauce ($25). Leave room to finish with a delicious piece of Saskatoon berry pie ($5). An impressive wine list is dominated by Canadian offerings. Breakfast is good also. Choose hot oatmeal and a warmed bagel ($6), an egg-white omelet ($8.50), or the best eggs Benedict ($9.25) in southern Alberta.

Along the main street, the selection of places to eat is varied, but none are outstanding. If

SOUTHERN ALBERTA

you're looking for a decent family restaurant, **Zum's** (116 Waterton Ave., 403/859-2388, daily 8 A.M.–9 P.M.) is a good choice. The burgers are tasty and come in all forms (including with buffalo patties) for $6–9, with fries extra. Wash it down with a milk shake ($5).

Tuscana (113 Waterton Ave., 403/859-0003, daily 11 A.M.–10 P.M.), with as many tables outside as in and live music on weekend nights, offers satisfying pastas ($16–21).

High tea is a tradition at the landmark **Prince of Wales Hotel** (403/859-2231), but it's an overpriced one. Sure, it's tasty and memorable—think finger sandwiches, pastries and cakes, tea, coffee, and other beverages served up on white linen at tables with the best view in town—but as any self-respecting Brit will tell you, it's more of an *afternoon* tea rather than the more substantial *high* tea. It's served in the lobby daily 2–4 P.M. and costs $30 per person.

The big windows at the hotel's **Royal Stewart Dining Room** (summer daily 6:30–10 A.M., 11:30 A.M.–2 P.M., and 5–9:30 P.M.) allow you to gaze down along Upper Waterton Lake while soaking up an Old World elegance unequaled in the park. A simple breakfast buffet every morning ($15 per person) is worth attending for the views alone. The rest of the day the menu is mostly old-fashioned, but with choices like pork tenderloin roasted in a mushroom and stout cream sauce ($28), no one complains. Prices are similar to any big-city restaurant of the same standard—for dinner, expect to pay around $100 for two without alcoholic drinks.

INFORMATION AND SERVICES

On the main access road opposite the Prince of Wales Hotel, the **Waterton Visitor Centre** (403/859-5133, June–Aug. daily 9 A.M.–8 P.M., May and early Sept. daily 9 A.M.–5 P.M., closed the rest of the year) provides general information on the park, sells fishing licenses, and issues Wilderness Use Permits. The park's administration office on Mount View Road (403/859-2224, year-round weekdays 8 A.M.–4 P.M.) offers the same services as the visitors center. For more information on the park, write

© ANDREW HEMPSTEAD

All services in Waterton are within the townsite, which occupies a prime lakefront position.

to Superintendent, Waterton Lakes National Park, Waterton Park, AB T0K 2M0. The Parks Canada website is www.pc.gc.ca. For general tourist information, the local chamber of commerce website, www.watertonchamber.com, provides plenty of current information and links to accommodations.

Waterton has no banks, but travelers checks are accepted at most businesses, and ATMs are scattered throughout town.

The post office is beside the fire station on Fountain Avenue. A launderette on Windflower Avenue is open daily 8 A.M.–10 P.M.

The closest hospitals are in Cardston (403/653-4411) and Pincher Creek (403/627-3333). The park's 24-hour emergency number is 403/859-2636. For the **RCMP,** call 403/859-2244.

Books and Maps

Tamarack Outdoor Outfitters (Mount View Rd., 403/859-2378, daily 8 A.M.–8 P.M.) has a section devoted to books, with field and recreation guides dominating. The **Waterton Natural History Association,** based in the Waterton Heritage Centre (117 Waterton Ave., 403/859-2624, May–Sept. 10 A.M.–5 P.M., July–Aug. until 8 P.M.), stocks every book ever written about the park (except this one), as well as many titles pertaining to western Canada in general.

Although the free park maps handed out at the Waterton Visitor Centre suffice for hiking any of the trails detailed in this book, I highly recommend picking up the Gem Trek map (available at any of the park bookstores; $9), which puts the varied topography in perspective and helps identify natural features of note.

Supplies

Tamarack Outdoor Outfitters (Mount View Rd., 403/859-2378, www.watertonvisitor services.com, daily 8 A.M.–8 P.M.) is a five-generation family business that stocks a little of everything. Here you'll find a good range of outdoor clothing and equipment, fishing tackle, books, a currency exchange, and picnic supplies.

GETTING THERE AND AROUND

The nearest commercial airport is at Lethbridge, 140 kilometers (87 mi) away. It is served by Air Canada's regional connector and has Budget, Hertz, and National rental cars. The closest **Greyhound** buses come to the park is Pincher Creek, 50 kilometers (31 miles) away. From the depot (1015 Hewetson St., 403/627-2716), a cab to the park (call **Crystal Taxi,** 403/627-4262) will run around $70 each way.

Tamarack Outdoor Outfitters (Mount View Rd., 403/859-2378, www.watertonvisitor services.com) operates hiker shuttle services to various trailheads within the park. Cameron Lake, the starting point for the Carthew-Alderson Trail (which ends back in town), is a popular drop-off point; $10 one-way. You could take one of these shuttles then return on the bus later in the day if driving the steep mountain roads doesn't appeal to you. The company also offers a shuttle along the Chief Mountain Highway.

Pat's (Mount View Rd., 403/859-2266) rents mountain bikes for $8 for the first hour then $6 per hour thereafter to a maximum of $38 per day. Motorized scooters are $25 per hour or $80 per day.

SOUTHERN ALBERTA

Crowsnest Pass and Vicinity

The Municipality of Crowsnest Pass is along Highway 3 between Pincher Creek and the Continental Divide in the southwestern corner of the province. The municipality encompasses a handful of once-bustling coal-mining communities, including Bellevue, Hillcrest, Frank, Blairmore, and Coleman. Many topographic features in the area are named Crowsnest, including a river, a mountain, and the actual pass (1,396 m/4,580 ft) on the Continental Divide. From Pincher Creek, it is 62 kilometers (39 mi) to the pass. Continuing west from there, the highway (known as the Crowsnest Highway, of course) descends into British Columbia to the coal-mining and logging towns of Sparwood and Fernie, then on to the major population center of Cranbrook. The area is worth exploring for its natural beauty and recreation opportunities alone; the Crowsnest River reputedly

offers some of Canada's best trout fishing. But a trip through this area wouldn't be complete without visiting the historic towns and mines along the route.

History

The tumultuous history of the pass is one of strikes, disasters, and, in more recent times, unemployment, as the coal mines have closed one by one. The first mines began operation after the Canadian Pacific Railway (CPR) opened its southern line through the pass in 1898. Many of the thousands of workers and their families that flocked to the new mining communities were immigrants who brought expectations of high wages and a secure future. But the area's entire economy revolved around just one industry—coal mining. Unfortunately for the miners, the coal here turned out to be of

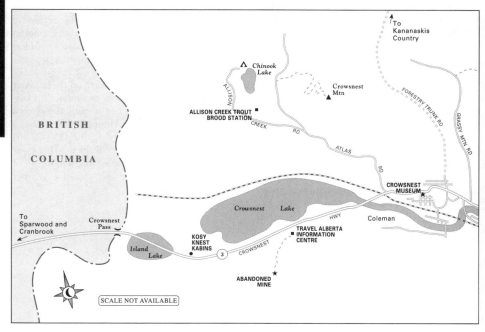

poor quality and located in seams at steep angles, making extraction difficult. In addition, most of the mining companies were severely undercapitalized, leading to serious problems. The CPR was the mining companies' largest customer, but because the coal was inferior to that from the British Columbia mines, the price paid was considerably less. The first mine closed in 1915, and the others followed suit one by one. After decades in the doldrums, things are looking up for the pass. City slickers are arriving keen to take advantage of low housing prices, an unhurried lifestyle, and the wide range of recreation. Developers are also beginning to target the region, with the Bridgegate project on Crowsnest Lake making headlines for its $1.5 billion price tag.

PINCHER CREEK AND VICINITY

The town of Pincher Creek, in a shallow valley 211 kilometers (131 mi) south of Calgary and 70 kilometers (43 mi) north of the U.S. border, is surrounded by some of the country's best cattle land and is reputed to be the windiest spot in Alberta. The town has an interesting historic park and it's easy to spend time exploring the Oldman River Dam area, but Pincher Creek also makes a central base for exploring the Crowsnest Pass and Waterton Lakes National Park.

The NWMP established a horse farm at what is now known as Pincher Creek in 1876. They found that oats and hay, the horses' main source of sustenance, grew much better here in the foothills than at their newly built post at Fort Macleod. The story goes that a member of the detachment found a pair of pincers near the river—lost many years earlier by prospectors from Montana—and the name stuck. Word of this fertile agricultural land quickly spread, and soon the entire area was settled. As was so often the case for towns across the west, the CPR bypassed Pincher Creek and built a siding to the north called Pincher Station. Most towns either

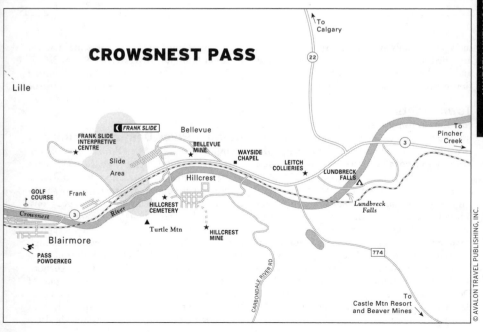

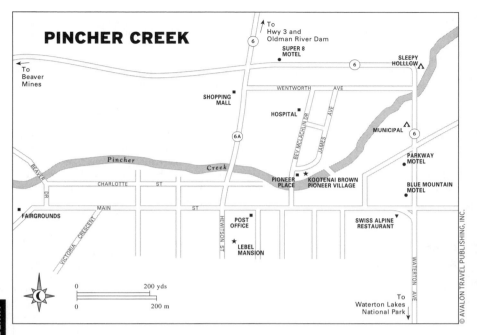

PINCHER CREEK

To Hwy 3 and Oldman River Dam 6

SUPER 8 MOTEL

SLEEPY HOLLLOW

6

To Beaver Mines

WENTWORTH AVE

SHOPPING MALL

HOSPITAL

BEV MCLACHLIN DR

JAMES AVE

MUNICIPAL 6

6A

Pincher Creek

PARKWAY MOTEL

BEAVER DR

CHARLOTTE ST

PIONEER PLACE ★ KOOTENAI BROWN PIONEER VILLAGE

BLUE MOUNTAIN MOTEL

MAIN ST

FAIRGROUNDS

HEWITSON ST

POST OFFICE

SWISS ALPINE RESTAURANT

VICTORIA CRESCENT

★ LEBEL MANSION

WATERTON AVE

0   200 yds

0   200 m

To Waterton Lakes National Park

© AVALON TRAVEL PUBLISHING, INC.

moved to the railway or struggled for a few years and died, but not Pincher Creek; it stayed put and has thrived ever since, with today's population sitting at a little under 4,000.

Town Sights

In addition to providing a home for the local information center, **Pioneer Place,** a large log structure across the river from Main Street, is the gateway to **Kootenai Brown Pioneer Village** (1037 Bev McLachlin Dr., 403/627-3684, June–Aug. daily 10 A.M.–6 P.M., Sept.–May. Mon.–Fri. 10 A.M.–4:30 P.M., adult $6, senior $4, child $3). Within the park are numerous historic buildings moved to the site. Highlights include the cabin of legendary mountain man Kootenai Brown (see *History* in the previous *Waterton Lakes National Park* section), a sprawling 1894 ranch house, a blacksmith workshop, Doukhobor barn, a sod hut, and a NWMP barn dating to 1878. All of the buildings are open for viewing, each restored to period settings.

Overlooking Pincher Creek's main street is **Lebel Mansion** (696 Kettles St., 403/627-5272, summer daily 9 A.M.–5 P.M.), a dignified 1910 brick house that has been restored by the Allied Arts Council. Inside is a small art gallery and cultural center.

Oldman River Dam and Vicinity

Completed in 1991, the Oldman River Dam, north of Pincher Creek below the confluence of the Crowsnest, Castle, and Oldman Rivers, is the latest attempt to irrigate regions of southern Alberta not normally able to produce crops. The 25-kilometer-long (15.5-mile-long) reservoir is held back by one of Alberta's highest dam walls (76 m/250 ft); Highway 785, which branches north from Highway 3 three kilometers (1.9 mi) east of the Pincher Creek turnoff, crosses the wall and allows access to the base of the spillway, where there's camping, excellent fishing for rainbow trout, and a specially built kayaking course. The reservoir above is also a

CHINOOK WINDS

On many days in the dead of winter, a distinctive arch of clouds forms in the sky over the southwestern corner of the province as a wind peculiar to the Rockies swoops down over the mountains. The warm wind, known as a chinook (a native word meaning "snow eater"), can raise temperatures by up to 20°C (36°F) in an hour and up to 40°C (72°F) in a 24-hour period. The wind's effect on the environment is profound. One story tells of a backcountry skier who spent the better part of a day traversing to the summit of a snow-clad peak on the front range of the Canadian Rockies. As he rested and contemplated skiing down, he realized that the slope had become completely bare!

Chinooks originate over the Pacific Ocean when warm, moist air is pushed eastward by prevailing westerlies. The air pressure of these winds is less than at lower elevations, and therefore as the air moves down the front ranges of the Canadian Rockies, it is subjected to increased pressure. This increasing air pressure warms the winds, which then fan out across the foothills and prairies. The "chinook arch" is formed as the clear air clashes with the warmer cloud-laden winds. The phenomenon is most common in southern Alberta but occurs to a lesser degree as far north as the Peace River Valley. Pincher Creek experiences around 35 chinooks each winter.

popular recreation spot for windsurfing, boating, and fishing.

Beyond the dam wall, **Heritage Acres** (403/627-2082, May–Sept. daily 8 A.M.–6 P.M., donation), a museum run by the Heritage Acres Antique Equipment and Threshing Club, is signposted to the south. In addition to a large collection of antique farm machinery, it includes a schoolhouse, a grain elevator, a Doukhobor barn, and Crystal Village—a collection of buildings made entirely from glass telephone insulators (200,000 of them).

Beauvais Lake Provincial Park

Located deep in the foothills 20 kilometers (12.5 mi) southwest of Pincher Creek, Beauvais Lake Provincial Park is a wilderness area with a rich history of early settlement. Foundations of buildings are all that remain of the first homesteaders' efforts to survive in what was then a remote location. The park's most famous settler was James Whitford, one of General Custer's scouts at the famous Battle of Little Bighorn. He is buried at Scott's Point, accessed from the end of the road along the lake's north side. Most of the 18-kilometer network of hiking trails are at the other end of the lake, including a short walk to a beaver pond. The lake is also good for boating and is stocked annually with rainbow and brown trout. The main campground (403/382-4097, $15–20), at the lake's western end, is open year-round. It's fairly primitive (pit toilets, no showers), but a few powered sites were added in 2007. If you're tent camping, continue beyond the summer cabins to a group of roadside walk-in sites.

Castle Mountain Resort

Alberta's fifth-largest alpine resort, Castle Mountain (403/627-5101, www.skicastle.ca) is also one of its best-kept secrets; plans to turn this quiet ski area into a four-season resort have been on the drawing board for years. Currently, the vertical rise is an impressive 860 meters (2,800 ft). Much of its 61 runs traverse intermediate and advanced terrain, with the Chutes, down the backside of the resort, holding the most challenge. Aside from the odd chinook, the skiing and snowboarding is some of the best a $50 lift ticket ($33 for seniors) can buy. It's 47 kilometers (29 mi) southwest of Pincher Creek along Highways 507 and 774. Check the resort website for on-hill lodging that costs $25 per person for a dorm bed and from $80 s or d in a private room.

Events

The mid-June **Cowboy Poetry Gathering** (403/627-5855) is a celebration of cowboy poetry and Western art held at the local fairgrounds (west end of Main Street). The Gathering isn't

a festival or competition—just a group of cowboys who come together each year to entertain each other. Poems are recited on Friday and Saturday; those known by heart are greeted with the most appreciation. On Saturday night, a huge barbecue takes place, with more beef than you could poke a brand at. This feast gets everyone in the mood to kick up their heels at the dance. Demonstrations and sales of traditional Western arts and crafts take place throughout the weekend.

On the third weekend of August, the fairgrounds come alive again, this time for the **Pincher Creek Fair & Rodeo.**

Accommodations and Camping

Pincher Creek's older motels are spread along a four-block strip of Highway 6 east of downtown, including a real cheapie—the **Blue Mountain Motel** (981 Main St., 403/627-5335, $58 s, $62 d). On the same block, the **Parkway Motel** (1070 Waterton Ave., 403/627-3344 or 888/209-9902, www.parkway motel.ca, $75–95 s or d) is slightly nicer. **Super 8 Motel** (1307 Freebairn Ave., 403/627-5671 or 800/800-8000, www.super8.com, $98 s, $113) at the north entrance to Pincher Creek has 48 modern, air-conditioned rooms and extras such as wireless Internet.

South of town off Highway 6 (call for directions) is **(Valley Blue Ranch** (403/627-2382, www.valleyblueranch.com, $85 s or d), which is primarily in business as a cattle ranch, but opens the door of its modern ranch house to visitors throughout the year. The two guest rooms have a bright country-style ambience, while the main living area and breakfast room have sweeping views across the rolling foothills. Rates include a full breakfast.

The **Municipal Campground** (May–Oct., tents $5, unserviced sites $12, powered sites $17) is in a residential area on Wentworth Avenue, just off Highway 6, and linked to Kootenai Brown Pioneer Village via a riverside trail. Rates include the use of showers and an unlimited supply of firewood. On the northeast side of town on Highway 6 is **Sleepy Hollow Campground** (403/627-2033),

with lots of permanent trailers, full hookups, and showers. Unserviced sites are $18, serviced ones $21–24.

Much nicer than these in-town options, if you don't need hookups, is **(Cottonwood Campground** (May–Oct., $15), 500 meters (0.3 mi) downstream of the Oldman River Dam 10 kilometers (6.2 mi) northeast of town. The 82 sites are spread throughout stands of towering cottonwood trees and all have easy river access. Fishing for rainbow trout is great in the river, but there's also a stocked trout pond. Along Highway 3 eight kilometers (five mi) west of Pincher Creek is **Castle River Campground** ($13), and to the southwest toward Beaver Mines is **Beauvais Lake Provincial Park** ($15–20). Both have pit toilets, kitchen shelters, and firewood.

Food

The **Swiss Alpine Restaurant** (988 Main St. at Waterton Ave., 403/627-5079, 11 A.M.–10 P.M.) is a longtime favorite with locals and savvy travelers in the know. The lounge displays lots of taxidermy and a Western-style atmosphere, and the dining area has good food, including Alberta beef and lamb, delicious salads (the Alpine salad is especially good), and traditional Swiss dishes such as fondue. Most entrées are more than $12, but portions are generous.

You'll pass **Twin Butte General Store** (Hwy. 6 24 km/15 mi south of Pincher Creek, 403/627-4035, daily 10 A.M.–8 P.M.) on the drive to Waterton Lakes, but it's also worth a detour for lunch or dinner. Stuck in the middle of what is seemingly nowhere, the store has a small restaurant attached to one side. The specialty is simple Mexican dishes, all inexpensive and served with a smile.

Information

Pincher Creek Tourist Information Centre (1037 Bev McLachlin Dr., 403/627-5855 or 888/298-5855, www.pinchercreek.ca, June–Aug. daily 10 A.M.–6 P.M., Sept.–May. Mon.–Fri. 10 A.M.–4:30 P.M.) is in Pioneer Place, an impressive log building across the river from downtown.

PINCHER CREEK TO LEITCH COLLIERIES

The first worthwhile stop as Highway 3 begins its westward climb to the Crowsnest Pass from Pincher Creek is **Lundbreck Falls** (signposted from the highway), where the Crowsnest River plunges 12 meters (40 ft) into the canyon below. At the top of the falls is a viewpoint, with trails leading down to the base of the canyon and downstream along the river. This is a favorite fishing spot for rainbow and brown trout downstream of the falls and for rainbows and whitefish upstream. Below the falls is **Lundbreck Falls Recreation Area** (May–Oct., unserviced sites $12, powered sites $17), where 65 campsites are spread out along two loops, one right by the river.

From the falls, Highway 3 passes the junction of Highway 22, which heads north to Kananaskis Country and Calgary. The next community west on Highway 3 is **Burmis,** which is well known for the **Burmis Tree,** a photogenic limber pine beside the north side of the highway.

Buildings from the coal-mining days litter Crowsnest Pass. This is the remains of Leitch Collieries, just west of Pincher Creek.

Leitch Collieries

At the turn of the 20th century, Leitch Collieries was the largest mining and coking operation in Crowsnest Pass and the only one that was Canadian-owned. In 1915, it became the first operation to cease production. Now it's a series of picturesque ruins with one of the most informative interpretive exhibits in the area. The collieries opened in 1907, mining a steep coal seam south of the ruins. The Number 2 Mine, beside the highway, commenced operation in 1909. To house workers, a town named Passburg was built east of the mine. Today this site is the most accessible of the area's "ghost towns," although nothing more than a few depressions remains; most buildings were moved after the mine closed. The early development of the site included a sandstone manager's residence, a powerhouse used to supply electricity to Passburg, a row of 101 coke ovens, and a huge tipple. A boardwalk through the mine ruins leads to "listening posts" (where recorded information is played) and interpretive signs.

The site is open year-round, with guided tours running daily 9 A.M.–5 P.M. in summer.

BELLEVUE

A French company, West Canadian Collieries, had been prospecting in the pass since 1898 and had bought 20,000 acres of land. Fortunately, the most impressive coal seams it found were right beside the main CPR line, which became the site of the **Bellevue Mine.** At 8 P.M. on December 9, 1910, an explosion rocked the mine and destroyed the ventilation fan. Thirty men died as a result of the accident. Most of them survived the initial blast but died after inhaling "afterdamp," the carbon dioxide and carbon monoxide left after fire has burned the oxygen from the air. The mine reopened soon after the tragedy, and at one time employed 500 men, but the gradual decline in the demand for coal led to the mine's closure in 1962.

The original town of Bellevue was built in

© ANDREW HEMPSTEAD

SOUTHERN ALBERTA

© ANDREW HEMPSTEAD

At the entrance to Bellevue, this little chapel holds sermons throughout summer – but only to eight people at a time.

1905, before the mine disaster. The townsite centered around two streets: Front Street (now 213th St.) and Main Street (now 212th St.). The earliest single-story wood-framed buildings had false facades to make them appear taller and more important than they really were. Two fires, in 1917 and 1921, destroyed many of the town's buildings, but these were soon replaced by more permanent structures, many of which still stand.

On Highway 3 beside Bellecrest Campground is the **Wayside Chapel,** which seats eight people. Recorded sermons are held throughout summer, and the doors are always open. During the last weekend in June, the town celebrates Bellecrest Days with a parade, pancake breakfasts, a mud-bog race, and a Jell-O-eating contest.

Bellevue Underground Mine Tour

The Bellevue Mine (21814 28th Ave., 403/564-4700, adult $7, senior and child $6) is the only mine in Alberta that is open for underground tours. The tour is as realistic as possible without actually making you shovel dirt. The mine is cold, dark, and damp. Before entering you are given a hard hat and a headlamp, which you can attach to your hat or carry by hand. The guides carry blankets for those visitors who get cold—the average temperature in the mine is 7°C (45°F). The tour runs mid-May–August 10 A.M.–5:30 P.M. every half hour. To get to the mine, follow the signs down the hill from the top end of 213th Street.

HILLCREST

Named after Charles Plummer Hill, one of the pass's earliest prospectors, Hillcrest is best remembered for Canada's worst mine disaster. The Hillcrest Coal and Coke Company began operations in 1905 and shortly thereafter laid out a townsite. Before long, the town had its own railway spur, school, hotel, and store. Then disaster struck. At 9:30 A.M. on June 19, 1914, with 235 men working underground, an explosion tore apart the tunnels of the Hillcrest Mine. The blast was so powerful that it destroyed a concrete-walled engine house located 30 meters from the mine entrance. Many of those who survived the initial explosion were subsequently asphyxiated by the afterdamp (residual carbon monoxide and carbon dioxide). Rescue teams from throughout the pass rushed to the mine but were forced back by gas and smoke. The final death toll was 189. The mine reopened and produced 250,000 tons of coal annually until closing in 1939 for economic reasons.

Many of the original miner residences still stand in Hillcrest, which is now a quiet town with a population of 1,000. The town has no services but two historically interesting sights. The **Hillcrest Mine** is accessible along a rough, unpaved road that branches left off 230th Street beyond the trailer court (it's easy to miss—the road runs along the trailer court's back fence). The ruins are extensive—look for the sealed mine entrance at the rear of the ruins, half-hidden by trees. Through town to the west (this road joins back up to Highway 3) is **Hillcrest Cemetery,** off 8th Avenue. Many of the mine-

disaster victims could not be identified. They were wrapped in white cloth and buried in the cemetery one foot apart in mass graves.

FRANK

Frank, two kilometers (1.2 mi) west of Bellevue, is probably the most famous (or infamous) town in the Crowsnest Pass area. In 1901, two Americans acquired mineral rights to the area directly below Turtle Mountain. Within months, their company, the Canadian-American Coal and Coke Company, had established a mine and laid out the townsite of Frank. The mine, when operational, became the first to sell coal in the pass and continued to thrive along with the town of Frank, whose population swelled to 600.

The original townsite of Frank is now an industrial park. To get to it, cross the rail line at 150th Street (just west of the turnoff for the interpretive center). Take the first left and look for a rusty fire hydrant to the right. This landmark, which once stood on Dominion Avenue, Frank's main street, is all that remains of the ill-fated town. Directly behind it was the grand Imperial Hotel, which is now just a depression in the ground with a tree growing in it. This road then continues across Gold Creek and into the slide area. A memorial was erected here by Delbert Ennis, whose entire family survived the slide—and they lived on the south side of Gold Creek! This road was the main route through the area before the slide and has since been cleared. It eventually joins up with the Hillcrest access road. The mine entrance is partially visible on the northern edge of the slide area, just above Frank Lake. For those with a sense of adventure, it is possible to climb Turtle Mountain (2,093 m/6,870 ft). The trailhead is in East Blairmore on Pipeline Road. The trek to the summit is actually easier than it looks because the trail follows the mountain's northwest ridge. Only the last 20 meters (66 ft) along an exposed section are tricky. Allow two to three hours each way.

◖ Frank Slide

It was before dawn early in the 20th century.

Everything in town was quiet, and the night shift was hard at work deep inside Turtle Mountain. Then, without warning, a gigantic chunk of the north face of the mountain sheared off, thundering into the valley below and burying part of Frank. It was the world's most destructive rock slide, burying 68 of the town's residents. Amazingly, none of the 20 working coal miners were killed. After being trapped for 14 hours, they dug themselves out.

In times of tragedy, there are usually heroes, and the hero of the Frank Slide was Sid Choquette. After realizing that the rail line had been covered, he scrambled over the still-moving mass of boulders and flagged down the morning express, stopping it before it reached the slide. As a token of appreciation, the CPR gave Choquette $25 and a letter of commendation. Within three weeks, the tracks were dug out and the railway reopened. One week later, the mine reopened. Most of Frank was intact, but fear of another slide led to the relocation of all the buildings across the railway line to a safer location. The mine closed in 1917.

It is impossible to calculate the amount of rock that fell from the mountain. It has been estimated at 82 million tons by some, 30 million cubic meters (one billion cubic ft) by others. Looking at the north face of Turtle Mountain will give you a visual idea of the slide, but the full extent doesn't become apparent until you actually drive through the slide area or view the fan of limestone boulders that spread more than three kilometers (1.9 mi) from the base of the mountain and more than two kilometers (1.2 mi) to the east and west. Scientists to this day puzzle over what caused the slide and the vast spread. Most experts believe that several factors contributed to the initial slide, and the weakening of the mountain by mining operations was only a small part of it. Regarding the spread of rock, one theory put forward by scientists is "air lubrication": as the huge mass of rock slid downward, it compressed and trapped air on which it rode across the valley. Today, Turtle Mountain is monitored daily with some of the world's most

© ANDREW HEMPSTEAD

Viewing the Frank Slide is the only way to appreciate the enormity of this geological catastrophe.

advanced seismographic equipment but has shown no sign of moving since.

Frank Slide Interpretive Centre (403/562-7388, mid-May–mid-Sept. 9 A.M.–6 P.M., the rest of the year 10 A.M.–5 P.M., adult $9, senior $8, child $5), on a slight rise at the northern edge of the slide area, is an excellent place to learn more about the history of the valley, its settlers, and its tragedies. The audiovisual presentation *In the Mountain's Shadow* is a particularly moving account of the terrible working and social conditions in the valley. A 1.5-kilometer (0.9-mi) self-guided trail leads down into the slide. Better still, scramble up the slope behind the parking lot and walk along the ridge for a view of the entire slide area.

No tourist services are available in Frank, but who wants to camp under Turtle Mountain anyway?

BLAIRMORE AND VICINITY

With a population of 1,900, Blairmore is the largest of the Crowsnest Pass communities. The town had only a small mine itself, but when the Frank Mine opened in 1901, Blairmore thrived. It became a main center for the surrounding mines and a supply point for the other towns. Real estate brokers, insurance agents, doctors, and barristers all made their homes here, and in 1907, West Canadian Collieries—which owned the Lille and Bellevue mines—relocated its offices to Blairmore. A brickyard opened, and many of the wooden-front buildings along the main street were replaced by impressive brick structures that remain to this day.

Sights and Recreation

Most of Blairmore's historic redbrick buildings can be viewed along Main Street (20th Ave.). The most impressive is the three-story 1912 **Cosmopolitan Hotel,** where an ever-obliging publican had his liquor license revoked many times for serving thirsty miners after hours.

Crowsnest Pass Golf and Country Club (across Highway 3 from downtown Blairmore, 403/562-2776) is the only golf course in the pass. Greens fees on the rolling 18-hole course are $23 for nine holes, $42 for 18.

The annual **Rum Runner Days** on the second weekend of July is a rip-roaring celebration of the town's seedy past. It kicks off with a pancake breakfast and parade on Saturday, followed by a barbecue and music in Bandstand Park. The weekend culminates with live music on the local ski hill.

Lille

The foundations of Lille, once a thriving coal-mining community of 400 north of Blairmore, are accessible only on foot. The hike is short, but the rewards are ample. Its isolation from the railway and poor quality of coal forced the mines to close in 1913, with the population moving out soon after. Most of the building materials have been salvaged throughout the years, leaving only foundations. To reach Lille, turn north on Grassy Mountain Road just east of Crowsnest Pass Golf and Country Club and follow it for eight kilometers (five mi) to an intersection. The road to the right leads to Lille, but from the intersection you're on foot; it's a three-kilometer (1.9-mi) hike along an old railway grade to the abandoned townsite in a grassy meadow; allow one hour each way. To the right of the path, you'll pass an impressive row of 50 coke ovens and the foundations of a once-grand hotel. Scattered through the meadow on the left-hand side of the trail are the ruins of the miners' cottages, schools, and even a couple of rusty fire hydrants. A four-wheel-drive track leads east (left) through the meadow to two of the mines, which require some bushwhacking to find. On the south (right) side of this road are the foundations of the bakery, butcher shop, general store, and hospital.

Accommodations and Camping

The historic **Cosmopolitan Hotel** (13001 20th Ave., 403/562-7321, $55 s, $75–95 d) has 16 guest rooms. They're still basic, and some share bathrooms, but the price is right. Continuing west along the main street is the **Highwood Motel** (11373 20th Ave., 403/562-8888 or 888/562-8881, $55 s, $70 d), which has a restaurant and pub on the premises.

Lost Lemon Campground (11001 19th Ave., 403/562-2932, www.lostlemon.com, Apr.–Oct.) is a private facility across the railway tracks at the west end of town. It has showers, an outdoor swimming pool, a hot tub, a playground, and a laundry room and is situated right beside the Crowsnest River, making it the perfect overnight stop for anglers. Tent sites are $18, hookups $22–26, and cabins with kitchens are $85 s or d.

Food and Drink

The best place in Blairmore for a meal is **C Stone's Throw Cafe** (13047 20th Ave., 403/562-2230, Mon. and Wed.–Sat. 6:30 A.M.–6 P.M., Sun. 10 A.M.–4 P.M.), in a restored heritage building overlooking main street. Everything is made fresh, including breakfast wraps ($5), delicious pita melts ($5), soup & sandwich deals ($5), and fruit smoothies ($3.25). The coffee is the best in the pass, or choose from one of the many teas. Wireless Internet is another plus.

The bar in the **Cosmopolitan Hotel** is always busy, although a little rough around the edges—don't ask for an umbrella in your drink and you should be alright.

COLEMAN

Westernmost of the Crowsnest Pass communities is Coleman, which is 15 kilometers (nine mi) from the British Columbia border. The town expanded rapidly at the turn of the 20th century, and by 1904 it had two hotels, two churches, and several stores along Main Street. The 1950s were a time of amalgamation among the coal-mining companies in the pass, enabling the Coleman Colliery to remain open until 1983, long after all other operations had closed. Many of the town's miners joined the ranks of the unemployed, some found work in the British Columbia mines, and others packed up their belongings and left the pass completely. The effect on the town has been devastating. A walk down Coleman's 17th Avenue gives you an idea of what the main street of Bellevue, Frank, Passburg, and Lille must have looked like after their respective mines

Coleman Journal building

had closed. Many of the buildings are boarded up, with some businesses having relocated to the highway.

Downtown

Located in the old Coleman High School building is the **Crowsnest Museum** (7701 19th Ave., 403/563-5434, summer daily 10 A.M.–6 P.M., the rest of the year Mon.–Fri. 10 A.M.–noon and 1–4 P.M., adult $6, senior $5, child $4). With two floors crammed full of exhibits and artifacts from throughout the region, the museum requires at least an hour of your time. The adjacent schoolyard has displays of farming, mining, and firefighting equipment. Across the street is the *Coleman Journal* **building.** The *Coleman Journal* was a Pulitzer Prize–winning weekly newspaper that was published until 1970. After extensive restoration, the building has been opened to the public. Interpretive panels explain the slow process of early newspaper publishing. It's open the same hours as the museum. Many other buildings that remain are of historical signifi-

cance and across the railway tracks at the west end of 17th Avenue are the remains of the coke ovens, the most complete in the pass.

Accommodations and Food

Up on the highway through town, the **Stop Inn Motel** (8322 20th Ave., 403/562-7381, $48 s, $52 d) has clean, basic rooms, each with cable TV and a small fridge. Also on the highway, the newer **Valley View Motel** (403/563-5600, $66 s, $68 d) has 25 small but modern rooms, some of which are air-conditioned. On the north side of the highway three kilometers (1.9 mi) west of Coleman is **Crowsnest Mountain Resort** (4210 21st Ave., 403/562-7993, www.albertaresort.com, $100 s, $115 d), a combination of five modern chalets, a restaurant, an RV park (seasonal pad rentals only), and real estate development. Each chalet has a simple yet practical layout, kitchenette, full bath, covered porch with barbecue, and in-floor heating. Continuing west, 12 kilometers (7.5 mi) west of town, is **Kosy Knest Kabins,** (403/563-5155, $54 s, $62 d), where all 10 units have kitchenettes and TVs but the decor hasn't changed much since the 1960s.

While most of downtown Coleman's businesses have relocated to the highway, **Chris's Restaurant** (7802 17th Ave., 403/563-3093, Mon.–Fri. 6 A.M.–10 P.M., Sat.–Sun. 8 A.M.–8 P.M.) manages to hang on. Choose from hamburgers, cheeseburgers, bacon burgers, and loaded burgers. The menu might be limited, but the burgers are good and start at just $3. Up on the highway is **Cinnamon Bear Bakery** (8342 20th Ave., 403/562-2443, daily 7:30 A.M.–5:30 P.M.), a sweet-smelling café where coffee is under $2, a double iced chai is just $3.50, and a made-to-order soup and sandwich combo is $8.

WEST OF COLEMAN
Crowsnest Mountain

From Coleman, the British Columbia border is only 15 kilometers (9.3 mi) away, but there's no rush because you have a mountain to climb. Crowsnest Mountain (2,785 m/9,100 ft) is the symbol of the pass, and although it's a

fairly difficult ascent with an elevation gain of 1,030 meters (3,380 ft), it can be hiked by anyone with a good level of fitness. Snow may be encountered until July, and a certain amount of scrambling across scree slopes is required. Atlas Road spurs north three kilometers (1.9 mi) west of Coleman past one of Alberta's few outcrops of igneous rock (to the north just before the junction). Follow this road for 10.5 kilometers (6.5 mi), staying right at the first fork. The trailhead is marked, and a little farther is the parking lot—well, a place to park your vehicle anyway. At first the trail climbs steadily through a subalpine forest of pine and spruce before crossing a stream. At the first scree slope, below the north face of the mountain, is an impressive view of the Seven Sisters to the northeast. The trail through the scree slope is not always obvious, but try to follow it anyway because it's the easiest route. At the base of the cliff, go right and climb up the wide gully to approximately 20 meters (66 ft) before the top of the rise, then veer sharply to the left. If you have difficulties scrambling up this section, turn back; if not, continue up three more gullies (the route is fairly obvious), from which the trail levels out and continues to the summit. The view from here is spectacular, extending well into British Columbia to the west and to the Porcupine Hills to the east. A canister attached to one of the summit markers contains a notepad in which to sign your name and prove you made it. It is only five kilometers (3.1 mi) to the summit, but you should allow between 3.5 and five hours each way. Check the weather forecast before heading out.

To the Border

Also accessed via Atlas Road is **Allison Creek Trout Brood Station** (403/563-3385, July–Aug. Wed.–Sun. 10 A.M.–noon and 1–3 P.M.), where you can take a self-guided tour to learn how brown, brook, and rainbow trout are reared to provide eggs for trout hatcheries around the province. From the hatchery, Allison Creek Road spurs left to **Allison/Chinook Recreation Area,** with a network of forested hiking trails concentrated around Chinook Lake. The lake itself is a pretty body of water, with Crowsnest Mountain forming an imposing backdrop. It takes around 30 minutes to walk around the lake (a little longer if you stop to marvel at the osprey), or you can just relax on the sandy beach. The park also has a largish campground (403/563-5395, www.rockymountain camping.ca, $12–14) with limited facilities.

Back on Highway 3, the **Travel Alberta Information Centre** (403/563-3888, mid-May–mid-June 10 A.M.–6 P.M., mid-June–Aug. 9 A.M.–6 P.M.) has a spectacular view of Crowsnest Mountain. The center is difficult to see coming from the east—look for a blue roof on the south side of the road. Behind the information center, an old road now accessible only on foot leads three kilometers (1.9 mi) to an abandoned mine. The road crosses a small creek several times before coming to an intersection. Continue straight ahead (follow the creek) past an old car and into a grassy meadow. Head one kilometer (0.6 mi) farther to the mine slag heap and scramble to the top for a view of the mine and some log cabins. Allow one hour each way.

Continuing west is the convoluted shoreline of **Crowsnest Lake,** popular with locals for fishing (boat required), but a little cool for swimming. The best stopping point is a large pullout beside a short rocky beach. Beyond this point, the ambitious Bridgegate site will eventually include 2,000 condos, a casino, a five-star hotel, and Canada's largest resort conference center. From here, Highway 3 crosses Island Lake before crossing the Continental Divide and entering British Columbia, which is another day and another book. (Naturally, I recommend *Moon British Columbia.*)

WEST OF CALGARY

Although many people traveling west from Calgary head straight for the famous Banff National Park, there are interesting detours worth considering en route. The idea behind this chapter, then, is to encourage you to delay your inevitable arrival in Banff by describing how you can saddle up at western Canada's only unguided horseback riding ranch, walk the fairways of a golf course regularly described as the best value in North America, follow in the footsteps of Olympians, and more. Lots more.

The term West of Calgary is very broad, so this chapter has been broken down into three distinct sections, each a different travel experience but linked by location and sense of place. While each of the three is within day-tripping distance of Calgary, or could be linked together as a way of traveling between Calgary and Banff, they deserve more time. The region's popularity becomes apparent in summer, when Calgarians escaping the city fill the local campgrounds, teahouses, and hiking trails.

Ranching was Alberta's first major industry, and the earliest of the major spreads were established through the Ranchlands. The very first ranch was at Cochrane, just west of Calgary, but the entire southern foothills have been used for running cattle for more than a century. You'll see tracts of endless farmland, but many of the biggest ranches have been broken up over the years, into hobby farms and even subdivisions filled with estate-style homes. You may also recognize some of the scenery, which has starred in movies such as the 2000 Jackie Chan hit *Shanghai Noon;* the Oscar-winning *Unforgiven,* starring Clint Eastwood; *Legends*

HIGHLIGHTS

⟨ Millarville: Make your way to the Millarville Racetrack on a summer's Saturday morning for one of the province's most colorful farmers markets (page 172).

⟨ Bar U Ranch National Historic Site: Step back in time at this historic foothills ranch, where the past is bought to life through interpreters dressed in period costumes (page 173).

⟨ The Big Rock: These two massive rocks, deposited in the foothills during the last ice age, are the world's largest erratics (page 175).

⟨ Kananaskis Country Golf Course: Non-golfers won't be too impressed, but if you do golf and plan on playing just one round in Alberta, book a tee time here (page 180).

⟨ Highwood Pass: In Peter Lougheed Provincial Park, you'll find one of the only places in Canada where you can drive to an area of alpine meadows (page 183).

⟨ Rawson Lake: Hikers visit this lake for a variety of reasons – to go fishing, to admire the wildflowers, or simply to soak up magnificent mountain scenery. Regardless of your own interests, add this destination to your hiking agenda (page 185).

⟨ Grassi Lakes: A short walk is required to reach these two crystal-clear lakes, which are natural highlights of the Canmore region (page 193).

⟨ Oh Canada Eh!: Slightly tacky, but good fun nevertheless, this dinner-theater production brings Canada's best-known symbols to life (page 197).

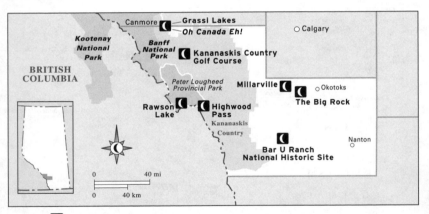

LOOK FOR **⟨** TO FIND RECOMMENDED SIGHTS, ACTIVITIES, DINING, AND LODGING.

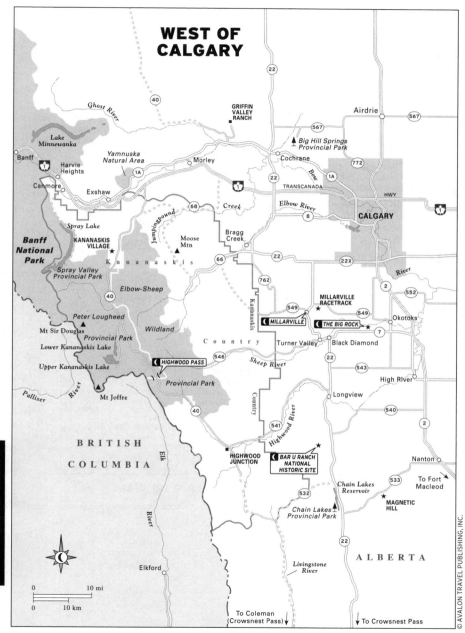

WEST OF CALGARY

of the Fall, starring Brad Pitt; the Kevin Costner western *Open Range; Brokeback Mountain,* where the Ranchlands stood in for Wyoming; and the 2007 Brad Pitt–driven *The Assassination of Jesse James by the Coward Robert Ford.*

Kananaskis Country is a vast tract of land set aside by the Alberta government as a multiuse recreation area. It is mostly protected as a series of parks, each with a varying level of services, including visitors centers, campgrounds, and summer interpretive programs. Mountainous terrain prevents a linked network of roads, but this is a good thing. The main thoroughfare is Highway 40, which hits many of the highlights, but you can also explore west from, for example, the Ranchlands town of Turner Valley, and find yourself on a road that dead-ends in a narrow valley. Although the region's emphasis is on the outdoors and camping, luxurious accommodations are available in Kananaskis Village (good enough for George W. Bush and Co. at the 2002 G8 Summit), which along with the adjacent alpine resort of Nakiska were built for the 1988 Winter Olympic Games.

The third component of this chapter is Canmore, a bustling mountain town at the northern edge of Kananaskis Country, and at the entrance to Banff National Park. The surrounding mountains provide Canmore's best recreation opportunities, while the town itself has extensive visitor facilities to match. Hiking is excellent on trails that lace the valley and mountainside slopes, with many high viewpoints easily reached. Flowing though town, the Bow River offers great fishing, kayaking, and rafting; golfers flock to three scenic courses; and nearby Mount Yamnuska has become the most developed rock-climbing site in the Canadian Rockies.

PLANNING YOUR TIME

You can include the region west of Calgary in your itinerary in a variety of ways, including as a detour between Calgary and Banff, as a day trip from either of these places, or as a destination in itself. Looping through the Ranchlands region on a day trip, you could plan to visit both **The Big Rock** and **Bar U Ranch National Historic Site** before heading through Kananaskis Country to Canmore and Banff. If it's a Saturday, you won't want to miss the rural fun at the farmers market in **Millarville.**

A single day isn't enough time to explore both the Ranchlands and Kananaskis/Canmore, so consider an overnight stay (there are lots of camping options through this region). After a day in the Ranchlands, plan on heading into the mountains. The trail to **Rawson Lake** is one of the more scenic walks, but to reach the alpine meadows of **Highwood Pass** you don't even need to get out of the car. Combine these two with a tee time at **Kananaskis Country Golf Course** and you'll still have plenty of time for an evening drive through Peter Lougheed Provincial Park.

Regardless of whether or not you stay in Canmore, there's plenty to do in the town itself, including hiking trails such as the one to **Grassi Lakes,** golfing, shopping, and being entertained at *Oh Canada Eh!*

Ranchlands

If you have ever dreamed of being a cowboy for a day or a week, this is the place to do it. The area also offers enough museums, teahouses, antiques emporiums, and events to keep even the most saddle-sore city slicker busy all summer. The Ranchlands region extends from Cochrane south to the ranching and farming communities of Okotoks and High River, and then west through the Porcupine Hills to the mountains of the Canadian Rockies. For those that live on the land, the western edge of the Ranchlands is as far west as their cattle run, which includes up low valleys that would otherwise be regarded as being within the Canadian Rockies. Highway 2 follows the eastern flanks of these foothills south from Calgary. Other roads crisscross the region and lead to communities that are rich in heritage, many of which have recently been discovered by artisans and craftspeople who now call them home.

COCHRANE

The foundation of Alberta's cattle industry was laid down here in the 20th century, when Senator Matthew Cochrane established the first of the big leasehold ranches in the province. Today's town of Cochrane (population 15,000), 38 kilometers (24 mi) northwest of downtown Calgary along Highway 1A, has seen its population increase by over 10 percent annually since the mid-1990s. Although ranching is still important to the local economy, Cochrane is growing as a "bedroom" suburb of Calgary. The business district, in the older section of town between Highway 1A and the rail line, is a delightful pocket of false-fronted buildings holding cafés, restaurants, and specialty shops.

Cochrane Ranche

To prevent the lawlessness that existed across the U.S. West extending into Canada, the government began granting huge grazing leases across the prairies. One of the original takers was Matthew Cochrane, who established the first real ranch west of Calgary, bringing herds of cattle from Montana to his 76,500-hectare (189,000-acre) holding in 1881. After two harsh winters, he moved his herds south again. A small piece of Cochrane's land holding is now preserved as Cochrane Ranche Provincial Historic Site. Almost completely surrounded by development, the 61-hectare (150-acre) site straddles Big Hill Creek one kilometer (0.6 mi) west of downtown along Highway 1A. A short trail leads up to a bluff and Malcolm MacKenzie's **Men of Vision,** a statue of a rider and his horse looking over the foothills. An old log cabin by the parking lot is used as an interpretive center (403/932-1193, mid-May–Sept. 9 A.M.–5 P.M.) and picnic tables dot the grounds.

Big Hill Springs Provincial Park

Protecting the end of a massive coulee, this small 26-hectare (64-acre) park is 16 kilometers (10 mi) northeast of Cochrane along Highway 22, then east along Highway 567. It provides an example of vegetation that was once widespread across the prairies. The park centers on a steep-walled valley with a stream flowing through it, cascading over several rocky terraces. A two-kilometer (1.2-mi) trail loops up the creek to its bubbling source, then back down a treed hillside. This short hike is an excellent way to escape the heat of the prairie.

Recreation

Immerse yourself in the Western lifestyle at **Griffin Valley Ranch** (403/932-7433), one of the few places in Alberta that allows unguided horseback riding. Trails lead through this historic 1,800-hectare (4,500-acre) ranch along creeks, through wooded areas and open meadows, and to high viewpoints where the panorama extends west to the Canadian Rockies. Horse rentals are similarly priced to trail riding (one hour $30, two hours $50, three hours $70); the catch is that at least one member of your party must be a "member" of the ranch (simply sign a waiver and pay the $50 annual fee). To get to the ranch, follow Highway 1A west from

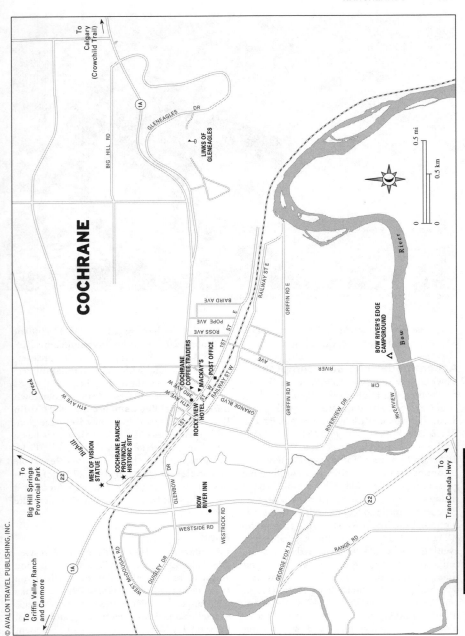

COCHRANE

To
Calgary
(Crowchild Trail)

GLENEAGLES DR

1A

BIG HILL RD

LINKS OF
GLENEAGLES

Creek

Bighill

4TH AVE W

To
Big Hill Springs
Provincial Park

22

MEN OF VISION
STATUE

COCHRANE RANCHE
PROVINCIAL
HISTORIC SITE

1ST ST

4TH AVE W

3RD AVE W

COCHRANE
COFFEE TRADERS

RAILWAY ST W

MACKAY'S

POST OFFICE

ROCKY VIEW
HOTEL

GRANDE BLVD

BAIRD AVE

POPE AVE

ROSS AVE

1ST ST

RAILWAY ST E

GRIFFIN RD E

AVE

GRIFFIN RD W

RIVERVIEW DR

RIVER

CIR

RIVERVIEW

Bow

River

BOW RIVER'S EDGE
CAMPGROUND

GLENBOW DR

BOW
RIVER INN

WESTSIDE RD

WESTROCK RD

WEST McDOUGAL RD

QUIGLEY DR

1A

To
Griffin Valley Ranch
and Canmore

RANGE RD

GEORGE FOX TR

22

To
TransCanada Hwy

0.5 mi

0.5 km

0

0

WEST OF CALGARY

WEST OF CALGARY

© ANDREW HEMPSTEAD

Malcolm MacKenzie's *Men of Vision* statue, Cochrane

Cochrane for 18 kilometers (11 mi), take Highway 40 north, then follow the signs.

Accommodations and Camping

The best local lodging, 16 kilometers (10 mi) northeast along Highway 22, then east along Highway 567 beyond the entrance to Big Hill Springs Provincial Park, is **Big Springs Estate Bed & Breakfast** (403/948-5264 or 888/948-5851, www.bigsprings-bb.com, $149–279 s or d). Set on 14 hectares (35 acres), this luxurious accommodation comprises five comfortable guest rooms, a cheerful breakfast room, a large sitting area, and extensive gardens. The Springs Executive Suite ($249) comes with a freestanding jetted tub and a wood-burning fireplace. All rates include a gourmet breakfast and light evening snacks such as homemade chocolate fudge and other niceties such as slippers and robes. Back in town, you'll find western style on a budget at the **Rocky View Hotel** (1st St. and 2nd Ave. W, 403/932-2442, $50–70 s or d). Rooms are very basic, with shared bathroom facilities and no phones. **Bow River Inn**

(Hwy. 22, south of Hwy. 1A, 403/932-7900 or 866/663-3209, www.bowriverinn.com, $109 s or d, kitchenette $129) is a pleasant, reasonably priced motel with a choice of family restaurants within walking distance.

Two kilometers (1.2 mi) south of downtown is **Bow RiversEdge Campground** (900 Griffin Rd., 403/932-4675, www.bowriversedge.com, mid-April–mid-Oct., $31–35), which has a wealth of modern facilities that include Wi-Fi, a playground, and a laundry. **Ghost Reservoir Provincial Recreation Area** (22 km/14 mi west of town along Hwy. 1A, May–Oct., $17) has a pleasant lakefront location, but the site can get windy.

Food

◖ Cochrane Coffee Traders (114 2nd Ave., 403/932-4395, daily from 7:30 A.M.) is as good as any place to start the day, especially if you snag one of the outdoor tables. Choose from a wide range of specialty coffees and sweet treats, as well as a healthy selection of sandwiches. Back on 1st Street is the two-story wooden-

RANCHING IN ALBERTA

The ranching tradition that Alberta so proudly claims started in the late 1800s. The massive herds of bison that once roamed the foothills had been devastated, the indigenous peoples had been moved to reservations, and the Canadian Pacific Railway had completed the link to the eastern provinces. A huge tract of land in the foothills now stood empty, and the Canadian government was convinced by Senator Mathew Cochrane to establish leases set at a minimal payment of one cent per acre, with the senator himself leasing a 100,000-acre spread immediately west of Calgary. It didn't take long for word to get out. Cowboys from Montana, Wyoming, and Texas came hootin' and hollerin' as they drove thousands of head of cattle north. They brought with them a new spirit, craving the open spaces and the hardships associated with living on the land. Many of the cattle barons who invested in the land were wealthy Americans and eastern Canadians who rarely, if ever, visited their holdings. Even English royalty became involved. Edward, Prince of Wales, who abdicated the throne to marry Wallis Simpson, purchased a 25,000-acre spread in 1919.

Ranching is still an important part of the province's economic base, with four million head of cattle worth $1.6 billion in annual income for Alberta. Facts and figures aside, there's plenty of opportunity for visitors to experience ranching traditions, including at **Bar U Ranch,** a National Historic Site where the traditions of life in the saddle live on through working displays and demonstrations of ranching skills, or by taking a vacation at one of many ranches offering accommodations and activities.

---

fronted **Rocky View Hotel** (403/932-2442) which houses the **Canyon Rose Restaurant,** a popular all-day dining spot, and the **Stageline Saloon.** Of the many eateries lining Cochrane's downtown 1st Street, the most popular on a hot summer's afternoon is **Mackay's** (403/932-2455), an ice-cream parlor dating to 1948. A blackboard displays up to 50 flavors, but I'm told the favorites are still vanilla, chocolate, and strawberry.

BRAGG CREEK

Bragg Creek is a rural hamlet nestled in the foothills of the Canadian Rockies, 34 kilometers (21 mi) south of Cochrane and 40 kilometers (25 mi) west of Calgary. To the east is the Sarcee Indian Reservation and to the west is Kananaskis Country. The **Stony Trail,** an Indian trading route that passed through the area, had been in use for generations when the first white people arrived in the early 1880s. Much of the surrounding forest had been cleared by fire, encouraging farmers to settle in the isolated region and eke a living from the land. Improved road access in the 1920s

encouraged families from Calgary to build weekender homes in town. Today many of Bragg Creek's 1,000 residents commute daily to nearby Calgary. The ideal location and quiet lifestyle have attracted artists and artisans—the town claims to have more painters, potters, sculptors, and weavers than any similarly sized town in Alberta.

Sights and Recreation

Arriving along Highway 22 from either the north or south, you'll be greeted upon arrival in Bragg Creek by a slightly confusing four-way-stop intersection with a treed triangle of land in the middle. Take the option along the north (right) side of the distinctive polished log Bragg Creek Trading Post II to access the main shopping center, a western-themed collection of basic town services interspersed with craft shops and cafés. White Avenue, also known as **Heritage Mile** and originally the main commercial strip, has more of the same and leads through an appealing residential area. This road continues southwest to 122-hectare (300-acre) **Bragg Creek Provincial Park,** a day-use

area alongside the Elbow River. With a basket of goodies from one of Bragg Creek's many food outlets, leave the main parking lot behind to enjoy a picnic lunch at one of the many riverside picnic tables.

Accommodations and Food

Although lacking motels and campgrounds (the closest camping is along the Elbow River Valley in Kananaskis Country), Bragg Creek is a popular overnight escape for folks from Calgary. Best of a bunch of bed-and-breakfasts is **Countryside Inn** (call for directions, 403/949-2805), a large country-style house nestled among stands of trees within walking distance of both the river and village. The home has three comfortable guest rooms—one with its own hot tub—a spacious sitting room, a billiards room, and an outdoor hot tub. A hearty breakfast is included in the rates of $125 s, $140 d.

Bragg Creek Shopping Centre holds a wide variety of eateries as well as most services, including a gas station, bakery, grocery store, and post office. Around the corner, at the main intersection, is the **Cinnamon Spoon** (Bragg Creek Trading Post II, 403/949-4110, Mon.–Fri. 6 A.M.–5 P.M., Sat.–Sun. 6 A.M.– 5 P.M.), with the best coffee in town, as well as pastries, cakes, smoothies, and sandwiches made to order. At the **Steak Pit** (43 White Ave., 403/949-3633, daily from 11:30 A.M.), the setting is early Canadian, yet elegant. The dining room, decorated with hand-hewn cedar furniture, is only a small part of the restaurant, which also has a café, lounge, sports bar, and gift shop. Eating here isn't cheap (mains $22–36) but *is* comparable to Calgary restaurants. The menu sets out to prove great steaks don't necessitate fancy trimmings, and does so with the best cuts of Alberta beef and great spuds.

BRAGG CREEK TO TURNER VALLEY

From Bragg Creek, it's 70 kilometers (43 mi) southeast to Okotoks. The most scenic route south from Bragg Creek is along Highway 762 through Millarville.

◀ Millarville

Millarville is not a town as such, but rather a collection of estate-style homes in the foothills of the Canadian Rockies. **Millarville Racetrack,** five kilometers (3.1 mi) northeast of the hamlet, is a hive of activity each Saturday morning, when huge crowds gather for the **Millarville Farmer's Market** (June–early Oct. 8:30 A.M.–noon). In addition to more than 160 local vendors, live entertainment and wagon rides are provided. The **Millarville Rodeo** was first held in 1997, but it has already gained a following among the local population. It's held the last weekend of May. The Canada Day (July 1) tradition of the **Millarville Races** goes back a lot farther, to 1905. The main race involves locals on stock horses vying for a silver cup and belt buckle. Head out to the racetrack to join the action.

TURNER VALLEY

Turner Valley, a quiet town of 1,800 straddling the Sheep River 69 kilometers (43 mi) southwest of Calgary, is synonymous with the oil-and-gas industry in Alberta. In 1914, Canada's first major crude-oil discovery was made here, but gas, not oil, first sparked interest in the valley. In 1903, a farmer named Bill Herron found gas seeping from fissures on his land. He had it tested and, to his surprise, was told it was petroleum gas. He was having trouble convincing anyone to back an oil-related enterprise and, so the story goes, he finally persuaded two oilmen to become involved by taking them to the site of the gas, lighting it, and cooking them a fried breakfast on the flame. Shortly after, the Calgary Petroleum Products Company was formed and started sinking wells, which was the beginning of an economic boom. During the oil boom, gas was burned off in an area known as Hell's Half Acre east of Turner Valley. It is estimated that 28 billion cubic meters (990 billion cubic ft) of excess gas were flared off in the first 10 years.

Turner Valley Gas Plant

This National Historic Site is not set up as a tourist attraction, and is currently closed for

reclamation, but head over to **Hell's Half Acre Bridge,** which crosses the Sheep River southeast of downtown, from where gas flares that still burn 24 hours a day can be viewed. The Municipal Centre (Main St., 403/933-4944) has information on the site and shows a documentary on demand.

Practicalities

Turner Valley Lodge (112 Kennedy Dr., 403/933-7878, www.turnervalleylodge.com, $66 s, $72 d) is the town's only motel. The 27 rooms are plainly furnished, but offer air-conditioning. **Turner Valley Campground** (May–Oct.) is right downtown beside the Municipal Centre and an outdoor swimming pool; unserviced sites $12, powered sites $14. You'd be better off heading west into Kananaskis Country, though, for more enjoyable surroundings.

Coyote Moon Café (202 Main St., 403/933-3363, Mon.–Fri. 7:30 A.M.–5 P.M., Sat.–Sun. 9 A.M.–7 P.M.) is a fantastic little café, always bustling and with wonderful smells coming from the kitchen. Even though this is cowboy country, the coffee choices are city style all the way. One block south, **【 Route 40 Soup Co.** (146 Main St., 403/933-7676, Mon.–Tues. 11 A.M.–5 P.M., Wed.–Thurs. 10 A.M.–8 P.M., Fri.–Sat. 11 A.M.–9 P.M.) is a real find. The soups ($8 per bowl) are rich, thick, and full of locally sourced produce. Just west of Turner Valley's only traffic light is the Quonset-shaped **Chuckwagon Café** (105 Sunset Blvd., 403/933-0003, daily for breakfast, lunch, and dinner). It's a typical small-town diner, with the $3.99 breakfast special an especially good value, although the portion isn't huge.

The **tourist information center** (Main St., 403/933-4944, summer daily 10 A.M.–6 P.M.) is in the Municipal Centre.

BLACK DIAMOND

This town of 1,900 on the banks of the Sheep River, four kilometers (2.5 mi) east of Turner Valley, was named for the coal once mined nearby. James A. McMillan, a government land surveyor, was digging an irrigation ditch when he uncovered a rich seam of coal. Within a few years, a mine had become operational, and the coal, which was of excellent quality, was used in households throughout the region. The coal mines have long since closed. Most residents work in the nearby oil fields or commute the 65 kilometers (40 mi) to Calgary.

Practicalities

The town center is a bustling little strip along Centre Avenue. Highway 22 enters town from the west along Centre Avenue, then spurs south along Government Road to Longview. At the main intersection is the **Black Diamond Hotel** (403/933-4656), which has been modernized on the outside, but on the inside retains a classic small-town pub atmosphere that rocks with country music each weekend. Three blocks south, the **Triple "A" Motel** (322 Government Rd., 403/933-4915) has basic rooms for $45 s, $55 d. **Lions Campground,** in Centennial Park, is a great little spot by the Sheep River (access via 5th St. off Centre St.). It has showers, a kitchen shelter, and firewood; unserviced sites $12, powered sites $14–18.

Wonders (130 Government Rd., 403/933-2347, July–Aug. 6:30 A.M.–10 P.M.), a small gift shop, is the unofficial tourist information center, but it's worth dropping by just to enjoy coffee on the outdoor deck.

HIGHWAY 22 SOUTH
【 Bar U Ranch National Historic Site

Established in 1882, the Bar U Ranch (31 km/19 mi south of Black Diamond, 403/395-2212 or 800/568-4996, June–early Oct. daily 9 A.M.–5 P.M., adult $7.50, senior $6, child $3.50) was one of western Canada's top ranches in the late 1800s. It was a corporate ranch, run by the Northwest Cattle Company and stocked with more than 3,000 cattle driven north from Montana. The company was renowned throughout North America as a leading breeder of Percherons, a type of draft horse that originated in the Perche region of France. Like most of the big ranches in North America, the Bar U was broken up over time. Today a 145-hectare (360-acre) parcel of the original

WEST OF CALGARY

spread has been preserved, with hundreds of Percherons running free through its rolling fields. Many of the old buildings have been restored; there's an orientation center, a small theater, a blacksmith's shop, and a general store. Ranching skills are also demonstrated. In the **Roadhouse Restaurant,** the menu reflects the food that ranch hands of days gone by would have enjoyed after a long day in the saddle: buffalo burgers, sourdough breads, hearty soups, and stew are all offered.

Chain Lakes Provincial Park

Continuing south, the next worthwhile stop is Chain Lakes Provincial Park, sitting in the Willow Creek Valley between the Canadian Rockies and Porcupine Hills. The park was named for a series of spring-fed lakes that have since been dammed. The park is in a transition zone; therefore, plant and animal species are varied. Birdlife is especially prolific, with shorebirds, waterfowl, and osprey all present. In the north end of the park are some high bluffs, offering good views of the surrounding land. Fishing is excellent for rainbow trout, and more than 60,000 bull trout have been released in recent years as part of an ambitious program to restore the species to its once-prolific numbers. The campground and day-use area are at the southern end of the reservoir, close to a boat launch and beach. Campsites (unserviced $15, powered sites $20) along three loops have some privacy, but facilities are limited to picnic tables and pit toilets.

East to Nanton

Views of the Canadian Rockies in the rearview mirror are spectacular as you head east on Highway 533 from Chain Lakes Provincial Park through the northern reaches of the Porcupine Hills. At a high point in the hills is **Magnetic Hill,** where an optical illusion creates a bizarre misimpression: put your car in neutral and it will slowly roll *up* the hill! As you descend into a valley east from the hill, you'll pass the old holdings of the A 7 Ranch, which was once one of Alberta's largest ranches. Its original owner, A. E. Cross, helped finance the

first Calgary Stampede in 1912. The ranch has now been subdivided but remains in the same family. From this point, it's 35 kilometers (22 mi) to Nanton and Highway 2, where you can head north to High River, Okotoks, and Calgary, or south to Fort Macleod.

HIGH RIVER

In the heart of the province's ranching country, 45 kilometers (28 mi) south of Calgary, High River has grown steadily from its beginnings as a rest stop on the Macleod Trail. Originally it was known as the Crossing because it was the only possible place to ford the Highwood River. A period of severe drought at the turn of the 20th century was followed by many years of ample rainfall, and the community slowly grew to its current population of 8,000.

Highway 2A runs north–south through High River. At the south edge of town, 12th Avenue heads east to a major intersection with Highway 2. Downtown High River is a compact collection of staid old buildings west across the railway tracks from Highway 2A (Centre St.). Housed in a restored Canadian Pacific Railway (CPR) station, the **Museum of the Highwood** (406 1st St. W, 403/652-7156, summer Mon.–Sat. 10 A.M.–5 P.M., Sun. 1–5 P.M., $3) is chock-full of displays portraying early Western life. Of particular interest is the exhibit cataloging chuck wagon racing, a sport that has special significance to locals since the area boasts many champions. Better still, if you're visiting on the third weekend of June, plan on attending the **North American Chuckwagon Championships** at the fairgrounds.

Practicalities

Of the three motels in town, the **Super 8** (1601 13th Ave., 403/652-4448 or 866/831-8558, www.super8.com, from $99 s, $109 d) has the newest facilities, including an indoor pool and waterslide, a fitness room, and Internet access. The local campground is within a few blocks of downtown. It's in **George Lane Memorial Park** (west along 5th Ave. SW, 403/652-2529, May–Oct.). Sites are well-spaced and some

enjoy riverside positioning. Facilities include showers and kitchen shelters; unserviced sites $16, powered sites $22.

In a restored 1947 rail car beside the museum is the **Whistle Stop Café** (1st St. SW, 403/652-7026, Mon. 10 A.M.–2 P.M., Tues.–Sat. 10 A.M.–4 P.M., Sun. 11 A.M.–4 P.M.). You won't find anything too fancy here, just salads and sandwiches under $8 and slices of delicious berry pie for $4.

OKOTOKS AND VICINITY

The fast-growing town of Okotoks is in the Sheep River Valley 34 kilometers (21 mi) south of Calgary and just minutes from Highway 2 to the east. It is the largest population base between Calgary and Lethbridge, and many of its 14,000 residents, up from 5,000 just 20 years ago, commute into Calgary to work. The town began as a rest stop along the Macleod Trail, which linked Fort Calgary to Fort Macleod last century. Many old buildings still stand and have been incorporated into a walking tour, with maps available at the tourist information

center. Along similar lines is the **Okotoks Art Walk,** which links downtown businesses displaying the works of local artists. The starting point is the **Station Cultural Centre** (53 N. Railway St., 403/938-3204), through downtown in a restored railway station. **Okotoks Bird Sanctuary,** located east of town, attracts ducks, geese, and other waterfowl visible from a raised observation deck.

◖ The Big Rock

The name Okotoks came from the Blackfoot word *okatak* (rock), probably in reference to the massive boulders seven kilometers (4.3 mi) west of town along Highway 7. Known as erratics, they are the largest such geological formation in the world. During the last ice age, a sheet of ice up to one kilometer (0.6 mi) thick crept forward from the north. A landslide in what is now Jasper National Park deposited large boulders on top of the ice. The ice continued moving south, carrying the boulders with it. Many thousands of years later, as temperatures warmed and the ice melted, the

Cafés and galleries dot the main street of Okotoks.

© ANDREW HEMPSTEAD

boulders were deposited far from their source (hence the name "erratic").

Practicalities

The best accommodations in town are provided at **Okotoks Country Inn** (on Hwy. 2A, 403/938-1999 or 877/938-3336), with 40 climate-controlled motel rooms, modern facilities, and rates of $82 s, $92 d that include a light breakfast. Municipally operated **Sheep**

River Campground (403/938-4282, May–Oct., tents $18, hookups $21–30) has a delightful riverside location just a short walk from town off Highway 2A.

Take Elizabeth Street east from Highway 2A and continue through downtown to reach **Okotoks Visitor Information Centre** (53 N. Railway St., 403/938-3204, May–early Aug. daily 9 A.M.–5 P.M.). The chamber of commerce website is www.okotoks.ca.

Kananaskis Country

During Alberta's oil-and-gas boom of the 1970s, oil revenues collected by the provincial government were channeled into various projects aimed at improving the lifestyle of Albertans. One lasting legacy of the boom is Kananaskis Country (pronounced can-AN-a-skiss), a sprawling 4,250-square-kilometer (1,640-square-mile) wilderness area west of Calgary that has been developed with an emphasis on providing recreation opportunities for as many people as possible. Although Kananaskis Country lacks the famous lakes and glaciated peaks of Banff and Jasper National Parks, in many ways it rivals them. Wildlife is abundant, and opportunities for observation of larger mammals are superb. The region has large populations of moose, elk, black bears, bighorn sheep, and mountain goats. Wolves, grizzly bears, and cougars are present, too, but are less likely to be seen.

Geographically, Kananaskis Country can be divided into eight areas, each with its own distinct character. They include **Bow Valley Provincial Park**, a small park between the TransCanada Highway and Bow River; **Kananaskis Valley**, home to a golf course, ski resort, and the accommodations of Kananaskis Village; **Peter Lougheed Provincial Park**, which rises from fish-filled lakes to the glaciated peaks of the Continental Divide; **Spray Valley Provincial Park**, named for a massive body of water nestled below the Continental Divide; **Sibbald**, an integrated recreation area where horseback riding is permitted; **Elbow**

River Valley and adjacent **Sheep River Valley**, sections of the foothills that rise to Elbow-Sheep Wildland Provincial Park; and in the far south the **Highwood/Cataract Creek** areas, where the rugged landscape ranges from forested valleys to snowcapped peaks.

Access and Information

The main access to Kananaskis Country is 80 kilometers (50 mi) west of Calgary off the TransCanada Highway (see the following *Old Banff Road* section). Other points of access are south from Canmore; at Bragg Creek on the region's northeast border; west from Longview in the southeast; or along the Forestry Trunk Road from the south.

For more information, contact the regional Parks and Protected Areas division of the provincial government, in the Provincial Building at 800 Railway Avenue, Canmore, 403/678-5508; or surf the Internet to www.cd.gov.ab.ca, and click on the Enjoying Alberta link. Another good source of information is **Friends of Kananaskis Country** (403/678-5593, www.kananaskis.org), a nonprofit organization that advertises educational programs, is involved in a variety of hands-on projects, and promotes Kananaskis Country in partnership with the government.

Old Banff Road

The original route from Calgary into the mountains has long been bypassed, but for those with

The severely folded and faulted south face of Mount Kidd is one of the most distinctive geological features in Kananaskis Country.

a little extra time, it remains as a pleasant alternative to the TransCanada Highway. Also known as Highway 1A, the easiest place to join it is at Cochrane, an important ranching center west of Calgary (see the *Ranchlands* section earlier in this chapter). From there, Highway 1A follows the north side of the Bow River to Highway 40, the main entrance to Kananaskis Country. The first major junction is with Highway 940, which spurs northwest to **Ghost River Wilderness Area.** Soon after this junction, the highway passes **Ghost Lake,** which was created by damming the Bow River for hydroelectricity. Continuing west, the impressive face of **Mount Yamnuska,** a popular rock-climbing spot, is visible to the north. Along this route, Highway 40 crosses the TransCanada Highway and heads south into Kananaskis Country.

BOW VALLEY PROVINCIAL PARK

This park, at the north end of Kananaskis Country, sits at the confluence of the Kananas-

kis and Bow Rivers and extends as far south as Barrier Lake. The entrance to the park is four kilometers (2.5 mi) west of Highway 40 (the main access into Kananaskis Country). It was originally part of Rocky Mountains Park (now Banff National Park), but the area became separated when park boundaries were reduced in 1930, excluding areas zoned for further industrial development.

The Bow Valley was gouged by glaciers during a succession of ice ages, leaving the typical U-shaped glacial valley surrounded by towering peaks. Three vegetation zones are found within the park, but evergreen and aspen forest predominates. To the casual motorist driving along the highway, the park seems fairly small, but more than 300 species of plants have been recorded, and 60 species of birds are known to nest within its boundaries. The abundance of wildflowers, birds, and smaller mammals can be enjoyed along four short interpretive trails. Other popular activities in the park include fishing for a variety of trout and whitefish in

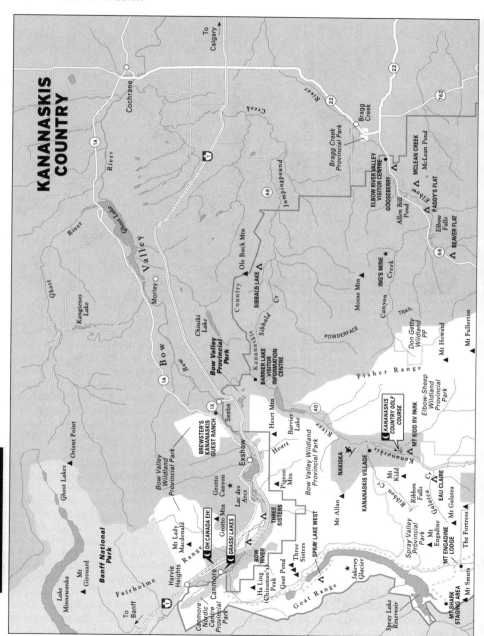

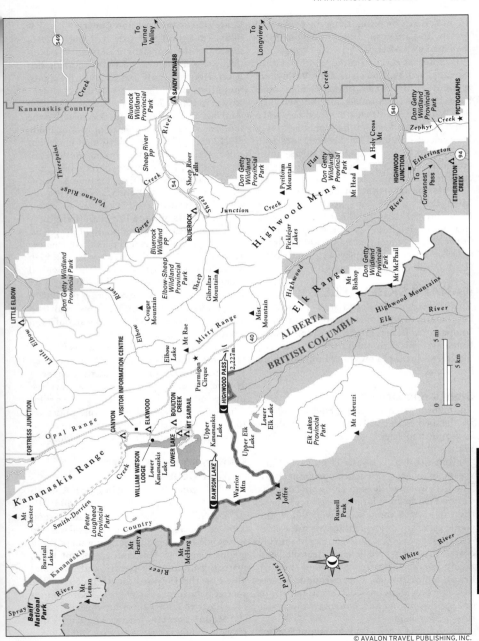

the Bow River, bicycling along the paved trail system, and attending interpretive programs presented by park staff.

Facilities at the two campgrounds within the park, **Willow Rock** and **Bow Valley,** are as good as any in the province. They both have showers, flush toilets, and kitchen shelters. Willow Rock also has powered sites and a coin laundry and is open for winter camping. Unserviced sites are $20, powered sites $30. Reservations can be made for both campgrounds at 403/673-2163, www.bowvalley campgrounds.com.

A **visitor information center** (summer Mon.–Fri. 8 A.M.–8 P.M., the rest of the year Mon.–Fri. 8:15 A.M.–4:30 P.M.) is at the park entrance on Highway 1X. It offers general information on the park and Kananaskis Country, as well as interpretive displays. A 2.2-kilometer (1.4-mi) hiking trail also begins here.

KANANASKIS VALLEY

This is the most developed area of Kananaskis Country, yet summer crowds are minimal compared to Banff. Highway 40 follows the Kananaskis River through the valley between the TransCanada Highway and Peter Lougheed Provincial Park.

Sights and Drives

The following sights are along Highway 40 and are detailed from the TransCanada Highway in the north to Peter Lougheed Provincial Park in the south.

From the TransCanada Highway, Highway 40 branches south across open rangeland. The first worthwhile stop along this route is **Canoe Meadows,** a large day-use area above the sparkling Kananaskis River. Below the picnic area, whitewater enthusiasts use a short stretch of river as a slalom course. Manmade obstacles and gates challenge recreational and racing kayakers; upstream (around the first bend), the man-made Green Tongue creates a steep wave, allowing kayakers to remain in one spot, spinning and twisting while water rushes past them.

South from Canoe Meadows, stop at **Barrier**

Lake Visitor Information Centre (403/673-3985, June–mid-Sept., daily 9 A.M.–6 P.M., the rest of the year daily 9 A.M.–4 P.M.). Nestled between Highway 40 and the Kananaskis River, riverside trails lead in both directions, including two kilometers (1.2 mi) downstream to Canoe Meadows. Barrier Lake itself is farther along Highway 40, dominated to the south by the impressive peak of Mount Baldy (2,212 m/7,257 ft). The lake is man-made, but still a picture of beauty. From the south end of Barrier Lake, Highway 40 continues south to a spot that will be of particular interest to anglers, **Mount Lorette Ponds,** stocked annually with rainbow trout.

Kananaskis Village lies just off Highway 40 four kilometers (2.5 mi) south of the ponds. The village, the epicenter of action during the 1988 Winter Olympic Games, sits on a high bench below Nakiska—where the downhill events of the games were held—and overlooks a golf course. The village comprises two hotels, restaurants, and other service shops set around a paved courtyard complete with waterfalls and trout-stocked ponds.

From the village, it's 15 kilometers (9.3 mi) farther south to the border of Peter Lougheed Provincial Park. Just beyond the village is **Wedge Pond.** Originally dug as a gravel pit during golf course construction, it is now filled with water and encircled by a one-kilometer (0.6-mi) trail offering fantastic views to towering 2,958-meter (9,700-ft) Mount Kidd.

◖ Kananaskis Country Golf Course

Regularly voted Best Value in North America by *Golf Digest,* this 36-hole layout (403/591-7272 or 877/591-2525, www.kananaskisgolf .com) is bisected by the Kananaskis River and surrounded by magnificent mountain peaks. It comprises two 18-hole courses: **Mount Kidd,** featuring undulating terrain and an island green on the 197-yard fourth hole, and the shorter (which is a relative term—both courses measure over 7,000 yards from the back markers) **Mount Lorette,** where water comes into play on 13 holes. Greens fees are $80 (Alberta

In addition to being inexpensive, Kananaskis Country Golf Course is generally regarded as one of the most scenic in North America – the perfect combination for keen golfers.

residents pay $60) and a cart is an additional $15 per person. Golfers enjoy complimentary valet parking and use of the driving range, as well as a restaurant and bar with awesome mountain views and a well-stocked golf shop.

Winter Recreation
Nakiska (403/591-7777 or 800/258-7669, www.skinakiska.com) is a state-of-the-art alpine resort built to host the alpine skiing events of the 1988 Winter Olympic Games. Great cruising and fast fall-line skiing on runs cut specially for racing will satisfy the intermediate-to-advanced crowd. The resort has a total of 28 runs and a vertical rise of 735 meters (2,410 ft). Lift tickets are adult $54, senior and youth $44, child $22. Check the website for accommodation packages and transportation schedules from Canmore.

The most accessible of Kananaskis Country's 200 kilometers (124 mi) of cross-country trails are in the Ribbon Creek area. Most heavily used are those radiating from Kananaskis

Village and those around the base of Nakiska. Most trails are easy to intermediate, including a five-kilometer (3.1-mi) track up Ribbon Creek. Rentals are available in the Village Trading Post in Kananaskis Village.

Accommodations
A magnet for families, the privately owned **Sundance Lodges** (403/591-7122, www.sundancelodges.com, mid-May–Sept.) is a wonderful option for travelers looking to try camping or who want something a little more adventurous than a regular motel room. Campsites cost $21 per night, with rentals including tents, camp stoves, sleeping bags, and utensil kits available for minimal charge. Next up are the tepees ($49–65), 12 of them, each with colorfully painted canvas walls rising from wooden floors. Inside are mattresses, a heater, and a lantern. Finally, you can stay in one of 18 Trapper Tents ($69 s or d), which are larger but have similar interior fittings and a canvas-covered awning over a picnic table. When you

tire of hiking and biking on surrounding trails, return to the lodge for fishing in a manmade pond, horseshoes, badminton, and volleyball. Other amenities include a general store, hot showers, a laundry, and Internet access. Sundance sits beside the Kananaskis River, just off Highway 40, 22 kilometers (13.7 miles) south of the TransCanada Highway.

Built for the 1988 Winter Olympic Games, **Kananaskis Village** was again in the world spotlight when eight of the world's most powerful men met here during the G8 Summit in June 2002. The village is home to two resortlike hotels set around a cobbled courtyard. Outdoor seating from various eateries spills onto the terrace, and biking and hiking trails radiate out in all directions. All in all, a good place to base yourself for an overnight hotel stay.

Executive Resort at Kananaskis (403/591-7500 or 888/388-3932, www.executivehotels .net) is the smaller and more personal of the two hotels, with guest rooms that combine natural colors with dramatic contemporary styling. Some of the rooms are bedroom lofts with gas fireplaces, kitchenettes, large bathrooms, and sitting rooms ($260 s or d); the others are standard-size hotel rooms that begin at $230. Extras include the Mountain Spa facility, a fitness center, an indoor pool, and a restaurant and pub.

The 321-room **Delta Lodge at Kananaskis** (403/591-7711 or 866/432-4322, www.delta hotels.com) is part of an upscale Canadian hotel chain. It offers two distinct types of rooms. In the main lodge are 251 moderately large Delta Rooms, many with mountain views, balconies, and fireplaces. Connected by a covered walkway are 70 Signature Club (a Delta designation) rooms, each boasting elegant Victorian-era charm, a mountain view, a luxurious bathroom complete with bathrobes, extra large beds, and many extras, such as CD players. Guests in this wing also enjoy a private lounge and continental breakfast. All guests have use of the Summit Spa and Fitness Centre, which comprises a full-facility health club, an indoor swimming pool, whirlpool, steam room, sauna, and a beauty salon with tanning beds. Summer

rates for Delta Rooms are $220 s or d, while Signature Club rooms start at $340.

Camping

Mount Kidd RV Park (403/591-7700, www .mountkiddrv.com) is a commercial campground nestled below the sheer eastern face of Mount Kidd, along Highway 40 south of Kananaskis Village and the golf course. The campground's showpiece is the Campers Center, containing the main registration area and all the usual bathroom facilities as well as whirlpools, saunas, a wading pool, a game room, a lounge, groceries, a concession area, and a laundry room. Outside are two tennis courts, picnic areas by the river, and many paved biking and hiking trails. Most of the 229 campsites are hookups, but the few tenting sites are a good value at $22 per night. Powered sites are $28, with power and water $30, and full hookups are $35.

Those who can survive without such luxuries should continue 6.5 kilometers (four miles) south beyond Mount Kidd RV Park to **Eau Claire Campground** (late June–mid-Sept., $20), operated by Kananaskis Camping (403/591-7226, www.kananaskiscamping.com). Facilities are limited to 51 sites (those on the outside of the loop afford the most privacy), each with a picnic table and fire pit, along with pump water, pit toilets, and a playground.

Food

The Delta Lodge (403/591-7711) contains four restaurants and two bars. For a warm, relaxed atmosphere, head to the **Bighorn Lounge** (daily from 11 A.M.), near the arcade's main entrance. It features a bistro-style menu highlighted by a wide variety of inexpensive appetizers perfect for sharing, such as cheese platters. **Obsessions Deli** serves up light snacks, including healthy sandwiches and rich, handmade truffles. Also in the arcade is the **◖ Fireweed Grill** (daily 6 A.M.–10 P.M.), offering a casual Western-style atmosphere. The setting here is particularly appealing with floor-to-ceiling windows and an adjoining outdoor patio used during summer. Breakfast is served buffet-style daily until

10 A.M. The country-style **Brady's Market** (summer daily for lunch and breakfast, $15–28) features seasonal produce prepared in traditional European dishes. **Seasons Dining Room** (June–Oct. Tues.–Sat. 6–9:30 P.M.), in the Signature Club wing, is the village's most elegant restaurant. French-Canadian cuisine is served on sterling silver as a pianist plays in the background; expect to pay $20–33 for an entrée.

Food is also available at **Wildflower Restaurant**, at the adjacent Executive Resort, or at the golf course, where the restaurant offers a casual atmosphere and stunning valley views.

PETER LOUGHEED PROVINCIAL PARK

This park is a southern extension of the Kananaskis Valley and protects the upper watershed of the Kananaskis River. It is contained within a high mountain valley and dominated by two magnificent mountain bodies of water—**Upper** and **Lower Kananaskis Lakes**. The 500-square-kilometer (193-square-mile) wilderness is the second-largest provincial park in Alberta.

Highway 40 is the main route through the park. The most important intersection to make note of is five kilometers (3.1 mi) along Highway 40 from the park's north boundary. At this point, Kananaskis Lakes Road branches off to the west, accessing Upper and Lower Kananaskis Lakes. These two lakes are the center of boating and fishing in the park, and opportunities abound for hiking and camping nearby.

◀ Highwood Pass

In the southeastern corner of the park, Highway 40 climbs to Highwood Pass (2,227 m/7,310 ft), the highest road pass in Canada. On the way up to the pass, a pleasant detour is Valley View Trail, a five-kilometer (3.1-mi) paved road whose route higher up the slopes of the Opal Range allows views across the entire park to the Continental Divide. The pass itself is right at the tree line, one of the most accessible alpine areas in all the Canadian Rockies. Simply step out of your vehicle and follow the interpretive trails through the

Highwood Meadows. In the vicinity, the **Rock Glacier Trail,** two kilometers (1.2 mi) north of Highwood Pass, leads 150 meters (0.1 mi) to a unique formation of moraine rock.

From the pass, Highway 40 descends into the Highwood/Cataract Creek areas of Kananaskis Country (Highwood Junction is 35 km/22 mi from the pass). **Note:** The road over the Highwood Pass is in critical wildlife habitat and is closed December 1–June 15.

Recreation

Hiking (see *Peter Lougheed Hiking* later in this chapter) is the most popular activity in the park, but by no means the only one. The **Bike Trail** is a 20-kilometer (12.5-mi) paved trail designed especially for bicycles that begins behind the visitor information center and follows Lower Kananaskis Lake to Mount Sarrail Campground. Many other trails are designated for mountain-biking use; inquire at the visitor information center, 403/591-6344. **Boulton Creek Trading Post** (403/591-7058) rents mountain bikes during summer ($10 per hour, $40 per day). Upper and Lower Kananaskis Lakes have fair fishing for a variety of trout and whitefish. A nightly interpretive program takes place in campground amphitheaters throughout the park. Look for schedules posted on bulletin boards, or check with the visitor information center.

Camping

Within the park are six auto-accessible campgrounds that hold a total of 507 sites. All are on Kananaskis Lakes Road and are linked by bicycle and hiking trails. **Boulton Creek Campground** ($20–30) has coin-operated showers just beyond the registration gate (complete with rack for those who have a bike), flush toilets, a few of the 118 sites with power, and an interpretive amphitheater, and is within walking distance of a restaurant and grocery store. **Elkwood Campground** ($20) is the largest of the park's campgrounds, with 130 sites. It offers showers ($1 for five minutes) along each of four loops, flush toilets, a playground, and an interpretive amphitheater. **Canyon, Lower**

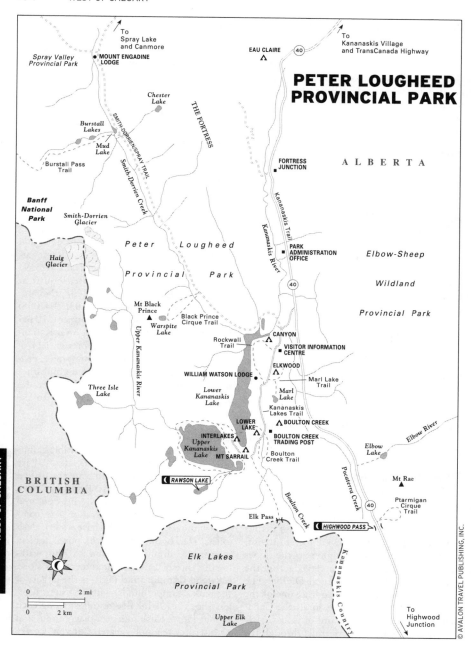

To
Spray Lake
and Canmore

EAU CLAIRE
⋏

To
Kananaskis Village
and TransCanada Highway

Spray Valley
Provincial Park

● MOUNT ENGADINE
LODGE

40

PETER LOUGHEED
PROVINCIAL PARK

Chester
Lake

THE FORTRESS

Burstall
Lakes

SMITH-DORRIEN/SPRAY TRAIL

Mud
Lake

FORTRESS
JUNCTION

A L B E R T A

Burstall Pass
Trail

Smith-Dorrien Creek

**Banff
National
Park**

Smith-Dorrien
Glacier

Kananaskis Trail

Haig
Glacier

P e t e r   L o u g h e e d

Kananaskis River

PARK
ADMINISTRATION
OFFICE

Elbow-Sheep

P r o v i n c i a l   P a r k

40

Wildland

Provincial Park

Mt Black
Prince ▲

Black Prince
Cirque Trail

Warspite
Lake

Upper Kananaskis River

Rockwall
Trail

CANYON
⋏

VISITOR INFORMATION
CENTRE

ELKWOOD
⋏

WILLIAM WATSON LODGE ●

*Lower
Kananaskis
Lake*

Marl Lake
Trail

Marl
Lake

Three Isle
Lake

*Kananaskis
Lakes Trail*

LOWER
LAKE ⋏

⋏ BOULTON CREEK

INTERLAKES ⋏
*Upper
Kananaskis
Lake* ⋏
MT SARRAIL

BOULTON CREEK
TRADING POST

Elbow
Lake

Elbow River

Boulton
Creek Trail

**B R I T I S H
C O L U M B I A**

◖ RAWSON LAKE ◗

Mt Rae ▲

Ptarmigan
Cirque
Trail

Pocaterra Creek

40

Elk Pass

◖ HIGHWOOD PASS ◗

Boulton Creek

0   2 mi

0   2 km

Elk Lakes

Provincial Park

Kananaskis Country

To
Highwood
Junction

*Upper Elk
Lake*

Lakes, and **《 Interlakes Campgrounds** ($20) are more rustic, with only pit toilets, pump water, and picnic tables (Interlakes has some great water-view sites). **Mt. Sarrail Campground** ($18) is described as a "walk-in" campground for tenters, but some sites are right by the main parking lot. All campgrounds in Peter Lougheed Provincial Park are operated by Kananaskis Camping Inc. (403/591-7226, www.kananaskiscamping.com).

Information and Services

At the excellent visitor information center (four km/2.5 mi along Kananaskis Lakes Rd. from Hwy. 40, 403/591-6322, summer daily 9 A.M.– 7 P.M., the rest of the year Mon.–Fri. 9 A.M.– 5 P.M. and weekends 9 A.M.–5 P.M.), exhibits catalog the natural and cultural history of the park through photographs, videos, and hands-on displays. The knowledgeable staff hides hordes of literature under the desk—you have to ask for it. Also ask them to put on a movie or slide show in the theater; most revolve around the park. The movie *Bears and Man* is a classic 1970s flick dealing with public attitude toward bears—one of the first documentaries to do so. A large lounge area that overlooks the valley to the Opal Range is used mainly in winter by cross-country skiers but is always open for trip planning or relaxing.

Located along Kananaskis Lakes Road, 10 kilometers (6.2 mi) south of Highway 40, **Boulton Creek Trading Post** (mid-May–mid-Oct. 9 A.M.–6 P.M., until 10 P.M. in July and August) is the park's only commercial center. It sells groceries, basic camping supplies, fishing tackle and licenses, propane, and firewood. The store also rents bikes. Next door is an unremarkable family-style restaurant serving up pasta, burgers, and the like. A cooked breakfast is $8 (although it's not open until 9 A.M.). It also has an ice-cream window and serves coffee.

PETER LOUGHEED HIKING

The park offers a number of interesting interpretive trails and more strenuous hikes. Most trailheads are located along Kananaskis Lakes Road, a paved road that leads off Highway 40 to Upper and Lower Kananaskis Lakes.

Rockwall Trail, from the visitor information center, and **Marl Lake Trail,** from Elkwood Campground, are wheelchair accessible. The following are some of the park's most popular interpretive and day hikes.

Boulton Creek

- Length: 4.9 kilometers/3 miles (90 minutes) round-trip

- Elevation gain: Minimal

- Rating: Easy

- Trailhead: Boulton Bridge, Kananaskis Lakes Road, 10 kilometers (6.2 mi) from Highway 40

A booklet, available at the trailhead or at the visitor information center, corresponds with numbered posts along this interpretive trail. The highlighted stops emphasize the valley's human history. After a short climb from a riverside parking lot below the Boulton Creek Trading Post, the trail reaches a cabin built in the 1930s as a stopover for forest-ranger patrols. The trail then follows a high ridge and loops back along the other side of the creek to the trailhead.

《 Rawson Lake

- Length: 3.5 kilometers/2.2 miles (1.5 hours) one-way

- Elevation gain: 305 meters/1,000 feet

- Rating: Moderate

- Trailhead: Upper Lake day-use area, Kananaskis Lakes Road, 13 kilometers (eight mi) from Highway 40

This picturesque subalpine lake is one of the most rewarding half-day hiking destinations in Kananaskis Country. Sitting in a high cirque and backed by a towering yet magnificently symmetrical headwall, it's easy to spend an hour or two soaking up your surroundings once you reach the end of the trail. Snow lies along the trail well into July and the lake doesn't open for fishing until July 15, but it is nevertheless a popular destination throughout

© ANDREW HEMPSTEAD

Easily reached from the valley floor, Rawson Lake is one of the park's premier hiking destinations.

summer. Make your way to the farthest parking lot at Upper Lake (through the middle of the main parking lot) and begin the trek by taking the Upper Kananaskis Lake Circuit Trail. Sarrail Creek Falls is passed at the one-kilometer (0.6-mi) mark, 150 meters (0.1 mi) before the Rawson Lake cutoff. Taking the uphill option, you're faced with almost two kilometers (1.2 mi) of switchbacks. The trail then levels out, with boardwalks constructed over boggy sections of trail suddenly emerging at the lake's outlet.

Elbow Lake

- Length: 1.3 kilometers/.8 miles (30 minutes) one-way

- Elevation gain: 135 meters/440 feet

- Rating: Easy

- Trailhead: Elbow Pass day-use area, Highway 40, 13 kilometers (eight mi) south of Kananaskis Lakes Road

The official trail is a wide road that climbs quickly into the bowl holding shallow Elbow Lake. The lake is a popular spot, especially for summer picnics; campsites are spread around the south shore. An interesting side trip is to Rae Glacier, a small glacier on the north face of Mount Rae. The trail starts on the east shore of the lake, gaining 400 meters (1,310 ft) of elevation in just over two kilometers (1.2 mi).

Ptarmigan Cirque

- Length: 5.6 kilometers/3.5 miles (two hours) round-trip

- Elevation gain: 230 meters/750 feet

- Rating: Moderate

- Trailhead: Highwood Pass, Highway 40, 17 kilometers (10.5 mi) south of Kananaskis Lakes Road

The trailhead for this steep interpretive walk is across the road from the parking lot at Highwood Pass. A booklet, available at the trailhead or at the visitor information center, corresponds with numbered posts along the trail. As you climb into the alpine zone, magnificent panoramas unfold. Along the trail you are likely to see numerous small mammals. Columbian ground squirrels, pikas, least chipmunks, and hoary marmots are all common. At higher elevations the meadows are home to bighorn sheep, mountain goats, and grizzly bears.

SPRAY VALLEY PROVINCIAL PARK

The creation of 35,800-hectare (88,460-acre) Spray Valley Provincial Park in 2001 provided the final link in continuous protection between bordering Peter Lougheed Provincial Park in the south and Willmore Wilderness Park beyond the northern reaches of Jasper National Park in the north. The park's dominant feature is **Spray Lake Reservoir,** a 16-kilometer-long (10-mi-long) body of water that provides a variety of recreational opportunities.

The **Smith-Dorrien/Spray Trail** is the only road through the park. This 60-kilometer (37-mi) unpaved (and often dusty) road links Peter

© ANDREW HEMPSTEAD

Rarely is the vast body of Spray Lake totally calm, but on a windless morning the scene is postcard perfect.

Lougheed Provincial Park in the south to Canmore in the north. From the south, the road climbs up the Smith-Dorrien Creek watershed, passing Mud Lake and entering Spray Valley Provincial Park just south of Mount Engadine Lodge. Around three kilometers (1.9 mi) farther north is **Buller Pond** (on the west side of the road), from where the distinctive "Matterhorn" peak of Mount Assiniboine can be seen on a clear day. The road then parallels the eastern shoreline of Spray Lake for over 20 kilometers (12.5 mi), passing three lakefront picnic areas. Beyond the north end of Spray Lake, the road passes **Goat Pond** and the Goat Creek trailhead, then descends steeply into the Bow Valley and Canmore.

Accommodations and Camping

☾ Mount Engadine Lodge (403/678-4080, www.mountengadine.com, mid-June–mid-Oct. and early Feb.–mid-Apr.) offers a particularly lovely setting on a ridge overlooking an open meadow and small creek at the turnoff

to the Mount Shark staging area. The main lodge has a dining room, a comfortable lounge area, and a beautiful sundeck holding a hot tub. Breakfast is served buffet-style, lunch can be taken at the lodge or packed for a picnic, and dinner is served in multiple courses of European specialties. Rates for lodge rooms range from $135 per person for a room with a shared bathroom to $169 per person in room with an en suite. Cabins are $169 per person. All meals are included in these nightly rates.

The park's only campground is **Spray Lake West** (June–Sept., $18), a rustic facility spread out along the western shoreline of Spray Lake. Many of the 50-odd sites are very private, but facilities are limited to picnic tables, fire pits, and pit toilets.

SIBBALD, ELBOW RIVER VALLEY, AND SHEEP RIVER VALLEY REGIONS

The northeastern section of Kananaskis Country spans the Sibbald, Jumpingpound, Elbow

WEST OF CALGARY

COUGARS

Elusive and rarely encountered by casual hikers, cougars (also known as mountain lions, pumas, and catamounts) measure up to 1.5 meters (five ft) long, with the average male weighing 75 kilograms (165 lbs) and the female 40–55 kilograms (88–121 lbs). Their athletic prowess puts Olympians to shame. They can spring forward over eight meters from a standstill, leap four meters into the air, and safely jump from a height of 20 meters (66 ft).

Cougars are versatile hunters whose acute vision takes in a peripheral span in excess of 200 degrees. They typically kill a large mammal such as an elk or deer every 12–14 days, eating part of it and caching the rest. Their diet also includes chipmunks, ground squirrels, snowshoe hares, and occasionally porcupines.

The cougar is a solitary animal with distinct territorial boundaries. This limits its population density, which means that its overall numbers are low. On the other hand, its traditional western range is expanding east across North America. It is estimated that Alberta is home to around 1,000 cougars, mostly in the mountains or foothills, with one occasionally sighted within Calgary city limits.

Cases of cougars stalking humans have increased over the last decade, but actual attacks are rare (one fatality has been recorded in Alberta since 1970). Cougar-human encounters usually occur when the cougar has been surprised or if it's particularly hungry. When hiking or cross-country skiing in cougar country, look behind and above frequently and keep dogs on a leash. If approached by a cougar, never turn your back or start running; instead, maintain eye contact and back away slowly. Do not play dead – fight back if it comes to that.

© ANDREW HEMPSTEAD

River, and Sheep River Valleys. The valleys start in the west among the high peaks of the Opal Range. As they cut east through the foothills, they gradually open up, ending at the prairie. At higher elevations, elk, bighorn sheep, and bears make their home. In the foothills, visitors are likely to see mule and white-tailed deer, elk, and moose. This area of Kananaskis Country also has a relatively high population of cougars, but these shy cats are rarely sighted.

At the entrance to the Elbow River and Sheep River Valleys are information centers that are open in summer only (use **Barrier Lake Visitor Information Centre,** described earlier in the *Kananaskis Valley* section, for Sibbald). The only other facilities are campgrounds, which are generally primitive and open mid-May to September.

Sibbald

The Sibbald Creek Trail (Hwy. 68) traverses the rolling foothills of the Sibbald and Jumpingpound Valleys and is accessible from the TransCanada Highway, intersecting Highway 40 south of the Barrier Lake Visitor Information Centre. Fishing is popular in **Sibbald Lake** and **Sibbald Meadows Pond.** A couple of short trails begin at the picnic area at Sibbald Lake, including the 4.4-kilometer (2.7-mi) **Ole Buck Loop,** which climbs a low ridge.

Sibbald Lake Campground offers 134 sites spread around five loops (Loop D comes closest to the lake). Amenities include pit toilets, drinking water, and a nightly interpretive program; $20 per site. For camping information contact Elbow Valley Campgrounds (403/949-3132, www.evcamp.com).

Elbow River Valley

The main access road into the Elbow River Valley is Highway 66 west from Bragg Creek. It climbs steadily along the Elbow River, passing **McLean Pond** and **Allen Bill Pond** (both are stocked with rainbow trout) and six-meter-high (20-ft-high) **Elbow Falls,** before climbing through an area devastated by wildfire in 1981, then descending to a campground 42 kilometers (26 mi) from Bragg Creek.

Five campgrounds with a combined total of 551 sites lie along the Elbow River Valley. The most developed of the five is **McLean Creek Campground,** 12 kilometers (7.5 mi) west of Bragg Creek. At the campground entrance is the Camper Centre with groceries, coin showers, and firewood ($6 per bundle). Unserviced sites are $23 per night, powered sites $30. For reservations contact Elbow Valley Campgrounds (403/949-3132, www.evcamp.com). The other campgrounds and their distances from Bragg Creek are **Gooseberry** (10 km/6.2 mi), **Paddy's Flat** (20 km/12.4 mi), **Beaver Flat** (30 km/18.6 mi), and, at the very end of the road, **Little Elbow** (50 km/31 mi). Each of these campgrounds has only basic facilities—pit toilets and hand-pumped drinking water—but, still, sites are $20 per night.

Sheep River Valley

The Sheep River Valley lies immediately south of the Elbow River Valley, in an area of rolling foothills between open ranchlands to the east and the high peaks bordering **Elbow-Sheep Wildland Provincial Park** to the west. Access is from the town of Turner Valley (take Sunset Blvd. west from downtown), along Highway 546. The highway passes through **Sheep River Provincial Park** (which protects the wintering ground of bighorn sheep) and **Sheep River Falls,** and ends at a campground 46 kilometers (29 mi) west of Turner Valley.

Along Highway 546, west from Turner Valley, are two campgrounds. **Sandy McNabb Campground,** the larger of the two, is a pleasant walk from the river right by the entrance to Kananaskis Country. All sites are $20 per night. Both facilities are operated by High Country Camping (403/558-2373 or 866/366-2267, www.campingalberta.com). All sites are filled on a first-come, first-served basis.

Highwood/Cataract Creek

The Highwood/Cataract Creek areas stretch from Peter Lougheed Provincial Park to the southern border of Kananaskis Country. This is the least developed area in Kananaskis Country. The jagged peaks of the Highwood

Mountains, mostly protected by remote **Don Getty Wildland Provincial Park,** are the dominant feature; high alpine meadows among the peaks are home to bighorn sheep, elk, and grizzlies. Lower down, spruce and lodgepole pine forests spread over most of the valley, giving way to grazing lands along the eastern flanks. The main access from the north is along Highway 40, which drops 600 vertical meters (1,970 ft) in the 35 kilometers (22 mi) between **Highwood Pass** and **Highwood Junction.** From the east, Highway 541 west from Longview joins Highway 40 at Highwood Junction. The main summer activities in this area of Kananaskis Country are hiking, horseback riding, climbing, and fishing. Winter use is primarily by snowmobilers.

All three campgrounds in the Highwood/Cataract Creek areas are south of Highwood Junction. Open May–November, **Etherington Creek** is seven kilometers (4.3 mi) south of the junction; **Cataract Creek** is a further five kilometers (3.1 mi) south and is open mid-May to early September. Both offer primitive facilities including water, pit toilets, firewood, fire pits, and picnic tables; $18 per night. Continuing south, along Highway 532 up and over Plateau Mountain Ecological Reserve, is 16-site **Indian Graves Campground.** It's open mid-May to mid-September and costs $16 per night. Reservations are taken for camping at Etherington Creek only; contact High Country Camping (403/558-2373 or 866/366-2267, www.campingalberta.com).

Canmore

The town of Canmore lies in the Bow Valley, 103 kilometers (64 miles) west of Calgary, 28 kilometers (17 miles) southeast of Banff, and on the northern edge of Kananaskis Country. Long perceived as a gateway to the mountain national parks, the town is very much a destination in itself these days, with world-class golfing, a profusion of mountain trails, and the home of the Alpine Club of Canada. Its location close to Calgary and the freedom it enjoys from the strict development restrictions that apply in the nearby parks have made Canmore the fastest-growing town in Canada, with the population having tripled in the last 20 years. The permanent population is 11,500, with the most recent Census showing 4,000 non-permanent residents (that is, folks who own a home in town but whose permanent address is elsewhere).

History

The Canadian Pacific Railway chose the Bow Valley as the route through the mountains, with the first divisional point west of Calgary at what is now Canmore. Mining on the Three Sisters and Mount Rundle commenced soon after. Hotels and businesses were established, and a hospital, a North West Mounted Police (NWMP) post, and an opera house were built. The last mine closed in 1979.

Canmore is now in the middle of its second boom, which combines tourism and residential development. In 1979, the population stood at 3,500; in the last 20 years that number has more than tripled, with estimates pegging the population to top out at 20,000 in less than 20 years. Resort and residential projects costing over $2 billion are underway throughout the town. The largest of these is **Three Sisters Mountain Village.** When completed, the 840-hectare (2,080-acre) project will include 3,600 residential units, 500 hotel rooms, and three golf courses along an 11-kilometer (6.8-mi) stretch of the Bow River between Pigeon Mountain and Chinaman's Peak.

Canmore is a popular spot for moviemakers; big-budget movies filmed in and around town have included *Grizzly Falls, Mystery Alaska, The Edge, The Last of the Dogmen, Legends of the Fall, Snow Dogs,* and the 2007 Brad Pitt film *The Assassination of Jesse James by the Coward Robert Ford.*

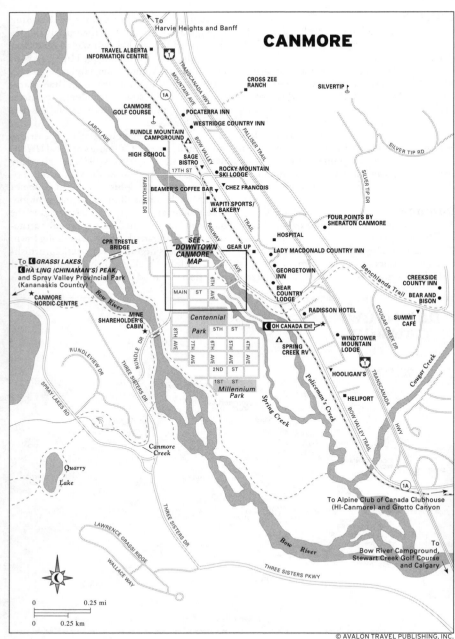

To
Harvie Heights and Banff

CANMORE

TRAVEL ALBERTA
INFORMATION CENTRE

TRANSCANADA HWY

MOUNTAIN AVE

1A

CROSS ZEE
RANCH

SILVERTIP

CANMORE
GOLF COURSE

POCATERRA INN

WESTRIDGE COUNTRY INN

LARCH AVE

BOW VALLEY

PALLISER TRAIL

SILVER TIP RD

RUNDLE MOUNTAIN
CAMPGROUND

HIGH SCHOOL

SAGE
BISTRO

17TH ST

ROCKY MOUNTAIN
SKI LODGE

SILVER TIP DR

FAIRHOLME DR

BEAMER'S COFFEE BAR

CHEZ FRANCOIS

WAPITI SPORTS/
JK BAKERY

TRAIL

FOUR POINTS BY
SHERATON CANMORE

RAILWAY

CPR TRESTLE
BRIDGE

HOSPITAL

*SEE
"DOWNTOWN
CANMORE"
MAP*

GEAR UP

LADY MACDONALD COUNTRY INN

To **GRASSI LAKES,
HA LING (CHINAMAN'S) PEAK,**
and Spray Valley Provincial Park
(Kananaskis Country)

Bow River

AVE

MAIN ST

6TH AVE

GEORGETOWN
INN

Benchlands Trail

CREEKSIDE
COUNTY INN

BEAR AND
BISON

CANMORE
NORDIC CENTRE

MINE
SHAREHOLDER'S
CABIN

BEAR
COUNTRY
LODGE

COUGAR CREEK DR

SUMMIT
CAFÉ

RADISSON HOTEL

*Centennial
Park*

5TH ST

OH CANADA EH!

WINDTOWER
MOUNTAIN
LODGE

Cougar Creek

RUNDLEVIEW DR

RUNDLE DR

8TH AVE

7TH
AVE

6TH
AVE

5TH
AVE

4TH
AVE

SPRING
CREEK RV

Policeman's Creek

TRANSCANADA HWY

THREE SISTERS DR

2ND ST

HOOLIGAN'S

SPRAY LAKES RD

1ST ST

*Millennium
Park*

Spring Creek

BOW VALLEY TRAIL

HELIPORT

Canmore
Creek

Quarry
Lake

To Alpine Club of Canada Clubhouse
(HI-Canmore) and Grotto Canyon

1A

LAWRENCE GRASSI RIDGE

THREE SISTERS DR

Bow River

To
Bow River Campground,
Stewart Creek Golf Course
and Calgary

WALLACE WAY

THREE SISTERS PKWY

0   0.25 mi

0   0.25 km

WEST OF CALGARY

SIGHTS

Canmore is spread across both sides of the TransCanada Highway, with downtown Canmore occupying an island in the middle of the Bow River. Although development sprawls in all directions, large tracts of forest remain intact, including along the river, where you'll find paths leading beyond built-up areas and into natural areas. The most expansive of these is 32,600-hectare (80,550-acre) **Bow Valley Wildland Provincial Park,** which has been designated in pockets along the valley floor as well as most of the surrounding mountain slopes along both sides of the valley.

Downtown

Through booming times, the original core of Canmore, on the southwestern side of the TransCanada Highway, has managed to retain much of its original charm. Many historical buildings line the downtown streets,

while other buildings from the coal-mining days are being preserved at their original locations around town. The best way to get downtown from the TransCanada Highway is to take Railway Avenue from Highway 1A and drive down 8th Street, the main drag (parking is easiest one street back along 7th Street, where one parking lot—at 6th Avenue—is designated for RVs).

The first building of interest at the east end of the main street is Canmore's original **NWMP post** (609 8th St., 403/678-1955, summer daily 9 A.M.–6 P.M., the rest of the year Mon.–Fri. noon–4 P.M., free), built in 1892. It is one of the few such posts still in its original position, even though at the time of its construction the building was designed as a temporary structure to serve the newly born coal-mining town. The interior is decorated with period furnishings, while out back is a thriving garden filled with the same food crops planted by the post's

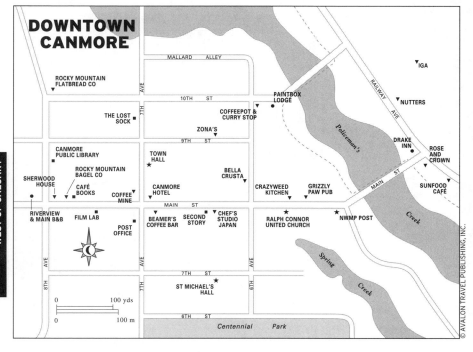

DOWNTOWN CANMORE

The 1871 North West Mounted Police post is Canmore's oldest building.

original inhabitants. Canmore Hotel, on the corner of 8th Street and 7th Avenue, was built in 1891 (at a time when three hotels already operated) and is still open for thirsty townsfolk and travelers alike.

Around the corner from the hotel, inside the impressive Civic Centre complex, is **Canmore Museum and Geoscience Centre** (907 7th Ave., 403/678-2462, Mon.–Fri. 9 A.M.–5 P.M., adult $3, senior and child $2). This facility highlights the region's rich geological history and its importance to the growth of the town and related industries. Geological formations along three local hikes are described, which, along with a small fossil display, microscopes, and computer resources, make this facility an interesting rainy-day diversion.

West of Downtown

Several scenic and historic sights lie across the Bow River from downtown, including the remains of various mining operations. To get there, walk south along 8th Avenue for 500 me-

ters (0.3 mile) to the Bow River. With a pedestrian-only bridge and paved paths on both sides of the river leading in either direction, this is a good point to stop and get oriented. A pleasant loop can be made by walking north and crossing the river at the old **CPR trestle bridge,** which once served local mines. Follow the trail back downstream, past the **Mine Shareholders' Cabin,** a log structure built in 1914.

In the same vicinity, a trail leads off from Three Sisters Drive up Canmore Creek, passing the remains of a mine site that was first worked in 1891. Beyond the visible coal seam and crumbling concrete foundations is a picturesque waterfall tucked below residential development. Backtrack 300 meters (0.2 mile) from the end of the trail and climb the wooden steps, crossing Spray Lakes Road to **Quarry Lake.** This small lake lies in an open meadow and is a popular sunbathing and swimming spot.

HIKING

The hiking trails around Canmore are usually passed by in favor of those of its famous neighbors, but some interesting trails do exist. Paved paths around town are suitable for walking, bicycling, and, in winter, skiing. They link Policeman's Creek with the golf course, Nordic center, and Riverview Park on the Bow River.

◖ Grassi Lakes

- Length: 2 kilometers/1.2 miles (40 minutes) one-way

- Elevation gain: 300 meters/980 feet

- Rating: Easy/moderate

- Trailhead: Spray Village, beyond the Nordic center, six kilometers (3.7 mi) west of downtown off Spray Lakes Road

This historical trail climbs to two small lakes below Chinaman's Peak. From the parking lot just off Spray Lakes Road, take the left fork 150 meters (0.1 mile) along the trail. It climbs steadily to stairs cut into a cliff face before leading up to a bridge over Canmore Creek and to the lakes. Interpretive signs along the trail point out interesting aspects of the Bow

hoodoo on the north side of Canmore

Valley and detail the life of Lawrence Grassi, who built the trail in the early 1920s. With Chinaman's Peak as a backdrop, these gin-clear, spring-fed lakes are a particularly rewarding destination. Behind the upper lake, an easy scramble up a scree slope leads to four pictographs (native rock paintings) of human figures. They are on the first large boulder in the gorge. An alternate return route is down a rough access road between the hiking trail and Spray Lakes Road, passing a broken-down log cabin along the way.

Ha Ling (Chinaman's) Peak

- Length: 2.2 kilometers/1.4 miles (90 minutes) one-way

- Elevation gain: 740 meters/2,430 feet

- Rating: Moderate/difficult

- Trailhead: Goat Creek parking lot, Spray Lakes Road, nine kilometers (5.6 mi) west of Canmore

Ha Ling Peak is the impressive pinnacle of rock that rises high above Canmore to the southwest. While the sheer eastern face is visible from town, this trail winds up the backside of the mountain and ends with stunning views across the Bow Valley. Leaving your vehicle at the Goat Creek Trailhead, cross the road, then walk up to and over the canal to search out the trail, which begins from behind a small workshed. The trail climbs steadily through subalpine forest of Engelmann spruce before breaking out above the tree line, where views north extend down the glacially carved Goat Creek Valley. The trail then forks; the left fork climbs unforgivingly to Chinaman's Peak, but hikers are rewarded with views no less spectacular by continuing to the right along a lightly marked trail that ends at a saddle. On a clear day, the panorama afforded from this viewpoint is worth every painful step. Take care on the return journey; stay high and to the right and watch for rock cairns and colored flagging to ensure you enter the trees at the right spot.

Cougar Creek

- Length: 9.5 kilometers/6 miles (four hours) one-way

- Elevation gain: 550 meters/1,800 feet

- Rating: Moderate

- Trailhead: Corner of Benchlands Trail and Elk Run Boulevard, east side of TransCanada Highway

This unofficial trail follows a valley carved deeply into the Fairholme Range by Cougar Creek. The length and elevation gain listed are to a high ridge on the boundary of Banff National Park. Few hikers reach this point, with most content to turn around within an hour's travel. The first section of trail runs alongside a manmade channel that acts as a conduit for runoff in years of high snowfall. It's dry most of summer, but extra care should be taken in spring. Cross just before the mouth of the canyon. From this point the rough trail crosses the creek bed 10 times in the first three kilometers (1.9 km) to a major fork. Stay within the left valley, continuing up and around the base of

Mount Charles Stewart. From this point, the valley walls close in and it's a steep climb up to the boundary of Banff National Park. On the return journey, continue beyond the parking lot to the Summit Café, where you can relax on the patio with a cool drink.

Mount Lady Macdonald

- Length: 3.5 kilometers/2.1 miles (90 minutes) one-way

- Elevation gain: 850 meters/2,790 feet

- Rating: Moderate/difficult

- Trailhead: Corner of Benchlands Trail and Elk Run Boulevard, east side of TransCanada Highway

Named for the wife of Canada's first prime minister, this peak lies immediately north of Canmore. Follow Cougar Creek to where the canyon begins, and look for a faint trail winding up a grassy bank to the left. Once on the trail, take the steepest option at every fork, then a sharp right 300 meters (0.2 mile) after the trail bursts out into a cleared area. This section is steep, climbing through a rock band to the mountain's southern ridge, which you'll follow the rest of the way. The distance and elevation listed are to an unused helipad below the main summit. It's a steep, unrelenting slog, but views across the Bow Valley are stunning. From this point, the true summit is another 275 vertical meters (900 vertical feet) away, along an extremely narrow ridge that drops away precipitously to the east.

Grotto Canyon

- Length: 2 kilometers/1.2 miles (40 minutes) one-way

- Elevation gain: 60 meters/200 feet

- Rating: Easy

- Trailhead: Grotto Pond, Highway 1A, 12 kilometers (7.5 mi) east of Canmore

This is one of the most interesting trails around Canmore. From Grotto Pond, this trail first follows a powerline road behind the Baymag plant.

Then at a signed intersection it takes off through the woods to the mouth of the canyon. No official trail traverses the canyon; hikers simply follow the creek bed through the towering canyon walls. Around 300 meters (0.2 mile) into the canyon, look for pictographs to the left. At the two-kilometer (1.2-mile) mark, the canyon makes a sharp left turn at Illusion Rock, where water cascades through a narrow chasm and into the main canyon. Many hikers return from this point, but through the next section of canyon, the valley opens up, passing hoodoos and a cave. It's 6.5 kilometers (four miles) from the trailhead to the end of the valley, with most of the 680 meters (2,230 feet) of elevation gained in the last two kilometers (1.2 miles).

Heli-Hiking

Heli-hiking is the summer alternative to heli-skiing—a helicopter does the hard work, and you get to hike in a remote, alpine region that would usually entail a long, steep hike to access. **Alpine Helicopters** (403/678-4802) offers options starting at $300 per person, which includes 10 minutes of flight time and 3–4 hours of hiking. The company is flexible, with ground time and destinations chosen by the clients. Flightseeing (no landing) costs $180 for 25 minutes of airtime. The heliport is along Highway 1A south of downtown. Try to book ahead for these trips; they're very popular with travelers staying in Banff, where there is no flightseeing.

OTHER RECREATION
Canmore Nordic Centre

This sprawling complex on the outskirts of Canmore was built for the 1988 Winter Olympic Games. The cross-country skiing and biathlon (combined cross-country skiing and rifle shooting) events were held here, and today the center remains a world-class training ground for Canadian athletes in a variety of disciplines. The operation was privatized in 1997 and pronounced a provincial park in 2000. Even in summer, long after the snow has melted, the place is worth a visit. An interpretive trail leads down to and along the west bank

of the Bow River to the barely visible remains of Georgetown, a once-bustling coal-mining town. Many other trails lead around the grounds, and it's possible to hike or bike along the Bow River all the way to Banff. **Mountain biking** is extremely popular on 70 kilometers (43.5 miles) of trails. Bike rentals are available at **Trail Sports** (below the day lodge, 403/678-6764, daily 9 A.M.–6 P.M.); rates are $8 per hour and $30 per day for a front-suspension bike, $15 and $45, respectively, for a full suspension bike. Snowmaking guarantees a ski season running from December through late March, with rentals and instruction available through Trail Sports. The day lodge (403/678-2400, daily 8 A.M.–4:30 P.M.) is open year-round and has lockers, a lounge area, a café (daily 10 A.M.–4 P.M.), and an information desk.

Fishing

The **Bow River** has good fishing for brown and brook trout, including right downtown between the old railway bridge and Rundle Drive. Follow Highway 1A east from town to access the best river fishing, as well as **Gap Lake** and **Grotto Pond;** the latter is stocked with rainbow trout. The Bow River is renowned for its rainbow trout fishing. This occurs downstream of Canmore toward Calgary and beyond **Ghost Lake,** which holds healthy populations of lake, rainbow, and brown trout.

For all your fishing needs, head to **Wapiti Sports** (1506 Railway Ave., 403/678-5550), which stocks bait and tackle and sells licenses.

Golf

As with golfing elsewhere in the Canadian Rockies, book all tee times well in advance, but also try to be flexible, because two of Canmore's three courses offer weekday and twilight discounts.

Silvertip (403/678-1600 or 877/877-5444, www.silvertipresort.com) spreads across a series of wide benches between the valley floor and the lower slopes of Mount Lady Macdonald. The layout is challenging, with the most distinct feature being an elevation change of 200 meters (660 feet) between the lowest and high-

est points on the course. Adding to this challenge are narrow, sloping, tree-lined fairways, numerous water hazards, 74 bunkers, and a course length of a frightening 7,300 yards from the back markers. High-season greens fees are $150 Sunday through Wednesday and $160 Thursday to Saturday, which includes a mandatory cart (each cart has GPS to help golfers judge distances) and use of the driving range.

Stewart Creek Golf Club (403/609-6099 or 877/993-4653, www.stewartcreekgolf.com), another newer layout, lies across the valley in the Three Sisters Mountain Village development. It is shorter than Silvertip but still measures more than 7,000 yards from the back tees. The fairways are relatively wide, but positioning of tee shots is important, and the course is made more interesting by hanging greens, greenside exposed rock, and historic mine shafts. Greens fees are $155–175, with twilight rates of $100. These rates include use of a power cart and practice facility.

Canmore Golf & Curling Club (403/678-4785), built in the 1920s as a nine-hole course at the north end of 8th Avenue, has developed into an 18-hole course with a modern clubhouse and a practice facility that includes a driving range. It is an interesting layout, with scenic panoramas and water on some holes. Greens fees are $101 inclusive of a power cart and lunch voucher.

Horseback Riding

Nestled on a wide bench on the northeastern side of town, **Cross Zee Ranch** (403/678-4171) has been guiding visitors through the valley since the 1950s. From expansive stables, rides pass through thickly wooded areas, along colorful meadows, and to high lookouts. Options include Ranger Ridge and Bone Gully (one hour, $32 per person), Sunny Bench (90 minutes, $46), and the Great Aspens ride (two hours, $54).

Climbing

Hundreds of climbing routes have been laid out around Canmore. **Mount Yamnuska,** which rises 900 meters (2,950 feet) above the

ALPINE CLUB OF CANADA

The Alpine Club of Canada (ACC), like similar clubs in the United States and Great Britain, is a nonprofit mountaineering organization whose objectives include the encouragement of mountaineering through educational programs, the exploration and study of alpine and glacial regions, and the preservation of mountain flora and fauna.

The club was formed in 1906, mainly through the tireless campaign of its first president, Arthur Wheeler. A list of early members reads like a Who's Who of the Canadian Rockies – Bill Peyto, Tom Wilson, Byron Harmon, Mary Schäffer – names familiar to all Canadian mountaineers. Today the club membership includes 3,000 alpinists from throughout Canada.

The club's ongoing projects include operating the Canadian Alpine Centre (Lake Louise Hostel), maintaining a system of 20 huts throughout the backcountry of the Canadian Rockies, and publishing the annual *Canadian Alpine Journal* – the country's only record of mountaineering accomplishments. A reference library of the club's history is kept at the Whyte Museum of the Canadian Rockies in Banff.

For further information and membership details, visit association headquarters (along Hwy. 1A on the eastern edge of Canmore, 403/678-3200, www.alpineclubofcanada.ca).

---

valley floor east of town along Highway 1A, is the most developed site. Climbers also flock to **Ha Ling (Chinaman's) Peak, Cougar Creek,** the area behind **Grassi Lakes,** and **Grotto Canyon.** Canmore is home to many qualified mountain guides.

Yamnuska (403/678-4164 or 866/678-4164, www.yamnuska.com) offers basic rock-climbing courses and instruction for all ability levels on ice climbing, mountaineering, and trekking. A good introduction to rock climbing is the weekend-long Outdoor Rock Intro course, which costs $250. Unique to the company are three-month-long courses that take in all aspects of mountain-oriented skills.

ENTERTAINMENT AND EVENTS
◖ *Oh Canada Eh!*
Popularized across the country at Niagara Falls, this musical dinner show (125 Kananaskis Way, off Bow Valley Trail, 403/609-0004 or 800/773-0004) provides a rip-roaring evening of fun and food in a modern building decorated as a cavernous log cabin. It's unashamedly cheesy, but the parade of costumed Canadian characters—such as lumberjacks, natives, Mounties, and even Anne of Green Gables—will keep you laughing as they sing and dance across the floor. The food is surprisingly good, with Canadian favorites such as Alberta beef, salmon, and maple chocolate cake served buffet-style. Performances are nightly through summer at 6:30 P.M., and the all-inclusive cost is adult $60, child 6–16 $29.

Nightlife
The **Sherwood House** (838 8th St., 403/678-5211) has a beer garden that catches the afternoon sun and is especially busy on weekends. At the other end of the main street is the **Drake Inn** (909 Railway Ave., 403/678-5131), with a small outdoor patio and a nonsmoking section with comfortable lounges. Across the road, at the **Rose and Crown** (749 Railway Ave., 403/678-5168), you'll find a beer garden. All these bars have midweek drink specials, and the latter two have a couple of pool tables. The Drake Inn has a band playing Wednesday–Saturday nights, as does the Rose and Crown, and the Sherwood House has an occasional Sunday-afternoon jam session.

The **Grizzly Paw Brewing Company** (622 8th St., 403/678-9983) brews its own beer, with six ales produced in-house (look for special winter brews around Christmas). Most are heavy, English-style beers, but the lighter Grumpy Bear Honey Wheat Ale suits most tastes.

Canmore's only nightclub is **Hooligan's** (Bow Valley Trail, 403/609-2662), and there's live music somewhere in town every weekend.

Festivals and Events

Canmore's small-town pride lives on through a busy schedule of festivals and events, which are nearly always accompanied by parades of flag-waving kids, free downtown pancake breakfasts, and an evening shindig somewhere in town.

On the middle weekend of May, it's all about the kids at the **Canmore Children's Festival** (403/678-1875, www.canmorechildrensfestival.com), where the fun and frivolity centers on the local high school grounds off 17th Street. Expect lots of music, live theater, story-telling, and educational presentations. **ArtsPeak** (www.artspeakcanmore.com) is a mid-June celebration hosted at venues throughout town. As the name suggests expect lots of art-oriented festivities, including workshops, displays, and walking tours.

Canada Day is celebrated with a pancake breakfast, parade, various activities in Centennial Park, and 10:30 P.M. fireworks. On the first weekend of August, Canmore hosts a **Folk Music Festival** (www.canmorefolk festival.com), which starts on Saturday and runs through Monday evening. This event, which attracts more than 14,000 fans, features national and international acts performing in Centennial Park, and musical workshops. Canmore Nordic Centre hosts a variety of mountain-biking events each summer, highlighted by a late August stop on the **24 Hours of Adrenalin** tour (www.24hoursofadrenalin.com) in which 1,500 racers complete as many laps as they can in a 24-hour period, either in teams or as solo riders.

The first Sunday of September is the **Canmore Highland Games** (www.canmore highlandgames.ca), a day of dancing, eating, and caber tossing, culminating in a spectacular and noisy parade of pipe bands throughout the grounds of Centennial Park that attracts more than 10,000 spectators. The grand finale is the *ceilidh,* a traditional Scottish celebration involving loud beer-drinking, foot-stomping music, which takes place under a massive tent

set up in the park for the occasion. Fall's other major gathering is for the **Festival of the Eagles** (www.eaglewatch.ca), on the middle weekend of October and coinciding with the southbound migration of golden eagles. Viewing scopes are set up at the high school grounds off 17th Street; scheduled events include talks, slide shows, and field trips.

ACCOMMODATIONS AND CAMPING

Canmore's population boom has been mirrored by the construction of new hotels and motels. Most of the newer lodgings are on Bow Valley Trail (Highway 1A). As with all resort towns in the Canadian Rockies, reservations should be made as far in advance as possible in summer.

Under $50

HI-Canmore (403/678-3200, www.hihostels .ca) is an excellent hostel-style accommodation at the base of Grotto Mountain. Affiliated with Hostelling International, the lodge is part of headquarters for the Alpine Club of Canada, the country's national mountaineering organization. In addition to sleeping up to 46 people in seven rooms, it has a kitchen, an excellent library, a laundry room, a bar, a sauna, and a lounge area with a fireplace. Rates are $20 per night for members of Hostelling International or the Alpine Club, while everyone else pays $27. Private rooms are $60 s or d for members, $81 for nonmembers. To get there from downtown, follow Bow Valley Trail southeast; it's signposted to the left, 500 meters (0.3 mile) after passing under the TransCanada Highway.

$50-100

For travelers who have budgeted around $100 for a room, it's hard to go past **Riverview and Main** (918 8th St., 403/678-9777, www.river viewandmain.com, $85–120 s or d), centrally located half a block beyond the end of the downtown core. The rooms are decently sized and brightly decorated, and each has access to a deck. The guest lounge centers on a river-stone

BED-AND-BREAKFASTS

Over 40 bed-and-breakfasts operate in Canmore. They are all small, family-run affairs with only one or two rooms (a local town bylaw limits the number of guest rooms in private homes). During summer, they fill every night. Check the website of the **Canmore Bow Valley Bed and Breakfast Association** (www.bbcanmore.com) for a full list of bed-and-breakfasts.

wood-burning fireplace. Rates include a selection of hot and cold breakfast items.

$100-150

Named for one of the valley's original coal-mining communities, the **⒞ Georgetown Inn** (1101 Bow Valley Trail, 403/678-3439 or 800/657-5955, www.georgetowninn.ab.ca) is set up as a country inn of times gone by, complete with a cozy dining room open daily for breakfast and dinner (closed Mon.–Tues. in winter). Each of the 20 guest rooms has its own individual charm, with a modern twist on decor that features lots of English antiques. The best values are the Victoria Rooms, each with a separate sitting area and electric fireplace ($159). Complimentary nonalcoholic drinks and a delicious cooked breakfast are included in midweek rates ranging $119–169 s or d and weekend rates of $139–199 s or d.

Windtower Mountain Lodge (160 Kananaskis Way, 403/609-6600 or 866/609-6600, www.windtower.ca) provides hotel and suite accommodations within a much larger condominium development. Facilities include a picnic and barbecue area, a fitness center, an outdoor hot tub, a café, and underground parking. Hotel-style rooms range $129–169, depending on size, while suites feature separate bedrooms as well as a full kitchen, private balcony, laundry room, and large well-equipped living area for $199–299 s or d. Either way—and not taking into account perpetually dis-

counted rooms advertised on the website—this is an excellent value, especially for families or small groups.

At the edge of Canmore's downtown core is the **Drake Inn** (909 Railway Ave., 403/678-5131 or 800/461-8730, www.drakeinn.com). It offers bright and cheerfully decorated motel rooms for $119 s, $129 d. Well worth an extra $10 are the Creekside Rooms, featuring private balconies overlooking Policeman's Creek. The adjoining bar opens daily at 7 A.M. for the best-value breakfast in town at only $5.

Not only can you rent one- and two-bedroom units with full kitchens at **Rocky Mountain Ski Lodge** (1711 Bow Valley Trail, 403/678-5445 or 800/665-6111, www.rockymtnskilodge.com), there's plenty of outdoor space for kids to run around, including a playground. Also on the property are a barbecue and picnic area, and a laundry. The self-contained suites, some with loft bedrooms, start at $150. Standard rooms, some with kitchens, are $120–130.

The 30-room **Bear Country Lodge** (1002 Bow Valley Trail, 403/678-1000 or 888/678-1008, www.bearcountrylodge.com) features eye-catching timber and river-stone styling outside and throughout an impressive lobby, but stops short of continuing to the standard motel rooms, which are unremarkable ($129 s or d, $149 with a kitchenette). Honey Bear Suites, however, reflect the decor of the public areas, with pine log furnishings, gas fireplaces, and hot tubs ($189 s or d). Rates include a continental breakfast buffet in a pleasant downstairs dining room. The Bear Country kicks off the trend of more expensive hotels that heavily discount rooms outside of summer, with rates from just $79.

$150-200

Lady Macdonald Country Inn (1201 Bow Valley Trail, 403/678-3665 or 800/567-3919, www.ladymacdonald.com, $150–240 s or d) exudes a welcoming atmosphere and personalized service not experienced in the larger properties. Its 12 rooms are all individually furnished, with the smallest, the Palliser Room, featuring

elegant surroundings and a magnificent wrought-iron bed. The largest of the rooms is the Three Sisters, which has welcoming pastel-colored decor, a king-size bed, two-way gas fireplace, hot tub, and uninterrupted views of its namesake. Rates include a hearty hot breakfast in a country-style breakfast room.

(Creekside Country Inn (709 Benchlands Trail, 403/609-5522 or 866/609-5522, www.creeksidecountryinn.com) is a modern mountain-style lodge featuring lots of exposed timber. The 12 rooms are elegant in their simplicity; eight have lofts. Facilities include a lounge with roaring log fire, a small exercise room, a whirlpool, and a steam room. Rates are $149–199 ($89–129 outside of summer), which includes a gourmet continental breakfast that will set you up for the day. Children under 12 stay and eat free.

Over $200

(Bear and Bison (705 Benchlands Trail, 403/678-2058, www.bearandbisoninn.com) is an elegant lodging with nine guest rooms in three different themes. Timber and stone surroundings are complemented by rich heritage tones throughout. Each room has a king-size four-poster bed, a jetted tub, a fireplace, and a private balcony or patio. The lounge has a high vaulted ceiling, a welcoming open fire, and panoramic picture windows. Guests also enjoy an inviting library and a private garden complete with an oversized hot tub. Rates of $275–350 s or d include baked goods on arrival, pre-dinner drinks, and a breakfast you will remember for a long time. Outside of summer, rates run $175–295.

Paintbox Lodge (629 10th St., 403/609-0482 or 888/678-6100, www.paintboxlodge .com, $239–369 s or d) has the same upscale charm as the Bear and Bison but enjoys a more central location, just one block from the main street. The lobby itself—exposed hand-hewn timbers, slate tiles, and unique pieces of mountain-themed art—is an eye-catching gem. The upscale mountain decor continues through the eight large guest rooms, each lavishly decorated with muted natural colors and a tasteful se-

© ANDREW HEMPSTEAD

The Bear and Bison is one of Canmore's finest lodgings.

lection of heritage artifacts. Rooms also boast beds draped with the finest linens, bathrooms anchored by a deep soaker tub, and high-speed Internet access for those who can't leave their work behind. The more expensive rooms have fireplaces and balconies.

At the base of Silvertip Resort, across the TransCanada Highway from downtown, is **Four Points by Sheraton Canmore** (1 Silvertip Trail, 403/609-4422 or 888/609-4422, www.fourpointscanmore.com, from $215 s or d), Canmore's most luxurious chain hotel. It is a full-service property, complete with 99 contemporary guest rooms, 13 suites, in-room high-speed Internet access, a fitness center, an outdoor hot tub, a casual Italian restaurant and adjacent bar, and a gift store.

Harvie Heights

If you don't need the restaurants and shopping of Canmore, consider basing yourself in the small hamlet of Harvie Heights, eight kilometers (five miles) west of Canmore and less than one kilometer (0.6 mile) from the entrance to Banff National Park. The least expensive option at Harvie Heights is a standard motel room at the **Gateway Inn** (800 Harvie Heights Rd., 403/678-5396 or 877/678-1810, www.gatewayinn.ca), which ranges $75–95 s or d. Self-contained cabins, each with a kitchenette and adjacent fire pit, are $99–165 s or d, with the more expensive ones having three bedrooms; cabins also have a two-night minimum. You'll also find a playground, picnic area, and communal fire pit for evening relaxation.

Rundle Ridge Chalets (1100 Harvie Heights Rd., 403/678-5387 or 800/332-1299, www.chalets.ab.ca) is one of the mountains' original bungalow camps, with 37 self-contained cedar chalets scattered around a pleasant two-hectare (five-acre) property. Summer rates range $139–215 s or d. The cabins are winterized, and rates drop as low as $90 from mid-September to mid-June.

Banff Boundary Lodge (1000 Harvie Heights Rd., 403/678-9555 or 877/678-9555, www.banffboundarylodge.com) has less outdoor space than the two options detailed above,

but is a newer property. The 42 units each have one or two bedrooms, a comfortable lounge area with TV/VCR, and a full kitchen. Other facilities include an outdoor hot tub, barbecue area, and laundry. In summer, units are $199–229 per night, but the rest of the year rates drop as low as $120, an excellent value.

Deadman's Flats

Deadman's Flats, seven kilometers (4.3 miles) east of Canmore along the TransCanada Highway, is little more than a truck stop, but it has motels, a bed-and-breakfast, and 24-hour dining at a Husky gas station.

Big Horn Motel (403/678-2290 or 800/892-9908, www.bighornmotel.com, $79–99 s or d) offers 27 surprisingly modern, mostly nonsmoking rooms. All have TVs and phones, some have kitchens and balconies, and a couple are wheelchair accessible.

In an alpine-style two-story chalet, the **Kiska Inn** (110 1st Ave., 403/678-4041 or 866/678-4041, www.kiska.ab.ca) offers six guest rooms. Each is spacious and features a subtle theme (the Canmore Room is particularly appealing, $130–140 s or d includes breakfast). Guest amenities include a shared kitchen, a comfortable lounge room with TV/VCR combo, a backyard barbecue area, and Internet access. The adjacent Mexican restaurant has good food and a surprisingly welcoming ambience.

Camping

Spring Creek RV Campground (502 3rd Ave., 403/678-5111, www.springcreekrv.ca) enjoys a central location off 8th Street in downtown Canmore. The site is slated for residential development, but will be welcoming campers while still providing a home for permanent residents until 2010. The best sites are situated along a stretch of grass that parallels Policeman's Creek. Unserviced sites are $29, hookups $32–44, self-contained cabins $150 s or d.

East of Canmore are three government campgrounds operated by **Bow Valley Campgrounds** (403/673-2163, www.bowvalleycampgrounds.com). Each has pit toilets,

kitchen shelters, and firewood for sale at $6 per bundle. None have hookups. **Bow River Campground** (open late Apr.–early Sept.) is three kilometers (1.9 miles) east of Canmore at the Three Sisters Parkway overpass; **Three Sisters Campground** (mid-Apr.–Oct.) is accessed from Deadman's Flats, a further four kilometers (2.5 miles) east, but it has a pleasant treed setting; **Lac des Arcs Campground** (late Apr.–mid-Sept.) slopes down to the edge of a large lake of the same name seven kilometers (4.3 miles) farther toward Calgary. All sites are $20 and reservations are taken from April 1.

FOOD

The restaurant scene has come a long way in Canmore in the last decade. While you can still get inexpensive bar meals at the many pubs, other choices run the gamut, from the lively atmosphere of dining in the front yard of a converted residence to vegetarian with a view.

Cafés

The **Rocky Mountain Bagel Company** (830 8th St., 403/678-9978, daily 6:30 A.M.–10 P.M.) is a popular early-morning gathering spot. With a central location, it's always busy but manages to maintain an inviting atmosphere. It's the perfect place to start the day with a good strong coffee and fruit-filled muffin.

Down one block, **Beamer's Coffee Bar** (737 7th Ave., 403/609-0111, daily 6:30 A.M.–10 P.M.) is a smaller space with equally good coffee. Out on the Bow Valley Trail (between Dairy Queen and Boston Pizza) is another **Beamer's Coffee Bar** (403/678-3988), this one anchored by a long comfortable couch wrapped around a fireplace—the perfect place to relax with one of Beamer's complimentary daily papers.

Just off Main Street, the **Coffeepot & Curry Stop** (637 10th St., 403/678-2688, Mon.–Fri. 6:45 A.M.–6 P.M., Sat. 10 A.M.–5 P.M.) starts the day by serving up locally roasted coffee then moves on to a lunchtime menu of simple but delicious curries ($8).

Away from downtown, near where Cougar Creek enters Canmore from the Fairholme Range, is the **Summit Café** (1001 Cougar Creek Dr., 403/609-2120, daily 6:30 A.M.– 6 P.M.; kitchen closes at 4 P.M.). It features a health-conscious menu including lots of salads, but many people come just to soak up the sun on the outside deck or relax with the daily paper and a cup of coffee.

Gourmet

Bella Crusta (702 6th Ave., 403/609-3366, Mon.–Sat. 10 A.M.–6 P.M.) is the purveyor of the best gourmet pizza in the Bow Valley. Heated slices to go are $5, or pay $13–15 for a family-sized version and heat it yourself on a barbecue as the friendly staff recommends.

 Crazyweed Kitchen (626 8th St., 403/609-2530, daily 11 A.M.–7 P.M., $4–24) dishes up creative culinary fare that gets rave reviews from even cultured Calgarians. Behind the glass counter is a wide choice of freshly made dishes, which may include Thai chicken wraps or curried seafood. Healthy portions are served at tables inside or out, or packed to go.

Tucked away in an industrial park beyond the south end of Bow Valley Trail is **Valbella Meats** (104 Elk Run Blvd., 403/678-3637, Mon.–Fri. 8 A.M.–6 P.M., Sat. 9 A.M.–5:30 P.M.). Valbella mainly supplies gourmet meats to Bow Valley restaurants and grocery stores; head there for Canadian specialties such as buffalo, venison, and salmon; fresh cuts of marinated Alberta beef, lamb, chicken, and pork; and cured sausages.

Canadian

Canmore has seen many top-notch restaurants open in the last few years, but the decade-old **Zona's** (710 9th St., 403/609-2000, daily 11 A.M.–2 A.M., for dinner only outside summer) continues to garner rave reviews. The food is great, but so is the restaurant itself—earthy tones, hardwood floors, rustic furniture, bamboo blinds, and kiln-fired clay crockery create an inviting ambience unequaled in Canmore. The menu takes its roots from around the world, with an emphasis on healthy eating and freshly prepared Canadian produce. Choose from dishes such

as Moroccan molasses lamb curry ($17) or a filet of salmon baked and smothered in a maple and whiskey sauce ($20.50). Zona's also serves homemade lemonade and a wide selection of slightly overpriced wines and beers. A large deck provides much-needed extra seating in summer.

Off the top end of Main Street, the **Rocky Mountain Flatbread Co.** (838 10th St., 403/609-5508, summer Fri.–Sat. 11 A.M.– 2 P.M. and daily 5–10 P.M., the rest of the year Wed.–Sun. 5–10 P.M.) is a lovely space of natural tones dominated by a clay wood-fired oven in one corner. The oven is also the main attraction when it comes to the food— gourmet flatbread-style pizzas in the $14–20 range. My advice: start with a bowl of made-from-scratch chicken noodle soup ($6), then move on to the prosciutto, mango, mushroom, and avocado pizza (the $16 size is enough for two people).

I'd recommend dining at **☕ Sage Bistro** (1712 Bow Valley Trail, 403/678-4878, Sun.– Thurs. 8 A.M.–10 P.M., Fri.–Sat. 8 A.M.–11 P.M.) simply because it's one of the few restaurants in Canada that makes shepherd's pie the way it should be—with lamb. But this nuance aside, the innovative Canadian-oriented cuisine and flawless presentation make Sage an excellent choice for dinner. Starters include sweet-potato fries ($7) and Dungeness crab cakes ($12), while mains include familiar favorites with a local twist: grilled bison short ribs ($23) and venison meatloaf ($22). Even if my shepherd's pie recommendation doesn't appeal to you, finish up with maple syrup crème brûlée (trust me, you'll love it). The deck is a wonderful place for lunch.

Spanish

Tapas (Paintbox Lodge, 633 10th St., 403/609-0583, summer daily 7 A.M.–11:30 P.M., the rest of the year daily 5–9 P.M.) offers a truly Spanish tapas menu in a jazzed-up heritage home with tables inside, upstairs, and out back. Most dishes fall in the $6–12 range, or order *platos* style and get a thoughtful selection of small dishes for two ($30–38).

Vegetarian

The prime location of **Sunfood Cafe** (743 Railway Ave., 403/609-2613; daily 9 A.M.–9 P.M.) won't become apparent until you climb the steps from busy Railway Avenue to the sun-drenched patio and admire the surrounding mountains. I'm a meat lover, but still, I have my favorites at this vegetarian eatery: French onion soup ($5.50) as a starter, then green Thai coconut curry ($15) as a main. I then reward myself with Kahlua mocha chocolate cake ($6.50) for dessert.

INFORMATION AND SERVICES

The best source of pre-trip information (apart from this book, of course) is **Tourism Canmore** (403/678-1295 or 866/226-6673, www.tourismcanmore.com). A **Travel Alberta Information Centre** (403/678-5277, May–Sept. 8 A.M.–8 P.M., Oct. 9 A.M.–6 P.M.), just off the TransCanada Highway on the west side of town, provides plenty of information about Canmore and Banff.

The *Rocky Mountain Outlook* and *Canmore Leader* are both filled with local issues and entertainment listings; both are available free on stands throughout the valley. **Canmore Public Library** (950 8th Ave., 403/678-2468) is open Monday–Thursday 11 A.M.–8 P.M., Friday–Sunday 11 A.M.–5 P.M. At the top end of the main street, **Café Books** (826 Main St., 403/678-0908, Mon.–Sat. 10 A.M.–6 P.M., Sun. 10 A.M.–5 P.M., later hours in summer) stocks an excellent selection of Canadiana, including hiking guides, coffee table–style pictorials, Rocky Mountain cookbooks, and calendars, as well as nonfiction by local authors. With a huge collection of used books, **Second Story** (713 8th St., 403/609-2368) hasn't been on the second floor since the weight of the books forced a move downstairs to the basement of the same address.

The post office is on 7th Avenue, beside Rusticana Grocery. **The Lost Sock** laundry (in the small mall on 7th Ave. at 10th St.) is open 24 hours daily and has Internet access. **Canmore Hospital** (403/678-5536) is along Bow Valley Trail. For the **RCMP,** call 403/678-5516.

one of many appealing gift stores along the main street of Canmore

All the hotels and motels have some kind of guest Internet access, or stop by **Canmore Public Library** (700 9th St., 403/678-2468, Mon.–Thurs. 11 A.M.–8 P.M., Fri.–Sun. 11 A.M.–5 P.M.).

GETTING THERE AND AROUND

The following companies offer door-to-door service on routes that link Calgary International Airport and Banff: **Banff Airporter** (403/762-3330, www.banffairporter.com) and **Rocky Mountain Sky Shuttle** (403/762-5200, www.rockymountainskyshuttle.com). The cost from Calgary is around $47–51 one-way. Adjacent desks at the airport's Arrivals level take

bookings, but you can reserve a seat by booking over the phone or online in advance.

Greyhound pulls into 701 Bow Valley Trail (403/678-3807) and offers regular services to Calgary, Banff, and beyond.

The most enjoyable way to get around Canmore is on foot or bike, on the extensive trail network winding throughout the town. **Gear Up** (1302 Bow Valley Trail, 403/678-1636) rents front- and full-suspension mountain bikes, as well as canoes and kayaks. For a cab, call **Apex** (403/609-0030). **Budget,** based at the Canmore Inn & Suites (1402 Bow Valley Trail, 403/609-3360), is Canmore's only rental-car outlet. As with Banff rental companies, included mileage is limited to 150 kilometers per day.

BANFF NATIONAL PARK

This 6,641-square-kilometer (2,564-square-mi) national park encompasses some of the world's most magnificent scenery. The snow-capped peaks of the Canadian Rockies form a spectacular backdrop for glacial lakes, fast-flowing rivers, endless forests, and two of North America's most famous resort towns, Banff and Lake Louise. The park's vast wilderness is home to deer, moose, elk, mountain goats, bighorn sheep, black and grizzly bears, wolves, and cougars. Many of these species are commonly sighted from roads in the park, others forage within town, and some remain deep in the backcountry. The human species is concentrated mainly in the picture-postcard town of Banff, near the park's southeast gate, 128 kilometers (80 mi) west of Calgary. Northwest of Banff, along the TransCanada Highway, is Lake Louise, regarded as one of the seven natural wonders of the world, rivaled for sheer beauty only by Moraine Lake, just down the road. Just north of Lake Louise, the Icefields Parkway begins its spectacular course alongside the Continental Divide to Jasper National Park.

Banff National Park is only one component of a complex geological and natural area consisting of four adjacent national parks that together have been declared a World Heritage Site by UNESCO. (The others are Jasper to the north and Kootenay and Yoho to the west in British Columbia.)

One of Banff's greatest draws is the accessibility of its natural wonders. Most highlights are close to the road system. For more adventurous travelers, an excellent system of

© ANDREW HEMPSTEAD

HIGHLIGHTS

◖ Fairmont Banff Springs: You don't need to book a room here to enjoy the many wonders of one of the world's great mountain resorts – join a guided tour, enjoy a meal, or simply wander through the grandiose public areas (page 217).

◖ Bourgeau Lake: A steep trail leads to this lake's beautiful, yet remote rocky shores, populated by colonies of pikas (page 226).

◖ Lake Louise: Famous Lake Louise has hypnotized visitors with her beauty for over 100 years. Visitors can rent canoes from the boathouse (page 249).

◖ Moraine Lake: If anywhere in the Canadian Rockies qualified as a double must-see, it would be this deep-blue body of water surrounded by glaciated peaks (page 250).

◖ Lake Agnes: You won't completely escape the crowds by hiking to this scenic tarn from Lake Louise, but you will leave most of them behind (page 254).

◖ Larch Valley: This walk is a good introduction to hiking in the Canadian Rockies, especially in fall when the larch trees have turned a brilliant gold (page 255).

◖ Bow Lake: Although you can soak up this lake's beauty from the Icefields Parkway, walk along its northern shoreline early in the morning to make the most of this scenic gem (page 263).

◖ Peyto Lake: Another one of Banff's famous lakes. The main difference here is the perspective from which it is viewed – a lookout high above its shoreline (page 263).

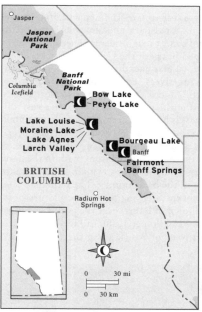

LOOK FOR ◖ TO FIND RECOMMENDED SIGHTS, ACTIVITIES, DINING, AND LODGING.

hiking trails leads to alpine lakes, along glacial valleys, and to spectacular viewpoints where crowds are scarce and human impact has been minimal. Summer in the park is busy. In fact, the park receives nearly half of its four million annual visitors in just two months—July and August. The rest of the year, crowds outside the town of Banff are minimal. In winter, three world-class alpine resorts—Ski Norquay, Sunshine Village, and Lake Louise—crank up their lifts. Being low-

season, hotel rates are reasonable. And if you tire of downhill skiing or snowboarding, you can try cross-country skiing, ice-skating, or snowshoeing; take a sleigh ride; soak in a hot spring; or go heli-skiing across the mountains in British Columbia.

The park is open year-round, although roads on mountain passes along the park's western boundary occasionally close in winter because of avalanche-control work and snowstorms.

Park Entry

Permits are required for entry into Banff National Park. A **National Parks Day Pass** is adult $9, senior $7.75, child $4.50, to a maximum of $18 per vehicle. It is interchangeable between parks and is valid until 4 P.M. the day following its purchase. If you'll be traveling in the parks extensively, consider an annual **National Parks of Canada Pass,** good for entry into national parks across Canada, for adult $63, senior $54, to a maximum of $125 per vehicle. Passes can be bought at the eastern park gate on the TransCanada Highway, the park information centers in Banff or Lake Louise, and at campground kiosks. For more information, check online at the Parks Canada website (www.pc.gc.ca).

PLANNING YOUR TIME

If you are planning to visit Alberta, it is almost inevitable that your itinerary will include Banff National Park, both for its many and varied outdoor attractions and for its central location. The park can be anything you want

it to be, depending on the time of year you visit and what your interests are. The main population center is Banff, which has all the services of a large town, as well as attractions such as landmark **Fairmont Banff Springs.** The park holds four lakes that you won't want to miss for their scenic beauty: **Lake Louise, Moraine Lake, Bow Lake,** and **Peyto Lake.** All four are easily accessible by road but also offer surrounding hiking, and the former two have canoe rentals. Hiking is the park's biggest attraction, and many visitors plan their itinerary around walking. I'd suggest mixing it up—choosing from the hikes that reflect your fitness level and combining them with visits to the major natural attractions. For example, when in the vicinity of Lake Louise, walk the **Lake Agnes Trail,** and while at Moraine Lake, plan on visiting **Larch Valley.** For the more adventurous, **Bourgeau Lake** is a stunning day-hike destination.

You can book one accommodation for your entire stay or spend an equal number of nights in Banff and Lake Louise. If you have a family

© ANDREW HEMPSTEAD

Black bears are common throughout the park.

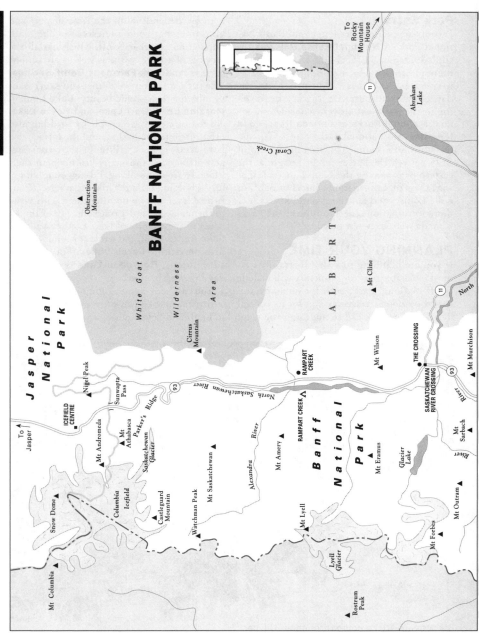

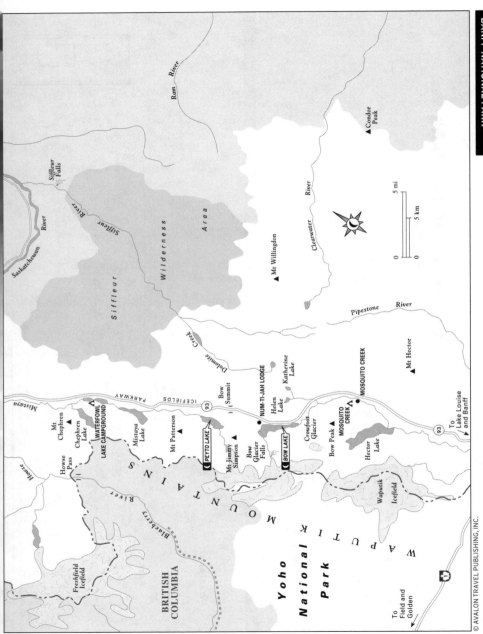

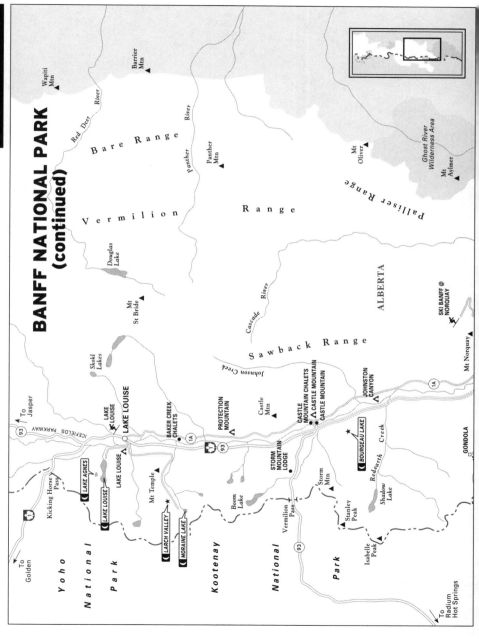

BANFF NATIONAL PARK (continued)

Wapiti Mtn

Barrier Mtn

Red Deer River

Bare Range

Panther River

Panther Mtn

Mt Oliver

Ghost River Wilderness Area

Mt Aylmer

Vermilion Range

Palliser Range

Douglas Lake

Mt St Bride

Cascade River

ALBERTA

SKI BANFF @ NORQUAY

Skoki Lakes

Sawback Range

Johnson Creek

Mt Norquay

To Jasper

Lake Louise

LAKE LOUISE

BAKER CREEK CHALETS

1A

PROTECTION MOUNTAIN

Castle Mtn

CASTLE MOUNTAIN CHALETS

CASTLE MOUNTAIN

JOHNSTON CANYON

1A

ICEFIELDS PARKWAY

93

GONDOLA

LAKE AGNES

Kicking Horse Pass

LAKE LOUISE

LAKE LOUISE

Mt Temple

LARCH VALLEY

MORAINE LAKE

Boom Lake

STORM MOUNTAIN LODGE

Storm Mtn

Vermilion Pass

BOURGEAU LAKE

Redearth Creek

Shadow Lake

Stanley Peak

To Golden

Yoho National Park

Kootenay National Park

93

Isabelle Peak

To Radium Hot Springs

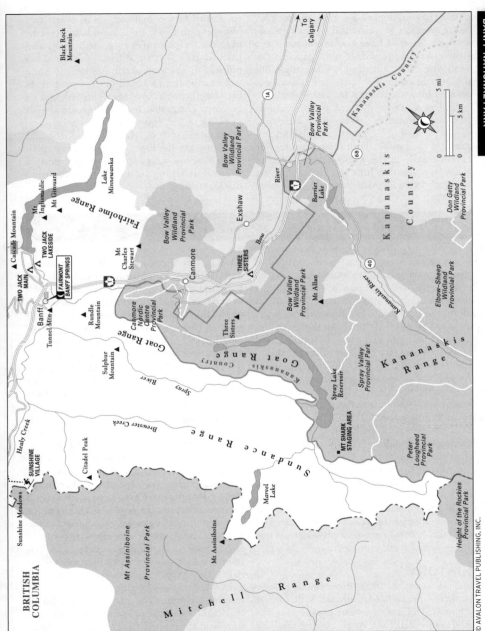

or like the convenience of staying put for your entire vacation, it is practical to book a room in either Banff or Lake Louise and use it as a base—spending your days in the park but also venturing farther afield, with, for example, one day scheduled for the Icefields Parkway and another for a Canmore/Kananaskis combo.

Unless you're a diehard skier or snowboarder, summer is definitely the best time of year to visit. The months of July and August are the busiest, with crowds decreasing exponentially in the weeks before and after these two months. June and September are wonderful times to visit the park. Aside from the crowd factor, in June, wildflowers start blooming and wildlife is abundant. September sees temperatures ripe for hiking, and the turning colors are at their peak. In either month, discounted accommodations are a welcome bonus. In May and the stretch from October through November, the park is at its quietest. The park's three alpine resorts begin opening in December and remain in operation until April or May. While skiing and boarding are the big wintertime draw, plan on expanding your experience by joining a sleigh ride, trying snowshoeing, or heading out ice-fishing.

Town of Banff

Many visitors to the national park don't realize that the town of Banff is a bustling commercial center with 7,700 permanent residents. The town's location is magnificent. It is spread out along the Bow River, extending to the lower slopes of Sulphur Mountain to the south and Tunnel Mountain to the east. In one direction is the towering face of Mount Rundle, and in the other, framed by the buildings along Banff Avenue, is Cascade Mountain. Hotels and motels line the north end of Banff Avenue, and a profusion of shops, boutiques, cafés, and restaurants hugs the south end. Also at the south end, just over the Bow River, is the Park Administration Building. Here the road forks—to the right is the historic Cave and Basin Hot Springs, to the left the Banff Springs Hotel and Sulphur Mountain Gondola. Some people are happy walking along the crowded streets or shopping in a truly unique setting, but visitors who are more interested in some peace and quiet can easily slip into pristine wilderness just a five-minute walk from town.

HISTORY
On November 8, 1883, three young railway workers—Franklin McCabe and William and Thomas McCardell—went prospecting for gold on their day off. After crossing the Bow River by raft, they came across a warm stream and traced it to its source at a small log-choked basin of warm water that had a distinct smell of sulphur. Nearby, they detected the source of the foul smell coming from a hole in the ground. Nervously, one of the three men lowered himself into the hole and came across a subterranean pool of aqua-green warm water. The three men had found not gold but something just as precious—a hot mineral spring that in time would attract wealthy customers from around the world. Word of the discovery soon got out, and the government encouraged visitors to the Cave and Basin as an ongoing source of revenue to support the new railway.

A small reserve was established around the springs on November 25, 1885, and two years later the reserve was expanded and renamed **Rocky Mountains Park.** It was primarily a business enterprise centered around the unique springs and catering to wealthy patrons of the railway. The Banff Springs Hotel, the world's largest hotel at the time, opened in 1888. Enterprising locals soon realized the area's potential and began opening restaurants and offering guided hunting and boating trips. By 1900, the bustling community of Banff had eight hotels and had become Canada's best-known tourist resort, attracting visitors from around the world.

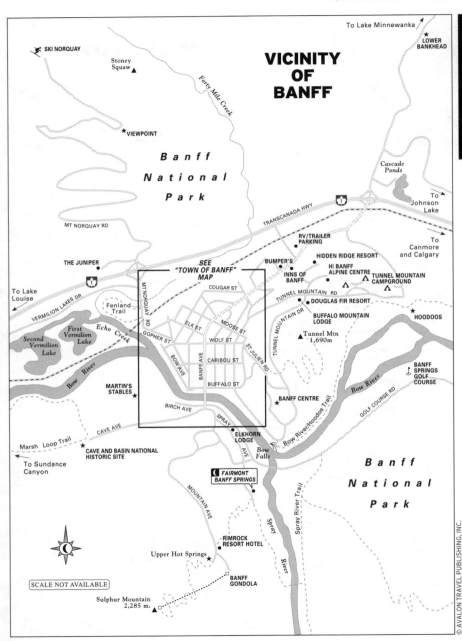

VICINITY OF BANFF

To Lake Minnewanka

★ LOWER BANKHEAD

✕ SKI NORQUAY

Stoney Squaw ▲

Forty Mile Creek

★ VIEWPOINT

**B a n f f
N a t i o n a l
P a r k**

Cascade Ponds

TRANSCANADA HWY

1

To Johnson Lake

MT NORQUAY RD

To Canmore and Calgary

RV/TRAILER PARKING

HIDDEN RIDGE RESORT

THE JUNIPER

1

SEE "TOWN OF BANFF" MAP

BUMPER'S

INNS OF BANFF

HI BANFF ALPINE CENTRE

TUNNEL MOUNTAIN CAMPGROUND

To Lake Louise

Fenland Trail

COUGAR ST

TUNNEL MOUNTAIN RD

DOUGLAS FIR RESORT

VERMILION LAKES DR

First Vermilion Lake

Echo Creek

MT NORQUAY RD

ELK ST

MOOSE ST

GOPHER ST

WOLF ST

ST JULIEN RD

BUFFALO MOUNTAIN LODGE

HOODOOS

Second Vermilion Lake

TUNNEL MOUNTAIN DR

▲ Tunnel Mtn 1,690m

Bow River

BANFF AVE

CARIBOU ST

BOW AVE

BUFFALO ST

BANFF SPRINGS GOLF COURSE

MARTIN'S STABLES ★

BIRCH AVE

Bow River

GOLF COURSE RD

★ BANFF CENTRE

Bow River/Hoodos Trail

CAVE AVE

SPRAY AVE

Marsh Loop Trail

CAVE AND BASIN NATIONAL HISTORIC SITE

ELKHORN LODGE

Bow Falls

**B a n f f
N a t i o n a l
P a r k**

To Sundance Canyon

🌙 FAIRMONT BANFF SPRINGS

MOUNTAIN AVE

Spray River Trail

Spray River

RIMROCK RESORT HOTEL

Upper Hot Springs ★

BANFF GONDOLA

SCALE NOT AVAILABLE

Sulphur Mountain 2,285 m. ▲

© AVALON TRAVEL PUBLISHING, INC.

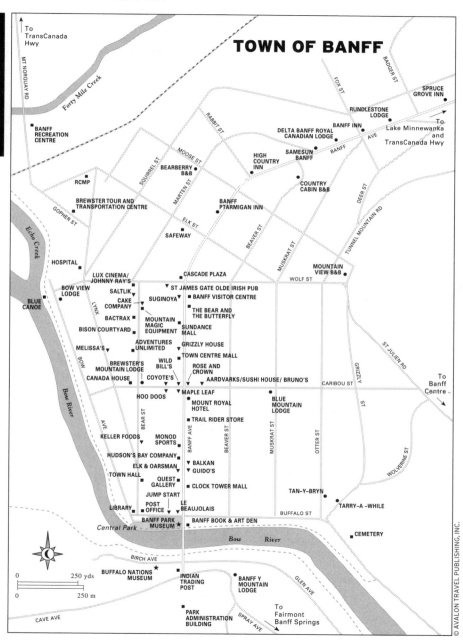

TOWN OF BANFF

To
TransCanada
Hwy

MT NORQUAY RD

Forty Mile Creek

BADGER ST

FOX ST

SPRUCE
GROVE INN

RUNDLESTONE
LODGE

BANFF INN

To
Lake Minnewanka
and
TransCanada Hwy

BANFF
RECREATION
CENTRE

RABBIT ST

DELTA BANFF ROYAL
CANADIAN LODGE

BANFF AVE

MOOSE ST

HIGH
COUNTRY
INN

SAMESUN
BANFF

SQUIRREL ST

BEARBERRY
B&B

MARTEN ST

COUNTRY
CABIN B&B

RCMP

DEER ST

BREWSTER TOUR AND
TRANSPORTATION CENTRE

BANFF
PTARMIGAN INN

GOPHER ST

ELK ST

TUNNEL MOUNTAIN RD

SAFEWAY

BEAVER ST

Echo Creek

HOSPITAL

MUSKRAT ST

MOUNTAIN
VIEW B&B

BLUE
CANOE

BOW VIEW
LODGE

LUX CINEMA/
JOHNNY RAY'S

CASCADE PLAZA

WOLF ST

SALTLIK

ST JAMES GATE OLDE IRISH PUB

LYNX

CAKE
COMPANY

SUGINOYA

BANFF VISITOR CENTRE

BACTRAX

MOUNTAIN
MAGIC
EQUIPMENT

THE BEAR AND
THE BUTTERFLY

BISON COURTYARD

SUNDANCE
MALL

ST JULIEN RD

MELISSA'S

ADVENTURES
UNLIMITED

GRIZZLY HOUSE

Bow

BREWSTER'S
MOUNTAIN LODGE

WILD
BILL'S

TOWN CENTRE MALL

CANADA HOUSE

COYOTE'S

ROSE AND
CROWN

GRIZZLY ST

To
Banff
Centre

AARDVARKS/SUSHI HOUSE/ BRUNO'S

CARIBOU ST

Bow River

HOO DOOS

MAPLE LEAF

MOUNT ROYAL
HOTEL

BLUE
MOUNTAIN
LODGE

BEAR ST

TRAIL RIDER STORE

AVE

KELLER FOODS

BANFF AVE

BEAVER ST

MUSKRAT ST

OTTER ST

WOLVERINE ST

MONOD
SPORTS

HUDSON'S BAY COMPANY

ELK & OARSMAN

BALKAN

TOWN HALL

GUIDO'S

QUEST
GALLERY

CLOCK TOWER MALL

TAN-Y-BRYN

JUMP START

LIBRARY

POST
OFFICE

LE
BEAUJOLAIS

TARRY-A-WHILE

BUFFALO ST

BANFF PARK
MUSEUM

BANFF BOOK & ART DEN

Central Park

CEMETERY

Bow   River

BIRCH AVE

0   250 yds

0   250 m

BUFFALO NATIONS
MUSEUM

INDIAN
TRADING
POST

BANFF Y
MOUNTAIN
LODGE

GLEN AVE

To
Fairmont
Banff Springs

CAVE AVE

PARK
ADMINISTRATION
BUILDING

SPRAY AVE

Changing Attitudes

At the turn of the 20th century, Canada had an abundance of wilderness; it certainly didn't need a park to preserve it. The only goal of Rocky Mountains Park was to generate income for the government and the Canadian Pacific Railway (CPR). In 1902, the park boundary was again expanded to include 11,440 square kilometers (4,420 square mi) of the Canadian Rockies. This dramatic expansion meant that the park became not just a tourist resort but also home to existing coal-mining and logging operations and hydroelectric dams. Government officials saw no conflict of interest, actually stating that the coalmine and township at **Bankhead** added to the park's many attractions. As attitudes began to change, the government set up a Dominion Parks Branch, whose first commissioner, J. B. Hawkins, believed that land set aside for parks should be used for recreation and education. Gradually, resource industries were phased out. Hawkins's work culminated in the National Parks Act of 1930, which in turn led Rocky Mountains Park to be renamed Banff National Park.

Development and the Future

For the first century of its existence, the town of Banff was run as a service center for park visitors by the Canadian Parks Service in Ottawa—a government department with plenty of economic resources but little idea about how to handle the day-to-day running of a midsized town. Any inconvenience this arrangement caused park residents was offset by cheap rent and subsidized services. In June 1988, Banff's residents voted to sever this tie, and on January 1, 1990, Banff officially became an incorporated town, no different than any other in Alberta (except that Parks Canada controls environmental protection within town limits).

SIGHTS AND DRIVES
Banff Park Museum

Although displays of stuffed animals are not usually associated with national parks, the Banff Park Museum (93 Banff Ave., 403/762-1558, mid-May–late Sept. daily 10 A.M.–6 P.M.,

the rest of the year daily 1–5 P.M., adult $4, senior $3.50, child $3) provides an insight into the park's early history. Visitors during the Victorian era were eager to see the park's animals without actually having to venture into the bush. A lack of roads and scarcity of large game resulting from hunting meant that the best places to see animals, stuffed or otherwise, were the game paddock, the zoo, and this museum, which was built in 1903. In its early years, the Banff Zoo and Aviary occupied the grounds behind the museum. The zoo kept more than 60 species of animals, including a polar bear. The museum itself was built before the park had electricity, hence the railroad pagoda design using skylights on all levels. While the exhibits still provide visitors with an insight into the intricate workings of various park ecosystems, they are also an interesting link to the park's past. Staff lead a guided tour through the facility Monday–Friday at 3 P.M. and Saturday–Sunday at 2:30 P.M. The museum also has a Discovery Room, where touching the displays is encouraged, and a reading room is stocked with books on the park.

Whyte Museum of the Canadian Rockies

The Whyte Foundation was established in the mid-1950s by local artists Peter and Catharine Whyte to help preserve artistic and historical material relating to the Canadian Rockies. Their museum (111 Bear St., 403/762-2291, daily 10 A.M.–5 P.M., adult $6, senior and child $3.50) opened in 1968 and has continued to grow ever since. It now houses the world's largest collection of Canadian Rockies literature and art. Included in the archives are more than 4,000 volumes, oral tapes of early pioneers and outfitters, antique postcards, old cameras, manuscripts, and a large photography collection. The highlight is the photography of Byron Harmon, whose black-and-white studies of mountain geography have shown people around the world the beauty of the Canadian Rockies. The downstairs gallery features changing art exhibitions. The museum also houses the library and archives of the Alpine

Club of Canada. On the grounds are several heritage homes formerly occupied by local pioneers, including Bill Peyto (see sidebar "Wild Bill Peyto" later in this chapter) and a backcountry cabin used by wardens.

Cascade Gardens and Canada Place

Across the river from downtown, Cascade Gardens offers a commanding view along Banff Avenue and of Cascade Mountain. The gardens are immaculately manicured, making for enjoyable strolling on a sunny day. The stone edifice in the center of the garden is the **Park Administration Building,** which dates to 1936. It replaced a private spa and hospital operated by one of the park's earliest entrepreneurs, Dr. R. G. Brett. Known as Brett's Sanatorium, the original 1886 structure was built to accommodate guests drawn to Banff by the claimed healing qualities of the hot springs' water.

In addition to providing a park headquarters, the administration building is home to Canada Place (mid-May–Aug. daily 10 A.M.–6 P.M., Sept.–mid-Oct. daily noon–5 P.M., mid-Oct.–mid-May Wed.–Sun. 1–4 P.M., free), a small room filled with hands-on exhibits that focus on the country's heritage and how this history was shaped by the vastness of the land. You can also watch a nationalistic video presentation, and make a recording of what the country means to you.

Buffalo Nations Museum

Looking like a stockade, this museum (1 Birch Ave., 403/762-2388, summer daily 10 A.M.–6 P.M., the rest of the year daily 1–5 P.M., adult $8, senior $6, child $2.50) overlooks the Bow River across from Central Park. It is dedicated to the heritage of the natives who once inhabited the Canadian Rockies and adjacent prairies. The museum was developed by prominent local resident Norman Luxton in the early 1900s. At that time it was within the Indian Trading Post, an adjacent gift shop that still stands. The museum contains memorabilia from Luxton's lifelong relationship with Stoney natives, including an elaborately deco-

rated tepee, hunting equipment, arrowheads dating back 4,000 years, stuffed animals, original artwork, peace pipes, and traditional clothing. Various aspects of native culture—such as ceremonial gatherings, living in a tepee, and weaving—are also displayed. The adjacent Indian Trading Post is now one of Banff's better gift shops and is definitely worth a browse.

Cave and Basin National Historic Site

At the end of Cave Avenue, this historic site (403/762-1566, summer daily 9 A.M.–6 P.M., the rest of the year Mon.–Fri. 11 A.M.–4 P.M. and Sat.–Sun. 9:30 A.M.–5 P.M., adult $4, senior $3.50, child $2.50) is the birthplace of Banff National Park and of the Canadian National Parks system. After its discovery in 1883—lounging in the hot water was considered a real luxury in the Wild West—bathhouses were installed, and bathers paid 10 cents for a swim. The pools were eventually lined with concrete, and additions were built onto the original structures. Ironically, the soothing minerals in the water that had attracted millions of people to bathe here eventually caused the pools' demise. The minerals, combined with chlorine, produced sediments that ate away at the concrete structure until the pools were deemed unsafe. After closing in 1975, the pools were restored to their original look at a cost of $12 million. They reopened in 1985 only to close again in 1993 for the same reasons, coupled with flagging popularity.

Although the pools are now closed for swimming, the center is still one of Banff's most popular attractions. Interpretive displays describe the hows and whys of the springs. A narrow tunnel winds into the dimly lit cave, and short trails lead from the center to the cave entrance and through a unique environment created by the hot water from the springs. Interpretive tours run four times daily in summer.

Banff Upper Hot Springs

These springs (Mountain Ave., 403/762-1515, summer daily 9 A.M.–11 P.M., the rest of the year daily 10 A.M.–10 P.M.), toward the Banff

Gondola, were first developed in 1901. The present building was completed in 1935, with extensive renovations made in 1996. Water flows out of the bedrock at 47°C (116.6°F) and is cooled to 40°C (104°F) in the main pool. Once considered for privatization, the springs are still run by Parks Canada and are popular throughout the year. Swimming is $7.50 adults, $6.50 seniors and children; lockers and towel rental are a couple of dollars extra. Within the complex is **Pleiades Massage & Spa** (403/760-2500), offering a wide range of therapeutic treatments, including massages from $50 for 30 minutes as well as body wraps, aromatherapy, and hydrotherapy.

Banff Gondola

The easiest way to get high above town without breaking a sweat is on this gondola (403/762-2523, summer 7:30 A.M.–9 P.M., shorter hours the rest of the year, closed for two weeks in January, adult $23.50, child $11.75). The modern four-person cars rise 700 meters (2,300 ft) in eight minutes to the summit of 2,285-meter (7,500-ft) **Sulphur Mountain**. From the observation deck at the upper terminal, the breathtaking view includes the town, Bow Valley, Cascade Mountain, Lake Minnewanka, and the Fairholme Range. Bighorn sheep often hang around below the upper terminal. The short **Vista Trail** leads along a ridge to a restored weather observatory. Between 1903 and 1931, long before the gondola was built, Norman Sanson was the meteorological observer who collected data at the station. During this period he made more than 1,000 ascents of Sulphur Mountain, all in the line of duty.

The **Summit Restaurant** (403/762-7486, hours vary widely, so check ahead, $6–22) serves up cafeteria-style food combined with priceless views. Above this eatery is the **Panorama Room** (403/762-7486, early June–early Sept. daily 7:30 A.M.–9 P.M., early Sept. to mid-Oct. daily 8:30 A.M.–6:30 P.M., breakfast $15, lunch $20, dinner $28), dishing up more of the same, but buffet-style, and the Chinese **Regal View Restaurant** (403/762-7486, hours vary widely, so check ahead, $12–25).

From downtown, the gondola is three kilometers (1.9 mi) along Mountain Avenue. May–October **Brewster** (403/762-6767) provides shuttle service to the gondola from downtown hotels.

A 5.5-kilometer (3.4-mi) hiking trail to the summit begins from the Upper Hot Springs parking lot. Although it's a long slog, you'll be rewarded with a discounted gondola ride down ($10 one way).

Fairmont Banff Springs

On a terrace above the Bow River is the **Fairmont Banff Springs,** one of the largest, grandest, and most opulent mountain resort hotels in the world. What better way to spend a rainy afternoon than to explore this turreted 20th-century castle, seeking out a writing desk overlooking one of the world's most-photographed scenes and penning a long letter to the folks back home?

When the hotel opened in 1888, it immediately became one of North America's most popular accommodations for wealthy guests. But don't let the hotel's opulence keep you from spending time here. Visit the hotel between 11:30 A.M. and 1:30 P.M. to enjoy a huge buffet lunch combined with a 30-minute **Historical Hotel Tour** for $28 per person. Call 403/762-2211 for details. Otherwise wander through on your own, admiring the 5,000 pieces of furniture and antiques (most "antiques" in public areas are reproductions), paintings, prints, tapestries, and rugs. Take in the medieval atmosphere of Mt. Stephen Hall with its lime flagstone floor, enormous windows, and large oak beams; take advantage of the luxurious spa facility (see *Spas* under *Other Recreation and Entertainment* in this chapter), or relax in one of 12 eateries or four lounges.

The hotel is a 15-minute walk southeast of town, either along Spray Avenue or via the trail along the south bank of the Bow River. **Banff Transit** buses leave Banff Avenue for the Springs twice an hour; adult $2, child $1. Alternatively, horse-drawn buggies take passengers from the Trail Rider Store (132 Banff Ave., 403/762-4551) to the Springs for around $80 for two passengers.

A CASTLE IN THE WILDERNESS

The Fairmont Banff Springs, "The Springs," as it's best known, has grown with the town of Banff and is an integral part of local history. William Cornelius Van Horne, vice president of the Canadian Pacific Railway, decided that the best way of encouraging customers to travel on his newly completed rail line across the Rockies was to build a series of luxurious mountain accommodations. The largest of these was begun in 1886, as close as possible to Banff's newly discovered hot springs. The location chosen had magnificent views and was only a short carriage ride from the train station. Money was no object, and architect Bruce Price began designing a mountain resort the likes of which the world had never seen. At some stage of construction his plans were misinterpreted, and much to Van Horne's shock the building was built back to front. The best guest rooms faced the forested slopes of Sulphur Mountain while the kitchen had panoramic views of the Bow Valley.

When it opened on June 1, 1888, it was the largest hotel in the world, with 250 rooms beginning at $3.50 per night including meals. Water from the nearby hot springs was piped into the hotel's steam baths (rumor has it that when the pipes were blocked, water from the Bow River was used, secretly supplemented by bags of sulphur-smelling chemicals). Overnight, the quiet community of Banff became a destination resort for wealthy guests from around world. Every room was booked every day during the short summer seasons. In 1903, a wing was added, doubling the hotel's capacity. The following year a tower was added to the hotel. Additions made over the years were never able to keep up with demand, so in 1911, when guest numbers reached 22,000, construction of a new hotel designed by Walter Painter began.

The original design – an 11-story tower joining two wings in a baronial style – was reminiscent of a Scottish castle mixed with a French country château. This concrete-and-rock-faced, green-roofed building stood as it did at its completion in 1928 until 1999, when an ambitious multiyear program of renovations commenced. The most obvious change to those who have visited before will be the new lobby, moved to a more accessible frontside location. The Canadian Pacific moniker remained part of the Banff Spring's official name until 2000, when the hotel and all other Canadian Pacific hotels became part of the Fairmont Hotels and Resorts chain.

© ANDREW HEMPSTEAD

Bow Falls

Small but spectacular Bow Falls is below the Fairmont Banff Springs, only a short walk from downtown. The waterfall is the result of a dramatic change in the course of the Bow River brought about by glaciation. At one time the river flowed north of Tunnel Mountain and out of the mountains via the valley of Lake Minnewanka. As the glaciers retreated, they left terminal moraines, forming natural dams and changing the course of the river. Eventually the backed-up water found an outlet here between Tunnel Mountain and the northwest ridge of Mount Rundle. The falls are most spectacular in late spring when runoff from the winter snows fills every river and stream in the Bow Valley watershed.

To get there from town, cross the bridge at the south end of Banff Avenue, scramble down the grassy embankment to the left, and follow a pleasant trail along the Bow River to a point above the falls. This easy walk is one kilometer (0.6 mile); 20 minutes each way. By car, cross the bridge and follow Golf Course signs.

Banff Centre

On the lower slopes of Tunnel Mountain is Banff Centre, whose surroundings provide inspiration as one of Canada's leading centers for postgraduate students in a variety of disciplines, including Mountain Culture, Arts, and Leadership Development. The Banff Centre opened in the summer of 1933 as a theater school. Since then it has grown to become a prestigious institution attracting artists of many disciplines from throughout Canada. The Centre's **Walter Phillips Gallery** (St. Julien Rd., 403/762-6281, Wed.–Sun. noon–5 P.M.) presents changing exhibits of visual arts from throughout the world.

Activities are held on the grounds of the Banff Centre year-round. Highlights include a summer educational program, concerts, displays, live performances, the Playbill Series, the Banff Arts Festival, and Banff Mountain Festivals, to name a few (see *Festivals and Events* later in this chapter). Call 403/762-6100 for a program, go to the website www.banff

centre.ca, or check the *Crag and Canyon* (published weekly on Wednesday).

Vermilion Lakes

This series of shallow lakes forms an expansive montane wetland supporting a variety of mammals and 238 species of birds. Vermilion Lakes Drive, paralleling the TransCanada Highway immediately west of Banff, provides the easiest access to the area. The level of **First Vermilion Lake** was once controlled by a dam. Since its removal, the level of the lake has dropped. This is the beginning of a long process that will eventually see the area evolve into a floodplain forest such as is found along the Fenland Trail. **Second** and **Third Vermilion Lakes** have a higher water level that is controlled naturally by beaver dams. Near First Vermilion Lake is an active osprey nest. The entire area is excellent for wildlife-viewing, especially in winter when it provides habitat for elk, coyote, and the occasional wolf.

Mount Norquay Road

One of the best views of town accessible by vehicle is on this road, which switchbacks steeply to the base of Ski Norquay, the local hangout for skiers and boarders. On the way up are several lookouts, including one near the top where bighorn sheep often graze.

To Lake Minnewanka

Lake Minnewanka Road begins where Banff Avenue ends at the northeast end of town. After passing under the TransCanada Highway, **Cascade Falls** is obvious off to the left beyond the airstrip. The base of the falls can be easily reached in five minutes (climbing higher without the proper equipment is dangerous). In winter, these falls freeze and you'll often see ice climbers slowly making their way up the narrow thread of frozen water. Directly opposite is a turn to **Cascade Ponds,** a popular day-use area where families gather on warmer days to swim, sunbathe, and barbecue.

Continuing straight ahead at the first intersection, the next turnout along this road is at **Lower Bankhead.** During the early 1900s,

BANFF'S ELK

Few visitors leave Banff without having seen elk, which are easily distinguished by their white rumps. Elk were reported passing through the park early in the 20th century but have never been indigenous. In 1917, 57 elk were moved to the park from Yellowstone National Park. Two years later, 20 more were transplanted and the new herd multiplied rapidly. Coyotes, cougars, and wolves were being slaughtered under a predator-control program, leaving the elk relatively free from predators. The elk proliferated and soon became a problem because they took to wintering in the range of bighorn sheep, deer, moose, and beaver. Between 1941 and 1969, controlled slaughters of elk were conducted in an attempt to reduce the population.

Today, the elk population has stabilized at about 2,800. In summer, look for them in open meadows along the Bow Valley Parkway, along the road to Two Jack Lake, and at Vermilion Lakes. In fall, you'll find hundreds of elk grazing on the golf course until the first snow flies. Fall is rutting season, and the bull elk become dangerous as they gather their harems. In winter, small herds find a home on the edge of town.

© ANDREW HEMPSTEAD

Bankhead was a booming mining town producing 200,000 tons of coal a year. The poor quality of coal and bitter labor disputes led to the mine's closure in 1922. Soon after, all the buildings were moved or demolished. Although for many years the mine had brought prosperity to the park, perceptions changed. The National Parks Act of 1930, which prohibited the establishment of mining claims in national parks, was greeted with little animosity.

From the parking lot at Lower Bankhead, a 1.1-kilometer (0.7-mi) interpretive trail leads through the industrial section of the town and past an old mine train. The town's 1,000 residents lived on the other side of the road at what is now known as **Upper Bankhead.** Just before the Upper Bankhead turnoff, the foundation of the Holy Trinity Church can be seen on the side of the hill to the right. Not much remains of Upper Bankhead. It is now a day-use area with picnic tables, kitchen shelters, and firewood. Through the meadow to the west of here are some large slag heaps, concealed mine entrances, and various stone foundations.

Lake Minnewanka

Minnewanka (Lake of the Water Spirit) is the largest body of water in Banff National Park. Mount Inglismaldie (2,964 m/9,720 ft) and the Fairholme Range form an imposing backdrop. The reservoir was first constructed in 1912, and additional dams were built in 1922 and 1941 to supply hydroelectric power to Banff. Even if you don't feel up to an energetic hike, it's worth parking at the facility area and going for a short walk along the lakeshore. You'll pass a concession selling snacks and drinks, then the tour-boat dock, before entering an area of picnic tables and covered cooking shelters—the perfect place for a picnic. Children will love exploring the rocky shoreline and stony beaches in this area, but you should continue farther around the lake, if only to escape the crowds. **Lake Minnewanka Boat Tours** (403/762-3473) has a 90-minute cruise to the far reaches of the lake, passing the Devil's Gap formation. It departs from the dock mid-May to the end of September 3–5 times daily (first sailing is 10:30 A.M. and costs adult $37, child $18). **Brewster** (403/762-6767) offers this cruise combined with a bus tour from Banff for $48 per person. Easy walking trails lead along the western shore. The lake is great for fishing (lake trout to 15 kg/33 lb) and is the only one in the park where motorboats are allowed.

dawn at the Lake Minnewanka marina

Lake Minnewanka Boat Tours rents aluminum boats with small outboard engines and represents local fishing guides.

From Lake Minnewanka the road continues along the reservoir wall, passing a plaque commemorating the Palliser Expedition. You'll often have to slow down along this stretch of road for bighorn sheep. The road then descends to **Two Jack Lake** and a small day-use area. Take the turn-off to **Johnson Lake** to access a lakeside trail, good swimming, and picnic facilities with views across to Mount Rundle.

BOW VALLEY PARKWAY

Two roads link Banff to Lake Louise. The TransCanada Highway is the quicker route, more popular with through traffic. The other is the more scenic 51-kilometer (32-mi) Bow Valley Parkway, which branches off the Trans-Canada Highway five kilometers (3.1 mi) west of Banff. Cyclists will appreciate this road's two long, divided sections and low speed limit (60 kph/37 mph). Along this route are several impressive viewpoints, interpretive displays,

picnic areas, good hiking, great opportunities for viewing wildlife, a hostel, three lodges, campgrounds, and one of the park's best restaurants, The Bistro (see *Accommodations* and *Food* later in this chapter). Between March and late June, the southern end of the parkway (as far north as Johnston Canyon) is closed daily 6 P.M.–9 A.M. for the protection of wildlife.

As you enter the parkway, you pass the quiet, creekside **Fireside** picnic area, where an interpretive display describes how the Bow Valley was formed. **Muleshoe** wetland consists of oxbow lakes that were formed when the Bow River changed its course and abandoned its meanders for a more direct path. Across the parkway is a one-kilometer (0.6-mi) trail that climbs to a viewpoint overlooking the valley. (The slope around this trail is infested with wood ticks during late spring/early summer, so be sure to check yourself carefully after hiking in this area.) Beyond Muleshoe, the road inexplicably divides for a few car lengths. A large white spruce stood on the island until it blew down in 1984. The story goes that while the road was being constructed, a surly foreman was asleep in the shade of the tree and, not daring to rouse him, workers cleared the roadway around him. The road then passes through particularly hilly terrain, part of a massive rockslide that occurred approximately 8,000 years ago.

Continuing down the parkway you'll pass the following sights.

Johnston Canyon

Johnston Creek drops over a series of spectacular waterfalls here, deep within the chasm it has carved into the limestone bedrock. The canyon is not nearly as deep as Maligne Canyon in Jasper National Park—30 meters (100 ft) at its deepest, compared to 50 meters (165 ft) at Maligne—but the catwalk that leads to the lower falls has been built through the depths of the canyon rather than along its lip, making it seem just as spectacular. The lower falls are one kilometer (0.6 mi) from Johnston Canyon Resort, while the equally spectacular upper falls are a further 1.6 kilometer (one mi)

© ANDREW HEMPSTEAD

Upper Falls, Johnston Canyon

but he was known to everyone as Joe. In 1887, when Silver City came under the jurisdiction of the National Parks Service, Joe was allowed to remain. He did so and was friendly to everyone, including Stoney Indians, Father Albert Lacombe (who occasionally stopped by), well-known Banff guide Tom Wilson, and of course to the animals who grazed around his cabin. By 1926, he was unable to trap or hunt due to failing eyesight, and many people tried to persuade him to leave. It wasn't until 1937 that he finally moved to a Calgary retirement home, where he died soon after.

Castle Mountain to Lake Louise

After you leave the former site of Silver City, the aptly named Castle Mountain comes into view. It's one of the park's most recognizable peaks and most interesting geographical features. The mountain consists of very old rock (approximately 500 million years old) sitting atop much younger rock (a mere 200 million years old). This unusual situation occurred as the mountains were forced upward by pressure below the earth's surface, thrusting the older rock up and over the younger rock in places.

The road skirts the base of the mountain, passes Castle Mountain Village (which has gas, food, and accommodations), and climbs a small hill to Storm Mountain Viewpoint, which provides more stunning views and a picnic area. The next commercial facility is **Baker Creek Chalets and Bistro,** an excellent spot for a meal. Then it's on to another viewpoint at Morant's Curve, from where Temple Mountain is visible. After passing another picnic area and a chunk of Precambrian shield, the road rejoins the TransCanada Highway at Lake Louise.

upstream. Beyond this point are the **Ink Pots,** mineral springs whose sediments reflect sunlight, producing a brilliant aqua color. While in the canyon, look for nesting great gray owls and black swifts.

Silver City

At the west end of **Moose Meadows,** a small plaque marks the site of Silver City. At its peak this boomtown had a population of 2,000, making it bigger than Calgary at the time. During its heady days, five mines were operating, extracting not silver but ore rich in copper and lead. The town had a half-dozen hotels, four or five stores, two real-estate offices, and a station on the transcontinental rail line when its demise began. Two men, named Patton and Pettigrew, salted their mine with gold and silver ore to attract investors. After selling 2,000 shares at $5 each, they vanished, leaving investors with a useless mine. Investment in the town ceased, mines closed, and the people left. Only one man refused to leave. His name was James Smith,

HIKING

After experiencing the international thrills of Banff Avenue, many people want to see the *real* Banff—the reason that millions of visitors flock here, thousands take low-paying jobs just to stay here, and those who become severely addicted cut ties with the outside world, raise families, and live happily ever

after here. Although many landmarks can be seen from the roadside, to really experience the park's personality you'll need to go for a hike. One of the best things about Banff's approximately 80 hiking trails is the variety. From short interpretive walks originating in town to easy hikes rewarded by spectacular vistas to a myriad of overnight backcountry opportunities, Banff's trails offer something for everyone. Before attempting any hikes, however, you should visit the **Banff Visitor Centre** (224 Banff Ave., 403/762-1550, mid-June–Aug. daily 8 A.M.–8 P.M., mid-May–mid-June and Sept. daily 8 A.M.–6 P.M., the rest of the year daily 9 A.M.–5 P.M.), where staff can advise you on the condition of trails and closures and a small gift store sells hiking books, including the recommended *Canadian Rockies Trail Guide.*

Most of the trails listed below start in or near town; the last four start out of town, on the way toward Lake Louise.

A trail along the shoreline of Lake Minnewanka requires a crossing of Stewart Canyon.

Fenland

- Length: Two kilometers/1.2 miles (30 minutes) round-trip

- Elevation gain: None

- Rating: Easy

- Trailhead: Forty Mile Creek Picnic Area, Mount Norquay Road, 300 meters (0.2 mi) north of the rail crossing

If you've just arrived in town, this short interpretive trail provides an excellent introduction to the Bow Valley ecosystem. A brochure, available at the trailhead, explains the various stages in the transition between wetland and floodplain spruce forest, visible as you progress around the loop. This fen environment is prime habitat for many species of birds. The work of beavers can be seen along the trail, and elk are here during winter. This trail is also a popular shortcut for joggers and cyclists heading for Vermilion Lakes.

Tunnel Mountain

- Length: 2.3 kilometers/1.4 miles (30–60 minutes) one-way

- Elevation gain: 300 meters/990 feet

- Rating: Easy/moderate

- Trailhead: St. Julien Road, 350 meters (0.2 mi) south of Wolf Street

Accessible from town, this short hike is an easy climb to one of the park's lower peaks. It ascends the western flank of Tunnel Mountain through a forest of lodgepole pine, switchbacking past some viewpoints before reaching a ridge just below the summit. Here the trail turns northward, climbing through a forest of Douglas fir to the summit and views across town to Vermilion Lakes.

Bow River/Hoodoos

- Length: 4.8 kilometers/3 miles (60–90 minutes) one-way

- Elevation gain: Minimal

- Rating: Easy

SUNSHINE MEADOWS

Sunshine Meadows, straddling the Continental Divide, is a unique and beautiful region of the Canadian Rockies. It's best known as home to Sunshine Village, a self-contained alpine resort accessible only by gondola from the valley floor. But for a few short months each summer, the area is clear of snow and becomes a wonderland for hiking. Large amounts of precipitation create a lush cover of vegetation – over 300 species of wildflowers alone have been recorded here.

From Sunshine Village, trails radiate across the alpine meadow, which is covered in a colorful carpet of fireweed, glacier lilies, mountain avens, white mountain heather, and forget-me-nots (the meadows are in full bloom late July to mid-August). The most popular destination is **Rock Isle Lake,** an easy 2.5-kilometer (1.6-mi) jaunt from the upper village that crosses the Continental Divide while only gaining 100 meters (330 ft) of elevation. Mount Assiniboine (3,618 m/11,870 ft), known as the "Matterhorn of the Rockies," is easily distinguished to the southeast. Various viewpoints punctuate the descent to an observation point overlooking the lake. From here, options include a loop around Larix Lake and a traverse along Standish Ridge.

If the weather is cooperating, it won't matter which direction you head (so long as it's along a formed trail); you'll experience the Canadian Rockies in all their glory.

It's possible to walk the six-kilometer (3.7-mi) restricted-access road up to the meadows, but a more practical alternative is to take the Sunshine Meadows Alpine Shuttle along a road closed to public traffic. This service is operated by **White Mountain Adventures** (403/678-4099 or 800/408-0005, www.white mountainadventures.com). Through a June–September season, buses depart Banff (daily at 8:30 A.M., adult $43, child $23 round-trip) and the Sunshine Village parking lot (daily on the hour 9 A.M.–5 P.M., adult $23, child $13 round-trip). The shuttle returns from the meadows 2:30–5:30 P.M., with the 2:30 P.M. and 5:30 P.M. departures continuing to Banff. For $25 extra, you can explore the meadows with a naturalist, who will lead you through all the highlights. Advance reservations are required for both the bus and guided hike. To get to the base of the gondola from Banff, follow the TransCanada Highway nine kilometers (5.6 mi) west to Sunshine Village Road, which continues a similar distance along Healy Creek to the Sunshine Village parking lot.

© ANDREW HEMPSTEAD

Rock Isle Lake

• Trailhead: Surprise Corner, Tunnel Mountain Drive

From a viewpoint famous for the Fairmont Banff Springs outlook, the trail descends to the Bow River, passing under the sheer east face of Tunnel Mountain. It then follows the river a short distance before climbing into a meadow where deer and elk often graze. From this perspective the north face of Mount Rundle is particularly imposing. As the trail climbs you'll hear the traffic on Tunnel Mountain Road long before you see it. The trail ends at hoodoos, strange limestone-and-gravel columns jutting mysteriously out of the forest. An alternative to returning the same way is to catch the **Banff Transit** bus from Tunnel Mountain Campgrounds. It leaves every half hour ($2).

Sundance Canyon

• Length: 4.4 kilometers/2.7 miles (90 minutes) one-way

• Elevation gain: 100 meters/330 feet

• Rating: Easy

• Trailhead: Cave and Basin National Historic Site

Sundance Canyon is a rewarding destination across the river from downtown. Unfortunately the first three kilometers (1.9 mi) are along a paved road closed to traffic (but not bikes) and hard on your soles. Occasional glimpses of the Sawback Range are afforded by breaks in the forest. The road ends at a shaded picnic area from where the 2.4-kilometer (1.5-mi) Sundance Loop begins. Sundance Creek was once a larger river whose upper drainage basin was diverted by glacial action. Its powerful waters have eroded into the soft bedrock, forming a spectacular overhanging canyon whose bed is strewn with large boulders that have tumbled in.

Cascade Amphitheatre

• Length: 6.6 kilometers/4.1 miles (2–3 hours) one-way

• Elevation gain: 610 meters/2,000 feet

• Rating: Moderate/difficult

• Trailhead: Day lodge, top of Mount Norquay Road, six kilometers (3.7 mi) from town

This hike into the enormous cirque and the subalpine meadows directly behind Cascade Mountain is one of the most demanding around Banff. Starting from the day lodge, the trail skirts the base of a number of ski lifts and follows an old road to the floor of Forty Mile Valley. Keep right at all trail junctions. One kilometer (0.6 mi) after crossing Forty Mile Creek, the trail begins switchbacking up the western flank of Cascade Mountain through a forest of lodgepole pine. Along the way are breathtaking views of Mount Louis's sheer east face. After the trail levels off it enters a magnificent U-shaped valley and the amphitheater begins to define itself. The trail becomes indistinct in the subalpine meadow, which is carpeted in colorful wildflowers during summer. Farther up the valley, vegetation thins out as boulder-strewn talus slopes cover the ground. If you sit still long enough on these rocks, marmots and pikas will slowly appear, emitting shrill whistles before disappearing again.

Cory Pass

• Length: 5.8 kilometers/3.6 miles (2.5 hours) one-way

• Elevation gain: 920 meters/3,020 feet

• Rating: Moderate/difficult

• Trailhead: Fireside Picnic Area, Banff end of the Bow Valley Parkway

This strenuous hike has a rewarding objective—a magnificent view of dogtoothed Mount Louis. The towering slab of limestone rises more than 500 meters (1,640 ft) from the valley below. Just over one kilometer (0.6 mi) from the trailhead, the trail divides. The left fork climbs steeply across an open slope to an uneven ridge that it follows before ascending yet another steep slope to Cory Pass—a wild, windy, desolate area surrounded in jagged peaks dominated by Mount Louis. An alternative to returning along the same trail is continuing down into Gargoyle

Valley, following the base of Mount Edith before ascending to Edith Pass and returning to the junction one kilometer (0.6 mi) from the picnic area. Total distance for this trip is 13 kilometers (eight mi), a long day considering the steep climbs and descents involved.

◖ Bourgeau Lake

- Length: 7.6 kilometers/4.7 miles (2.5 hours) one-way

- Elevation gain: 730 meters/2,400 feet

- Rating: Moderate

- Trailhead: Signposted parking lot, Trans-Canada Highway, three kilometers (1.9 mi) west of Sunshine Village Junction

This trail follows Wolverine Creek to a small subalpine lake nestled at the base of an impressive limestone amphitheater. Although the trail is moderately steep, plenty of distractions along the way are worthy of a stop (and rest). Across the Bow Valley, the Sawback Range is easy to distinguish. As the forest of lodgepole pine turns to spruce, the trail passes under the cliffs of Mount Bourgeau and crosses Wolverine Creek (below a spot where it tumbles photogenically over exposed bedrock). After strenuous switchbacks, the trail climbs into the cirque containing Bourgeau Lake. As you continue around the lake's rocky shore, you'll hear the colonies of noisy pikas, even if you don't see them.

Rockbound Lake

- Length: 8.4 kilometers/5.2 miles (2.5 hours) one-way

- Elevation gain: 760 meters/2,500 feet

- Rating: Moderate/difficult

- Trailhead: Castle Mountain Junction, Bow Valley Parkway, 30 kilometers (18.6 mi) west of Banff

This strenuous hike leads to a delightful little body of water tucked behind Castle Mountain. For the first five kilometers (3.1 mi) the trail follows an old fire road along the south-ern flanks of Castle Mountain. Early in the season or after heavy rain, this section can be boggy. Glimpses of surrounding peaks ease the pain of the steady climb as the trail narrows. After eight kilometers (five mi) you'll come to Tower Lake, backed by grassed slopes, which the trail skirts to the right before climbing a steep slope. From the ridge, Rockbound Lake comes into view and the reason for its name immediately becomes apparent. A scramble up any of the nearby slopes will reward you with good views.

Castle Lookout

- Length: 3.7 kilometers/2.3 miles (90 minutes) one-way

- Elevation gain: 520 meters/1,700 feet

- Rating: Moderate

- Trailhead: Lake Louise, four kilometers (2.5 mi) from TransCanada Highway

However you travel through the Bow Valley, you can't help but be impressed by Castle Mountain rising proudly from the forest. This trail takes you above the tree line on the mountain's west face. From the Bow Valley Parkway, the trail follows a wide pathway for 1.5 kilometers (0.9 mi) to an abandoned cabin in a forest of lodgepole pine and spruce. It then becomes narrower and steeper, switchbacking through a meadow before climbing through a narrow band of rock and leveling off near the lookout site. Magnificent panoramas of the Bow Valley spread out before you in both directions. Storm Mountain can be seen directly across the valley.

OTHER RECREATION AND ENTERTAINMENT
Mountain Biking

Whether you have your own bike or you rent one from the many bicycle shops in town, cycling in the park is for everyone. Loop roads through the golf course and past Lake Minnewanka are popular, as is the Bow Valley Parkway, while Mount Norquay Road is a steep grunt favored by local riders for the exercise.

Several routes into the backcountry have been designated as mountain bike trails. These include Sundance (3.7 km/2.3 mi one-way), Rundle Riverside to Canmore (15 km/9.3 mi one-way), and Spray River Loop (via Goat Creek, 48 km/30 mi round-trip). Before heading into the backcountry, pick up the *Trail Bicycling Guide* from the Banff Visitor Centre.

Abominable (229 Wolf St., 403/762-5065), **Bactrax** (225 Bear St., 403/762-8177), and **Banff Adventures Unlimited** (211 Bear St., 403/762-4554) rent front- and full-suspension mountain bikes for $7–12 per hour and $25–48 per day. Rates include a helmet, lock, and biking map. Bactrax also offers mountain-bike tours, including to Vermilion Lakes and along Sundance Canyon. Tours cost $20 per person per hour.

Horseback Riding

Jim and Bill Brewster led Banff's first paying guests into the backcountry on horseback more than 100 years ago. Today visitors are still able to enjoy the park on this traditional form of transportation. **Warner Guiding & Outfitting** (www.horseback.com) offers a great variety of trips. Their main office is downtown in the **Trail Rider Store** (132 Banff Ave., 403/762-4551), although trips depart from either **Martin's Stables** (403/762-2832), behind the recreation grounds on Birch Avenue, or **Banff Springs Corral** (403/762-2848), along Spray Avenue. From Martin's Stables, the one-hour trip departs on the hour daily 9 A.M.–6 P.M. and takes in a pleasant circuit around the Marsh Loop ($34). A two-hour trip around the Sundance Loop ($62) departs four times daily. Other longer trips include the three-hour Mountain Morning Breakfast Ride, featuring a hearty breakfast along the trail (departs 9 A.M., adult $88, child $68); Explorer Day Ride, a seven-hour ride up the lower slopes of Sulphur Mountain (departs 9 A.M., $162); and the Evening Steak Fry, a three-hour ride with a suitably Western steak-and-baked-bean dinner along the trail (departs 5 P.M., adult $88, child $68). For those not comfortable on horseback, the morning and evening trips come with the

option to ride in a wagon ($78 per person). In addition to day trips, Warner runs a variety of overnight rides that stay in backcountry lodges or tent camps. The main accommodation is Sundance Lodge, an easy three-hour ride from Banff, which has 10 rooms, a large living area, and even hot showers. The shortest option is an overnight trip departing Saturday through summer for $464 per person inclusive of meals. A three-day trip is $696.

White-Water Rafting and Canoeing

Anyone looking for white-water-rafting action will want to run the **Kicking Horse River,** which flows down the western slopes of the Canadian Rockies into British Columbia. Many operators provide transportation from Banff and Lake Louise. **Rocky Mountain Raft Tours** (403/762-3632) offers one-hour ($32) and two-hour ($50) float trips down the Bow River, beginning just below Bow Falls and ending along the golf course loop road. No rapids are involved, so you'll stay dry.

On a quiet stretch of the Bow River, at the north end of Wolf Street, **Blue Canoe** (403/762-3632 or 403/760-5007, May–Sept. daily 9 A.M.–9 P.M.) rents canoes for use on the river from where it's an easy paddle upstream to the Vermilion Lakes and Forty Mile Creek; $25 one hour, $40 two hours, or $50 for a full day of paddling.

Fishing and Boating

The finest fishing in the park is in Lake Minnewanka, where lake trout as large as 15 kilograms (33 lb) have been caught. One way to ensure a good catch is through **Lake Minnewanka Boat Tours** (403/762-3473), which offers fishing trips in a heated cabin cruiser; trolling and downrigging are preferred methods of fishing the lake. A half-day's fishing (3.5 hours) is $275 for one or two persons. The company also rents small aluminum fishing boats with outboard motors for $40 for the first hour, then $16 for every extra hour to a maximum of $120 per day.

The most experienced of local fishing

guides is Dan Bell of **Upper Bow Fly Fishing** (403/760-7668, www.upperbowflyfishing .com). Bell has been fishing and guiding in the Banff area for more than 20 years and has represented Canada as a member of the National Fly-Fishing Team on multiple occasions. His purpose-built drift boats are perfect for chasing brown trout along the Bow River downstream from Banff, with regular stops made for fly-casting from the banks. He'll also take interested anglers to high alpine lakes chasing cutthroat trout. Rates start at $240 per person for a half day on the river and include guiding, gear, and lessons.

Before fishing anywhere in the park you need a national park fishing license ($10 per week, $35 per year), available from the Banff and Lake Louise visitors centers and sport shops throughout the park.

Golf

Spread out along the Bow River below Mount Rundle is the **Banff Springs Golf Course,** considered one of the world's most scenic. The course dates to 1928 and was designed by famed Canadian architect Stanley Thompson. An additional nine holes opened in 1989. Not only is the course breathtakingly beautiful, but it's also challenging for all levels of golfers. Pick up a copy of the book *The World's Greatest Golf Holes,* and you'll see a picture of the fourth hole on the Rundle Nine. It's a par three, over Devil's Cauldron 70 meters (230 ft) below, to a small green backed by the sheer face of Mount Rundle rising vertically more than 1,000 meters (3,280 ft) above the putting surface. Another unique feature of the course is the abundance of wildlife. There's always the chance of seeing elk feeding on the fairways, or coyotes, deer, or black bears scurrying across in front of you as you putt. Greens fees (including cart and driving-range privileges) are $200 for the main course, discounted to $125 in May and from late September to early October. The Tunnel 9 offers the same spectacular challenges as Thompson's original layout but lacks the history; nine holes cost $40–60, depending on the season. Free shuttle

Banff Springs Golf Course

© ANDREW HEMPSTEAD

buses run from the Fairmont Banff Springs to the clubhouse. There you'll find club rentals ($50–65), putting greens, a driving range, a pro shop, two chipping greens (one hidden up in the trees with surrounding bunkers), and a restaurant with a stunning wraparound deck. Booking tee times well in advance is essential; call 403/762-6801.

Tours

The Whyte Museum hosts interesting walking tours through summer. The most popular of these is the **Historic Banff Walk**, which departs from the museum daily at 2:30 P.M., taking around 90 minutes to traverse the historic parts of downtown; $7 per person. The **Heritage Homes Tour** allows an opportunity for visitors to take a closer look at the historic residences located in the trees behind the museum, including that of Peter and Catharine Whyte. This tour departs in summer daily at 2:30 P.M. and also costs $7 per person. Around 40 minutes is spent visiting the home of a prominent Banff family on the Luxton Home & Garden Tour. Departures are summer only, daily at 1:30 P.M.; $7.

Brewster (403/762-6767 or 877/791-5500, www.brewster.ca) is the dominant tour company in the area. The three-hour Discover Banff bus tour takes in downtown Banff, Tunnel Mountain Drive, the hoodoos, the Cave and Basin, and Banff Gondola (gondola fare included). This tour runs in summer only and departs from the bus depot daily at 8:30 A.M.; call for hotel pickup times. Adult fare is $68, children half price. Brewster also runs several other tours. A four-hour tour to Lake Louise departs select Banff hotels daily; $55. In winter this tour departs Tuesday and Friday mornings, runs five hours, and includes Banff sights; $53. During summer, the company also offers tours from Banff to Lake Minnewanka ($52, includes two-hour boat cruise), and Columbia Icefield ($100, Ice Explorer extra).

Discover Banff Tours (Sundance Mall, 215 Banff Ave., 403/760-5007 or 877/565-9372, www.banfftours.com) is a smaller company, with smaller buses and more personalized service. Its tour routes are similar to Brewster's: a three-hour Discover Banff tour visits Lake Minnewanka, the Cave and Basin, the Fairmont Banff Springs, and the hoodoos for $49 adults, $27 children; a full-day trip to the Columbia Icefield is $132 adults, $34 children; and a two-hour Evening Wildlife Safari is $39 adults, $22 children. This company offers a good selection of other tours throughout the year, including a wintertime Icewalk in frozen Johnston Canyon (adult $59, child $30).

Swimming and Fitness Centers

Many of Banff's bigger hotels have fitness rooms, and some have indoor pools. A popular place to swim and work out is in the **Sally Borden Fitness & Recreation Facility** (Banff Centre, St. Julien Road, 403/762-6450, daily 6 A.M.–11 P.M.), which holds a wide range of fitness facilities, climbing gym, squash courts, a 25-meter-long heated pool, a wading pool, and a hot tub. General admission is $9.50, or pay $4.25 to swim only. Go to www.banffcentre .ca/sbb for a schedule.

The **Banff Upper Hot Springs** (Mountain Ave., 403/762-1515, daily 10 A.M.–10 P.M., $7.50) were developed in 1901 as an alternative to those at the Cave and Basin, and are still run by Parks Canada. Most folks come for a relaxing soak, but massages are available for an additional charge.

Banff's only water slide is in the **Douglas Fir Resort** (Tunnel Mountain Dr., 403/762-5591, Mon.–Fri. 4–9:30 P.M., Sat.–Sun. 10 A.M.–9:30 P.M.). The two slides are indoors, and the admission price of $7.50 (free for kids younger than age five) includes use of a hot tub and exercise room.

Spas

The luxurious **Willow Stream** spa facility in the Fairmont Banff Springs (403/762-2211, daily 6 A.M.–10 P.M.) is the place to pamper yourself. Opened in 1995 at a cost of $12 million, it sprawls over two levels and 3,000 square meters (0.7 acres) of a private corner of the hotel. The epicenter of the facility is a circular mineral pool capped by a high glass-topped

ceiling and ringed by floor-to-ceiling windows on one side and on the other by hot tubs fed by cascading waterfalls of varying temperatures. Other features include outdoor saltwater hot tubs, private solariums, steam rooms, luxurious bathrooms, a café featuring light meals, and separate male and female lounges complete with fireplaces and complimentary drinks and snacks. Numerous other services are offered, including facials, body wraps, massage therapy, salon services, and hydrotherapy. Entry to Willow Stream is included in some package rates for guests at the hotel. Admission is $59 per day for hotel guests, which includes the use of a locker and spa attire, with almost 100 services available at additional cost (most of these include general admission, so, for example, you can spend the day at Willow Stream and receive a one-hour massage for $145).

Pleiades Massage & Spa is located in the Banff Upper Hot Springs complex. See *Banff Upper Hot Springs* earlier in this chapter for more information.

Bowling and Cinema

Fairmont Banff Springs (403/762-2211) has a four-lane, five-pin bowling center; games are $4.25 per person. The **Lux Cinema Centre** (229 Bear St., 403/762-8595) screens new releases for $12 ($8 on Tuesday).

WINTER RECREATION

Banff National Park transforms itself into a winter playground covered in an impossibly white blanket of snow November until May. Of Alberta's six major ski areas, three are in Banff National Park. Apart from an abundance of snow, the resorts have something else in common—spectacular views—which alone are worth the price of a lift ticket. If skiing or snowboarding aren't your thing, you'll still always find something to do: cross-country skiing, ice-skating, snowshoeing, or just relaxing. Crowds are nonexistent, and hotels reduce rates by up to 70 percent (except Christmas holidays), which is reason enough to venture into the mountains. Lift and lodging packages begin at $80 per person.

Ski Norquay

Visible from town, the steep eastern slopes of Mount Norquay are home to a small resort (403/762-4421, www.banffnorquay.com) with a big reputation. Since Canada's first chairlift was installed in 1948, the resort has had an experts-only reputation, mainly because of terrain serviced by the North American Chair (including the famous double-black-diamond Upper Lone Pine run), but out of sight from the valley floor is a variety of intermediate terrain that has made the resort a favorite with shredders and cruisers alike. Snowboarders congregate at a half-pipe and terrain park. A magnificent post-and-beam day lodge nestled below the main runs is surrounded on one side by a wide deck that catches the afternoon sun while inside is a cafeteria, restaurant, and bar. Lift tickets are adult $52, youth and senior $40, child $17; lift, lesson, and rental packages cost about the same. Hourly passes provide some flexibility (two hours $26, three hours $30, etc.). A few runs are lit for night skiing and boarding on Friday evening; $24 adults, $22 seniors, $12 children. A shuttle bus makes pickups from Banff hotels for the short six-kilometer (3.7-mi) ride up to the resort; $6.

Sunshine Village

The skiing and boarding at Sunshine (403/762-6500 or 877/542-2633, www.skibanff.com) has lots going for it—over six meters (20 ft) of snow annually (no need for snowmaking up here), wide-open bowls, a season stretching for nearly 200 days, skiing and boarding in two provinces, and the only slope-side accommodations in the park. A gondola whisks skiers and snowboarders six kilometers (3.7 mi) from the valley floor to the alpine village while eight high-speed quads (including the world's fastest) constructed in the last decade have opened up an amazing amount of terrain. Some of Canada's steepest lift-served runs—including Delirium Dive and the Wild West—require skiers and boarders to be equipped with a transceiver, shovel, probe, and partner, but you'll have bragging rights that night at the bar (especially if you've descended the Delirum Dive's Bre-X line).

© ANDREW HEMPSTEAD

uncrowded slopes at Sunshine Village

Aside from Delirium Dive, the area is best known for its excellent beginner and intermediate terrain, which covers 60 percent of the mountain. The total vertical rise is 1,070 meters (3,510 ft) and the longest run (down to the lower parking lot) is eight kilometers (five mi). Day passes are adult $65, senior $54, youth $50, child $25, and those younger than six ride free. Two days of lift access and one nights' lodging at slope-side Sunshine Inn cost $160 per person in high season—an excellent deal. The inn has a restaurant, lounge, game room, and large outdoor hot tub. Transportation from Banff, Canmore, or Lake Louise to the resort is $12 round-trip; check the website or inquire at major hotels for the timetable.

Rentals and Sales

Each resort has ski and snowboard rental and sales facilities, but getting your gear down in town is often easier. **Abominable Ski & Sportswear** (229 Banff Ave., 403/762-2905) and **Monod Sports** (129 Banff Ave., 403/762-4571) have been synonymous with Banff and

the ski industry for decades, and while the **Rude Boys Snowboard Shop** (downstairs in the Sundance Mall, 215 Banff Ave., 403/762-8480) has only been around since the 1980s, it is *the* snowboarder hangout. Other shops with sales and rentals include **Banff Springs Ski & Mountain Sports** (Fairmont Banff Springs, 405 Spray Ave., 403/762-5333), **Mountain Magic Equipment** (224 Bear St., 403/762-2591), **Ski Hub** (119 Banff Ave., 403/762-4754), **Ski Stop** (203 Bear St., 403/760-1650), and **Snow Tips** (225 Bear St., 403/762-8177). Basic packages—skis, poles, and boots—are $25–30 per day, while high-performance packages range $35–50. Snowboards and boots rent for $25–50 per day.

Cross-Country Skiing

No better way of experiencing the park's winter delights exists than skiing through the landscape on cross-country skis. Many summer hiking trails are groomed for winter travel. The most popular areas are Johnson Lake, Golf Course Road, Spray River, Sundance Canyon,

on Lake Louise, Moraine Lake Road, and in Skoki Valley at the back of Lake Louise Ski Area. The booklet *Cross-Country Skiing—Nordic Trails in Banff National Park* is available for $1 from the Banff and Lake Louise visitors centers. Weather forecasts (403/762-2088) and avalanche hazard reports (403/762-1460) are posted at both centers.

Rental packages are available from **Snow Tips** (225 Bear St., 403/762-8177) and **Mountain Magic Equipment** (224 Bear St., 403/762-2591). Expect to pay $15–25 per day. **White Mountain Adventures** (403/678-4099 or 800/408-0005) offers lessons for $50 per person.

Ice-Skating

Rinks are located on the **Bow River** along Bow Street, and on the golf-course side of the **Fairmont Banff Springs.** The latter rink is lit after dark, and a raging fire is built beside it— the perfect place to enjoy a hot chocolate. Early in the season (check conditions first), skating is possible on **Vermilion Lakes** and **Johnson Lake.** Rent skates from **Banff Springs Ski & Mountain Sports** (Fairmont Banff Springs, 403/762-5333) for $5 per hour.

Sleigh Rides

Warner Guiding and Outfitting (403/762-4551) offers sleigh rides on the frozen Bow River throughout winter ($25 per person).

NIGHTLIFE

Like resort towns around the world, Banff has a deserved reputation as a party town, especially among seasonal workers, the après-ski crowd, and young Calgarians. Crowds seem to spread out, with no particular bar being more popular than another or being a place where you can mingle with fellow travelers. Given the location and vacation vibe, drink prices are as high as you may expect, with attitude thrown in for free.

Banff is a nonsmoking town; smoking is limited to outdoor areas. Also note that the RCMP (police) patrol Banff all night, promptly arresting anyone who even looks like trouble, including anyone drunk or drinking on the streets.

Bars

Wild Bill's (upstairs at 201 Banff Ave., 403/762-0333) is named for Banff guide Bill Peyto and is truly legendary. This frontier-style venue attracts the biggest and best bands of any Banff venue, with bookings that vary from local faves to washed-up rockers such as Nazareth; as a general rule, expect alternative music or underground country early in the week and better-known rock or pop Thursday–Sunday. Across the road, the **Maple Leaf** (137 Banff Ave., 403/760-7680) has a stylish space set aside as a bar. The **Elk & Oarsman** (119 Banff Ave., 403/762-4616) serves up beer and more in a clean, casual atmosphere that is as friendly as it gets in Banff. Across the road from Wild Bill's is the **Rose and Crown** (202 Banff Ave., 403/762-2121), serving British beers and hearty pub fare. It also features a rooftop patio and rock 'n' roll bands a few nights a week, but there's not much room for dancing. Also down the main drag is **Tommy's** (120 Banff Ave., 403/762-8888), a perennial favorite for young seasonal workers and those who once were and now consider themselves locals.

Away from busy Banff Avenue is **Melissa's** (218 Lynx St., 403/762-5776), which is a long-time favorite drinking hole for locals. It has a small outdoor patio, a long evening happy hour, a pool table, and multiple TVs. From "Mel's," cut down Bear Street to reach **Saltlik** (221 Bear St., 403/762-2467), best known as an upscale (and upstairs) steakhouse. At street level, the lounge opens to a street-side patio. Around the corner, the **St. James Gate Olde Irish Pub** (207 Wolf St., 403/762-9355) is a large Irish-style bar with a reputation for excellent British-style meals and occasional appearances by Celtic bands.

Hotel Hangouts

Many Banff hotels have lounges open to guests and nonguests alike. They are generally quieter than the bars listed previously and often offer abbreviated menus from adjacent restaurants. For Old World atmosphere, nothing in town comes close to matching the regal atmosphere of the **Sir William Wallace Room,** in

the Fairmont Banff Springs (403/762-2211, daily 4 P.M.–midnight). Also in the hotel is the **Rundle Lounge** (Fairmont Banff Springs, 403/762-2211, daily noon–1 A.M.), an open space with views extending to the golf course. Below the hotel is the **Waldhaus Pub** (Fairmont Banff Springs, 403/762-2211, summer daily from 4 P.M.). It has the best deck in town, but it's mainly the haunt of locals coming off the golf course or savvy visitors (such as those who've read this book).

Downtown, the **Mount Royal Hotel** (corner of Banff Ave. and Caribou St., 403/762-3331) has a small lounge off the lobby, while below, accessed from farther up Banff Avenue, is the **Buffalo Paddock** (138 Banff Ave., 403/762-3331), with pool tables. At the opposite end of the style scale is the lounge in the **Voyager Inn** (555 Banff Ave., 403/762-3301), which is worth listing for the fact that it has the cheapest beer in town and drink specials every night (and a liquor store with cheaper prices than downtown). Just past the Voyager Inn is **Bumpers** (603 Banff Ave., 403/762-2622), a steakhouse with a small bar and pool table in a cozy upstairs loft.

Nightclubs

Banff has two nightclubs. Cavernous **Aurora** (downstairs in the Clock Tower Mall at 110 Banff Ave., 403/760-5300) was formerly an infamous gathering place known as Silver City, but renovations in the late 1990s added some class to Banff's clubbing scene. It's respectable early in the evening but becomes one obnoxiously loud, overpriced smoky pickup joint after midnight. The other option is **HooDoos** (at 137 Banff Ave. but enter from Caribou St., 403/762-8434), a stylish setup with similar city-like surroundings.

FESTIVALS AND EVENTS
Spring

Most of the major spring events take place at local alpine resorts, including a variety of snowboard competitions that are great fun for spectators. One long-running spring event is the **Slush Cup,** which takes place at Sunshine

Village in late May. Events include kamikaze skiers and boarders who attempt to jump an ice-cold pit of water.

During the second week of June, the **Banff Television Festival** (403/678-9260, www.bannftvfest.com) attracts the world's best television directors, producers, writers, and even actors for meetings, workshops, and awards, with many show screenings open to the public.

Summer

Summer is a time of hiking and camping, so festivals are few and far between. The main event is the **Banff Arts Festival** (403/762-6214 or 800/413-8368, www.banffcentre.ca), a three-week (mid-July–early Aug.) extravaganza presented by professional artists studying at the Banff Centre. They perform dance, drama, opera, and jazz for the public at locations around town.

On July 1, Banff celebrates **Canada Day** with a pancake breakfast, a parade down Banff Avenue, and an afternoon of fun and frivolity in Central Park that includes events such as a stupid-pet-tricks competition.

Each summer the national park staff presents an extensive **Park Interpretive Program** at locations in town and throughout the park, including downstairs in the visitors center daily at 8:30 P.M. All programs are free and include guided hikes, nature tours, slide shows, campfire talks, and lectures. For details, consult *The Mountain Guide* available at the Banff Visitor Centre (403/762-1550), or look for postings on campground bulletin boards.

Fall

Fall is the park's quietest season, but busiest in terms of festivals and events. First of the fall events, on the last Saturday in September, **Melissa's Road Race** (www.melissas roadrace.ca) attracts more than 2,000 runners (the race sells out months in advance) in 10- and 22-kilometer races. The **International Banff Springs Wine and Food Festival** is hosted by the Fairmont Banff Springs at the end of October. To encourage tourism during the quietest time of the year, **Winterstart**

(Nov.–mid-Dec.) features cheap lodging and a host of fun events. This coincides with the opening of lifts at the park's three winter resorts beginning in mid-November.

One of the year's biggest events is the **Banff Mountain Film Festival,** held on the first weekend of November. Mountain-adventure filmmakers from around the world submit films to be judged by a select committee. Films are then shown throughout the weekend to an enthusiastic crowd of thousands. Exhibits and seminars are also presented, and top climbers and mountaineers from around the world are invited as guest speakers. Tickets to the Banff Mountain Film Festival go on sale one year in advance and sell out quickly. Tickets for daytime shows start at $45 (for up to 10 films). Night shows are from $32, and all-weekend passes cost around $150 (weekend passes with two nights' accommodations and breakfasts start at a reasonable $250). Films are shown in the two theaters of the Banff Centre. For more information, contact the festival office (403/762-6675); for tickets, call the Banff Centre box office (403/762-6301 or 800/413-8368, www.banffcentre.ca). If you miss the actual festival, it hits the road on the Best of the Festival World Tour. Look for it in your town, or check out the listed website for venues and dates.

Starting in the days leading up to the film festival, then running in conjunction with it, is the **Banff Mountain Book Festival,** which showcases the work of publishers, writers, and photographers whose work revolves around the world's great mountain ranges. Tickets can be bought to individual events ($16–30), or there's a Book Festival Pass ($130) and a pass combining both festivals ($250).

Winter

Santa Claus makes an appearance on Banff Avenue at noon on the last Saturday in November; if you miss him there, he usually goes skiing at each of the local resorts on Christmas Day. Events at the resorts continue throughout the long winter season, among them **World Cup Downhill** skiing at Lake Louise in late November. **Banff/Lake Louise Winter Festival** is a 10-day celebration at the end of January that has been a part of Banff's history since 1917. Look for ice sculpting on the frozen lake in front of the Chateau Lake Louise, the Lake Louise Loppet, barn dancing, and the Town Party, which takes place in the Fairmont Banff Springs.

SHOPPING
Canadiana and Clothing

Few companies in the world were as responsible for the development of a country as was the **Hudson's Bay Company** (HBC) in Canada. Founded in 1670, the HBC established trading posts throughout western Canada, many of which attracted settlers, forming the nucleus for towns and cities that survive today, including Alberta's capital, Edmonton. HBC stores continue their traditional role of providing a wide range of goods in towns big and small across the country. In Banff, the HBC store is at 125 Banff Ave. (403/762-5525).

Another Canadian store, this one famous for its fleeces, sweaters, and leather goods, and as supplier to the Canadian Olympic teams, is **Roots** (227 Banff Ave., 403/762-9434). For belts, buckles, and boots, check out the **Trail Rider Store** (132 Banff Ave., 403/762-4551). Pick up your Canadian-made Tilley Hat and other Tilley Endurables from **Piccatilley Square,** on the main floor of the Cascade Plaza (317 Banff Ave., 403/762-0302). Check out the **Rude Boys** (215 Banff Ave., 403/762-8480), a snowboard and skate shop downstairs in the Sundance Mall, but don't expect to find anything suitable for your grandparents.

Camping and Outdoor Gear

Inexpensive camping equipment and supplies can be found in **Home Hardware** (221 Bear St., 403/762-2080) and in the low-ceilinged downstairs section of the **Hudson's Bay Company** (125 Banff Ave., 403/762-5525). More specialized needs are catered to at **Mountain Magic Equipment** (224 Bear St., 403/762-2591). The store stocks a large range of top-quality

outdoor and survival gear (including climbing equipment) and rents tents ($20 per day), sleeping bags ($12), backpacks ($10), and boots ($10). Mountain Magic Equipment also sells and repairs all types of bikes.

Two of the best spots to shop for outdoor apparel are locally owned **Abominable Ski & Sportswear** (229 Banff Ave., 403/762-2905) and **Monod Sports** (129 Banff Ave., 403/762-4571).

Gifts and Galleries

Banff's numerous galleries display the work of mostly Canadian artists. **Canada House Gallery** (201 Bear St., 403/762-3757) features a wide selection of Canadian landscape and wildlife works and native art. The **Quest Gallery** (105 Banff Ave., 403/762-2722) offers a diverse range of affordable Canadian paintings and crafts as well as more exotic pieces such as mammoth tusks from prehistoric times and Inuit carvings from Nunavut. Across the Bow River from downtown, browse through traditional native arts and crafts at the **Indian Trading Post** (1 Birch Ave., 403/762-2456).

Bookstores

Banff Book & Art Den (94 Banff Ave., 403/762-3919, www.banffbooks.com, summer daily 9 A.M.–9 P.M., the rest of the year 10 A.M.–7 P.M.) is the largest bookstore in the Canadian Rockies, with reading material spread over a split-level hardwood floor. It stocks a large collection of park literature, wilderness guides, coffee-table books, travel guides, and the entire range of Gem Trek maps. The Book & Art Den has a second store in Fairmont Banff Springs, located beyond the front lobby. **The Bear and the Butterfly** (214 Banff Ave., 403/762-8911), operated by the nonprofit Friends of Banff organization, holds a thoughtful selection of nature and recreation books. They also have a smaller store within the Banff Visitor Centre (224 Banff Ave., 403/762-8918). The **Whyte Museum Bookstore** (111 Bear St., 403/762-2291, daily 10 A.M.–5 P.M.) specializes in regional natural and human history.

ACCOMMODATIONS

Banff has a few accommodations right downtown, but most are strung out along Banff Avenue, an easy walk from the shopping and dining precinct. Nearby Tunnel Mountain is also home to a cluster of accommodations. Under this accommodations section, I also include three excellent options between Banff and Lake Louise.

Finding a room in Banff in summer is nearly as hard as trying to justify its price. By late afternoon just about every room and campsite in the park will be occupied, and basic hotel rooms begin at around $150. Fortunately, many alternatives are available, including backpacker lodges; bed-and-breakfast rooms in private homes; and cabins, which are cost-effective for families or small groups. Wherever you decide to stay, it is vital to book well ahead during summer and the Christmas holidays. The park's off-season is October–May, and hotels offer huge rate reductions during this period.

All rates quoted below are for a standard room in the high season (June to early September).

Banff Central Reservations

Banff Central Reservations (403/705-4020 or 877/542-2633, www.banffreservations.com) is tied in with Sunshine Village, but has been providing an excellent booking and reservation service for many years.

Under $50

HI-Banff Alpine Centre (801 Hidden Ridge Way, 403/762-4123 or 866/762-4122, www.hihostels.ca) is just off Tunnel Mountain Road three kilometers (1.9 mi) from downtown. This large, modern hostel sleeps 216 in small two-, four-, and six-bed dormitory rooms as well as four-bed cabins. The large lounge area has a fireplace, and other facilities include a recreation room, public Internet access, bike and ski/snowboard workshop, large kitchen, self-service café/bar, and laundry. In summer, members of Hostelling International pay $29 per person per night (nonmembers $33) for a

dorm bed or $83 s or d ($88 for nonmembers) in a private room. The rest of the year, dorm beds are $23 (nonmembers $27) and private rooms $71 s or d (nonmembers $79). During July and August, reserve at least one month in advance to be assured of a bed. The hostel is open all day, but check-in isn't until midday. To get there from town, ride the Banff Transit bus ($2), which passes the hostel twice an hour during summer. The rest of the year the only transportation is by cab, about $8 from the bus depot.

A one-time hospital, **Banff Y Mountain Lodge** (102 Spray Ave., 403/762-3560 or 800/813-4138, www.ymountainlodge.com) has undergone massive renovations to create an excellent centrally located choice for budget travelers. Facilities include the casual Sundance Bistro (7 A.M.–10 P.M.), a laundry facility, and the Great Room, a huge living area where the centerpiece is a massive stone fireplace; writing desks and shelves stocked with books are scattered throughout. A bed in the dormitory is $31 per person, a private room that shares bathroom facilities is $70 s or d, and an en suite is $90–105 s or d. These rates are reduced outside of summer.

Along the main strip of accommodations and a five-minute walk to downtown is **Samesun Banff** (449 Banff Ave., 403/762-5521 or 877/562-2783, www.samesun.com). As converted motel rooms, each small dormitory has its own bathroom. Guest amenities include a hot tub, sauna, large communal kitchen, game room with a pool table, TV room, activities desk, bike rentals, courtyard, and laundry. Dorm beds are $31 per person, with a number of private twin (two single beds) rooms for $89 s or d.

Thirty-two kilometers (20 mi) from Banff along the Bow Valley Parkway, **HI-Castle Mountain** is near several interesting hikes and across the road from a general store with basic supplies. This hostel sleeps 28 in two dorms and has a kitchen, octagonal common room with wood-burning fireplace, hot showers, and bike rentals. Members of Hostelling International pay $23, nonmembers $27. Make book-

ings through the association's reservation line (403/760-7580 or 866/762-4122) or book online (www.hihostels.ca). Check-in is 5–10 P.M.

$50-100

Accommodations in this price range are limited to private rooms at the three backpacker lodges (above) and at a few bed-and-breakfasts. The best value of these is **Mountain View B&B** (347 Grizzly St., 403/760-9353, www.mountainviewbanff.ca, May–Sept., $85–120 s or d), on a quiet residential street three blocks from the heart of downtown. The two guest rooms are simply furnished, each with a double bed, TV, sink, and bar fridge. They share a bathroom and a common area that includes basic cooking facilities (microwave, toaster, kettle) and opens to a private deck. Off-street parking and a light breakfast round out this excellent choice.

Mrs. Cowan has been offering budget accommodation at the 1926 **Tan-Y-Bryn** (118 Otter St., 403/762-3696) residence for many years. Although furnishings are sparse at best and bathrooms shared, the price is unequaled in town: $50–65 s, $55–75 d includes a light breakfast.

$100-150

[Blue Mountain Lodge (137 Muskrat St., 403/762-5134, www.bluemtnlodge.com, $105–109 s, $129–149 d) is a rambling, older-style lodge with 10 guest rooms, each with a private bath, TV, and telephone. The Trapper's Cabin room is the most expensive, but the gabled ceiling, walls decorated with snowshoes and bearskin, and an electric fireplace create a funky, mountain feel. All guests have use of shared kitchen facilities, a lounge, and Internet access while enjoying an expansive cold buffet breakfast to set you up for a day of hiking.

The eight guest rooms at the **Elkhorn Lodge** (124 Spray Ave., 403/762-2299 or 877/818-8488, www.elkhornbanff.ca) are nothing special, but travelers on a budget who aren't fans of bed-and-breakfasts will find this older lodge suitable. The four small sleeping rooms—each with a bathroom, TV, and coffeemaker—are $110 s or d, while larger rooms

© ANDREW HEMPSTEAD

Blue Mountain Lodge

with fridges are $195–265. Rates include a light breakfast. It's halfway up the hill to the Fairmont Banff Springs.

Across a quiet road from the river and three blocks from downtown is the old-style **Bow View Lodge** (228 Bow Ave., 403/762-2261 or 800/661-1565, www.bowview.com), which has an outdoor pool, making it a good choice for families. Moderately sized rooms are priced $140 s or d, $160 with a filtered river view. A two-bedroom family suite is $205.

Bumper's Inn is at the far end of the motel strip (603 Banff Ave., 403/762-3386 or 800/661-3518, www.bumpersinn.com). The property is best known for its steakhouse, but behind the restaurant are 39 older-style rooms facing a courtyard for $145 s or d (from $85 in winter).

The wilderness setting at **Johnston Canyon Resort** (403/762-2971 or 888/378-1720, www.johnstoncanyon.com, mid-May–early Oct.), 26 kilometers (16 mi) west of Banff, is unequalled by any of the other choices in this price range. The rustic cabins are older, and some have kitchenettes. On the grounds are

tennis courts, a barbecue area, and a general store. Resort dining options are as varied as munching on a burger and fries at the counter of an old-time cafeteria to enjoying Asian-style Chilean sea bass in a dining room that oozes alpine charm. Basic two-person duplex cabins are $129, two-person cabins with a gas fireplace and sitting area are $169, and they go up in price all the way to $284 for a Classic Bungalow complete with two bedrooms, cooking facilities, and heritage-style furnishings.

$150-200

Dating to 1917, **C Tarry-A-While** (117 Grizzly St., 403/762-0462, www.tarry.ca) was built for one of the Canadian Rockies' most famous residents, Mary Schäffer, by her outfitter husband, Billy Warren. It is currently owned by the Peter and Catharine Whyte Foundation, allowing a lucky few to soak up mountain heritage in its most pure form. Guests choose from three rooms, each with its own character. The simply furnished Billy Warren Room is particularly appealing. It features fir-paneled walls,

a solid pine bed, and a clawfoot tub in the en suite bathroom. High season (mid-May–mid-Oct.) rates of $150–175 s or d include an expansive breakfast spread and use of two sitting rooms piled high with local literature.

Some of Banff's private residences have cabins for rent. One of the reasons that **Country Cabin Bed & Breakfast** (419 Beaver St., 403/762-3591, www.banffmountain country.com/cabin) is the best of these is the quiet location off busy Banff Avenue but still within easy walking distance of downtown. The log cabin has a separate bedroom, a full bathroom with log and tile features surrounding a jetted tub, and a living area equipped with a fold-out futon and a TV/VCR combo. If you don't feel like dining downtown, you can cook up a storm on the barbecue supplied. Summer rates of $150 s or d, $85 the rest of the year, include a continental breakfast delivered to your door.

The rooms at the **Banff Inn** (501 Banff Ave., 403/762-8844 or 800/667-1464, www.banffinn.com, $160–170 s or d) are no-frills modern in appearance. Each of the 99 rooms has a log-trimmed balcony, and the facade is Rundlestone (quarried locally and named for Mount Rundle). Pluses include underground heated parking, a day spa, a guest lounge with fireplace and plasma TV, and free continental breakfast.

Spruce Grove Inn (545 Banff Ave.) is a modern mountain-style lodge and relatively good value at $185 s or d (upgrade to a king bed for $200 s or d or a Loft Suite that sleeps four for $225). Make reservations and check in at the adjacent Banff Voyager Inn (403/762-3301 or 800/879-1991, www.banffvoyagerinn.com).

Toward downtown from the Spruce Grove is the **High Country Inn** (419 Banff Ave., 403/762-2236 or 800/293-5142, www.banff highcountryinn.com, from $180 s or d), which has a heated indoor pool, spacious hot tubs, a cedar-lined sauna, and the ever-popular Ticino Swiss/Italian restaurant. All rooms are adequately furnished with comfortable beds and an earthy color scheme.

The **Rundlestone Lodge** (537 Banff Ave.,

403/762-2201 or 800/661-8630, www.rundle stone.com) features mountain-style architecture with an abundance of raw stonework and exposed timber inside and out. At street level is a comfortable sitting area centered on a fireplace, as well as an indoor pool, a lounge-style bar, and a restaurant. Furniture and fittings in the 96 rooms are elegant, and all come with high-speed Internet access and a TV/DVD combo. Many rooms have small balconies and gas fireplaces; some are wheelchair accessible. Rooms begin at $185 s or d; suites range $220–315.

$200-250

More than 100 years since Jim and Bill Brewster guided their first guests through the park, their descendants are still actively involved in the tourist industry, operating the central and very stylish **Brewster's Mountain Lodge** (208 Caribou St., 403/762-2900 or 888/762-2900, www.brewstermountainlodge.com). The building features an eye-catching log exterior with an equally impressive lobby and adjoining lounge in a prime downtown location. The Western theme is continued in the 77 upstairs rooms. Superior rooms feature two queen-size beds or one king-size bed ($220), deluxe rooms offer a private balcony ($240), and loft suites have hot tubs (from $280). All rates include breakfast, and if you don't feel like dining out you can order room service from noon onward. Packages provide good value here, while off-season rates are slashed up to 50 percent.

The 134-room **Banff Ptarmigan Inn** (337 Banff Ave., 403/762-2207 or 800/661-8310, www.bestofbanff.com) is a slick full-service hotel with tastefully decorated rooms, down comforters on all beds, a restaurant, heated underground parking, wireless Internet, and a variety of facilities to soothe sore muscles, including a spa, a whirlpool, and a sauna. The 134 rooms start at $230 s or d.

A 15-minute downhill walk to town, **Douglas Fir Resort** (Tunnel Mountain Rd., 403/762-5591 or 800/661-9267, www.douglas fir.com, from $220 s or d) offers 133 large condo-style units, each with a kitchen and a lounge with fireplace. Other facilities include

© ANDREW HEMPSTEAD

Brewster's Mountain Lodge

a hot tub, an exercise room, squash and tennis courts, a grocery store, and a laundry. Infinitely more important if you have children are the two indoor water slides and heated pool.

Better still, stay outside town limits at **(Baker Creek Chalets** (403/522-3761, www.bakercreek.com), along the Bow Valley Parkway 40 kilometers (25 mi) northwest of Banff and just 10 kilometers (6.2 mi) from Lake Louise. Each of the log chalets (from $245 s or d) has a kitchenette, loft, fireplace, and outside deck (complete with cute woodcarvings of bears climbing over the railings). The Trapper's Cabin ($315) is a huge space with a log bed, antler chandelier, wood-burning fireplace, double-jetted tub, and cooking facilities. A lodge wing has eight luxurious suites, each with richly accented log work, a deck, a microwave and fridge, and a deluxe bathroom; $215 s or d, $245 with a double-jetted tub, and $310 with a loft. (Check the website for great off-season deals.) The restaurant here is highly recommended.

Constructed by the Canadian Pacific Railway in 1922, **(Storm Mountain Lodge** (Hwy. 93,

403/762-4155, www.stormmountainlodge.com, early Dec.–mid-Oct., $199–255) reopened in 2003 after a major restoration project that saw 14 historic cabins returned to their former rustic glory. Each has its original log walls, along with a log bed, covered deck, a wood-burning fireplace, and bathroom with clawfoot tub. They don't have phones or TVs, so there's little to distract you from the past. Off-season deals include a breakfast and dinner package (mid-Apr.–mid-June) for $225 d. Outside, the wilderness beckons, with Storm Mountain as a backdrop. The lodge is at Vermilion Pass, a 25-minute drive from Banff or Lake Louise (head west from the Castle Mountain interchange). Storm Mountain Lodge Restaurant (daily 5–10 P.M.) is one of my favorite places to eat in the park (see *Food* later in this chapter).

$250-300

In the heart of downtown Banff, the venerable redbrick **Mount Royal Hotel** (138 Banff Ave., 403/762-3331 or 877/442-2623, www.mount royalhotel.com) dates to 1908. Today guests

© ANDREW HEMPSTEAD

Baker Creek Chalets

are offered 135 tastefully decorated rooms with high-speed Internet access and the use of a large health club with hot tub. Also on the premises are a restaurant and small lounge. Rates are from $250 s or d but are discounted as low as $100 in the shoulder seasons. For a splurge, you won't find better than the one-bedroom suites ($350–500).

The best rooms along the motel strip are at **Delta Banff Royal Canadian Lodge** (459 Banff Ave., 403/762-3307 or 888/778-5050, www.deltahotels.com, from $290 s or d), which opened in the summer of 2000. It features 99 luxuriously appointed rooms, heated underground parking, a lounge, a dining room where upscale Canadian specialties are the highlight, a large spa/pool complex, and a landscaped courtyard.

Bed-and-breakfast connoisseurs will fall in love with **Bearberry B&B** (417 Marten St., 403/762-3750, www.bearberry.com), a purpose-built lodging within walking distance of downtown. The home itself is a beautiful timber-and-stone structure; inside, guests soak up

mountain-style luxury in the living area with vaulted ceiling, which comes complete with a stone fireplace, super-comfortable couches, and a library of local books. The spacious rooms come with niceties such as pillow-top mattresses, TV/DVD combos, heated bathroom floors, and bathrobes. Bearberry is also the only local bed-and-breakfast with heated underground parking. Summer rates are $295 s or d, discounted to $200 the rest of the year.

At **Buffalo Mountain Lodge,** a 15-minute walk from town on Tunnel Mountain Road (at Tunnel Mountain Dr., 403/762-2400 or 800/661-1367, www.crmr.com), you'll notice the impressive timber-frame construction, as well as the hand-hewn construction of the lobby, with its vaulted ceiling and eye-catching fieldstone fireplace. The 108 rooms, chalets, and bungalows all have fireplaces, balconies, large bathrooms, and comfortable beds topped by feather-filled duvets; many have kitchens. And you won't need to go to town to eat—one of Banff's best restaurants, Cilantro Mountain Café, is adjacent to the main lodge. Rack rates

start at $300, but book in advance and online to pick up summer rates around $250. (The lodge takes its name from Tunnel Mountain, which early park visitors called Buffalo Mountain for its shape.)

At Castle Junction, 32 kilometers (20 mi) northwest of Banff, is **Castle Mountain Chalets** (403/762-3868 or 877/762-2281, www.decorehotels.com). Set on 1.5 hectares (four acres), this resort is home to a collection of magnificent log chalets. Each has high ceilings, beautifully handcrafted log interiors, at least two beds, a stone fireplace, a full kitchen with dishwasher, a bathroom with hot tub, and satellite TV. Rates range $255–335 s or d. At the back of the grounds are several older cabins offered in summer ($190 s or d). Part of the complex is a grocery store, barbecue area, and the only gas between Banff and Lake Louise.

Over $300

The **Fairmont Banff Springs** (403/762-2211 or 800/257-7544, www.fairmont.com) is one of the world's great mountain resort hotels. The rooms have recently been modernized—think Internet access and air-conditioning—although many date to the 1920s, and as is common in older establishments, these accommodations are small (Fairmont Rooms are 14.4 square m/155 square ft). But room size is only a minor consideration when staying in this historic gem. With 12 eateries, four lounges, a luxurious spa facility, a huge indoor pool, elegant public spaces, a 27-hole golf course, tennis courts, horseback riding, and enough twisting, turning hallways, boardwalks, towers, and shops to warrant a detailed map, you'll not be wanting to spend much time in your room. Unless, of course, you are in the presidential suite, located in the central tower. It has eight rooms, a canopy bed, a hot tub, a baby grand piano, a private pool, and your own private elevator linking each of the three floors. During summer, rack rates for a regular Fairmont room are $639 s or d, discounted to around $350 the rest of the year. Some Fairmont rooms have valley views ($679), while the larger Signature rooms ($759) have upgraded furnishings and a

stylish heritage feel. Many summer visitors stay as part of a package—the place to find these is on the website, www.fairmont.com. Finally, at any time of year, call a day in advance or even stop by the day of—if rooms are available they are sold at up to 50 percent off the rack rate.

On Mountain Avenue, a short walk from the Upper Hot Springs, is **Rimrock Resort Hotel** (403/762-3356 or 888/746-7625, www.rimrockresort.com), a full-service luxury resort dating to the mid-1990s. Guest amenities include two restaurants, two lounges, a health club, an outdoor patio, and a multistory parking garage. Each of 345 well-appointed rooms is decorated with earthy tones offset by brightly colored fabrics. They also feature picture windows, a king-size bed, a comfortable armchair, a writing desk, two phones, a mini-bar, and a hair dryer. This hotel caters to disabled persons as well as any in the park. Since it's set high above the Bow Valley, views for the most part are excellent. Prices range $405–480 depending mostly on the views. Regular shuttle buses make the short run to town during summer.

CAMPING

Within Banff National Park, 13 campgrounds hold more than 2,000 sites. Although the town of Banff has five of these facilities with more than 1,500 sites in its immediate vicinity, all fill by early afternoon. The three largest campgrounds are strung out over 1.5 kilometers (0.9 mi) along Tunnel Mountain Road, with the nearest sites 2.5 kilometers (1.6 mi) from town. A percentage of sites at Tunnel Mountain Campground can be reserved through the **Parks Canada Campground Reservation Service** (877/737-3783, www.pccamping.ca), and it's strongly recommended that you do reserve if you require power hookups. Although plenty of sites are available for those without reservations, they fill fast each day (especially in July and August). The official checkout time is 11 A.M., so plan on arriving at your campground of choice earlier in the day than this to ensure getting a site. When the main campgrounds fill, those unable to secure a site will be directed to an overflow area along

Minnewanka Lake Road. This glorified parking lot provides few facilities and no hookups. Open fires are permitted in designated areas throughout all campgrounds, but you must purchase a Firewood Permit ($8 per site per night) to burn wood, which is provided at no cost. For general camping information, stop at the Banff Visitor Centre (224 Banff Ave., 403/762-1550) or go the Parks Canada website (www.pc.gc.ca) and follow the links to Banff National Park.

Tunnel Mountain

Closest to town is **Tunnel Mountain Campground,** which is three campgrounds rolled into one. The location is a lightly treed ridge east of downtown, with views north to Cascade Mountain and south to Mount Rundle. From town, follow Tunnel Mountain Road east, to beyond the Douglas Fir Resort (which is within walking distance for groceries, booze, and laundry). If you're coming in off the Trans-Canada Highway from the east, bypass town completely by turning left onto Tunnel Mountain Road at the Banff Rocky Mountain Resort. Approaching from this direction, the first campground you pass is the park's largest with 622 well-spaced, relatively private sites ($26 per site), each with a fire ring and picnic table. Other amenities include drinking water, hot showers, and kitchen shelters. This campground has no hookups. It is open mid-May to early September. Less than one kilometer (0.6 mi) farther along Tunnel Mountain Road toward town is a signed turnoff ("Hookups") that leads to a registration booth for two more campgrounds. Unless you have a reservation (see above), you'll be asked whether you require an electrical hookup ($30 per site) or a site with power, water, and sewer ($36 per site), then sent off into the corresponding campground. The power-only section (closest to town) stays open year-round, the other from mid-May to September. Both have hot showers but little privacy between sites.

Lake Minnewanka Road

Along Lake Minnewanka Road northeast of town are two campgrounds offering fewer services than the others, but with sites that offer more privacy. The pick of the two is **(Two Jack Lakeside Campground** (June–mid-Sept., $26 per site), the best of Banff's campgrounds with 80 sites tucked into trees at the south end of Two Jack Lake, an extension of Lake Minnewanka. Facilities include hot showers, kitchen shelters, drinking water, and flush toilets. It's just over six kilometers (3.7 mi) from the TransCanada Highway underpass. The much larger **Two Jack Main Campground** (mid-June–mid-Sept., $21 per site) is a short distance farther along the road, with 381 sites spread throughout a shallow valley. It offers the same facilities as Two Jack Lakeside, sans showers.

Bow Valley Parkway

Along Bow Valley Parkway between the town of Banff and Lake Louise are three campgrounds. Closest to Banff is **Johnston Canyon Campground** (early June–mid-Sept., $26 per site), between the road and the rail line 26 kilometers (16 mi) west of Banff. It is the largest of the three campgrounds, with 140 sites, and has hot showers but no hookups. Almost directly opposite is Johnston Canyon Resort, with groceries and a restaurant, and the beginning of a trail to the park's best-known waterfalls.

Continuing eight kilometers (five mi) toward Lake Louise, **Castle Mountain Campground** (early June–early Sept., $21 per site) is also within walking distance of a grocery store (no restaurant), but it has just 44 sites and no showers. Services are limited to flush toilets, drinking water, and kitchen shelters.

Protection Mountain Campground (July–Aug., $21 per site), a further 14 kilometers (8.7 mi) west and just over 20 kilometers (12.5 mi) from Lake Louise, opens as demand dictates, usually by late June. It offers 89 sites, along with flush toilets, drinking water, and stove-equipped kitchen shelters.

FOOD

Banff has more than 100 dining establishments—more per capita than any town or city across Canada. From lobster to linguini, alli-

gator to à la carte, and fajitas to fudge, there's something to suit the budget of anyone who spends time in the park. In July and August, the most popular restaurants don't take reservations and you can expect a wait.

While the quality of food is most people's number one priority when dining out, the level of service (or lack of it) also comes into play in Banff, especially if you are paying big bucks for fine dining. Getting it all right—good food, top-notch service, and a memorable ambience—in a tourism-oriented town is rare. Which leads to the restaurants I've recommended below, the best of a very varied bunch.

Groceries

Banff has two major grocery stores. In addition to a wide selection of basic groceries, **Keller Foods** (122 Bear St., 403/762-3663, 7 A.M.–10 P.M.) has a good deli with pre-made salads and sandwiches, preheated soup, and hot chickens. At the other end of downtown, **Safeway** (318 Marten St., 403/762-5329) is open 8 A.M.–11 P.M.

Cafés

The **Cake Company** (220 Bear St., 403/762-8642) serves great coffee and delicious pastries, muffins, and cakes baked daily on the premises. **Evelyn's Coffee Bar** (201 Banff Ave., 403/762-0352) has good coffee and huge sandwiches. The few outside tables—on the busiest stretch of the busiest street in town—are perfect for people-watching. **Jump Start** opposite Central Park (206 Buffalo St., 403/762-0332) has a wide range of coffee concoctions as well as homemade soups (from $5.50) and sandwiches ($7) that are delicious.

Banff's lone bakery is **Wild Flour** (Bison Courtyard, 211 Bear St., 403/760-5074, daily 7 A.M.–6 P.M.), and it's a good one (albeit a little pricey). Organic ingredients are used whenever possible, and everything is freshly baked daily. The result is an array of healthy breads, mouthwatering cakes and pastries, and delicious meat pies.

The main reasons for visiting the Banff Centre include attending the many events, exercis-

ing at the fitness facility, or wandering through the grounds. Add to this list having a casual meal at the **Gooseberry Juice Bar** (Banff Centre, Tunnel Mountain Dr., 403/762-6100, daily 8 A.M.–10 P.M.), overlooking the swimming pool within the Sally Borden Building. Sandwiches are made to order, or try a mini-pizza or bowl of steaming soup.

Cheaper Eats

Of the many Banff drinking holes that offer predictable pub-style menus, **Wild Bill's** (201 Banff Ave., 403/762-0333) is a standout. Named for one of Banff's most famed mountain men, the decor is suitably Western, with a menu to match. The Nachos Grande ($9.50) with a side of guacamole ($3) is perfect to share. Later in the day, steaks and spit-roasted chicken are traditional favorites ($15–30). Wild Bill's is open daily from 11 A.M. until well after midnight, but plan on dining before 9 P.M.

A town favorite that has faithfully served locals for many years is **Melissa's** (218 Lynx St., 403/762-5511, 7:30 A.M.–10 P.M.). Breakfast is busiest, while lunch and dinner are casual affairs—choose from a wide variety of generously sized burgers, freshly prepared salads, and mouthwatering Alberta beef.

At the back of the Clock Tower Mall, **Pad Thai** (110 Banff Ave., 403/762-4911, lunch and dinner daily) is a real find. The namesake pad Thai is $8, curries are all around the same price, and delicious spring rolls are $4. You can eat in or take out.

Alberta Beef

Even though **Bumper's** (603 Banff Ave., 403/762-2622, 4:30–10 P.M.) is away from the center of Banff, it's worth leaving the shopping strip and heading out to this popular steakhouse. Large cuts of Alberta beef, an informal atmosphere, efficient service, and great prices keep people coming back. Favorite choices are the slabs of Roast Prime Rib of Beef, in four sized cuts and cooked to order. Prices range from $18 for the Ladies cut to $29 for the Man Mountain cut, which includes unlimited trips to a small salad bar.

Banff's most fashionable steakhouse is **Saltlik** (221 Bear St., 403/762-2467, from 11 A.M.). It's big and bold and the perfect choice for serious carnivores with cash to spare. The concrete-and-steel split-level interior is complemented with modish wood furnishings. Facing the street, glass doors fold back to a terrace for warm-weather dining. The specialty is AAA Alberta beef, finished with grain feeding to enhance the flavor, then flash-seared at 650°C (1,200°F) to seal in the juices, and served with a side platter of seasonal vegetables. Entrées are priced comparably to those at a city steakhouse ($18–35), but the cost creeps up as you add side dishes.

Canadian

Occupying the prime position on one of Banff's busiest corners is the **Maple Leaf** (137 Banff Ave., 403/760-7680, daily 11 A.M.–11 P.M.). Take in the dramatic Canadian-themed decor—exposed river stone, polished log work, a two-story interior rock wall, and a moose head (tucked around the corner from the street-level lounge). Some tables surround a busy area by the bar and kitchen, so try to talk your way into the upstairs back corner. The cooking uses modern styles with an abundance of Canadian game and produce. The lunch menu has an Atlantic salmon burger, along with lots of lighter salads and stir-fries ($10–17). Some of Canada's finest ingredients appear on the dinner menu: herb-and-citrus-crusted halibut and the bison tenderloin are standouts. Treat yourself to a glass of Canadian ice wine to accompany dessert.

Interesting decor sees chic-industrial blending with mountain rustic at ◖ **The Bison** (Bison Courtyard, Bear St., 403/762-5550, daily for lunch and dinner). Tables are inside or out at this upstairs dining room, and almost all have a view of the open kitchen. The food is solidly Canadian, with a menu that takes advantage of wild game, seafood, and Alberta beef. Starters are mostly under $14 and mains reasonably priced at $16–28. Also of note is the wine list, which again is extremely well priced, compared to other Banff restaurants.

Buffalo Mountain Lodge Restaurant at a lodge of the same name (Tunnel Mountain Road, 403/762-2400, daily 7 A.M.–10 P.M.) features a distinctive interior of hand-hewn cedar beams and Old World elegance—complete with stone fireplace and a chandelier made entirely from elk antlers—along with large windows that frame the surrounding forest. The featured cuisine is referred to as Rocky Mountain, reflecting an abundance of Canadian game and seafood combined with native berries and fruits. The least expensive way to dine on this uniquely Canadian fare is by visiting at lunch and ordering the Rocky Mountain Game Platter, costing $20 for two people. Dinner entrées range $24–33 and include fare like elk sirloin that's given an exotic touch with accompanying quince compote.

European

A longtime favorite with the casual crowd is **Guido's** (upstairs at 116 Banff Ave., 403/762-4002, from 5:30 P.M.). Prices are a little higher than they should be for the dated surroundings, but diners return here for the homemade pasta cooked to perfection in a variety of classic Italian sauces, rather than for the ambience.

If you are staying up on Tunnel Mountain—or even if you're not—**Cilantro Mountain Café** (Buffalo Mountain Lodge, 403/760-3008, summer daily 11 A.M.–11 P.M., the rest of the year Wed.–Sun. 5–10 P.M., closed mid-Sept.–mid-Dec.) is an excellent choice for a casual, well-priced meal. You can choose to dine inside the cozy log cabin that holds the main restaurant and open kitchen, or out on the patio. Starters are dominated by seafood options, but the flatbread, baked to order and delivered with choice of dips ($8), is a good choice to share. The thin-crust, wood-fired pizza for one ($15–17) is the highlight, with a small but varied selection of other mains ($22–31) that change as seasonal produce becomes available.

Even if you've tried exotic meats, you probably haven't had them in a restaurant like the ◖ **Grizzly House** (207 Banff Ave., 403/762-4055, daily 11:30 A.M.–midnight), which provides Banff's most unusual dining experience.

The decor is, to say the least, eclectic (many say eccentric)—think lots of twisted woods, a motorbike hanging from the ceiling, a melted telephone on the wall. Each table has a phone for across-table conversation, or you can put a call through to your server, the bar, a cab, diners in the private booth, or even those who spend too long in the bathroom. The food is equally unique and the service as professional as anywhere in town. The menu hasn't changed in decades, and this doesn't displease anyone. Most dining revolves around traditional Swiss fondues, but with nontraditional dipping meats such as rattlesnake, alligator, shark, ostrich, scallops, elk, and wild boar. Four-course table d'hôte fondue dinners are $38–56 per person, which includes soup or salad, followed by a cheese fondue, then one of six meat and sea-food fondue (or hot rock) choices, and finally a fruity chocolate fondue.

Ticino (High Country Inn, 415 Banff Ave., 403/762-3848, daily 5–10 P.M.) is a park in-stitution that reflects the heritage of the park's early mountain guides, with solid timber fur-nishings, lots of peeled and polished log work, and old wooden skis, huge cowbells, and an alpenhorn decorating the walls. It's named for the southern province of Switzerland where the cuisine has a distinctive Italian influence. The Swiss chef is best known for a creamy wild mushroom soup, unique to the region; his beef and cheese fondues ($17–27 per person); juicy cuts of Alberta beef; and veal dishes (such as veal scaloppini, $27). Save room for one of Ti-cino's sinfully rich desserts. Also of note is the professional service.

You'll think you've swapped continents when you step into ❿ **Le Beaujolais** (212 Buffalo St., 403/762-2712, from 6 P.M.), a Canadian leader in French cuisine. With crisp white linens, old-style stately decor, and immacu-late service, this elegant room has been one of Banff's most popular fine-dining restaurants for 20 years. Its second-floor location ensures great views of Banff, especially from window tables. The dishes feature mainly Canadian produce, prepared and served with a traditional French flair. Entrées begin at $31, but the ex-tent of your final tab depends on whether you choose à la carte items or one of the three- to six-course table d'hôte menus ($55–85)—and also on how much wine you consume. Nation-alism shows through in the 10,000-bottle cel-lar, with lots of reds from the Bordeaux and Burgundy regions of France.

Asian

A couple of doors off Banff Avenue, **Sushi House Banff** (304 Caribou St., 403/762-2971, daily for lunch and dinner) is a tiny space with a dozen stools set around a moving miniature railway that has diners picking sushi and other delicacies from a train as it circles the chef, who loads the carriages as quickly as they empty.

More expensive is **Suginoya** (225 Banff Ave., 403/762-4773, daily 11 A.M.–10:30 P.M.). Choose from the sushi bar, *ozashiki* booths, or regular tables. Traditional *shabu-shabu* and sea-food teriyaki are staples. The number of Jap-anese diners here is indicative of the quality. Expect to pay at least $13 for entrées, $19–25 for one of the combination dinners.

Fairmont Banff Springs

Whether guests or not, most visitors to Banff drop by to see one of the town's biggest tourist attractions, and a meal here might not be as ex-pensive as you think. If you are in the mood for a snack such as chili and bread or sandwiches to go, head to the Lobby Level and the **Castle Pantry,** which is open 24 hours daily. Impres-sive buffets are the main draw at the **Bow Valley Grill,** a pleasantly laid out dining room that seats 275. Each morning 6:30 A.M.–10:30 P.M. an expansive buffet of hot and cold delicacies is laid out for the masses ($26 per person). Lunch (daily 11:30 A.M.–5:30 P.M.) offers a wide-rang-ing menu featuring everything from salads to seafood. Through the busiest months of sum-mer, pay for the buffet lunch (11:30 A.M.–2 P.M., until 4 P.M. Sat., $29) and you'll be invited to a walking tour of the property. In summer, eve-ning diners (6–9 P.M., $17–28) order from a menu that appeals to all tastes, while the rest of the year dinner is offered as a buffet, with a different theme each night. The hotel's Sunday

brunch, served in the Bow Valley Grill (11 A.M.–2:30 P.M., $38), is legendary, with chefs working at numerous stations scattered around the dining area and an enormous spread not equaled for variety anywhere in the mountains. Reservations are required for Sunday brunch (as far in advance as possible) and dinner.

Ensconced in an octagonal room of the Manor Wing, **Castello Ristorante** (daily 6–9 P.M., Jan.–May closed Tues.–Wed.) is a seductive dining room with a modern, upscale ambience. The menu is dominated by Italian favorites, with pastas in the $18–26 range and specialties from $22. The **Rundle Lounge** (daily midday–1 A.M.) is a long, narrow piano bar, where most tables offer views down the Bow Valley. The à la carte menu offers no surprises. **Grapes** (daily 6–9 P.M.) is an intimate yet casual wine bar noted for its fine cheeses and pâtés. More substantial meals such as fondues are also offered.

The hotel's most acclaimed restaurant is the ◖ **Banffshire Club** (Tues.–Sat. 6–10 P.M.), which seats just 76 diners. Like its predecessor, the Rob Roy Room, this fine-dining restaurant is a bastion of elegance, which begins as a harp player serenades you through a gated entrance. Inside, extravagantly rich wood furnishings, perfectly presented table settings, muted lighting, and kilted staff create an atmosphere as far removed from the surrounding wilderness as is imaginable. Most diners choose one of four table d'hôte menus, which range from $100 per person for two courses to $225 for nine courses accompanied by specially selected wines. Reservations and a jacket are required.

Two restaurants lie within the grounds surrounding the hotel, and both are worthy of consideration. Originally the golf course clubhouse, the **Waldhaus Restaurant** (daily 6–9 P.M., closed Apr.) is nestled in a forested area directly below the hotel. The big room is dominated by dark woods and is warmed by a roaring fire. The menu features German specialties, with mains from $17. Below this restaurant is a pub of the same name, with a pub-style dinner menu offered in a casual atmosphere. The **Golf Course Clubhouse** is a seasonal restaurant on the golf course proper that serves light breakfasts, lunch buffets, and more formal dinners. A shuttle bus runs every 30 minutes between the main lobby and the clubhouse.

For all Fairmont Banff Springs dining reservations, call 403/662-6860 or, after 5 P.M., 403/762-2211. During the summer months a desk in the main lobby has all menus posted and takes reservations.

Out-of-Town

◖ **Muk-a-Muk Bistro** (The Juniper, Norquay Rd., 403/763-6205, daily 7 A.M.–9:30 P.M.) is well worth searching out for both Canadian cuisine and unparalleled views across town to Mount Rundle and the Spray Valley. The stylish interior may be inviting, but in warmer weather, you'll want to be outside on the patio, where the panorama is most spectacular. The menu blends traditional tastes with Canadian produce. If your taste runs toward seafood, there are sweet-potato crab cakes ($11) as a starter. For those looking for something a little more local, the bison Bolognese ($24) is a good choice. Most breakfasts are under $10, while at lunch beer-braised bison ribs smothered in blueberries ($19) are a treat.

The first of two noteworthy restaurants along the Bow Valley parkway is **Bridges** (Johnston Canyon Resort, 26 km/16 mi from Banff, 403/762-2971). With a historic atmosphere and views out to a creek, it opens nightly at 6 P.M. for a wide-ranging menu that includes a jambalaya pasta served with a generous quantity of shrimp ($13–21).

Also well worth the drive is ◖ **The Bistro** (Baker Creek Chalets, 40 km/24.7 miles northwest of town along the Bow Valley Parkway, 403/522-2182, Sat.–Sun. 7 A.M.–2 P.M., Mon.–Fri. noon–2 P.M. and daily 5–9:30 P.M.). Dining is in a small room that characterizes the term "mountain hideaway," in an adjacent lounge bar, or out on a small deck decorated with pots of colorful flowers. The menu isn't large, but dishes feature lots of Canadian game and produce, with favorites like medallions of venison served with an orange and gin sauce ($29) and roasted duck breast with a cream-based cranberry sauce ($24).

The food at **⟪ Storm Mountain Lodge** (Hwy. 93, 403/762-4155, early Dec.–mid-Oct. Fri.–Sun. 5–9 P.M., summer daily 11:30 A.M.–3:30 P.M. and 5–9 P.M.) is excellent, but it's the ambience you'll remember long after leaving—an intoxicating blend of historical appeal and rustic mountain charm. The chef uses mostly organic produce with seasonally available game and seafood—bison, venison, wild salmon, and the like—to create tasty and interesting dishes well suited to the I-must-be-in-the-Canadian-wilderness surroundings. Storm Mountain Lodge is a 25-minute drive northwest from Banff; take the TransCanada Highway toward Lake Louise and head west at the Castle Mountain interchange.

INFORMATION

Many sources of information are available on the park and its commercial facilities. Once you've arrived, the best place to make your first stop is the **Banff Visitor Centre** (224 Banff Ave., mid-June–Aug. daily 8 A.M.–8 P.M., mid-May–mid-June and Sept. daily 8 A.M.–6 P.M., the rest of the year daily 9 A.M.–5 P.M.). On the right-hand side is a desk staffed by Parks Canada employees. They will answer all of your queries regarding Banff's natural wonders and advise you of trail closures. Anyone planning an overnight back-country trip should register here and obtain a camping pass ($10 per person per night). Here you can also pick up park brochures, or wander down the back to peruse park maps, view a free slide show, and watch videos about the park. The Parks Canada website (www.pc.gc.ca) also has park information. Across the floor is a desk for the **Banff/Lake Louise Tourism Bureau.** This organization represents businesses and commercial establishments in the park. Here you can find out about accommodations and restaurants and have any other questions answered. To answer the most frequently asked question, the restrooms are downstairs. For general tourism information, contact the Banff/Lake Louise Tourism Bureau (P.O. Box 1298, Banff, AB T1L 1B3, 403/762-8421, www.banff.ca).

Banff Public Library (opposite Central Park at 101 Bear St., 403/762-2661, Mon.–

Thurs. 10 A.M.–8 P.M., Fri. 10 A.M.–6 P.M., Sat. 11 A.M.–6 P.M., Sun. 1–5 P.M.) boasts an extensive collection of nonfiction books, many about the park and its environs, which makes it an excellent rainy-day hangout. It also has a large collection of magazines and newspapers. Internet access is free, but book ahead.

SERVICES

The post office (Mon.–Fri. 9 A.M.–5:30 P.M.) is on the corner of Buffalo and Bear Streets opposite Central Park.

All the major hotels have guest Internet access of some kind or another, and the library has free access. You can also head downstairs to the **Cyberweb Internet Cafe** (Sundance Mall, 215 Banff Ave., 403/762-9226, daily 9 A.M.–midnight).

Major banks can be found along Banff Avenue and are generally open Monday–Thursday 10 A.M.–4 P.M. and Friday 9 A.M.–4:30 P.M. **Freya's Currency Exchange** is in the Clock Tower Mall (108 Banff Ave., 403/762-4652).

The only downtown launderette is **Cascade Coin Laundry,** on the lower level of the Cascade Plaza (daily 7:30 A.M.–10 P.M.). **Chalet Coin Laundry** is on Tunnel Mountain Road at the Douglas Fir Resort, within walking distance of all Tunnel Mountain accommodations (daily 8 A.M.–10 P.M.).

Along Banff Avenue you'll find a handful of photo shops with digital imaging capabilities; check around for the cheapest because many have special offers. The most competitive and reliable is the **Banff Camera Shop** (101 Banff Ave., 403/762-3562).

Mineral Springs Hospital (301 Lynx St., 403/762-2222) has 24-hour emergency service. **Rexall Drug Store,** on the lower level of the Cascade Plaza (317 Banff Ave., 403/762-2245), is open daily until 9 P.M.

GETTING THERE AND AROUND
Getting There
Calgary International Airport, 128 kilometers (80 mi) east, is the closest airport to Banff National Park. **Brewster** (403/762-6767 or

800/661-1152, www.brewster.ca) is one of many companies offering shuttles between the airport and Banff National Park. Its service leaves the airport twice daily, stopping at Banff then continuing to Lake Louise. Calgary to Banff is adult $48, child $24. This shuttle delivers guests to all major Banff hotels as well as the park's main bus terminal, the **Brewster Tour and Transportation Centre,** a five-minute walk from downtown Banff at 100 Gopher Street. The depot has a ticket office, lockers, a café, and a gift shop. It's open daily 7:30 A.M.–10:45 P.M. Other airporter buses are **Banff Airporter** (403/762-3330 or 888/449-2901, www.banffairporter.com) and **Rocky Mountain Sky Shuttle** (403/762-5200 or 888/762-8754, www.rockymountainskyshuttle.com). The advantage of traveling with these two companies is that they offer door-to-door service for around the same price. Adjacent desks at the airport's Arrivals level take bookings, but reserve a seat by booking over the phone or online in advance. The earliest service back to the airport departs Banff at 4:30 A.M.

Greyhound (403/762-1092 or 800/661-8747, www.greyhound.ca) offers scheduled service from the Calgary bus depot at 877 Greyhound Way SW, five times daily to the Brewster Tour and Transportation Centre at 100 Gopher Street and Samson Mall, Lake Louise. Greyhound buses leave Vancouver from the depot at 1150 Station Street three times daily for the scenic 14-hour ride to the park.

Getting Around

Most of the sights and many trailheads are within walking distance of town. **Banff Transit** (403/760-8294) operates bus service along two routes through the town of Banff: one from the Fairmont Banff Springs to the RV and trailer parking area at the north end of Banff Avenue, the other from the Fairmont Banff Springs to the Tunnel Mountain Campgrounds. Mid-May to September, buses run

twice an hour between 7 A.M. and midnight. From October to December, the two routes are merged as one, with buses running hourly midday to midnight. No local buses run the rest of the year. Travel costs $2 per sector.

Cabs around Banff are reasonably priced—flag drop is $4, then it's $2 per kilometer. From the Banff bus depot to Tunnel Mountain accommodations will run around $8, same to the Fairmont Banff Springs, more after midnight. Companies are **Banff Taxi** (403/762-4444) and **Taxi Taxi** (403/762-8000).

The days when a row of horse-drawn buggies eagerly awaited the arrival of wealthy visitors at the CPR Station have long since passed, but the **Trail Rider Store** (132 Banff Ave., 403/762-4551) offers visitors rides around town in a beautifully restored carriage ($11 per person for 15 minutes). Expect to pay $22 per carriage for a short loop along the Bow River.

Plan on renting a vehicle elsewhere before you reach the park. In addition to high pricing for walk-in customers, the main catch with local companies is that they don't offer unlimited mileage. The most you'll get is a free 150 kilometers per day, and then expect to pay $0.25 per kilometer. Agencies and their local contact numbers are: **Avis** (Cascade Plaza, 317 Banff Ave., 403/762-3222), **Budget** (Brewster's Mountain Lodge, 208 Caribou St., 403/762-4565), **Hertz** (Fairmont Banff Springs, Spray Ave., 403/762-2027), and **National** (corner of Lynx and Caribou Sts., 403/762-2688). Reservations for vehicles in Banff should be made well in advance, especially in July and August.

The Banff and Lake Louise Visitor Centres are wheelchair accessible—restrooms, information desks, and theater are all barrier free. Once inside, use the handy Touchsource monitors for a full listing of all barrier-free services within the park. An all-terrain wheelchair is available at the Cave and Basin National Historic Site for use on park trails. To reserve, call 403/762-1566.

Lake Louise and Vicinity

As the first flush of morning sun hits Victoria Glacier, and the impossibly steep northern face of Mount Victoria is reflected in the sparkling emerald-green waters of Lake Louise, you'll understand why this lake is regarded as one of the world's seven natural wonders. Overlooking the lake is one of the world's most photographed hotels, Chateau Lake Louise. Apart from simply viewing the lake, the area has plenty to keep you busy. Some of the park's best hiking, canoeing, and horseback riding are nearby. And only a short distance away is Moraine Lake, not as famous as Lake Louise but rivaling it in beauty.

Lake Louise is 56 kilometers (35 mi) northwest of Banff along the TransCanada Highway, or a little bit farther if you take the quieter Bow Valley Parkway. The hamlet of Lake Louise, composed of a small mall, hotels, and restaurants, is located in the Bow Valley, just west of the TransCanada Highway. The lake is 200 vertical meters (660 ft) above the valley floor, along a winding four-kilometer (2.5-mi) road. Across the valley is Canada's second-largest ski area, Lake Louise, a world-class facility renowned for its diverse terrain, abundant snow, and breathtaking views.

From Lake Louise, the TransCanada Highway continues west, exiting the park over Kicking Horse Pass and passing through Yoho National Park to Golden. Highway 93, the famous Icefields Parkway, begins just north of the village and heads northwest through the park's northern reaches to Jasper National Park.

History

During the summer of 1882, Tom Wilson, an outfitter, was camped near the confluence of the Bow and Pipestone Rivers when he heard the distant rumblings of an avalanche. He questioned Stoney Indian guides and was told the noises originated from the "Lake of Little Fishes." The following day, Wilson, led by a native guide, hiked to the lake to investigate. He became the first white man to lay eyes on

what he named Emerald Lake. Two years later, the name was changed to Lake Louise, honoring Princess Louise Caroline Alberta, daughter of Queen Victoria.

A railway station known as Laggan was built where the rail line passed closest to the lake, six kilometers (3.7 mi) away. Until a road was completed in 1926, everyone arrived by train. The station's name was changed to Lake Louise in 1913 to prevent confusion among visitors. In 1890, a modest two-bedroom wooden hotel replaced a crude cabin that had been built on the shore of the lake as word of its beauty spread. After many additions, a disastrous fire, and the addition of a concrete wing in 1925, the château of today took shape. Recreational mountaineering has been popular in the park for more than 100 years, and most of the early climbing was done on peaks around Lake Louise. Following the 1896 death of P. S. Abbot (North America's first mountaineering fatality) the CPR began employing Swiss mountain guides to satisfy the climbing needs of wealthy patrons of the railway and to make the sport safer.

SIGHTS
◖ Lake Louise

In summer, around 10,000 visitors a day make the journey from the Bow Valley floor up to Lake Louise. By noon the tiered parking lot is often full. An alternative to the road is one of two hiking trails that begin in the village and end at the public parking lot (see *Hiking* later in the *Lake Louise* section). From here a number of paved trails lead to the lake's eastern shore. From these vantage points the dramatic setting can be fully appreciated. The lake is 2.4 kilometers (1.5 mi) long, 500 meters (1,640 ft) wide, and up to 90 meters (295 ft) deep. Its cold waters reach a maximum temperature of 4°C (39°F) in August. The snow-covered peak at the back of the lake is **Mount Victoria** (3,459 m/11,350 ft), which sits on the Continental Divide. Amazingly, its base is over 10 kilometers (6.2 mi) from the eastern

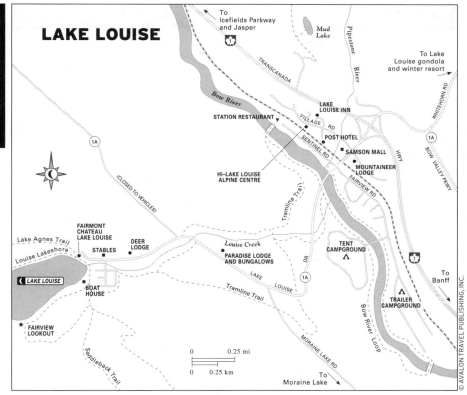

LAKE LOUISE

To Icefields Parkway and Jasper

Mud Lake

Pipestone River

To Lake Louise gondola and winter resort

WHITEHORN RD

Bow River

TRANSCANADA

LAKE LOUISE INN

STATION RESTAURANT

VILLAGE RD

1A

POST HOTEL

SENTINEL RD

SAMSON MALL

1A

HWY

BOW VALLEY PKWY

HI-LAKE LOUISE ALPINE CENTRE

MOUNTAINEER LODGE

FAIRVIEW RD

(CLOSED TO VEHICLES)

Tramline Trail

FAIRMONT CHATEAU LAKE LOUISE

Lake Agnes Trail

DEER LODGE

Louise Creek

TENT CAMPGROUND

Louise Lakeshore

STABLES

PARADISE LODGE AND BUNGALOWS

DR

To Banff

LAKE LOUISE

LAKE LOUISE

1A

BOAT HOUSE

Tramline Trail

TRAILER CAMPGROUND

1

FAIRVIEW LOOKOUT

Bow River Loop

Saddleback Trail

MORAINE LAKE RD

0   0.25 mi

0   0.25 km

To Moraine Lake

© AVALON TRAVEL PUBLISHING, INC.

end of the lake. Mount Victoria, first climbed in 1897, remains one of the park's most popular peaks for mountaineers. Although the difficult northeast face (facing the château) was first successfully ascended in 1922, the most popular and easiest route to the summit is along the southeast ridge.

Fairmont Chateau Lake Louise is a tourist attraction in itself. Built by the CPR to take the pressure off the popular Fairmont Banff Springs, the château has seen many changes in the last 100 years, yet it remains one of the world's great mountain resorts. No one minds the hordes of camera-toting tourists who traipse through each day—and there's really no way to avoid them. The immaculately manicured gardens between the château and the lake make an interesting foreground for the millions of Lake Louise photographs taken each year. Aside from soaking up the view, hiking is one of the few activities you don't have to pay for. At the lakeshore boathouse, canoes can be rented for $40 per hour, or you can take a trail ride from **Lake Louise Stables** (403/522-3511) for $38 per hour.

◀ Moraine Lake

Although less than half the size of Lake Louise, Moraine Lake is just as spectacular and worthy of just as much film. It is located up a winding road 13 kilometers (eight mi) off Lake Louise Drive. Its rugged setting, nestled in the Valley of the Ten Peaks among the towering mountains of the main ranges, has provided inspiration for

© ANDREW HEMPSTEAD

Lake Louise will take your breath away.

millions of people from around the world since Walter Wilcox became the first white man to reach its shore in 1899. Wilcox's subsequent writings—such as "no scene has given me an equal impression of inspiring solitude and rugged grandeur"—guaranteed the lake's future popularity. Although Wilcox was a knowledgeable man, he named the lake on the assumption that it was dammed by a glacial moraine deposited by the retreating Wenkchemna Glacier. In fact, the large rock pile that blocks its waters was deposited by major rockfalls from the Tower of Babel to the south. The lake often remains frozen until June, and the access road is closed all winter. A trail leads along the lake's northern shore, and canoes can be rented for $28 per hour from the lakeside concession.

Sightseeing Gondola

During summer the main ski lift at Lake Louise Mountain Resort (403/522-3555) whisks visitors up the face of Mount Whitehorn to Whitehorn Lodge in either open chairs or enclosed gondola cars. The view from the top—

at an altitude of more than two kilometers (1.2 mi) above sea level across the Bow Valley, Lake Louise, and the Continental Divide—is among the most spectacular in the Canadian Rockies. Short trails lead through the forests, across open meadows, and, for the energetic, to the summit of Mount Whitehorn, more than 600 vertical meters (1,970 vertical ft) above. Visitors are free to walk these trails, but it pays to join a guided walk ($5–7) if you'd like to learn about the surrounding environment. After working up an appetite (and working off breakfast), head to the teahouse in the Whitehorn Lodge, try the outdoor barbecue, or, back at the base area, enjoy lunch at the Lodge of the Ten Peaks, the resort's impressive post-and-beam day lodge. The lift operates May to September daily 9 A.M.–4 P.M. with extended summer hours of 8:30 A.M.– 6 P.M.; adult $23, child $11.50. Ride-and-dine packages are an excellent deal. Pay an extra $2 per person and have a buffet breakfast (8–11 A.M.) included with the gondola ride or $6 extra for the buffet lunch (11:30 A.M.–

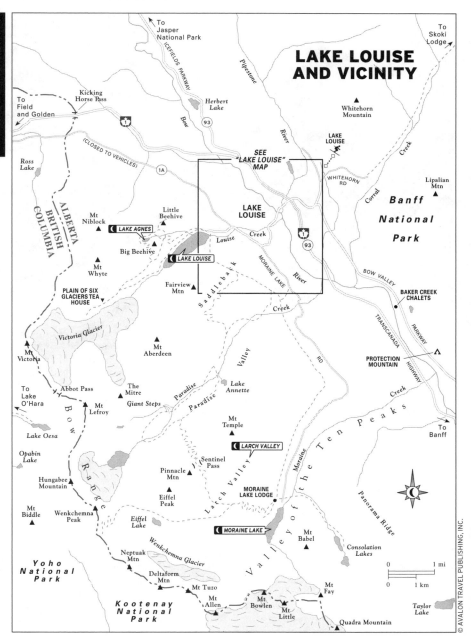

LAKE LOUISE AND VICINITY

To Jasper National Park

To Skoki Lodge

Kicking Horse Pass

To Field and Golden

Herbert Lake

Whitehorn Mountain

LAKE LOUISE

Ross Lake

SEE "LAKE LOUISE" MAP

WHITEHORN RD

Lipalian Mtn

Mt Niblock

Little Beehive

(LAKE AGNES

LAKE LOUISE

Banff

National

Park

Big Beehive

Louise

Creek

(LAKE LOUISE

Mt Whyte

PLAIN OF SIX GLACIERS TEA HOUSE

Fairview Mtn

Saddleback

MORAINE LAKE

River

BOW VALLEY

BAKER CREEK CHALETS

Victoria Glacier

Creek

Mt Aberdeen

TRANSCANADA

PARKWAY

Mt Victoria

Valley

RD

PROTECTION MOUNTAIN

HIGHWAY

To Lake O'Hara

Abbot Pass

The Mitre

Mt Lefroy

Giant Steps

Paradise

Lake Annette

Paradise

Creek

To Banff

Bow

Lake Oesa

Mt Temple

Ten

Peaks

Opabin Lake

Range

(LARCH VALLEY

Hungabee Mountain

Pinnacle Mtn

Sentinel Pass

Larch Valley

Mt Biddle

Wenkchemna Peak

Eiffel Peak

MORAINE LAKE LODGE

Moraine

Panorama Ridge

Eiffel Lake

(MORAINE LAKE

Mt Babel

Consolation Lakes

Wenkchemna Glacier

Valley of the

Neptuak Mtn

Deltaform Mtn

Mt Tuzo

Mt Fay

Yoho National Park

Mt Allen

Mt Bowlen

Mt Little

Taylor Lake

Kootenay National Park

Quadra Mountain

0   1 mi

0   1 km

© AVALON TRAVEL PUBLISHING, INC.

© ANDREW HEMPSTEAD

Moraine Lake

2:30 P.M.). Free shuttles run from Lake Louise accommodations to the day lodge.

HIKING

The variety of hiking opportunities in the vicinity of Lake Louise and Moraine Lake is surely equal to any area on the face of the earth. The region's potential for outdoor recreation was first realized in the late 1800s, and it soon became the center of hiking activity in the Canadian Rockies. This popularity continues today; trails here are among the most heavily used in the park. Hiking is best early or late in the short summer season. Head out early in the morning to miss the strollers, high heels, dogs, and bear-bells that you'll surely encounter during the busiest periods.

The two main trailheads are at Fairmont Chateau Lake Louise and Moraine Lake. Two trails lead from the village to the château (a pleasant alternative to driving the steep and very busy Lake Louise Drive). Shortest is the 2.7-kilometer (1.7-mi) **Louise Creek Trail.** It begins on the downstream side of the point

where Lake Louise Drive crosses the Bow River, crosses Louise Creek three times, and ends at the Lake Louise parking lot. The other trail, **Tramline,** is 4.5 kilometers (2.8 mi) longer but not as steep. It begins behind the railway station and follows the route of a narrow-gauge railway that once transported guests from the CPR line to Chateau Lake Louise.

Bow River Loop

- Length: 7-kilometer/4.3-mile loop (1.5–2 hours)
- Elevation gain: Minimal
- Rating: Easy
- Trailheads: Various points throughout Lake Louise Village, including behind Samson Mall

This loop follows both banks of the Bow River southeast from the railway station. Used by joggers and cyclists to access various points in the village, the trail also links the station to the Lake Louise Alpine Centre, Post Hotel, Samson Mall, both campgrounds, and the Louise Creek and Tramline trails to Lake Louise. Interpretive signs along its length provide information on the Bow River ecosystem.

Louise Lakeshore

- Length: Two kilometers/1.2 miles (30 minutes) one-way
- Elevation gain: None
- Rating: Easy
- Trailhead: Lake Louise, four kilometers (2.5 mi) from TransCanada Highway

Probably the busiest trail in all of the Canadian Rockies, this one follows the north shore of Lake Louise from in front of the château to the west end of the lake. Here numerous braided glacial streams empty their silt-filled waters into Lake Louise. Along the trail's length are benches to sit and ponder what English mountaineer James Outram once described as "a gem of composition and of coloring…perhaps unrivalled anywhere."

Fairmont Chateau Lake Louise, from along the Louise Lakeshore Trail

Plain of the Six Glaciers

• Length: 5.3 kilometers/3.3 miles (90 minutes) one-way

• Elevation gain: 370 meters/1,215 feet

• Rating: Easy/moderate

• Trailhead: Lake Louise

Hikers along this trail are rewarded not only with panoramic views of the glaciated peaks of the main range, but also with a rustic trail's-end teahouse serving homemade goodies baked on a wooden stove. For the first two kilometers (1.2 mi), the trail follows Louise Lakeshore Trail to the western end of the lake. From there it begins a steady climb through a forest of spruce and subalpine fir. It enters an open area where an avalanche has come tumbling down (now a colorful carpet of wildflowers), then passes through a forested area into a vast wasteland of moraines produced by the advance and retreat of Victoria Glacier. Views of surrounding peaks continue to improve until

the trail enters a stunted forest. After switchbacking up through this forest, the trail arrives at the teahouse (July to early September). The trail continues one kilometer (0.6 mi) beyond the teahouse to the narrow top of a lateral moraine. From here the trail's namesakes are visible. From left to right the glaciers are Aberdeen, Upper Lefroy, Lower Lefroy, Upper Victoria, Lower Victoria, and Pope's. Between Mount Lefroy (3,441 m/11,290 ft) and Mount Victoria (3,459 m/11,350 ft) is Abbot Pass, where it's possible to make out Abbot Hut on the skyline. When constructed in 1922, this stone structure was the highest building in Canada.

◖ Lake Agnes

• Length: 3.6 kilometers/2.2 miles (90 minutes) one-way

• Elevation gain: 400 meters/1,312 feet

• Rating: Moderate

• Trailhead: Lake Louise

This moderately strenuous hike is one of the park's most popular. It begins in front of the château, branching right near the beginning of the Louise Lakeshore Trail. For the first 2.5 kilometers (1.6 mi), the trail climbs steeply, switchbacking through a forest of subalpine fir and Engelmann spruce, crossing a horse trail, passing a lookout, and leveling out at tiny Mirror Lake. Here the old, traditional trail veers right (use it if the ground is wet or snowy) while a more direct route veers left to the Plain of the Six Glaciers. The final elevation gain along both trails is made easier by a flight of steps beside Bridal Veil Falls. The trail ends beside a rustic teahouse overlooking Lake Agnes, a subalpine lake nestled in a hanging valley. The teahouse offers homemade soups, healthy sandwiches, and a wide assortment of teas.

From the teahouse a one-kilometer (0.6-mi) trail leads to Little Beehive and impressive views of the Bow Valley. Another trail leads around the northern shore of Lake Agnes, climbing to the **Big Beehive,** a total of five kilometers (3.1 mi) from the château. This is

a great place to admire the uniquely colored waters of Lake Louise directly below.

Paradise Valley

- Length: 18 kilometers/11.2 miles (6 hours) round-trip

- Elevation gain: 380 meters/1,250 feet

- Rating: Moderate

- Trailhead: Moraine Lake Road, 3.5 kilometers (2.2 mi) from Lake Louise Drive

This aptly named trail makes for a long day hike, but it's possible to make a shorter trip by not completing the full loop. The trail climbs steadily for the first five kilometers (3.1 mi), crossing Paradise Creek numerous times and passing the junction of a trail that climbs the Sheol Valley to Saddleback. After five kilometers (3.1 mi) the trail divides again, following either side of the valley to form a 13-kilometer (eight-mi) loop. **Lake Annette** is 700 meters (0.4 mi) along the left fork. It's a typical subalpine lake in a unique setting—nestled against the near-vertical 1,200-meter (3,940-ft) north face of snow-and ice-capped **Mount Temple** (3,549 m/11,645 ft), one of the 10 highest peaks in the Canadian Rockies. The lake is a worthy destination in itself. Allow yourself four hours round-trip from the trailhead. For those completing the entire loop, continue beyond the lake into an open avalanche area that affords views across Paradise Valley. Look and listen for pikas and marmots among the boulders. The trail then passes through Horseshoe Meadow, crosses Paradise Creek, and heads back down the valley. Keep to the left at all trail crossings and you'll quickly arrive at a series of waterfalls known as the Giant Steps. From the base of these falls, it is eight kilometers (five mi) back to the trailhead.

◖ Larch Valley

- Length: 2.9 kilometers/1.8 miles (60 minutes) one-way

- Elevation gain: 400 meters/1,310 feet

- Rating: Moderate

- Trailhead: Moraine Lake, 13 kilometers (eight mi) from Lake Louise Drive

In fall, when the larch trees have turned a magnificent gold and the sun is shining, few spots in the Canadian Rockies can match the beauty of this valley. But don't expect to find much solitude (and don't be too disappointed if the trail is closed in fall—it often is due to wildlife). Although the most popular time for visiting the valley is fall, it is a worthy destination all summer, when the open meadows are filled with colorful wildflowers. The trail begins just past Moraine Lake Lodge and climbs fairly steeply with occasional glimpses of Moraine Lake below. After reaching the junction of the Eiffel Lake Trail, keep right, passing through an open forest of larch and into the meadow beyond. The range of larch is restricted within the park and this is one of the few areas where they are prolific. Mount Fay (3,235 m/10,615 ft) is the dominant peak on the skyline, rising above the other mountains that make up the Valley of the Ten Peaks. Note: Hiking in Larch Valley is prone to restrictions due to grizzly-bear activity. In recent years, a compromise to closing the area completely has been to restrict hikers to parties of six or more.

Eiffel Lake

- Length: 5.6 kilometers/3.5 miles (2 hours) one-way

- Elevation gain: 400 meters/1,310 feet

- Rating: Moderate/difficult

- Trailhead: Moraine Lake

Eiffel Lake is small, and looks even smaller in its rugged and desolate setting, surrounded by the famed Valley of the Ten Peaks. For the first 2.4 kilometers (1.5 mi), follow the Larch Valley Trail (see previous listing), then fork left. Most of the elevation gain has already been made, and the trail remains relatively level before emerging onto an open slope from where each of the 10 peaks can be seen, along with Moraine Lake far below. Eiffel lake itself soon comes into view. It lies in a depression formed by a rockslide from Neptuak Mountain. The

lake is named for **Eiffel Peak,** a rock pinnacle behind it, which with a little imagination could be compared to the Eiffel Tower in Paris.

Consolation Lakes

* Length: Three kilometers/1.9 miles (1 hour) one-way

* Elevation gain: 65 meters/213 feet

* Rating: Easy/moderate

* Trailhead: Beside the washrooms at Moraine Lake parking lot

This short trail begins with a crossing of Moraine Creek at the outlet of Moraine Lake and ends at a pleasant subalpine lake. The first section of the trail traverses a boulder-strewn rock pile—the result of rock slides on the imposing Tower of Babel (3,100 m/10,170 ft)—before entering a dense forest of Engelmann spruce and subalpine fir and following Babel Creek to the lower lake. The wide valley affords 360-degree views of the surrounding jagged peaks, including Mount Temple back down the valley and Mounts Bident and Quandra at the far end of the lakes. After eating a picnic lunch (from Laggans, in the Samson Mall) while perched on one of many boulders, you could continue to Upper Consolation Lake by crossing Babel Creek and following a usually wet and muddy trail along the lake's eastern shore.

WINTER RECREATION

Lake Louise is an immense winter playground offering one of the world's premier alpine resorts, unlimited cross-country skiing, ice-skating, sleigh rides, and nearby heli-skiing. Between November and May, accommodation prices are reduced by up to 70 percent (except Christmas holidays). Lift and lodging packages begin at $60 per person, and you'll always be able to get a table at your favorite restaurant.

Lake Louise Mountain Resort

Canada's answer to U.S. mega-resorts such as Vail and Killington is Lake Louise (403/522-3555 or 877/253-6888, www.skilouise.com),

which opens in November and operates until mid-May. The nation's second-largest winter resort (behind only Whistler/Blackcomb) comprises 1,700 hectares (4,200 acres) of gentle trails, mogul fields, long cruising runs, steep chutes, and vast bowls filled with famous Rocky Mountain powder.

The resort is made up of four distinct faces. The front side has a vertical drop of 1,000 meters (3,280 feet) and is served by eight lifts, including four high-speed quads, and western Canada's only six-passenger chairlift. Resort statistics are impressive: a 990-meter (3,250-foot) vertical rise, 1,700 hectares (4,200 acres) of patrolled terrain, and more than 100 named runs. The four back bowls are each as big as many midsize resorts and are all well above the tree line. Larch and Ptarmigan faces have a variety of terrain, allowing you to follow the sun as it moves across the sky or escape into trees for protection on windy days. Each of the three day lodges has a restaurant and bar. Ski and snowboard rentals, clothing, and souvenirs are available in the Lodge of the Ten Peaks, a magnificent post-and-beam day lodge that overlooks the front face.

Lift tickets are $69 per day adults, $56 seniors, $50 youth, and $20 children younger than 12. Free guided tours of the mountain are available three times daily—inquire at customer service. Free shuttle buses run regularly from Lake Louise accommodations to the hill. From Banff you pay $14 round-trip for transportation to Lake Louise. For information on packages and multi-day tickets that cover all three park resorts, go to www.skibig3.com.

Cross-Country Skiing

The most popular cross-country skiing areas are on Lake Louise, along Moraine Lake Road, and in Skoki Valley at the back of the Lake Louise ski area. For details and helpful trail classifications, pick up a copy of *Cross-Country Skiing–Nordic Trails in Banff National Park,* from the Lake Louise Visitor Centre. Before heading out, check the weather forecast at the visitors center or call 403/762-2088. For avalanche reports, call 403/762-1460.

Ice-Skating and Sleigh Rides

Of all the skating rinks in Canada, the one on frozen Lake Louise, in front of the château, is surely the most spectacular. Spotlights allow skating after dark, and on special occasions hot chocolate is served. Skates are available in the château at **Monod Sports** (403/522-3837); $12 for two hours.

Brewster Lake Louise Sleigh Rides (403/522-3511) offers rides in traditional horse-drawn sleighs along the shores of Lake Louise beginning from in front of the château. Although blankets are supplied, you should still bundle up. The one-hour ride is $24 per person, $16 for children. Reservations are necessary. The rides are scheduled hourly from 11 A.M. on weekends and from 3 P.M. weekdays with the last ride between 6 and 9 P.M.

NIGHTLIFE

The lounge in the **Post Hotel** (200 Pipestone Dr., 403/522-3989) oozes mountain style and upscale charm. It's cozy, quiet and the perfect place to relax in front of a fire with a cocktail before moving on to the adjacent fine-dining restaurant. Not your scene? Hang out with seasonal workers at the smoky **Lake Louise Grill & Bar** (upstairs in Samson Mall, 403/522-3879) then move across the road with your newfound friends to **Charlie's Pub** (Lake Louise Inn, 403/522-3791) for dancing to recorded music until 2 A.M. Up at the Fairmont Chateau Lake Louise (403/522-3511) is **The Glacier Saloon** (daily from 6 P.M.), where on most summer nights a DJ plays music ranging from pop to Western.

ACCOMMODATIONS AND CAMPING

In summer, accommodations at Lake Louise are even harder to come by than in Banff, so it's essential to make reservations well in advance. Any rooms not taken by early afternoon will be the expensive ones.

Under $50

With beds for $100 less than anyplace else in the village, the 164-bed **C HI-Lake Louise**

Alpine Centre (403/522-2200 or 866/762-4122, www.hihostels.ca) is understandably popular. Of log construction, with large windows and high vaulted ceilings, the lodge is a joint venture between the Alpine Club of Canada and the Hostelling International Canada–Pacific Mountain Region. Beyond the large reception area is **Bill Peyto's Cafe,** the least expensive place to eat in Lake Louise. Upstairs is a large lounge area and guide's room—a quiet place to plan your next hike or browse through the large collection of mountain literature. Other amenities include Wi-Fi, a laundry, a games room, and a wintertime ski shuttle. Members of Hostelling International pay $34 per person per night (nonmembers $38) for a dorm bed or $99 s or d ($106 for nonmembers) in a private room. Rates are discounted to $27 for a dorm and $78 s or d for a private room ($31 and $86, respectively, for nonmembers) October through May, including throughout the extremely busy winter season. The hostel is open year-round, with check-in after 3 P.M. In summer and on weekends during the winter season, advance bookings (up to six months) are essential. The hostel is on Village Road, less than one kilometer (0.6 mi) from Samson Mall.

$150-200

An excellent option for families and those looking for old-fashioned mountain charm is **C Paradise Lodge and Bungalows** (403/522-3595, www.paradiselodge.com, mid-May to early October). This family-operated lodge provides excellent value in a wonderfully tranquil setting. Spread out around well-manicured gardens are 21 attractive cabins in four configurations. Each has a rustic yet warm and inviting interior, with comfortable beds, a separate sitting area, and a recently renovated bathroom. Each cabin has a small fridge, microwave, and coffeemaker, while the larger ones have full kitchens and separate bedrooms. Instead of television, children are kept happy with a playground that includes a sandbox and jungle gym. On Wednesday and Sunday nights, a local naturalist presents an

outdoor interpretive program for interested guests. The least expensive cabins—complete with a classic cast-iron stove/fireplace combo are $199 s or d, or pay $40 extra for a big deck with soaring valley views. Twenty-four luxury suites, each with a fireplace, TV, one or two bedrooms, and fabulous mountain views, start at $270, or $290 with a kitchen. The Honeymoon Suite, with all of the above as well as a large hot tub, is $320. To get there from the valley floor, follow Lake Louise Drive toward the Fairmont Chateau Lake Louise for three kilometers (1.9 mi); the lake itself is just one kilometer (0.6 mi) farther up the hill.

Historic **Deer Lodge** (403/410-7417 or 800/661-1595, www.crmr.com) began life in 1921 as a teahouse, with rooms added in 1925. Facilities include a rooftop hot tub with glacier views, game room, restaurant (breakfast and dinner), and bar. The least expensive rooms ($175 s or d) are small and don't have phones. Rooms in the $200–250 range are considerably larger, or pay $270 for a heritage-themed Tower Room. Deer Lodge is along Lake Louise Drive, up the hill from the village, and just a five-minute walk from the lake itself.

On the valley floor, **Mountaineer Lodge** (403/522-3844, www.mountaineerlodge.com, May–mid-Oct.) charges from $180 s or d for large, functional guest rooms, many with mountain views and all with Wi-Fi. On the downside, the rooms have no phones or air-conditioning, and there is no elevator. Rates are halved during the first and last months of the operating season.

$200-250

Aside from the château, the **Lake Louise Inn** (210 Village Rd., 403/522-3791 or 800/661-9237, www.lakelouiseinn.com) is the village's largest lodging, with more than 200 units spread throughout five buildings. Across from the lobby, in the main lodge, is a gift shop and an activities desk, and beyond here is a pizzeria, a restaurant, a bar, and a large indoor pool. Standard rooms are $210 s or d, rising well above $300 for a suite with a fireplace. Most rates booked online include breakfast.

Over $250

Originally called Lake Louise Ski Lodge, the ◖ **Post Hotel** (403/522-3989 or 800/661-1586, www.posthotel.com) is one of only a handful of Canadian lodges that have been accepted into the prestigious Relais & Châteaux organization. Bordered to the east and south by the Pipestone River, it may lack views of Lake Louise, but it is as elegant, in a modern, woodsy way, as the château. Each bungalow-style room is furnished with Canadian pine and has a balcony. Many rooms have whirlpools and fireplaces, while some have kitchens. Other facilities include the upscale Temple Mountain Spa, an indoor pool, a steam room, and a library. The hotel has 17 different room types, with 26 different rates depending on the view. Rates start at $335 s or d per night. Between the main lodge and the Pipestone River are four sought-after cabins, each with a wood-burning fireplace; $380–1,300 s or d.

At the lake for which it's named, four kilometers (2.5 mi) from the valley floor, is super-luxurious **Moraine Lake Lodge** (403/522-3733 or 877/522-2777, www.morainelake.com, June–Sept.). Designed by renowned architect Arthur Erickson, the lodge is a bastion of understated charm, partially obscured from the masses of day-trippers who visit the lake and yet taking full advantage of its location beside one of the world's most-photographed lakes. The decor reflects the wilderness location, with an abundance of polished log work and solid, practical furnishings in heritage-themed rooms. The rooms have no TVs or phones; instead guests take guided nature walks, have unlimited use of canoes, and are pampered with complimentary afternoon tea and evening liqueurs. Lodge rooms are $395 s or d, King Cabins $495.

The famously fabulous **Fairmont Chateau Lake Louise** (403/522-3511 or 800/257-7544, www.fairmont.com), a historic 500-room hotel on the shore of Lake Louise, has views equal to any mountain resort in the world. But all this historic charm and mountain scenery comes at a price. During the summer season (late June to mid-Oct.), the rack rate for rooms *without* a

lake view is $659 s or d, while those with a view are $829. Rooms on the Fairmont Gold Floor come with a private concierge and upgraded everything for a little over $1,000. As at the company's sister property in Banff, most guests book a room as part of a package, either online at www.fairmont.com or through a travel agent, and end up paying closer to $400 for a room in peak summer season. Official rates drop as low as $250 s or d outside of summer, with accommodation and ski pass packages often advertised for around $250 d. Children younger than 18 sharing with parents are free, but if you bring a pet it'll be an extra $25.

Backcountry Accommodations

If you're prepared to lace up your hiking boots for a true mountain experience, consider spending time at ⟨ **Skoki Lodge** (403/256-8473 or 800/258-7669, www.skoki.com), north of the Lake Louise ski resort and far from the nearest road. Getting there requires an 11-kilometer (6.8-mi) hike or ski, depending on the season. The lodge is an excellent base for exploring nearby valleys and mountains. It dates to 1931, when it operated as a lodge for local Banff skiers, and is now a National Historic Site. Today it comprises a main lodge, sleeping cabins, and a wood-fired sauna. Accommodations are rustic—propane heat but no electricity—but comfortable, with mostly twin beds ($169 per person) in the main lodge and cabins that sleep up to five ($185–200 per person). Rates include three meals daily, including a picnic lunch that guests build from a buffet-style layout before heading out hiking or skiing. The dining room and lounge center on a wood-burning fire, where guests come together each evening to swap tales from the trail and mingle with the convivial hosts. The operating season is mid-June to mid-October and mid-December to mid-April.

Camping

Exit the TransCanada Highway at the Lake Louise interchange, 56 kilometers (35 mi) northwest of Banff, and take the first left beyond Samson Mall and under the railway bridge to reach **Lake Louise Campground,** within easy walking distance of the village. The campground is divided into two sections by the Bow River, but linked by the Bow River Loop hiking trail that leads into the village along either side of the Bow River. Individual sites throughout are close together, but some privacy and shade are provided by towering lodgepole pines. Just under 200 powered (called "serviced" by Parks Canada) sites are grouped together at the end of the road. In addition to hookups, this section has showers and flush toilets; $32. Across the river are 216 unserviced sites, each with a fire ring and picnic table. Other amenities include kitchen shelters and a modern bathroom complex complete with hot showers. These cost $28 per night. A dump station is near the entrance to the campground ($8 per use). An interpretive program runs throughout summer nightly (except Tues.) at 9 P.M. in the outdoor theater. Sites can be booked in advance by contacting the **Parks Canada Campground Reservation Service** (877/737-3783, www.pccamping.ca). The many sites available on a first-come, first-served basis fill fast in July and August, so plan on arriving early in the afternoon to ensure a spot. The serviced section of this campground is open year-round, the unserviced section mid-May to September.

FOOD

Other guidebooks encourage readers to "eat at your hotel." Not only is this unhelpful, it's misleading—the village of Lake Louise may exist only to serve travelers, but there are good dining options serving all budgets.

Breakfast

Please don't eat breakfast at the gas station restaurant simply because it is the first place you spot coming off the highway. If you don't feel like a cooked breakfast, start your day off at ⟨ **Laggan's Mountain Bakery** (Samson Mall, 403/552-2017, daily 6 A.M.–8 P.M.), *the* place to hang out with a coffee and a freshly baked breakfast croissant, pastry, cake, or muffin. The chocolate brownie is delicious (order

two slices to save having to line up twice). If the tables are full, order take-out and enjoy your feast on the riverbank behind the mall.

Across the TransCanada Highway, the **Lodge of the Ten Peaks,** at the base of Lake Louise Mountain Resort (403/522-3555), is open in summer daily 7:30–10:30 A.M. for a large and varied breakfast buffet that costs a super-reasonable adult $10.50, child $7.50. An even better deal is to purchase a breakfast/gondola ride combo for $25 (the gondola ride alone is $23). The buffet lunch (11:30 A.M.–2:30 P.M.) is $17, or $29 with the gondola ride.

If you made the effort to rise early and experienced the early-morning tranquility of Moraine Lake, the perfect place to sit back and watch the tour bus crowds pour in is from the dining room of ◖ **Moraine Lake Lodge** (403/522-3733, June–Sept. daily from 7:30 A.M.). Staying overnight at the lodge may be an extravagant splurge, but breakfast isn't. A simple, well-presented continental buffet is just $13, while the hot version is a reasonable $16.

Canadian Contemporary

One hundred years ago visitors departing trains at Laggan Station were keen to get to the Chateau Lake Louise as quickly as possible to begin their adventure. Today, guests from the château, other hotels, and even people from as far away as Banff are returning to dine in the ◖ **Lake Louise Railway Station Restaurant** (200 Sentinel Rd., 403/522-2600), which combines a dining room in the actual station (daily 11:30 A.M.–9 P.M.) with two restored dining cars (summer daily 6–9 P.M.). Although the menu is not extensive, it puts an emphasis on creating imaginative dishes with a combination of Canadian produce and Asian ingredients. Lighter lunches include a Caesar salad topped with roasted-garlic dressing ($8.50)—perfect for those planning an afternoon hike. In the evening, expect starters such as pear and prosciutto bruschetta ($11) and entrées like a memorable pan-seared salmon smothered in roasted-corn salsa ($29).

European

In 1987, the ◖ **Post Hotel** was expanded to include a luxurious new wing. The original log building was renovated as a rustic, timbered dining room (403/522-3989, daily 11:30 A.M.–2 P.M. and 5–9:30 P.M.) linked to the rest of the hotel by an intimate lounge. Although the dining room isn't cheap, it's a favorite of locals and visitors alike. The chef specializes in European cuisine, preparing several Swiss dishes (such as veal zurichois) to make owner George Schwarz feel less homesick. But he's also renowned for his presentation of Alberta beef, Pacific salmon, and Peking duck. Main meals start at $25. The 28,500-bottle cellar is one of the finest in Canada. Reservations are essential for dinner.

Fairmont Chateau Lake Louise

Within this famous lakeside hotel is a choice of eateries and an ice cream shop. For all château dining reservations, call 403/522-1817.

The **Poppy Brasserie** has obscured lake views and is the most casual place for a meal. Breakfasts (daily 7–11:30 A.M.) are offered buffet-style ($25 per person), a little expensive for light eaters. Lunch and dinner (daily 11:30 A.M.–8:30 P.M.) are à la carte. The **Walliser Stube** (daily 6–9 P.M.) is an elegant two-story wine bar decorated with rich wood paneling and solid oak furniture. It offers a simple menu of German dishes from $18.95 as well as cheese fondue. The **Lakeview Lounge** (daily noon–9 P.M.) is along floor-to-ceiling windows with magnificent lake views. Choose this dining area for afternoon tea (daily noon–4 P.M., reservations required, $27 per person, or $35 with a glass of champagne).

The **Victoria Room** (July–Aug. daily 7–9 A.M., May–Sept. daily 6–9 P.M.) enjoys excellent views across the lake to the mountain for which it's named. This restaurant combines the elegance of a European ballroom with a charming alpine allure. It's open for breakfast, Sunday brunch, and evening dining with choices that range from traditional British dishes to innovative Pacific Northwest fare.

The **Fairview Dining Room** (daily 6–9 P.M.) has a lot more than just a fair view. As the châ-

© ANDREW HEMPSTEAD

Fairmont Chateau Lake Louise

teau's signature dining room, it enjoys the best views and offers the most elegant setting. Appetizers start at $7, while entrées combine Canadian produce with classic European cooking styles (mains $24–37).

INFORMATION AND SERVICES

The **Lake Louise Visitor Centre** (403/522-3833, mid-June–Aug. daily 8 A.M.–8 P.M., mid-May–mid-June and Sept. daily 8 A.M.–6 P.M., the rest of the year daily 9 A.M.–4 P.M.) is beside Samson Mall on Village Road. This excellent Parks Canada facility has interpretive displays, slide and video displays, and staff on hand to answer questions, recommend hikes suited to your ability, and issue camping passes to those heading out into the backcountry. Look for the stuffed (literally) female grizzly and read her fascinating, but sad, story.

A small postal outlet in Samson Mall also serves as a bus depot and car-rental agency. Although Lake Louise has no banks, there's a currency exchange in the Fairmont Chateau Lake Louise and a cash machine in the grocery store. The mall also holds a busy launderette (summer daily 8 A.M.–8 P.M., shorter hours the rest of the year). Camping supplies and bike

rentals are available from **Wilson Mountain Sports** (403/522-3636, daily 9 A.M.–9 P.M.).

Pipestone Photo (403/522-3617, daily 9 A.M.–7 P.M.) has a range of photographic supplies unequaled in all of the Canadian Rockies. It's relatively well priced and has one-hour photo developing.

The closest hospital is in Banff (403/762-2222). For the local **RCMP,** call 403/522-3811.

Bookstores

Woodruff & Blum (Samson Mall, 403/522-3842, daily 9 A.M.–10 P.M.) offers an excellent selection of books on the natural and human history of the park, as well as animal field guides, hiking guides, and general western Canadiana. In the Fairmont Chateau Lake Louise, **Mountain Lights Gift Shop** (403/522-3734) has a similar albeit smaller collection.

GETTING THERE AND AROUND

Calgary International Airport is the closest airport to Lake Louise. **Brewster** (403/762-6767 or 800/661-1152, www.brewster.ca), **Banff Airporter** (403/762-3330 or 888/449-2901, www.banffairporter.com), and **Rocky**

Mountain Sky Shuttle (403/762-5200 or 888/762-8754, www.rockymountainskyshuttle .com) offer at least a couple of shuttles per day that continue beyond Banff to Lake Louise from the airport. All charge around the same—$60 each way, with a slight round-trip discount.

Greyhound (403/522-3870, www.grey hound.ca) leaves the Calgary bus depot (877 Greyhound Way SW) five times daily for Lake Louise. The fare is less than that charged by Brewster, and the Banff–Lake Louise portion only is around $14. From Vancouver, it's a 13-hour ride to Lake Louise aboard the Greyhound bus.

Samson Mall is the commercial heart of Lake Louise village. If the parking lot out front is full, consider leaving your vehicle across the road behind the Esso gas station, where one area is set aside for large RVs. The campground, alpine center, and hotels are all within easy walking distance of Samson Mall. Fairmont Chateau Lake Louise is a 2.7-kilometer (1.7-mi) walk from the valley floor. The only car-rental agency in the village is **National** (403/522-3870). The agency doesn't have many vehicles; you'd be better off picking one up at Calgary International Airport. **Lake Louise Taxi & Tours** (Samson Mall, 403/522-2020) charges $3 for flag drop, then $1.85 per kilometer. From the mall to Fairmont Chateau Lake Louise runs around $12, to Moraine Lake $25, and to Banff $130. **Wilson Mountain Sports** (Samson Mall, 403/522-3636) has mountain bikes for rent from $15 per hour or $39 per day (includes a helmet, bike lock, and water bottle). They also rent camping, climbing, and fishing gear.

Icefields Parkway – Banff

The 230-kilometer (143-mi) Icefields Parkway, between Lake Louise and Jasper, is one of the most scenic, exciting, and inspiring mountain roads ever built. From Lake Louise, it parallels the Continental Divide, following in the shadow of the highest, most rugged mountains in the Canadian Rockies. The first 122 kilometers (76 mi) to Sunwapta Pass (the boundary between Banff and Jasper National Parks) can be driven in two hours, and the entire parkway in four. But you'll probably want to spend at least one day, and probably more, stopping at each of the 13 viewpoints, hiking the trails, watching the abundant wildlife, and just generally enjoying one of the world's most magnificent landscapes. Along the section within Banff National Park are two lodges, three hostels, three campgrounds, and one gas station.

Although the road is steep and winding in places, it has a wide shoulder, making it ideal for an extended bike trip. Allow seven days to pedal north from Banff to Jasper, staying at hostels or camping along the route. This is the preferable direction to travel by bike because the elevation at the town of Jasper is more than 500 meters (1,640 ft) lower than either Banff or Lake Louise.

The parkway remains open year-round, although winter brings with it some special considerations. The road is often closed for short periods for avalanche control, so check road conditions in Banff or Lake Louise before setting out. And fill up with gas, because no services are available between November and April.

History

Banff guide Bill Peyto led American explorer Walter Wilcox up the Bow Valley in 1896, to the high peaks along the Continental Divide northeast of Lake Louise. The first complete journey along this route was made by Jim Brewster in 1904. Soon after, A. P. Coleman made the arduous journey, becoming a strong supporter for the route aptly known as "The Wonder Trail." During the Great Depression of the 1930s, as part of a relief-work project, construction began on what was to become the Icefields Parkway. It was completed in 1939, and the first car traveled the route in 1940. In tribute to the excellence of the road's

early construction, when upgraded to its present standard in 1961, the original roadbed was followed nearly the entire way.

SIGHTS

The Icefields Parkway forks right from the TransCanada Highway just north of Lake Louise. The impressive scenery begins immediately. Just three kilometers from the junction is **Herbert Lake,** formed during the last ice age when retreating glaciers deposited a pile of rubble—known as a moraine—across a shallow valley and water filled in behind it. The lake is a perfect place for early-morning or -evening photography when the **Waputik Range** and distinctively shaped **Mount Temple** are reflected in its waters.

Traveling north, you'll notice numerous depressions in the steep, shaded slopes of the Waputik Range across the Bow Valley. The cooler climate on these north-facing slopes makes them prone to glaciation. Cirques were cut by small "local glaciers." On the opposite side of the road, **Mount Hector** (3,394 m/11,100 ft), easily recognized by its layered peak, is soon visible.

Hector Lake Viewpoint is 16 kilometers (10 mi) from the junction. Although the view is partially obscured by trees, the emerald-green waters nestled below a massive wall of limestone form a breathtaking scene. **Bow Peak,** seen looking northward along the highway, is only 2,868 meters (9,400 ft) high but is completely detached from the Waputik Range, making it a popular destination for mountain climbers. As you leave this viewpoint, look across the northeast end of Hector Lake for glimpses of **Mount Balfour** (3,246 m/10,650 ft) on the distant skyline.

Crowfoot Glacier

The aptly named Crowfoot Glacier can best be appreciated from north of Bow Lake. From the viewpoint, 17 kilometers (10.6 mi) north of Hector Lake, it is easy to see how this and other glaciers are formed. It sits on a wide ledge near the top of Crowfoot Mountain, from where its glacial "claws" cling to the mountain's steep slopes. The retreat of this glacier has been dra-

matic. Only 50 years ago, two of the claws extended to the base of the lower cliff.

◖ Bow Lake

The sparkling, translucent waters of Bow Lake are among the most beautiful that can be seen from the Icefields Parkway. The lake was created when moraines, left behind by retreating glaciers, dammed subsequent meltwater. On still days, the water reflects the snowy peaks, their sheer cliffs, and the scree slopes that run into the lake. You don't need to take a photography class to take good pictures here! At the southeast end of the lake is a day-use area with waterfront picnic tables and a trail that leads to a swampy area at the lake's outlet. At the upper end of the lake is a lodge and the trailhead for a walk to Bow Glacier Falls (see *Hiking* later in the *Icefields Parkway—Banff* section).

The road leaves Bow Lake and climbs to **Bow Summit.** Looking back, the true color of Bow Lake becomes apparent, and the Crowfoot Glacier reveals its unique shape. At an elevation of 2,069 meters (6,790 ft), this pass is one of the highest points crossed by a public road in Canada. It is also the beginning of the Bow River—the one you camped beside at Lake Louise, photographed flowing through the town of Banff, and strolled along in downtown Calgary.

◖ Peyto Lake

From the parking lot at Bow Summit, a short, paved trail leads to one of the most breathtaking views you could ever imagine. Far below the viewpoint is Peyto Lake, an impossibly intense green-colored lake whose hues change according to season. Before heavy melting of nearby glaciers begins (June to early July), the lake is dark blue. As summer progresses, meltwater flows across a delta and into the lake. This water is laden with fine particles of ground-rock debris known as "rock flour," which remains suspended in the water. The mineral content of the rock flour is not responsible for the lake's unique color, but rather the particles reflecting the blue-green sector of the light spectrum. Therefore, as the amount of suspended rock flour changes, so does the color of the lake.

© ANDREW HEMPSTEAD

Bow Lake

The lake is one of many park landmarks named for early outfitter Bill Peyto. In 1898, he was part of an expedition camped at Bow Lake. Seeking solitude (as he was reportedly wont to do), he slipped off during the night to sleep near this lake. Other members of the party coined the name "Peyto's Lake," and it stuck.

Three kilometers farther along the parkway is a viewpoint from where **Peyto Glacier** is visible at the far end of Peyto Lake Valley. This glacier is part of the extensive **Wapta Icefield,** which straddles the Continental Divide and extends into the northern reaches of Yoho National Park in British Columbia.

Beside the Continental Divide

From Bow Pass, the parkway descends to a viewpoint directly across the Mistaya River from **Mount Patterson** (3,197 m/10,490 ft). **Snowbird Glacier** clings precariously to the mountain's steep northeast face, and the mountain's lower, wooded slopes are heavily scarred where rock and ice slides have swept down the mountainside.

As the parkway continues to descend and crosses **Silverhorn Creek,** the jagged lime-stone peaks of the Continental Divide can be seen to the west. **Mistaya Lake** is a three-kilometer-long (1.9-mi-long) body of water that sits at the bottom of the valley between the road and the divide, but it can't be seen from the parkway. The best place to view this panorama is from the **Howse Peak Viewpoint** at Upper Waterfowl Lake. From here, the high ridge that forms the Continental Divide is easily distinguishable. Seven peaks can be seen from here, including, of course, **Howse Peak** (3,290 m/10,800 ft). At no point along this ridge does the elevation drop below 2,750 meters (9,000 ft). From Howse Peak, the Continental Divide makes a 90-degree turn to the west. One dominant peak that can be seen from Bow Pass to the north of the Saskatchewan River Crossing is **Mount Chephren** (3,268 m/10,720 ft). Its distinctive shape and position away from the main ridge of the Continental Divide make it easy to distinguish (directly north of Howse Peak).

To Saskatchewan River Crossing

Numerous trails lead around the swampy shores of **Upper and Lower Waterfowl Lakes,**

© ANDREW HEMPSTEAD

If you make just one stop along the Icefields Parkway, do it at the Peyto Lake lookout.

providing one of the park's best opportunities to view moose, who feed on the abundant aquatic vegetation that grows in Upper Waterfowl Lake. Rock and other debris that has been carried down from nearby valley systems has built up, forming a wide alluvial fan, nearly blocking the **Mistaya River** and creating Upper Waterfowl Lake.

Continuing north is **Mount Murchison,** on the east side of the parkway. Although not one of the park's highest mountains, this gray-and-yellow massif of Cambrian rock includes 10 individual peaks.

From a parking lot 14 kilometers (8.7 mi) northeast of Waterfowl Lake Campground, a short trail descends into the montane forest to **Mistaya Canyon.** Here, the effects of erosion can be appreciated as the Mistaya River leaves the floor of Mistaya Valley, plunging through a narrow-walled canyon into the North Saskatchewan Valley. The area is scarred with potholes where boulders have been whirled around by the action of fast-flowing water, carving deep depressions into the softer limestone bedrock below.

The **North Saskatchewan River** posed a major problem for early travelers and later for the builders of the Icefields Parkway. This swiftly running river eventually drains into Hudson Bay. In 1989, it was named a Canadian Heritage River. A panoramic viewpoint of the entire valley is located one kilometer past the bridge. From here, the Howse and Mistaya Rivers can be seen converging with the North Saskatchewan at a silt-laden delta. This is also a junction with Highway 11 (also known as David Thompson Highway), which follows the North Saskatchewan River to Rocky Mountain House and Red Deer. From this viewpoint, numerous peaks can be seen to the west. Two sharp peaks are distinctive: **Mount Outram** is the closer, and the farther is **Mount Forbes** (3,630 m/11,900 ft), the highest peak in Banff National Park (and the sixth-highest in the Canadian Rockies).

To Sunwapta Pass

On the north side of the North Saskatchewan River is the towering hulk of **Mount Wilson,** named for Banff outfitter Tom Wilson. The Icefields Parkway passes this massif on its western flanks. A pullout just past Rampart Creek Campground has good views of Mount

WILD BILL PEYTO

"... Rarely speaking – his forte was doing things, not talking about them." These words from a friend sum up one of Banff's earliest characters. These attributes, combined with his knowledge of the Canadian Rockies, earned Bill Peyto status as one of Banff's greatest guides. In 1886, at the tender age of 18, Ebenezer William Peyto left England for Canada. After traveling extensively he settled in Banff and was hired as an apprentice guide for legendary outfitter Tom Wilson. Wearing a tilted sombrero, fringed buckskin coat, cartridge belt, hunting knife, and a six-shooter, he looked more like a gunslinger than a mountain man. As his reputation as a competent guide grew, so did the stories. While guiding clients on one occasion, he led them to his cabin. Before entering, Peyto threw stones in the front door until a loud snap was heard. It was a bear trap that he'd set up to catch a certain trapper who'd been stealing his food. One of the guests commented that if caught, the trapper would surely have died. "You're damned right he would have," Bill replied. "Then I'd have known for sure it was him."

In 1900 Peyto left to fight in the Boer War and was promoted to corporal for bravery. This rank was revoked before it became official because they learned he'd "borrowed" an officer's jacket and several bottles of booze for the celebration. Returning to a hero's welcome in Banff, he established an outfitting business and continued prospecting for copper in Simpson Pass. Although his outfitting business thrived, the death of his wife left him despondent. "Ain't it Hell," the name of the house he built on Banff Avenue, summed up his view of life. In his later years, after being wounded in World War I, he became a warden in the Healy Creek–Sunshine district, where his exploits during the 1920s added to his already legendary name. After 20 years of service he retired, and in 1943, at the age of 75, he passed away. One of the park's most beautiful lakes is named after him, as is a glacier and one of Banff's popular watering holes – Wild Bill's, a designation that he would have appreciated. His face also adorns the large signs welcoming visitors to Banff.

Amery to the west and Mounts Sarbach, Chephren, and Murchison to the south. Beyond here is the **Weeping Wall,** a long cliff of gray limestone where a series of waterfalls tumbles more than 100 meters (330 ft) down the steep slopes of **Cirrus Mountain.** In winter, this wall of water freezes, becoming a mecca for ice climbers. After climbing quickly, the road drops again before beginning the long climb to Sunwapta Pass. Before ascending to the pass, the road makes a sweeping curve over an alluvial plain of the North Saskatchewan River. Halfway up the 360-vertical-meter climb is a viewpoint well worth stopping for. Cyclists will definitely appreciate a rest. From here, views extend down the valley to the slopes of Mount Saskatchewan and, on the other side of the parkway, Cirrus Mountain. Another viewpoint, farther up the road, has the added attraction of **Panther Falls** across the valley. A cairn at **Sunwapta Pass** (2,023 m/6,640 ft)

marks the boundary between Banff and Jasper National Parks. It also marks the divide between the North Saskatchewan and Sunwapta Rivers, whose waters drain into the Atlantic and Arctic Oceans respectively.

HIKING
Helen Lake

- Length: 6 kilometers/3.7 miles (2.5 hours) one-way

- Elevation gain: 455 meters/1,500 feet

- Rating: Moderate

- Trailhead: Across the Icefields Parkway from Crowfoot Glacier Lookout, 33 kilometers (20 mi) northwest from the junction with the TransCanada Highway

The trail to Helen Lake is one of the easiest ways to access a true alpine environment from the southern end of the Icefields Parkway. The trail

climbs steadily through a forest of Engelmann spruce and subalpine fir for the first 2.5 kilometers (1.6 mi) to an avalanche slope, reaching the tree line and the first good viewpoint after three kilometers (1.9 mi). The view across the valley is spectacular, with Crowfoot Glacier visible to the southwest. As the trail reaches a ridge, it turns and descends into the glacial cirque where Helen Lake lies. Listen and look for hoary marmots around the scree slopes along the lakeshore.

For those with the time and energy, it's possible to continue an additional three kilometers (1.9 mi) to Dolomite Pass; the trail switchbacks steeply up a further 100 vertical meters (330 vertical ft) in less than one kilometer (0.6 mi), then descends steeply for a further one kilometer (0.6 mi) to Katherine Lake and beyond to the pass.

Bow Glacier Falls

- Length: 3.4 km/2.1 miles

- Elevation gain: 130 meters/430 feet

- Rating: Easy

- Trailhead: Num-ti-jah Lodge, Bow Lake, 36 kilometers (22.3 mi) northwest from the TransCanada Highway

This hike skirts one of the most beautiful lakes in the Canadian Rockies before ending at a narrow but spectacular waterfall. From a parking lot in front of Num-ti-jah Lodge, follow the shore through Willow Flats to a gravel outwash area at the end of the lake. Across the lake are reflected views of Crowfoot Mountain and, farther west, a glimpse of Bow Glacier among the jagged peaks of the Waputik Range. The trail then begins a short but steep climb up the rim of a canyon before leveling out at the edge of a vast moraine of gravel, scree, and boulders. This is the end of the trail, although it's possible to reach the base of Bow Glacier Falls by picking your way through the 800 meters (0.5 mi) of rough ground that remains.

Chephren Lake

- Length: 4 kilometers/2.5 miles (60–90 minutes) one-way

- Elevation gain: 100 meters/330 feet

- Rating: Easy

- Trailhead: Waterfowl Lakes Campground, Icefields Parkway, 57 kilometers (35 mi) northwest from the TransCanada Highway

The trail to this pale-green body of water (pronounced kef-ren) is one of my favorites along the parkway, mostly for the scenery but also for the lack of crowds. The official trailhead is a bridge across the Mistaya River at the back of Waterfowl Lakes Campground (behind site 86). If you're not registered at the campground, park at the end of the unpaved road running along the front of the campground, and walk 300 meters (0.2 mi) down the well-worn path to the river crossing. Across the river, the trail dives headlong into a subalpine forest, reaching a crudely signposted junction after 1.6 kilometers (one mi). Take the right fork. This leads 2.4 kilometers (1.5 mi) to Chephren Lake, descending steeply at the very end (this stretch of trail is often muddy). The lake is nestled under

© ANDREW HEMPSTEAD

Chephren Lake, a moderately easy four-kilometer (2.5-mile) hike from the Icefields Parkway

the buttresses of Mount Chephren. To the left—farther up the lake—is Howse Peak.

Parker's Ridge

- Length: 2.4 kilometers/1.5 miles (one hour) one-way
- Elevation gain: 210 meters/690 feet
- Rating: Easy/moderate
- Trailhead: Icefields Parkway, four kilometers (2.5 mi) south of Sunwapta Pass

From the trailhead on the west side of the highway, this wide path gains elevation quickly through open meadows and scattered stands of subalpine fir. This fragile environment is easily destroyed, so it's very important that you stay on the trail. During the short alpine summer, these meadows are carpeted with red heather, white mountain avens, and blue alpine forget-me-nots. From the summit of the ridge, you look down on the two-kilometer-wide (1.2-

© ANDREW HEMPSTEAD

Mountain goats are often sighted at higher elevations, including the area around Helen Lake and Parker's Ridge.

mi-wide) Saskatchewan Glacier spreading out below. Beyond is Castleguard Mountain, renowned for its extensive cave system.

ACCOMMODATIONS AND CAMPING
Under $50

North of Lake Louise, four and a half hostels are spread along the Icefields Parkway, two in Banff and two in Jasper National Park (the "half" is Hilda Creek Wilderness Hostel, north of Rampart Creek, which has been closed indefinitely after being mostly destroyed by fire in 2002). Facilities at all four are limited, and beds should be reserved as far in advance as possible. For reservations, call 403/670-7580 or 866/762-4122, or book online (www.hihostels.ca). The first, 24 kilometers (15 mi) from Lake Louise, is **HI-Mosquito Creek,** which is near good hiking and offers accommodations for 32 in four- and six-bed cabins. Facilities include a kitchen, wood-heated sauna, and a large common room with fireplace. Although the hostel has no showers, guests are permitted to use those at the nearby Lake Louise Alpine Centre. Rates are $23 per night for members of Hostelling International; nonmembers pay $27. Check-in is 5–10 P.M., and it's open year-round.

HI-Rampart Creek, a further 64 kilometers (40 mi) along the parkway, is nestled below the snowcapped peak of Mount Wilson, with views across the North Saskatchewan River to even higher peaks along the Continental Divide. Like Mosquito Creek, it's near good hiking and has a kitchen and sauna. Its four cabins have a total of 24 bunk beds. Members pay $23 per night, nonmembers $27. It's open nightly mid-April to mid-October and weekends only mid-November to mid-April. Check-in is 5–10 P.M.

$100-150

The Crossing (403/761-7000, www.thecrossing resort.com, mid-Mar.–Nov.) is a large complex 87 kilometers (54 miles) north of Lake Louise and 45 kilometers (28 miles) south of Columbia Icefield. It's also one kilometer (0.6 mile) north of Saskatchewan River Crossing, where

Highway 11 spurs east along Abraham Lake to Rocky Mountain House and Red Deer. The rooms offer a good combination of size and value but lack the charm of those at Num-ti-jah to the south and the views enjoyed by those at the Columbia Icefield Centre to the north. Each of 66 units has a phone and television. The least expensive rooms, with two double beds, are $129 s, $139 d. Add $10 per room for a mountain view. The larger Family Rooms are $169. All rates are heavily discounted outside of June–September. In addition to overnight rooms, the Crossing has the only gas between Lake Louise and Jasper, a self-serve cafeteria, a restaurant, a pub with a cook-your-own-steak grill, and a supersized gift shop.

Over $150

Pioneer guide and outfitter Jimmy Simpson built **《 Simpson's Num-ti-jah Lodge** (403/522-2167, www.num-ti-jah.com), on the north shore of Bow Lake, 40 kilometers (25 mi) north of Lake Louise, as a base for his outfitting operation in 1920. In those days, the route north from Lake Louise was nothing more than a horse trail. The desire to build a large structure when only short timbers were available led to the unusual octagonal shape of the main lodge. Simpson remained at Bow Lake, a living legend, until his death in 1972 at the age of 95. The rustic mountain ambience has changed little since Simpson's passing, and an overnight stay at Num-ti-jah is a memorable experience. Just don't expect the conveniences of a regular motel. Under the distinctively red steep-pitched roof of the main lodge are 25 rooms, some that share bathrooms, and there's not a TV or phone in sight. Downstairs, guests soak up the warmth of a roaring log fire while mingling in a comfortable library filled with historical mountain literature. A dining room lined with historical memorabilia is open throughout the day, serving up a breakfast buffet and evening delicacies such as shellfish fettuccini ($20). Depending on the view, rates are $210–230 s or d for a room with shared bath,

$260–305 s or d for an en suite. It's open year-round (except Nov.), with rates reduced 40 percent outside of summer.

Camping

Beyond Lake Louise, the first camping along the Icefields Parkway is at **Mosquito Creek Campground** (year-round, $17), 24 kilometers (15 mi) from the TransCanada Highway. Don't be perturbed by the name, though; the bugs here are no worse than anywhere else. The 32 sites are nestled in the forest, with a tumbling creek separating the campground from a hostel. Each site has a picnic table and fire ring, while other amenities include pump water, pit toilets, and a kitchen shelter with an old-fashioned woodstove. If you're camping at Mosquito Creek and want a break from the usual camp fare, consider traveling 17 kilometers/10.6 miles up the highway to the convivial dining room at Num-ti-jah Lodge (403/522-2167) to feast on Canadian-inspired cuisine in a historic dining room.

《 Waterfowl Lake Campground (late June–mid-Sept., $23) is 33 kilometers (20 mi) north along the Icefields Parkway from Mosquito Creek. It features 116 sites between Upper and Lower Waterfowl Lakes, with a few sites in view of the lower lake. Facilities include pump water, flush toilets, and kitchen shelters with wood-burning stoves. Rise early to watch the first rays of sun hit Mount Chephren from the shoreline of the lower lake, then plan on hiking the four-kilometer (2.5-mi) trail to Chephren Lake—you'll be first on the trail and back in time for a late breakfast.

Continuing toward Jasper, the Icefields Parkway passes the Crossing, a good place to gas up and buy last-minute groceries before reaching **Rampart Creek Campground** (late June–early Sept., $17 per site), 31 kilometers (19 mi) beyond Waterfowl Lake and 88 kilometers (55 mi) from Lake Louise. With just 50 sites, this campground fills early. Facilities include kitchen shelters, pit toilets, and pump water.

JASPER NATIONAL PARK

Snowcapped peaks, vast ice fields, beautiful glacial lakes, soothing hot springs, thundering rivers, and the most extensive backcountry trail system of any Canadian national park make Jasper a stunning counterpart to its sister park, Banff. A 3.5-hour drive west of Alberta's provincial capital of Edmonton, Jasper extends from the headwaters of the Smoky River in the north to the Columbia Icefield (and Banff National Park) in the south. To the east are the foothills, and to the west is the Continental Divide, which marks the Alberta–British Columbia border. This 10,900-square-kilometer (4,208-square-mi) wilderness is a haven for wildlife; much of the park is traveled only by wolves and grizzlies.

Although the peaks of Jasper National Park are not particularly high, they are among the most spectacular along the length of the Rocky Mountains. While the mountains will get your immediate attention, it is the lakes and glaciers within that create the beauty. A natural highlight is the expansive Columbia Icefield, a remnant of the last ice age. Glacial silt suspended in bodies of water such as Maligne Lake produce amazing emerald, turquoise, and amethyst colors; early artists who painted these lakes had trouble convincing people that their images were accurate. One of Jasper's main draws is the abundance of wildlife, which follows an annual cycle of sorts. During winter, larger mammals move to lower elevations where food is accessible. By June, most of the snow cover at lower elevations has melted, the crowds haven't arrived, and animals can be seen feeding along the

© ANDREW HEMPSTEAD

HIGHLIGHTS

◖ **Columbia Icefield:** Don't miss one of the world's most accessible glacial areas. Take the Ice Explorer tour to get a close-up view of this natural wonder (page 274).

◖ **Wilcox Pass:** Escape the crowds lingering around the Icefield Centre on this hike, where the panorama of the Columbia Icefield is laid out in all its glory (page 278).

◖ **Mount Edith Cavell and Cavell Meadows:** Although Mount Edith Cavell is visible from various points within the park, no vantage point is as memorable as that from its base, reachable by road from Highway 93A (page 285). For an awesome, neck-straining view, take the Cavell Meadows Trail (page 289).

◖ **Maligne Canyon:** Easy access makes this natural attraction extremely popular, along with its many unique geological features. Visit before 9 A.M. to miss the tour bus crowd (page 286).

◖ **Maligne Lake:** This is the most famous body of water in Jasper National Park. And for good reason – it's simply stunning. Take a tour boat to Spirit Island or hike the Lake Trail (Mary Schäffer Loop) along the lake's eastern shore (page 286).

◖ **Opal Hills:** The vast majority of visitors to Maligne Lake don't travel past the lake's shoreline. Go beyond the ordinary on this trail, which provides stunning views of the whole Maligne Valley from alpine meadows (page 291).

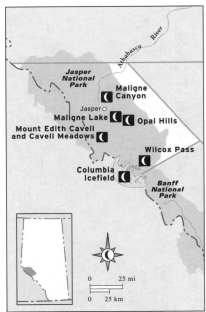

LOOK FOR ◖ TO FIND RECOMMENDED SIGHTS, ACTIVITIES, DINING, AND LODGING.

valley floor. In fall, tourists move to warmer climates, the rutting season begins, bears go into hibernation, and a herd of elk moves into Jasper town for the winter. Smaller critters are common around campgrounds, but it's hoofed residents, such as the hundreds of elk in and around town, that provide the easiest big game–viewing. Drive the Icefields Parkway in spring and you're almost guaranteed to see black bears feeding on dandelions. But it is often the unexpected that creates the best memories—the call of a loon on Pyramid Lake, the sight of reclusive caribou on a hike

in the Opal Hills, or a beaver busy at work along the Athabasca River wetlands.

The park's most spectacular natural landmarks can be admired from the Icefields Parkway. Regarded as one of the world's great mountain drives, this highway connects the town of Jasper in the north to Banff National Park in the south. The town is the park's main service center, a smaller, less commercial version of Banff, where you'll find accommodations to suit all budgets, restaurants, gas stations, and the usual array of touristy shops. The town is also the starting point for scenic

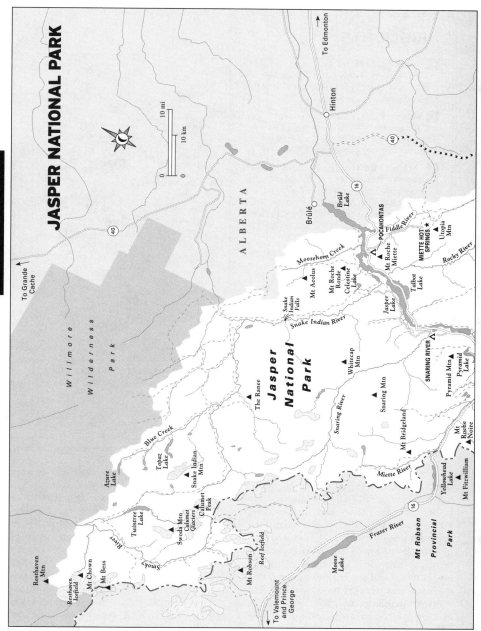

JASPER NATIONAL PARK

10 mi

10 km

To Grande
Cache

ALBERTA

Willmore

Wilderness

Park

To Edmonton

Hinton

Brûlé
Lake

Brûlé

POCAHONTAS

Moosehorn Creek

Mt Roche
Ronde

Mt Aeolus

Celestine
Lake

Fiddle River

MIETTE HOT
SPRINGS ★

Mt Roche
Miette

Utopia
Mtn

Rocky River

Snake
Indian
Falls

Snake Indian River

Jasper
Lake

Talbot
Lake

The Ranee

Jasper

National

Park

Whitecap
Mtn

Snaring Mtn

SNARING RIVER

Pyramid Mtn

Pyramid
Lake

Snaring River

Mt Bridgeland

Mt
Roche
Noire

Blue Creek

Topaz
Lake

Snake Indian
Mtn

Miette River

Yellowhead
Lake

Mt Fitzwilliam

Azure
Lake

Twintree
Lake

Calumet
Glaciers

Calumet
Peak

Swoda Mtn

Mt Robson

Reef Icefield

Fraser River

Mt Robson

Provincial

Park

Moose
Lake

Resthaven
Mtn

Resthaven
Icefield

Mt Chown

Mt Bess

Smoky River

To Valemount
and Prince
George

To Valemount
and Prince
George

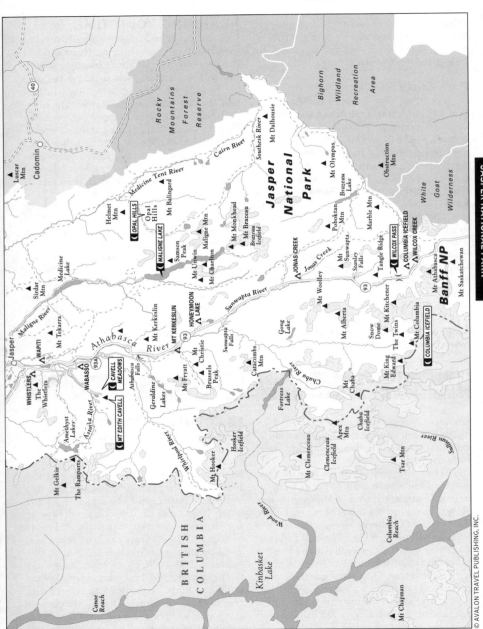

JASPER NATIONAL PARK

drives to the base of Mount Edith Cavell and Maligne Lake, as well as a base for fishing, boating, downhill skiing, golfing, horseback riding, and white-water rafting.

Park Entry

Permits are required for entry into Jasper National Park. A **National Parks Day Pass** is adult $9, senior $7.75, child $4.50, up to a maximum of $18 per vehicle. It can also be used in neighboring Banff National Park if you're traveling down the Icefields Parkway and is valid until 4 P.M. the day following its purchase. An annual **National Parks of Canada Pass**—good for entry into all of Canada's national parks—is $63 adults and $54 seniors, up to a maximum of $125 per vehicle.

Both types of pass can be purchased at the park information center, at the booth along the Icefields Parkway a few kilometers south of the town of Jasper, and at campground kiosks. If you're traveling north along the Icefields Parkway, you'll be required to stop and purchase a park pass just beyond Lake Louise (Banff National Park). The Parks Canada website (www.pc.gc.ca) has detailed pass information.

PLANNING YOUR TIME

It's a cliché, but backcountry enthusiasts could spend a full summer exploring Jasper and still not see everything. If you're planning to visit Jasper, I'm assuming you *do* enjoy the outdoors—hiking, fishing, watching wildlife, and the like—but maybe not with a backpack full of provisions strapped to your back. Keeping this in mind, I'd recommend spending four days in the park. The best choices for accommodations are the summer-only cabin complexes, so book for three nights and spend your days exploring natural attractions such as **Mount Edith Cavell, Maligne Canyon,** and **Maligne Lake.** If you're traveling up from Lake Louise, plan on spending the first day along the Icefields Parkway, arriving at **Columbia Icefield** before the crowds. If your time in Jasper is limited to two days and one night, you should have enough time to visit each of the natural attractions I mark as must-see sights, walk a couple of the shorter trails (**Wilcox Pass,** overlooking the Columbia Icefield, and **Cavell Meadows** are my top picks, with the **Opal Hills** a close third), and even squeeze in a rafting trip or golf game.

Icefields Parkway – Jasper

Sunwapta Pass (2,040 m/6,690 ft), four kilometers (2.5 mi) south of the Columbia Icefield, marks the boundary between Banff and Jasper National Parks.

The following sights along the Icefields Parkway are detailed from south to north, from the Icefield Centre to the town of Jasper, a distance of 105 kilometers (65 mi). The scenery along this stretch of road is no less spectacular than the other half through Banff National Park, and it's easy to spend at least a full day en route.

No gas is available along this stretch of the Icefields Parkway. The nearest gas stations are at Saskatchewan River Crossing (Banff National Park) and in the town of Jasper, a total distance of 150 kilometers (93 mi), so keep your tank topped off to be safe.

◖ COLUMBIA ICEFIELD

The largest and most accessible of 17 glacial areas along the Icefields Parkway is 325-square-kilometer (125-square-mi) Columbia Icefield, beside the Icefields Parkway at the south end of the park, 105 kilometers (65 mi) south from Jasper and 132 kilometers (82 mi) north from Lake Louise. It's a remnant of the last major glaciation that covered most of Canada 20,000 years ago, and it has survived because of its elevation at 1,900–2,800 meters (6,230–9,190 ft) above sea level, cold temperatures, and heavy snowfalls. From the main body of the ice cap, which sits astride the Continental Divide, six glaciers creep down three main valleys. Of these, **Athabasca Glacier** is the most accessible and

© ANDREW HEMPSTEAD

Brewster's Ice Explorers drive right onto the icefield for a close look.

can be seen from the Icefields Parkway; it is one of the world's few glaciers that you can drive right up to. It is an impressive 600 hectares (1,480 acres) in area and up to 100 meters (330 ft) deep. The speed at which glaciers advance and retreat varies with the long-term climate. Athabasca Glacier has retreated to its current position from across the highway, a distance of over 1.6 kilometers (one mi), in a little more than 100 years. Currently it retreats up to two meters (six ft) per year. The rubble between the toe of Athabasca Glacier and the highway is a mixture of rock, sand, and gravel known as "till," deposited by the glacier as it retreats.

Exploring the Icefield

From the Icefields Parkway, an unpaved road leads down through piles of till left by the retreating Athabasca Glacier to a parking area beside Sunwapta Lake. An interesting alternative is to leave your vehicle beside the highway and take the 1.6-kilometer (one-mi) hiking trail through the lunarlike landscape to the

parking area. From this point, a short path leads up to the toe of the glacier. (Along the access road, look for the small markers showing how far the toe of the glacier reached in years gone by; the farthest marker is across the highway beside the stairs leading up to the Icefield Centre.)

The ice field can be dangerous for unprepared visitors. Like all glaciers, the broken surface of the Athabasca is especially hazardous because snow bridges can hide its deep crevasses. The crevasses are uncovered as the winter snows melt. The safest way to experience the glacier firsthand is on specially developed vehicles with balloon tires that can travel over the crevassed surface. The Ice Explorers are operated by **Brewster** (780/852-6550 or 877/423-7433, www.brewster.ca). The 90-minute tour of Athabasca Glacier includes time spent walking on the surface of the glacier. The tour, which begins with a ride in a regular bus from the Icefield Centre, costs adult $34, child $17, and operates from mid-April to mid-October 9 A.M.–5 P.M. (try to plan your tour for

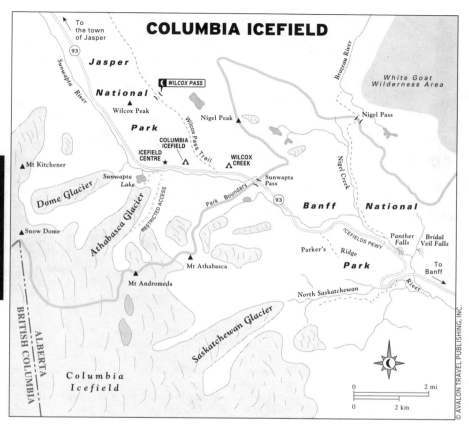

COLUMBIA ICEFIELD

To the town of Jasper

Jasper

Sunwapta River

Breteau River

White Goat Wilderness Area

WILCOX PASS

National

▲ Wilcox Peak

Nigel Peak ▲

Nigel Pass

Wilcox Pass Trail

Park

COLUMBIA ICEFIELD
ICEFIELD CENTRE ★

WILCOX CREEK

▲ Mt Kitchener

Sunwapta Lake

Sunwapta Pass

Nigel Creek

Dome Glacier

Athabasca Glacier

RESTRICTED ACCESS

Park Boundary

Banff

National

ICEFIELDS PKWY

Panther Falls

Bridal Veil Falls

Parker's Ridge

▲ Snow Dome

Park

To Banff

▲ Mt Athabasca

North Saskatchewan

▲ Mt Andromeda

River

Saskatchewan Glacier

ALBERTA

BRITISH COLUMBIA

Columbia Icefield

0   2 mi

0   2 km

© AVALON TRAVEL PUBLISHING, INC.

before 10 A.M. or after 3 P.M., after the tour buses have departed for the day). The ticketing office is on the main floor of the Icefield Centre (no reservations are taken), with the surrounding area resembling an airport departure lounge—check the television screens for departure times and ensure you make your way to the correct gate. Early in the season the glacier is still covered in a layer of snow and is therefore not as spectacular as during the summer. If you're in Banff or Jasper without transportation, consider Brewster's day trip to the Columbia Icefield, which lasts nine hours and costs adult $131, child $66, including the Ice Explorer excursion.

Icefield Centre

The magnificent Icefield Centre is nestled at the base of Mount Wilcox, overlooking the Athabasca Glacier. In this remote location, the building is as environmentally friendly as possible: lights work on motion sensors to reduce electricity, some water is reused, suppliers must take their packaging with them after deliveries, and the entire building freezes in winter.

The center is the staging point for Ice Explorer tours, but before heading out onto the ice field, don't miss the **Glacier Gallery** on the lower floor. This large display area details all aspects of the frozen world, including the story of glacier formation and movement.

Tangle Falls

The centerpiece is a scaled-down fiberglass model of the Athabasca Glacier, which is surrounded by hands-on displays and audiovisual presentations.

Back on the main floor of the center you'll find a Parks Canada desk (780/852-6288)—a good source of information for northbound visitors—along with the Ice Explorer ticketing desk, restrooms, and the obligatory gift shop. Upstairs you'll find the cavernous **Columbia Café,** with snacks and hot drinks to go on the right and an overpriced cafeteria-style restaurant to the left. Both are open daily 9 A.M.–6 P.M. Across the hallway is the **Glacier Dining Room,** open daily 7–10 A.M. for a breakfast buffet, reopening 6–9:30 P.M. for ordinary Chinese-Canadian fare (mains range $17–30). The only redeeming feature of these dining options has nothing to do with the food—the view from both inside and out on the massive deck is stupendous. (For northbound travelers, my advice is to pick up lunch at Laggan's Mountain Bakery in Lake Louise.)

The entire Icefield Centre closes down for the winter in mid-October, reopening the following year in mid-April. During summer, the complex (including display area) is open daily 9 A.M.–11 P.M. with reduced hours outside of July and August.

Between the Columbia Icefield and Sunwapta Falls

Sunwapta Lake, at the toe of the Athabasca Glacier, is the source of the **Sunwapta River,** which the Icefields Parkway follows for 48 kilometers (30 mi) to Sunwapta Falls. Eight kilometers (five mi) north from the Icefield Centre, the road descends to a viewpoint for **Stutfield Glacier.** Most of the glacier is hidden from view by a densely wooded ridge, but the valley floor below its toe is littered with till left by the glacier's retreat. The main body of the Columbia Icefield can be seen along the clifftop high above, and south of the glacier you can see Mount Kitchener.

Six kilometers (3.7 mi) farther down the road is **Tangle Ridge,** a grayish-brown wall of limestone over which Beauty Creek cascades. At this point the Icefields Parkway runs alongside the Sunwapta River, following its braided course through the **Endless Range,** the eastern wall of a classic glacier-carved valley.

A further 41 kilometers (25 mi) along the road a 500-meter (0.3-mi) spur at Sunwapta Falls Resort leads to **Sunwapta Falls.** Here the Sunwapta River changes direction sharply and drops into a deep canyon. The best viewpoint is from the bridge across the river, but it's also worth following the path on the parking-lot side of the river downstream along the rim of the canyon. Two kilometers (1.2 mi) farther downstream the river flows into the much-wider Athabasca Valley.

Goat Lookout

After following the Athabasca River for 17 kilometers (11 mi), the road ascends to a lookout with picnic tables offering panoramic river views. Below the lookout is a steep bank of exposed glacially ground material containing natural deposits of salt. The local mountain

goats spend most of their time on the steep slopes of Mount Kerkeslin, to the northeast, but occasionally cross the road and can be seen searching for the salt licks along the riverbank, trying to replenish lost nutrients.

Athabasca Falls

Nine kilometers (5.6 mi) beyond Goat Lookout and 32 kilometers (20 mi) south of Jasper, the Icefields Parkway divides when an old stretch of highway (Hwy. 93A) crosses the Athabasca River and continues along its west side for 25 kilometers (15.5 mi) before rejoining the Parkway seven kilometers (4.3 mi) south of the town. At the southern end of this loop the Athabasca River is forced through a narrow gorge and over a cliff into a cauldron of roaring water. As the river slowly erodes the center of the riverbed, the falls will move upstream. Trails lead from a day-use area to various viewpoints above and below the falls. The trail branching under Highway 93A follows an abandoned river channel before emerging at the bottom of the canyon. Facilities at the Athabasca Falls include picnic tables and toilets.

Continuing North to Jasper

Take Highway 93A beyond Athabasca Falls to reach Mount Edith Cavell, or continue north along the Icefields Parkway to access the following sights. The first worthwhile stop along this route is **Horseshoe Lake,** reached along a 350-meter (0.2-mi) trail from a parking lot three kilometers (1.9 mi) north of Athabasca Falls. The southern end of this delightful little body of water is ringed by a band of cliffs (popular with locals in summer as a cliff-diving spot), but many private (unofficial) picnic spots line its western shoreline.

Two kilometers (1.2 mi) north of the Horseshoe Lake parking lot are a couple of lookouts with spectacular views across the Athabasca River to **Athabasca Pass,** used by David Thompson on his historic expedition across the continent. To the north of the pass lies Mount Edith Cavell. From this lookout it is 26 kilometers (16 mi) to the town of Jasper.

HIKING
◖ Wilcox Pass

- Length: Four kilometers/2.5 miles (90 minutes) one-way

- Elevation gain: 340 meters/1,115 feet

- Rating: Moderate

- Trailhead: Wilcox Creek Campground, three kilometers (1.9 mi) south of the Icefield Centre

Views of the Columbia Icefield from the Icefields Parkway pale in comparison with those achieved along this trail on the same side of the valley as the Columbia Icefield Centre. This trail was once used by northbound outfitters because, 100 years ago, Athabasca Glacier covered the valley floor and had to be bypassed. Beginning from the north side of Wilcox Creek Campground, the trail climbs to a ridge with panoramic views of the valley, Columbia Icefield, and surrounding peaks. Ascending gradually from there, the trail enters a fragile environment of alpine meadows. From the pass, most hikers return along the same trail.

Geraldine Lakes

- Length: Five kilometers/3.1 miles (2 hours) one-way

- Elevation gain: 410 meters/1,350 feet

- Rating: Moderate

- Trailhead: Geraldine Fire Road, off Highway 93

The first of the four Geraldine Lakes is an easy two-kilometer (1.2-mi) hike from the end of the 5.5-kilometer (3.4-mi) Geraldine Fire Road. The forest-encircled lake reflects the north face of Mount Fryatt (3,361 m/11,030 ft). The trail continues along the northwest shore, climbs steeply past a scenic 100-meter-high (330-ft-high) waterfall, and traverses some rough terrain where the trail becomes indistinct; follow the cairns. At the end of the valley is another waterfall. The trail climbs east of the waterfall to a ridge above the second of the lakes, five kilometers (3.1

© ANDREW HEMPSTEAD

Buck Lake (signposted along the Icefields Parkway) is one of many bodies of water accessible by hiking trail.

mi) from the trailhead. Two other lakes, accessible only by bush-bashing, are located farther up the valley.

Valley of the Five Lakes

- Length: 2.3 kilometers/1.4 miles (40 minutes) one-way

- Elevation gain: 60 meters/200 feet

- Rating: Easy

- Trailhead: Icefields Parkway, 10 kilometers (6.2 mi) south of the town Jasper

These lakes, nestled in an open valley, are small but make a worthwhile destination. From the trailhead, 10 kilometers (6.2 mi) south of town along the Icefields Parkway, the trail passes through a forest of lodgepole pine, crosses a stream, and climbs a ridge from where you'll have a panoramic view of surrounding peaks. As the trail descends to the lakes, turn left at the first intersection to a point between two of the lakes. These lakes are linked to Old Fort

Point by a tedious 10-kilometer (6.2-mi) trail through montane forest.

ACCOMMODATIONS AND CAMPING

Two lodges and two hostels lie along the Icefields Parkway proper. A number of other accommodations and the park's main campgrounds are along the parkway, but within close proximity to the town of Jasper. These are covered under the *Town of Jasper* section of this chapter.

Under $50

Reservations for the two hostels can be made by contacting HI–Canada (780/852-3215 or 877/852-0781, www.hihostels.ca). At both facilities, check-in is 5–11 P.M., but the main lodges are open all day.

HI-Beauty Creek, 17 kilometers (10.5 mi) north of Columbia Icefield, 144 kilometers (90 mi) north from Lake Louise, and 88 kilometers (55 miles) south of Jasper, is nestled in a

small stand of Douglas fir between the Icefields Parkway and the Sunwapta River. Each of its separate male and female cabins has 12 beds, a woodstove, and propane lighting. A third building holds a kitchen and dining area. There are no flush toilets or showers. Members $15, nonmembers $20. Open May–September.

Farther north is the equally rustic **HI-Athabasca Falls,** 32 kilometers (20 mi) south of the town Jasper and 198 kilometers (123 mi) north from Lake Louise. It is larger than the one at Beauty Creek and has electricity. Athabasca Falls is only a few minutes' walk away. Members of Hostelling International pay $15, nonmembers $20. It's closed Tuesdays October–April and all of November.

$150-200

Historic **Sunwapta Falls Resort** (780/852-4852 or 888/828-5777, www.sunwapta.com, May–mid-Oct.) is 55 kilometers (34 mi) south of the town of Jasper and within walking distance of the picturesque waterfall for which it is named. It features 52 motel-like units, with either two queen beds or one queen bed and a fireplace; some have balconies. Rates are $179–199 s or d, reduced to $100–130 outside of the busy July to mid-September period. In the main lodge is a lunchtime self-serve restaurant popular with passing travelers. In the evening this same room is transformed into the Endless Chain Restaurant, featuring simply prepared Canadian game and seafood in the $18–26 range and a delectable wild-berry crumble for $6.

The **Icefield Chalet** (780/852-6550 or 877/423-7433, www.brewster.ca, May–Sept.), the top story of Columbia Icefield Centre, lies in a stunning location high above the tree line and overlooking the Columbia Icefield, 105 kilometers (65 mi) south of the town of Jasper and

132 kilometers (82 mi) north of Lake Louise. It features 29 standard rooms, 17 of which have glacier views, and three larger, more luxurious corner rooms. All units have satellite TV and phones. Rates June to mid-September range $215–225 s or d, while in May and the last two weeks of September rates start at $110. (For the view alone, the more expensive rooms are well worth the extra $10.) Because of the remote location, dining options are limited to the in-house café and restaurant. The **Glacier Dining Room** opens daily at 7 A.M. for a breakfast buffet, reopening 6–9:30 P.M. for dinner. On the same level is a cafeteria-style café and a snack bar. All food outlets are designed around the basic needs of passing highway travelers.

Camping

Aside from Whistlers and Wapiti Campgrounds at the top end of the Icefields Parkway (detailed under *Town of Jasper* in this chapter), there are five campgrounds along this stretch of road, all of which are managed by Parks Canada. None of them take reservations. **Wilcox Creek** and **Columbia Icefield Campgrounds** are within two kilometers (1.2 mi) of each other at the extreme southern end of the park, just over 100 kilometers (62 mi) south of the town of Jasper and around 125 kilometers (78 mi) north of Lake Louise. Both are primitive facilities with pit toilets, cooking shelters, and fire rings; all sites are $15. Smallish sites at Columbia Icefield Campground are set in a stunted subalpine forest of aspen and spruce, with views extending across to the Athabasca Glacier. Immediately to the south, Wilcox Creek offers larger sites, better suited to RVs and trailers, but with no hookups. Continuing north is **Jonas Creek** and then **Honeymoon Lake** and **Mt. Kerkeslin Campgrounds.** All cost $15 per night and have only primitive facilities.

Town of Jasper

At the top end of the Icefields Parkway, 280 kilometers (174 mi) north of Banff and a 3.5-hour drive west of the provincial capital, Edmonton, the town of Jasper is the service center of the park. For you, the visitor, Jasper is the wonderfully underrated counterpart to its neighbor, Banff. Jasper is home to around half the population of Banff, but it's also less commercialized and its streets are a lot quieter. Part of the town's charm is its location at the confluence of the Athabasca and Miette Rivers, surrounded by the rugged, snowcapped peaks of Jasper National Park.

Connaught Drive, the town's main street, parallels the rail line as it curves through town. Along here, you'll find the park information center, the bus depot, the rail terminal, restaurants, motels, and a series of parking lots. Behind Connaught Drive is Patricia Street (one-way northbound), which has more restaurants and services and leads to more hotels and motels on Geikie Street. Behind this main commercial core are rows of neat houses—much less pretentious than those in Banff—and all the facilities of a regular town, including a library, a school, a swimming pool, and a hospital.

HISTORY

The first white man to enter the Athabasca River Valley was David Thompson, one of Canada's greatest explorers. He was looking for a pass through the mountains to use as access to the Pacific Ocean. The gap he eventually found—Athabasca Pass, south of Mount Edith Cavell—became the main route used by the North West and Hudson's Bay Companies to cross the Rockies. While Thompson was making his crossing, some of his party remained in the Athabasca River Valley and constructed a small settlement east of the present town. Used for many years as a supply depot for fur traders, the post office was run by a clerk named Jasper Hawes, and in time the settlement became known as Jasper's House.

In 1907, the federal government officially declared the boundaries of Jasper Forest Park and bought all the land within it, except for one homestead owned by Lewis Swift. (This parcel remained privately owned until 1962, long after the stubborn Mr. Swift had passed away.) When the Grand Trunk Pacific Railway was completed in 1911, visitors flocked into the remote mountain park settlement, and its future was ensured. The first accommodation for tourists was 10 tents on the shore of Lac Beauvert, which became known as Jasper Park Camp. In 1921, the tents were replaced by the original Jasper Park Lodge. By the summer of 1928, a road was completed from Edmonton, and a golf course was built.

Incorporation

Although the infrastructure of the town began developing in the 1960s, it was run from Ottawa by Parks Canada until 2002. In that year, Jasper was incorporated as a "town," with locally elected residents serving as mayor and council members. Decisions made by the council must still balance the needs of living in a national park, but also represent locals who call the park home. On the surface, obvious visible changes of this autonomy are a new emergency-services building, a new wastewater-treatment plant, and improvements to an ever-increasing downtown parking problem. One thing hasn't changed, and that's the basic premise of the town's existence: more than 50 percent of Jasper's 5,200 residents work in the hospitality industry, serving the needs of two million visitors annually.

SIGHTS AND DRIVES

With all the things to do and see in the park, it's amazing how many people hang out in town. July and August are especially busy; much-needed improvements to the parking situation have had little impact on the traffic—try for a parking spot in the lot along the railway line. The best way to avoid the problem

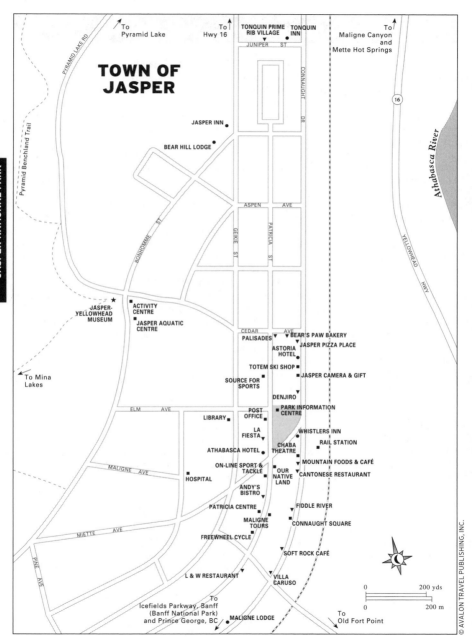

TOWN OF JASPER

To Pyramid Lake

To Hwy 16

TONQUIN PRIME RIB VILLAGE

TONQUIN INN

To Maligne Canyon and Mette Hot Springs

JUNIPER ST

CONNAUGHT DR

JASPER INN

BEAR HILL LODGE

ASPEN AVE

GEIKIE ST

PATRICIA ST

BONHOMME ST

PYRAMID LAKE RD

Pyramid Benchland Trail

Athabasca River

16

YELLOWHEAD HWY

★ JASPER-YELLOWHEAD MUSEUM

ACTIVITY CENTRE

JASPER AQUATIC CENTRE

CEDAR AVE

To Mina Lakes

PALISADES

BEAR'S PAW BAKERY

JASPER PIZZA PLACE

ASTORIA HOTEL

TOTEM SKI SHOP

JASPER CAMERA & GIFT

SOURCE FOR SPORTS

DENJIRO

ELM AVE

LIBRARY

POST OFFICE

PARK INFORMATION CENTRE

LA FIESTA

WHISTLERS INN

RAIL STATION

CHABA THEATRE

ATHABASCA HOTEL

ON-LINE SPORT & TACKLE

MOUNTAIN FOODS & CAFÉ

MALIGNE AVE

HOSPITAL

OUR NATIVE LAND

CANTONESE RESTAURANT

ANDY'S BISTRO

PATRICIA CENTRE

FIDDLE RIVER

MALIGNE TOURS

CONNAUGHT SQUARE

MIETTE AVE

FREEWHEEL CYCLE

SOFT ROCK CAFÉ

PINE AVE

L & W RESTAURANT

VILLA CARUSO

To Icefields Parkway, Banff (Banff National Park) and Prince George, BC

MALIGNE LODGE

To Old Fort Point

0   200 yds

0   200 m

© AVALON TRAVEL PUBLISHING, INC.

MARY SCHÄFFER

In the early 1900s, exploration of mountain wilderness areas was considered a man's domain. However, a spirited and tenacious woman entered that domain and went on to explore areas of the Canadian Rockies that no white man ever had. Mary Sharples was born in 1861 in Pennsylvania and raised in a strict Quaker family. Mary was introduced to Dr. Charles Schäffer on a trip to the Rockies, and in 1889 they were married. His interest in botany drew them back to the Rockies, where Charles collected, documented, and photographed specimens until his death in 1903. Mary also became apt at these skills. After hearing Sir James Hector (the geologist on the Palliser Expedition) reciting tales of the mountains, her zest to explore the wilderness increased. In 1908, with Billy Warren guiding, Mary, her dog, and a small party set out for a lake that no white man had ever seen but that the Stoney Indians knew as Chaba Imne, or "Beaver Lake." After initial difficulties, they succeeded in finding the elusive body of water now known as Maligne Lake. In Mary's words, "there burst upon us... the finest view any of us have ever beheld in the Rockies." In 1915 Mary married Billy Warren, continuing to explore the mountains until her death in 1939. Her success as a photographer, artist, and writer was equal to the success of any of her male counterparts. But it is her unwavering love of the Rockies – her "heaven of the hills" – for which she is best remembered.

Pyramid Lake Rd., 780/852-3013, mid-June–Sept. daily 10 A.M.–9 P.M., the rest of the year Thurs.–Sun. 10 A.M.–5 P.M., adult $4, child $3), as unstuffy as any museum could possibly be and well worth a visit even for nonmuseum types. The main gallery features colorful, modern picture boards with exhibits that take visitors along a timeline of Jasper's human history through the fur trade, the coming of the railway, and the creation of the park. Documentaries are shown on demand in a small television room. The museum also features extensive archives, including hundreds of historical photos, manuscripts, documents, maps, and videos.

The Den (corner of Connaught Dr. and Miette Ave., 780/852-3361, daily 9 A.M.–10 P.M.), in the darkened bowels of the Whistlers Inn, is a throwback to a bygone era, when displays of stuffed animals were considered the best way to extol the wonders of nature. "See animals in their natural setting" cries museum advertising, but the shrubbery looks suspiciously like fake Christmas trees and the bull elk seems to be screaming "Get me out of here!" Yep, they even charge you for it—exchange $3 for a token at the Whistlers' reception desk.

Patricia and Pyramid Lakes

A winding road heads through the hills at the back of town to these two picturesque lakes, formed when glacial moraines dammed shallow valleys. The first, to the left, is Patricia; the second, farther along the road, is Pyramid, backed by **Pyramid Mountain** (2,765 m/9,072 ft). Both lakes are popular spots for picnicking, fishing, and boating. Boat rentals are available at **Pyramid Lake Boat Rentals** (780/852-4900). Canoes, rowboats, paddleboats, and kayaks are $30 for the first hour and $20 for each additional hour. Motorboats are $45 per hour. From the resort, the road continues around the lake to a footbridge, which leads to an island popular with picnickers.

Jasper Tramway

This tramway (780/852-3093, adult $23, child 5–14 $11.50) climbs more than 1,000 vertical meters (3,280 ft) up the steep north face of **The**

is to avoid town during the middle of the day. The park information center, on Connaught Drive, is the only real reason to be in town. The shaded park in front of the center is a good place for people-watching.

Museums

At the back of town is the excellent **Jasper-Yellowhead Museum and Archives** (400

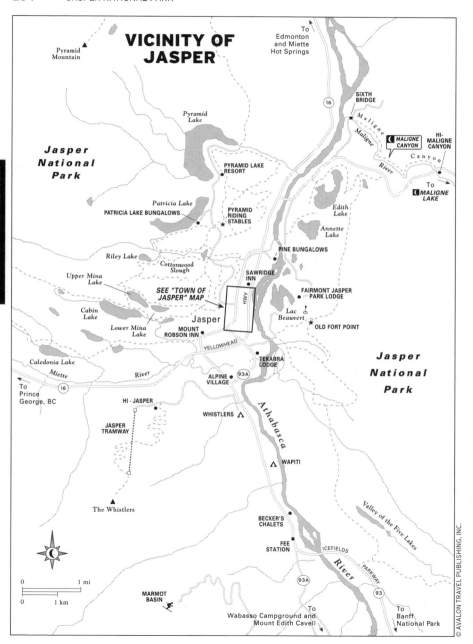

VICINITY OF JASPER

To Edmonton and Miette Hot Springs

Pyramid Mountain

SIXTH BRIDGE

Pyramid Lake

Jasper National Park

Maligne

Maligne

MALIGNE CANYON

HI- MALIGNE CANYON

PYRAMID LAKE RESORT

Canyon

River

To MALIGNE LAKE

Patricia Lake

PATRICIA LAKE BUNGALOWS

PYRAMID RIDING STABLES

Edith Lake

Annette Lake

Riley Lake

Cottonwood Slough

PINE BUNGALOWS

Upper Mina Lake

SAWRIDGE INN

SEE "TOWN OF JASPER" MAP

HWY

FAIRMONT JASPER PARK LODGE

Cabin Lake

Jasper

Lac Beauvert

Lower Mina Lake

MOUNT ROBSON INN

OLD FORT POINT

YELLOWHEAD

Jasper National Park

Caledonia Lake

Miette

River

TEKARRA LODGE

To Prince George, BC

ALPINE VILLAGE

93A

HI - JASPER

JASPER TRAMWAY

WHISTLERS

WAPITI

Athabasca

The Whistlers

BECKER'S CHALETS

Valley of the Five Lakes

FEE STATION

ICEFIELDS

River

PARKWAY

0   1 mi

0   1 km

MARMOT BASIN

93A

93

To Banff National Park

To Wabasso Campground and Mount Edith Cavell

© AVALON TRAVEL PUBLISHING, INC.

Whistlers, named for the hoary marmots that live on the summit. The tramway operates two 30-passenger cars that take seven minutes to reach the upper terminal, during which time the conductor gives a lecture about the mountain and its environment. From the upper terminal, a 1.4-kilometer (0.9-mi) trail leads to the 2,470-meter (8,104-ft) true summit. The view is breathtaking; to the south is the Columbia Icefield, and on a clear day you can see Mount Robson (3,954 m/12,970 ft)—the highest peak in the Canadian Rockies—to the northwest. Free two-hour guided hikes leave the upper terminal for the true summit daily at 10 A.M., 11 A.M., 2 P.M., and 3 P.M. You should allow two hours on top and, on a clear summer's day, two more hours in line at the bottom. The tramway is three kilometers (1.9 mi) south of town on Highway 93 (Icefields Parkway) and then a similar distance up Whistlers Road. It operates in summer daily 8:30 A.M.–10 P.M., shorter hours April–June and September to mid-October, closed the rest of the year.

(Mount Edith Cavell

The original Icefields Parkway (Hwy. 93A), which followed the southeast bank of the Athabasca River, has been bypassed by a more direct route on the other side of the river. Along the original route, known also as the Athabasca Parkway, a 14.5-kilometer (nine-mi) road winds its way up to a parking area below the northeast face of 3,363-meter (11,033-ft) Mount Edith Cavell, the park's most distinctive peak. It can be seen from many vantage points in the park, including the town and the gold course, but none is more impressive than directly below it. On this face, **Angel Glacier** lies in a saddle on the mountain's lower slopes. From the parking area, the **Path of the Glacier Trail** (one hour round-trip) traverses moraines deposited by the receding Angel Glacier and leads to some great viewpoints. For other local hiking opportunities, see *Hikes near Mount Edith Cavell* later in this chapter.

Edith and Annette Lakes

These two lakes along the road to Jasper Park Lodge—across the Athabasca River from town—are perfect for a picnic, a swim, or a pleasant walk. They are remnants of a much larger lake that once covered the entire valley floor. The lakes are relatively shallow; therefore, the sun warms the water to a bearable temperature. In fact, they have the warmest waters of any lakes in the park. The 2.5-kilometer (1.6-mi) **Lee Foundation Trail** encircles Lake Annette and is wheelchair accessible. Both lakes have day-use areas with beaches and picnic areas.

Jasper Park Lodge

Accommodations are not usually considered "sights," but then this is the Rockies, where three grand railway hotels attract as many visitors as the more legitimate natural attractions. Jasper Park Lodge has been the premier accommodation in the park since it opened in 1921. Back then, it was a single-story structure, reputed to be the largest log building in the world. It burned to the ground in 1952 but was rebuilt. Additional bungalows were

Mount Edith Cavell

© ANDREW HEMPSTEAD

JASPER NATIONAL PARK

erected along Lac Beauvert, forming a basis for today's lodge. Rows of cabins radiate from the main lodge, which contains restaurants, lounges, and the town's only covered shopping arcade. Today, up to 900 guests can be accommodated in 442 rooms. A large parking area for nonguests is on Lodge Road, behind the golf clubhouse; you're welcome to walk around the resort, play golf, dine in the restaurants, and, of course, browse through the shopping promenade, even if you're not a registered guest. From the main lodge, a hiking trail follows the shoreline of Lac Beauvert and links up with other trails from Old Fort Point. To walk from town takes one hour.

(Maligne Canyon

To get here, head northeast from town and turn right onto Maligne Lake Road. The canyon access road veers left 11 kilometers (6.8 mi) from Jasper. This unique geological feature has been eroded out of the easily dissolved limestone bedrock by the fast-flowing Maligne River. Surface water here is augmented by underground springs; therefore, it seems that more water flows out of the canyon than into it. The canyon is up to 50 meters deep, yet so narrow that squirrels often jump across. At the top of the canyon, opposite the teahouse, are large potholes in the riverbed. These potholes are created when rocks and pebbles become trapped in what begins as a shallow depression, and under the force of the rushing water the rocks carve jug-shaped hollows into the soft bedrock.

An interpretive trail winds down from the parking lot, crossing the canyon six times. The most spectacular sections of the canyon can be seen from the first two bridges, at the upper end of the trail. In summer, a teahouse operates at the top of the canyon. To avoid the crowds at the upper end of the canyon, an alternative would be to park at Sixth Bridge, near the confluence of the Maligne and Athabasca Rivers, and walk *up* the canyon (see the *Hiking Around Town* section).

Medicine Lake

From the canyon, Maligne Lake Road climbs

to Medicine Lake, which does a disappearing act each year. The water level fluctuates because of an underground drainage system known as karst. At the northwest end of the lake, where the outlet should be, the riverbed is often dry. In fall, when runoff from the mountains is minimal, the water level drops, and by November the lake has almost completely dried up. Early Indians believed that spirits were responsible for the phenomenon, hence the name.

(Maligne Lake

At the end of the road, 48 kilometers (30 mi) from town, is Maligne Lake, the largest glacier-fed lake in the Canadian Rockies and second-largest in the world. The first paying visitors were brought to the lake in 1929, and it has been a mecca for camera-toting tourists from around the world ever since. Once at the lake, tourists have plenty of activities to choose from. But other than taking in the spectacular vistas, the only thing you won't need your wallet for is hiking one of the numerous trails in the area.

The most popular tourist activity at the lake is a 90-minute narrated cruise up the lake on a glass-enclosed boat to oft-photographed **Spirit Island.** Cruises leave in summer every hour on the hour 10 A.M.–5 P.M., with fewer sailings in May and September; adult $41, child $20. Many time slots are booked in blocks by tour companies; therefore, reservations are suggested. Rowboats and canoes can be rented at the Boat House, a provincial historic site dating to 1929, for $27 per hour or $81 per day. Double sea kayaks go for $33 per hour and $97 per day. The lake also has excellent trout fishing (for details, see *Other Recreation* later in the *Town of Jasper* section).

All commercial operations to and around the lake are operated by **Maligne Tours** (616 Patricia St., 780/852-3370 or 866/625-4463, www.malignelake.com), based in downtown Jasper. At the lake itself, in addition to the cruises and boat rentals, Maligne Tours operates a souvenir shop and large café with a huge area of tiered outdoor seating overlooking the

BIGHORN SHEEP

Bighorn sheep are some of the most distinctive mammals of the Canadian Rockies. Easily recognized by their impressive horns, they are often seen grazing on grassy mountain slopes or at salt licks beside the road. The color of their coat varies with the season; in summer it is a brownish gray with a cream-colored belly and rump, turning lighter in winter. At seven years of age, males are fully grown and can weigh up to 120 kilograms (265 lbs). Females generally weigh around 80 kilograms (180 lbs).

© ANDREW HEMPSTEAD

Both sexes possess horns, rather than antlers like moose, elk, and deer. Unlike antlers, horns are not shed each year and can grow to astounding sizes. The horns of rams are larger than those of ewes and curve up to 360 degrees. The spiraled horns of an older ram can measure over one meter (three ft) and weigh as much as 15 kilograms (33 lbs). As the horns grow, they become marked by an annual growth ring. By counting the rings it is possible to determine the approximate age of the animal. In fall, during the mating season, a hierarchy is established among them for the right to breed with ewes. As the males face off against each other to establish dominance, their horns act as both weapons and buffers against the head-butting of other rams. The skull structure of the bighorn, rams in particular, has become adapted to these clashes, allowing them to avoid serious concussions.

These animals are particularly tolerant of humans and often approach parked vehicles; although they are not dangerous, as with all mammals in the park, you should not approach or feed them.

lake. The **Maligne Lake Shuttle** runs from the Maligne Tours office and from various hotels out to the lake 3–4 times daily from mid-May to late September. The first shuttle leaves for the lake each morning at 8:30 A.M.; $32.10 round-trip.

To Miette Hot Springs

From Jasper, it's 50 kilometers (31 mi) to the park's eastern boundary along Highway 16, following the Athabasca River the entire way. Beyond the turnoff to Maligne Lake, Highway 16 enters a wide valley flanked to the west by the Palisade and to the east by the Colin Range. Along **Jasper Lake,** 20 kilometers (12 mi) from town, are a number of viewpoints and picnic areas. Four kilometers (2.5 mi) from the north end of the lake is **Disaster Point,** a great spot for viewing bighorn sheep that often gather at an area of exposed mineral salts beside the road.

After curving, swerving, rising, and falling many times, Miette Hot Springs Road ends 18 kilometers (11 mi) from Highway 16 at the warmest springs in the Canadian Rockies (780/866-3939, mid-May–mid-Oct. 10:30 A.M.–9 P.M., extended to 8:30 A.M.–10:30 P.M. in summer). In the early 1900s, these springs were one of the park's biggest attractions. In 1910, a packhorse trail was built up the valley and the government constructed a bathhouse. The original hand-hewn log structure was replaced in the 1930s with pools that remained in use until new facilities were built

in 1985. Water that flows into the pools is artificially cooled from 54°C (128°F) to a soothing 39°C (100°F). A newer addition to the complex is a cool-water plunge pool. Admission is $6.25 for a single swim or $8.75 for the day (senior and child $5.25 and $7.75, respectively).

HIKING NEAR TOWN

The 1,200 kilometers (745 mi) of hiking trails in Jasper are significantly different than those in the other mountain national parks. The park has an extensive system of interconnecting backcountry trails that, for experienced hikers, can provide a wilderness adventure rivaled by few areas on the face of the earth. The most popular trails for extended backcountry trips are the **Skyline Trail,** between Maligne Lake Road and Maligne Lake (44.5 km/27.6 mi, three days each way); the trails to **Amethyst Lakes** in the Tonquin Valley (19 km/11.8 mi, one day each way), and the **South Boundary Trail,** which traverses a remote section of the front ranges into Banff National Park (160 km/100 mi, 10 days each way).

The following section highlights only the very best day hikes, leaving longer trails to Brian Patton and Bart Robinson to describe in their excellent book *The Canadian Rockies Trail Guide.* Trails in the immediate vicinity of the town have little elevation gain and lead through montane forest to lakes. The trails around nearby Maligne Lake and at the base of Mount Edith Cavell have more rewarding objectives and are more challenging.

Before setting off on any hikes, whatever the length, go to the **park information center** in downtown Jasper for trail maps, trail conditions, and trail closures.

Pyramid Benchland

- Length: Seven kilometers/4.3 miles (5 hours) round-trip
- Elevation gain: 120 meters/400 feet
- Rating: Easy
- Trailhead: Jasper-Yellowhead Museum, Pyramid Lake Road

Numerous official and unofficial hiking trails weave across the benchland immediately west of the town of Jasper. From the far corner of the parking lot beside the museum, a well-marked trail climbs onto the benchland. Keep right, crossing Pyramid Lake Road, and you'll emerge on a bluff overlooking the Athabasca River Valley. Bighorn sheep can often be seen grazing here. If you return to the trailhead from here, you will have hiked seven kilometers (4.3 mi). The trail continues north, disappearing into the montane forest until arriving at Pyramid Lake. Various trails can be taken to return to town; get a map at the park information center before setting out.

Patricia Lake Circle

- Length: Five-kilometer/3.1-mile loop (90 minutes)
- Elevation gain: Minimal
- Rating: Easy
- Trailhead: Two kilometers (1.2 mi) along Pyramid Lake Road

Beginning across the road from the riding stables, this trail traverses a mixed forest of aspen and lodgepole pine—prime habitat for a variety of larger mammals such as elk, deer, and moose. The second half of the trail skirts Cottonwood Slough, where you'll see a number of beaver ponds. Unlike the name suggests, this trail doesn't encircle Patricia Lake, but instead just passes along a portion of its southern shoreline.

The Jasper-Yellowhead Museum is the starting point for a maze of trails which link up with the Patricia Lake Circle. **Lower and Upper Mina Lakes** are reached after a 2.5-kilometer (1.5-mi) hike from the museum, from where the variety of options for continuing to Patricia Lake becomes apparent only after looking at a map.

Old Fort Point

- Length: 6.5-kilometer/4-mile loop (2 hours)
- Elevation gain: 60 meters/200 feet

© ANDREW HEMPSTEAD

Lower Mina Lake

- Rating: Easy
- Trailhead: Take Highway 93A south from downtown; follow the first left after crossing Highway 16 and park beside the Athabasca River.

Old Fort Point is a distinctive knoll above the Athabasca River to the east of town. Although it is not likely a fort was ever located here, the first fur-trading post in the Rockies, Henry House, was located just downstream. It's easy to imagine fur traders and early explorers climbing to this summit for 360-degree views of the Athabasca and Miette Rivers. From the parking lot beyond the single-lane vehicle bridge over the Athabasca River, climb the wooden stairs, take the left trail to the top of the knoll, and then continue back to the parking lot along the north flank of the hill.

HIKING NEAR MOUNT EDITH CAVELL

Cavell Road begins 13 kilometers (eight mi) south from town along Highway 93A and ends

after 14.5 kilometers (nine mi) at the trailhead for the Cavell Meadows Trail, one of most scenic in the park. The Astoria River trail into the Tonquin Valley is one of the overnight treks that was mentioned earlier as beyond the scope of this book, but this one is just too good to pass by.

【 Cavell Meadows

- Length: Four kilometers/2.5 miles (1.5 hours) one-way
- Elevation gain: 380 meters/1,250 feet
- Rating: Moderate
- Trailhead: Parking lot at the end of Cavell Road, 27.5 kilometers (17 mi) south of town

Renowned local author of the *Canadian Rockies Trail Guide,* Brian Patton, says of this trail, "I am always amazed such a wildly spectacular setting can be reached so easily." And you'll agree after making the short journey from the parking lot beneath Mount Edith Cavell to an alpine meadow and panoramic views of Angel Glacier. The trail begins by following the paved Path of the Glacier Loop, then branches left, climbing steadily through a subalpine forest of Engelmann spruce and then stunted subalpine fir to emerge facing the northeast face of Mount Edith Cavell and Angel Glacier. The view of the glacier from this point is nothing less than awesome, as the ice spills out of a cirque, clinging to a 300-meter-high (980-ft-high) cliff face. The trail continues to higher viewpoints and an alpine meadow that, by mid-July, is filled with wildflowers.

Astoria River

- Length: 19 kilometers/11.8 miles (6–7 hours) one-way
- Elevation gain: 450 meters/1,480 feet
- Rating: Moderate
- Trailhead: Opposite the hostel on Cavell Road

From Cavell Road, this trail descends through a forest on the north side of Mount Edith Cavell for five kilometers (3.1 mi), then crosses the

Astoria River and begins a long ascent into spectacular Tonquin Valley. Amethyst Lakes and the 1,000-meter (3,280-ft) cliffs of the Ramparts first come into view after 13 kilometers (eight mi). At the 17-kilometer (10.5-mi) mark the trail divides. To the left it climbs into Eremite Valley, where there is a campground. The right fork continues following Astoria River to Tonquin Valley, Amethyst Lakes, and a choice of four campgrounds and two lodges.

HIKING IN THE MALIGNE LAKE AREA

Hikes in the vicinity of Maligne Lake, 48 kilometers (30 mi) from the town of Jasper, provide many opportunities to view the lake and explore its environs. To get there, take Highway 16 east for four kilometers (2.5 mi) from town and turn south on Maligne Lake Road. The first three hikes detailed are along the access road to the lake; the others leave from various parking lots at the northwest end of the lake.

Maligne Canyon

- Length: 3.7 kilometers/2.3 miles (90 minutes) one-way

- Elevation gain: 125 meters/410 feet

- Rating: Moderate

- Trailhead: Turn off to 6th Bridge 2.5 kilometers (1.6 mi) along Maligne Lake Road from Highway 16

Maligne Canyon is one of the busiest places in the park, yet few visitors hike the entire length of the canyon trail. By beginning from the lower end of the canyon, at the confluence of the Maligne and Athabasca Rivers, you'll avoid starting your hike alongside the masses and you'll get to hike downhill on your return (when you're tired). To access the lower end of the canyon, follow the one-kilometer (0.6-mi) spur off Maligne Lake Road to 6th Bridge. Crowds will be minimal for the first three kilometers (1.9 mi) to 4th Bridge, where the trail starts climbing. By the time

One of Jasper's most famous scenes, Maligne Lake with Spirit Island in the foreground, is accessible by tour boat.

© ANDREW HEMPSTEAD

you get to Third Bridge, you start encountering "adventurous" hikers coming down the canyon, and soon thereafter you'll meet the real crowds, high heels, bear bells, and all. Upstream of here the canyon is deepest and most spectacular.

Jacques Lake

- Length: 12 kilometers/7.5 miles (3–3.5 hours) one-way
- Elevation gain: 100 meters/330 feet
- Rating: Moderate
- Trailhead: Beaver Lake Picnic Area, 28 kilometers (17.4 mi) from Highway 16 along Maligne Lake Road

The appeal of this trail, which begins from the southeast end of Medicine Lake, is its lack of elevation gain and the numerous small lakes it skirts as it travels through a narrow valley. On either side, the severely faulted mountains of the Queen Elizabeth Ranges rise steeply above the valley floor, their strata tilted nearly vertical.

Lake Trail (Mary Schäffer Loop)

- Length: 3.2-kilometer/2-mile loop (1 hour)
- Elevation gain: Minimal
- Rating: Easy
- Trailhead: Boathouse, Maligne Lake

This easy, pleasant walk begins from beside the boathouse, following the eastern shore of Maligne Lake through an open area of lakeside picnic tables to a point known as **Schäffer Viewpoint,** named for the first white person to see the valley. Across the lake are the aptly named Bald Hills, the Maligne Range, and to the southwest, the distinctive twin peaks of Mount Unwin and Mount Charlton. After dragging yourself away from the spectacular panorama, continue along a shallow bay before following the trail into a forest of spruce and subalpine fir, then looping back to the middle parking lot.

◖ Opal Hills

- Length: 8.2-kilometer/5.1-mile loop (3 hours)
- Elevation gain: 455 meters/1,500 feet
- Rating: Moderate
- Trailhead: North corner, upper parking lot, Maligne Lake

This is one of the best trails in the park. It begins from behind the information board in the corner of the parking lot, climbing steeply for 1.5 kilometers (0.9 mi) to a point where it divides. Both options end in the high alpine meadows of the Opal Hills; the trail to the right is shorter and steeper. Once in the meadow, stunning views of the entire Maligne Valley are yours to enjoy.

Bald Hills

- Length: 5.2 kilometers/3.2 miles (2 hours) one-way
- Elevation gain: 495 meters/1,620 feet
- Rating: Moderate
- Trailhead: Picnic area at the very end of Maligne Lake Road

This trail follows an old fire road for its entire distance, entering an open meadow near the end. This was once the site of a fire lookout. The 360-degree view takes in the jade-green waters of Maligne Lake, the Queen Elizabeth Ranges, and the twin peaks of Mount Unwin and Mount Charlton. The Bald Hills extend for seven kilometers (4.3 mi), their highest summit not exceeding 2,600 meters (8,530 ft). A herd of caribou summers in the hills.

Moose Lake

- Length: 1.4 kilometers/.9 miles (30 minutes) one-way
- Elevation gain: Minimal
- Rating: Easy
- Trailhead: Picnic area at the very end of Maligne Lake Road

If you're looking for a quick jaunt away from the crowds, take this short trail that begins 200 meters (0.1 mi) along the Bald Hills Trail, spurring left along the Maligne Pass Trail (signposted). One kilometer (0.6 mi) along this trail a rough track branches left, leading to Moose Lake—a quiet body of water where moose are sometimes seen. To return, continue along the trail as it descends to the shore of Maligne Lake, a short stroll from the picnic area.

OTHER RECREATION

A number of booking agents represent the many recreation-tour operators in Jasper. The **Jasper Adventure Centre** (Chaba Theatre, 604 Connaught Dr., 780/852-5595, www.jasper adventurecentre.com) takes bookings for all the activities below, as well as for accommodations and for transportation to various points in the park and beyond. **Maligne Tours** (616 Patricia St., 780/852-3370, www.malignelake.com) operates all activities in the Maligne Lake area, including the famous lake cruise.

Horseshoe Lake is a popular swimming hole south of town.

Mountain Biking

Biking in the park continues to grow in popularity: The ride between Banff and Jasper, along the Icefields Parkway, attracts riders from around the world. In addition to the paved roads, many designated unpaved bicycle trails radiate from the town. One of the most popular is the Athabasca River Trail, which begins at Old Fort Point and follows the river to a point below Maligne Canyon. Cyclists are particularly prone to sudden bear encounters; make noises when passing through heavily wooded areas. The brochure *Mountain Biking Trail Guide* lists designated trails and is available from the information center and all local sport shops. Rental outlets include **On-line Sport & Tackle** (600 Patricia St., 780/852-3630), **Source for Sports** (406 Patricia St., 780/852-3654), **Freewheel Cycle** (618 Patricia St., 780/852-3898), **Vicious Cycle** (630 Connaught Dr., 780/852-1111), and the **Activity Centre** at Jasper Park Lodge (780/852-5708). Expect to pay $6–10 per hour or $24–40 for any 24-hour period, which includes a helmet and lock.

Horseback Riding

On the benchlands immediately behind the town of Jasper is **Pyramid Riding Stables** (Pyramid Lake Rd., 780/852-7433). The stables offer one-, two-, and three-hour guided rides for $38, $60, and $80, respectively. The one-hour trip follows a ridge high above town, providing excellent views of the Athabasca River Valley. **Skyline Trail Rides** (Jasper Park Lodge, 780/852-4215) offers a one-hour guided ride around Lake Annette ($39 per person) and a two-hour ride along the Valleyview Trail ($60 per person). Both companies operate between mid-April and October.

Overnight pack trips consist of 4–6 hours of riding per day, with a few nights spent at a remote mountain lodge where you can hike, boat, fish, or ride. Rates start at $180 per person per day for meals, accommodation, and a horse, of course. For details, contact **Skyline Trail Rides** (780/852-4215 or 888/852-7787, www.skylinetrail.com) or **Tonquin Valley Adventures** (780/852-1188, www.tonquinadventures.com).

White-Water Rafting

Within the park, the **Athabasca** and **Sunwapta Rivers** are run by a half dozen outfitters, while across the border in British Columbia, the **Fraser River** is another option for a guided rafting trip. On the Athabasca River, the Mile 5 Run is an easy two-hour float that appeals to all ages. Farther upstream, some operators offer a trip that begins from below Athabasca Falls, on a stretch of the river that passes through a narrow canyon; this run takes three hours. The boulder-strewn rapids of the Sunwapta and Fraser Rivers offer more thrills and spills—these trips are for the more adventurous and last 3–4 hours. Most companies offer a choice of rivers and provide transportation to and from downtown hotels. Expect to pay $50–62 for trips on the Athabasca and $75 for the Sunwapta and Fraser. The following companies run at least two of three rivers: **Maligne Rafting Adventures** (780/852-3370 or 866/625-4463), **Raven Adventures** (780/852-4292), **Rocky Mountain River Guides** (780/852-3777), and **White Water Rafting** (250/566-4879 or 888/566-7238). **Jasper Raft Tours** (780/852-2665 or 888/553-5628) floats a 16-kilometer (10-mi) stretch of the Athabasca River in large, stable inflatable rafts; $50 adults, $20 children.

Fishing

Fishing in the many alpine lakes—for rainbow, brook, Dolly Varden, cutthroat, and lake trout, as well as pike and whitefish—is excellent. Many outfitters offer guided fishing trips. Whether you fish with a guide or by yourself, you'll need a national park fishing license ($10 per week, $35 per year), available from the park information center.

Stable 5.5-meter (18-ft) Freighter canoes with a small electric motor are the preferred fishing boat on Maligne Lake. They are available at the lakeside **Boat House** (780/852-3370, June–Aug. daily 8:30 A.M.–6:30 P.M.) for $106 per day, with rod and reel rentals extra. Guided fishing trips on the lake are offered from the Boat House by **Maligne Tours** (780/852-3370); half-day $150 per person for two people, full-day $200 per person for two.

Currie's Guiding (780/852-5650) offers trips to Maligne Lake (full-day $210 per person) and to Talbot Lake, a shallow body of water east of town renowned for its pike fishing. Rates include equipment and instruction. **Source for Sports** (406 Patricia St., 780/852-3654) and **On-line Sport & Tackle** (600 Patricia St., 780/852-3630) sell and rent fishing tackle and also have canoe and boat rentals.

Golf

The world-famous **Jasper Park Lodge Golf Course** (780/852-6090) was designed by renowned golf-course architect Stanley Thompson. The course opened in 1925, after 200 men had spent an entire year clearing trees and laying out the holes to Thompson's design. Today, the old-fashioned layout is consistently ranked as one of the top 10 courses in Canada. The 18-hole, 6,670-yard course takes in the contours of the Athabasca River Valley as it hugs the banks of turquoise-colored Lac Beauvert. It is a true test of accuracy, and with holes named the Maze, the Bad Baby, and the Bay, you'll need lots of balls. Greens fees for 18 holes vary with the season: $195 mid-June to September, $140 mid-May to mid-June, and $110 in early May and from October 1 through closing (usually mid-October). These rates are discounted for Canadian residents. A power cart is $40 per round. Golfing after 5 P.M. is discounted to just over $100—a great deal during the long days of June and July. Other facilities include a driving range, club rentals ($35–55), a restaurant, and a lounge.

Tours

Brewster (780/852-3332) offers a four-hour Discover Jasper tour taking in Patricia and Pyramid Lakes, Maligne Canyon, and Jasper Tramway (ride not included in fare). It departs April–October daily at 8:30 A.M. from the railway station; $48. **Maligne Tours** (616 Patricia St., 780/852-3370, www.malignelake.com) schedules a variety of tours, including a six-hour trip to Maligne Lake ($85, includes cruise).

Jasper Adventure Centre, in the Chaba Theatre (604 Connaught Dr., 780/852-5595, www.jasperadventurecentre.com) operates several well-priced tours, including the following: Mount Edith Cavell (departs 2 P.M., three hours, $50), Maligne Valley (departs 9:30 A.M., five hours, $90, including boat tour), and Miette Hot Springs (departs 6 P.M., four hours, $57). Similarly priced tours take in historical sites and local wildlife.

Swimming and Fitness Centers

Jasper Aquatic Centre (401 Pyramid Lake Road, 780/852-3663) has an Olympic-size swimming pool; admission is $5.60. The adjacent **Jasper Activity Centre** (780/852-3381) has squash courts, indoor and outdoor tennis courts, a climbing wall, a weight room, and an indoor skate park; admission $6.50.

WINTER RECREATION

Winter is certainly a quiet time in the park, but that doesn't mean there's a lack of things to do. Marmot Basin offers world-class alpine skiing; many snow-covered hiking trails are groomed for cross-country skiing; portions of Lac Beauvert and Pyramid Lake are cleared for ice-skating; horse-drawn sleighs travel around town; and Maligne Canyon is transformed into a magical, frozen world. Hotels reduce rates by 40–70 percent through winter and many offer lodging and lift tickets for under $80 per person.

Marmot Basin

The skiing at Marmot Basin (780/852-3816 or 800/363-3078, www.skimarmot.com) is highly underrated. The best terrain for adventurous skiers and boarders is Charlie's Basin, a massive powder-filled bowl, and the open bowls and lightly treed glades off the summit of Eagle Ridge. Marmot Basin now has seven lifts servicing 600 hectares (1,500 acres) of terrain and a vertical rise of 900 meters (2,940 ft). The longest run is 5.6 kilometers (3.5 mi). Marmot doesn't get the crowds of the three resorts in Banff National Park, so lift lines are uncommon. The season runs from early December to late April. Lift tickets are adult $60, senior and child $48. (Throughout Jasper in January celebrations, adult tickets are just $45.) Rentals are available at the resort or in town at **Totem Ski Shop** (408 Connaught Dr., 780/852-3078).

Cross-Country Skiing

For many, traveling Jasper's hiking trails on skis is just as exhilarating as on foot. An extensive network of 300 kilometers (185 mi) of summer hiking trails is designated for skiers, with around 100 kilometers (62 mi) groomed. The four main areas of trails are along Pyramid Lake Road, around Maligne Lake, in the Athabasca Falls area, and at Whistlers Campground. A booklet available at the park information center details each trail and its difficulty. Weather forecasts and avalanche-hazard reports are posted here also.

Rental packages are available from **Source for Sports** (406 Patricia St., 780/852-3654), the rental shop at **Jasper Park Lodge** (780/852-3433), and **Totem Ski Shop** (408 Connaught Dr., 780/852-3078), which also offers repairs and sales.

Maligne Canyon

By late December, the torrent that is the Maligne River has frozen solid. Where it cascades down through Maligne Canyon the river is temporarily stalled for the winter, creating remarkable formations through the deep limestone canyon. **Jasper Adventure Centre** (306 Connaught Dr., 780/852-5595) offers exciting three-hour guided tours into the depths of the canyon throughout winter, daily at 9 A.M., 1 P.M., and 6 P.M.; adult $40, child $20.

ENTERTAINMENT, EVENTS, AND SHOPPING
Nightlife

The most popular nightspot in town is the **Atha-B,** in the Athabasca Hotel (510 Patricia St., 780/852-3386), where bands play some nights. It gets pretty rowdy with all the seasonal workers, but it's still enjoyable; minimal cover charge. This hotel also has a large lounge and a bar with a pool table and a popular 5–7 P.M. happy hour. **Pete's Club** (upstairs at 614 Patri-

cia St., 780/852-6262) has a jam on Tuesday night and bands playing Friday–Sunday. The music varies—it could be blues, rock, or Celtic. The **De'd Dog Bar and Grill,** in the Astoria Hotel (404 Connaught Dr., 780/852-3351), is a large, dimly lit sports bar with pool tables and plenty of locals drinking copious amounts of beer, especially during the 5–7 P.M. happy hour. Right downtown, the **Whistle Stop Pub,** in the Whistlers Inn (105 Miette Ave., 780/852-3361), has a great atmosphere with a classic wooden bar and memorabilia everywhere.

Escape the smoky bar scenes at the **Downstream Bar** (620 Connaught Dr., 780/ 852-9449), a nonsmoking place that opens at 4 P.M. and has live music Friday and Saturday. You don't need to be a guest of Jasper's finest hotel, the Jasper Park Lodge (780/852-3301), to enjoy the ambience of its three lounges: the **Emerald Lounge** has comfortable indoor seating and a long outdoor terrace overlooking Lac Beauvert; **Tent City** is a sports-style bar with a relaxed atmosphere and two pool tables; while **Palisade's** is a winter-only bar attracting the après-ski crowd each evening. Most of Jasper's other large hotels, including the Amethyst Lodge, Jasper Inn, and Marmot Lodge, also have lounges.

Festivals and Events

Summer is prime time on the park's events calendar. **Canada Day** (July 1) celebrations begin with a pancake breakfast and progress to a flag-raising ceremony (in front of the information center) and a parade along Connaught Drive. Live entertainment and a fireworks display end the day. The **Jasper Heritage Rodeo** (www.jasperheritagerodeo.com), on the second weekend of August, dates from 1926 and attracts pro cowboys from across Canada. Apart from the traditional rodeo events, the fun includes a mechanical bull, a children's rodeo, a casino, pancake breakfasts, the ever-popular stick-pony parade, and the crowning of Miss Rodeo Jasper. Most of the action takes place in the arena at the Jasper Activity Centre, behind town on Pyramid Lake Road.

On the other side of the calendar, winter is

not totally partyless—**Jasper in January** is a two-week celebration that includes fireworks, special evenings at local restaurants, a chili cook-off, discounted lift tickets at Marmot Basin, and all the activities associated with winter.

Shopping

Jasper certainly doesn't provide the shopping experience found in Banff, but a number of interesting shops beckon on rainy days. **Our Native Land** (601 Patricia St., 780/852-5592) is a large shop chock-full of authentic arts and crafts produced by artisans from throughout western Canada. Search out everything from moose-hide moccasins to masks (check out the musk-ox head near the back of the store). They also stock Inuit soapstone carvings from the Canadian Arctic. **Bearberry** (612 Connaught Dr., 780/852-1112) features a good cross-section of Canadiana. Beyond the information center, **Pine Cones & Pussy Willow** (308 Connaught Drive, 780/852-5310) is a little less tacky than your average souvenir shop, with furry toys and plastic rulers complemented by the works of local artists.

Head to the **Friends of Jasper** store (780/852-4767) in the park information center or the **museum** for a good selection of books on the park's natural and human history. A larger selection of literature, including lots of western Canadiana, can be found at **Jasper Camera and Gift** (412 Connaught Dr., 780/852-3165, daily 9 A.M.–10 P.M.). **Maligne Lake Books** (Jasper Park Lodge, 780/852-4779) has a good selection of coffee-table books.

ACCOMMODATIONS

In summer, motel and hotel rooms here are expensive. Most of the motels and lodges are within walking distance of town and have indoor pools and restaurants. Luckily, alternatives to staying in $200-plus hotel rooms do exist. The best alternatives are the lodges scattered around the edge of town. Open in summer only, each offers a rustic yet distinct style of accommodation in keeping with the theme of staying in a national park. Additionally, many private residences have rooms for rent in summer; three hostels are close

PRIVATE-HOME ACCOMMODATIONS

At last count, Jasper had over 100 residential homes offering accommodations. Often they supply nothing more than a room with a bed, but the price is right – $50-100 s or d. Often a bathroom is shared with other guests or the family; few have kitchens and only a few supply light breakfast. In most cases, don't expect too much from the lower-priced choices. The positive side, apart from the price, is that your hosts are usually knowledgeable locals and downtown is only a short walk away. For a full listing that includes the facilities at each approved property, check the Jasper Home Accommodation Association website, www.stayinjasper.com. The Park Information Centre has a board listing private-home accommodations with rooms available for the upcoming night.

to town; and there's always camping in the good ol' outdoors.

Under $50

Staying in hostels isn't for everyone, but it's the only type of accommodation in the park that comes close to falling into this price category. Hostelling International–Canada operates five hostels in Jasper National Park, but none right in downtown Jasper. Reservations are highly recommended at all hostels during July and August. Make these by calling 780/852-3215 or 877/852-0781, going online to www.hihostels.ca, or through other major hostels such as those in Lake Louise, Banff, Calgary, or Edmonton.

On the road to the Jasper Tramway, seven kilometers (4.3 mi) south from town off the Icefields Parkway, is **HI-Jasper,** which has 84 beds in men's and women's dorms, a large kitchen, a common room, showers, a laundry, public Internet access, an outdoor barbecue area, and mountain-bike rentals. Members of Hostelling International pay $22, nonmem-

bers $27. Private rooms are $60 and $70 s or d respectively. In the summer months this hostel fills up every night. The front desk is open daily noon–midnight. Cab fare between downtown Jasper and the hostel is $20.

HI-Maligne Canyon is on Maligne Lake Road, beside the Maligne River and a short walk from the canyon. Although rustic, it lies in a beautiful setting. The 24 dorm beds are in two cabins; other amenities include electricity, a kitchen, and a dining area. Rates are $15 for members, $20 for nonmembers. Check-in is between 5 P.M. and 11 P.M. The hostel is closed on Wednesday October–April.

❰ HI-Mount Edith Cavell (mid-June to mid-Oct.) offers a million-dollar view for the price of a dorm bed. It's 13 kilometers (eight mi) up Cavell Road off Highway 93A, and because of the location there's usually a spare bed. Opposite the hostel are trailheads for hiking in the Tonquin Valley, and it's just a short walk to the base of Mount Edith Cavell. The hostel is rustic (no showers and only pit toilets) but has a kitchen, dining area, and outdoor wood sauna. Members pay $15 per night, nonmembers pay $20. Check-in is 5–11 P.M.

$50-100

If you're simply looking for somewhere to rest your head, consider Jasper's least expensive hotel rooms at the downtown **Athabasca Hotel** (510 Patricia St., 780/852-3386 or 877/542-8422, www.athabascahotel.com), which dates to 1928. The cheapest of its 61 rooms share bathrooms and are above a noisy bar, but the price is right—$75–89 s or d. This hotel also has more expensive rooms, each with a vaguely Victorian decor and private bathrooms ($129–159 s or d).

The cheapest motel-style units at **Patricia Lake Bungalows** (780/852-3560 or 888/499-6848, www.patricialakebungalows.com, May–mid-Oct.), a five-minute drive north from Jasper along Pyramid Lake Road, fall into this price range (from $95 per night), but it is worth paying extra for a freestanding unit. Comfortable but older cottages with kitchens and TVs start at $155 s or d, rising to $170 for

those with either a lake view or fireplace. Suites ($170–250) are a good value in relation to similar-sized rooms elsewhere in town.

$100-150

With a variety of cabin layouts and a central location, **(Bear Hill Lodge** (100 Bonhomme St., 780/852-3209, www.bearhilllodge.com, mid-Apr.–mid-Oct.) makes a great base camp for travelers who want the cabin experience within walking distance of downtown. The original cabins are basic, but each has a TV, bathroom, gas fireplace, and coffee-making facilities ($148 s or d, $168 with a kitchenette). Chalet Rooms are larger and more modern, and each has a wood-burning fireplace but no kitchen ($179). Colin Rooms are more spacious still; each has a jetted tub, gas fireplace, and limited cooking facilities ($210). Units are discounted 40 percent during the first and last months of operation. Breakfasts ($8 per person) feature a wide selection of freshly baked items, fruit, and cereals. Other amenities include a jetted tub, a barbecue area, a launderette, and Internet access.

Typifying a bungalow camp of the 1950s, **Pine Bungalows** (780/852-3491, www.pinebungalows.com, May–mid-Oct.) lies on a secluded section of the Athabasca River opposite the northern entrance to town. Individual wooden cabins with kitchens and fireplaces begin at $135 s or d (most cabins face the river, but numbers 1 and 3 enjoy the best views) while more modern two-bedroom log cabins are $195. A three-night minimum applies in July and August.

Farther south along the Icefields Parkway, **(Becker's Chalets** (780/852-3779, www.beckerschalets.com, May–mid-Oct.) is spread along a picturesque bend on the Athabasca River six kilometers (3.7 mi) south of town. This historic lodging took its first guests more than 50 years ago and continues to be a park favorite for many guests who make staying here an annual ritual. Moderately priced chalets, each with kitchenette, gas fireplace, and double bed ($145, or $175 for those on the riverfront), are an excellent deal. Deluxe log duplexes featuring all the modern conveniences, including color TV, start at a reasonable $170 s or d and go up to $380 for a unit that sleeps eight. Also available are a few one-bed sleeping rooms ($105). Becker's also boasts one of the park's finest restaurants.

$150-200

The lure of **(Tekarra Lodge** (Hwy. 93A, 1.6 km/one mi south from downtown, 780/852-3058 or 888/962-2522, www.tekarralodge.com, mid-May–early Oct.) is its historic log cabins and forested setting above the confluence of the Miette and Athabasca Rivers. Each cabin has been totally modernized yet retains a cozy charm, with comfortable beds, fully equipped kitchenettes, wood-burning fireplaces, and smallish but adequate bathrooms. High season rates start at $190 with the spacious Athabasca Cabins best suited for small families. An on-site restaurant is open for breakfast (7:30–11 A.M.) and dinner (5–11 P.M.).

A short distance south along Highway 93A from Tekarra Lodge, at the junction of the Icefields Parkway three kilometers (1.9 mi) south of town, is **(Alpine Village** (780/852-3285, www.alpinevillagejasper.com, late Apr.–mid-Oct.). This resort is laid out across well-manicured lawns, and all buildings are surrounded by colorful gardens of geraniums and petunias. After a day exploring the park, guests can soak away their cares in the outdoor hot pool or kick back on a row of Adirondack chairs scattered along the Athabasca River, directly opposite the resort. The older sleeping cabins have been renovated ($180 s or d, $195 with a kitchen and fireplace), while the newer deluxe one-bedroom log cabins feature stone fireplaces and modern furnishings ($280). The Deluxe Family Cabins ($340) sleep up to five, with two beds in an upstairs loft, a fireplace, and a full kitchen.

Right downtown is the **Astoria Hotel** (404 Connaught Dr., 780/852-3351 or 800/661-7343, www.astoriahotel.com). This European-style lodging was built in 1924 and has been kept in the same family since. Rooms are brightly furnished and each has a fridge, TV, and VCR. Standard rooms are $180 s or d,

JASPER NATIONAL PARK

cabin accommodation, Alpine Village

while much larger Superior rooms, complete with full bath, are $200. Outside of summer, these same rooms cost from $110. Note that there is no elevator in this four-story hotel.

$200-250

Near the end of Pyramid Lake Road, north from downtown, it's impossible to miss the sprawling grounds of **Pyramid Lake Resort** (780/852-4900 or 888/962-2522, www.pyramidlake resort.com), the only lodging away from town (besides Jasper Park Lodge) that is open year-round. Plenty of water-based activities and rentals (across the road), an interpretive program, a fitness center, and a large barbecue area make the resort a good choice for families. Summer-only cabins, with separate bedrooms, full baths, and lake views, range $209–239 s or d. In addition to lake views, motel-style units feature gas fireplaces and kitchenettes for $285 (discounted below $150 in the off-season).

Hotel choices barely over the $200 mark include the **Tonquin Inn** (100 Juniper St., 780/852-4987 or 800/661-1315, www.tonquin

inn.com, $211–398 s or d), with an indoor pool, an outdoor hot tub, laundry facilities, a steakhouse restaurant, and a sunny lounge bar; and **Maligne Lodge** (780/852-3143 or 800/661-1315, www.malignelodge.com, $204–271 s or d), also with an indoor pool. These places are worth considering outside of summer, when the cabin accommodations are closed and rates are discounted substantially.

Jasper Inn (98 Geikie St., 780/852-4461 or 800/661-1933, www.jasperinn.com) is a modern château-style lodging of brick and red cedar. Many rooms have private balconies, and more than 100 are self-contained suites with kitchenettes and fireplaces. Other features include a large indoor pool and a sundeck overlooking a Japanese rock garden. Rates start at $237 s or d, with kitchen units starting at $242. The Upper Loft Suites, complete with kitchen, fireplace, and—as the name suggests—a bedroom in the loft, are a much better deal at $249 s or d (from $114 outside of summer).

The **Sawridge Inn** (82 Connaught Dr., 780/852-5111 or 800/661-6427, www.sawridge

jasper.com) offers 154 air-conditioned rooms built around a large atrium and indoor pool. Also contained within the atrium is a fine-dining restaurant and lounge. Smartly decorated rooms overlooking the atrium are $235 s or d, outward-facing rooms with big balconies are $260, or pay $310 for an extra-spacious room with a king bed. Rates are reduced up to 60 percent outside of the busiest mid-June to September period.

$250-350

Chateau Jasper (96 Geikie St., 780/852-5644 or 800/661-1315, www.chateaujasper.com) is one of Jasper's nicest lodgings. Guest rooms are spacious and elegantly finished with maple furnishings and low ceilings that give them a cozy feel. Bathrooms are particularly well equipped, with guests also enjoying the use of plush bathrobes. Summer rates start at $296 s or d, but as you move into these higher priced places, off-season discounts become steeper—in this case, rooms throughout the winter season are just $135 s or d. The in-house dining room, Le Petit Marché, combines a café that pours some of Jasper's finest coffee with a bistro-style restaurant.

Over $350

C Jasper Park Lodge (780/852-3301 or 800/257-7544, www.fairmont.com) lies along the shore of Lac Beauvert (meaning "beautiful green lake" in French) across the Athabasca River from downtown. This is the park's original resort and its most famous. It's a sprawling resort, with plenty of activities. The best-known of these is the golf course, but guests also enjoy walking trails, horseback riding, canoeing, tennis, and swimming in an outdoor heated pool that remains open year-round. The main lodge features stone floors, carved wooden pillars, and a high ceiling. This building contains multiple restaurants and lounges, an activity booking desk, a fitness room, a games room, and Jasper's only covered shopping arcade. The 446 rooms vary in configuration and are spread out over the expansive property. All have coffee-makers, TVs, telephones, and Internet access. The least expensive Fairmont Rooms ($489 s

or d) are smallish, hold two twin beds, and offer limited views. Also away from the lake are larger Deluxe Rooms ($549 s or d); each has a patio or balcony. Junior Suites ($629 s or d) have a distinct country charm, and each has either a sitting room and balcony or patio with lake views. Moving up to the more expensive options, Lakeview Suites ($759 s or d) overlook Lac Beauvert and are backed by the 18th fairway of the golf course. Each features a patio or balcony, fireplace, and two TVs. For a super-splurge, consider the cabins starting from $800. Most guests don't pay the summer rack rates quoted here. The cost of lodging is usually included in one of the plethora of packages offered (click on the "Package Finder" link on the Fairmont website for all the options). Outside of summer, Jasper Park Lodge becomes a real bargain, with rooms with lake views (remember it'll be frozen in winter) for less than $200.

Backcountry Accommodations

Jasper's two backcountry lodges are southwest of Jasper in the spectacular Tonquin Valley. Accessible only on foot or horseback or, in winter, by skiing, both lodges are open to hikers (with advance reservations); most guests stay as part of a package that includes horseback riding.

Dating to 1939, **Tonquin Amethyst Lake Lodge** (780/852-1188, www.tonquinadventures.com) was extensively upgraded in the early 1990s. Private cabins have wood-burning heaters, twin log beds with thick blankets, oil lanterns, and a spectacular view. Tonquin Adventures offers a number of well-priced packages, including riding into the lodge on horses, accommodations, three hearty ranch-style meals, and use of small boats and fishing gear (three days, $480; four days, $750; five days, $925). Rates are reduced in winter, when guests ski in under their own power. Regardless of the season, getting there involves a 19-kilometer (11.8-mile) journey from a trailhead opposite HI–Mount Edith Cavell.

Nearby **Tonquin Valley Backcountry Lodge** (780/852-3909, www.tonquinvalley.com) offers a similar setup, with most guests arriving

by horseback on a pre-arranged ride from the nearest road. In this case, the departure point is along Marmot Basin Road, from a parking lot at Portal Creek. Rates are $150 per person per night, with a five-night package—inclusive of horse rental—costing $900 per person.

CAMPING

Campgrounds in Jasper begin opening in mid-June, and all but Wapiti are closed by mid-October. All campsites have a picnic table and fire ring, with a fire permit costing $8 (includes firewood). A percentage of sites in the most popular campgrounds can be reserved through the Parks Canada Campground Reservation Service (877/737-3783, www.pccamping.ca) for a nominal fee. If you're traveling in July or August, know which dates you'll be in Jasper, and require electrical hookups, it is strongly advised to take advantage of this service.

© ANDREW HEMPSTEAD

Golden-mantled ground squirrels are common campground visitors. Resist the urge to feed them.

Near the Town of Jasper

Whistlers Campground, at the base of Whistlers Road, three kilometers (1.9 mi) south of town, has 781 sites, making it the largest campground in the Canadian Rockies. It is divided into four sections; prices vary with the services available—walk-in sites $22, unserviced sites $26, powered sites $30, full hookups $36. Each section has showers. Whistlers is open May to mid-October.

Two kilometers (1.2 mi) farther south along the Icefields Parkway is **Wapiti Campground,** which offers 366 sites and has showers; unserviced sites $26, powered sites $30. This is the park's only campground open year-round, with serviced winter camping $20 per night.

Sites at **Wabasso Campground,** along Highway 93A approximately 16 kilometers (10 mi) south of town, are set among stands of spruce and aspen; $21 per night.

East Along Highway 16

East of town, off Highway 16, are two smaller, more primitive campgrounds. **Snaring River Campground,** 17 kilometers (11 mi) from Jasper on Celestine Lake Road, is $15 (overflow camping is $10); **Pocahontas Campground,** 45 kilometers (28 mi) northeast, is $21. Both are open mid-May to early September.

FOOD

It's easy to get a good, or even great, meal in Jasper. Connaught Drive and Patricia Street are lined with cafés and restaurants. Considering this a national park, menus are reasonably well priced. You should expect hearty fare, with lots of beef, game, and a surprising selection of seafood.

Coffeehouses and Cafés

You'll smell the wonderful aroma of freshly baked bread even before entering **◖ Bear's Paw Bakery** (4 Cedar Ave., 780/852-3233, daily from 7 A.M.). The European-style breads are perfect for a picnic lunch, but not as tempting as the cakes and pastries. You can also order soup and sandwiches.

The **Soft Rock Cafe** (632 Connaught Dr.,

780/852-5850, daily 7:30 A.M.–6:30 P.M.) occupies a sunny spot along Jasper's main thoroughfare. It is one of the most popular places in town to start the day. Seating is inside or out, and you order at the counter. Breakfast options include omelets and skillet dishes (all around $10). If the cinnamon buns are still in the oven, you'll have to come back later in the day—they're gigantic! The variety of coffee concoctions here is mind-boggling, and all prices are reasonable.

Back toward the heart of downtown, **Mountain Foods & Café** (606 Connaught Dr., 780/852-4050, daily for breakfast and lunch) offers a full cooked breakfast for $6 and healthy wraps, rolls, and sandwiches the rest of the day. In the railway station is **Trains & Lattes** (607 Connaught Dr., 780/852-7444, daily 6 A.M.–7 P.M.), a small espresso bar.

Casual

Pizza lovers congregate at **Jasper Pizza Place** (402 Connaught Dr., 780/852-3225, daily for lunch and dinner). It's a large and noisy restaurant with bright furnishings, a concrete floor, exposed heating ducts, and walls lined with photos from Jasper's earliest days. Regular thick-crust pizzas are available from 11 A.M., but it's not until 5 P.M., when the wood-fired oven begins producing thin-crust pizzas with adventurous toppings, that this place really shines. One side is order-at-the-counter style, the other has waitperson service, as does the rooftop patio.

On the same side of town as Jasper Pizza Place is one of Jasper's oldest restaurants, **Papa George's** (Astoria Hotel, 406 Connaught Dr., 780/852-3351, daily 7 A.M.–10 P.M.), which has been dishing up hearty fare to park visitors since 1925. The setting is old-fashioned, with east-facing windows taking in the panorama of distant mountain peaks. Breakfast is $4–8, while lunch and dinner feature burgers, pasta, and steaks; daily specials are $12–19 and include soup and salad. The small dessert bar is a few dollars extra.

Canadian

One of Jasper's best restaurants, **⟨ Becker's**

Gourmet Restaurant (780/852-3535, May–mid-Oct. daily 8–11 A.M. and 5:30–10 P.M.) is six kilometers (3.7 mi) out of town to the south along the Icefields Parkway, but well worth the short drive. From this cozy dining room where the atmosphere is intimate or the adjacent enclosed conservatory, the views of Mount Kerkeslin and the Athabasca River are inspiring. This restaurant is a throwback to days gone by, with an ever-changing menu of seasonal game and produce that includes a daily wild-game special. A menu staple is the baked rack of lamb smothered with apricot glaze. Hot and cold starters range $9–13, while no main is more than $30. For dessert, the raspberry crisp is a delight. The breakfast buffet costs $15.

Back toward town from Becker's, on Highway 93A, is the dining room of historic **Tekarra Lodge** (780/852-4624, May–Sept. daily 8–11 A.M. and 5:30–10 P.M.). The setting may be mountain-style rustic, but the cooking appeals to modern preferences with combinations like banana-crusted chicken breast with sweet mango curry sauce ($22); most mains are less than $30.

Steak

⟨ Villa Caruso (640 Connaught Dr., 780/852-3920, daily 11 A.M.–midnight) is a steakhouse with a modern mountain vibe. The upstairs location—request a balcony table if the weather's warm—allows great views across the valley. The menu features a wide variety of Alberta beef dishes, including a massive 16-ounce T-bone for $35. But there's a lot more than steak on offer, including chicken, seafood, and pasta dishes from $16.50.

Prime Rib Village (Tonquin Inn, 100 Juniper St., 780/852-4966, daily from 5 P.M.) has been a longtime Jasper favorite. Charbroiled steaks and hearty servings of prime rib cost $27–34, but the prime rib sandwich ($21), with a plate-load of extras, will fill any carnivorous cravings for a few dollars less. This restaurant also offers a surprisingly good selection of seafood.

Seafood

Fiddle River Seafood Restaurant (upstairs

JASPER NATIONAL PARK

at 620 Connaught Dr., 780/852-3032, daily 5–10 P.M.) is a long way from the ocean and not particularly coastal in feel, but it offers a wide variety of seafood. The striking decor matches dark polished wood with forest-green furnishings, and large windows provide mountain views (reservations are needed for windowside tables). Trout, arctic char, red snapper, ahi tuna, and halibut all make regular appearances on the blackboard menu. Expect to pay about $50 per person for a three-course meal.

European

C Andy's Bistro (606 Patricia St., 780/852-4559, daily 5–9:30 P.M.) is an elegantly casual eatery offering a wide range of uncomplicated dishes using Canadian game and produce prepared with Swiss-influenced cooking styles. Start with a plate piled high with Prince Edward Island steamed mussels ($12, but enough for two people), then choose between dishes such as pan-seared ostrich medallions ($24) or halibut cheeks with crystallized ginger sauce ($22). Andy's has an extensive cellar of wines but no official wine list. Instead, diners are encouraged to choose from red wines set along the bar and white wines from the fridge. At the unique *stammtisch,* a large table, up to 10 diners can be seated at once, free to come and go as they please. It's the perfect place to mingle with fellow travelers. Also notable at Andy's is the staff, who seem experienced and knowledgeable.

Miss Italia Ristorante (610 Patricia St., 780/852-4002), upstairs in the Patricia Centre Mall, features bright and breezy interior decor with tables also set on a narrow terrace bedecked in pots of colorful flowers. Cooked breakfasts (from 8 A.M.) are $6–9. The rest of the day, pastas made fresh daily average $15, a baked filet of Atlantic salmon is $17, and souvlaki with a side of salad and pita bread is just $16. Check out the daily specials before ordering—they are taken from the regular menu but discounted a couple of bucks and come with soup or salad.

Directly behind the park information center, **La Fiesta** (504 Patricia St., 780/852-0404,

Mon.–Sat. 11:30 A.M.–9 P.M.) is a small eatery where the Mediterranean meets Mexico. It offers a tapas-style menu of Mexican dishes ranging $6.50–13, as well as adventurous delights such as pork kebabs served with a fig-and-pine-nut relish and mussels steamed in a tequila broth. This is also the best place in town for a martini.

Asian

The **Cantonese Restaurant** (608 Connaught Dr., 780/852-3559, daily noon–10 P.M.) is the place to go for Chinese; combo specials are $9–13, and set five-course menus for two start at $28.

Denjiro (410 Connaught Dr., 780/852-3780, daily 5–11:30 P.M.) features a traditional sushi bar and eight tatami booths for eating the Japanese cuisine; combination dinners average $19 per person.

Jasper Park Lodge

Jasper's premier accommodation, across the river from downtown, offers a choice of casual or elegant dining in a variety of restaurants and lounges. Across from the reception area is a dedicated dining reservation desk, staffed in summer daily 11 A.M.–8 P.M., or call 780/852-6052. Reservations are required for the Edith Cavell and Moose's Nook dining rooms.

Downstairs in the shopping arcade, **Meadows Restaurant** is a casual room open for a breakfast buffet daily 6–11:30 A.M. and then in the evening for a dinner buffet 6–9 P.M. The turnover of food is quick, meaning everything remains fresh. Request a table away from the buffet for a quieter dining experience.

The **Emerald Lounge** (daily 11:30 A.M.–10 P.M.) takes pride of place in the expansive lobby of the main building. Table settings of various configurations are spread throughout the room while also sprawling out and along the **Emerald Outdoor Patio,** from where views over picturesque Lac Beauvert to distant mountains are uninterrupted. Both lunch and dinner menus feature imaginative modern Canadian cuisine, but with dinner (from 5:30 P.M.) being decidedly more expensive. At

© ANDREW HEMPSTEAD

terrace dining, Jasper Park Lodge

Canadian game and seafood, the classic cuisine is served with a French flair. Prices for two-, three-, and four-course table d'hôte combos are a relatively reasonable $55, $70, and $80, respectively. Dress code is "business casual": no t-shirts or jeans; a jacket and tie are "recommended but not required." The Sunday brunch, served between 10 A.M. and 12:30 P.M., costs $30 and is especially popular.

INFORMATION AND SERVICES
Information
The residence of Jasper's first superintendent, a beautiful old stone building dating to 1913 located right downtown, is now used by Parks Canada as the **Park Information Centre** (Connaught Dr., 780/852-6176, www.pc.gc.ca, summer daily 8 A.M.–7 P.M., the rest of the year daily 9 A.M.–5 P.M.). The staff provides general information on the park and can direct you to hikes in the immediate vicinity. Also within the building is the **Parks Canada Trail Office** (780/852-6177), which handles questions for those going into the backcountry and issues the relevant passes. **Jasper Tourism and Commerce** (780/852-3858, www.jaspercanadianrockies.com) also has a desk in the building, and the friendly staff never seem to tire of explaining that all the rooms in town are full. As well as providing general information on the town, they have a large collection of brochures on activities, shopping, and restaurants. Beside the main Parks Canada desk is the **Friends of Jasper National Park** outlet selling topographic maps, books, and local publications. Look for notices posted out front with the day's interpretive programs.

Housed in Jasper's original Royal Canadian Mounted Police detachment building, small **Jasper Municipal Library** (500 Robson St., 780/852-3652, Mon.–Thurs. 11 A.M.–8 P.M., Fri.–Sat. 10 A.M.–5 P.M.) holds just about everything ever written about the park.

Jasper's weekly newspaper, *The Booster,* is available throughout town on Wednesday. As well as newsworthy stories, it includes a list of upcoming events, trail reports, and a town map

lunch, salads ranging $8–13 can be made into a full meal by adding extras such as smoked salmon and slices of chicken breast, or stick to mains such as the bison burger ($15). Generous dinner mains range $18–34—the Alberta rib eye roasted in red-pepper butter is typical.

The elegantly rustic **Moose's Nook Northern Grill** (daily 6–9 P.M.) is a good place to enjoy traditional Canadian fare, such as grilled wild boar chops, whiskey-flamed arctic char, or a chargrilled Albertan rib eye steak. Mains range $25–34. Be sure to leave room for dessert—the chestnut-crusted cheesecake smothered in maple syrup is incredible.

The **Edith Cavell** (daily 6–9 P.M.) is the finest fine-dining restaurant in Jasper. Its dark oak walls contrast with the white linens and large, bright windows overlooking Lac Beauvert and the mountains beyond. Even though the restaurant has changed little over time, its overly pretentious atmosphere has softened and service has become more comfortable. Still, this is seriously cultured dining, unequaled in Jasper. With an emphasis on local produce and

JASPER NATIONAL PARK

JASPER NATIONAL PARK

© ANDREW HEMPSTEAD

Park Information Centre

with funky little symbols highlighting the locations of various "crimes."

The official Town of Jasper website (www
.jasper-alberta.com), with lists of current
events, weather conditions, and loads of helpful links, is also worth checking out.
Jasper National Park Radio is on the AM
band at 1490. For weather conditions in the
park, call 780/852-6176.

Services

The post office (502 Patricia St.) is behind the
park information center. Mail to be picked up
here should be addressed General Delivery,
Jasper, AB T0E 1E0. **More Than Mail** (620
Connaught Dr., 780/852-3151, daily 9 A.M.–
10 P.M.) offers a wide range of communication services, including regular post, public
Internet access, fax and copying facilities, a
work area for laptops, international calling,
and currency exchange.

Send and receive email and surf the Internet at the following Jasper locations: **Digital
Den** (upstairs at 610 Patricia St., 780/852-
9765, daily 9 A.M.–10 P.M.); **Jasper Municipal
Library** (Elm Ave., 780/852-3652, Mon.–
Thurs. 11 A.M.–8 P.M., Fri.–Sat. 10 A.M.–
5 P.M.); **More Than Mail** (620 Connaught Dr.,
780/852-3151, daily 9 A.M.–10 P.M.); and **Soft
Rock Café** (632 Connaught Dr., 780/852-
5850, daily 8 A.M.–10 P.M.).

The two laundries on Patricia Street are
open 6 A.M.–11 P.M. and offer showers that
cost $2 for 10 minutes (quarters).

The hospital is at 518 Robson Street (780/852-
3344). For the **RCMP,** call 780/852-4848.

GETTING THERE

Getting to Jasper by public transportation is easy,
although the closest airport handling domestic
and international flights is at Edmonton, 360
kilometers (224 mi) to the east. The **VIA Rail
station** and the **bus depot** (used by both Greyhound and Brewster) are in the same building,
central to town at 607 Connaught Drive. The
building is open 24 hours daily in summer (the
rest of the year Mon.–Sat. 7:30 A.M.–10:30 P.M.,
Sun. 7:30–11 A.M. and 6:30–10:30 P.M.). Lock-

ers are available for $1 per day. Car-rental agencies and a café are here, too.

Rail

Jasper is on the Canadian route, the only remaining transcontinental passenger rail service in the country. Trains run either way three times weekly. To the west the line divides, going to both Prince Rupert and Vancouver; to the east it passes through Edmonton and all points beyond. For all rail information, contact **VIA Rail** (800/561-8630, www.viarail.ca). Another rail option is offered by **Rocky Mountaineer Vacations** (604/606-7245 or 877/460-7245, www.rockymountaineer.com). This company operates a luxurious summer-only rail service between Vancouver and Jasper with an overnight in Kamloops (British Columbia).

Bus

Greyhound buses (780/852-3926 or 800/661-8747, www.greyhound.ca) depart Jasper for all points in Canada (except Banff), including Vancouver (three times daily, 12–13 hours, $126 one-way), Edmonton (five times daily, 4.5 hours, $59 one-way) with connections to Calgary, and Prince Rupert (once daily, 18 hours, $171 one-way).

The main carrier up the Icefields Parkway from Calgary and Banff is Banff-based **Brewster** (780/852-3332 or 800/661-1152, www.brewster.ca). This company operates a shuttle to and from Calgary International Airport daily May through mid-October ($100 each way). It also offers a year-round tour (May–Oct. daily, Nov.–Apr. Sat. only) between Banff and Jasper. The trip takes nine hours and costs $114 one-way. The round-trip requires an overnight in Jasper. In winter, **Sun Dog Tours** (780/852-4056 or 888/786-3641, www.sundogtours.com) operates a skier shuttle between Calgary and Jasper once daily in each direction. Sample fares to Jasper are: from Calgary, $105; from Banff, $59; and from Lake Louise, $53.

GETTING AROUND

The **Maligne Lake Shuttle** (780/852-3370) runs out to Maligne Lake mid-May–September, three to four times daily ($32.10 round-trip) from its depot (616 Patricia St.). Stops are made at Maligne Canyon and HI–Maligne Canyon. Other pickup points include the Jasper Inn and Jasper Park Lodge.

Rental cars start at $60 per day with 150 free kilometers. The following companies have agencies and their local numbers are: **Avis** (780/852-3970), **Budget** (780/852-3222), **Hertz** (780/852-3888), and **National** (780/852-1117).

Cabs in town are not cheap. Most drivers will take you on a private sightseeing tour or to trailheads if requested; try **Jasper Taxi** (780/852-3600 or 780/852-3146).

JASPER NATIONAL PARK

CENTRAL ALBERTA

The central sector of the province is a diverse region extending from the peaks of the Canadian Rockies in the west through the foothills and aspen parkland to the prairies in the east. **Rocky Mountain Forest Reserve** occupies much of the heavily forested western foothills, nestled against the folded and faulted front ranges of the Canadian Rockies. Most of this large coniferous forest is committed for nonrenewable resource development, although two designated wilderness areas in the reserve are totally protected from development. The entire reserve is a recreation playground: perfect for camping, fishing, hiking, and other outdoor activities. Rocky Mountain House, a medium-size town on Highway 11, is the gateway to the foothills. The North West and Hudson's Bay Companies once used trading posts here as a

jumping-off point into the mountain wilderness to the west.

The 290-kilometer (180-mi) route between Calgary and Edmonton through central Alberta on Highway 2 takes about three hours to drive straight through. Those with a little more time can explore the many historic towns along the way or visit a buffalo jump used by natives to stampede herds of bison to their deaths. Halfway between Calgary and Edmonton is Red Deer, a city of 80,000 that was once an important way station for travelers on the Calgary Trail (or Edmonton Trail, depending on which direction they were going).

North and east of Red Deer is the aspen parkland, a biome with characteristics unique to Canada's prairie provinces. Long, straight country roads link primarily agricultural towns

© ANDREW HEMPSTEAD

HIGHLIGHTS

◖ Rocky Mountain House National Historic Site: Not much remains of the original trading posts, but as an important part of Canada's fur-trading history this site is well worth a visit (page 312).

◖ Nordegg: This town was abandoned in the 1950s; there are now tours of the "ghost town" and coal-mining infrastructure. Even if history isn't your thing, there's enough surrounding wilderness to fill an entire vacation (page 314).

◖ Markerville: This tiny village, which gets my vote for "Alberta's prettiest town," is home to a restored creamery serving up traditional Icelandic fare (page 322).

◖ Lacombe Corn Maze: Get lost in this unique family-operated attraction (page 330).

◖ Alberta Prairie Railway Excursions: It's all aboard for this steam-train ride back in time (page 332).

◖ Reynolds-Alberta Museum: Filled to overflowing with an amazing collection of machinery, this museum stands tall as one of the province's finest (page 333).

◖ Miquelon Lake Provincial Park: An unexpected surprise, this park has an interesting natural history, lots of wildlife, one of Alberta's better beaches, and excellent camping facilities (page 337).

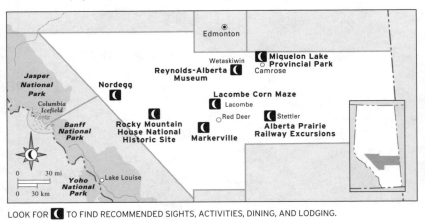

LOOK FOR ◖ TO FIND RECOMMENDED SIGHTS, ACTIVITIES, DINING, AND LODGING.

along three main highways that extend east into the neighboring province of Saskatchewan. Highlights of this section of parkland include five provincial parks, one of Canada's last remaining passenger steam trains at Stettler, and a fantastic museum dedicated to machinery at Wetaskiwin.

PLANNING YOUR TIME

The region covered by this chapter encompasses a wide swathe of the province, so rather than planning a visit to central Alberta, the ideal scenario would be to include as many highlights as possible as you make your way between Calgary or Edmonton, or as a detour from the Icefields Parkway between Banff and Jasper. If it's the latter and you have a spare day, a side trip along the David Thompson Highway is highly recommended. This route heads east out of the mountains, but doesn't leave the stunning scenery behind. There's also lots of history to soak up at places like the coal-mining ghost town of

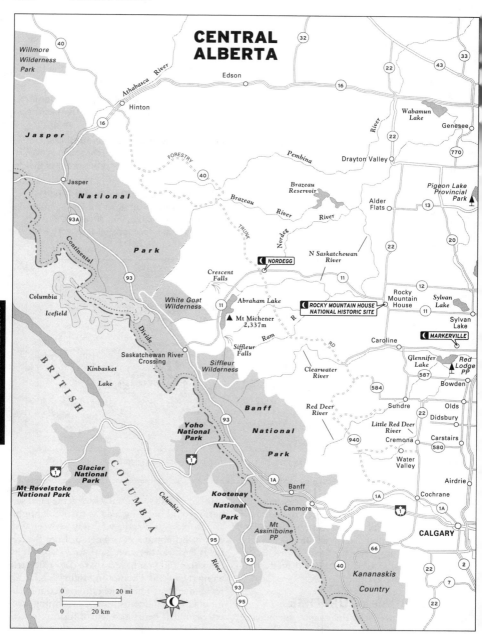

CENTRAL ALBERTA

Willmore
Wilderness
Park

Edson

Hinton

Jasper

Athabasca River

FORESTRY

Jasper

National

93A

Park

Continental

93

Columbia

Icefield

Divide

White Goat
Wilderness

Crescent
Falls

◖ NORDEGG

Abraham Lake

▲ Mt Michener
2,337m

◖ ROCKY MOUNTAIN HOUSE
NATIONAL HISTORIC SITE

Siffleur
Falls

Saskatchewan River
Crossing

Kinbasket

Lake

Siffleur
Wilderness

B R I T I S H

Pembina

Brazeau

Brazeau
Reservoir

River

Brazeau
River

River

Nordegg

TRUNK

N Saskatchewan
River

Drayton Valley

Alder
Flats

Wabamun
Lake

Genesee

Pigeon Lake
Provincial
Park

13

20

22

Rocky
Mountain
House

12

11

Sylvan
Lake

Sylvan
Lake

◖ MARKERVILLE

Caroline

Ram R

RD

Clearwater
River

Glennifer
Lake

587

Red
Lodge
PP

Bowden

Banff

Red Deer
River

National

Park

Yoho
National
Park

93

C O L U M B I A

Glacier
National
Park

Mt Revelstoke
National Park

Columbia

Kootenay
National
Park

Canmore

1A

Banff

Mt
Assiniboine
PP

95

93

River

93

95

Little Red Deer
River

940

Cremona

Sundre

584

Olds

Didsbury

Carstairs

580

Water
Valley

Airdrie

Cochrane

1A

1A

1A

CALGARY

66

40

*Kananaskis
Country*

22

7

22

2

40

16

22

32

33

43

16

22

770

Edson

Hinton

0   20 mi

0   20 km

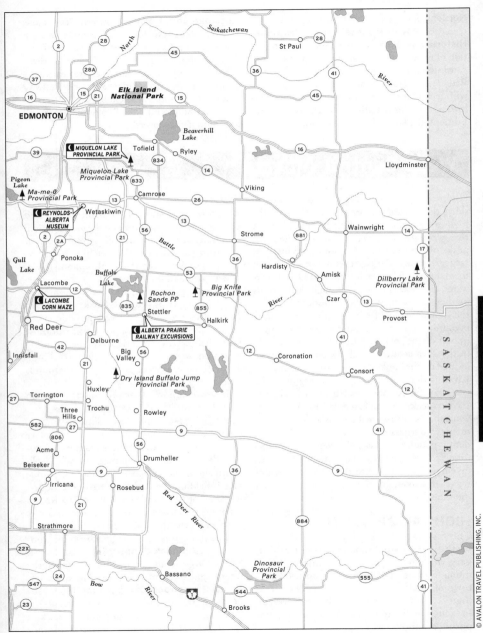

Nordegg and the former fur-trading posts protected by **Rocky Mountain House National Historic Site.** If you're leaving the northern portion of the province for another trip, you could continue east from Rocky Mountain House to Red Deer via **Markerville,** an enchanting village with Icelandic origins. If your itinerary only allows one day for the drive between Calgary and Edmonton, plan on finding your way out of the **Lacombe Corn Maze** and into the **Reynolds-Alberta Museum** for its celebration of man and machine. Central Alberta east of Highway 2 is the domain of those with plenty of time. With two weeks to explore the entire province, a steam-train ride with **Alberta Prairie Railway Excursions** should be included on your itinerary, while **Miquelon Lake Provincial Park** will appeal to nature lovers.

West-Central Alberta

Highway 2 between Calgary and Edmonton skirts the edge of the prairie—just west of the highway, a region of foothills begins. The hills rise gradually, eventually reaching the lofty peaks of the front ranges adjoining Banff and Jasper National Parks. Several rivers—among them the North Saskatchewan, Red Deer, Clearwater, and Brazeau—slice through the foothills on their cascading descent from sources high in the Canadian Rockies. Fur trading was once a booming industry here, but the greatest human impact on the area came from coal mining early in the 20th century. Rocky Mountain House, located on the bank of the North Saskatchewan River, is the largest town in the region and a good base for exploring. Further west is a lightly traveled region of the Canadian Rockies. Here you can hike in two wilderness areas, camp in many wilderness campgrounds, fish in abundantly populated lakes and rivers, explore historic sites, raft the North Saskatchewan River, take horseback trips into the hills, cross-country ski in winter, or just admire the spectacular mountain scenery.

HIGHWAY 22 NORTH

This highway follows the eastern flanks of the foothills from Cochrane, northwest of Calgary, through the small communities of Cremona, Sundre, and Caroline, and the larger town of Rocky Mountain House. The Canadian Rockies dominate the western horizon for much of the route and are especially imposing around Sundre.

Sundre

This town of 2,300, on the banks of the Red Deer River, is the quintessential Albertan town. Sundre is surrounded by rolling foothills that are historically tied to the ranching industry; oil and gas now keep the local economy alive. The town has a popular Sunday farmers market, a good golf course, and is also a jumping-off point for trips into the Rocky Mountain Forest Reserve. Nearby rivers provide excellent white-water rafting opportunities for those with their own craft. Highway 584, heading west from town, links up with Forestry Trunk Road, providing access to many campgrounds and fishing spots.

In town, Sundre's **Pioneer Village Museum** (130 Centre St., 403/638-3233, June–Aug. daily 1–5 P.M., Sept.–May Thurs.–Sat. 1–4 P.M., adult $5, senior and child $3) displays a large collection of artifacts from early pioneer days, including farm machinery, a blacksmith shop, and an old schoolhouse. A canoe race is held on the Red Deer River on the last weekend of May, and the **Sundre Pro Rodeo** (403/638-3055, www.sundrerodeo.com) comes to town on the third weekend of June.

The most appealing of Sundre's four motels is the **Chinook Country Inn** (120 2nd St. SW, 403/638-3300, $64 s, $68 d), where the rates include a light breakfast. The town-operated **Greenwood Campground** (403/638-2680, mid-May–mid-Sept., unserviced sites $20, hookups $25–30), on the west bank of the Red Deer River within walking distance

© ANDREW HEMPSTEAD

The First Nations people built dome-shaped sweat lodges out of brush and covered them in buffalo robes. This example can be seen at Rocky Mountain House National Historic Site.

of downtown, has clean facilities that include showers and a covered cooking shelter complete with a woodstove. East of town is **Tall Timber Leisure Park** (403/638-3555, www.talltimber .net, May–mid-Oct., $25–30), a full-service RV park with an indoor pool, but tenters aren't welcome. **Outlaw's** (250 Main Ave., 403/638-2882, daily for lunch and dinner) is the only place in town to get a decent meal. Lunch specials are $5–7, including a salad bar, and the weekend hot breakfast buffet, served until noon, is $10.95.

Sundre Visitor Information Centre (403/638-3245, summer daily 10 A.M.–6 P.M., the rest of the year Mon.–Fri. 10 A.M.–4 P.M.) is on the east bank of the Red Deer River.

Caroline

Named after the daughter of one of the town's earliest settlers, Caroline depended on agriculture and forestry to support its economy until the mid-1990s, when Alberta's largest sour gas discovery was made south of town. Now Shell Canada's processing plant at the site also contributes to the area's livelihood.

Four-time World Men's Figure Skating champion (and four-time professional champion) Kurt Browning was born and raised on a ranch just west of town. His portrait adorns local tourist literature, and the town's **Kurt Browning Arena** (48th Ave., Mon.–Fri. 8 A.M.–4 P.M.) houses Kurt's Korner, a display of personal memorabilia.

Caroline Municipal RV Park (east end of town, 403/722-2210, mid-May–mid-Sept., $14–16) has showers and powered sites.

Forestry Trunk Road

At regular intervals along Highway 22, gravel roads lead west to the Forestry Trunk Road—a well-graded gravel road that parallels the Rockies for more than 1,000 kilometers (620 mi). Along the route are plenty of campgrounds, beautiful scenery, and a degree of solitude not found along roads through the national parks farther west. The middle section of the trunk road begins at

its intersection with Highway 1A, 13 kilometers (eight mi) west of Cochrane. Heading north from there, the first services available are 265 kilometers (165 mi) away at Nordegg, on Highway 11. Opportunities to exit and enter the road are found west of Cremona, Sundre, Caroline, and Rocky Mountain House.

ROCKY MOUNTAIN HOUSE AND VICINITY

This town of 6,600, best known simply as Rocky, straddles the North Saskatchewan River and is surrounded by gently rolling hills in a transition zone between aspen parkland and mountains. Highway 11 (also known as David Thompson Highway) passes through town on its way east to Red Deer (82 km/51 mi) and west to the northern end of Banff National Park (170 km/106 mi).

History

Between 1799 and 1875, four fur-trading posts were built at the confluence of the Clearwater and North Saskatchewan Rivers, west of the present townsite. The forts were used not only for trading but also as bases for exploring the nearby mountains. David Thompson, one of western Canada's greatest explorers, was a regular visitor. In 1821, after the two major fur-trading companies merged, the community that had grown around the forts was christened Rocky Mountain House. In the early 1900s, settlers began arriving. Today, the town's economy relies on forestry, natural-gas processing, agriculture, and tourism.

◀ Rocky Mountain House National Historic Site

This National Historic Site commemorates the important role fur trading played in Canada's history. The first trading post, or fort, was built on the site in 1799. By the 1830s, beaver felt was out of fashion in Europe, and traders turned to buffalo robes. By the 1870s, the

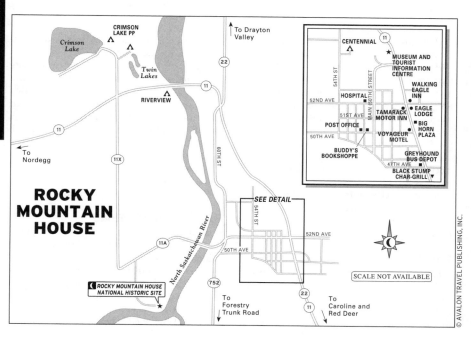

massive herds of buffalo that had roamed the plains for thousands of years were gone. This signaled an end to the fur trade, an industry that had opened up the West and had been the natives' main source of European goods, such as clothing, horses, and guns. The last post at Rocky Mountain House closed soon after and, by the early 1900s, was reduced to two brick chimneys. In 1926, the forts were declared National Historic Sites. Today, the protected areas include the sites of five forts, a buffalo paddock, and a stretch of riverbank where the large voyageur canoes would have come ashore to be loaded with furs bound for Europe.

The **visitors center** is the best place to begin a visit to the site; its interpretive displays detail the history of the forts, the fur trade, and exploration of the West. Two trails lead along the north bank of the river. The longer of the two, a 3.2-kilometer (two-mi) loop, passes the site of the two original forts. Frequent "listening posts" along the trail play a lively recorded commentary on life in the early 1800s. All that remains of the forts are depressions in the ground, but through the commentary and interpretive displays, it is easy to get a good idea of what the forts looked like. To the north of the fort site is an observation deck for viewing a small herd of buffalo that may or may not be visible. The other trail leads one kilometer (0.6 mi) to two chimneys, remnants of the later forts.

The park is open year-round on weekdays 10 A.M.–6 P.M., although the visitors center is open only late May to August, daily 10 A.M.–5 P.M. It's seven kilometers (4.3 mi) west of Rocky Mountain House on Highway 11A, 403/845-2412. Admission is adults $2.50, seniors $2, children $1.50.

Rocky Mountain House Museum

This museum (5406 48th St., 403/845-2332, July–Aug. daily 9 A.M.–8 P.M., June and Sept. daily 9 A.M.–5 P.M., the rest of the year weekdays only, adult $3, child $1) is in the same complex as the information center. Exhibits include an array of pioneer artifacts, including an early Forest Service cabin, a one-room schoolhouse, and an interesting rope-making machine.

Recreation

The best way to appreciate the history of the area, see some great river scenery, and generally have a good time is to take a float trip with **Voyageur Ventures** (403/845-7878) down the North Saskatchewan River. The voyageur canoes used are replicas of those used by early explorers; they are large and stable, requiring little paddling skill. Half-day trips, which include a stop at the National Historic Site and lunch, are $76; a full day with cooked lunch—prepared along the riverbank while you take a short hike or rest in the sun—is $126. Overnight river trips start at $280.

Another center of water-based activities is **Crimson Lake Provincial Park,** northwest of town. Crimson Lake is great for boating and canoeing (rentals available), whereas nearby Twin Lakes, also in the park, is stocked with rainbow trout. The undeveloped northwest side attracts many species of waterfowl, including loons, herons, grebes, sandhill cranes, and a variety of ducks.

Accommodations and Camping

Many motels are spread out along Highway 11 east of town. The least expensive is the **Voyageur Motel** (403/845-3381 or 888/845-5569), which has large clean rooms with fridge and microwave from $50 s, $65 d, or pay an extra $10 for a kitchenette. **Walking Eagle Inn** (4819 45th St., 403/845-2804 or 866/845-2131, www.walkingeagle.net), easily recognized by its striking log exterior, has comfortable rooms, a steakhouse restaurant, and a steam room. Rates start at $99 s or d and rise to $159 for a suite with full kitchen. Under the same management is the adjacent, and similarly priced, **Eagle Lodge** (4915 45th St., 403/844-4412 or 866/845-2131, www.walkingeagle.net).

Riverview Campground (Hwy. 11, 403/845-4422, unserviced sites $15, hookups $22–25), on the North Saskatchewan River, is the only commercial facility in town. The unserviced sites are tucked in among a grove of trees on the riverbank, and above them are serviced sites, with spectacular views along the valley. The campground has a small grocery store, a

launderette, showers, and free firewood. Another recommended spot is **(Crimson Lake Provincial Park** (403/845-2330), northwest of town along an access road off Highway 11, where you'll find two campgrounds; sites along the bank of Crimson Lake are $20–23, whereas those beside Twin Lakes are $17. Finally, **Centennial Park Campground** (off 54th St., 403/845-3720, mid-May–Sept., $13) has a central location within walking distance of the information center. Showers and firewood are supplied.

Food

The only restaurants in town are those in the strip of family-style and fast-food places along Highway 11 and 52nd Avenue. The restaurant in the **Tamarack Motor Inn** (4904 45th St., 403/845-5252, daily 6 A.M.–11 P.M.) offers a large range of choices, including hearty cooked breakfasts for $6–9, a Friday-night buffet, and Sunday brunch. Also in the hotel is Duffers Pub, with nightly food specials. **Walking Motor Inn** (4819 45th St., 403/845-2804), on the other side of the highway, also has a restaurant, **Grillers Steakhouse,** open daily for lunch and dinner. Finally, there's the **Black Stump Char-Grill** (4504 48th Ave., 403/844-8432, daily 11 A.M.–10 P.M.), with the same name (and identical logo) to a chain of steakhouse restaurants in Australia. But the similarities end there—it's a mix of Canadian and Greek dishes here in Rocky, with dinner mains in the $14–24 range.

Information and Services

Make your first stop in town the tourist information center (54th Ave., 403/845-5450 or 800/565-3793, www.rockychamber.org/vic), beside Highway 11 north of downtown. The center is open late May–August Monday–Saturday 9 A.M.–8 P.M., Sunday 10 A.M.–6 P.M.; the rest of the year Monday–Friday 9 A.M.–5 P.M.

The post office is downtown at 4912 47th Avenue. **Buddy's Bookshoppe** (4928 50th St., 403/845-3168, Mon.–Fri. 9:30 A.M.–5:30 P.M., Sat. 10 A.M.–5 P.M.) has a great selection of new local literature, as well as many used books.

Rocky Mountain House General Hospital (403/845-3347) is at 5016 52nd Avenue.

Getting There and Around

The **Greyhound** bus depot is in the Shell gas station (4504 47th Ave., 403/845-2650, www.greyhound.ca). Greyhound operates a daily service between Calgary and Rocky, but you must change buses in Red Deer. For a taxi, call **Rocky Cabs** (403/845-4000).

(NORDEGG

Westbound Highway 11 climbs slowly from the aspen parkland around Rocky Mountain House into the dense forests on the eastern slopes of the Canadian Rockies. The only community between Rocky and Banff National Park is Nordegg, 85 kilometers (53 mi) west of Rocky. Nordegg was once a booming coal-mining town of 3,500, but the town was abandoned when the mines closed. Now fewer than 100 souls call the town home. The original townsite has mostly disappeared, but remaining mine structures are preserved as a National Historic Site.

History

Early in the 20th century, Martin Nordegg staked a claim at a site near where his namesake town is today. Soon after, he established **Brazeau Collieries** and struck a deal with the Canadian National Railway; if they would extend the line to his mines, he would have 100,000 tons of coal waiting. He kept his end of the deal and the railway kept theirs, completing the rail line in 1914. The town of Nordegg became the first "planned" mining town in Alberta. The streets were built in a semicircular pattern, centered around the railroad station and shops. Fifty miners' cottages were built, all painted in pastel colors. Gardens were planted, two churches and a hospital were built, and a golf course was developed—miners had never had it better. In 1923, production peaked at nearly half a million tons of coal. By the 1930s, most of the coal was being converted to briquettes, which were easy to handle and burned better than raw coal. By the early 1940s, with

four briquette presses, Nordegg had one of the largest such operations in North America. But the success soon turned to ash. In 1941, an explosion killed 29 men, and in 1950, fire destroyed many structures. Then trains began converting to diesel fuel and home heating went to natural gas. Brazeau Collieries ceased operations in January 1955. Many miners had spent their entire lives working the mine and had raised families in the remote mining community. By the summer of 1955, the town had been abandoned.

Sights and Recreation
The Nordegg Historical Society, made up of many former residents of the mining community, operates the **Nordegg Heritage Centre** (403/721-2625, mid-May–Sept. daily 9 A.M.– 5 P.M.), a two-story former school building along the main street. Among many interesting museum displays are newspaper articles telling of the town's ups and downs and extensive photo archives. Also in the building is a gift shop and café. Beyond the heritage center is the original townsite, now with only a few buildings still standing, including a boarding house, hotel, general store, and church (still used). Visitors are free to wander around the townsite, but ask at the heritage center for a map. Beyond the townsite is the mine infrastructure, much of which still remains. The only access to this section of Nordegg is on a guided tour. These depart twice daily through summer, and are booked through the heritage center. Neither tour goes underground but the longer version ($8) takes in the briquette-processing plants and mine entrances. Call ahead for a schedule.

In the 1990s, a group of locals decided to restore the original 1916 **Nordegg Golf Course** (403/721-2003, May–Sept.), where nature had taken over since the town was deserted 40 years previously. Today, it costs $12 to golf all day, rentals are available, and you can get a beer and burger at the end of your round.

Practicalities
A good option for budget travelers is **HI-Nordegg** (403/721-2140, www.hihostels.ca),

also known as Shunda Creek Hostel. Affiliated with Hostelling International, this huge log chalet in a wilderness setting has a fully equipped kitchen, a dining room, a fireplace, hot showers, and an outdoor hot tub. Members of Hostelling International pay $20 per night, nonmembers $25. The hostel is along Shunda Creek Recreation Area Road, just west of Nordegg. Check-in is after 4 P.M. and it's open year-round.

Nordegg Lodge (403/721-3757 or 800/408-3294, $82 s, $92 d) is the only accommodation in town itself, and is a motel rather than a lodge. The 38 rooms are nothing special, but the lodge has a restaurant (daily 7 A.M.–9 P.M.), a lounge, a laundry room, mini-golf, and an adjacent grocery store/gas station.

Campers here have many choices, with provincial recreation-area campgrounds north and south along the Forestry Trunk Road, and east and west along Highway 11. All sites are primitive but have pit toilets, firewood, and kitchen shelters and are usually beside a creek or lake. Expect to pay $11–17 per night. Closest to town is **Upper Shunda Creek,** three kilometers (1.9 mi) west of Nordegg.

The motel has a dining room, but the food at the **Miner's Café** (Nordegg Heritage Centre, 403/721-2625, mid-May–Sept. daily 9 A.M.–5 P.M.) is much better. The soup and sandwich special is $8, and the sandwiches are stacked and delicious. Freshly made fruit pies are an easy choice for dessert.

WEST FROM NORDEGG
The **Forestry Trunk Road** crosses Highway 11 three kilometers (1.9 mi) west of Nordegg. This road, used mainly to maintain the forest, is well traveled by those going fishing, hiking, and camping. From Highway 11, it is 190 kilometers (118 mi) north to Hinton and 265 kilometers (165 mi) south to Cochrane. No services are available along either route, but the scenery is spectacular, the fishing great, and the crowds nonexistent.

From this junction, Highway 11 veers southwest. Twenty-three kilometers (14 mi) from Nordegg, it passes a side road to **Crescent Falls** and **Bighorn Canyon.** Five kilometers (3.1 mi)

© ANDREW HEMPSTEAD

enjoying a sweeping panorama of
Abraham Lake

farther, a gravel road leads south to the eastern end of **Abraham Lake,** one of Alberta's largest reservoirs, on the North Saskatchewan River. An information center (403/721-3952, summer daily 8:30 A.M.–4:30 P.M.) at the dam describes its construction. Back on the highway, the main body of Abraham Lake quickly comes into view, its brilliant turquoise water reflecting the front ranges of the Canadian Rockies. Don't stop for a photo session just yet, though, because the views improve farther west. Across the lake is **Michener Mountain** (2,337 m/7,670 ft).

Accommodations along Highway 11

◖ **Aurum Lodge** (45 km/28 mi west of Nordegg, 40 km/25 mi east of the Banff National Park, 403/721-2117, www.aurumlodge.com, $160–230 s or d) trades on an eco-friendly stance and wonderfully scenic location overlooking Abraham Lake. Owners Alan and Madeleine Ernst used recycled materials wherever possible during construction, natural light streams into all corners, the kitchen

uses a wood-fired stove, and much of the waste is recycled. But don't imagine some backwoods cabin without running water—it's a comfortable and modern lodge. Rooms in the main lodge are simply decorated, but bright and immaculately kept. Cozy self-contained cottages offer a bathroom, kitchen with woodstove, and lots of privacy. Spend some time on the sun-drenched deck or curled up in front of the fireplace with a book—you won't even realize there are no televisions. Check the website for meal inclusions and packages, or pay $22 per person extra for dinner.

David Thompson Resort (three km/1.9 mi west of Aurum Lodge, 403/721-2103, www.davidthompsonresort.com, May–mid-Oct.) provides a variety of lodging options. Its full-service RV park charges $23.50 for unserviced sites, $28.50–37.50 for hookups. Older motel rooms and cabins with propane lights and no running water are available for $100 s or d. The bathroom facilities were in need of an upgrade at the time of our research trip for this edition, but as a trade off there's a unique open-sided bar that opens for karaoke each night and then again in the morning for a pancake breakfast. Other facilities include a playground with massive slides, Frisbee-golf course, restaurant, and gas station.

Kootenay Plains Ecological Reserve

Located at the south end of Abraham Lake, this reserve protects a unique area of dry grasslands in the mountains. As Mary Schäffer noted during her historic journey north to Maligne Lake, "to gain full appreciation of the plains you must leave the road and pause in their midst." The climate in this section of the valley is unusually moderate, the warmest in the Rockies. June grass and wheat grass, usually associated with the prairies of southeastern Alberta, thrive here. The valley is a prime wintering area for elk, mule deer, bighorn sheep, and moose. For thousands of years, the Kootenay peoples would cross the mountains from the Columbia River Valley to hunt these mammals and the bison that were

DAVID THOMPSON

David Thompson, one of Canada's greatest explorers, was a quiet, courageous, and energetic man who drafted the first comprehensive and accurate map of western Canada. He arrived in Canada from England as a 14-year-old apprentice clerk for the Hudson's Bay Company. With an inquisitive nature and a talent for wilderness navigation, he quickly acquired the skills of surveying and mapmaking. Natives called him Koo-koo-sint, which translates as "The Man Who Looks at Stars."

Between 1786 and 1808 Thompson led four major expeditions into what is now Alberta – the first for the Hudson's Bay Company and the last three for its rival, the North West Company. The most important one was the fourth, from 1806 to 1808, during which he discovered the Athabasca Pass through the Continental Divide. For many years, this was the main route across the Canadian Rockies to the Pacific Ocean.

In 1813 Thompson began work on a master map covering the entire territory that the North West Company controlled. It was four meters (13 ft) long and two meters (six ft) wide, detailing over 2.4 million square kilometers (1.5 million square mi). On completion it was hung out of public view in the council hall of a company fort in the east. It was years later, after his death in 1857, that the map was "discovered" and Thompson became recognized as one of the world's greatest land geographers.

White Goat Wilderness Area

Two designated wilderness areas near the west end of Highway 11—White Goat and Siffleur—afford hikers the chance to enjoy the natural beauty and wildlife of the Canadian Rockies away from the crowds associated with the mountain national parks. No horses or motorized vehicles are allowed within wilderness-area boundaries, and hunting and fishing are prohibited, as is all construction. This, ironically, gives these lightly traveled regions (an unnamed 15-year resident of adjoining Banff National Park had never heard of them) more protection than the national parks. The drawback, however, and the reason so few people explore these areas, is that wilderness really means *wilderness,* sans roads, bridges, or campsites. In fact, no roads even lead to the areas' boundaries; the only access is on foot.

White Goat comprises 44,500 hectares (110,000 acres) of high mountain ranges, wide valleys, hanging glaciers, waterfalls, and high alpine lakes. It lies north and west of Highway 11, abutting the north end of Banff National Park and the south end of Jasper National Park. The area's vegetation zones are easily recognizable: subalpine forests of Engelmann spruce, subalpine fir, and lodgepole pine; alpine tundra higher up. Large mammals here include a large population of bighorn sheep, as well as mountain goats, deer, elk, woodland caribou, moose, cougars, wolves, coyotes, black bears, and grizzly bears.

The most popular hike is the **McDonald Creek Trail,** which first follows the Cline River, then McDonald Creek to the creek's source in the heart of the wilderness area. McDonald Creek is approximately 12 kilometers (7.5 mi) from the parking area on Highway 11, but a full day should be allowed for this section as the trail crosses many streams. From where McDonald Creek flows into the Cline River, it is 19 kilometers (11.8 mi) to the McDonald Lakes, but allow another two full days; the total elevation gain for the hike is a challenging 1,222 meters (4,000 ft). Other hiking possibilities include following the Cline River to its source and crossing Sunset Pass into Banff National Park, 17 kilometers

then prolific. Because of the dry microclimate and its associated vegetation, mammals are not abundant in summer.

Westward from Kootenay Plains, Highway 11 continues climbing, past a parking area (from where a trail leads to a whirlpool on the North Saskatchewan River) and on into Banff National Park. It ends on the Icefields Parkway at Saskatchewan River Crossing. From here, it is 153 kilometers (95 mi) north to Jasper and 127 kilometers (79 mi) south to Banff.

(10.6 mi) north of Saskatchewan River Crossing, or heading up Cataract Creek and linking up with the trails in the Brazeau River area of Jasper National Park.

White Goat Wilderness Area has no facilities and is for experienced hikers only. For more information contact the **Department of Sustainable Resource Development** (780/944-0313, www.srd.gov.ab.ca).

Siffleur Wilderness Area

Siffleur, like White Goat Wilderness Area, is a remote region of the Canadian Rockies, completely protected from any activities that could have an impact on the area's fragile ecosystems, including road and trail development. No bridges have been built over the area's many fast-flowing streams, and the few old trails that do exist are not maintained. Elk, deer, moose, cougars, wolverines, wolves, coyotes, black bears, and grizzly bears roam the area's four main valleys, whereas higher, alpine elevations harbor mountain goats and bighorn sheep.

The area is on the opposite (south) side of Highway 11 from White Goat Wilderness and borders Banff National Park to the west and south. The main trail into the 41,200-hectare (101,800-acre) wilderness begins from a parking area two kilometers (1.2 mi) south of the Two O'Clock Creek Campground at Kootenay Plains. The area's northeastern boundary is a seven-kilometer (4.3 mi) hike from here. Even if you're not heading right into Siffleur, the first section of this trail, to **Siffleur Falls,** is worth walking. Along the first section, the trail crosses the North Saskatchewan River via a swinging bridge, then at the two-kilometer (1.2-mi) mark crosses the Siffleur River, reaching the falls after four kilometers (2.5 mi); allow 70 minutes one-way. These are the official Siffleur Falls, but others lie further upstream at the 6.2-kilometer (3.9-mi) and 6.9-kilometer (4.3-mi) marks.

Once inside the wilderness area, the trail climbs steadily alongside the Siffleur River and into the heart of the wilderness. Ambitious hikers can continue through to the Dolomite

Grizzly bears inhabit the remote mountains west of Nordegg, but are rarely sighted.

© ANDREW HEMPSTEAD

Creek Area of Banff National Park, finishing at the Icefields Parkway, seven kilometers (4.3 mi) south of Bow Summit. Total length of this trail is 68 kilometers (42 mi), a strenuous five-day backcountry expedition. Another access point for the area is opposite Waterfowl Lake Campground in Banff National Park. From here it is six kilometers (3.7 mi) up Noyes Creek to the wilderness area boundary; the trail peters out after 4.5 kilometers (2.8 mi) and requires some serious scrambling before descending into Siffleur. This trail—as with all others in the wilderness area—is for experienced hikers only.

Two O'Clock Creek Campground lies two kilometers (1.2 mi) from the park's main trailhead in Kootenay Plains Provincial Recreation Area. It is a primitive facility, with 24 sites each with a picnic table and fire pit, a picnic shelter, free firewood, and drinking water. Sites are $12 per night. For more information, contact the **Department of Sustainable Resource Development** (780/944-0313, www.srd.gov.ab.ca).

NORTH FROM ROCKY MOUNTAIN HOUSE

Pigeon Lake

East of Alder Flats along Highway 13, this lake is a popular recreation area for residents of Edmonton, 105 kilometers (65 mi) to the northeast. The lake is reputed to be the best swimming lake in Alberta and offers good fishing for walleye, pike, and whitefish. At the southeastern end of the lake is the little hamlet of **Ma-me-o,** where the streets are lined with a colorful array of summer cottages. The beach here is good and is backed by a few shops, including a restaurant. In the heart of the town is Alberta's smallest provincial park, **Ma-me-o Provincial Park** (1.5 hectares/3.7 acres). It is a day-use area only.

Pigeon Lake gets very busy in summer. Most visitors are "cottagers," but you can also enjoy the resortlike atmosphere of the area by spending time at **By the Lake Bed and Breakfast** (86 Grandview, 780/586-3598, www.bythe lakebnb.com, $85–120 s or d). Two rooms are offered in this modern lakeside home, one in the main house, another in an adjacent building. Both have an inviting atmosphere, ensuites, and plenty of privacy. In addition to their separate sitting rooms, a patio off the main house opens to gardens and the waterfront. Rates include a gourmet breakfast. The property is signposted off Highway 771 northwest of Westerose.

Also along the western shoreline is **Pigeon Lake Provincial Park.** At the main 300-site campground, you'll find a beach, show-ers, kitchen shelters, firewood, and the start of an 11-kilometer (6.8-mi) trail system; unserviced sites $25, powered sites $31. **Zeiner Campground,** a little farther north, has powered sites, kitchen shelters, firewood, groceries, canoe rentals, and showers, but less shade around the campsites; unserviced sites $25, powered sites $31. For reservations at either campground, call 780/586-2644.

Drayton Valley and Vicinity

Drayton Valley is a town of 5,200 at the base of the foothills and at the western edge of Alberta's extensive oil and gas fields, 110 kilometers (68 mi) north of Rocky Mountain House. It is located on what is known as the **subcontinental divide:** a high point of land dividing the Arctic Ocean–bound Pembina River System from the Atlantic Ocean–bound North Saskatchewan River System. To the southwest, along Highway 620, is **Brazeau Reservoir,** whose waters are used to supply hydroelectric power to nearby industry.

East of Drayton Valley, 40 kilometers (25 mi) along Highway 39 then 25 kilometers (16 mi) north on Highway 770, are the **Genesee Fossil Beds.** Each year the North Saskatchewan River erodes its banks here, exposing often perfectly preserved 60-million-year-old fossilized plants. To get to the site from the hamlet of Genesee, head west three kilometers (1.9 mi), south 1.6 kilometers (one mi), then west again a similar distance to a small creek. A partially defined trail leads down to the much larger river and to the fossil beds.

Calgary to Red Deer

The main route out of Calgary is the Deerfoot Trail, which becomes Highway 2 as it heads through outlying suburbs and onto the prairies. To the west are the foothills and, more than 100 kilometers (62 mi) away, dominating the horizon, the Canadian Rockies. They remain in view for much of the 145-kilometer (90-mi) run to the city of Red Deer, located halfway to Edmonton. The Calgary and Edmonton Railway Company built the first permanent link between Alberta's two largest centers in 1891, following a trail that had been used for generations by natives, early explorers, traders, and missionaries. With the coming of the automobile, a road was built. The original road (Hwy. 2A) is now paralleled the entire length by Highway 2, a four-lane divided highway that makes the trip an easy three-hour drive. Highway 2A is still maintained in some sections, passing through small ranching and farming communities. A longer but more interesting alternative is to take Highways 9 and 21, to the east of Highway 2, passing through the southern edge of the aspen parkland to a buffalo jump used by natives 2,000 years ago.

VIA HIGHWAY 2A

Airdrie

This fast-growing city (pop. 30,000) is mostly residential, with many local folks commuting to Calgary. It began as the first stopping house on the Calgary and Edmonton Railway and has grown ever since. The town's **Nose Creek Valley Museum** (1701 Main St. S, 403/948-6685, summer daily 9 A.M.–5 P.M., adult $2) has an interesting exhibit of artifacts from the Blackfoot and Shoshoni tribes, who fought many battles in the area, vying for dominance as buffalo herds declined.

Along Highway 2 are all the usual chain motels and family-style eateries, but if you're looking for a reason to stop, do so for a meal at the **Homestead Restaurant** (525 Woodside Dr., 403/948-7416, daily for lunch and dinner). Overlooking the Woodside Golf Course, the outlook is an oasis of green in the middle of seemingly endless housing estates. Adding to the charm is the food, with well-prepared dishes a notch above the usual clubhouse fare. Think chicken Thai salad ($8.50) or Spolumbo sausage (a Calgary delicacy) fettuccine Alfredo ($9.50) for lunch and perfectly cooked Alberta rib eye with soup or salad ($18.50) for a dinner main.

Carstairs and Vicinity

Carstairs is a small farming, dairy, and ranching center 67 kilometers (42 mi) north of Calgary. The town's tree-lined streets are dotted with grand old houses, and the grain elevators associated with all prairie towns stand silhouetted against the skyline. Although a small museum is located at 1138 Nanton Street, the main attractions are outside of town. **PaSu Farm** (10 km/6.2 mi west of town, 403/337-2800, Tues.–Sat. 10 A.M.–5 P.M., Sun. noon–5 P.M.) is a working farm with a dozen breeds of sheep. It also displays a wide variety of sheepskin and wool products, as well as weavings from Africa. The farm's restaurant serves light lunches plus scones, homemade apple pie, and various teas Tuesday–Saturday noon–4 P.M., along with a Sunday (noon–2:30 P.M.) lunch.

Much of the wool from PaSu Farm is sold to **Custom Woolen Mills** (403/337-2221, Mon.–Fri. 9 A.M.–3 P.M.), on the other side of Carstairs, 20 kilometers (12.5 mi) east on Highway 581 and 4.5 kilometers (2.8 mi) north on Highway 791. At this working museum, the raw wool is processed on clunky-looking machines—some of which date to the 1880s—into wools and yarns ready for knitting (and sale). A self-guided tour is offered.

Olds

Olds is a little more than halfway between Calgary and Red Deer. Surrounded by rich farmland, it's the home of **Olds College** (403/556-8281), which has been a leader in the development of Canadian agriculture for the last 100 years. Visitors are free to wander

The gardens at Olds College are open to the public.

around the campus, admiring colorful beds of well-tended prairie-hardy plants. The 600-hectare (1,480-acre) campus is along Highway 2, south of the main street. Also on the main drag is **Mountain View Pizza** (4513 52nd Ave., 403/556-1069, Mon.–Tues. 7:30 A.M.–5:30 P.M., Wed.–Fri. 7:30 A.M.–8:30 P.M., Sat. 9:30 A.M.–5:30 P.M.). But instead of making the cut for its pizza, this place gets a nod for superb coffee, roasted in-house and served in a café-like atmosphere.

Red Lodge Provincial Park
This small park is 14 kilometers (8.7 mi) west of **Bowden** on the **Little Red Deer River.** An English settler built a large log house on the river's edge and then painted the logs red, hence the name. The park is situated within a heavily wooded strip of land that extends east from the foothills well into central Alberta, an ideal habitat for deer and moose. The campground has a kitchen shelter, coin-operated showers, and firewood, and the river is good

for swimming, floating, and fishing. It gets busy on summer weekends; $20, no reservations accepted.

Innisfail
It was from Antler Ridge, just north of Innisfail (pop. 7,000), that in 1754 Anthony Henday became the first white man to see the Canadian Rockies. Highway 54, named the Anthony Henday Highway in his honor, begins in town and branches west, passing the turnoff to Markerville and continuing to Caroline and the Forestry Trunk Road.

Innisfail Historical Village (in the fairgrounds at 42nd St. and 52nd Ave., 403/227-2906, summer daily 11 A.M.–5:30 P.M., donation) has re-created historic buildings, including a stopping house, a school, a store, a Canadian Pacific Railway (CPR) station, and a blacksmith's shop, on a one-hectare (1.5-acre) site. The Royal Canadian Mounted Police (RCMP) **Police Dog Service Training Centre**

The main reason to stop at Innisfail is to watch a performance at the RCMP dog training facility.

(four km/2.5 mi south of town, 403/227-3346) is where police dog handlers and their four-legged companions come from across Canada to receive training in obedience, agility, and criminal apprehension. Through summer, public demonstrations are given every Wednesday at 2 P.M. Bookings are not required, but the small grandstand is usually full by start time, so arrive early for the best seats.

◖ Markerville

This town, 16 kilometers (10 mi) west then three kilometers (1.9 mi) north of Innisfail, was originally settled in the 1880s by Icelandic people, who had settled in eastern Canada but after finding the land unproductive continued west. Today, around 100 people—most that trace their heritage back to the original settlers—call Markerville home. It's a pretty village, with smartly painted homes and well-kept gardens. The only official attraction is **Markerville Creamery** (403/728-3006, mid-May–early Sept. Mon.–Sat. 10 A.M.–5:30 P.M., Sun. noon–5:30 P.M.). Between 1902 and the time of its closure in 1972, the creamery won many awards for its fine-quality butters, as you'll learn on a self-guided tour ($2) of the butter-making process. Part of the creamery has been converted to a *kaffistofa* (café) with a choice of Icelandic specialties.

The most famous of the Icelandic immigrants was Stephan A. Stephansson, one of the Western world's most prolific poets. He spent the early part of his life in his homeland; most of his poetry was written in Canada. Just north of Markerville is his restored 1927 home, the distinctive pink-and-green **Stephansson House** (403/728-3929, mid-May–Aug. daily 10 A.M.–6 P.M., $2). Interpretive panels beside the parking lot tell the story of Stephansson and his fellow immigrants while a short trail leads through a grove of trees to the house itself.

THE BACK WAY

The area east of Highway 2, immediately north of Calgary, was once covered in aspen. But over time, the trees have given way to cereal agricul-

Markerville is one of Alberta's most attractive towns.

ture and large dairy farms. Stands of trees are now limited to the valleys of tributaries of the Red Deer River, the region's main watershed. The landscape is generally flat, but along the main route north (via Highways 9 and 21) are interesting towns and a buffalo jump.

To Three Hills

Highway 9 intersects Highway 1 approximately 31 kilometers (19 mi) east of Calgary and heads north to **Irricana.** Two kilometers (1.2 mi) northwest of town, **Pioneer Acres** (403/935-4357, May–Sept. daily 9 A.M.–5 P.M., $5) displays a large collection of working farm machinery and holds a festival early in August, with demonstrations of pioneer farming and homemaking activities.

North of Irricana is **Beiseker,** where a CPR station, built in 1910, has been restored and now houses a museum (403/947-3774). From here, Highway 9 heads east, passing the junction with Highway 21 and continuing on to Drumheller (see the *Dinosaur Valley* chapter).

Torrington

Torrington, on Highway 27, 25 kilometers (15.5 mi) west of Highway 21, has more gophers than residents. This wouldn't be unusual for a prairie town, except that Torrington's gophers are all stuffed. The town made world headlines in 1997 with the opening of the **Gopher Hole Museum** (208 1st St., 403/631-3931, June–Sept. daily 10 A.M.–5 P.M., $2), which, as the brochure describes, is "a whimsical portrayal of daily life in our tranquil village." Approximately 40 dioramas house stuffed gophers in various poses, including gophers in love, gophers playing sports, trailer-court gophers, and even gophers wearing shirts declaring that animal rights activists, who were incensed at the idea of the museum, should "Go stuff themselves." Admission includes a copy of the words to the *Torrington Gopher Call Song,* which wafts through the quiet streets of the village whenever the museum is open.

Trochu

Continuing north along Highway 21 from Three Hills is Trochu, where an **arboretum** (just off Hwy. 21 on North Rd., 403/442-2111, mid-May–mid-Oct. daily 9 A.M.–8 P.M., $2) showcases the flora of southern Alberta. Pathways lead through the gardens, where more than 100 different plant species attract a variety of birds.

St. Ann Ranch (King Georges Ave., 403/442-3924 or 888/442-3924, www.stann ranch.com) was established in 1905 by a group of aristocratic French settlers and is now a Provincial Historic Site. A French settlement, including a school, a church, and a post office, grew around it. The thriving community suffered a blow during World War II when many townsmen returned to France to defend their country. Descendants of an original settler now operate the main residence as a country-style inn. There are nine guest rooms in all, each decked out in period antiques; the more expensive ones have fireplaces. Rates of $50–70 s, $75–95 d include breakfast. It's over the railway tracks on the south side of town.

Dry Island Buffalo Jump

This 1,180-hectare (2,900-acre) park is named for both an isolated mesa in the Red Deer River Valley and the site where natives stampeded bison over a cliff approximately 2,000 years ago. The buffalo jump—a 50-meter (164-ft) drop—is much higher than other jumps in Alberta and is in an ideal location; the approach to the jump is uphill, masking the presence of a cliff until the final few meters. Below the prairie benchland, cliflike valley walls and banks of sandstone have been carved into strange-looking badlands by wind and water erosion. A great diversity of plantlife grows in the valley; more than 400 species of flowering plants have been recorded. The park is a day-use area only; apart from a picnic area and a few trails, it is undeveloped. Access is along a gravel road east from Highway 21. From the park entrance, at the top of the buffalo jump, the road descends steeply for 200 vertical meters (660 ft) into the valley (it can be extremely slippery after rain) to the bank of the Red Deer River.

CENTRAL ALBERTA

Red Deer

This city of 80,000 (Alberta's third-largest) is on a bend of the Red Deer River, halfway between the cities of Calgary and Edmonton, which are 145 kilometers (90 mi) south and 148 kilometers (92 mi) north, respectively. From the highway, Red Deer seems to be all industrial estates and suburban sprawl, but an extensive park system runs through the city, and many historic buildings have been restored.

History

The name Red Deer was mentioned on maps by explorer David Thompson in the early 1800s. The Cree name for the river is *Waskasoo* (elk); scholars believe that Thompson translated the word incorrectly, confusing these animals with the red deer of Scotland.

Permanent settlement began in 1884 at a site where the busy trail linking Calgary to Edmonton crossed the Red Deer River. Most of the early settlement was centered around Fort Normandeau, at the river crossing. But the Calgary and Edmonton Railway Company built its line and a station farther east, and the town slowly grew in around it. Initially, the economy was based on agriculture, but it profited from the oil-and-gas boom after World War II. By the 1970s, Red Deer was one of Canada's fastest-growing cities, and things haven't slowed down yet, with surrounding tracts of land being broken up for residential and industrial subdivisions.

SIGHTS

If you're arriving in Red Deer from either the north or south, stay on Highway 2 until the large red-and-white **Red Deer Visitor and Convention Bureau** building comes into view (from the north, take the 32nd Street exit and loop back onto Highway 2 northbound). In addition to being a good source of information about the city, it is home to an interesting sports museum. From this complex, duck through the Heritage Ranch parking lot to get downtown.

Alberta Sports Hall of Fame and Museum

Being halfway between Calgary and Edmonton, Red Deer is a good home for this sporting museum (Hwy. 2, in the same building as the Red Deer Visitor and Convention Bureau, 403/341-8614, summer daily 9 A.M.–6 P.M., the rest of the year daily 10 A.M.–5 P.M., adult $3). Displays highlight the feats of local sporting heroes such as hockey legend Wayne Gretzky, multiple-time World Figure Skating Champion Kurt Browning, and Red Deer skater Jamie Sale, who, with partner David Pelletier, was belatedly awarded a skating gold medal at the 2002 Winter Olympics after the infamous judging controversy. But it's not all about winter sports—you can also admire the achievements of Albertans like Sharon Wood (the first North American woman to summit Mount Everest) and Jason Zuback (multiple-time world champion in long drive golfing). In addition to a "Highlights of History" exhibit, the museum has a computerized honor roll, film footage of great sporting moments, and a variety of interactive sports booths that let you test hockey, baseball, and skiing skills.

Downtown

The downtown **Red Deer and District Museum** (4525 47A Ave., 403/309-8405, July and Aug. Mon.–Fri. 10 A.M.–5 P.M. and Sat.–Sun. 1–5 P.M., the rest of the year daily noon–5 P.M., donation) tells the story of the area from prehistoric times to the present, with emphasis on the growth and development of the last 100 years. If you have youngsters in tow, head for the interactive Children's Zone; if you have a love of the tacky and wacky, search out the display of the World's Most Boring Postcard, a title bestowed on a postcard depicting the museum exterior. The museum is also the starting point for two historical walking tours—ask here for a map. Adjacent to the museum is **Heritage Square,** a collection of historic structures, including the Stevenson-Hall Block, Red Deer's

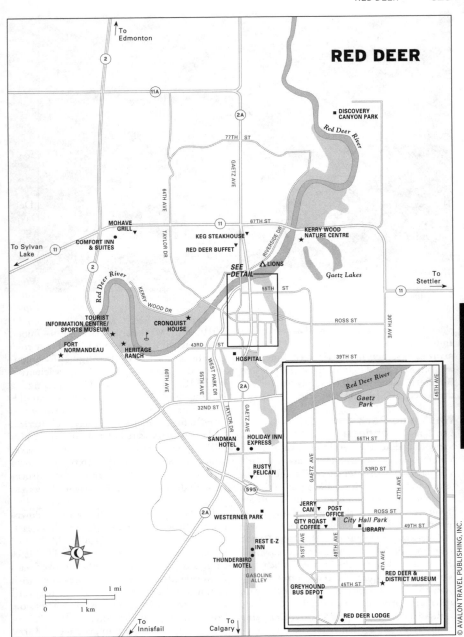

RED DEER

To Edmonton

DISCOVERY CANYON PARK

Red Deer River

77TH ST

GAETZ AVE

2A

64TH AVE

TAYLOR DR

11A

11

67TH ST

KEG STEAKHOUSE

RED DEER BUFFET

MOHAVE GRILL

COMFORT INN & SUITES

To Sylvan Lake

RIVERSIDE DR

KERRY WOOD NATURE CENTRE

SEE DETAIL

LIONS

Gaetz Lakes

55TH ST

ROSS ST

30TH AVE

To Stettler

Red Deer River

KERRY WOOD DR

TOURIST INFORMATION CENTRE/ SPORTS MUSEUM

CRONQUIST HOUSE

FORT NORMANDEAU

HERITAGE RANCH

43RD ST

HOSPITAL

60TH AVE

WEST PARK DR

55TH AVE

39TH ST

2A

32ND ST

TAYLOR DR

GAETZ AVE

SANDMAN HOTEL

HOLIDAY INN EXPRESS

RUSTY PELICAN

595

2A

WESTERNER PARK

REST E-Z INN

THUNDERBIRD MOTEL

GASOLINE ALLEY

0   1 mi

0   1 km

To Innisfail

To Calgary

Detail

Red Deer River

Gaetz Park

45TH AVE

55TH ST

GAETZ AVE

53RD ST

47TH AVE

ROSS ST

JERRY CAN

POST OFFICE

CITY ROAST COFFEE

City Hall Park

LIBRARY

51ST AVE

49TH AVE

47A AVE

49TH ST

RED DEER & DISTRICT MUSEUM

GREYHOUND BUS DEPOT

45TH ST

RED DEER LODGE

CENTRAL ALBERTA

Cronquist House

oldest building, and a re-created Norwegian log-and-sod farmhouse, typical of those in which many early settlers in Alberta lived. One block west, on Ross Street in front of City Hall, is **City Hall Park,** where 45,000 flowering plants create the perfect spot for a relaxing rest.

Waskasoo Park and Fort Normandeau

Sprawling along the Red Deer River is 11-kilometer-long (seven-mi-long), Waskasoo Park. The park has a 75-kilometer (47-mi) trail system, which is good for walking or biking in summer and cross-country skiing in winter. If you've stopped at the highway-side information center, it's possible to drive through the one-way gate to adjacent **Heritage Ranch** (403/347-4977), but there's no access from the ranch back out to the highway. The ranch is primarily an equestrian center offering trail rides ($20 per hour). From the ranch, walk upstream through the wooded river valley, or drive back out along 32nd Street, crossing Highway 2, to Fort Normandeau (403/346-

2010, mid-May–June daily noon–5 P.M., July–Aug. daily noon–8 P.M.). This replica is built on the site of the original fort, constructed in the spring of 1885 in anticipation of the Riel Rebellion—a Métis uprising led by Louis Riel. As protection against marauding natives, a hotel by the river crossing was heavily fortified. Its walls were reinforced, lookout towers were erected, and the entire building was palisaded. The fort was never attacked and was moved to an outlying farm in 1899. Beside the fort is an interpretive center with displays depicting early settlement at the crossing.

On the opposite side of the river from downtown is **Cronquist House** (take 55th St. east, then Taylor Dr., 403/346-0055, Mon.–Fri. 9 A.M.–4 P.M. and Sun. 1–4 P.M.). This 1911 three-story Victorian farmhouse overlooks Bower Ponds. When it was threatened with demolition, enterprising locals waited until winter and moved it piece by piece across the frozen lake to its present site.

Continuing downstream, you'll find **Kerry**

Sylvan Lake marina

Wood Nature Centre (6300 45th Ave., 403/ 346-2010, daily 10 A.M.–5 P.M.), which has various exhibits and videos on the natural history of the river valley and provides access to a paved walking trail through the adjacent 118-hectare (292-acre) **Gaetz Lakes Sanctuary.** Protected since 1924, this parkland of spruce and poplar interspersed with marshes is home to 128 recorded species of birds and 25 species of mammals.

Sylvan Lake
This lake, 22 kilometers (14 mi) west of Red Deer, has been one of Alberta's most popular summer resorts since the turn of the 20th century. It has more than five kilometers (three mi) of sandy beaches, clean warm water, a large marina, and plenty of recreation facilities. **Wild Rapids** (Lakeshore Dr., 403/887-3636, June–Aug., daily 11 A.M.–7 P.M., adult $25, under 48 inches $18) offers 11 water slides, a heated pool, and sailboard and paddleboat rentals. Other facilities at and around the lake include boat rentals from **Sylvan**

Marina (403/887-2950), three golf courses, and a greyhound track (403/887-5782) that hosts Saturday races through summer.

RECREATION AND EVENTS
The city's park system provides a range of recreational facilities. Paddleboats and canoes can be rented at Bower Ponds (403/347-9777). At Heritage Ranch (403/347-4977), trail riding, horseback-riding lessons, and wagon and sleigh rides are offered.

Children will love **Discovery Canyon Park** (403/343-8311, summer daily 9 A.M.–8 P.M.), which is all about discovering fun rather than learning. The highlight is a natural stream that has been modified into a waterslide, complete with rapids and a big pool at one end. Admission is free and tube rental is $3. To get there, follow 30th Avenue four kilometers (2.5 mi) north from 67th Street.

Most city events take place at **Westerner Park** (403/343-7800, www.westerner.ab.ca), a sprawling complex at the far south end of the city. The park is also home to the Red

Deer Rebels hockey team, which plays in the Western Hockey League. **Westerner Days** begins in mid-July, the weekend that the Calgary Stampede ends; festivities include a parade, a midway, livestock displays, chuckwagon races, an arts pavilion, and a casino. In early November, Red Deer hosts a large **Agri-Trade.** The **Red Deer International Air Show** (403/340-2333, www.rdairshow.com), held on the weekend closest to August 1, is one of Canada's most spectacular aerial events.

ACCOMMODATIONS AND CAMPING

Red Deer's location between Alberta's two largest cities makes it a popular location for conventions and conferences, so the city has a lot of hotels. The larger hotels are generally full of conventioneers during the week; weekend rates and Web specials usually bring rates down below $100 a night.

$50-100

The **Thunderbird Motel** is in "Gasoline Alley," the southernmost commercial strip (Hwy. 2 S, 403/343-8933, $60 s, $65 d), and as you can guess from the name, it's an older place. The 40 rooms are set around an outdoor pool and barbecue area. In the same vicinity is the unremarkable **Rest E-Z Inn** (Hwy. 2 S, 403/343-8444 or 800/424-9454, $62 s, $65 d), where a continental breakfast is included in the price.

$100-150

The **Holiday Inn Express** is south of downtown on the northbound side of the road (2803 Gaetz Ave., 403/343-2112, www.hiexpress.com, $119 s or d). The rooms are spacious, modern, and well furnished. Breakfast is included in the rates, as is access to an indoor saltwater pool. Directly across the road is the **Sandman Hotel Red Deer** (2818 Gaetz Ave., 403/343-7400 or 800/726-3626, www.sandmanhotels.com, $109–129 s or d). It features 143 smartly decorated guest rooms, an indoor pool, a fitness center, a lounge, and a restaurant.

    Red Deer Lodge (4311 49th Ave., 403/346-8841 or 800/661-1657, www.reddeerlodge.net,

$119–149 s or d) is a seven-story, 230-room downtown hostelry set up for conventioneers. This full-service establishment has rooms set around a huge tropical atrium where there's an indoor pool, a restaurant, and two lounges.

    My pick of the Red Deer accommodations is the **Comfort Inn & Suites** (6846 66th St., 403/348-0025 or 866/348-0025, www.comfort innreddeer.com, $139 s or d), just off Highway 2 at the north end of town. Opened in late 2005, the spacious rooms are filled with modern conveniences, a light breakfast is included in the rates, and there's an indoor pool with a waterslide. Another reason to stay is this motel's eco-friendly design, which includes a roof covered in solar power panels.

Camping

Red Deer has good city camping at the treed **Lions Campground,** on the west side of the river (4759 Riverside Dr., 403/342-8183, May–Sept., unserviced sites $18, powered sites $27). To get there, follow Gaetz Avenue north through town and turn right after crossing the Red Deer River. The campground has showers, full hookups, and a laundry room.

FOOD

Downtown, head to **City Roast Coffee** (4940 Ross St., 403/347-0893, Mon.–Sat. 7:30 A.M.– 6 P.M.). It's a big-city-style coffeehouse offering coffees from around the world and light snacks such as soups and sandwiches. Around the corner, a very different type of eatery, the **Jerry Can** (5005 50th Ave., 403/347-9417, daily for breakfast or lunch), attracts a strange collection of locals who come for the inexpensive meals and to catch up on gossip.

    Fast-food and family-style restaurants line 50th (Gaetz) Avenue north and south of downtown, including the **Red Deer Buffet** (Village Mall, 403/342-5555, daily 11 A.M.–10 P.M.), your quintessential Chinese all-you-can-eat with way too many choices and minimal service. But the price is right—$9.95 at lunch and $12.95 at dinner. In the vicinity is the **Keg Steakhouse** (6365 50th Ave., 403/309-5499, daily for lunch and dinner) with a cool atmo-

sphere and professional yet friendly service. A few blocks west is **Mohave Grill** (6608 Orr Dr., 403/340-3463, daily for lunch and dinner), which is beside the Comfort Inn. The setting is in-your-face Southwestern, but the menu is well priced, with dinner mains such as a half chicken roasted in barbecue sauce for $16, a meaty jambalaya for $15, and rich chocolate cheesecake for $6.

For Red Deer's most distinguished dining experience plan on eating at the **◖ Rusty Pelican** (2079 50th Ave., 403/347-1414, daily 11 A.M.–10 P.M.). Mains range from the semi-exotic (Cajun-style red snapper) to the traditional (prime rib of beef with Yorkshire pudding) and all are within the $13–30 range. A menu filled with seafood starters, a sensibly priced wine list, and melt-in-your-mouth strawberry cheesecake round out this top pick.

Surrounded by tropical greenery, **Botanica Restaurant** takes pride of place within a huge atrium at the Red Deer Lodge (4311 49th Ave., 403/346-8841). It's open daily for breakfast (daily buffet), lunch, and dinner (the Saturday prime rib buffet is worthwhile).

INFORMATION AND SERVICES

The Red Deer Visitor and Convention Bureau operates the excellent tourist information center (403/346-0180 or 800/215-8946, www.tourismreddeer.net, year-round Mon.–Fri. 9 A.M.–5 P.M., Sat.–Sun. 10 A.M.–5 P.M., until 6 P.M. in summer) on Highway 2 between the main north and south entrances to the city. It's on the city side of the highway (if you're arriving from the north, take the 32nd Street exit and loop back onto Highway 2 northbound). In addition to providing a load of information, the center has a gift shop, a concession area, and restrooms, and is adjacent to a picnic area.

Red Deer Public Library is an excellent facility housed in a single-story, redbrick building behind City Hall (4818 49th St., 403/346-4576, Mon.–Thurs. 9:30 A.M.–8:30 P.M., Fri.–Sat. 9:30 A.M.–5:30 P.M., Sun. 1:30–5 P.M.). **Chapters** (5250 22nd St., 403/309-2427) is part of a chain of Canadian megabookstores. The **Red Deer Book Exchange** (6791 50th Ave., 403/342-4883, closed Sun.) features a wide variety of used books and magazines.

Services you may need include the post office (4909 50th St.), the **Lost Sock Laundromat** (6350 67th St., 403/347-9274, daily 8:30 A.M.–10 P.M.), **Red Deer Regional Hospital** (3942 50th Ave., 403/343-4422) and the **RCMP** (403/341-2000).

GETTING THERE AND AROUND

Two scheduled bus services link Red Deer to Calgary and Edmonton. **Greyhound** departs from the depot (4303 Gaetz Ave., 403/343-8866, www.greyhound.ca) throughout the day for both cities. **Red Arrow** offers a more luxurious service, with complimentary beverages and snacks. Their buses depart north of downtown at 5315 54th Street four times daily for Calgary and Edmonton; call 403/343-2356 or visit www.redarrow.pwt.ca.

For a taxi, call **Associated Cabs** (403/346-2222) or **Chinook Cabs** (403/341-7300).

East of Highway 2: The Aspen Parkland

The aspen parkland lying east of Highway 2, between Red Deer and Edmonton, is a transition zone between the prairies to the south and the boreal forest to the north. Here, groves of aspen and, to a lesser degree, balsam poplar grow around sloughs and pothole-like depressions left by the retreating ice sheet at the end of the last ice age. Much of the original vegetation was burned by native peoples in order to attract grazing bison. In the last 100 years, the land has been given over to agriculture, changing its ecological makeup forever. Although much of the forest has been cleared and cultivated, the region is still home to mammals such as fox, coyote, lynx, white-tailed deer, beaver, and muskrat. The lakes and sloughs attract more than 200 species of birds, including literally millions of ducks that can be seen in almost all bodies of water.

From Red Deer, halfway between Calgary and Edmonton, Highway 2 continues north, providing access to outdoor recreation opportunities along the way. Sylvan, Gull, and Pigeon Lakes are popular summer resort areas west of the highway. To the east are the historic towns of Lacombe, Ponoka, and Wetaskiwin, home of the large Reynolds-Alberta Museum. Highways 12, 13, and 14 are the main routes east. Along each are many small towns with interesting museums and quiet provincial parks. Camrose, on Highway 13, hosts one of North America's largest gatherings of country-music superstars each August.

LACOMBE

Lacombe, 30 kilometers (19 mi) north of Red Deer and three kilometers (1.9 mi) east of Highway 2, is a historic town of 9,000 that is the site of provincial and federal agricultural stations. At the turn of the 20th century, the town was a bustling commercial center of 1,000, where an important spur of the Calgary and Edmonton Railway headed east. After a devastating 1906 fire, the town implemented a bylaw dictating that all new buildings were to be constructed using brick or stone. Today, many Edwardian-era buildings stand in the main business district. One block from the main street (50th Ave.), at 5036 51st Street, is **Michener House** (403/782-3933, summer Monday–Friday, noon–4 p.m., donation). This small wooden house dating to 1896 is the birthplace of Roland Michener, Canadian governor-general between 1967 and 1974.

Big-hitting golfers should consider a stop at the **Nursery Golf & Country Club** (Range Rd. 27-0, 403/782-5400, green fees $38), which is home to Canada's longest golf hole. It's the 11th hole, a Par 6 stretching to 782 yards from the back markers. Turn off Highway 2 four kilometers (2.5 mi) north of town.

◀ Lacombe Corn Maze

Only open when the corn reaches a height of six feet, the Lacombe Corn Maze (Hwy. 12, 403/782-4653, late July–Aug. Mon.–Sat. 11 a.m.–9 p.m., Sept.–mid-Oct. Wed.–Sat. 4–8 p.m., adult $8.50, child $6.50) is a rural highlight of central Alberta, even for adults. Cut in a different design each year, it's only one of two such mazes in the province (members of the same family operate both) and takes at least an hour to get through, with a "cheat sheet" for those who get truly lost. Also on site is a petting zoo, a tire horse carousel, a corn cannon, a jumping pillow, and miniature train rides to keep the young ones amused for a bit longer.

Practicalities

Between Highway 2 downtown is a campground and an information center (www.lacombetourism.com), but for motel accommodations, stay on the highway to reach **Wolf Creek Inn** (Hwy. 2, 403/782-4716, $59 s, $69 d). Set a little way back from the highway and overlooking a small lake, it's home to 20 adequate motel rooms overlooking a small lake. Arrive around noon or early evening and you'll find a full parking lot and busy restaurant, packed with highway

THE CANADA GOOSE

Each spring and fall the skies of central Alberta come alive with the honking of the Canada goose, a remarkable bird whose migratory path takes it clear across the North American continent. Each spring, family units migrate north to the same nesting site. These are spread throughout Canada, from remote wetlands of northern Alberta to desolate islands in the Arctic Ocean. Groups of families migrate together in flocks, the size of the flock varying according to the region, subspecies, and season. Preparation for long flights includes hours of preening and wing-flexing. Once in the air they navigate by the sun, moon, and stars, often becoming disoriented in fog or heavy cloud cover. They are intensely aware of air pressure and humidity. In spring Canada geese hitch a ride north on the strong winds produced by low-pressure systems rolling up from the southwest. In fall they take advantage of Arctic fronts that roar south. If weather conditions aren't right, the geese will rest for a while, usually in farmers' fields (taking advantage of freshly sown crops). The V formation for which the geese are famous serves a very specific purpose: Each bird positions itself behind and slightly to the side of the bird immediately ahead. In this way every goose in the flock has a clear view, and all but the leader benefit from the slipstream of the birds ahead.

If, during migration, a goose becomes ill or is crippled by a hunter's bullet, family members will remain with the bird, delaying their flight and leaving the injured bird only if it dies or if their own survival is in jeopardy.

© ANDREW HEMPSTEAD

travelers in the know looking to avoid fast-food joints. The advertising claims the dining room is famous for its cheese toast (which comes with all meals), and it is good. But you also find solid small-town cooking, reasonable prices, and friendly service. Access is only from Highway 2 southbound, so if you're heading toward Edmonton, take the second exit and loop back south via the overpass.

BETWEEN HIGHWAY 2 AND STETTLER

From Lacombe, it's 70 kilometers (43 mi) west to Stettler, and then another 200 kilometers (124 mi) to the Saskatchewan border. The first stretch of highway passes the south side of **Buffalo Lake,** a large, shallow body of water surrounded by a hummocky area created by receding ice during the last ice age. The lake itself is used by migrating waterfowl such as great blue herons and Canada geese each spring and fall, and supports a large population of northern pike.

North of Erskine is the lakeside village of **Rochon Sands.** Follow the road through town to reach **Rochon Sands Provincial Park,** protecting a sandy beach with good swimming. Enjoy a picnic lunch in the shaded day-use area or camp for $17 per night. Another nearby camping option is ◖ **Ol' MacDonalds Resort** (off Hwy. 835, 403/742-6603, www.olmacdonalds.com, May–Sept.), a sprawling lakefront campground offering over 300 treed sites and an amazing array of things to do. Aside from

the beach with shallow, warm water, there's watercraft rentals, evening wagon rides, a petting zoo, indoor mini-golf within a museum, an antique carousel, a café, and bike and buggy rentals. Camping costs range from $24 for an unserviced site away from the water to $37.50 for a full hookup.

STETTLER

Stettler (pop. 5,200) is along Highway 12, 72 kilometers (45 mi) east of Highway 2 in the middle of a farming and ranching area well known for its purebred livestock.

◖ Alberta Prairie Railway Excursions

A highlight of a visit to Stettler is actually *leaving* town—aboard one of Canada's last remaining passenger steam trains. Operated by Alberta Prairie Railway Excursions (403/742-2811, www.absteamtrain.com), the trains run between Stettler's historic railway station and Big Valley to the south. A rollicking good time is had by all, with live music, the occasional train robbery, and a hearty meal served at the turnaround point. Check the website for a schedule; the train runs each weekend May through October (and Thurs. and Fri. in July and Aug.). The fare is adult $81, youth $61, child $33.

Other Sights

It is estimated that in the early 1900s Alberta had around 1,700 wooden grain elevators, but today only 50 remain, including one beside the departure point for the Alberta Prairie Railway Excursions. This one dates to the 1920s and was in use until as recently 2003. Also unique is the adjacent coal shed, where coal delivered via the railway was stored before delivery to local residents.

Stettler also offers the **Town and Country Museum** (44th Ave., 403/742-4534, May–early Sept. daily 10 A.M.–5:30 P.M., adult $3, senior and child $2), a surprisingly large complex comprising over two dozen buildings spread over three hectares (7.5 acres). Highlights include the imposing courthouse, a railway station, and a small farmhouse that provided a home for three generations of the same family.

Practicalities

The nicest of five accommodations in town is **Stettler Ramada** (Hwy. 12, at the west entrance to town, 403/742-6555 or 800/272-6232, www.ramada.com, $119 s or d), a solid four-story chain hotel that opened in 2007. **Stettler Lions Campground** is adjacent to the golf course on the west side of town (off Hwy. 12 on 62nd St.). It has showers and hookups for $14–20 per night and is open May–October.

Most restaurants are along Highway 12; try **White Goose Restaurant** (5778 47th Ave., 403/742-2544, daily for breakfast, lunch, and dinner), a family-style eatery with inexpensive seafood dishes. In the older section of downtown, the **Little House of Coffee** (5109 51st St., 403/742-5282, daily for breakfast and lunch) pours a delicious cup of chai tea, as well as coffee, of course.

Stettler Tourist Information Centre (Hwy. 12, 403/742-3181, www.stettler.net, Mon.–Fri. 9 A.M.–7 P.M., Sat. 9 A.M.–6 P.M., Sun. 10 A.M.–5 P.M.) is beside Tim Hortons at the west entrance to town.

CONTINUING EAST ALONG HIGHWAY 12
Big Knife Provincial Park

Legend has it that Big Knife Creek was named after a fight between two long-standing enemies—one Cree, the other Blackfoot—that resulted in the death of both men. Recent history is no less colorful. A local farmer named One-eyed Nelson ran a moonshine operation here. His hooch was in demand throughout the prairies; he even exported the popular brew to Montana. Thirty years after he'd left the area, park rangers found the remains of his still in the side of the creek bank.

The small campground at the park has limited facilities, but the Battle River flows through the park, making for good swimming and canoeing. Sites are situated among towering cottonwood trees; $17. To get to the park

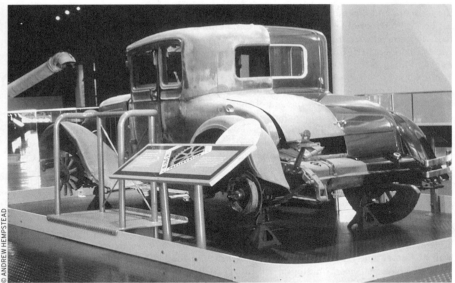

© ANDREW HEMPSTEAD

This display at the Reynolds-Alberta Museum shows the amount of work it takes to restore an antique vehicle.

from Stettler, head east along Highway 12 approximately 40 kilometers (25 mi) to Halkirk, then north on Highway 855 another 20 kilometers (12.5 mi).

Gooseberry Lake Provincial Park

This small park, 14 kilometers (8.7 mi) north of Consort, is on the shore of a tree-encircled lake and is made up of rolling grassland and a series of alkaline ponds. Many birds, including the northern phalarope, use the lake as a staging area along their migratory paths. The campground is between the lake and a nine-hole golf course and has powered sites, a kitchen shelter, and firewood. Unserviced sites are $20, powered sites $22. To the north are the **Neutral Hills,** which, according to legend, the Great Spirit raised to prevent the Cree and Blackfoot from fighting.

Nearby **Consort** is the birthplace of Katherine Dawn Lang, best known to the country/pop/dance music world as Grammy-winning star k. d. lang.

WETASKIWIN

This town, halfway between Red Deer and Edmonton on Highway 2A, was founded as a siding on the Calgary and Edmonton Railway and has developed into a wheat-farming and cattle-ranching center of 11,000. In the language of the Cree, *Wetaskiwin* (Where Peace was Made) is a reference to nearby hills where a treaty between the Cree and Blackfoot was signed in 1867.

◀ Reynolds-Alberta Museum

Usually, museums of this caliber are located in major cities. But here in the rolling hills two kilometers (1.2 mi) west of Wetaskiwin, a world-class facility cataloging the history of all types of machinery rises like a mirage from the rural prairie landscape. (After donating his original collection to start off the museum, local Stan Reynolds went right on collecting. Hundreds of old cars, tractors, military vehicles, aircraft, steam engines, and assorted farm machinery strewn about in varying states of repair between

the museum and downtown are testament to his hobby.) Surrounding the main exhibition hall, the complete history of transportation in Alberta is re-created, from horse-drawn carriages to luxurious 1950s automobiles. Over 1,000 vehicles have been fully restored, but some, such as the handmade snowmobile, are in their original condition. At the end of the display, you can peer into a large hall where the restoration takes place. The transportation displays encircle a large area where traditional farm machinery is on show, from the most basic plow to a massive combine harvester. The museum is open year-round daily 10 A.M.–5 P.M. (closed Mon. Sept.–May). Admission is adult $9, senior $7, child $5. For further information, call 780/361-1351.

Behind the museum lies an airstrip and a large hangar that houses **Canada's Aviation Hall of Fame.** The Hall of Fame recognizes those who have made contributions to the history of aviation and contains several vintage aircraft. Admission is included with a ticket to the Reynolds-Alberta Museum. Hours are also the same. Operating out of the Hall of Fame, **Central Aviation** (780/352-9689) offers a 10-minute flight in an old biplane for $109; weekends only.

Accommodations and Food

Set on two hectares (five acres) of mature gardens, **☾ Country Pleasures** (5712 45th Ave., 780/352-4335, $75–85 s or d) is a delightful bed-and-breakfast that wouldn't look out of place in the English countryside, except it's one block from the bright lights of Wetaskiwin's ubiquitous commercial strip. Common areas include a cozy living room, but on a warm evening it's hard to pass up one of the garden benches for some quiet time. Each of three guest rooms has an ensuite. Opt for Henry's Den and you'll enjoy a fireplace, claw-foot bathtub, and private patio. Looking for a regular motel room? Try the **Super 8 Motel** (3820 56th St., 780/361-3808 or 800/800-8000, www.super8.com, $99–109 s or d), a newer place that is within walking distance of the museum. Rates include continental breakfast.

Opposite the local golf course, **Wetaskiwin Lions RV Campground** (2.5 km/1.6 mi east of town along Hwy. 13, 780/352-7258, May–Sept., unserviced sites $15, hookups $20–24) has free showers, a laundry room, a cooking shelter, a stocked trout pond, and mini-golf.

Grandma Lee's Bakery (5103 50th Ave., 780/352-7711, Mon.–Sat. 7:30 A.M.–5 P.M.) is enduringly popular with locals for its small-town atmosphere as much as its food. Recommended are the meat pies and tasty pastries. A few doors away, the **Stanley Café** (5015 50th Ave., 780/352-3633, daily noon–8 P.M.) is a plain diner with westernized Chinese food at low prices (mains all under $10). Opposite the information center is **Runway Lunch** (5505 50th Ave., 780/352-3777, Mon.–Fri. 7:30 A.M.–4 P.M.), where the home-style cooking is a welcome respite from the blandness of the fast-food joints lining nearby 56th Street.

Information

At the junction of Highway 2A and 50th Avenue, the local tourist information center (4910 55th St., 780/352-8003, year-round Mon.–Fri. 9 A.M.–5 P.M., as well as summer weekends 9 A.M.–3 P.M.) is impossible to miss—just look for the colorful water tower across the road.

CAMROSE

Camrose, 40 kilometers (25 mi) east of Wetaskiwin, is a town of 15,000 that has greatly benefited from the oil-and-gas boom, yet retains its agricultural base.

Sights

As a tribute to early Norwegian settlers, a nine-meter (30-ft) scaled-down replica of a Viking longship is on display in the **Bill Fowler Centre** (5402 48th Ave., 780/672-4217, summer Mon.– Fri. 8:30 A.M.–7:30 P.M. and Sat.–Sun. 9:30 A.M.–5:30 P.M., the rest of the year Mon.–Fri. 8:30 A.M.–4:30 P.M.). Overlooking Mirror Lake, the center is also home to the local **tourist information center** and the start of a 10-kilometer (6.2-mi) trail system that encircles the lake (2.2 km/1.4 mi) and follows Camrose Creek south to the campground.

Camrose & District Museum (4522 53rd St., 780/672-3298, summer Tues.–Sun. 10 A.M.– 5 P.M., free) presents a working model of a steam threshing machine, a log church, a blacksmith's shop, and many other outdoor displays.

Big Valley Jamboree

Canada's largest annual gathering of country-music superstars is the Big Valley Jamboree (780/672-0224 or 888/404-1234, www.bigvalley jamboree.com), held on the first weekend of August at the Exhibition Grounds east of Camrose. In addition to the main stage, live performances take place in the massive beer garden and on a smaller indoor stage. Between acts, there are rodeo performances, a midway, a trade show, and lots of drinking and dancing. Most fans camp out, with one area set aside especially for

families. Daily passes are approximately $75, and a three-day weekend pass goes for $185; camping is $65 for as long as you can handle the heat, the noise, and the booze (actually, it's not that bad—a great time is had by all).

Accommodations and Camping

Just a couple of blocks from Mirror Lake, the centrally located **Camrose Motel** (6116 48th Ave., 780/672-3364, from $70 s or d) has 20 basic rooms, each with a microwave and a small fridge. Across town, the much larger **Hotel Marada** (3911 48th Ave., 780/672-7741, $80 s, $85 d) has large rooms, a café, a restaurant, and a lounge.

The town-operated **Valleyview Campground** (5204 50th Ave., May–Sept., $13–16) has powered sites, showers, a kitchen shelter, and

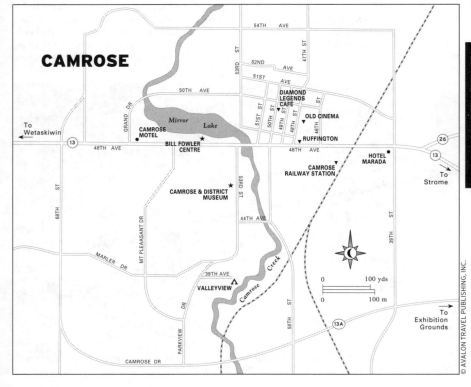

CENTRAL ALBERTA

firewood. To get there, follow 53rd Street south from Highway 13 for two kilometers (1.2 mi) and turn left on 39th Avenue. Within view of the camping area is a massive ski jump and a biathlon range, two sports brought to the area by Norwegian settlers over 100 years ago.

Food

A former residence converted to a teahouse, the **Ruffington** (4803 48th St., 780/672-4500, summer Mon.–Sat. 10 A.M.–5:30 P.M., Sun. noon–5 P.M.) comes with all the decorations but no pretensions. The menu offers a selection of teas (and coffee), plus full-blown lunches such as quiche and a delicious selection of fudges to finish off. It's along Highway 13, just east of the downtown turnoff. The friendly, country-style atmosphere is similar at **Camrose Railway Station** (44th St., 780/672-3099, Thurs.–Fri. 1–5 P.M., Sat. 10 A.M.–5 P.M.). It's typical tearoom fare in a restored station. Call ahead for a Saturday schedule— often it's a theme with links to Camrose's past (German, Ukrainian, Native, etc).

Downtown, **Diamond Legends Café** (4971 50th St., 780/608-2111, daily for breakfast and lunch) stands out for healthy soups and sandwiches (combos for $7). The café owners are also involved in the World's Longest Barbeque, serving Alberta beef for up to 10,000 people over a week in late June. Also downtown, a two-tiered movie theater has been transformed into a unique restaurant called the **Old Cinema** (4917 48th St., 780/672-4804, daily for dinner). Downstairs is a lounge and stage where live entertainment is presented on weekends. The dining area is upstairs on the balcony, surrounded in greenery. Expect to pay $28 for a three-course meal.

HIGHWAY 13 EAST

This part of Alberta is dominated by the **Battle River,** which flows from Pigeon Lake, in the foothills west of Wetaskiwin, through heavily developed agricultural land to Wainwright, then into Saskatchewan, where it drains into the North Saskatchewan River. Buffalo herds once congregated along the banks of the river, drawing Cree from the north and Blackfoot

Camrose Railway Station is home to a friendly little tearoom.

from the south, who fought over the right to hunt them—hence the river's name.

In **Strome,** the **Sodbuster's Museum** (5029 Main St., 780/376-3546, May–Sept. daily 11 A.M.–4 P.M., $2) is dedicated to the ingenuity of pioneer families who claimed homesteads in the region. The museum also has various native artifacts and a six-meter-long (20-ft-long) chunk of petrified wood.

Continuing east, Highway 13 descends to the Battle River and **Hardisty,** which is home to a feedlot with the capacity to feed 15,000 cattle. **Hardisty Lake,** at the west edge of town, is stocked with rainbow trout and has a beach, a golf course, and a campground (780/888-2700, May–Oct. $19–28) with hookups, showers, and free firewood.

From Hardisty, the highway continues east through **Amisk** (a nearby Hutterite colony welcomes visitors) to **Czar** and the **Prairie Panorama Museum** (780/857-2155, Apr.–Sept. Sun. 2–6 P.M.), which is known throughout the land for its collection of more than 1,000 salt- and pepper-shakers.

The small town of **Provost** is 20 kilometers (12.5 mi) from the Alberta-Saskatchewan border. Ten kilometers (6.2 mi) south of town is **St. Norbert's Church,** a magnificent Gothic structure built in 1926.

HIGHWAY 14 EAST
◀ Miquelon Lake Provincial Park

Originally a bird sanctuary, this 906-hectare (2,240-acre) park lies 30 kilometers (19 mi) north of Camrose on Highway 833. It is part of the massive 650-square-kilometer (250-square-mi) **Cooking Lake Moraine,** a hummocky, forested region dotted with lakes that extends north to Elk Island National Park. At the end of the last ice age, as the sheet of ice that covered much of the continent receded, it occasionally stalled, as it did in this area. Chunks of ice then broke off and melted, depositing glacial till in mounds. Between the mounds are hollows, known as kettles, which have filled with water. The **Knob and Kettle Trail System** starts behind the baseball diamond and is a series of short interconnecting

CENTRAL ALBERTA

© ANDREW HEMPSTEAD

The Ruffington is a small-town teahouse in a converted home.

trails through this intriguing landscape. Being heavily wooded, the area attracts many birds and animals; most ponds house a beaver family, and moose and deer can often be seen feeding at dawn and dusk. The draw for most visitors is the wide beach fronting a warm and shallow bay. Other amenities include a sparkling new visitors center (2006), a large playground, and an adjacent golf course (780/672-7308). The **C** **park campground** (780/672-7308, May–Sept., unserviced sites $22, powered sites $25) is the best in the region with modern washrooms, kitchen shelters, and firewood.

Tofield

In recent years, Tofield's biggest attraction, **Beaverhill Lake,** has undergone a transformation. Up to 18 kilometers (11 mi) long and 10 kilometers (6.2 mi) wide yet only an average of one meter (three ft) deep, the lake has receded dramatically. Western Canada's only shorebird reserve, **Beaverhill Natural Area,** 10 kilometers (6.2 mi) east of Tofield, is still an official designation, even though bird numbers have dropped considerably from highs of 50,000 birds at any given time in the late 1990s. Many of the 250 recorded species that once used its unspoiled islands and rich marshes as a stopover have changed their migration patterns to take in other bodies of water. It's still worth a stop in town at the **Beaverhill Lake Nature Centre** (403/662-3191, summer Mon.–Fri. 10 A.M.–6 P.M., Sat. noon–5 P.M., Sun. 1–4 P.M.), an interpretive center with maps of the area and bird checklists.

The **Beaverhill Motel** (403/662-3396) has basic rooms for $55 s or d. Campers gravitate to **Lindbrook Star Gazer Campground** (51123 Range Rd. 200, 780/662-4439, May–Oct., tenting $22, powered sites $25), which has an outdoor swimming pool. To get there from Tofield, head 10 kilometers (6.2 mi) west on Highway 14 then three kilometers (1.9 mi) north on SH 630.

Ryley

If you need an excuse to stop in Ryley, visit **George's Harness & Saddlery** (5020 50th St., 403/663-3611, Mon.–Fri. 8 A.M.–5 P.M., Sat. 8 A.M.–4 P.M., free), a working museum that produces saddles, chuckwagon harnesses, and other equine accessories. Most artifacts are made with antique tools and stitching machines. The goings-on in the large workshop are visible from the shop, but if the staff aren't busy filling orders, they'll happily show you around.

Viking Rib Stones

Southeast of Viking in a farmer's field are the two "rib stones," carved with a design resembling bison ribs that have been dated at 1,000 years old. The stones held special significance for generations of Plains Indians, whose lives revolved around the movement of bison herds. They believed that by conducting certain ceremonial rites and by leaving gifts of beads or tobacco around the stones, their luck in hunting would improve. They then gave thanks by leaving more gifts after a successful hunt. The site is not well marked. Fourteen kilometers (8.7 mi) east of Viking on Highway 14 is a historical marker. A little farther east is a gravel road to the south; follow this road two kilometers (1.2 mi) to Highway 615, turn east (left), then take the first gravel road to the south (right) and follow it for 2.5 kilometers (1.5 mi) to a low knoll surrounded by fields. A provincial historic cairn marks the site.

Wainwright

The last town along Highway 14 before Saskatchewan, Wainwright is best known for the military's 400-square-kilometer (154 square mi) **CFB/ASU Wainwright,** a training facility used mostly by reservists that includes four villages used to simulate battle scenarios. It is on what once was Buffalo National Park, the site of probably the most unusual chain of events ever to take place in a Canadian national park. Originally created in 1908 to protect 3,000 plains bison, **Buffalo National Park** was also home to elk, moose, and deer. Experiments within the park cross-bred bison with cattle, trying to create a more resilient farm stock. Meanwhile, bison parts were sold for pemmican. All that may seem odd enough to begin with, but then a

© ANDREW HEMPSTEAD

rib stones near Viking

Hollywood film crew paid officials to stampede a herd of bison and slaughter part of the herd for a movie scene. Shortly afterward, the bison were struck by tuberculosis and were secretly shot, along with every ungulate in the park. The only reminder of this sad and sorry story is a small herd of bison, which can be viewed in **Bud Cotton Buffalo Paddock** beside the base's main gate (turn left at the guarded entrance, then right down the fence line for best viewing opportunities). The base is two kilometers (1.2 mi) south of town along 1st Street.

Wainwright Museum (403/842-3115, daily 9 A.M.–5 P.M.) is a restored Canadian National Railway station at the end of Main Street, with displays on the railway and the ill-fated national park. Further along the line is **Wainwright Rail Park** (780/842-3138, June–Aug. daily 10 A.M.–4 P.M., donation), the re-creation of a working railyard, complete with a distinctive snowplow railcar.

A local restaurant, the **(Honey Pot Eatery & Pub** (825 2nd Ave., 780/842-4094, Mon.–Sat. 11 A.M.–11 P.M., Sun. 11 A.M.–2 P.M.), is worthy of a mention for the fact that it has been

serving up healthy food for much longer than it has been trendy. It's been open since 1979, serving hungry locals and travelers alike dishes as varied as grilled Arctic char and elk smothered in Saskatoon berries, both a reasonable $18.

Dillberry Lake Provincial Park

This park is on the Alberta/Saskatchewan border, 50 kilometers (31 mi) southeast of Wainwright in the transition zone between aspen parkland and prairie. Of the many lakes within the park, Dillberry is the largest. It's surrounded by sandy beaches and low sand dunes (the biggest dunes are at the southeastern end of the lake), and its clear spring-fed waters are good for swimming. The aspen that do grow around the lake are somewhat stunted, a result of having adapted to the windy environment of the prairie. The diverse habitat creates excellent bird-watching opportunities—140 species have been recorded. The park's 200-site campground (780/858-3824, May–Sept., unserviced sites $20, powered sites $23) is behind the park's finest beach and has showers, kitchen shelters, and firewood.

EDMONTON

Edmonton, Alberta's capital, sits in the center of the province, surrounded by the vast natural resources that have made the city unabashedly wealthy. It's a vibrant cultural center and a gateway to the north, but its reputation as a boomtown may be its defining characteristic. Boomtowns are a phenomenon unique to the West—cities that have risen from the surrounding wilderness, oblivious to hardship, pushed forward by dreams of the incredible wealth to be made overnight by pulling riches from the earth. Most boomtowns disappear as quickly as they rise, but not Edmonton. The proud city saw not one but three major booms in the 20th century and has grown into one of the world's largest northerly cities. Its population has mushroomed to over 700,000 (930,000 if the surrounding area is included), making it the sixth-largest city in Canada. Although Calgary is the administrative and business center of the province's billion-dollar petroleum industry, Edmonton is the technological, service, and supply center.

The **North Saskatchewan River Valley** winding through the city has been largely preserved as a 27-kilometer (17-mi) greenbelt—the largest urban park system in Canada. Rather than the hodgepodge of slums and streets you might expect in a boomtown, the modern city of Edmonton has been extremely well designed and well built, with an eye toward the future. The downtown area sits on a spectacular bluff overlooking the river-valley park system. Silhouetted against the deep-blue sky, a cluster of modern glass-and-steel highrises makes a

HIGHLIGHTS

◖ **Muttart Conservatory:** Four glass pyramids make up this interesting attraction across from downtown. It's especially fun to visit in winter, to feel the humidity of the jungle pyramid while snow covers the outside grounds (page 351).

◖ **Fort Edmonton Park:** Immerse yourself in the past at this sprawling riverside attraction, where costumed interpreters add to the historic atmosphere (page 352).

◖ **Old Strathcona:** Edmonton's best-preserved historical district centers on Whyte Avenue, a continuous strip of trendy boutiques, funky cafés, and interesting bookstores (page 354).

◖ **Royal Alberta Museum:** Exhibits in one of Canada's premier museums cover Alberta's one billion years of natural and human history (page 354).

◖ **West Edmonton Mall:** Simply put, there is no place like it in Canada – the world's largest shopping and indoor amusement complex truly does have something for everyone (page 357).

◖ **River Valley Park System:** Escape from the mall and other indoor attractions by spending time within a system of interconnecting parks along the North Saskatchewan River (page 363).

LOOK FOR ◖ TO FIND RECOMMENDED SIGHTS, ACTIVITIES, DINING, AND LODGING.

dynamic contrast to the historic granite Alberta Legislature Building and the lush valley floor below.

Edmonton is home to the University of Alberta, and it's hosted events such as the 1978 Commonwealth Games, 1983 World University Games, 1996 World Figure Skating Championships, and the 2001 World Championships in Athletics. So it comes as no surprise that Edmonton has some of Canada's best cultural facilities. Each week during summer, a festival of some sort takes place within the city. But the city's biggest attrac-tion is the ultimate shopping experience of **West Edmonton Mall,** the world's largest shopping and amusement complex.

ORIENTATION

Highway 2 from Calgary enters Edmonton from the south and divides just north of Gateway Park Tourist Information Centre. At that point, it becomes known as **Gateway Boulevard** (also called **103rd Street**). Southbound, it's **Calgary Trail (104th Street).** From the south, you can get to West Edmonton Mall and Highway 16 West without going through

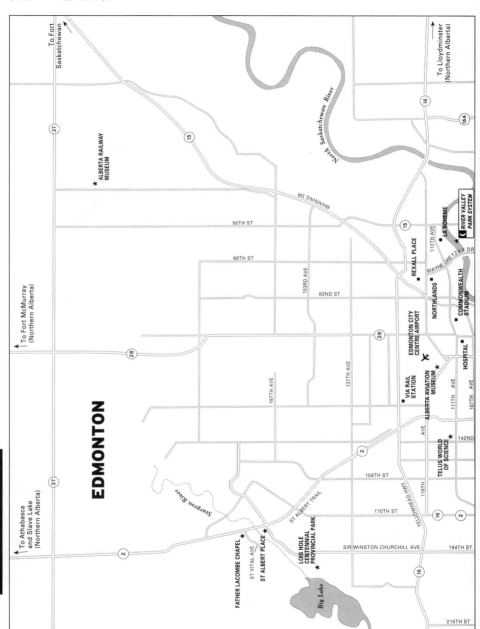

EDMONTON

To Fort Saskatchewan

To Lloydminster (Northern Alberta)

To Fort McMurray (Northern Alberta)

To Athabasca and Slave Lake (Northern Alberta)

North Saskatchewan River

Sturgeon River

MANNING DR

WAYNE GRETZKY DR

ST ALBERT TRAIL

YELLOWHEAD HWY

SIR WINSTON CHURCHILL AVE

★ ALBERTA RAILWAY MUSEUM

★ FATHER LACOMBE CHAPEL

★ ST ALBERT PLACE

■ REXALL PLACE

■ NORTHLANDS

■ LA BOHEME

■ COMMONWEALTH STADIUM

■ HOSPITAL

■ VIA RAIL STATION

★ ALBERTA AVIATION MUSEUM

EDMONTON CITY CENTRE AIRPORT

■ TELUS WORLD OF SCIENCE

RIVER VALLEY PARK SYSTEM

LOIS HOLE CENTENNIAL PROVINCIAL PARK

Big Lake

50TH ST
66TH ST
153RD AVE
82ND ST
137TH AVE
167TH AVE
112TH AVE
111TH AVE
107TH AVE
142ND
118TH
156TH ST
170TH ST
184TH ST
215TH ST
ST VITAL AVE

37
15
16
16A
15
28
28
2
2
16
2
16

EDMONTON

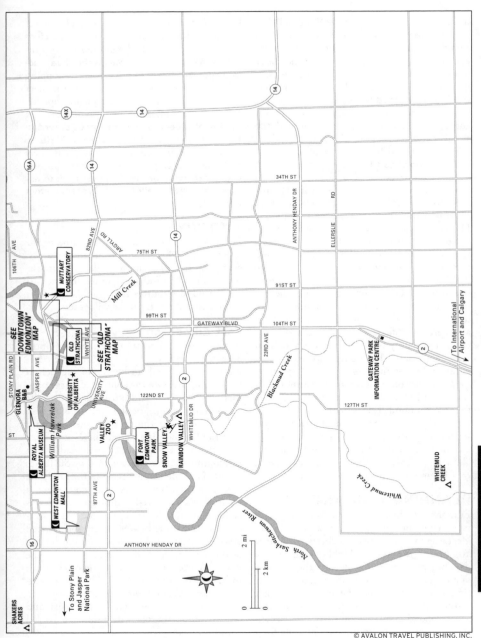

SHAKERS
ACRES

To Stony Plain
and Jasper
National Park

ANTHONY HENDAY DR

87TH AVE

WEST EDMONTON
MALL

ROYAL
ALBERTA MUSEUM

GLENORA
B&B

William Hawrelak
Park

VALLEY
ZOO

FORT
EDMONTON
PARK

SNOW VALLEY

RAINBOW VALLEY

UNIVERSITY
OF ALBERTA

UNIVERSITY AVE

122ND ST

JASPER AVE

STONY PLAIN RD

106TH AVE

MUTTART
CONSERVATORY

SEE
"DOWNTOWN
EDMONTON"
MAP

OLD
STRATHCONA

WHYTE AVE

SEE "OLD
STRATHCONA"
MAP

ARGYLL RD

82ND AVE

Mill Creek

75TH ST

99TH ST

GATEWAY BLVD

104TH ST

91ST ST

23RD AVE

WHITEMUD DR

Blackmud Creek

GATEWAY PARK
INFORMATION CENTRE

127TH ST

2

To International
Airport and Calgary

WHITEMUD
CREEK

Whitemud Creek

North Saskatchewan River

34TH ST

ANTHONY HENDAY DR

ELLERSLIE RD

14

14X

14

16A

14

16

2 mi

2 km

0

0

EDMONTON

downtown, by taking **Anthony Henday Drive,** which crosses the North Saskatchewan River southwest of downtown. You can also head east along this ring road to access the northeast portion of the city. From the Anthony Henday intersection, Gateway Boulevard continues north to **Whitemud Drive,** an inner ring road providing access to Fort Edmonton Park, the zoo, and the mall, and then passes through **Old Strathcona,** crossing the North Saskatchewan River directly south of downtown.

The **Yellowhead Highway** passes through the city east to west, north of downtown. To get downtown from the east, take 97th Street. From downtown, Jasper Avenue changes to Stony Plain Road as it heads west, eventually joining Highway 16 at the city's western limits.

Since the early 1900s, Edmonton streets have been numbered. Avenues run east to west, numbered from 1st Avenue in the south to 259th Avenue in the north. Streets run north to south, numbered from 1st Street in the east to 231st Street in the west. Even-numbered addresses are on the north sides of the avenues and west sides of the streets. The center of the city is crossed by both 101st Street and 101st Avenue, the latter having retained its original name of **Jasper Avenue.**

When vast outlying areas were annexed by the city in 1982, new additions had to be made to the street-numbering system. First Street was renamed Meridian Street and 1st Avenue was renamed Quadrant Avenue. The entire existing city now lies within the northwest quadrant, allowing for easy numbering of new streets as the city grows to the south and east.

PLANNING YOUR TIME

Edmonton is the perfect place to soak up city-type attractions, which makes a stop here an ideal way to break up your Alberta adventure. You can zip through the highlights in a single day, but that somewhat defeats the purpose of a break from an otherwise outdoorsy vacation. Instead, plan to spend at least one night in the capital, spoiling yourself at an upscale accommodation (the Union Bank Inn if a central location is important, the Varscona for a boutique splurge, or the Fantasyland Hotel if you have kids) and dining at one of the city's many fine restaurants. Regardless of your interests, **West Edmonton Mall** is the one attraction you won't want to miss. Even if shopping malls are not your idea of a vacation, the sheer excess of it all is an unforgettable eye-opener. In order of importance, plan on also visiting the **Royal Alberta Museum, Fort Edmonton Park,** and **Muttart Conservatory.** Visits to these four main attractions should fill a day and a half, leaving time to explore the historic **Old Strathcona** precinct and get back to nature in the **River Valley Park System** on foot or on a bike.

HISTORY

For at least 3,000 years, natives came to the river valley where Edmonton now stands, searching for quartzite to make stone tools. They had no knowledge of, or use for, the vast underground resources that would eventually cause a city to rise from the wilderness.

Fort Edmonton

European fur traders, canoeing along the North Saskatchewan River, found the area where Edmonton now stands to be one of the richest fur-bearing areas on the continent. Large populations of beavers and muskrats lived in the surrounding spruce, poplar, and aspen forest. In 1795, William Tomison, a Scotsman, built a sturdy log building beside the North West Company's Fort Augustus. He named it Fort Edmonton after an estate owned by Sir James Winter Lake, deputy governor of the Hudson's Bay Company. Both forts stood on the site of the present legislature-building grounds. It was an ideal location for trading. Cree and Assiniboine could trade beaver, otter, and marten pelts in safety, without encroaching on the territory of fierce Plains Indians, such as the Blackfoot. Yet the fort was far enough south to be within range of the Blackfoot—peaceable when outside their own territory—who came north to buy muskrat, buffalo meat, and other natural resources, which they later traded with Europeans.

After 100 years, the fur trade ended abruptly. Many of the posts throughout the West were abandoned, but Edmonton continued to be an important stop on the route north. Goods were taken overland from Edmonton to Athabasca Landing, where they were transferred to barges or steamers and taken north on the Athabasca River. Around this time, there was an increased demand for grains, and improving technology made agriculture more viable. This opportunity attracted settlers, who arrived through the 1880s to farm the surrounding land. Edmonton suffered a setback when the Canadian Pacific Railway (CPR) chose a southerly route through Calgary for the TransContinental Railway. A branch built by the Calgary and Edmonton Railway Company arrived in 1891, but it ended on the south side of the North Saskatchewan River, at Strathcona.

The Klondike Gold Rush

The most common images of the Klondike Gold Rush in the Yukon are of miners climbing the Chilkoot or White Pass Trails in a desperate attempt to reach Dawson City. Often, for financial reasons, various other routes were promoted as being superior. The merchants of Edmonton led a patriot cry to try the "All-Canadian Route," which would allow prospectors to buy their supplies in a Canadian city rather than in Seattle. The proposed route followed the Athabasca Landing Trail north to Athabasca, continued by boat down the Athabasca, Slave, and Mackenzie Rivers to just south of the Mackenzie Delta, and ended with a short overland trip to the goldfields. The route was impractical and very difficult. Approximately 1,600 people were persuaded to attempt the route. Of these, 50 died, many turned back, and only 700 reached the Yukon. None reached the goldfields before 1899, when the main rush was over, and few, if any, found gold. This slim connection to the gold rush is now celebrated in the annual **Edmonton's Klondike Days.**

Selecting the Capital

The provinces of Alberta and Saskatchewan were both inaugurated on September 1, 1905. Because Regina had been the capital of the Northwest Territories, it was only natural that

Government House

it continue as the capital of Saskatchewan. The decision about Alberta's capital did not come as easily, however. The Alberta Act made Edmonton the temporary capital, but it had plenty of competition. Other contenders were Athabasca Landing, Banff, Calgary, Cochrane, Lacombe, Red Deer, Vegreville, and Wetaskiwin. Each town thought it had a rightful claim: Banff because it could be fortified if war ever broke out, Vegreville for the clean air and a climate free of chinook winds. But the strongest claims were from the citizens of Calgary, who believed their city to be the financial and transportation center of the province. Heated debates on the subject took place in the Canadian capital of Ottawa and among rival newspaper editors, but Edmonton has remained the capital to this day. In 1912, Edmonton merged with Strathcona, giving the city a total population of 55,000. For the next 35 years, the city grew and declined according to the fortunes of agriculture.

Oil and a Growing City

Fur was Edmonton's first industry and coal was its second. Commercial coal-mining operations began as early as 1880, with mining concentrated in three areas of the city. The last of more than 150 operations closed in 1970, and much of the coal seam remains unmined below the downtown area. But Edmonton's future lay not in coal, but oil. Since the discovery of "black gold" in 1947 at nearby Leduc, Edmonton has been one of Canada's fastest-growing cities. The building of pipelines and refineries created many jobs, and the city became the center of western Canada's petrochemical industry. As demand continued to rise, hundreds of wildcat wells were drilled around Edmonton. Farmers' fields were filled with derricks, valves, and oil tanks, and by 1956, more than 3,000 producing wells were pumping within 100 kilometers (62 mi) of the city.

Edmonton experienced the same postwar boom of most major North American cities, as a major population shift from rural areas to the city began. By 1956, Edmonton's population had grown to 254,800, doubling in size since 1946. A 20-square-kilometer (eight-square-mi) area east of the city was filled with huge oil tanks, refineries, and petrochemical plants. Changes were also taking place within the city as the wealth of the oil boom began to take hold. Restaurants improved and cultural life flourished. The city's businesses were jazzed up, and the expanding business community began moving into the glass-and-steel skyscrapers that form the city skyline today. Various service industries also became important; West Edmonton Mall alone employs 23,500 people.

2000 and Beyond

Although the original boom is over, oil is still a major part of the city's economy. Planned developments in the surrounding oil patch service area total approximately $40 billion this decade, with Edmonton benefiting directly from spin-off infrastructure. A great deal of this development is associated with the **oil sands** of Fort McMurray, including four "upgraders" costing $2.5 billion each that are currently under construction within city limits. In addition to oil-related companies, Edmonton's low cost of living is attractive to many companies. Economic Development Edmonton (www.ede.org) is a city-sponsored department that promotes the city to the world. One of its innovations is the sprawling **Edmonton Research Park,** on the southern outskirts, which has become a focal point for up-and-coming information technology and science companies. Nanotechnology is also big news in Edmonton, with the University of Alberta leading the way in research of material many thousands of times smaller than a human hair.

Sights

DOWNTOWN

Looking at Edmonton's dynamic skyline, it's hard to believe that not much more than 100 years ago the main drag was lined with dingy saloons and rowdy dance halls. Since those heady days, the city has seen many ups and downs—its present look is a legacy of the 1970s oil boom. The well-planned city center, on the northern bank of the North Saskatchewan River, is a conglomeration of skyscrapers that seemingly rose overnight when oil money flooded the city. The downtown core is fairly compact and is within walking distance of many hotels and the bus depot. **Jasper Avenue** (101st Ave.) is downtown's main thoroughfare, lined with restaurants and shops. At the east end of Jasper Avenue is the **Shaw Conference Centre,** a glass-and-steel building that appears to cling to the wall of the river valley. One block north is the large and popular **City Centre** shopping complex. On 102nd Street is the 36-story ManuLife Place, Edmonton's tallest building. A few blocks east is the **Arts District,** comprising the provincial government buildings, including the futuristic city hall, and an array of performing arts centers. (The streets immediately east of 97th Street are a skid row with sleazy bars and suspicious-looking characters—not the place to linger at night.)

Throughout all of the development, several historic buildings managed to survive. Many can be seen along **Heritage Trail,** a route taken by early fur traders that linked the old town to Fort Edmonton. Today the trail begins at the Shaw Conference Centre, at the corner of Jasper Avenue and 97th Street, and ends at the legislature grounds. The route is easy to follow—the sidewalk is paved with red bricks and lined with period benches, replica lampposts, and old-fashioned street signs.

Arts District

This complex, in the heart of downtown, occupies six square blocks and is one of the city's showcases. Within its limits are the Stanley A.

Milner Library, the Edmonton Art Gallery, Sir Winston Churchill Square, City Hall, the Law Courts Building, the Shaw Conference Centre, and the performing arts community's pride and joy, the magnificent Citadel Theatre and adjacent Winspear Centre.

The **Edmonton Art Gallery** (northeast of Sir Winston Churchill Square on 99th St., 780/427-6223, Mon.–Wed. and Fri. 10:30 A.M.–5 P.M., Thurs. 10:30 A.M.–8 P.M., and Sat.–Sun. 11 A.M.–5 P.M., adult $5, senior $3, child $2) houses an extensive collection of 4,000 modern Canadian paintings as well as historical and contemporary art in all media. Various traveling exhibitions are presented throughout the year. The exhibit *From Sea to Sea: The Development of Canadian Art* catalogs the entire history of the country's art through well-designed displays.

City Hall, built on the site of the old city hall, is designed to be the centerpiece of civic buildings within the Arts District. The main public areas are located on the main floor.

THE PEDWAY SYSTEM

The pedway system is unique and necessary this far north. It's a complex system of enclosed walkways linking office buildings, hotels, plazas, the civic center, and public transportation stops. Using the pedways, you can get virtually anywhere downtown without ever having to step outside into the elements. At first it all seems a bit complicated, but if you're armed with a map, the system soon becomes second nature. Pedways are below, above, or at street level, and the excellent signage makes it easy to find your way. The walkways are spotlessly clean, well lit, and relatively safe, although you wouldn't want to loiter around the Central Light Rail Transit (LRT) Station at night.

EDMONTON

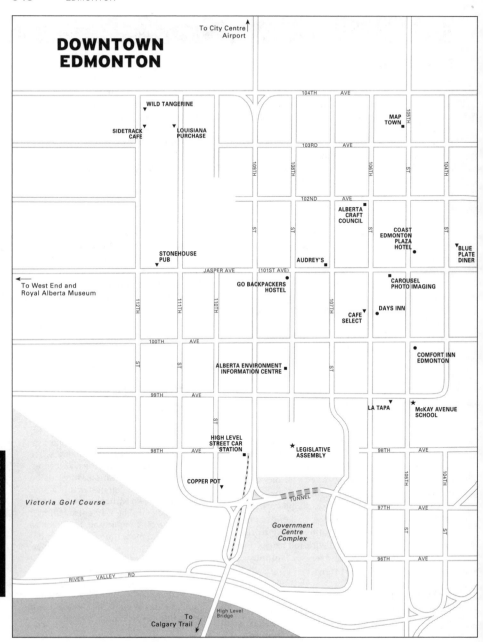

DOWNTOWN EDMONTON

To City Centre Airport

104TH AVE

WILD TANGERINE

SIDETRACK CAFE

LOUISIANA PURCHASE

103RD AVE

109TH ST

108TH ST

106TH ST

ST

104TH ST

MAP TOWN

105TH ST

102ND AVE

ALBERTA CRAFT COUNCIL

ST

ST

COAST EDMONTON PLAZA HOTEL

ST

BLUE PLATE DINER

STONEHOUSE PUB

AUDREY'S

JASPER AVE (101ST AVE)

To West End and Royal Alberta Museum

GO BACKPACKERS HOSTEL

CAROUSEL PHOTO IMAGING

112TH

111TH

110TH

107TH

CAFE SELECT

DAYS INN

100TH AVE

ST

ST

ST

COMFORT INN EDMONTON

ALBERTA ENVIRONMENT INFORMATION CENTRE

99TH AVE

ST

LA TAPA

McKAY AVENUE SCHOOL

HIGH LEVEL STREET CAR STATION

98TH AVE

LEGISLATIVE ASSEMBLY

98TH AVE

105TH ST

104TH ST

COPPER POT

Victoria Golf Course

TUNNEL

97TH AVE

Government Centre Complex

96TH AVE

ST

ST

RIVER VALLEY RD

To Calgary Trail

High Level Bridge

EDMONTON

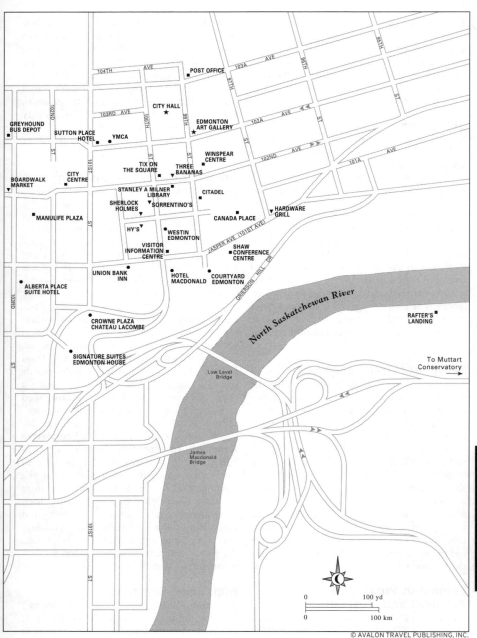

GREYHOUND
BUS DEPOT

SUTTON PLACE
HOTEL

YMCA

POST OFFICE

CITY HALL

EDMONTON
ART GALLERY

104TH   AVE

103RD   AVE

103A   AVE

102A   AVE

102ND   AVE

101A   AVE

BOARDWALK
MARKET

CITY
CENTRE

TIX ON
THE SQUARE

THREE
BANANAS

WINSPEAR
CENTRE

MANULIFE PLAZA

STANLEY A MILNER
LIBRARY

SHERLOCK
HOLMES

SORRENTINO'S

CITADEL

CANADA PLACE

HARDWARE
GRILL

HY'S

WESTIN
EDMONTON

VISITOR
INFORMATION
CENTRE

JASPER AVE (101ST AVE)

SHAW
CONFERENCE
CENTRE

UNION BANK
INN

HOTEL
MACDONALD

COURTYARD
EDMONTON

GRIERSON   HILL   DR.

ALBERTA PLACE
SUITE HOTEL

CROWNE PLAZA
CHATEAU LACOMBE

SIGNATURE SUITES
EDMONTON HOUSE

North Saskatchewan River

RAFTER'S
LANDING

To Muttart
Conservatory

Low Level
Bridge

James
Macdonald
Bridge

0   100 yd

0   100 km

EDMONTON

Tours of City Hall leave from the main lobby Monday, Wednesday, and Friday at 10:30 A.M. and 2:30 P.M. Immediately behind this area is the City Room, the building's main focal point. Its ceiling is a glass pyramid that rises eight stories. To the east are displays cataloging the city's short but colorful history.

Chinatown

An elaborate gateway designed by a master architect from China welcomes visitors to where Edmonton's small Chinatown *used* to be. The gate spans 23 meters (75 ft) across 102nd Avenue (also known as Harbin Rd.) at 97th Street. Eight steel columns painted the traditional Chinese color of red support it. Stretched across the center of the arch's roof is a row of ornamental tiles featuring two dragons, the symbol of power in China. The 11,000 tiles used in the gate were each handcrafted and glazed in China. In the last few years, Chinatown has moved up the road a few blocks. The archway now leads into an area of cheap boardinghouses and deserted parking lots but forms a colorful break from the pawnshops of 97th Street.

Fairmont Hotel Macdonald

This hotel (10065 100th St.) overlooking the river valley has long been regarded as Edmonton's premier luxury accommodation. For many years, it was the social center of the city. It was built in 1915 by the Grand Trunk Railway in the same château style used for many of the Canadian Pacific hotels across the country. After it closed in 1983, plans to tear it down were aborted; $28 million was spent on refurbishing it and the hotel reopened, as grand and elegant as ever. The main lobby has been totally restored and opens to the Confederation Lounge and the Library, a bar overlooking the river that has the feel of an Edwardian gentlemen's club. Ask at the reception desk for a map of the hotel.

Edmonton Public Schools Archives and Museum

Built in 1904, **McKay Avenue School** (on the Heritage Trail, 10425 99th Ave., 780/422-1970,

free) is Edmonton's oldest standing brick schoolhouse. It was the venue of the first two sittings of the provincial legislature in 1906. The building contains reconstructions of early classrooms and of the historic legislature assembly. Edmonton's first schoolhouse, a single-story wooden building dating to 1881, lies in back of the grounds, looking much as it would have to 19th-century students. It's open the same hours as early students attended, Tuesday–Friday 12:30–4 P.M., as well as Sunday 1–4 P.M.

Alberta Legislature Building

Home of the provincial government, this elegant Edwardian building overlooking the North Saskatchewan River Valley is surrounded by 24 hectares (59 acres) of formal gardens and manicured lawns. It officially opened in 1912 and, for many years, stood beside the original Fort Edmonton. Today it is one of western Canada's best examples of architecture from that era. Its 16-story vaulted dome is one of Edmonton's most recognizable landmarks. Many materials used in its construction were imported: sandstone from near Calgary; granite from Vancouver; marble from Quebec, Pennsylvania, and Italy; and mahogany from Belize. The interior features a wide marble staircase that leads from the spacious rotunda in the lobby to the chamber, and is surrounded by stained-glass windows and bronze statues.

Immediately north of the legislature building, beyond the fountains, is the **Legislative Assembly Interpretive Centre** (780/427-7362), which recounts the development of Alberta's political history and serves as the starting point for free tours of the legislature building. Between mid-May and October, tours depart on the hour in the morning and every 30 minutes in the afternoon weekdays 8:30 A.M.–5 P.M. and weekends 9 A.M.–5 P.M., the rest of the year hourly weekdays 9 A.M.–5 P.M. and weekends noon–5 P.M.

High Level Bridge

This bridge crosses the North Saskatchewan River at the bottom end of 109th Street. It was built in 1913, linking the new capital to

Strathcona. The bridge is 775 meters (2,500 ft) long and 53 meters (180 ft) above the river. It has been used as a tramway, a railway, a sidewalk, and a roadway. The rail line was in use until 1951, but in 2000 a local historical society began running a scheduled streetcar over the bridge. It runs from adjacent to the Grandin Light Rail Transit (LRT) Station across the bridge to as far south as Old Strathcona. The service operates 15 and 45 minutes past the hour Sunday–Friday 11 A.M.–4 P.M., Saturday 9 A.M.–4 P.M., and costs just $3 one-way.

In 1980, the **Great Divide Waterfall** was added to the bridge. When turned on, a curtain of water higher than Niagara Falls cascades down along the entire length of the bridge. It usually operates during special events such as Capital Ex, Canada Day, and on Sundays of long summer weekends.

Telephone Historical Centre

This museum (10440 108th Ave., 780/433-1010, Tues.–Fri. 10 A.M.–4 P.M., $3) catalogs the history of telecommunications in Edmonton from the introduction of telephones in 1885 to the present. It has many hands-on exhibits, including an early switchboard where you can make your own connections. Current technology is also displayed with exhibits of digital switching, fiberoptic cables, a talking robot, and cellular phones. A multimedia presentation in the small Alex Taylor Theatre traces telecommunications technology from its earliest days.

Ukrainian Sights

The **Ukrainian Canadian Archives and Museum** (9543 110th Ave., 780/424-7580, Tues.–Fri. 10 A.M.–5 P.M., Sat. noon–5 P.M., donation) exhibits artifacts from the lives of Ukrainian pioneers in Canada and has one of the largest archives in the country. Edmonton has 80,000 Canadians of Ukrainian descent, and as a result the city is home to a number of Ukrainian churches. One of the most impressive is **St. Josephat's Ukrainian Catholic Cathedral** (97th St. at 108th Ave.), which is well worth a look for its elaborate decorations and pastel wall paintings. In the same vicinity

© ANDREW HEMPSTEAD

St. Josephat's Ukrainian Catholic Cathedral

is the **Ukrainian Bookstore** (10215 97th St., 780/422-4255, www.ukrainianbookstore.com, closed Sun.).

SOUTHSIDE
◖ Muttart Conservatory

Nestled in the valley on the south side of the North Saskatchewan River are four large pyramid-shaped greenhouses that make up the Muttart Conservatory (9626 96A St. off 98th Ave., 780/496-8755, Mon.–Fri. 9 A.M.–5:30 P.M., Sat.–Sun. 11 A.M.–5:30 P.M., adult $7.75, senior $6.75, child $4.25). Three of the greenhouses contain the flora of specific climates. In the arid pyramid are cacti and other hardy plants found in desertlike conditions. The tropical pyramid holds a humid jungle, one of North America's largest orchid collections, and colorful and raucous exotic birds, who live among the palms. The temperate pyramid features plant species from four continents, none of which would grow naturally in Edmonton's harsh environment. The contents of the fourth pyramid change with the

EDMONTON

season but always feature colorful floral displays such as red, white, and yellow poinsettias at Christmastime. Take bus #85 or 86 south along 100th Street to get to the conservatory.

Edmonton Queen

The *Edmonton Queen* is a 52-meter (170-ft) paddlewheeler that cruises along the North Saskatchewan River from Rafter's Landing, near Muttart Conservatory. One-hour cruises depart late May to mid-September Thursday–Sunday at noon and 3 P.M. ($18, lunch extra), evening cruises depart at 7:30 P.M. ($48 including dinner), and the Sunday Brunch cruise departs 1 P.M. ($42). To get to Rafter's Landing, take 98th Avenue east along the south side of the river; 780/424-2628.

John Walter Museum

This historic site located near the Kinsmen Sports Centre consists of three houses—dating from 1875, 1884, and 1900—that were built by John Walter for his family. The first house was a stopping point for travelers using Walter's ferry service to cross the river. Walter also opened a carriage works, a lumber mill, and a coal mine, and at one time even built a steamship. For a time, the area was known as Walterdale, but with the completion of the High Level Bridge, the need for a ferry service ended. Today, all that remains are Walter's houses. Each house holds exhibits corresponding to the period of its construction and depicts the growth of Edmonton and the importance of the North Saskatchewan River. The buildings are open only February–mid-December Sunday 1–4 P.M., with bread-making demonstrations, old-fashioned games, and some other related activity scheduled to correspond with these hours. Admission is free and the grounds are pleasant to walk through at any time. The museum is at 10627 93rd Avenue. From downtown, take 101st Street south down Bellamy Hill and cross the river at the Walterdale Bridge. On foot, allow 30–60 minutes. By bus, jump aboard #9 west along 102nd Avenue or #52 from Old Strathcona. For further information, call 780/496-4852.

Rutherford House

Designated as a Provincial Historic Site, this elegant Edwardian mansion (11153 Saskatchewan Dr., 780/427-3995, summer daily 9 A.M.–5 P.M., the rest of the year Tues.–Sun. noon–5 P.M., adult $4, senior $3, child $2) was built in 1911 for Alexander C. Rutherford, Alberta's first premier. The Rutherford family lived in this house for 30 years. It was then used as a University of Alberta fraternity house before being restored to its original condition and furnished with antiques from the Edwardian period. You can wander throughout the two-story house and ask questions of the costumed interpreters. The covered sun porch operates as a tearoom in summer (Tues.–Sun. 11:30 A.M.–4 P.M.), serving lunch ($8–10) and afternoon tea ($5–10) using historical recipes from 1915 or earlier. It's on the University of Alberta campus. The easiest way to get there by public transport is on the LRT from downtown.

◖ Fort Edmonton Park

An authentic reconstruction of the early trading post from which Edmonton grew is only a small part of this exciting attraction (off Whitemud Dr. near Fox Dr., 780/496-8787, May–June Mon.–Fri. 10 A.M.–4 P.M. and Sat.–Sun. 10 A.M.–6 P.M., July–Aug. daily 10 A.M.–6 P.M., Sept. 10 A.M.–4 P.M., adult $10, senior $7.50, child $5), Canada's largest historic park. From the entrance, a 1919 steam locomotive takes you through the park to the Hudson's Bay Company Fort, which has been built much as the original fort would have looked in 1846—right down to the methods of carpentry used in its construction. Step outside the fort and walk forward in time—to 1885 Street, recreating downtown Edmonton between 1871 and 1891, when the West was opened up to settlers. The street is lined with wooden-facaded shops such as a bakery, a boat builder, a blacksmith, and a trading post. As you continue down the road, you round a corner and are on 1905 Street, in the time period 1892–1914, when the railway had arrived and Edmonton was proclaimed provincial capital. **Reed's Tea**

Step back in time at Fort Edmonton Park.

Room, near the far end of the street, serves English teas and scones noon–4 P.M. in a traditional atmosphere. By this time, you're nearly on 1920 Street, representing the years 1914–1929—a period of social changes when the business community was developing and the city's industrial base was expanding. Stop by Bill's Confectionary (noon– 4 P.M.) for a soda or sundae, hitch a lift aboard the streetcar, or plan an overnight stay at the Hotel Selkirk (see *Accommodations* later in this chapter) to round out the roaring '20s experience.

What really makes this park come alive are the costumed interpreters, immersed in life as it was in Edmonton of days gone by—preparing cakes and pastries for sale at the bakery, tending to carefully re-created vegetable plots, making butter beside the farmhouse, giving piano lessons to interested passersby, or just getting together for a friendly game of horseshoes. In addition, a constant variety of scheduled activities is offered; a weekly program is available from the main entrance or by calling 780/496-8787.

John Janzen Nature Centre

Beside Fort Edmonton Park (use the same parking lot) is John Janzen Nature Centre (780/496-2939, year-round Mon.–Fri. 9 A.M.– 4 P.M., longer hours and weekends in summer, adult $1.80, senior and child $1.55), which has hands-on exhibits, displays of local flora and fauna—both dead and alive—and a four-kilometer (2.5-mi) self-guided interpretive trail that leads through the river valley and loops back to the center. In one room, various natural environments have been simulated with displays of frogs, fish, snakes, salamanders, and a working beehive made from glass. Throughout the year, special events are held, films are shown, and Sunday nature walks are conducted.

Valley Zoo

Across the river from Fort Edmonton Park is the city zoo (end of Buena Vista Rd., off 142nd St., 780/496-6911, May–June daily 9:30 A.M.– 6 P.M., July–Aug. 9:30 A.M.–8 P.M., the rest of the year 9:30 A.M.–4 P.M., adult $8, senior $5.75, child $4), which holds approximately

EDMONTON

350 animals, representing all seven continents. It is designed mainly for kids, with a petting zoo, camel and pony rides, paddleboats, a miniature train, and cut-out storybook characters. To get there by bus, take #12 west along 102nd Avenue to Buena Vista Road and walk 1.6 kilometers (one mi) down to the park. On summer Sundays, bus #200 leaves on the hour from the University Transit Centre and goes right to the zoo.

◖ OLD STRATHCONA

When the Calgary and Edmonton Railway Company completed a rail line between the province's two largest cities, it decided to end it south of the North Saskatchewan River and establish a townsite there, rather than build a bridge and end the line in Edmonton. The town was named Strathcona, and it grew to a population of 7,500 before merging with Edmonton in 1912. Because of an early fire-prevention bylaw, buildings were built of brick. Today many still remain, looking much as they did at the turn of the 20th century. Old Strathcona is Edmonton's best-preserved historical district. In addition to the old brick buildings, the area has been refurbished with brick sidewalks and replica lampposts. The commercial core of Old Strathcona is centered along Whyte (82nd) Avenue west of the rail line. More than 75 residential houses built before 1926 are scattered to the north and west of Whyte Avenue.

Across from the rail line is the **Strathcona Hotel** (corner of 103rd St. and Whyte Ave.), one of the few wood-framed buildings surviving from the pre-1900 period. Before Strathcona had permanent churches, congregations worshiped in the hotel, and during Prohibition it was used as a ladies' college. The two blocks east of the hotel are lined with cafés and restaurants, used bookstores, and many interesting shops. One of these, and one of Old Strathcona's oldest businesses, is the **Hub Cigar and Newsstand** (10345 82nd Ave., 780/439-0144), which stocks more than 10,000 different newspapers and magazines from around the world. In a converted bus garage one block north is the **Old Strathcona Farmer's Market** (on

83rd Ave., year-round Sat. 8 A.M.–3 P.M.), with plenty of fresh produce, crafts, and homemade goodies for sale. Within walking distance of Whyte Avenue are several small museums.

The best way to get to Old Strathcona from downtown is aboard the **High Level Street Car** (780/437-7721), which runs from the west side of the Alberta Legislature Building to the 104th Street and 85th Avenue intersection in Old Strathcona. It departs downtown 15 and 45 minutes past the hour summer only, Sunday–Friday 11 A.M.–4 P.M., Saturday 9 A.M.–4 P.M., $3 one-way. From the station, wander south to bustling Whyte Avenue.

Many of the historic buildings have plaques at street level, but the brochures *A Walk Through Old Strathcona* and *Historical Walking and Driving Tour: Strathcona* make a stroll much more interesting. For more information on the district, contact the Old Strathcona Foundation (780/433-5866, www.strathcona.org).

C&E Railway Station Museum

Strathcona's original railway station was located just north of the CPR station. It was later moved farther along the line, then demolished and replaced with a replica that houses a railway museum. The museum (10447 86th Ave., 780/433-9739, summer Tues.–Sat. 10 A.M.–4 P.M., donation) relives the days of steam engines and settlers, when people streamed into the newly opened Canadian West from around the world.

WEST OF DOWNTOWN

From the city center, Jasper Avenue (101st Ave.) goes west through the **West End**—where many residential and commercial buildings date from the boom years of 1912–1914—and continues to **Glenora,** one of the city's oldest and most sought-after neighborhoods. Many streets are lined with elegant two-story mansions from the early 1900s. The neighborhood fountain in Alexander Circle (103rd Ave. and 133rd St.) is the center of the area.

◖ Royal Alberta Museum

The provincial museum (12845 102nd Ave.,

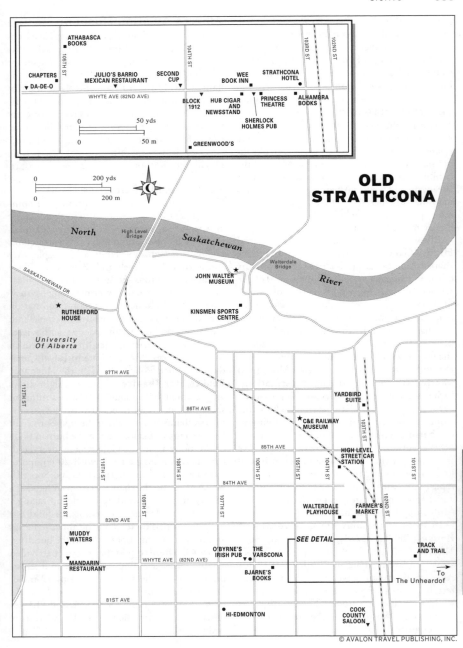

ATHABASCA
BOOKS

106TH ST
104TH ST
103RD ST
102ND ST

CHAPTERS
DA-DE-O

JULIO'S BARRIO
MEXICAN RESTAURANT

SECOND
CUP

WEE
BOOK INN

STRATHCONA
HOTEL

WHYTE AVE (82ND AVE)

BLOCK
1912

HUB CIGAR
AND
NEWSSTAND

PRINCESS
THEATRE

ALHAMBRA
BOOKS

SHERLOCK
HOLMES PUB

GREENWOOD'S

0   50 yds

0   50 m

0   200 yds

0   200 m

**OLD
STRATHCONA**

North

High Level
Bridge

Saskatchewan

Walterdale
Bridge

JOHN WALTER
MUSEUM

River

SASKATCHEWAN DR

RUTHERFORD
HOUSE

KINSMEN SPORTS
CENTRE

*University
Of Alberta*

87TH AVE

112TH ST

86TH AVE

YARDBIRD
SUITE

103TH ST

C&E RAILWAY
MUSEUM

85TH AVE

HIGH LEVEL
STREET CAR
STATION

110TH ST

108TH ST

106TH ST

105TH ST

104TH ST

101ST ST

84TH AVE

111TH ST

109TH ST

107TH ST

WALTERDALE
PLAYHOUSE

FARMER'S
MARKET

102ND ST

83ND AVE

MUDDY
WATERS

SEE DETAIL

TRACK
AND TRAIL

MANDARIN
RESTAURANT

WHYTE AVE   (82ND AVE)

O'BYRNE'S
IRISH PUB

THE
VARSCONA

To
The Unheardof

BJARNE'S
BOOKS

81ST AVE

HI-EDMONTON

COOK
COUNTY
SALOON

EDMONTON

780/453-9100, daily 9 A.M.–5 P.M., adult $10, senior $8, child $5) overlooks the river valley in the historic neighborhood of Glenora. It is one of Canada's largest (18,800 square meters/200,000 square feet) and most popular museums. Exhibits catalog one billion years of natural and human history. The highlight is most definitely the **Wild Alberta Gallery,** where a water setting and the province's four natural regions—mountain, prairie, parkland, and boreal forest—are re-created with incredible accuracy. Lifelike dioramas are only part of the appeal. Much of the exhibit encourages visitor interaction to solve the mystery of what is Alberta's most dangerous mammal, to touch the teeth of a grizzly bear, or soak up the sound of a bull moose calling in the female members of his species.

Elsewhere in the museum, the Natural History Gallery explains the forces that have shaped Alberta's land, describes the dinosaurs of the Cretaceous period and mammals of the ice age (such as the woolly mammoth), and displays a large collection of rocks and gems. Another section, the Syncrude Gallery of Aboriginal Culture, details Alberta's indigenous peoples, from their arrival 11,000 years ago to the way in which their traditions live on today through thousands of artifacts, Aboriginal interpreters, and audiovisual presentations. Other sections tell the story of the province's earliest explorers and the settlers who came from around the world to eke out a living in the harsh environment. The Bug Room, another favorite, displays insects dead and alive from around the world. The museum is well known for hosting traveling exhibits, making repeat visits worthwhile. The museum also has a gift shop and a café. To get there, take bus #100 along Jasper Avenue.

In front of the museum is **Government House** (780/427-2281, summer tours Sun. 11 A.M.–4:30 P.M., free), an impressive three-story sandstone structure built in 1913 for Alberta's lieutenant governor, who would entertain guests in the lavish reception rooms or in the surrounding gardens. The building was later used as a hospital, and then restored to its former glory in the 1970s.

Alberta Aviation Museum

This museum, adjoining Edmonton City Centre Airport (11410 Kingsway Ave., 780/451-1175, daily 10 A.M.–4 P.M., adult $7, senior $5, child $2), dates to World War II, when the hangars held British aircraft involved in training programs. Today the hangars contain 27 restored aircraft, including a favorite of early Canadian bush pilots—the Fairchild 71-C. One of the most recently completed projects was the on-site restoration of a WWII de Havilland Mosquito.

Telus World of Science

Completed in 1984, this multipurpose complex (11211 142nd St., 780/452-9100, daily 10 A.M.–5 P.M., summer until 9 P.M.) in Coronation Park is one of Edmonton's major attractions and most recognizable landmarks. Displays are spread over three levels and six galleries. They include a look into the future of communications; the chance to solve a crime along Mystery Avenue; the Robotics Lab; a ham radio station hooked up to similar stations around the world; a weather display that includes an audiovisual of the deadly tornado that hit Edmonton in the summer of 1987; a tribute to Royal Canadian Mounted Police (RCMP); the **Margaret Zeidler Star Theatre,** where laser light shows are presented daily noon–7 P.M. with a different show each hour; an interactive Eye-lusions exhibit; a chance to learn about the environment in Green's House; exploration of the human body in the Body Fantastic Gallery; Discoveryland, especially for kids; a room with 20 computer terminals linked to the Internet; and Sport II, which gives you the chance to try your hand at a variety of sports, including wheelchair racing.

A day pass (adult $11, senior $9, child $8) includes admission to all of the above galleries and theater presentations. Also in the building, an **IMAX Theatre** presents spectacular video productions—seemingly always of an interesting nature—projected onto a 13-by-19-meter (43-by-62-ft) screen; adult $11, senior $9, child $8 for the theater only; $16, $14, and $12, respectively, for admission to one IMAX feature and the other displays.

© ANDREW HEMPSTEAD

Telus World of Science has something for all ages.

Beside the complex is an **observatory,** which is open to the public daily 1–5 P.M. then 7–10 P.M. (weather permitting) for star-, moon-, and planet-gazing; no charge.

By bus from downtown take #125 west along Jasper Avenue to Westmount Station and hoof it through Coronation Park.

◖ WEST EDMONTON MALL

Feel like a trip to the beach to do some sunbathing and surfing? Would you like to play a round of golf? How about launching from the world's only indoor bungee jump? Do you like eating at Parisian cafés? Does watching a National Hockey League team in training seem like a good way to spend the afternoon? Do the kids like sea lion shows? And at the end of the day, would you like to sink into a hot tub, surrounded by a lush tropical forest? All of these activities are possible under one roof at West Edmonton Mall, the largest shopping and indoor amusement complex in the whole world. Calgary may have the greatest *outdoor* show on earth, but Edmonton has what can surely

be billed as the greatest *indoor* show on earth, a place that is visited by 22 million people annually. Much more than an oversized shopping mall, Edmonton's top tourist attraction is a shop-and-play four-season wonderland, where many visitors check into the 355-room luxury Fantasyland Hotel, stay a weekend, and never set foot outside the mall's 58 entrances.

Shopping is only one part of the mall's universal appeal. Prices are no less than anywhere else in the city, but the experience of having more than 800 stores (including more than 200 womenswear stores, 35 menswear stores, and 55 shoe shops) under one roof is unique.

Aside from the shops, many other major attractions fill the mall. **Galaxyland Amusement Park** is the world's largest indoor amusement park, with 25 rides, including Mindbender—a 14-story, triple-loop roller coaster (the world's largest indoor roller coaster)—and Space Shot, a 13-story, heart-pounding free fall. Off to one side, Galaxy Kids Playpark offers the younger generation the same thrills and spills in a colorful, fun-loving atmosphere. Admission is

EDMONTON

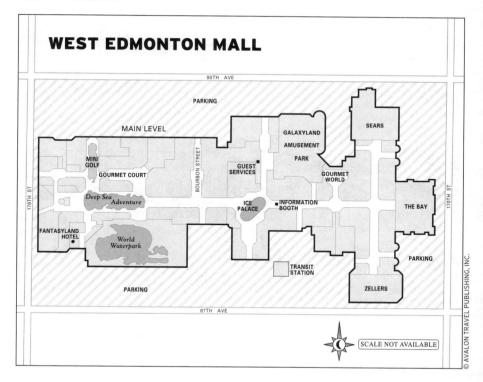

WEST EDMONTON MALL

90TH AVE

PARKING

MAIN LEVEL

GALAXYLAND
AMUSEMENT
PARK

SEARS

MINI
GOLF

GOURMET COURT

BOURBON STREET

GUEST
SERVICES

GOURMET
WORLD

178TH ST

170TH ST

*Deep Sea
Adventure*

FANTASYLAND
HOTEL

ICE
PALACE

INFORMATION
BOOTH

THE BAY

*World
Waterpark*

PARKING

TRANSIT
STATION

PARKING

ZELLERS

87TH AVE

SCALE NOT AVAILABLE

© AVALON TRAVEL PUBLISHING, INC.

EDMONTON

free, but the rides cost money. A Galaxyland day pass, allowing unlimited rides, is adult $29.95, families $79.95, senior or those under four feet $22.95.

In the two-hectare (five-acre) **World Waterpark,** you almost feel as though you're at the beach: the temperature is a balmy 30°C (85°F) and a long sandy beach (with special nonslip sand), tropical palms, colorful cabanas, a beach bar, and waves crashing on the shore all simulate the real thing. The computerized wave pool holds 12.3 million liters (3.2 million gallons) of water and is programmed by computer to eject "sets" of waves at regular intervals. Behind the beach are 22 water slides that rise to a height of 26 meters (85 ft). The World Waterpark also has the world's only indoor bungee jump, **Blue Thunder Bungee** ($79.95 including general waterpark access),

three whirlpools, and a volleyball court. On the second floor of the mall is a water-park viewpoint. Admission to World Waterpark is adult $29.95, families $79.95, senior or those under four feet $22.95.

At the same end of the mall as World Waterpark is the world's largest indoor lake. Here, you can gawk at the area along its entire 122-meter (400-ft) length from either the main or second floor of the mall. The most dominant feature of the lagoon is a full-size replica of Christopher Columbus's flagship, the *Santa Maria*. It was built in False Creek, Vancouver, and shipped across the Rockies to its new indoor home. You can jump aboard a bumper boat ($4 for five minutes); descend into the depths of the **Sea Life Caverns** ($8 per person, family $24) to view sharks, penguins, and a variety of colorful fish; or take a scuba-diving

WEST EDMONTON MALL TRIVIA

WEST EDMONTON MALL IS:

- the world's largest shopping and amusement complex, encompassing 483,000 square meters (5.3 million square ft) – that's equivalent to 115 football fields

WEST EDMONTON MALL HAS:

- over 800 stores
- over 110 eateries
- 58 entrances
- 21 movie screens
- 325,000 light bulbs
- five postal codes
- the world's largest parking lot (parking for 20,000 vehicles)

- the world's largest indoor amusement park
- the world's largest water park, covering two hectares (five acres) and containing 50 million liters (13.2 million gallons) of water
- the world's largest indoor lake (122 m/ 400 ft long)
- the world's only indoor bungee jump

WEST EDMONTON MALL:

- cost over one billion dollars to construct
- employs 23,500 people
- uses the same amount of power as a city of 50,000
- attracts 22 million people a year (over 60,000 per day)

West Edmonton Mall provides a shopping experience like no other.

© ANDREW HEMPSTEAD

EDMONTON

course. Beyond the indoor lake is **Playdium** (780/444-7529, daily 10 A.M.–midnight), opened in 2000 as part of the mall's Phase IV development. This state-of-the-art entertainment center offers more than 150 attractions, from "reality" sports to test your athletic prowess against the professionals to a Speed Zone, which is filled with the latest racing games.

Other major attractions in the mall include **Xorbitor,** a hydraulic capsule that simulates on-screen movements ($8 per ride); **Professor WEM's Adventure Golf** (adult $10, senior and child $7); and, smack in the middle of the mall, the **Ice Palace.** This NHL-size skating rink is the second home of the Edmonton Oilers, who occasionally practice here. It's open to the public year-round; adult $6 per session, senior or child $4, skate rental $4.

Other sights include an aviary with various exotic birds, a Chinese pagoda that was hand-carved by four generations of the same family, replicas of the British crown jewels, bronze statues commissioned especially for the mall, and a couple of aquariums. Three theme streets—**Europa Boulevard, Chinatown,** and the glitzy New Orleans–style **Bourbon Street**—hold some of the mall's 110 restaurants and eateries.

Hours and Other Practicalities

Shopping hours vary seasonally but are generally Monday–Saturday 10 A.M.–9 P.M., Sunday noon–6 P.M. Hours of the various attractions and restaurants vary. Many restaurants stay open later, and the nightclubs stay open to the early hours of the morning.

Mall maps color-code each of four phases to make finding your way around easier (shops and attractions use a phase number as part of their address). Maps are widely available throughout the mall. The two official information centers are both on the main level near the Ice Palace—a booth on the east side and Guest Services north toward Entrance 8. Staff will answer all commonly asked questions while the tech-savvy can download a Mobile Mall Map to their Palm PDA; both are open regular shopping hours. When your legs tire,

scooter rentals are available near the information booth; $6 for the first hour, $4 for each additional hour. For more information, contact West Edmonton Mall at 780/444-5200, www.westedmontonmall.com.

The mall is on 170th Street, between 87th and 90th Avenues. Parking is usually not a problem, but finding your car again can be, so remember which of the 58 entrances you parked near (a parking lot along 90th Ave. at 175th St. is designated for RVs). From downtown, take bus #100.

DEVON
Devonian Botanic Garden

These gardens (780/987-3054, July–Aug. daily 10 A.M.–9 P.M., Sept. daily 10 A.M.–6 P.M., Oct.–Nov. Sat.–Sun. 11 A.M.–4 P.M., adult $10.50, senior $8, child $6), developed by the University of Alberta, are located southwest of the city and five kilometers (3.1 mi) north of the small town of Devon, which was named for the Devonian rock formation in which nearby oil strikes were made during the late 1940s. The 70-hectare (173-acre) site has been developed around the natural contours of the land. The highlight is the **Kurimoto Japanese Garden,** one of the world's northernmost authentic Japanese gardens. The various natural elements are complemented by an ornamental gate, an arched bridge, and decorative lanterns. Other features are the large Alpine Garden, with examples of plants from mountainous regions; the Herb Garden, where in August the aroma is almost overpowering; the Peony Collection, which is at its most colorful in July; a greenhouse filled with plants unique to the Southern Hemisphere; and the Native People's Garden, which is surrounded by water and showcases plants used by the native people of Alberta.

STONY PLAIN
Multicultural Heritage Centre

West of Edmonton, the streets of Stony Plain, which was homesteaded before 1900, are lined with historic buildings, but the best place to learn more about the community's history is

FATHER ALBERT LACOMBE

Dressed in a tattered black robe and brandishing a cross, Father Albert Lacombe, known to natives as "the man with the good heart," dedicated his life to those with native blood – the

© ANDREW HEMPSTEAD

FATHER LACOMBE, O.M.I.
A MISSIONARY   UN MISSIONNAIRE
& PIONEER   & PIONNIER
OF THE NORTHWEST. DU NORD-OUEST.

Assiniboine, Blackfoot, Cree, and, in particular, the Métis. His travels, mainly associated with northern Alberta, took him as far south as Calgary, but his reputation extended to every corner of the province. He was a spokesman for the church, an effective influence on government policies, and, most importantly, he had a hand in just about every advance in the often-tense relationship between warring tribes and white men.

Father Lacombe originally came to what is now Alberta in 1852 to serve the Métis and natives who had moved to Fort Edmonton. In his time there he founded missions at what are now St. Albert and Brosseau. After a short stint in Manitoba, he returned as a traveling missionary, establishing Canada's first industrial school for natives. He also mediated a dispute between the C.P.R. and angry leaders of the Blackfoot over rights to build a rail line through a reserve, and he wrote the first Cree dictionary. The trust he built with native leaders was great; during one rebellion of the Blackfoot Confederacy, it is claimed that his influence prevented the slaughter of every white man on the prairies.

at this provincial historic site (5411 51st St., 780/963-2777, Mon.–Sat. 10 A.M.–4 P.M., Sun. 10 A.M.–6:30 P.M., free). On the grounds, the town's first high school houses a museum, a craft store, a library and archives, a candy store, and the **Heritage Kitchen**—a basement restaurant serving pioneer-style home-cooked meals at reasonable prices. Housed next door, in the historic residence of an early pioneer, is **Oppertshauser House,** Alberta's first rural public art gallery.

ST. ALBERT

The city of St. Albert (pop. 68,000)—northwest of Edmonton along the St. Albert Trail—is one of Alberta's oldest settlements but has today become part of Edmonton's sprawl. Albert Lacombe, a pioneering western Canadian priest, built a mansion overlooking the Stur-

geon River in 1861, when Fort Edmonton was only a small trading post. A sawmill and gristmill were constructed, and by 1870, St. Albert was the largest agricultural community west of Winnipeg. Father Lacombe's first log chapel, the **Father Lacombe Chapel** (west of Hwy. 2 on St. Vital Ave., 780/427-3995, mid-May–Aug. daily 10 A.M.–6 P.M., adult $2, senior and child $1.50), was built in 1861 and had a brick structure built around it in 1927. Now a Provincial Historical Site, it has been restored to its original appearance. Beside the chapel, a cast-iron statue of Father Lacombe that was made in France overlooks the city. Also on Mission Hill is the **Vital Grandin Centre,** an imposing three-story structure built in 1887 as a hospital.

In stark contrast to the historic buildings overlooking the Sturgeon River is City Hall in **St.**

EDMONTON

Albert Place on St. Anne Street, a contoured brick building designed by Douglas Cardinal. Inside is the **Musée Heritage Museum** (780/459-1528, Mon.–Sat. 10 A.M.–5 P.M., Sun. 1–5 P.M.), with displays telling the story of St. Albert's history and the people who made it happen. From this museum, walk along the river (three km/1.9 mi) or drive (take Sir Winston Churchill Ave. to Riel Dr.) to **Lois Hole Centennial Provincial Park,** protecting Big Lake and surrounding wetlands. Here, bird-watchers have the chance to see some 40 species of water and wading birds, including trumpeter swans.

St. Albert Information Centre (71 St. Albert Rd., 780/459-1724, Mon.–Fri. 8 A.M.–5 P.M., Sat.–Sun. 10 A.M.–5 P.M.) is in a large modern building beside Highway 2 on the south side of St. Albert (you can't miss it coming into the city from the south).

FORT SASKATCHEWAN AND VICINITY

In 1875—long after the fur-trading post of Fort Edmonton had been established—the North West Mounted Police (NWMP) marched north from Fort Macleod and established its northern divisional fort on the North Saskatchewan River, 30 kilometers (18.6 mi) northeast of Fort Edmonton. In the ensuing years, Fort Saskatchewan has grown into a large residential center, right at Edmonton's doorstep. To reach the town, take Highway 15 (Manning Dr.) out of Edmonton.

Fort Saskatchewan Museum and Historic Site

The site of the original fort overlooks the river from along 101st Street in downtown Fort Saskatchewan. A jail and courthouse replaced the original fort in 1909. The jail was demolished in 1994, but the two-story, red-brick courthouse still stands and now serves as a museum (10006 100th Ave., 780/998-1783, June–Sept. daily 10 A.M.–4 P.M., the rest of the year Tues.–Fri. 10 A.M.–4 P.M., adult $4, senior and child $3) cataloging the history of the site and the NWMP. Various other historic buildings have been moved to this picturesque site, including a restored log homestead, a blacksmith shop, and a one-room schoolhouse. A cairn marking the site of the NWMP guard room has been built from stones used in the original structure.

Alberta Railway Museum

If antique railway memorabilia interests you, consider stopping at this museum (24215 34th St., 780/472-6229, summer Tues.–Sun. 10 A.M.–5 P.M., adult $4, senior $2.50, child $1.25), a short detour from Highway 15 to Fort Saskatchewan. Or take 97th Street (Hwy. 28) north to Namao, turn east on Highway 37 and travel seven kilometers (4.3 mi), then go south on 34th Street for two kilometers (1.2 mi). It is well signposted from both directions. Featuring Canada's largest collection of Northern Alberta Railway (NAR) equipment, this museum also has rolling stock from the Canadian National Railway (CNR) and the CPR. More than 50 locomotive, passenger, and freight cars from 1877 to 1950 are displayed, some fully restored, others in the process of being so. Also exhibited are various railway artifacts, equipment, machinery, and the simple one-room flag-stop shelter from the rural hamlet of Opal.

Recreation

🔘 River Valley Park System

One of the first things you'll notice about Edmonton is its large amount of parkland. The city has more land set aside for parks, per capita, than any other city in Canada. Most parks interconnect along the banks of the North Saskatchewan River and in adjoining ravines, encompassing 7,400 hectares (18,300 acres) and comprising the largest stretch of urban parkland in North America. Within these parks are picnic areas, swimming pools, historic sites, golf courses, and many kilometers of walking and biking trails. One of the best ways to ensure you make the most of the park system is by referring to the brochure *Priceless Fun,* available from tourist information centers and online at the City of Edmonton website (www.edmonton.ca).

One of the larger individual parks is **William Hawrelak Park,** west of the university along Groat Road. A one-way road loops through the park, circling a manmade lake with paddleboats and fishing. There are many quiet picnic areas and an outdoor amphitheater that hosts a wide range of summer events. **River Valley Cycle** (6945 75th St., 780/465-3863) rents mountain bikes for $7.50 per hour, $30 per day, and leads organized rides during summer.

Swimming and Fitness Centers

It's often crowded, it's commercial, and it's not cheap, but Edmonton's ultimate swimming, sliding, and sunbathing experience awaits at **World Waterpark** in the West Edmonton Mall (170th St. and 87th Ave., 780/444-5200, adult $29.95, families $79.95, child under four feet $22.95).

Edmonton's outdoor swimming season lasts approximately three months beginning at the end of May. Of the five outdoor pools owned by the city, the one in **Queen Elizabeth Park** is in a particularly picturesque location among poplar trees and with a view of the city skyline over the river; access is from 90th Avenue. Another pool, close to the city center, is in **Mill Creek Park,** north of Whyte Avenue (82nd Ave.) on 95A Street. Admission to all outdoor pools is $4.

When the weather gets cooler, or to take advantage of more facilities, head to one of the city's many indoor pools, where admission includes the use of saunas, a hot tub, weight rooms, and water slides. Swimming events of the 1978 Commonwealth Games were held at the **Kinsmen Sports Centre** (9100 Walterdale Hill, 780/944-7400), in Kinsmen Park on the south bank of the North Saskatchewan River. Admission of $6 includes use of the pools, fitness center, sauna, and jogging track that were all given a thorough upgrade in early 2007. The cafeteria here has reasonably priced meals. For information on all city-operated pools, call 780/496-7946.

Golf

Edmonton has so many golf courses that you could play a different one each day for a month. One is within a three-iron shot of the city center, whereas others are along the North Saskatchewan River Valley and throughout outlying suburbs. Canada's oldest municipal course is the **Victoria Golf Course** (west of the legislature building along River Road, 780/496-4900, $34–41), which is still owned and operated by the city. This 18-hole course is only a little more than 6,000 yards in length but is made challenging by narrow fairways and smallish greens.

As a keen golfer, I can highly recommend the following courses that have opened in the last decade: 7,330-yard **RedTail Landing** (Hwy. 2 by the airport, 780/890-7888, $80), a links-style layout with well-placed bunkers and multiple water hazards, and **Jagare Ridge** (14931 9th Ave., 780/432-4030, $72), stretching along both sides of the Whitemud Creek Valley. West of the city, **The Ranch** (52516 Range Rd., Spruce Grove, 780/470-4700, $70) features a water-lined trio of finishing holes (and carts equipped with GPS and electronic

EDMONTON

scoring). Also in Spruce Grove, **The Links** (off Calahoo Rd., 780/962-4653, $49) is a well-maintained course with rolling fairways, large greens, and around 70 bunkers.

TOURS

If you are pressed for time, or even if you're not, a guided tour of Edmonton may be a good idea. The big tour companies bypass Edmonton, leaving a variety of small operators to offer personalized service and flexible schedules. As you'd expect from a former museum guide, Cameron Malcolm of **Out an' About Tours** (780/909-8687, www.outanabouttours.com) emphasizes the heritage and culture of Edmonton and Old Strathcona on his half-day city tours ($40), with the option to add a visit to Fort Edmonton Park ($65). **Magic Times** (780/940-7479, www.magictimes.ca) takes interested visitors on tours that concentrate on one area, such as Old Strathcona, or historic sites and Fort Edmonton Park. Expect to pay around $40 per person for a four-hour tour. Around 50 kilometers (31 mi) are covered in four hours with Peter Hominiuk of **Peter's Edmonton Tours** (780/469-2641), a personalized service that hits the major historic sites, the university, and the Royal Alberta Museum. Wayne Millar of **Birds & Backcountry Tours** (780/405-4880, www.birdsandbackcountry.com) leads visitors through urban parks. The Hawrelak Park morning tour includes breakfast for $45 per person. Wayne's forte is the areas east of Edmonton, including Elk Island National Park and the Cooking Lake Moraine; these tours leave on demand.

WINTER RECREATION
Downhill Skiing and Snowboarding

The closest major alpine resort is Marmot Basin, in Jasper National Park, but Edmonton has three small lift-serviced hills within the city limits and one just outside. All are great for beginners but won't hold the interest of other skiers or snowboarders for very long. Overlooking downtown from across the river is the **Edmonton Ski Club** (9613 96th Ave., 780/465-0852). It's open December–March,

with night skiing during the week. Lift tickets are $16. To get there, follow signs to the Muttart Conservatory. Also close to the city center is **Snow Valley** (southwest of downtown, where Whitemud Dr. crosses the river, 780/434-3991), which has a chairlift, a T-bar, and a small terrain park. Tickets are around the same price as the ski club.

Cross-Country Skiing

The River Valley Park System provides ample opportunity for cross-country skiing. More than 75 kilometers (47 mi) of trails are groomed from December to early March. The most popular areas are in William Hawrelak Park, up Mill Creek Ravine, and through Capilano Park. For details of trails, pick up the brochure *Cross-Country Ski Edmonton* from tourist information centers or download it from the City of Edmonton website (www.edmonton.ca). The **Kinsmen Sports Centre** has cross-country ski rentals; $12 for two hours, or $18 per day, including boots and poles.

SPECTATOR SPORTS
Hockey

Alberta's first major-league hockey team was the Alberta Oilers, who played in both Calgary and Edmonton. The team finally settled in Edmonton permanently for the 1973–1974 season. During the 1980s, when Wayne Gretzky was leading the **Edmonton Oilers,** the NHL's Stanley Cup resided just as permanently in Edmonton, "City of Champions." Since 1988, when Gretzky was sold to the L.A. Kings, the team has met with mixed success, although they did reach the Stanley Cup final in 2006. Home games are played September–April in Rexall Place (Wayne Gretzky Dr., 780/414-4625 or 866/414-4625, www.edmontonoilers.com). From downtown, the easiest way to get there is by LRT to the Coliseum station. Tickets cost from $45 and go all the way up to $100–150 for rink-side seats.

Football

The **Edmonton Eskimos** have a distinguished record in the Canadian Football League (CFL),

having won the Grey Cup 13 times—including five straight (1978–1982) and most recently in 2005. "Eskimos" was originally an insult, given to the team by a Calgary sportswriter in the team's early days, but the name stuck. Since 1948, the team has played in and won more Grey Cup games than any other team in the league. Two former Albertan premiers, Peter Lougheed and Don Getty, once starred for the team. The "Esks" play late June to November at Commonwealth Stadium (11000 Stadium Rd., 780/448-3757 or 800/667-3757, www.esks.com). Tickets are $28–50, with children half price.

Horse Racing

Harness racing takes place at **Northlands** (7300 116th Ave., 780/471-7210, www.northlands.com) from spring to mid-December. Thoroughbred racing takes place throughout summer at the same track. Racing is generally Friday at 6 P.M. and on weekends at 1 P.M. During Capital Ex celebrations, a full racing program is presented. Admission is nominal.

Arts, Entertainment, and Shopping

For details on theater events throughout the city, a listing of art galleries, what's going on where in the music scene, cinema screenings, and a full listing of festivals and events, pick up a free copy of *See Magazine* (www.seemagazine.com) or *Vue Weekly* (www.vueweekly.com). Both are published every Thursday and are available all around town, with all the same information presented on the respective websites. Tickets to most major performances are available from **Tix on the Square** (Sir Winston Churchill Square, 9930 102nd Ave., 780/420-1757, Mon.–Fri. 9:30 A.M.–6 P.M., Sat.–Sun. 9:30 A.M.–4 P.M.), a nonprofit outlet operated by the local arts council.

THE ARTS
Art Galleries

Scattered throughout the city are commercial art galleries, many of which exhibit and sell Canadian and native art. Eight galleries within six blocks of each other and the corner of Jasper Avenue and 124th Street have formed the **Gallery Walk Association** (www.gallery-walk.com). All are worth visiting, but the **Bearclaw Gallery** (10403 124th St., 780/482-1204) is of special note for those searching out the unique art of the First Nations. Among the shoe shops and souvenir stands in West Edmonton Mall is **Northern Images** (780/444-1995), also with a good collection of native and northern arts and crafts. Finally, headquarters for the **Alberta Craft Council** is the Edmonton store (10186 106th St., 780/488-6611).

Theater

Edmonton's 14 theater companies present productions at various locations all year long. For most companies, September–May is the main season.

The **Citadel** (9828 101A Ave., 780/425-1820 or 888/425-1820, www.citadeltheatre.com) is Canada's largest theater facility, taking up an entire downtown block. From the outside, it looks like a gigantic greenhouse; one entire side is glass, enclosing a magnificent indoor garden complete with walking paths and benches. The complex houses five theaters: the Maclab Theatre showcases the work of teens and children; the intimate Rice Theatre features mainly experimental and innovative productions; Zeidler Hall hosts films, lectures, and children's theater; Tucker Amphitheatre presents concerts and recitals across a pond and surrounded by tropical greenery, and often puts on small lunchtime stage productions; and Shoctor Theatre is the main stage for the Citadel's long-running subscription program ($22–55 per production). Tickets are available from the Citadel Box Office.

For slightly more adventurous productions and occasional international imports, see what's going on at the **Northern Light Theatre**

EDMONTON

(11516 103rd St., 780/471-1586, www.northern lighttheatre.com, $10–20). Edmonton's oldest theater is the **Walterdale Playhouse** (10322 83rd Ave., 780/439-2845, www.walterdale playhouse.com, from $8), in the heart of Old Strathcona, which presents historical and humorous material through an October–June season in a 1910 firehall.

Celebrations, in the Neighbourhood Inn (102-13103 Fort Rd., 780/448-9339), is a popular interactive dinner theater; the ticket price of $40–50 includes dinner. Open Wednesday–Sunday, reservations necessary, no jeans allowed, and you must be seated by 6 P.M. **Jubilations Dinner Theatre** (Phase III, West Edmonton Mall, 780/484-2424 or 877/214-2424, $46–56) is another such dinner theater, combining music and comedy. Shows start Wednesday–Saturday at 6:30 P.M. and Sunday at 5 P.M.

Music and Dance

In the heart of the Arts District is the magnificent **Winspear Centre** (corner of 99th St. and 102nd Ave., www.winspearcentre.com), a venue renowned as an acoustic wonder that is also capable of producing high-quality amplified sound. It is home to the **Edmonton Symphony Orchestra** (780/428-1414) and attracts a wide variety of national and international musical acts, ranging from choirs to classical performers. Contact the box office (780/428-1414 or 800/563-5081, $26–35) for tickets.

Both the **Edmonton Opera** (780/429-1000, www.edmontonopera.com) and the **Alberta Ballet** (780/428-6839, www.albertaballet .com) perform at the Jubilee Auditorium in the University of Alberta (11455 87th Ave.) between October and March. For performance dates and ticket information, call the box office numbers or Ticketmaster (780/451-8000).

Cinemas

Famous Players cinemas are located throughout the city, including 10233 Jasper Avenue (780/428-1307); 2950 Calgary Trail S (780/436-6977); and in West Edmonton Mall (780/444-2400). The historic **Princess**

Theatre (10337 82nd Ave., Old Strathcona, 780/433-0728) is an old-time movie house showing revivals, experiments, and foreign films. **Metro Cinema** (Zeidler Hall, The Citadel, 9828 101A Ave., 780/425-9212) shows classics, imports, and brave new films. The **Garneau Theatre** (8712 109th St., 780/433-0728) features mostly foreign films and those that have gained acclaim at film festivals. Admission is generally $9, except Mondays, when it's discounted to $5.

NIGHTLIFE
Casinos

Casinos in Alberta are all privately owned, but charitable organizations hold the actual gaming licenses (and keep the profits). Licenses allow slots to be turned on at 10 A.M. and table games to start at noon, with all the action coming to a close at 3 A.M. In addition to slots, the casinos offer blackjack, roulette, baccarat, Red Dog, and Sic Bo. The largest of Edmonton's five casinos is the western-themed **Casino Yellowhead** (Yellowhead Trail and 153rd St., 780/424-9467). **Palace Casino** (Phase II, West Edmonton Mall, 780/444-2112) has the advantage of location in tempting players to its tables.

Bars and Nightclubs

The **Sidetrack Cafe** (10333 112th St., 780/421-1326) is central to downtown, serves excellent food, and presents live entertainment nightly from 9 P.M. Shows change dramatically—one night it might be stand-up comedians, the next a blues band, then jazz—and the only thing you can rely on is that it will be busy. Monday is usually comedy night and Sunday variety night. Cover charges vary; $4–8 is normal. Downtown, the **Sherlock Holmes** (10012 101A Ave., 780/426-7784) serves a large selection of British and Irish ales and is the place to head for St. Patrick's Day (March 17). The rest of the year, drinkers are encouraged to join in nightly sing-alongs with the pianist. Sherlock Holmes also has locations in Old Strathcona (10341 82nd Ave., 780/433-9676) and along West Edmonton Mall's Bourbon Street

Head to the Cook County Saloon for live country music.

(780/444-1752). Old Strathcona is also home to **O'Byrne's Irish Pub** (10616 82nd Ave., 780/414-6766), where Celtic bands often play. The **Stonehouse Pub,** a few blocks west of downtown (11026 Jasper Ave., 780/420-0448), attracts an older crowd with classic rock 'n' roll pumping from the jukebox. It has an outdoor patio, plenty of pool tables, big-screen TVs, and nightly drink specials.

The **Confederation Lounge** (Fairmont Hotel Macdonald, 10065 100th St., 780/424-5181) oozes old-time style while **Bellamy's** (Crowne Plaza Chateau Lacombe, 10111 Bellamy Hill, 780/428-6611) is a quiet space with river views.

Cook County Saloon (8010 Gateway Blvd., 780/432-2665) is consistently voted Canada's Best Country Nightclub by the Canadian Country Music Association. Its mellow honky-tonk ambience draws crowds, and Canadian and international performers play here. Free two-step lessons are offered on selected weeknights, and on Friday and Satur-

day nights the action really cranks up, with live entertainment and a DJ spinning country Top 40 discs. On these two nights, the cover is $6 after 8 P.M. Beyond West Edmonton Mall is **Cowboys** (10102 180th St., 780/481-8739), with a Western theme but attracting a young, fratlike crowd with theme nights, popular promotions, white-hatted and scantily clad shooter girls, and a huge dance floor.

Top 40 and dance nightclubs change names, reputations, and locations regularly, but some are reliable fixtures. Even if the names change, the locations don't—Old Strathcona and West Edmonton Mall both offer a range of nightclubbing experiences. Your best bet for finding current hotspots is Edmonton's free entertainment rags, *See Magazine* and *Vue Weekly,* or the website www.clubvibes.com.

In West Edmonton Mall, **Red's** (780/481-6420) combines a billiards room, restaurant, cigar lounge, dance floor, and a stage that has been graced by some of the biggest names in country music. Also in the famous mall, **Rum Jungle** (780/486-9494) somehow makes an African safari theme hip, with jungle decor, vine-swinging servers, and a young groovy crowd; **Fever** (780/443-6666) combines a martini bar with a huge dance floor; and **Hooters** (780/444-9464) is, well, Hooters. On the same side of the city, but farther west, **Santannas Party House** (17930 Stony Plain Rd., 780/481-7625, Tues.–Sat.) is exactly that—a party house, with favorite hits from the last three decades blasting from massive sound systems.

Jazz and Comedy

The Edmonton Jazz Society is a volunteer-run organization that manages the **Yardbird Suite** (10203 86th Ave., 780/432-0428, www.yardbirdsuite.com). Live jazz fills the air September–June nightly 10 P.M.–2 A.M. Tuesday-night jam sessions are $2; on other nights admission is $5–18. Friday is nonsmoking night. The **Full Moon Folk Club** (780/438-6410, www.fmfc.org) sponsors visiting performers at a variety of venues, including St. Basil's Cultural Centre (10819 71st St.); tickets are well priced at approximately $15.

EDMONTON

At **Yuk Yuk's Komedy Kabaret** (Londonderry Mall, 6606 137th Ave., 780/481-9857, www.yukyuks.com), show times vary, but they offer at least one show nightly Wednesday–Saturday. Generally, Wednesday is amateur night, and the pros hit the stage the rest of the week. Tickets are $5–20.

SHOPPING
Plazas and Malls
Naturally, any talk of a shopping trip to Edmonton includes **West Edmonton Mall** (at 87th Ave. and 170th St.), the world's largest shopping and amusement complex; the mall is covered under *Sights* earlier in this chapter. Downtown's major shopping centers are **City Centre** and **ManuLife Place,** while on the southern outskirts **South Edmonton Common** (corner Gateway Blvd and 23rd Ave.) provides a home for 35 big box stores.

Camping Gear and Western Wear
Downtown, **Uniglobe Geo Travel** (10237 109th St., 780/424-8310) stocks a wide range of travel clothing and accessories, and also operates as a travel agency. **Mountain Equipment Co-op,** a Canadian outdoor equipment cooperative similar to REI in the United States, is west of the Royal Alberta Museum (12328 102nd Ave., 780/488-6614). Across the railway tracks from Old Strathcona is **Track 'n' Trail** (10148 82nd Ave., 780/432-1707), which carries a wide variety of cross-country skiing, camping, and climbing gear. In the same general area is **Totem Outdoor Outfitters** (7430 99th St., 780/432-1223), with more of the same as well as kayaks, canoes, and some used gear. West of downtown is the large **Campers Village** (10951 170th St., 780/484-2700), with camping equipment, fishing tackle, books, boots, and scuba-diving equipment.

Alberta's largest supplier of western wear is **Lammle's,** with five outlets throughout the city, including one in West Edmonton Mall (Phase I, 780/444-7877). The **Western Boot Factory** (10007 167th St., 780/489-0594) stocks thousands of styles of cowboy boots. You can't miss it because out front is

© ANDREW HEMPSTEAD

Western Boot Factory, near West Edmonton Mall, is home to the world's largest cowboy boot.

the world's largest cowboy boot. This store has another location at 3414 Gateway Boulevard, (780/435-3702). High-quality boots are also sold by **Diablo Boots** (3440 Gateway Blvd., 780/435-2592).

Bookstores
Audrey's (10702 Jasper Ave., 780/423-3487, Mon.–Fri. 9 A.M.–9 P.M., Sat. 9:30 A.M.–5:30 P.M., Sun. noon–5 P.M.) has the city's largest collection of travel guides, western Canadiana, and general travel writing on two vast floors. **Map Town** (10344 105th St., 780/429-2600, Mon.–Fri. 8 A.M.–5:30 P.M., Sat. 10 A.M.–5 P.M.) stocks the provincial 1:50,000 and 1:250,000 topographical map series along with city maps, world maps, Alberta wall maps, travel guides, atlases, and a huge selection of specialty maps. Map Town also has a solid selection of specialty guides for fishing, canoeing, climbing, and the like.

Old Strathcona is an excellent place for browsing through used bookstores. **Wee Book**

Inn (10310 82nd Ave., 780/432-7230) is the largest and stocks more recent titles and a large collection of magazines. **Alhambra Books** (upstairs at 10309 82nd Ave., 780/439-4195) specializes in Canadiana and has an extensive collection of Albertan material, including pamphlets and newspapers. **Athabasca Books** (8228 105th St., 780/431-1776) stocks mostly history and literature books. **Bjarne's Books** (10533 82nd Ave., 780/439-7123) has older books, including a large selection of hard-to-find western Canadiana and Arctic region material. The **Edmonton Bookstore,** west toward the university (11216 76th Ave., 780/433-1781), also has a large stock of out-of-print books from the region.

Old Strathcona's lone new-book stores are **Greenwood's** (7925 104th St., 780/439-2005), which stocks a lot of everything, and **Chapters** (10504 82nd Ave., 780/435-1290).

Festivals and Events

Spring

The **Alberta Book Festival** (780/426-5892), held in mid-March, is a three-day event with public workshops, readings, book signings, and a small midway. Many of the events are held in the Shaw Conference Centre.

The **Northern Alberta International Children's Festival** (780/459-1542, www.child fest.com) takes place the weekend closest to June 1 in the Arden Theatre, St. Albert. Acts from around the world include theater, music, dance, storytelling, and puppetry.

During the last week of June, the **Yardbird Jazz Festival** (780/432-0428, www.yard birdsuite.com) is held at various indoor and outdoor venues. Many foreign stars make special appearances.

The Works: Art & Design Festival (780/426-2122, www.theworks.ab.ca) features art exhibitions on the streets, in parks, and in art galleries through Old Strathcona for two weeks from late June.

Summer

For 10 days in early July, downtown's Winston Churchill Square comes alive during the **Edmonton Street Fest** (780/425-5162, www.edmontonstreetfest.com), with almost 1,000 performances by magicians, comics, jugglers, musicians, and mimes.

The 10-day **Capital Ex,** beginning on the third Thursday of each July, kicks off with a massive parade through downtown. Much of the activity is centered on Northlands (7300 116th St.), featuring a midway, casino, free music concerts, gold-panning, the Alberta Tattoo, the RCMP musical ride, thoroughbred racing, the Global Connections pavilion featuring an international marketplace, and a trade show of upscale arts and crafts. This is the city's biggest annual event, attracting approximately 800,000 visitors, so be prepared for big crowds everywhere. For more information, call organizers at 780/471-7210, or visit www.capitalex.ca. Running in conjunction with Capital Ex is **Taste of Edmonton** (Sir Winston Churchill Square, 780/423-2822, www.eventsedmonton.ca), where visitors can sample signature dishes from Edmonton's wide range of restaurants.

Fifty outdoor ethnic pavilions at Hawrelak Park are just a small part of **Edmonton Heritage Festival** (780/488-3378, www.heri tage-festival.com), which is held on the first weekend in August as a celebration of the city's multicultural roots. Visitors to the festival have the opportunity to experience international singing and dancing, arts-and-crafts displays, costumes, and cuisine from more than 60 cultures.

During the **Edmonton Folk Music Festival** (780/429-1999, www.edmonton-folkfest.org), held on the second weekend of August, Gallagher Park comes alive with the sound of blues, jazz, country, Celtic, traditional, and bluegrass music. Tickets are $45

EDMONTON

per day, although advance weekend passes are better value for keen folkies.

Quickly becoming one of the city's most popular events is the **Fringe Theatre Festival** (780/448-9000, www.fringetheatreadventures.ca), a 10-day extravaganza that begins on the second Thursday in August. It is held throughout Old Strathcona, in parks, on the streets, in parking garages, and in the area's historic restored theaters. With more than 1,000 performances and a crowd of half a million looking on, the festival has become North America's largest alternative-theater event, attracting artists from around the world. Tickets are generally inexpensive.

Symphony under the Sky (780/428-1414, www.edmontonsymphony.com), held on the weekend closest to August 31, is the last gasp in Edmonton's busy summer festival schedule. Led by the Edmonton Symphony Orchestra,

this five-day extravaganza of classical music takes place in William Hawrelak Park.

Fall and Winter

Farmfair International (780/471-7210, www.farmfairinternational.com) showcases some of North America's best livestock through sales and auctions, but exhibits, a trade show, the judging of Miss Rodeo Canada, and thousands of farm animals draw in casual visitors. The fair takes place at Northlands the second week of November. That same week, Rexall Place hosts the **Canadian Finals Rodeo** (780/471-7210, www.canadianfinalsrodeo.ca). This $500,000 event is the culmination of the year's work for Canada's top 10 money-earning cowboys and cowgirls in seven traditional rodeo events. The action takes place Wednesday–Sunday at 7 P.M. and 1 P.M. Sunday.

Accommodations and Camping

Nearly all of Edmonton's best hotels are located downtown. Other concentrations of motels can be found along Gateway Boulevard (Hwy. 2 from the south) and scattered along Stony Plain Road in the west. The towns of Leduc and Nisku have several motels close to Edmonton International Airport. Other options include many bed-and-breakfasts, a centrally located hostel, and camping (just five minutes from downtown, or in campgrounds west, east, or south of the city).

DOWNTOWN

All but two of the following accommodations (Glenora B&B Inn and La Boheme are the exceptions) are within walking distance of each other within the downtown core. As with city hotels around the world, parking is extra ($8–15), but may be included with weekend rates.

Under $50

Housed in one of the few older downtown hotels to escape the wrecking ball is **Go Backpackers**

Hostel (10815 Jasper Ave., 780/423-4146 or 877/646-7835, www.gohostels.ca), a few blocks from the heart of the city and surrounded by cafés, restaurants, and pubs. The hostelry has a total of 184 beds in eight-bed dorms ($22 per person), four-bed dorms ($26), private twin and double rooms ($70 s or d), and rooms with kitchenettes ($85 s or d). Facilities include two lounges, a communal kitchen, and public Internet access in the lobby.

$50-100

The **YMCA** has an outstanding location right downtown (10030 102A Ave., 780/421-9622, www.edmonton.ymca.ca, $46 s, $61 d). The rooms are small and sparsely furnished; each has a bed and desk, some have a sink, and the bathroom is down the hall. They are available to men, women, couples, and families. Downstairs is a café and guests have free access to the center's fitness facility (including a pool).

Between downtown and the Royal Alberta Museum, **Glenora B&B Inn** (12327

102nd Ave., 780/488-6766 or 877/453-6672, www.glenorabnb.com) is a home away from home a short walk from the galleries of 124th Street. The building that houses this bed-and-breakfast was built as a commercial enterprise in 1912 and has been completely renovated with the guest rooms above a guest parlor and street-level restaurant where a full breakfast is served (included in rates). The least expensive rooms share a bathroom ($70 s, $90 d), or pay extra for an ensuite (from $90 s, $110 d). For the same price as a mid-priced downtown hotel upgrade to a spacious Apartment Suite ($140 s, $160), complete with a kitchenette, canopied bed, and oversized bathroom.

Sure, it's a chain hotel, but **Comfort Inn Edmonton** (10425 100th Ave., 780/423-5611 or 888/384-6835, www.comfortinnedmonton .com) is a good choice. The 108 rooms are sensibly furnished for both leisure and business travelers. Parking, local calls, and in-room coffee are complimentary. Rack rates are $99 s or d, but the hotel website offers some great overnight packages.

The **Days Inn** (10041 106th St., 780/423-1925 or 800/329-7466, www.daysinn.com) is another solid choice in the same neighborhood. Parking is free. The in-house restaurant is open 6:30 A.M.–9 P.M. and a lounge stays open until midnight. Rates are $99 s or d, or book online and save up to $20 per night.

$100-150

Centrally located on the corner of Jasper Avenue and 99th Street, the **C Courtyard Edmonton** (1 Thornton Court, 780/423-9999 or 866/441-7591, www.marriott.com) is a modern and unpretentious hotel with spectacular views across the river valley. The 177 rooms that fill with natural light (or none at all if you close the heavy curtains) have plenty of space and big, modern bathrooms. Downstairs is a bistro with tables that spill onto a magnificent riverside patio. Rooms start at $149 s or d, or pay $179 for upgraded everything in a suite.

The lobby of the **Coast Edmonton Plaza Hotel** (10155 105th St., 780/423-4811 or

800/716-6199, www.coasthotels.com) has a distinct alpine feel, yet the rest of the property is nothing but city-style. Handsome rooms come with niceties—such as robes—that make you believe you're paying more than you are. You can pay more, for a Superior Room, and it will be money well spent. Facilities include an indoor pool, an exercise room, laundry service, a lounge, and a restaurant. Posted rates are $125 s, $135 d, but a quick check of the hotel website uncovered a $129 bed-and-breakfast package for two that included a $50 voucher for West Edmonton Mall—in July! At $8 per 24 hours, parking is well-priced compared to other downtown hotels.

No, it's not downtown, but it's close. **La Boheme** (6427 112th Ave., 780/474-5693, $95 s, $140 d) is in the historic Gibbard building, which originally held Edmonton's first luxury apartments. Today, La Boheme restaurant downstairs is one of the city's best, and six upstairs rooms have been graciously refurbished and are run as a bed-and-breakfast. The building is certainly charming, right down to its creaky floors. Each of the simply furnished rooms has a separate sleeping area. Rates include a continental breakfast.

If you plan to be in the city for a few days and want to cook your own meals, suite hotels (also called apartment hotels) offer a good value. **Alberta Place Suite Hotel** (10049 103rd St., 780/423-1565 or 800/661-3982, www.albertaplace.com) is one of the best choices. The 86 suites are large, and each has a well-equipped kitchen. Continental breakfast and daily papers are complimentary, a Hertz agent is on-site (discounted rentals for guests), and Jasper Avenue is only half a block away. Rates start at $109 s or d for a studio suite.

Signature Suites Edmonton House (10205 100th Ave., 780/420-4000 or 888/962-2522, www.edmontonhouse.com, $120–170 s or d) is slightly more expensive than Alberta Place, but each of the 300 rooms has a balcony with views of the valley or the city, and there's an indoor pool, a fitness room, a guest lounge and reading room, and shuttle service to West Edmonton Mall.

$150-200

If you're looking for accommodations in this price category, it's very hard to do better than the ◖ **Union Bank Inn** (10053 Jasper Ave., 780/423-3600 or 888/423-3601, www.union bankinn.com) for value, charm, and location. The inn is in a restored 1911 bank building in the heart of the city. The new owners have transformed the historic building into a luxurious boutique hotel, featuring a fireplace, down comforters, and bathrobes in each of 34 tastefully decorated rooms spread through two themed wings (heritage and contemporary). The rates of $179–299 per room also include a cooked breakfast, a wine-and-cheese tray presented to guests each evening, and free parking between 3 P.M. and 9 A.M.

Renovated in 1998, the 24-story **Crowne Plaza Chateau Lacombe** (10111 Bellamy Hill, 780/428-6611 or 800/661-8801, www.chateau lacombe.com) sits on Bellamy Hill, and its unusual cylindrical design distinguishes it against the skyline. The Chateau Lacombe features a fitness center, gift shop, a bar with river views, and a revolving restaurant that actually has decent food; $185 s or d (during summer, rooms are often advertised for less than $150, including breakfast).

Over $200

The **Fairmont Hotel Macdonald** (10065 100th St., 780/424-5181 or 866/540-4469, www.fair mont.com) is an Edmonton landmark that was originally part of the Canadian Pacific hotel chain (along with the Palliser Hotel in Calgary and the Banff Springs Hotel in Banff) but is now part of the Fairmont Hotels and Resorts chain. The 198 guest rooms come in several configurations (many are on the small side). A subtle air of Old World European elegance extends throughout the rooms and public areas such as the upmarket restaurant and the beautiful lounge overlooking the river valley. Rack rates for a standard Fairmont Room are $219 s or d. Packages offer better deals, or pay more for a suite.

Joined to the pedway system and very central, but still affording great river views, is the

Fairmont Hotel Macdonald is the grandest of Edmonton's downtown accommodations.

© ANDREW HEMPSTEAD

20-story **Westin Edmonton** (10135 100th St., 780/426-3636 or 800/937-8461, www.thewestin edmonton.com), one the city's best hotels. The 413 rooms are large, luxurious, and come with all the comforts of home; $225 s, $235 d, but weekend package deals are almost half price. Hotel facilities include a large indoor pool and a fitness center. The in-house eatery, Pradera, is a stylish space that spills into the cavernous lobby.

It's upscale all the way at the **Sutton Place Hotel** (10235 101st St., 780/428-7111 or 866/ 378-8866, www.suttonplace.com), in the financial district and linked to other buildings by the pedway system. In each of the 313 elegantly furnished rooms you'll find marble tabletops, walnut furniture, brass trimmings, a large work area, and a bay window. Other hotel facilities include an indoor pool, an exercise room, a lounge, and a restaurant notable for its chocolate buffet (Thurs.–Fri. at 5 P.M., $16). The rack rate is $304 s or d, but rooms sell for half this through the hotel website—even in midsummer.

SOUTH OF DOWNTOWN

Gateway Boulevard, an extension of Highway 2 as it enters the city from the south, offers a few cheap roadside motels just beyond Gateway Park, and is then dotted with chain hotels all the way to Old Strathcona. Remember when looking at addresses along this strip that Gateway Boulevard is Highway 2 northbound and Calgary Trail is Highway 2 southbound.

Under $50

HI-Edmonton (10647 81st Ave., 780/988-6836 or 877/467-8336, www.hihostels.ca) is sensibly located within walking distance of the hippest Edmonton neighborhood, Old Strathcona, with the best choice of restaurants, bars, and nightclubs. The building may seem a little clinical at first, but that feeling goes away when you begin to take advantage of the facilities offered. The lounge area is spacious and comfortable, and there's a quiet and private backyard, plenty of space in the kitchen, and off-street parking. Throughout summer, various trips and barbecues are put on, and a desk is set up in the lounge to take bookings for local sights and recreation. Most rooms are two-bed dorms ($26 per night for members of Hostelling International, $30 for nonmembers), but there are a few rooms with six beds ($22 and $26 respectively). Check-in is after 3 P.M. From the Greyhound bus depot, walk two blocks east to 101st Street and catch the #4, 6, 7, or 9 bus south. Get off at 82nd Avenue, then walk two blocks east and one south, and you're there.

$50-100

At the southern city limits, **Chateau Motel** (1414 Calgary Trail SW, 780/988-6661, $45–60 s, $55–70 d) has easy access to the airport and each room has a microwave and fridge.

Budget-conscious travelers enjoy the best of both worlds farther north at the **Southbend Motel** (5130 Gateway Blvd., 780/434-1418, www.southbendmotel.ca), where guests have access to the recreation facilities at the adjacent Cedar Park Inn while paying just $64 s, $73 d for accommodations.

$100-150

As you drive north along Calgary Trail, it's impossible to miss the 11-story, pastel-colored **Delta Edmonton South** (4404 Gateway Blvd., 780/434-6415 or 800/661-1122, www.deltahotels.com, $149 s or d) towering over the major intersection with Whitemud Drive. Guests are offered a wide variety of facilities and services, including an indoor pool, restaurant, lounge, airport shuttle, and valet parking.

Adjacent to the Delta is the **Coast Terrace Inn** (4440 Gateway Blvd., 780/437-6010 or 888/837-7223, www.coastterraceinn.com, from $109 s or d), another 200-room-plus, full-service hotel centered on a greenery-filled atrium.

Over $150

One of the city's finest accommodations is **《 The Varscona,** situated in the heart of Old Strathcona (8208 106th St., 780/434-6111 or 888/515-3355, www.varscona.com). The Varscona experience combines the personalized atmosphere of a boutique hotel with all the amenities you'd expect of an upscale chain. The 89 guest rooms are spacious and elegantly furnished in one of three pleasing styles. They all have king beds, large bathrooms, and niceties such as bathrobes and gourmet in-room coffee. Casual l'attitude is the Varscona's contribution to Old Strathcona's vibrant dining scene, while O'Byrne's Irish Pub is the place to relax with a pint. Midweek rates start at $270 s or d, but check online and you should find rooms from around $150. Either way, parking, a light breakfast, a daily newspaper, and an evening wine-and-cheese-tasting session are included.

Look no further than the **《 Hotel Selkirk** (780/496-7227 or 888/962-2522, www.maclabhotels.com) for a unique overnight experience with a historic twist. The original Hotel Selkirk along Jasper Avenue burnt down in 1962, but the historic property has been re-created in minute detail in Fort Edmonton Park, off Whitemud Drive southwest of downtown. The guest rooms have a cozy, Victorian feel but enjoy modern conveniences such as air-conditioning and Internet connections. Rates start at $118 s or d including breakfast and $190 d

EDMONTON

inclusive of dinner in the downstairs Johnson's Café. Drinks in the Mahogany Room, at a replica of Canada's longest bar, are extra.

WEST EDMONTON
$50-100
If you're on a budget and want to stay out by the mall, consider the **Yellowhead Motor Inn** (five km/3.1 mi away at 15004 Yellowhead Trail, 780/447-2400 or 800/661-6993, $69 d, $79 d), across from a casino and with an in-house restaurant and lounge.

Slightly more expensive, the next nearest accommodation is the three-story **West Harvest Inn** (17803 Stony Plain Rd., 780/484-8000 or 800/661-6993, www.westharvest.com, $85 s or d), offering 160 well-appointed air-conditioned rooms and a free mall shuttle.

$100-150
The pick within a cluster of choices along Stony Plain Road, a five-minute drive from the mall, is the **Sandman Hotel West Edmonton** (17635 Stony Plain Rd., 780/483-1385 or 800/726-3626, www.sandmanhotels.com).

The rooms are handsomely appointed in sharp tones and comfortable furnishings. The central atrium holds a pool and restaurant—a pleasant respite from the busy road out front. Pay $139 s or d for a standard room or $169 for a very spacious suite.

West Edmonton Mall Inn (17504 90th Ave., 780/444-9378 or 800/737-3783, www.west edmontonmall.com) lies across the road from its namesake. It features 88 well-appointed rooms, each with two comfortable beds, a coffeemaker, and a Sony PlayStation; from $120 s or d, or check the website for packages that include mall activities.

Over $150
Within West Edmonton Mall is the 355-room 【 **Fantasyland Hotel** (17700 87th Ave., 780/444-3000 or 800/737-3783, www.fantasy landhotel.com), famous for elaborately themed rooms that are way over the top. The hotel has 118 themed rooms, as well as over 200 regular rooms ($179 s or d) and a few extremely spacious Executive Suites with jetted tubs ($199 s or d), and three restaurants. But it's the theme

Theme rooms at the Fantasyland Hotel are an extravagant but memorable experience.

© WEST EDMONTON MALL

rooms that this hotel is known for. No catching a cab back to your hotel after a day of shopping here—just ride the elevator to the room of your wildest fantasy. Each floor has an over-the-top theme: the choice is yours—Hollywood, Roman, Polynesian, Victorian, African, Arabian, Igloo, Waterpark, Western, Canadian Rail, or Truck (where you can slumber in the bed of a real pickup truck). Each theme is carried out in minute detail. The Polynesian room fantasy, for example, begins as you walk along a hallway lined with murals depicting a tropical beach, floored with grass matting. You'll walk through a grove of palm trees before reaching your room. In the colorful room, an enormous hot tub is nestled in a rocky grotto, and the bed is shaped like a warrior's catamaran, with a sail as the headboard. This escapism comes at a cost, but maybe not as much as you'd expect—$269–339 s or d. (The theme rooms are very popular and are booked far in advance, especially on weekends.)

CAMPING
South
The best camping within the city limits is at the **Rainbow Valley Campground** (13204 45th Ave., 780/434-5531 or 888/434-3991, www.rainbow-valley.com, mid-Apr.–early Oct.). The location is excellent and, as far as city camping goes, the setting is pleasant. Facilities include free showers, a laundry room, a barbecue grill, a playground, and a cooking shelter. In summer, all sites are full by noon, so reserve ahead by credit card. Grassed tent sites are $22, powered sites $25. To get there, turn south off Whitemud Drive at 119th Street, then take the first right and follow it into the valley.

If you're coming into the city from the south, take Ellerslie Road west from Highway 2 to access **Whitemud Creek Golf and RV Park** (3428 156th St., 780/988-6800, www.whitemudcreek.com, $35). The 27 fully serviced sites are bunched together in the middle of a full-length, nine-hole golf course ($27), which is adjacent to a pleasant little creek. Facilities include a stocked trout pond, modern washrooms, a laundry room, and a clubhouse restaurant. To get there, follow Ellerslie Road three kilometers (1.9 mi) west from Highway 2, then take 127th Street for three kilometers (1.9 mi) south, then 40th Avenue west for a similar distance.

In the town of Devon, a 20-minute drive southwest of the city, is **River Valley Lions Campground** (780/987-4777, May–mid-Oct.), which lies alongside the North Saskatchewan River and beside a golf course. Tent sites are $18, hookups $23–27. To get there from Highway 2, take Highway 19 west; from out near West Edmonton Mall, take Highway 60 south from Highway 16.

West
Continue west from West Edmonton Mall to **Shakers Acres** (21530 103rd Ave., 780/447-3564 or 877/447-3924, www.shakersacres rvpark.com), on the north side of Stony Plain Road. Unserviced sites are $22 and hookups are $26–30.

Farther out, in Spruce Grove, is the **Glowing Embers Travel Centre** (26309 Hwy. 16, 780/962-8100 or 877/785-7275, www.glowing embersrvpark.com, Apr.–Oct., $30–36). All facilities are modern, and although tents are allowed, they may look out of place among the satellite-toting RVs. Facilities include a recreation hall, a grocery store, an RV wash, a launderette, and service bays with licensed technicians on hand.

East
Half Moon Lake Resort (21524 Hwy. 520, 780/922-3045, www.halfmoonlakeresort.com) is on the shore of a shallow lake, 30 kilometers (19 mi) from Edmonton. It has a large area set aside for tents ($30) and RVs and trailers ($33–38), but the emphasis is mainly on activities such as fishing, swimming, canoeing, boating, and horseback riding. To get there from downtown, head east on 82nd Avenue to Highway 21, three kilometers (1.9 mi) east of Sherwood Park, then south to Highway 520, then 10 kilometers (6.2 mi) east.

EDMONTON

Food

Eating out in Edmonton used to be identified with the aroma of good ol' Alberta beef wafting from the city's many restaurants, but things are changing. Today, 2,000 restaurants offer a balance of international cuisine and local favorites in all price brackets. From the legendary home-style cooking of Barb and Ernie's to the historic elegance of Madison's Grill, there's something to suit everyone's taste and budget. Restaurants are concentrated in a few main areas. Downtown in the plazas are food courts that fill with office workers, shoppers, and tourists each lunchtime. This part of the city also has some of Edmonton's finest dining establishments. Old Strathcona offers a smorgasbord of choices, with cuisine from all corners of the world. Gateway Boulevard and Calgary Trail, northbound and southbound, respectively, along Highway 2 south of downtown, are lined with family restaurants, buffets, and fast-food outlets.

DOWNTOWN
Cafés and Cheap Eats
Looking north to City Hall, **◖ Three Bananas** (9918 102nd Ave., 780/428-2200, Mon.–Fri. 7 A.M.–6 P.M., Sat. 10 A.M.–6 P.M., Sun. 11 A.M.–6 P.M.) is a bright, inspiring space in the heart of downtown. The menu features the usual array of coffee concoctions, single-serving pizzas, and grilled panini, all made to order.

Zenari's (10180 101st St., 780/423-5409 Mon.–Fri. 7 A.M.–6 P.M.) in ManuLife Plaza East is a trendy lunchtime deli hangout known for its variety of sandwiches and freshly prepared soups, as well as coffees from around the world, ground fresh to order. It's closed on Sunday.

Many of the city's downtown malls have food courts on their lower levels (10220 103rd St., City Centre Mall, at 102nd Ave. and 101st St. has the widest range), but worth searching out is the **Boardwalk Market** (corner of 102nd Ave. and 103rd St.), which is within a restored heritage building that was once a marketplace and now holds a good selection of food booths

with not a chain restaurant in sight. For me, the standout here is **Latin Delights,** where a delicious Chilean sandwich (grilled sirloin with green beans and hot sauce on thick bread made in-house) costs $5.

In an inconspicuous spot on the west side of downtown, **Blue Plate Diner** (10145 104th St., 780/429-0740, Mon.–Fri. 11 A.M.–10 P.M., Sat.–Sun. 9 A.M.–10 P.M.) is a welcoming place, with vegetarian choices that include a lentil and nut loaf doused with miso gravy. Everything except the ribs is under $15.

Pub Dining
Surrounded by the city's highest high-rises is the **Sherlock Holmes** (10012 101A Ave., 780/426-7784, Mon.–Sat. from 11:30 A.M.), a charming English-style pub with a shingled roof, whitewashed walls with black trim, and a white picket fence surrounding it. At lunchtime, it is packed with the office crowd. Try traditional British dishes such as Mrs. Hudson's Steak and Kidney Pie ($9), ploughmans ($9.50), liver and onions ($9.50), or fish and chips ($10.50), washed down with a pint of Newcastle ale or Guinness stout. Still hungry? The bread pudding ($5) is a delicious way to end your meal.

In the West End, the **Sidetrack Cafe** (10333 112th St., 780/421-1326, Mon.–Fri. from 7 A.M., weekends from 9 A.M.) has been a music hot spot for over two decades, but it also has a reputation for excellent food. Big, hearty breakfasts cost $4–7.50. Soups, salads, burgers, sandwiches, pizza, and world fare are all on the menu. The soup-and-sandwich lunch deal includes a bottomless bowl of soup. Dinners served 5–10 P.M. are mostly pub staples, but almost everything is under $10.

Canadian
The area along 97th Street has always been Edmonton's own little skid row, but this is changing. Now, it's home to the **◖ Hardware Grill** (9698 Jasper Ave., 780/423-0969, Mon.–Fri.

11:30 A.M.–2 P.M. and Mon.–Sat. from 5 P.M.), one of the city's finest restaurants. Located at the street level of an early 1900s redbrick building (once a hardware store), the white linen and silver table settings contrast starkly with the restored interior. The menu features dishes using a wide variety of seasonal Canadian produce, including pork, lamb, beef, venison, and salmon, all well prepared and delightfully presented. Lunches such as a grilled Thai chicken salad are less than $15, and dinner entrées run $27–37.

At **Madison's Grill** (Union Bank Inn, 10053 Jasper Ave., 780/423-3600, daily for breakfast, lunch, and dinner), the official-looking architecture of this former bank remains, with contemporary styling balancing columns and ornate ceiling. The kitchen features the best in Canadian ingredients, with the nightly Trio of Fish ($27–33) choices especially popular. The lunchtime grilled tuna on sourdough bread ($12) keeps up the seafood theme. Good food coupled with impeccable service makes Madison's the perfect place for a splurge.

Although the location at the base of an apartment building is unassuming, the **Copper Pot** (9707 110th St., 780/452-7800) is well worth searching out. It's across 109th Street from the legislature building, making it a great lunchtime diversion from seeing the sights of downtown. Seating is tiered, so no one misses out on the views across to the High Level Bridge and beyond, and the setting is bright and modern. At lunch, choose a soup-and-salad combination ($8) or one of the daily offerings ($14–17), which on my visit included pickerel (a sweet whitefish common in the northern waters of Alberta) pan-fried in an almond butter sauce. The dinner menu features lots of game and produce (mostly under $28) sourced from western Canada; bison from the prairies and trout from Great Slave Lake are tasty examples. Diners park for free in the underground lot accessed from 110th Street.

The city's hotels provide further dining options. In general, revolving restaurants are renowned for bad food as much as great views. But **La Ronde** (10111 Bellamy Hill, 780/428-6611), atop the Crowne Plaza Chateau La-

combe, is an exception. The Canadian-inspired menu features delicacies such as roasted Arctic char, braised caribou, and honey-glazed pickerel in the $20–34 range, or enjoy a three-course table d'hôte for $45.

The **Harvest Room** (Fairmont Hotel Macdonald, 10065 100th St., 780/429-6424), has the look of a cruise-ship dining room of yesteryear, but remains remarkably unstuffy. The food itself blends Canadian specialties with European influences and a very comprehensive wine list, to $40. High tea is served each summer afternoon (make reservations for weekend sittings); $22 per person includes a hotel tour.

Asian Fusion

Beside the famous Sidetrack Café (a good place for a pre-dinner drink), **Wild Tangerine** (10383 112th St., 780/429-3131, Mon.–Fri. 11:30 A.M.–10 P.M., Sat. 5–11:30 P.M.) boasts imaginative cooking in a casual, color-filled room. Many dishes have their origins in Asia, but have been given a modern makeover with local produce as a base (think grilled salmon dusted with lemon tea or mussels boiled open in red curry). Expect to pay $12–20 for a main and around $8 for dessert such as chocolate brownie covered in orange marmalade.

Steak

Steak, or, more precisely, Alberta beef, is the star at **Hy's Steak Loft** (10013 101A Ave., 780/424-4444, Mon.–Fri. from 11:30 A.M., daily from 5 P.M.), one of Canada's most renowned steakhouses. The elegant setting, centered around a Tiffany-style skylight, is slightly dated, but no one seems to mind. Only the best aged beef makes it to the table here. It's served in huge, tender cuts ranging from classic prime rib priced at $27–41 to an extravagant chateaubriand (the center cut of a tenderloin) carved tableside for $36 per person. Sides are extra, and of course the wine list is overloaded with good reds to match the meat.

European

Among the dozens of Italian restaurants in the city, one of the most popular is **Sorrentino's**

(780/424-7500, daily for lunch and dinner) with six city locations including downtown at 10162 100th Street. The decor at all locations is stylish, with a great Old World Italian charm. The food is simple and satisfying. Begin with gorgonzola (a blue cheese) baked in puff pastry, then move onto a traditionally rich pasta dish ($14–18), or something lighter such as the veal-and-wild-mushroom ravioli. The menu also features non-Italian choices, such as Australian lamb and Alberta beef.

As you descend the stairs to **The Creperie** below the Boardwalk Market (10220 103rd St., 780/420-6656, Mon.–Fri. for lunch and dinner, weekends dinner only), a great smell, wafting from somewhere in the depths of this historic building, hits you in the face. It takes a minute for your eyes to adjust to the softly lit dining area, but once you do, its inviting French provincial atmosphere is apparent. As you've probably guessed, crepes are the specialty. Choose from fillings as varied as the Canadian-influenced Crepe Pacific ($15), filled with shrimp, salmon, and asparagus, to the classic Crepe Suzette ($7) for dessert.

La Tapa (10523 99th Ave., 780/424-8272, weekdays for lunch, daily for dinner) is a modern, upbeat Spanish eatery in a restored two-story house. There are approximately 20 tapas to choose from, but I found it difficult to go past the *paella* ($18), a rice-based stew of meats and seafood. The wine list includes many Spanish wines, and Spanish beer is also offered.

Cafe Select (10018 106th St., 780/428-1629, Mon.–Fri. 11 A.M.–2 A.M., Sat.–Sun. 5 P.M.–2 A.M.), nestled below a parking garage just off Jasper Avenue, gives the first impression of being an upscale European-style bistro, and to a degree it is. The restaurant is elegant, soft music is played, and a bunch of intellectuals sip wine and eat oysters until two in the morning. But the food is well priced ($12–19 for pasta, steak, or fondue dishes), and no one seems to mind if you stick to just coffee and dessert. Try the chocolate torte ($6.50). The café is open daily until 2 A.M. (midnight on Sunday).

East Indian

My favorite East Indian restaurant in Edmonton is **Haweli** (10220 103rd St., 780/421-8100, daily for lunch and dinner), which has an enchantingly simple ambience, complete with silk curtains separating some tables and soothing background music. The food is traditional all the way, with a good-value lunch buffet ($13) and dinner mains mostly under $15.

OLD STRATHCONA AND VICINITY

This historic suburb south of downtown offers Edmonton's largest concentration of cafés and restaurants. There's a great variety of choices, and because it's a popular late-night hangout, many eateries are open to the wee hours.

Coffeehouses

Block 1912 (10361 82nd Ave., 780/433-6575) offers a great variety of hot drinks, cakes, pastries, and healthy full meals in an inviting atmosphere, which includes several comfortable lounges. Newspapers from around the world are available. **Muddy Waters** (8211 111th St., 780/433-4390) is a popular hangout with locals who really know their coffee. **Second Cup** (10402 82nd Ave., 780/439-8097) occupies the prime spot at a busy intersection. Farther west, upstairs in the **Chapters** bookstore (10504 82nd Ave., 780/435-1290) is a relaxing café away from the hustle and bustle of Whyte Avenue.

Mexican and Cajun

Julio's Barrio Mexican Restaurant (10450 Whyte Ave., 780/431-0774, daily for lunch and dinner until midnight), a huge restaurant decorated with earthy colors and Southwestern-style furniture, has a true Mexican ambience. The menu is appealing but limited. If you just want a light snack, try the warm corn chips with Jack cheese and freshly made Ultimate Salsa ($6.25); for something more substantial, consider the fajitas, presented in a cast-iron pan ($14). This place doesn't get really busy until after 9 P.M.

Da-de-o (10548 Whyte Ave., 780/433-0930,

11:30 A.M.–midnight) is styled on a 1950s diner in New Orleans. The menu features Cajun cuisine, including po'boys—Southern-style sandwiches using French bread and fillings such as blackened catfish and tequila salsa ($7.50 at lunch and all day Mon.–Tues., $10 otherwise)—as well as Southern fried chicken ($14), jambalaya ($14), and inexpensive dishes like barbecue beans and rice ($8) that have appeal to the money-watching college crowd. When the hip evening crowd arrives, service can be blasé at best.

Chinese

West of Old Strathcona, toward the University of Alberta, is **Mandarin Restaurant** (11044 82nd Ave., 780/433-8494, Mon.–Fri 11:30 A.M.–2 P.M. and daily for dinner from 4:30 P.M.), consistently voted as having the best Chinese food in the city, but you'd never know by looking at it. It's informal, noisy, family-style dining, and the walls are plastered with sporting memorabilia donated by diners. Most dishes are from northern China, which is known for traditionally hot food, but enough Cantonese dishes are offered to please all tastes. Expect to pay around $30 per person for a three-course meal.

Fine Dining

Located a few blocks east of the railway tracks, in a renovated shop, is one of Edmonton's most popular restaurants, the **Unheardof** (9602 82nd Ave., 780/432-0480, Tues.–Sun. from 5:30 P.M.). The main dining room is filled with antiques, and the tables are set with starched white linen and silver cutlery. The menu changes weekly, featuring fresh game such as buffalo tenderloin ($30), homemade chutneys, and relishes during fall, and chicken and beef dishes the rest of the year. Mains average $27–37 while desserts such as strawberry shortcake at $10 top off your meal. Although it's most obviously an upmarket restaurant, the service is comfortable, but most importantly, the food is absolutely mouthwatering. Reservations are essential.

A Local Legend

It feels uncomfortable placing this restaurant straight after the renowned Unheardof, especially since it's not even in Old Strathcona (it's a five-minute drive east then south), but **Barb and Ernie's** (9906 72nd Ave., 780/433-3242, Mon.–Fri. 11 A.M.–9 P.M., Sat.–Sun. 9 A.M.– 9 P.M.) needs to be included somewhere, and it doesn't fit anywhere else. Believe it or not, even here in the cultural capital of Canada getting a table at this restaurant sandwiched between auto-body shops nearly always entails a wait. Expect vinyl seats, silver chrome chairs, and photos of the owner with his hockey heroes. The home-style cooking is hearty and reasonably priced. Breakfast is busiest, with all the usual for under $8. The rest of the day, hamburgers begin at $3, and main meals such as roast duck with red cabbage run approximately $12.

Information and Services

Information Centers

For pre-trip planning, contact **Edmonton Tourism** (780/426-4715 or 800/463-4667, www.edmonton.com).

The most central source of tourist information is the main office of Edmonton Tourism downtown at 9990 Jasper Avenue (opposite the Fairmont Hotel Macdonald). If you're driving up to Edmonton from the south along Highway 2, move over to the right lane as you enter the city in preparation for a stop at Edmonton Tourism's **Gateway Park** information center (summer daily 8 A.M.–9 P.M., the rest of the year Mon.–Fri. 8:30 A.M.–4:30 P.M. and Sat.–Sun. 9 A.M.– 5 P.M.). Within this complex, you'll find interpretive displays on the oil industry, stands filled with brochures, and direct-dial phones for Edmonton accommodations. On the arrivals level of the **Edmonton International**

EDMONTON

Airport is another information center (year-round daily 7 A.M.–11 P.M.).

An excellent source of information on Alberta's provincial parks, forest reserves, and other protected areas is the **Alberta Environment Information Centre** (north of the legislature building at 9920 108th Street, 780/944-0313, www.albertaparks.ca, Mon.–Fri. 8:15 A.M.–4:30 P.M.).

Libraries

The Edmonton Public Library System (www .epl.ca) has 13 libraries spread throughout the city. The largest is the **Stanley A. Milner Library** (7 Sir Winston Churchill Square, 780/496-7000). It's open Monday–Friday 9 A.M.–9 P.M., Saturday 9 A.M.–6 P.M., and Sunday 1–5 P.M. This large, two-story facility, connected to the downtown core by pedways, is a great place to spend a rainy afternoon. It carries newspapers, magazines, and phone books from all corners of the globe, as well as rows and rows of western Canadiana. Throughout the week, author readings take place on the main level.

Post and Internet

The main post office is downtown at 9808 103A Avenue.

All downtown hotels have in-room Internet access, while most others have Wi-Fi or an Internet booth in the lobby. Public Internet access is free at all city libraries, or you can pay approximately $5 for 30 minutes downtown at the **Bohemia Cyber Café** (11012 Jasper Ave., 780/429-3442). In West Edmonton Mall, head to **Bytes Internet Café** (Bourbon St., 780/444-7873).

Banks

Main branches of most banks in the downtown area will handle common foreign-currency exchange transactions, as will **Currencies International** (780/484-3868), beside the Fantasyland Hotel lobby in West Edmonton Mall. Edmonton International Airport has a foreign exchange on the departures level.

Photography

Carousel Photo Imaging (10525 Jasper Ave., 780/424-7161) develops print film in an hour and E6 slide film in five hours; it's open Monday–Friday 7 A.M.–5:30 P.M. and Saturday 10 A.M.–4 P.M.

Laundry

On the west side of the city is **LaPerle Home-style Laundry** (9756 182nd St., 780/483-9200), which is handy to the hotels in the area and has large washers and dryers for sleeping bags. **The Laundry** (10808 107th Ave., 780/424-8981) is closer to downtown. The **Soap Time Laundromat** (7626 104th St., 780/439-3599) is open until 11:30 P.M.

Emergency Services

For medical emergencies, call 911 or one of the following hospitals: **Grey Nuns Community Hospital** (corner of 34th Ave. and 66th St., 780/450-7000), **Northeast Community Health Centre** (14007 50th St., 780/472-5000), **Royal Alexandra Hospital** (10240 Kingsway Ave., 780/477-4111), or **University of Alberta Hospital** (8440 112th St., 780/407-8822). For the **Edmonton Police Service,** call 780/945-5330.

Getting There and Around

GETTING THERE

Air

Edmonton International Airport (YEG) is beside Highway 2, 29 kilometers (18 mi) south of the city center. Canada's fifth-largest airport, it has undergone a transformation over the last decade with the construction of a new South Terminal and Central Hall linked to the original buildings, paid for in part by the Airport Improvement Fee ($15), built into all tickets for departing flights and still collected. On the arrivals level is a small information center (year-round daily 7:30 A.M.–11:30 P.M.). Also at the airport are car-rental desks, hotel courtesy phones, a restaurant, and a currency exchange. **Sky Shuttle** (780/465-8515 or 888/438-2342) departs the airport for downtown hotels every 20 minutes (every 30 minutes on weekends) on three different routes. One-way to downtown is $15, round-trip $25; check in at the counter beside the information center. The cab fare to downtown is set at $45 one-way.

Parking is $1 for 30 minutes to a maximum of $10 for any 24-hour period. Long-term parking is available at other places nearby as well. For a regular-size car, **Value Park** (780/890-8439) charges $8 per day or $37 for a full week. The Edmonton International Airport website (www.edmontonairports.com) links to airlines serving Edmonton and all transportation operators.

Rail

The **VIA Rail station** is a small, modern building beyond the west end of the City Centre Airport northwest of downtown (12360 121st St., 800/561-8630, www.viarail.ca). The ticket office is generally open 8 A.M.–3:30 P.M., later when trains are due. A Hertz rental outlet is also open for arriving and departing trains, but reservations are necessary. Trains leave Vancouver (1150 Station St.) and Prince Rupert three times weekly for the 23.5-hour trip to Edmonton (via Jasper), continuing on the Canadian route to the eastern provinces.

Bus

The **Greyhound** bus depot (10324 103rd St., 780/420-2400 or 800/661-8747, www.greyhound.ca) is within walking distance of the city center and many hotels. A cab to Edmonton International Hostel from the depot is $18. Within the depot is an A&W Restaurant, a small paper shop, a cash machine, and large lockers ($2). The depot is open Monday–Saturday 5:30 A.M.–midnight, Sunday 10 A.M.–6 P.M. Buses leave daily for all points in Canada, including Calgary (3.5 hours), Jasper (4.5 hours), and Vancouver (15–17 hours). As always with Greyhound, no seat assignments are given—just turn up, buy your ticket, and hop aboard. You can also buy discounted tickets seven days in advance. If you plan to travel extensively by bus, the Discovery Pass is a good deal.

Red Arrow (780/424-3339, www.redarrow.pwt.ca) buses leave Edmonton five to seven times daily for Red Deer and Calgary and once daily for Fort McMurray. The downtown office and pickup point is off to one side of the Holiday Inn Express (10014 104th St.).

GETTING AROUND

Bus

The **Edmonton Transit System** (780/496-1611, www.edmonton.ca) operates an extensive bus system that links the city center to all parts of the city and many major sights. Not all routes operate on Sunday. For many destinations south of the North Saskatchewan River, you'll need to jump aboard the Light Rail Transit (LRT) to the University Transfer Point. Bus fare anywhere within the city is adult $2.25, senior and youth $2; transfers are available on boarding and can be used for additional travel in any direction within 90 minutes. Day passes are $6.75. For more information and passes, go to the Customer Services Outlet at the Churchill LRT Station on 99th Street (weekdays 8:30 A.M.–4:30 P.M.).

EDMONTON

Light Rail Transit

The LRT has 12 stops (Canada's smallest subway system) running east–west along Jasper Avenue (101st Ave.), northeast as far as Whitemud Park, and south to Heritage Mall, with an extension to Century Park slated for completion in 2009. The LRT runs underground through the city center, connecting with many pedways. Travel between Grandin and Churchill is free Monday–Friday 9 A.M.–3 P.M. and Saturday 9 A.M.–6 P.M. LRT tickets are the same price as the bus, and tickets, transfers, and day passes are valid for travel on either the LRT or the bus system.

High Level Street Car

A great way to travel between downtown and Old Strathcona is on the High Level Street Car (780/437-7721, $3 one way). Trains and trams originally traveled this historic route over the High Level Bridge, but today a restored street car makes the journey from the west side of the Alberta Legislature Building to Old Strathcona every 30 minutes Sunday–Friday 11 A.M.–4 P.M. and Saturday 9 A.M.–4 P.M. One-way fare is $3.

Passengers with Disabilities

Edmonton Transit operates the Disabled Adult Transit System (DATS, 780/496-4570), which provides access to various points of the city for passengers with physical disabilities who are unable to use the regular transit system. The door-to-door service costs the same as Edmonton Transit adult tickets. Priority is given to those heading to work or for medical trips. A Pedway Information Sheet, detailing accessibility, is available from City Hall (780/424-4085).

Taxi

The standard flag charge for cabs is $2.75 plus approximately $1.65 per kilometer, but most companies have flat rates for major destinations within the city. Major companies are **Checker Cabs** (780/484-8888), **Alberta Co-op Taxi Line** (780/425-2525), **Prestige Cabs** (780/462-4444), and **Yellow Cab** (780/462-3456).

Car Rental

If you've just arrived in Edmonton, call around and compare rates. All major agencies include unlimited mileage and built-in charges for airport pickups. They also provide free pickup and drop-off at major Edmonton hotels and have outlets at the airport. Rental agencies and their local numbers are **Avis** (780/448-0066), **Budget** (780/448-2000), **Discount** (780/448-3888), **Enterprise** (780/440-4550), **Hertz** (780/415-5283), **National** (780/422-6097), **Rent-a-Wreck** (780/986-3335), and **Thrifty** (780/890-4555).

NORTHERN ALBERTA

The northern half of Alberta, from Highway 16 north to the 60th parallel, is a sparsely populated land of unspoiled wilderness, home to deer, moose, coyotes, foxes, lynx, black bears, and the elusive Swan Hills grizzly bear. For the most part, it is heavily forested, part of the boreal forest ecoregion that sweeps around the Northern Hemisphere, broken only by the Atlantic and Pacific Oceans. Much of the world's boreal forest has been devastated by logging, but in northern Alberta a good portion of the land is muskeg—low-lying bogs and marshes that make logging difficult and expensive. Only a few species of trees are adapted to the long, cold winters and short summer growing seasons characteristic of these northern latitudes. Conifers such as white spruce, black spruce, jack pine, fir, and larch are the most common.

This vast expanse of land is relatively flat, the only exceptions being the Swan Hills—which rise to 1,200 meters (3,900 ft)—and, farther north, the Birch and Caribou Mountains. The Athabasca and Peace River Systems are the region's largest waterways. Carrying water from hundreds of tributaries, they merge in the far northeastern corner of the province and flow north into the Arctic Ocean. A third major watercourse, the North Saskatchewan River, flows east from the Continental Divide, crossing northern Alberta on its way to Hudson Bay. Alberta's earliest explorers arrived along these rivers, opening up the Canadian West to the trappers, missionaries, and settlers who followed.

Northeast of Edmonton is the Lakeland region, where many early fur-trading posts were

HIGHLIGHTS

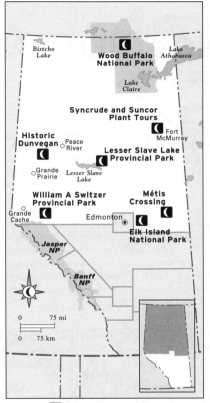

《 Elk Island National Park: Nowhere else in the province has the wildlife-viewing opportunities of this small park. Sightings of elk, moose, and bison are (almost) guaranteed (page 388).

《 Métis Crossing: This, Canada's largest Métis cultural center, spreads across a riverfront site important for its historical links to native peoples and fur traders (page 395).

《 Syncrude and Suncor Plant Tours: With more oil reserves than the rest of the world combined, it's no surprise that Fort McMurray is booming. The best way to take it all in is on one of these bus tours (page 406).

《 Wood Buffalo National Park: A visit to the world's second-largest national park requires time and money, but visitors will be rewarded with the sight of the world's largest free-roaming herd of bison (page 412).

《 Lesser Slave Lake Provincial Park: Alberta isn't renowned for its white sandy beaches and beautiful over-water sunsets, but this large park has both (page 419).

《 William A. Switzer Provincial Park: Dotted with fish-filled lakes and home to abundant big game, this park is a great place for outdoor enthusiasts to pitch a tent for a night or two (page 432).

《 Historic Dunvegan: Dating to 1885, the missionary buildings at this site are in beautiful condition. And if you're not a history buff, there's a colorful suspension bridge to admire (page 444).

LOOK FOR **《** TO FIND RECOMMENDED SIGHTS, ACTIVITIES, DINING, AND LODGING.

established. From there, Highway 63 heads north through boreal forest to Fort McMurray, an isolated city of 48,000, 450 kilometers (280 mi) north of its closest sizable neighbor, Edmonton. Oil is Fort McMurray's raison d'être—oil sands, to be precise. The Athabasca Oil Sands are the world's largest such deposit, and the city is booming.

North-central Alberta extends from Edmonton's outer suburbs north to the towns of Athabasca and Slave Lake, which are jumping-off points into the vast boreal forest. This area is a paradise for bird-watchers because it's at the confluence of three major flyways.

West of Edmonton, the Yellowhead Highway climbs into the Canadian Rockies, passing through Hinton, a town surrounded by natural wonders. From Hinton, travelers can continue on Highway 16 into Jasper National Park, or take Highway 40 northwest to Willmore Wilderness Park, a park usually ignored by tourists in favor of the neighboring national parks to the south. Continuing north on Highway 4, you come to Grande Prairie, one of northern Alberta's largest cities and a regional agriculture and service center. The Peace River Valley, north of Grande Prairie, leads travelers into the Northwest Territories via the Mackenzie Highway (Highway 35), which parallels the Peace and Hay Rivers.

With few regular "sights," northern Alberta receives fewer tourists than the rest of the province. Those who do venture north find solitude in a vast untapped wilderness with abundant wildlife and plenty of recreation—lakes and rivers to fish, historic sites to explore, rivers to float on, and gravel roads to drive just for the sake of it.

PLANNING YOUR TIME

The region covered in this chapter is similar in size to all the other chapters combined, and is relatively remote. One week in Alberta just isn't enough time to include this region, but with two weeks and a special interest (such as fishing or camping), you should plan on including at least a portion of the region in your itinerary. The exception to this is **Elk Island National Park,** close enough to Edmonton to make it part of a trip to that city. On a two- or three-day loop from the capital, you could include this park, plus cultural Lakeland highlights such as **Métis Crossing** while returning via the sandy beaches of **Lesser Slave Lake Provincial Park.** Fort McMurray is center of world attention for its oil sands, and although it's a long drive (or a short flight), a visit could be compared to spending time in a boomtown of a century ago, like Dawson City. But don't trek north without reservations for accommodation and a **Syncrude or Suncor plant tour.** If you dedicate a full week to Northern Alberta, plan on hitting the highlights already mentioned, and then heading west through Hinton to **William A. Switzer Provincial Park,** with its abundant wildlife and great fishing, and north to the Peace Country, where places like **Historic Dunvegan** have changed little since the days of the missionaries. The wilderness of **Wood Buffalo National Park,** in the northeast corner of the province, is only accessible by road through the Northwest Territories, making it a natural extension of a visit to that province. But those with a sense of adventure can fly north from Fort McMurray to Fort Chipewyan and reach the park by boat.

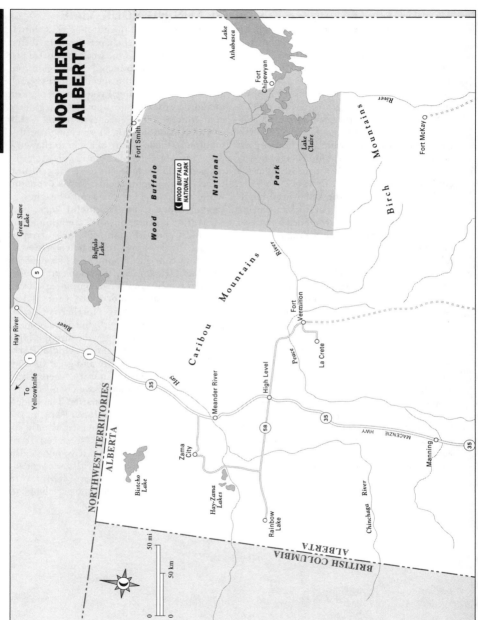

NORTHERN ALBERTA

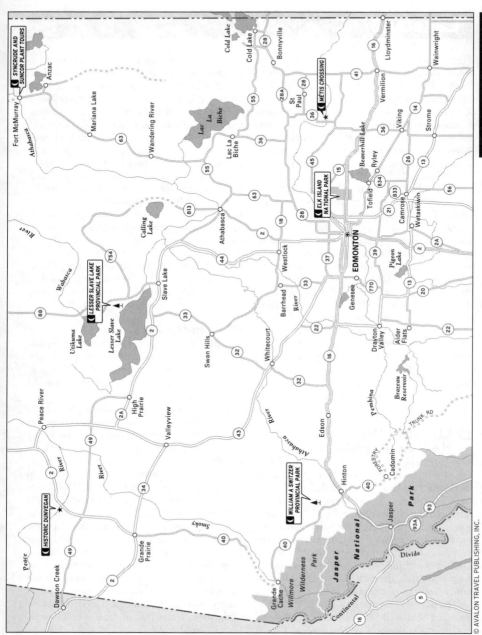

SYNCRUDE AND
SUNCOR PLANT TOURS

Anzac

Fort McMurray

Athabasca

Mariana Lake

63

Wandering River

Lac La Biche

55

Lac La Biche

36

Cold Lake

Cold Lake

28

Bonnyville

16

Lloydminster

Wainwright

41

Vermilion

28A

St Paul

28

MÉTIS CROSSING

36

14

Viking

Strome

Beaverhill Lake

36

26

13

55

63

813

Calling Lake

Athabasca

2

18

28

45

15

ELK ISLAND NATIONAL PARK

Tofield

834

Ryley

833

21

Camrose

56

Wetaskiwin

River

Wabasca

LESSER SLAVE LAKE PROVINCIAL PARK

754

Westlock

44

EDMONTON

37

2

2A

Slave Lake

Utikuma Lake

88

Lesser Slave Lake

2

33

Barrhead

River

33

Genesee

770

Pigeon Lake

39

13

20

22

Swan Hills

32

Whitecourt

32

16

Drayton Valley

Alder Flats

22

Brazeau Reservoir

High Prairie

2A

Valleyview

43

Athabasca River

Edson

Pembina

TRUNK RD

Peace River

49

River

River

River

34

Smoky

40

Grande Prairie

HISTORIC DUNVEGAN

49

Grande Prairie

2

Dawson Creek

Peace

River

WILLIAM A SWITZER PROVINCIAL PARK

Hinton

FORESTRY

Cadomin

40

Jasper

93

93A

93A

Divide

Park

National

Jasper

Wilmore

Wilderness

Park

40

Grande Cache

Continental

Divide

5

16

Lakeland

Highway 16, east from Edmonton, follows the southern flanks of a region containing hundreds of lakes formed at the end of the last ice age by a retreating sheet of ice nearly one kilometer (0.6 mi) thick. From its headwaters beneath the Columbia Icefield on the Continental Divide, the **North Saskatchewan River** flows east through Edmonton and the Lakeland region before eventually draining into Hudson Bay.

History buffs appreciate the legacies of early white settlers that dot the landscape here—restored fur-trading posts, missions, and the Ukrainian Village near Vegreville. Other visitors are attracted by the region's vast areas of unspoiled wilderness, including seven provincial parks. Anglers will feel right at home among the area's countless lakes, and wildlife-watchers are drawn to Elk Island National Park, which rivals Tanzania's Serengeti Plain for the population densities of its animal inhabitants.

The region's major population centers are Lloydminster (250 km/155 mi east of Edmonton), Canada's only town in two provinces; St. Paul, which has the world's only UFO landing pad; and Cold Lake, at the edge of the boreal forest, surrounded by vast reserves of untapped oil.

◖ ELK ISLAND NATIONAL PARK

Heading east from Edmonton on Highway 16, you'll reach Elk Island National Park in well under an hour. This small, fenced, 194-square-kilometer (75-square-mi) park preserves a remnant of the transitional grassland ecoregion—the aspen parkland—that once covered the entire northern flank of the prairie. It's also one of the best spots in Alberta for wildlife-watching; with approximately 3,000 large mammals, the park has one of the highest concentrations of big game in the world.

The park was originally set aside in 1906 to protect a herd of elk; it's Canada's only national park formed to protect a native species. The elk

here have never been crossbred and are probably the most genetically pure in the world. In addition to approximately 1,600 elk, resident mammals include moose, two species of bison, white-tailed and mule deer, coyotes, beavers, muskrats, mink, and porcupines. The many lakes and wetland areas in the park serve as nesting sites for waterfowl, and approximately 230 species of birds have been observed here.

A mosaic of mixed-wood forest—predominantly aspen and balsam poplar—covers the low, rolling Beaver Hills, slowly taking over the grassland. One slow-moving stream winds its way through the park, and many shallow lakes dot the landscape.

Park entry for one day is adult $7, senior $6, child $3.50 to a maximum of $14 per vehicle; if you've purchased an annual pass, you'll be waved straight through the fee station (but stop to pick up park information anyway).

Bison in the Park

Two different species of bison inhabit the park, and to prevent interbreeding, they are separated. All bison on the north side of Highway 16 are **plains bison,** whereas those on the south side are **wood bison.**

Before the late 1700s, 60 million plains bison lived on the North American plains. In less than a century, humanity brought these shaggy beasts to the brink of extinction. By 1880, incredibly, only a few hundred plains bison remained. A small herd, owned by ranchers in Montana, was brought north in 1907. They were held at what was then Elk Island Reserve until Buffalo National Park (since closed) at Wainwright was fenced. When it came time to move the animals from Elk Island, some couldn't be found, and today's herd descended from those well-hidden progenitors. A small part of the herd is kept in a large enclosure just north of the Park Information Centre, whereas others roam freely through the north section of the park. Today they number approximately 630 within the park.

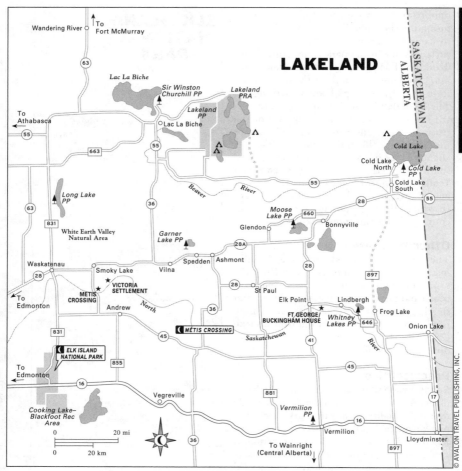

The wood bison, the largest native land mammal in North America, was thought to be extinct for many years—a victim of hunting, severe winters, and interbreeding with its close relative, the plains bison. In 1957, a herd of 200 was discovered in the remote northwestern corner of Wood Buffalo National Park. Some were captured and transported to the Mackenzie Bison Sanctuary in the Northwest Territories and to Elk Island National Park. The herd at Elk Island has ensured the survival of the species, and today it is the purest herd in the world. It is used as breeding stock for several captive herds throughout North America. To view the herd of 420, look south from Highway 16 or hike the Wood Bison Trail.

Hiking

Twelve trails, ranging in length from 1.4–18.5 kilometers (0.9–11.5 mi), cover all areas of the park and provide excellent

NORTHERN ALBERTA

opportunities to view wildlife. A park information sheet details each one. Make sure to carry water with you, though, because surface water in the park is not suitable for drinking. The paved **Shoreline Trail** (three km/1.9 mi one-way) follows the shore of Astotin Lake from the golf course parking lot. The **Lakeview Trail** (3.3 km/two mi round-trip) begins from the northern end of the recreation area and provides good views of the lake. Hike this trail in the evening for a chance to see beavers. The only trail on the south side of Highway 16 is the **Wood Bison Trail** (18.6 km/11.5 mi round-trip), which has an interpretive display at the trailhead. In winter, the trails provide excellent cross-country skiing and snowshoeing.

Other Recreation

The day-use area at **Astotin Lake,** 14 kilometers (8.7 mi) north of Highway 16, is the center of much activity. There's a pleasant beach and picnic area; canoes, rowboats, and small sailboats can be rented; and the rolling fairways of adjacent **Elk Island Golf Course** (780/998-3161, $36) provide an interesting diversion for golfers.

Practicalities

Sandy Beach Campground, on the north side of the Astotin Lake day-use area, is the only overnight facility within the park. It has fire pits, picnic tables, flush toilets, and showers; $25 per night plus $8 for a firewood permit. If you're traveling in the peak of summer (especially on weekends), it is strongly recommended to use the **Parks Canada Campground Reservation Service** (905/426-4648 or 877/737-3783, www.pccamping.ca, nonrefundable $11 reservation fee). The main campground is only open in summer; the rest of the year, primitive camping (no water, chemical toilets) is available at the boat-launch area. A concession selling fast food and basic camping supplies operates May–October at Astotin Lake, and the golf course (780/998-3161) has a casual restaurant.

If the weather isn't cooperating, there's

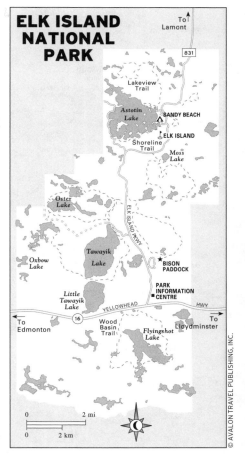

an alternative to camping—continue north through the park to the hamlet of Lamont, where **Archie's Motel** (5008 49th Ave., 780/895-2225) charges $50 s, $60 d in one of 10 basic rooms.

The **Park Information Centre** (780/992-5790, May–June weekends only, July–Aug. daily 10 A.M.–6 P.M.) is less than one kilometer (0.6 mi) north of Highway 16 on the Elk Island Parkway. For online information, click through the links on the Parks Canada website (www.pc.gc.ca).

bison

EAST ALONG THE YELLOWHEAD HIGHWAY

Blackfoot Recreation Area

South of Elk Island National Park is the 97-square-kilometer (34-square-mi) Cooking Lake–Blackfoot Recreation Area. It is an integrated resource management unit, meaning that it can be used for many purposes, including grazing, mineral exploration, hunting, and recreation. It is part of the massive Cooking Lake Moraine, formed during the last ice age as the retreating sheet of ice stalled for a time, leaving mounds and hollows that have since filled with water. Large natural areas of wetland and forest provide habitat for abundant wildlife, including moose, elk, white-tailed deer, coyotes, beavers, and more than 200 species of birds. Much of the well-posted trail system is for hikers only, but some parts are open to horses and mountain bikes. The **Blackfoot Staging Area,** off Highway 16, is the trailhead for a good selection of short hiking trails, but to really get into the heart of the area, head south along the southwestern border of Elk Island National Park to three other staging areas.

Ukrainian Cultural Heritage Village

This heritage village (50 km/31 mi east of Edmonton, 780/662-3640, late May–Aug. daily 10 A.M.–6 P.M., Sept. Sat.–Sun. 10 A.M.–6 P.M., adult $8, senior $7, child $4) is a realistic replica of a Ukrainian settlement, common in the rural areas of east-central Alberta at the turn of the 20th century. The first, and largest, Ukrainian settlement in Canada was located in this region. Driven from their homeland in Eastern Europe, Ukrainians fled to the Canadian prairies where, for many years, they dressed and worked in the ways of the Old World. These traditions are kept alive with costumed guides and a lively program of cultural events.

Vegreville

Although first settled by French farmers from Kansas, this town of 5,300 is best known for its Ukrainian heritage. Today Vegreville's

© ANDREW HEMPSTEAD

the world's largest *pysanka* – a Ukrainian Easter egg

biggest attraction is the world's largest **pysanka,** a giant, traditionally decorated Ukrainian Easter egg at the east end of town. It measures eight meters (26 ft) in length, weighs 2,270 kilograms (5,000 lbs), and can turn in the wind like a giant weathervane.

Vegreville celebrates its multicultural past on Canada Day (July 1) weekend with the **Ukrainian Pysanka Folk Festival.**

Vermilion

The reddish-colored iron deposits in a nearby river gave this town of 4,300 at the junction of Highways 16 and 41 its name. Many downtown buildings date to the 1919–1920 period after a fire destroyed the original main street (50th Avenue) in 1918. Made of locally fired brick, many have plaques detailing their history. Pick up a walking-tour brochure at the information center (summer daily 10 A.M.–6 P.M.) by the entrance to town. In a 1928 school building, **Vermilion Heritage Museum** (50th Ave. at 53rd St., 780/853-6211, mid-June–Aug. daily 11 A.M.–5 P.M.,

donation) holds an extensive photographic collection and native artifacts.

Vermilion Provincial Park is one of only two urban-area provincial parks in Alberta. The park encompasses 771 hectares (1,900 acres) of aspen parkland and grassland along the banks of the Vermilion River, an ancient glacial meltwater channel. To date, 20 species of mammals and 110 species of birds have been documented here. The park also has 15 kilometers (9.3 mi) of hiking trails and a campground with showers and a trout pond ($17–21). Access is from the west side of town, north along 62nd Street. This road winds around the back of a residential area, passes a 1905 CN railway station (relocated), and then descends to a riverside day-use area.

LLOYDMINSTER

North America has several twin cities that straddle borders (such as Minneapolis and St. Paul), but Lloydminster is the only one that has a single corporate body in two provinces (or states, depending on the case). Approximately 60 percent of the city's 23,000 residents live on the Alberta side, separated from their Saskatchewan neighbors by the main street.

Lloydminster was settled in 1903 by over 1,000 immigrants from Britain, who followed the Reverend George Lloyd to the site in search of good agricultural land. The community thrived, and when the provinces of Alberta and Saskatchewan were created out of the Northwest Territories in 1905, the town was divided by the new border, which ran along the fourth meridian. It functioned as two separate communities until 1930, when community leaders requested that the two halves be amalgamated into the City of Lloydminster. Farming and cattle ranching form the base of the regional economy, although oil and natural gas play an important role in the city's future.

Sights

The **Barr Colony Heritage Cultural Centre** (4515 44th St., 306/825-5655, July–Aug. daily 10 A.M.–8 P.M., the rest of the year Wed.–Sun. 1–5 P.M., adult $4, child $3) houses the

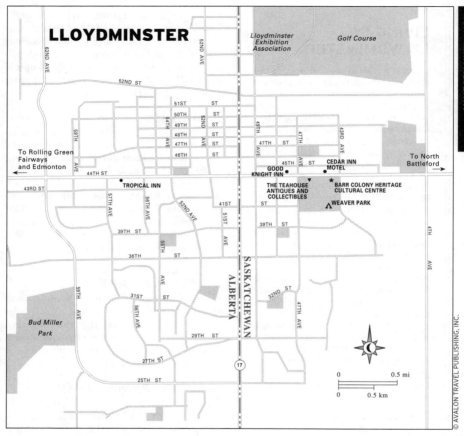

Richard Larsen Museum, featuring a collection of artifacts and antiques used by early settlers. Also here, the Imhoff Art Gallery contains more than 200 works of early-1900s artist Count Berthold Von Imhoff, a room is dedicated to describing oils sands technology, and a number of historic buildings dot the courtyard.

The 81-hectare (200-acre) **Bud Miller Park** (south of Hwy. 16 along 59th Ave., 780/875-4497, daily 7 A.M.–11 P.M.) offers several nature trails winding around a two-hectare lake and through stands of aspen. Canada's largest sundial, a tree maze, formal gardens, an arbo-

retum, a nature center, and boat rentals can also be found here.

Accommodations and Food

Although it looks decidedly untropical from outside, kids will love the **Tropical Inn** (5621 44th St., 780/825-7000 or 800/219-5244, www.tropical inns.com, $98–125) for its indoor water slide and pool complex. The 165 guest rooms are surprisingly appealing, with nice extras such as dry cleaning and high-speed Internet rounding out a good choice for overnight accommodations. A couple of cheapies on the Saskatchewan side of the border are **Cedar Inn Motel** (4526 44th

LIVING IN LLOYDMINSTER

Living in a town in two provinces can be confusing. Saskatchewan has a 5 percent provincial sales tax, but to make it more equitable for local businesses competing with those in a tax-free province that is literally across the road, the provincial government has exempted them from collecting the tax. The liquor store on the Alberta side is always busier – Alberta's booze is cheaper. The minimum drinking age is 19 in Saskatchewan, but 18-year-olds can just cross the road into Alberta to drink. Natural gas is supplied to all residents by an Alberta company, but only residents on the Alberta side get a government rebate. Albertans pay a monthly fee for health care (Saskatchewan residents get it for free), even though everyone goes to a hospital on the Saskatchewan side. The minimum wage is higher in Saskatchewan and vacations are longer, but income tax is higher. The best strategy might be to live in Alberta and work in Saskatchewan; houses on the Alberta side are up to 30 percent more expensive, but the province has lower taxes, and with a job in Saskatchewan – where the benefits are better – you'd come out in front eventually.

St., 306/825-6155, $50 s, $55 d) and the air-conditioned **Good Knight Inn** (4729 44th St., 306/825-0124, $58 s, $70 d).

Weaver Park Campsite (behind the Barr Colony Centre, 306/825-3726) has showers and a grocery store; unserviced sites $15, hookups $20–25. Much nicer is **Rolling Green Fairways** (780/875-4653, www.rollinggreens golf.ca, $22–27), two kilometers (1.2 mi) west of the city on Highway 16, then one kilometer (0.6 mi) north. Facilities include showers, a laundry room, free firewood, and, as the name suggests, an adjacent golf course.

The **Tea House** (south side of Hwy. 16, just east of the border post, 306/825-9498) was built in 1942 and is surrounded by well-established gardens. Afternoon tea and light lunches are served April–December Tuesday–Saturday 10 A.M.–6 P.M. Local favorites are the Irish pub and Tony Roma's restaurant in the **Tropical Inn** (5621 44th St., 780/825-7000); the latter is open for breakfast.

Information

The best source of information once you arrive in town is the provincially operated **Travel Alberta Information Centre** (one km/.6 mi east of town, mid-May–mid-June daily 9 A.M.–6 P.M., summer daily 8 A.M.–7 P.M.). The **Saskatchewan Visitor Reception Centre** (beside the Barr Colony Centre, 306/825-8690, summer daily 8 A.M.–8 P.M.) also has information on the town, but is mainly a source of information for those heading east.

HIGHWAY 28 TO SMOKY LAKE

Highway 28 leaves Edmonton heading north through the suburbs. After a series of 90-degree turns—first one way, then the other, then back again—it comes to **Waskatenau,** where it straightens out to pursue an easterly direction heading toward Cold Lake.

Long Lake Provincial Park

During the last ice age, the low-lying area occupied by this 764-hectare (1,890-acre) park was part of a deep glacial meltwater channel that has now filled with water. Today it's surrounded by boreal forest, although aspens predominate in the park because of fires over the years. Fishing is great here because the main body of water holds some lunker northern pike, as well as perch and walleye. Right on the lake is a 220-site campground (780/576-3959, April–Oct., unserviced sites $20, powered sites $25), with flush toilets, showers, a grocery store, and canoe rentals. To get there from Highway 28, head north from Waskatenau on Highway 831 for 48 kilometers (30 mi).

Immediately to the south of the park is the **White Earth Valley Natural Area,** a 2,055-hectare (5,080-acre) tract of land set aside to

protect the habitat of the abundant wildlife and waterfowl.

Smoky Lake

Named for a lake 93 kilometers (58 mi) west of St. Paul, where natives once rested and smoked pipes during hunts, this small town is home to the **Great White North Pumpkin Fair & Weigh-off** (www.smokylake.com), an annual competition to find the largest pumpkin. But don't waste time scanning the vegetable section at your local supermarket for a winner; you'll need a pumpkin weighing at least 340 kilograms (750 lbs) to take the day at Smoky Lake (the world record is 513 kg/1,130 lbs). For those who don't consider size important, there's always a prize for the ugliest pumpkin (officially, only "aesthetically challenged" pumpkins can be entered, appeasing the politically correct) and the pumpkin that's traveled the farthest. Celebrations take place the first weekend of October out at the agricultural complex at the junction of Highways 28 and 855. The official weigh-in takes place on Saturday at noon and is followed by a pig roast and, on Sunday, the Pumpkin Classic Golf Tournament.

VICTORIA TRAIL

Take Highway 855 south from Smoky Lake for 10 kilometers (6.2 mi) to reach Victoria Trail, an unpaved road along the north side of the North Saskatchewan River.

◖ Métis Crossing

At the junction of Highway 855 and Victoria Trail, Métis Crossing (780/656-2229, June–Aug. daily 11 A.M.–6 P.M., adult $5, senior and child $3) is the country's largest cultural center dedicated to the Métis, the descendants of those born as the result of relationships between French traders and native Cree women. George McDougall established a mission on the site in 1862 and within a decade it was surrounded by a bustling Métis community, who used the riverfront setting as a hub for trade. The restoration project is still in its infancy (the first phase opened in late 2006), but already there are plenty of things to do and see,

including a restored barn containing the story of the people's role in the fur trade and how a distinct culture emerged. Also on site are a craft store, playground, and campground.

Victoria Settlement

Victoria Settlement (7 km/4.3 mi east of Hwy. 855, 780/656-2333, mid-May–Aug. daily 10 A.M.–6 P.M., adult $3, senior $2, child $1.50) is the perfect compliment to Métis Crossing. In 1864, the Hudson's Bay Company established a fur-trading post at the site. The post closed in 1897 and was abandoned until the early 1900s, when groups of Ukrainian settlers moved to the area and the settlement became known as Victoria-Pakan. When the railway bypassed the settlement in 1918, businesses moved north to Smoky Lake, and the area was abandoned once again. Head to the 1906 Methodist church for a slideshow about the settlement or wander past the clerk's 1864 log cabin to the river and the graves of the founder's three daughters. Picnic tables are set among broad maple trees, which were planted during the fur-trading days.

From Victoria Settlement, you can continue south on Highway 855, which eventually intersects Highway 16 west of Vegreville. Along the way, you'll pass by **Andrew**, home of the world's largest mallard duck. Be careful not to rip your jeans climbing the fence to touch it.

ST. PAUL

This town of 5,000, 210 kilometers (130 mi) northeast of Edmonton, has spent many thousands of dollars developing an attraction that hasn't had a single official visitor in over 30 years. And the skeptics doubt it ever will. You guessed it (or maybe you didn't), St. Paul has the world's only **UFO landing pad**—a raised platform beside the main road forlornly waiting for a visitor from outer space. Beside the pad, the **tourist information center** (50th Ave. at 53rd St., 780/645-6800, daily 9 A.M.–5 P.M.) has interesting displays including photos of *real* UFOs as well as descriptions of some famous hoaxes. The building is a raised, UFO-shaped circular structure;

if approaching from outer space, look for the green flashing light on top.

The town's origins date to 1896, when Father Albert Lacombe, the famed Western missionary, established a settlement where Métis people—who had been largely ignored by the government during treaty talks—could live and learn farming skills. Lacombe extended an open invitation to all Métis in western Canada, but fewer than 300 responded. After 10 years of hardship, he opened the settlement to whites, attracting people from many cultures. The town's diverse background is cataloged at the **Musee Historique de St. Paul** (4537 50th Ave., 780/645-4800, summer Mon.–Fri. 8:30 A.M.–4:30 P.M.). At the south end of town (head down 47th St.) is **Upper Therien Lake.** More than 200 species of birds have been recorded around this and other nearby lakes. A large stretch of land along Lakeshore Drive has been set aside as a park with picnic shelters and paths leading out to the lake.

Accommodations

Rooms at the **King's Motel** (5638 50th Ave., 780/645-5656 or 800/265-7407, $55 s, $65 d) each come with a fridge and microwave. **St. Paul Overnight Trailer Park** (55th St. at 49th Ave., May–Sept., unserviced sites $12, powered sites $17), which has showers, is a short walk from the golf course. **Westcove Municipal Recreation Area** (16 km/10 mi north of St. Paul, 780/645-6688, May–mid-Sept., tents $9, unserviced sites $16, powered sites $18) is beside a beach on the shore of Vincent Lake and has all facilities.

ST. PAUL TO LLOYDMINSTER

Twenty-eight kilometers (17 mi) east of St. Paul, Highway 28 makes a 90-degree left turn at its junction with Highway 41 and resumes its northeasterly course toward Cold Lake (see *Northeast Toward Cold Lake* later in this chapter). Those heading back to Highway 16 can turn right at this junction and either beeline directly south on Highway 41 to Vermilion or wind around the backwoods to Lloydminster, taking in the following sights.

Nine kilometers (5.6 mi) south of the

Highway 28/41 junction is the hamlet of **Elk Point**—look for a large mural outlining the history of the area along 50th Avenue and an 11-meter (36-ft) statue of explorer Peter Fidler at the north end of town. Turn left (east) onto Highway 646, and soon you'll come to Fort George and the Buckingham House.

Fort George/Buckingham House

The site of these two fur-trading posts on the north bank of the North Saskatchewan River has been designated a Provincial Historical Site (13 km/eight mi east of Elk Point, 780/724-2611, mid-May–Aug. daily 10 A.M.–6 P.M., adult $3, senior $2, child $1.50). In 1792, soon after the North West Company had established Fort George, the Hudson's Bay Company followed suit a few hundred steps away with Buckingham House. Both posts were abandoned in the early 1800s and have long since been destroyed; depressions in the ground, piles of stone, and indistinct pathways are all that remain. Above the site is an interpretive center with audio and visual presentations explaining the rivalry between the two companies and the history of the forts. Interpretive trails lead from the center down to the river.

Lindbergh

Ever wondered where that salt on your dining table came from? Take a tour of the **Canadian Salt Company** (three km/1.9 mi east of Fort George/Buckingham House, 780/724-3745), owned by the Windsor Salt conglomerate, to find out. A vast reserve of salt left behind when the ocean that once covered Alberta receded lies deep below the earth's surface (1,000 m/3,300 ft underground) in the vicinity of Lindbergh. It is harvested via a simple yet effective process that pumps water into the bed of salt, creating a brine that is then brought to the surface and boiled to separate the salt from impurities. Hour-long tours of the facility are available on weekdays 9 A.M.–2 P.M. (free, reservations necessary).

Whitney Lakes Provincial Park

Whitney, Ross, Laurier, and Borden Lakes are the namesake attractions at this 1,490-hect-

are (3,680-acre) park on Highway 646. The fishing is excellent in all lakes but Borden. Because the park is in a transition zone, plant, mammal, and bird species are diverse. A mixed forest of aspen, white spruce, balsam poplar, and jack pine grows on the uplands, whereas black spruce and tamarack grow in lower, wetter areas. Beavers are common—look for their ponds on the north side of Laurier Lake. Other resident mammals include porcupines, white-tailed deer, coyotes, and, during berry season, black bears. Birds are abundant, especially waterfowl and shorebirds. A 1.5-kilometer (0.9-mi) interpretive trail starts at the day-use area at the northeast corner of Ross Lake. Fishing is best for northern pike, perch, and pickerel.

Within the park are two campgrounds with a total of more than 200 sites. **Ross Lake Campground** has 149 powered sites on six short loops around the south and eastern shore of the lake. Coin-operated showers are located between loops A and B. Whitney Lakes Campground is smaller and has no showers but does have power hookups. A trail along the shore links both campgrounds. Sites are $17–23 and no reservations are taken.

Frog Lake

On April 2, 1885, a band of Cree led by Chief Big Bear massacred nine whites in a remote Hudson's Bay Company post on Frog Lake. It was an act of desperation on the part of the Cree. The great buffalo herds had been devastated, and the fur trade was coming to an end. Big Bear had been forced into signing land treaties to prevent his people from starving. Life on reserves didn't suit the nomadic Cree, and they yearned to return to the old ways. Exactly what sparked the massacre remains unknown, but word of confrontations farther east may have encouraged the Cree. Historians believe the natives originally planned to take hostages, but when Tom Quinn, the post's Indian agent, refused native orders, a shooting spree took place.

The site is marked by a small graveyard and a series of interpretive panels outlining the events leading up to the massacre. To get there from Whitney Lakes, continue east on Highway 646 to its junction with Highway 897. Follow Highway 897 north to the small hamlet of Frog Lake. At the Frog Lake General Store, head east for three kilometers (1.9 mi) to a slight rise, then south at the crest.

To Lloydminster

From Frog Lake, get back on Highway 646 and follow it east to Highway 17 at the native community of **Onion Lake.** Highway 17 parallels the border 26 kilometers (16 mi) south to Lloydminster.

NORTHEAST TOWARD COLD LAKE

Highway 28A leaves Ashmont and bisects Upper and Lower Mann Lakes (best fishing is in Upper Mann Lake on the *south* side of the road).

Glendon

Twenty-five kilometers (15.5 mi) farther east is a turnoff to Glendon. This village's claim to fame takes the cake, or actually the pyrogy—it has the **world's largest pyrogy.** This important part of the Ukrainian diet (something like boiled potato- or onion-filled ravioli) can be sampled next to Pyrogy Park (free camping) in the Pyrogy Park Cafe, opposite the Pyrogy Motel (780/635-3002) on Pyrogy Drive.

Bonnyville

Originally called St. Louis de Moose Lake, this town of 5,500 is an agriculture center surrounded by many good fishing and swimming lakes, including **Moose Lake,** to the west, and **Muriel Lake,** to the south. The town is situated on the north shore of **Jessie Lake,** where more than 300 species of waterfowl and shorebirds have been recorded. Spring and fall are the best viewing times, although many species are present year-round, nesting in the marshes and aspen parkland surrounding the lake. Numerous viewing platforms, linked by the **Wetlands Nature Trail,** are scattered along Lakeshore Drive and Highway 41.

All of Bonnyville's tourist facilities, including motels, are along the main highway. The

tourist information center (780/826-3252, summer Mon.–Fri. 9 A.M.–8 P.M., Sat.–Sun. 10 A.M.–6 P.M.) is at the west end of town.

Moose Lake Provincial Park

Moose Lake is a large, shallow body of water west of Bonnyville between Highways 28A and 660. One of Alberta's earliest trading posts was built in 1789 on the shore of Moose Lake by Angus Shaw, of the North West Company. All that remains of the post is a pile of rocks and a depression just west of Moose Lake River (which forms the park's western boundary). In 1870, a smallpox epidemic wiped out the local Cree—they're buried on the west side of Deadman's Point. Access to the lake is possible from many directions, but the 736-hectare (1,820-acre) provincial park is on the lake's north shore. All but Deadman's Point has been affected by fire and is reforested with jack pine and dense forests of aspen and birch. Ground squirrels and coyotes are common, and black bears occasionally wander through. The park's namesake moose, however, are long gone. The lakeshore is a good place to explore, with trails leading either way from the day-use area to good sandy beaches. Another trail leads to the tip of Deadman's Point and to a bog that is home to many species of birds. Fishing in the lake is best for northern pike, perch, and walleye. The small campground has 59 sites on two loops, both of which have access to the beach; unserviced sites $20, powered sites $23.

COLD LAKE

At the end of Highway 28, a little less than 300 kilometers (186 mi) northeast of Edmonton, is Cold Lake (pop. 13,000). In 1997, the administration of three existing towns—Cold Lake, Grand Centre, and Medley—amalgamated; only seven kilometers (4.3 mi) separates what are now known as Cold Lake North and Cold Lake South but still collectively referred to as simply Cold Lake. The area you'll want to visit is Cold Lake North, on the south shore of Alberta's seventh-largest lake. This historic town has a large marina and is close to Cold Lake Provincial Park. The town that is still

marked on many maps as Medley—now part of Cold Lake South—is, in fact, only the name of the post office at **4 Wing Cold Lake,** Canada's largest air force base. Over 5,000 military personnel and their families live on the base, using an air-weapons range that occupies a large tract of wilderness to the north. The other part of Cold Lake South is a large service and residential area formerly known as Grand Centre. At the town's main intersection is a CF-104 Starfighter donated by the base in recognition of the ties between the communities.

Although the military has been present for over half a century, it is the **Cold Lake Oil Sands** that hold the key to the region's economic future. The heavy oil found north of Cold Lake is similar to that of the Athabasca Oil Sands at Fort McMurray, but the extraction process is different. The oil-rich sands lie in 50-meter-thick (160-ft-thick) underground reservoirs, making surface mining impractical. Instead, steam is pumped into the reservoirs, thinning out the tarlike bitumen, which is then pumped to the surface and piped to Edmonton. This process, known as "steam injection," is still in its developmental stages and is very expensive, but many of the major players in the North American oil market have leases around Cold Lake.

Alberta's Seventh-Largest Lake

Cold Lake is part of what was once a much larger lake, a remnant of the last ice age. Today the lake is approximately 22 kilometers (13.6 mi) wide, 27 kilometers (13.6 mi) long, and reaches depths of 100 meters (330 ft). Its surface is frozen for five months of the year and doesn't break up until early May; the tackle shop at the marina has a sheet pinned to the wall showing breakup dates for the last 50 years. Fishing in the lake is best for northern pike, lake trout, and walleye.

Cold Lake North, on the south shore, is the center of most activity on the lake. The 250-berth **marina** (at the end of the main street, 780/639-3535) rents boats and fishing tackle; small aluminum boats with outboard engines are $10 per hour and $70 per day. **Hook, Line, and Sinker Fishing Tours** (780/639-3474) of-

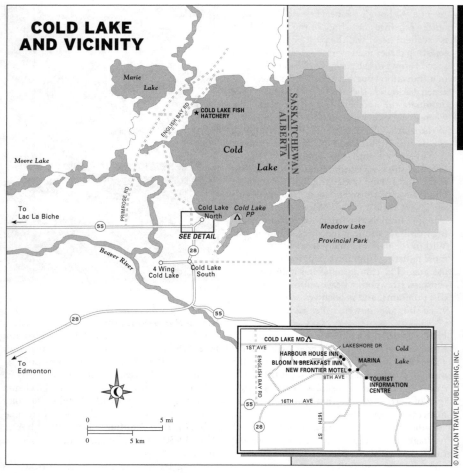

COLD LAKE
AND VICINITY

Marie
Lake

COLD LAKE FISH
HATCHERY

ENGLISH BAY RD

SASKATCHEWAN
ALBERTA

Cold

Lake

Moore Lake

PRIMROSE RD

To
Lac La Biche

55

Cold Lake   Cold Lake
North   PP

Cold Lake
North

SEE DETAIL

Meadow Lake
Provincial Park

Beaver River

28

4 Wing   Cold Lake
Cold Lake   South

28

55

To
Edmonton

0   5 mi

0   5 km

COLD LAKE MD

1ST AVE

LAKESHORE DR   Cold

HARBOUR HOUSE INN
BLOOM N BREAKFAST INN   MARINA   Lake
NEW FRONTIER MOTEL
8TH AVE
TOURIST
INFORMATION
CENTRE

ENGLISH BAY RD

55   16TH   AVE

28

16TH ST

fers varying packages in a modern 5.5-meter (18-ft) fishing boat. Charters are from $15 per person per hour for two people, but it's least expensive for four, when a full day of guided fishing is a reasonable $65 per person. The best beaches are on the northwestern shore of the lake at **English Bay. Kinosoo Beach,** along Lakeshore Drive, is also popular.

The **Cold Lake Fish Hatchery** (780/639-4087) is one of five facilities in Alberta where fish hatched at Calgary's Sam Livingston Fish Hatchery are raised to stock lakes throughout the province. It's open for self-guided tours daily 10 A.M.–3 P.M. To get there, take Highway 55 eight kilometers (five mi) west of Cold Lake, then Primrose Road 15 kilometers (nine mi) north, then head two kilometers (1.2 mi) east.

Cold Lake Provincial Park

This 5,855-hectare (14,470-acre) park is on a low isthmus of land east of town along 16th

Avenue. Although the beaches are much nicer on the northwestern shore of the lake, fishing is excellent here, and the park holds many interesting places to explore. A diversity of plant species grows in the park, thanks to its location in a transition zone between boreal forest and aspen parkland. Balsam fir and white spruce dominate the northern end of the peninsula, whereas stands of aspen and birch can be found to the south. The dominant natural feature of the park is **Hall's Lagoon**, on the northwest side of the isthmus. The lagoon is very shallow, and thick vegetation lines its banks. This is the best place for viewing birdlife, with an observation platform and identification boards set up for bird-watchers. More than 40 species of mammals also inhabit the area, including muskrats, mink, water shrews, and moose. Within the park are many short hiking trails, most radiating from the campground and day-use area. The campground has coin-operated showers, firewood, a beach, summer interpretive programs, and is open year-round; unserviced sites $20, powered sites $23.

Horn Music Festival

Each year, on the first weekend of September at a time when thousands of birds are migrating over Cold Lake and fall colors are at their most spectacular, the town hosts a weekend-long festival of horn music. Festivities include performances—by solo artists as well as groups—and a dinner featuring the best in local game. A package, including all events, accommodations, and meals, is $160 s, $220 d. For details, call 780/840-8000.

Accommodations and Camping

On the shore of Cold Lake, a short stroll from town, is the **C Harbour House Inn** (615 Lakeshore Dr., 780/639-2337, www.harbour houseinn.ca, $60–80 s, $70–100 d), one of Alberta's finest bed-and-breakfasts. Each of the 11 rooms is tastefully decorated in a unique theme. The Hearts Afire room is decorated in pastel colors and has a lake view, a fireplace, a bath, and a magnificent mahogany canopy bed. Along the same stretch of lakefront is

Harbour House Inn

© ANDREW HEMPSTEAD

Bloom N Breakfast Inn (607 Lakeshore Dr., 780/639-4730 or 877/307-8740, www.bloomn breakfast.com, $95 s, $99 d), a small bed-and-breakfast offering four guest rooms possessing individual charm—a couple with private balconies, another with a countrified feel, and a third-floor charmer with a bright-blue color scheme. Within walking distance of the marina is the **New Frontier Motel** (1002 8th Ave., 780/639-3030), with tolerable air-conditioned rooms for $60 s or d.

Along 1st Avenue, past Kinosoo Beach, is the **Cold Lake MD Campground** (780/639-4121, mid-May–mid-Sept.), popular with families who stay the summer; unserviced sites $13, powered sites $15, lakefront sites with power $20. Other options for campers are located east at **Cold Lake Provincial Park** (780/639-3341, May–Oct., $20–23) and west along Highway 55, where numerous gravel roads head north to primitive campgrounds (kitchen shelters, firewood, pit toilets); the best of the bunch is at **English Bay** on the northwest shore of Cold Lake.

Food

A pleasant walk along the lakeshore reaches the **(Espresso Bar** (615 Lakeshore Dr., 780/639-2337, Tues.–Sat. 11 A.M.–9 P.M.) contained within Harbour House Inn. It has great coffee, but is a lot more than a coffeeshop, with afternoon tea, light meals, and mouthwatering desserts.

Information and Services

Housed in an A-frame building on a low rise above the marina is **Cold Lake Information Centre** (780/594-7750 or 800/840-6140, www.coldlake.com, May–Aug. daily 9 A.M.–8 P.M., Sept.–Apr. Mon.–Fri. 9 A.M.–5 P.M.).

In Cold Lake North, the post office is at 913 8th Avenue. The only launderette is at the Husky gas station in Cold Lake South. **Cold Lake Health Centre** (314 25th St., 780/639-3322) is through Cold Lake North to the west.

Getting There

Greyhound buses depart daily from the Cold Lake South depot (5504 55th St., 780/594-2777, www.greyhound.ca) for the five-hour run to Edmonton.

LAC LA BICHE

The historic town of Lac La Biche (pop. 2,600) is located on the southern flanks of the boreal forest, 225 kilometers (140 mi) northeast of Edmonton. The town itself has little of interest, but nearby you'll find a restored mission, two interesting provincial parks, many excellent fishing lakes, and a gravel road that may or may not get you to Fort McMurray.

The town lies on a divide that separates the Athabasca River System, which drains into the Arctic Ocean, from the Churchill River System, which drains into Hudson Bay. The historic Portage La Biche, across this strip of land, was a vital link in the transcontinental route taken by the early fur traders. Voyageurs would paddle up the Beaver River from the east to Beaver Lake and portage the five kilometers (3.1 mi) to Lac La Biche, from where passage could be made to the rich fur-trapping regions along the Athabasca River. In 1798, David Thomp-

son built Red Deer Lake House for the North West Company at the southeast end of the lake. Soon after, Peter Fidler built Greenwich House nearby for the Hudson's Bay Company. By the early 1820s, this northern route across the continent was virtually abandoned for a shorter route along the North Saskatchewan River via Edmonton House. The mission is the best place to learn about the town's colorful past, but you can also get a taste at lakeside **McArthur Place** (Churchill Dr., 780/623-4323), which is a replica of the Lac La Biche Inn that once stood on the same site. Now functioning primarily as the town office, it also holds an information center, historic displays, and a stuffed cougar. Out front, a paved walking trail leads along the shoreline to a statue of explorer extraordinaire David Thompson.

Lac La Biche Mission

The mission was established beside the Hudson's Bay Company post in 1853 and was moved to its present site, 11 kilometers (6.8 mi) northwest of Lac La Biche, in 1855. It became a base for priests who had missions along the Athabasca, Peace, and Mackenzie Rivers and was used as a supply depot for voyageurs still using the northern trade route. The parish expanded, adding a sawmill, a gristmill, a printing press, and a boat-building yard. Today, the original buildings still stand, and services take place each Sunday in the church. A free, guided tour takes one hour, or you can wander around the buildings yourself (780/623-3274, mid-May–early Sept. daily 10 A.M.–5 P.M., adult $5, senior $4.25, child $3.50).

Accommodations and Camping

La Biche Inn (101st Ave., 780/623-4427 or 888/884-8886, $65 s, $75 d) has a restaurant and a nightclub where the disc jockey sits in a big rig. The closest campgrounds are east and north of town in the two provincial parks described in the following section. **Fish 'N Friends** (three km/1.9 mi east and a similar distance south off Hwy. 36, 780/623-9222, www.fish-nfriends.com, mid-May–Oct., $17–20) is a full-service RV park with a large

marina, boat rentals, a general store stocked with fishing tackle, and barbecues, perfect for cooking up freshly caught walleye.

VICINITY OF LAC LA BICHE
Sir Winston Churchill Provincial Park

Located on the largest of nine islands in Lac La Biche, this unique 239-hectare (590-acre) park was linked to the mainland in 1968 by a 2.5-kilometer (1.6-mi) causeway. A road around the island leads through a lush, old-growth coniferous forest. The trees on the island are much larger than those found on the mainland as a result of little disturbance from people and no major fires in more than 300 years. As they come to the end of their 65-year lifespan, the aspen and poplar that dominate younger boreal forests are replaced by balsam fir. Many fir trees are 150 years old and reach a height of 23 meters (74 ft). Along the loop road, short trails lead to sandy beaches (the best on the northeast side of the island), marshes rich with birdlife, and a bird-viewing platform where a mounted telescope lets you watch white pelicans and double-crested cormorants resting on a gravel bar. A campground (780/623-4144,

May to mid-Oct., $17–20) with showers includes a few powered sites on the south side of the island.

Lakeland Provincial Park and Recreation Area

Encompassing 60,000 hectares (148,000 acres) of boreal forest that is mostly in its natural state, this park and adjacent recreation area are a wildlife-watcher's paradise that includes 11 major lakes. Deer, moose, beavers, red foxes, lynx, coyotes, a few wolves and black bears, and more than 200 species of birds can be spotted in the area. A colony of great blue herons, Alberta's largest wading bird, lives at **Pinehurst Lake,** 27 kilometers (17 mi) off Highway 55. Fishing in the lakes is excellent for northern pike and walleye. Those with their own canoes can get out on the water for a real wilderness experience.

Campgrounds are located at **Pinehurst, Ironwood, Seibert,** and **Touchwood Lakes.** Each site has pit toilets and kitchen shelters, and firewood is available for sale; $13–18 per night. Several routes access the two areas; head east from Lac La Biche or north from Highway 55.

Fort McMurray and the Remote Northeast

It's a long drive up a one-way highway to reach Fort McMurray, 450 kilometers (280 mi) north of Edmonton, but it's far from a dead-end town. This city is a modern-day boomtown that revolves around the Athabasca Oil Sands, the world's greatest known deposit of oil. The city is awash with money—and workers spending it, but on a larger scale, the financial impact on the province and country is mind-blowing. So if you're not a construction worker or oilman, why should you make the long trek north? Actual "sights" are oil sands–related (tours through the mining operations are very popular), but nowhere in the world has so much economic development ever been concentrated in one place, which

makes simply being there an interesting study in socioeconomics.

To Fort McMurray

For many years, the only way to get to Fort McMurray was by airplane or the Muskeg Express, a rail service to Edmonton. Today, a paved highway (Hwy. 63), as good as any in the province, has replaced the rail line. It parallels, but never crosses, the Athabasca River, which cuts deeply into the boreal forest, covering the entire northern half of the province. From the highway's southern terminus (at the junction of Hwy. 55, between Lac La Biche and Athabasca) to Fort McMurray, only two small communities are found. The first is **Wandering River,**

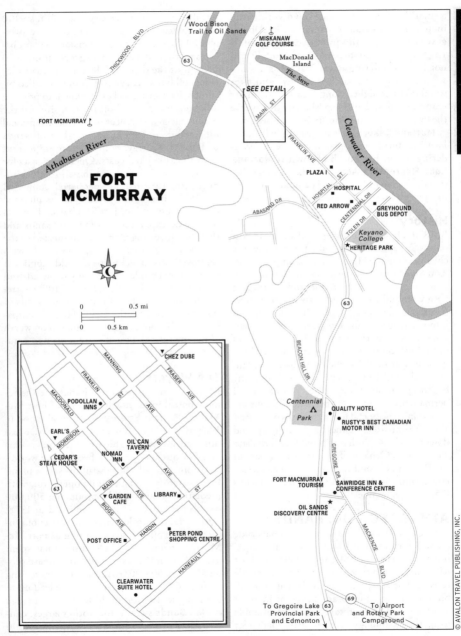

FORT MCMURRAY

Wood Bison Trail to Oil Sands

MISKANAW GOLF COURSE

MacDonald Island

The Snye

SEE DETAIL

MAIN ST

THICKWOOD BLVD

63

FORT MCMURRAY

Athabasca River

Clearwater River

FRANKLIN AVE

PLAZA I

HOSPITAL ST

HOSPITAL

ABASAND DR

RED ARROW

CENTENNIAL DR

GREYHOUND BUS DEPOT

TOLEN DR

Keyano College

HERITAGE PARK

0   0.5 mi
0   0.5 km

63

BEACON HILL DR

MANNING

CHEZ DUBE

FRANKLIN

FRASER AVE

ST

AVE

MACDONALD

PODOLLAN INNS

EARL'S

MORRISON

OIL CAN TAVERN

ST

CEDAR'S STEAK HOUSE

NOMAD INN

63

MAIN

GARDEN CAFE

AVE

LIBRARY

AVE

ST

BIGGS AVE

HARDIN

POST OFFICE

PETER POND SHOPPING CENTRE

HAINEAULT

CLEARWATER SUITE HOTEL

Centennial Park

QUALITY HOTEL

RUSTY'S BEST CANADIAN MOTOR INN

GREGOIRE DR

FORT MACMURRAY TOURISM

SAWRIDGE INN & CONFERENCE CENTRE

OIL SANDS DISCOVERY CENTRE

MACKENZIE BLVD

To Gregoire Lake Provincial Park and Edmonton

63

69

To Airport and Rotary Park Campground

a small lumber and service town with gas, a motel, and a 24-hour restaurant. The Alberta government maintains primitive campgrounds 13, 58, and 76 kilometers (8, 31, and 47 mi) north of Wandering River. Each has a water source, pit toilets, kitchen shelter, and firewood; $11 per night. Along the route are many roadside fens and areas ravished by fire, where the cycle of natural reforestation has begun.

Mariana Lake, a little more than halfway to Fort McMurray, has the same services as Wandering River. Just south of town is **Mariana Lake Recreation Area,** which, although beside the highway, has a good campground; also $11 per night.

History

In 1870, Henry Moberly opened a trading post on the Athabasca River and named it after the chief factor of the Hudson's Bay Company, William McMurray. The post quickly gained popularity as a transportation hub and for trading with Cree and Chipewyan natives. The natives first reported oil oozing from the sand here, but it took a long time for anyone to gain commercial success from extracting it. For the first half of the 20th century, the town experienced little growth. But in 1964, the first oil-sands plant was built, and 10 years later a second company began operation. Today the city has an air of permanence about it. As new subdivisions are carved into the boreal forest, suburbs of respectable three-bedroom homes have sprung up, and downtown looks similar to hundreds of midsize cities across Canada. The city is now part of the Region of Wood Buffalo, North America's largest municipality at 67,104 square kilometers (25,900 square miles).

ATHABASCA OIL SANDS

Only 800 billion barrels of conventional crude oil are known to remain on this entire planet, but the Athabasca Oil Sands, north of Fort McMurray, hold twice that amount in a single reserve. The accepted estimate is that only 315 billion barrels (more than is present in all of Saudi Arabia) of the total field are recoverable using the technology of today. Still, that's a lot

of oil and the math is easy—it will take 100 years to extract just 20 percent of the recoverable oil. Within 500 years, someone will probably have figured out a way to get at the other 80 percent of the deposit. The oil is not conventional oil but a heavy oil, commonly called bitumen. Extracting and processing it to produce a lighter, more useful oil is expensive. Of the many crucial differences between conventional oil reserves and the heavy, tar-like oil sands of Fort McMurray, none is more important than the associated costs. Operating costs for extracting and processing the oil sands' bitumen currently run at $12 per barrel, compared to Middle East crude, which can be pumped out of the ground for just $1 a barrel. Benefits include no exploration costs for oil sands and that the processing plants are connected to the insatiable U.S. market by pipelines. Still, with improvements in technology, world supplies of conventional crude slowly being depleted, and oil estimated to be selling for US$100 a barrel in the not too distant future, the oil sands of Fort McMurray are the focus of big oil companies with *big* money—some $100 billion worth of planned development is underway to complement existing infrastructure.

The Players

Massive mining operations punctuate the remote boreal forest north and east of Fort McMurray. **Suncor Energy** began production in 1967 after taking over the company that had initiated mining in the area three years earlier. The Suncor operation became the world's first commercially successful oil-sands plant. It is currently expanding its operation, with predictions that it will be producing 500,000 barrels per day by 2010. Established in 1978, **Syncrude,** the world's largest producer of synthetic crude oil, is also expanding its Fort McMurray operations. The company has spent $12 billion in the last decade to increase production to 260,000 barrels per day increasing to 460,000 barrels by 2008. In the lead up to pumping its first oil in 2002, Shell Canada's **Albian Sands** site was the world's largest construction project, employing up to 15,000

workers on-site at any one time. **Canadian Natural Resources** is one of many companies starting from scratch in the oil sands. Their Horizon site, slated to be pumping 230,000 barrels of oil per day by 2012, is costing $30 billion, making it the most ambitious construction project ever undertaken anywhere in the world by a private company.

All told, around $30 billion have been spent on oil-sands development since the mid-1990s, with the major players in the industry having collaborated on a development proposal that guarantees a combined regional investment of a further $70 billion over the next 15 years. The current total production rate of one million barrels a day is expected to increase to 2.2 million barrels by 2012.

The Process

As the name implies, the deposits are of highly compacted sand containing heavy oil or bitumen. The sands are mined in two different ways—deposits close to the surface are strip-mined, while the oil deeper down is extracted in situ (using steam injection). In the case of surface deposits, the size of the machinery used to scrape off the surface layer of muskeg and excavate the oil sands below it is mind-boggling. Syncrude's walking draglines are the largest pieces of land-bound machinery in the world. Each moves slowly, dropping buckets as large as a two-car garage into the ground and dragging them back on a boom the length of a football field. The process continues around the clock, with a constant stream of 170-ton heavy haulers taking the overburden to reclamation sites and the oil sands to conveyor belts bound for the processing plants.

Extracting oil sands that lie deep below the Earth's surface is very costly. A simplified explanation of the process is that the fields are tapped by parallel wells. Steam is injected in one, loosening then liquefying and separating the oil from the sand. A second, lower well, extracts the resulting oil. Around 80 percent of known deposits will require this type of extraction technique.

Once on the surface, it must be chemically al-

tered to produce a lighter, more useful oil. This process—in stark contrast to other operations where the oil is simply brought to the surface and shipped or piped around the world—requires an enormous amount of machinery and labor. Hot water and steam are used to separate the sand from the bitumen, which is then diluted with naphtha to make it flow more easily. The bitumen is heated to 500°C (930°F), producing vapors that, when cooled, condense at three levels. The sulfur and the gases produced during the process are all drawn off and put to use, but the liquid products are the most precious. By blending them and increasing the hydrogen content of the mix to make it "lighter," a high-quality synthetic crude oil is produced. This oil is piped to Edmonton and distributed around North America for use in vehicles, airplanes, and derivative products such as plastics.

The People

In 1974, the population of Fort McMurray was just 1,500. Today it stands at 65,000, having doubled since the mid-1990s. While the current permanent population is quoted at 65,000, this doesn't take into account the tens of thousands of temporary contract workers living in modular camps up at the actual oil sands. Factors these folks in and you have Alberta's third-largest city.

Workers are attracted to Fort McMurray for one reason: money. Local dishwashers make $50,000 a year, entry-level workers at the mines make over six figures, and the exotic dancers in town make the workers happy. With the super-high wages paid in the oil fields, downtown businesses are chronically understaffed, so much so that many offer retention awards or provide hiring bonuses to employees who find new workers. Up in the oil fields themselves, companies like Canadian Natural Resources have found it easiest to fly its construction workers into a private airstrip by charter plane from Edmonton. The province of Newfoundland and Labrador is a big supplier of labor, so much so that there are direct flights from Fort McMurray to St. John's, as well as a "Newfie" music hour on the local radio station and even

the only Mary's Brown's (a fast-food chain) outside of that eastern province.

The downside to high wages is a high cost of living. Incredibly, Fort McMurray currently has the hottest market in Canada, with trailers selling from $300,000 and single-family homes averaging $500,000. The rental vacancy rate is generally quoted at zero percent, and if something does come up, you can expect to pay around $1,800 per month for a one-bedroom apartment.

SIGHTS
Oil Sands Discovery Centre

For an insight into the history, geology, and technology of the Athabasca Oil Sands mining process, head to this large interpretive center (515 Mackenzie Blvd., 780/743-7167, mid-May–Aug. daily 9 A.M.–5 P.M., the rest of the year Tues.–Sun. 10 A.M.–4 P.M., adult $6, senior $5, child $4). Start your visit by watching *Quest for Energy,* a multimedia, big-screen presentation about the industry that has grown around the resource. The center houses an interesting collection of machinery and has interactive displays, hands-on exhibits, and interpretive presentations. Outside is the Industrial Equipment Garden, where an older-style bucket-wheel excavator and other machinery are displayed. To move the excavator to this site, it had to be disassembled, with some sections requiring a 144-wheel, 45-meter-long (150-ft-long) trailer for the 45-kilometer (28-mi) trip from the mine.

Syncrude and Suncor Plant Tours

Touring the oil-sands plants is the best way to experience the operation firsthand. The scope of the developments is overwhelming, while the size of the machinery is almost inconceivable. Two companies—Syncrude and Suncor—are involved in tour programs offered through Fort McMurray Tourism (780/791-4336 or 800/565-3947, www.fortmcmurray-tourism.com). Tours of the Syncrude site depart every Saturday in June, July–August Wednesday–Saturday, and September Friday–Saturday

at 9 A.M. The Suncor tour departs June Sunday–Monday, July–August Sunday–Tuesday at 1 P.M. Regardless of which tour you choose, the itinerary is similar. Departing from the Oil Sands Discovery Centre, the tours involve a bus ride north with stops at Wood Bison Trail Gateway and the Giants of Mining display, and then a tour of either the Syncrude or Suncor sites, with time set aside to get out of the bus at a lookout point. The round-trip takes around four hours. Tour cost is adult $25, senior and youth $20, which includes entry to the Discovery Centre and to Heritage Park (see listing later in this chapter). Children under 12 are not permitted and a security check is made before departure (have a photo ID ready). To join a tour you *must* make advance reservations. (The tourism office has put together some accommodation/tour packages that are an excellent deal—around $150 per person for two night's accommodation and a tour.)

Wood Bison Trail

Driving north from the city on Highway 63 gives you a chance to view the mining operations (albeit at a distance), plus make a few interesting stops. Up to 40,000 vehicles a day traverse this route, including 400 buses filled with workers, so be prepared for a lot of traffic.

Make your first stop 27 kilometers (17 mi) north of Fort McMurray at the **Wood Bison Trail Gateway,** where there is an impressive wood bison sculpture made from oil sands. Also on display is a 100-million-year-old cypress tree found fossilized in the oil sands. This pullout is also the starting point for the **Matcheetawin Discovery Trails,** two interpretive loops over a reclaimed mine now covered in a mixed forest of aspen and spruce. The longer of the two passes a lookout over the Syncrude development. Continuing north three kilometers (1.9 mi) you'll find a turn to the left that climbs to a viewpoint over a herd of 300 bison. The road then parallels a reclamation pond to the **Giants of Mining** exhibit, comprising some of the original machinery used in oil-sands development. This is the beginning of the Syncrude spread, and as the road

The Giants of Mining display is difficult to miss driving along the Wood Bison Trail.

tation to the city. Other displays include boats used on the river, a Northern Alberta Railway passenger car, and an early log mission, while another tells the story of local bush pilots.

Gregoire Lake Provincial Park

Southeast of the city 29 kilometers (18 mi) is Gregoire Lake, the only accessible lake in the Fort McMurray area. The 690-hectare (1,700-acre) park on the lake's west shore is a typical boreal forest of mixed woods and black-spruce bogs. Many species of waterfowl nest on the lake, and mammals such as moose and black bears are relatively common. Some short hiking trails wind through the park, and canoes are rented in the day-use area, which also has a sandy beach and playground.

RECREATION
Wilderness Tours

Majic Country Wilderness Adventures (780/743-0766, www.wildernesscountry.com) offers tours from Fort McMurray. The most popular

loops around the pond, you begin to get a feel for the scope of the operation. Around 55 kilometers (34 mi) from Fort McMurray, the road forks. To the left is Fort McKay, and to the right Highway 63 crosses the Athabasca River and continues 10 kilometers (6.2 mi) to a dock. Here, supplies such as petroleum and building materials are loaded onto barges and transported downstream (north) to remote communities such as Fort Chipewyan.

This is the end of the summer road. Between December and March, a winter road is built over the frozen muskeg and river 225 kilometers (140 mi) to Fort Chipewyan and up the Slave River to Fort Smith in the Northwest Territories.

Heritage Park

A two-hectare (five-acre) village, Heritage Park (1 Tolen Dr., 780/791-7575, mid-June–Aug. daily 9 A.M.–5 P.M., the rest of the year Mon.–Sat. noon–4 P.M., adult $3, senior and child $2) is made up of historic buildings linked by a boardwalk and houses artifacts that reflect the importance of fishing, trapping, and transpor-

The sandy beaches of Gregoire Lake Provincial Park provide a break from the monotony of the boreal forest.

outing for money-laden workers with a day off is chasing northern pike down the Clearwater River in a jet-boat ($500 per day for four people). Other jet-boat tours take in the Suncor site and a chunk of exposed oil sands from river level, or head out early for the best chance at spotting the abundant bird species drawn to local waterways. Other options include an overnight stay at a remote riverside cabin and horseback riding, or just rent a canoe ($35 per day) and set your own schedule.

Golf

Miskanaw Golf Course (north of downtown on MacDonald Island, 780/791-0070, $44) is a challenging 6,650-yard layout with plenty of hazards. **Fort McMurray Golf Club** (off Thickwood Blvd., 780/743-5577, $60) has rolling tree-lined fairways.

Swimming and Fitness Centers

The **MacDonald Island Recreation Complex** (McDonald Island, 780/791-0070, daily 8 A.M.–11 P.M.) has a modern exercise room, tennis courts, squash courts, and a swimming pool.

ARTS AND ENTERTAINMENT

As you'd expect, Fort McMurray has dozens of wild, noisy bars filled with workers that have more money than they know what to do with. Downtown, the **Oil Can Tavern** in the Oil Sands Hotel (10007 Franklin Ave., 780/743-2211) is legendary as a hard-drinking pub with weekend country or rock 'n' roll bands. Also in this hotel are a regular nightclub and a strip joint. A more subdued option would be to relax with a quiet drink on the leather sofas of the **Pillar Pub** at Podollan Inns (10131 Franklin Ave., 780/790-2000). South of downtown, the **Sawridge Inn and Conference Centre** (530 Mackenzie Blvd., 780/791-7900) has a pleasant lounge overlooking an indoor pool, or stop by the **Lions Den Pub** at the Quality Hotel (424 Gregoire Dr., 780/791-7200) to shoot some pool.

It's possible to find some big-city culture if you search it out. **Keyano College** (8115 Franklin Ave., 780/791-4990, www.keyano.ca) is a major learning center, with courses as di-verse as heavy-machinery operations and holistic healing. **Keyano Theatre** puts on a season of live performances September–May at the college while a small art gallery (Sept.–May Mon.–Fri. noon–2 P.M., Sat. 1–4 P.M.) opens during the school year.

ACCOMMODATIONS AND CAMPING

High demand dictates there are no bargains in Fort McMurray, and in fact just getting a room can be difficult. Therefore, if you're planning to stay indoors, it's imperative you book your Fort McMurray accommodations as far in advance as possible. Check with Fort McMurray Tourism (780/791-4336 or 800/565-3947, www.fortmcmurraytourism.com) for accommodation/tour package deals.

$100-150

Rusty's Best Canadian Motor Inn (385 Gregoire Dr., 780/791-4646, www.bestcdn.com, $94 s, $104 d) is one of a bunch of properties four kilometers (2.5 mi) south of downtown near the visitors center. All rooms have a fridge and some have kitchens, or dine in the hotel restaurant or lounge.

Across the road from Rusty's is the **Quality Hotel** (424 Gregoire Dr., 780/791-7200 or 800/582-3273). You'll do no better for value than the mid-sized Standard rooms ($149 s or d), or splurge on a Superior room ($219 s or d) that really is superior. On the bottom floor is a restaurant, lounge, and indoor swimming pool.

$150-200

An excellent alternative to the hotel options is **C Chez Dube** (10102 Fraser Ave., 780/790-2367 or 800/565-0757, www.chezdube.com, $150 s, $165 d), a turreted 14-room bed-and-breakfast surrounded by a well-tended garden that includes colorful flowerpots hanging from the verandah. The rooms each have a pastel color scheme, comfortable beds, en suite bathroom, Wi-Fi, and television. Rates include a full breakfast and use of a games room. It backs onto the riverfront park and is only a few blocks from the main street.

© ANDREW HEMPSTEAD

Chez Dube, a character-filled bed-and-breakfast in a city filled with regular motels

Fort McMurray's largest accommodation, with 190 rooms, is the **Sawridge Inn and Conference Centre** (530 Mackenzie Blvd., 780/791-7900 or 800/661-6567, www.sawridge.com, from $154 s, $169 d), which underwent a major revamp in 2003. Rooms have all the standard amenities business travelers demand, including wireless Internet, while the city's best breakfast (included in the rate) is served each morning in the downstairs restaurant. A lounge is spread around an indoor pool complex.

Downtown, the seven-story **Nomad Inn** (10006 MacDonald Ave., 780/791-4770 or 800/661-5029, www.thenomadinn.com, $159 s or d) was last revamped in 2000 (a long time ago for a place whose main customers are construction workers), but remains reasonably well kept. It also has underground parking, an airport shuttle, a reliable Keg Steakhouse restaurant, and a lively bar.

Podollan Inns (10131 Franklin Ave., 780/790-2000 or 888/448-2080, www.podollan.com, $169–249 s or d) is one of the newer downtown hotels. Extra-large guest rooms come with modern conveniences such as cardlock entry and high-speed Internet, while downstairs is one of the city's quieter lounges and heated underground parking. Rates include a light breakfast.

Even newer (2005) is **《 Clearwater Suite Hotel** (4 Haineault St., 780/799-7676 or 877/799-7676, www.clearwatersuitehotel.com, $175–180 s or d), which is aimed at long-term stays but is the nicest choice right downtown. Guest rooms are modern and come with 32-inch TVs, free Internet access, a washer/dryer combo, a kitchen, and free breakfast. It's well worth the few extra dollars for a King Suite.

Camping

All campgrounds are south of the city limits, and fill permanently through summer with workers. **Rotary Park Campground** (Hwy. 69, 780/790-1581, $20) offers showers, cooking facilities, and powered sites and is open year-round. The park is signposted but easy to miss; turn east along Highway 69 and look for the entrance to the left. **Centennial Park Campground** (395 Sakitaww Trail, 780/714-9790, $30) is a little more cramped, but has full hookups, showers, and a laundry.

Continuing beyond the airport is **Golden Eagle Resort** (Hwy. 69, 780/715-6970, www.goldeneagleresort.net, $24–35), with 80 campsites encircling a small body of water. While bathroom facilities were severely limited on my visit for this edition, it's a well laid out place, with a beach, canoe and paddleboat rentals, and a small café. This campground sets aside a few sites for casual visitors, so you should be able to get a space at short notice.

Furthest from town is the forested campground at **Gregoire Lake Provincial Park** (19 km/12 mi south on Hwy. 63 then 10 km/6.2 mi east on Hwy. 881, 780/334-2111, unserviced sites $17, powered sites $20), which has 140 fairly private sites, 60 with power hookups. Facilities include showers, firewood, and watercraft rentals.

FOOD

Even though wages in Fort McMurray are twice the national average, it doesn't mean the locals have fancy tastes. In fact, the city lacks any really good restaurants at all, with all the business going to fast-food restaurants and family-oriented chains. Also, local eateries find it very hard to find staff, which translates to service that is often adequate at best. It also means shortened hours simply because there is no one to work.

For breakfast, it's hard to pass up recommending the **◖ Hearthstone Grill** (Sawridge Inn and Conference Centre, 530 Mackenzie Blvd., 780/791-7900, daily from 6:30 A.M.), which has a surprisingly good buffet at even better price—just $10 including coffee. Adding to the appeal is an open dining space that is stylish and welcoming. Lunch is also served buffet style while dinner mains start at $16.

The **Keg Steakhouse** (Nomad Inn, 10006 MacDonald Ave., 780/791-4770, Mon.–Sat. 11 A.M.–midnight, Sun. 4–11 P.M.) is part of a Canadian chain renowned for fine cuts of Alberta beef served up in a stylish family-restaurant atmosphere. You can't go wrong by ordering the prime rib with horseradish sauce, boiled vegetables, and a roast potato ($18–25), or go creative and try the teriyaki sirloin ($28). **Earl's** (9802 Morrison St., 780/791-3275, daily for lunch and dinner) has a similar smart atmosphere and wide-ranging menu. A few pastas are under $17 and steak ranges $20–28.

Cedar's Steakhouse (10020 Biggs Ave., 780/743-1717, daily from 4 P.M.) is a dimly lit room attached to a bar. Locals may tell you this is where they go for a splurge, but in reality the food is no better than at the upscale chains like Earl's and the Keg. Expect to pay around $20 for a T-bone with salad and potato.

INFORMATION AND SERVICES

Fort McMurray Tourism (780/791-4336 or 800/565-3947, www.fortmcmurraytourism .com) does an excellent job of promoting the city to the world. They operate an information center south of downtown (June–Aug. Mon.–

Fort McMurray Public Library

© ANDREW HEMPSTEAD

Fri. 8 A.M.–6 P.M. and Sat.–Sun. 9 A.M.–5 P.M., Sept.–May Mon.–Fri. 8:30 A.M.–4 P.M.), just north of the Oil Sands Discovery Centre. In addition to having a wealth of information on the city, the organization represents many northern fly-in fishing lodges and offers overnight accommodation packages.

The post office is at 9521 Franklin Avenue. **Fort Laundromat** (Plaza I on Franklin Ave.) is open daily 9 A.M.–9 P.M. **Fort McMurray Public Library** is housed in a large rust-colored building (9907 Franklin Avenue, 780/743-7800, Mon. 5–9 P.M., Tues.–Wed. 10 A.M.–5 P.M., Thurs. 1–9 P.M., Fri.–Sat. 10 A.M.–5 P.M., Sun. 1–5 P.M.). It has free Internet access, or pay a few bucks an hour at **Frogz** (8706 Franklin Ave., 780/743-3839, Tues.–Sun. 3–10 P.M.).

For emergencies, contact **Fort McMurray Regional Hospital** (7 Hospital Street, 780/791-6161) or the **RCMP** (780/799-8888).

GETTING THERE AND AROUND
Getting There

It's a long 450-kilometer (280-mi) drive up to

Fort McMurray on a highway that is regarded as one of the most dangerous in the province (mostly due to the high volume of traffic), so many people prefer to fly. The **airport** is nine kilometers (5.6 mi) south, then six kilometers (3.7 mi) east of downtown. **Air Canada** (888/247-2262, www.aircanada.com), **Westjet** (800/538-5696, www.westjet.com), and **Air Mikisew** (780/743-8218 or 888/268-7112, www.airmikisew.com) fly daily between Edmonton and Fort McMurray, with Air Mikisew departing from the centrally located Edmonton City Centre Airport. Once at the airport, you'll find hotel phones, rental cars (make sure you have a reservation), and a line of cabs charging $30 to get downtown.

Greyhound (8220 Manning Avenue, 780/791-3664, www.greyhound.ca) has service three times daily to Edmonton. **Red Arrow** (8217 Franklin Ave., 780/791-2990 or 800/232-1958, www.redarrow.pwt.ca) offers a more luxurious service than Greyhound, with fewer stops, more legroom, and free coffee and snacks. Either way, it's a five-hour trip to Edmonton.

Getting Around

Wood Buffalo Express (780/743-7096) is a local transit service to outlying suburbs and the Oil Sands Discovery Centre. Buses run seven days a week and travel costs $1.25 per sector; seniors ride free. From downtown, a cab costs $13 to the Oil Sands Discovery Centre and $30 to the airport. Taxi companies include **Access Taxi** (780/799-3333), **Sun Taxi** (780/743-5050), and **United Class Cabs** (780/743-1234). The following car rentals are available in town, and all have airport counters: **Avis** (780/743-4773), **Budget** (780/743-8215), **Hertz** (780/743-4047), and **National** (780/743-6393).

FORT CHIPEWYAN

When the North West Company established a post on the west shore of Lake Athabasca in 1788, what is now Alberta was a wild land with no white settlers. Today, Fort Chipewyan (pop. 1,400), on the site of the original trading post (225 km/140 mi north of Fort McMurray),

holds the title of Alberta's most remote community. In summer, the only access is by river or air. After the winter freeze settles in, a winter road connects the community to the outside world. For fur traders, Fort Chip, as it's best known, was the ideal location for a post. The confluence of the Athabasca and Peace Rivers was nearby, and to the north were the Slave and Mackenzie Rivers. It became a way station for some of Canada's great explorers—Alexander Mackenzie, David Thompson, Simon Fraser, and Sir John Franklin—who rested and replenished supplies at the post.

Sights and Recreation

Set on a south-facing slope overlooking the lake, the town itself is worth a half-day exploration, but most visitors use it as a base for trips into nearby Wood Buffalo National Park and fishing on the lake and nearby rivers. At the east side of town is the **Bicentennial Museum** (Mackenzie Ave., 780/697-3844, year-round Sat.–Sun. 1–5 P.M., ask at your accommodation for weekday hours, donation), modeled on the original fur-trading post. It is a surprisingly interesting little museum, with highlights including a replica of the original fort, a winter coat made from buffalo hide, old outboard boat motors, handmade moccasins, as well as oddities such as the shell of a Pacific turtle that somehow made its way into Lake Athabasca. You can also purchase handicrafts by local artists. From the back of the museum, a walking trail with interpretive panels leads along the lakefront to a small docking area. Along the way is the 1874 **St. Paul's Anglican Church,** the oldest church in Alberta. The imposing buildings across the bay to the west are part of a Roman Catholic mission.

Athabasca Delta Interpretive Tours (780/697-3521) operates a lodge on Jackfish Lake that is reached by a short boat ride from Fort Chip. The emphasis is on the traditional lifestyle of the local Dene people; activities include wilderness trips, fishing, wildlife viewing, and native cooking. Rates are around $250 per day.

© ANDREW HEMPSTEAD

Established in 1874, the St. Paul's Anglican Church in Fort Chipewyan is the oldest church in Alberta.

Accommodations and Food

Perched atop barren rock overlooking Lake Athabasca, the location of **Fort Chipewyan Lodge** (780/697-3679 or 888/686-6333, www.fortchipewyanlodge.com) is nothing short of stunning. The 10 basic but comfortable rooms have bathrooms and TV, but don't take full advantage of the setting. The lodge also has a restaurant with great views and a wraparound deck, and an upstairs lounge that is mostly the domain of locals. Rates are $112 s, $122 d, but many package deals, including meals and tours into the delta, are offered. It takes around 10 minutes to walk downtown from the lodge.

The only other option is **Wah Pun Bed & Breakfast** (780/697-3030, wahpun@telusplanet.net, $95 s, $115 d), a modern log home through town to the west. Owned by former chief Archie Waquan and his wife Dawn, it's a good place to learn more about local issues. Guest rooms have private bathrooms and phones while communal areas include a lounge with a pool table and fireplace.

Fort Chipewyan Lodge has a restaurant (daily 8 A.M.–6 P.M., later in summer) with fantastic views over the lake. Unfortunately the food doesn't live up to the setting—choose from dishes such as pork chops and roast potato ($14) or steak and fries ($18). Downtown across from the municipal office, **Northern Nugget** (780/697-3777, daily 10 A.M.–7 P.M.) doesn't have a sign out front, but inside you'll find a few tables and dishes such as a roast beef sandwich ($10).

Getting There and Around

Operated by the local Cree nation, **Air Mikisew** (780/743-8218 or 888/268-7112, www.airmikisew.com) links Edmonton, Fort McMurray, and Fort Chipewyan with multiple daily scheduled flights. The fare is roughly $200 per sector, inclusive of taxes. Views of the oil sands on these flights are fantastic and will give you an idea of their scope.

Once at the airport, there are usually cabs waiting, including **Tuccaro's Taxi** (780/697-3400), which charges $8 to get into town.

Between mid-December and mid-March, a winter road constructed from Fort McMurray to Fort Smith passes through Fort Chip and is passable by two-wheel-drive vehicles; call 780/697-3778 for road conditions.

◖ WOOD BUFFALO NATIONAL PARK

In the far northeast corner of Alberta is Wood Buffalo National Park, the second-largest national park in the world (the largest is in Greenland). It is accessible by road only through the Northwest Territories or by charter from Fort McMurray. Throughout this 45,000-square-kilometer (17,400-square-mi) chunk of boreal forest, boreal plains, shallow lakes, and bogs flow two major rivers—the Peace and Athabasca. These drain into **Lake Claire,** forming one of the world's largest freshwater deltas. The Peace-Athabasca Delta is a mass of confusing channels, shallow lakes, and sedge meadows, surrounded by a wetland that is a prime wintering range for bison, rich in waterfowl, and home to beavers, muskrats, moose, lynx,

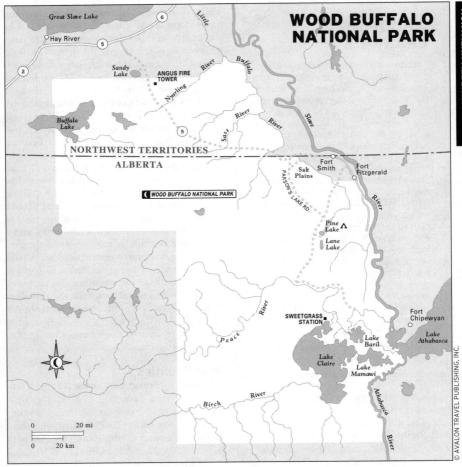

wolves, and black bears. From the delta, the Slave River, which forms the park's eastern boundary, flows north into Great Slave Lake.

Probably best known for being the last natural nesting habitat of the rare whooping crane, the park is also home to the world's largest free-roaming herd of bison. It has extensive salt plains and North America's finest example of gypsum karst topography—a phenomenon created by underground water activity. For all of these reasons, and as an intact example of the bo-real forest that once circled the entire Northern Hemisphere, the park was declared a UNESCO World Heritage Site in December 1983.

Sights

The expansive **Salt Plains** in the northeast of the park are one of Wood Buffalo's dominant natural features. Underground water flows through deposits of salt left behind by an ancient saltwater ocean, emerging in the form of salt springs. Large white mounds form at their

WHOOPING CRANES

Through a successful captive-breed-ing program, the whooping crane, *Grus americana*, has become a symbol of human efforts to protect endangered spe-cies in North America. Whoopers, as they are commonly called, have never been prolific. They stand 1.3 meters (four ft), have a wingspan of 2.4 meters (eight ft), and are pure white with long black legs. (They are often confused with the slightly smaller, reddish-brown-colored sandhill crane, which is common in the park.) Their naturally low reproduction rate coupled with severe degradation of their habitat caused their numbers to dip as low as 21 – a single flock that nested in Wood Buffalo National Park – in 1954. Today, the population of the highly publicized and heavily studied flock has increased to more than 200, more than half the num-ber that remain worldwide (most of those remaining are in captivity). The birds nest in a remote area of marshes and bogs in the northern reaches of Wood Buffalo far from human contact, migrating south to the Texas coast each fall.

source, and where the water has evaporated the ground is covered in a fine layer of salt. The best place to view this phenomenon is from the **Salt Plains Overlook,** 35 kilometers (22 mi) west of Fort Smith, then 11 kilometers (6.8 mi) south on Parson's Lake Road. The panoramic view of the plains is spectacular from this spot, but it's worth taking the one-kilometer (0.6-mi) trail to the bottom of the hill.

In the same vicinity, a bedrock of **gypsum karst** underlies much of the park. Gypsum is a soft, white rock that slowly dissolves in water. Underground water here has created large cavities beneath this fragile mantle. This type of terrain is known as karst, and this area is the best example of karst terrain in North America. As the bedrock continues to dissolve, the underground caves enlarge, eventually

collapsing under their own weight, forming large depressions known as **sinkholes.** The thousands of sinkholes here vary in size from three meters (10 ft) to 100 meters (330 ft) across. The most accessible large sinkhole is behind the Angus Fire Tower, 150 kilometers (93 mi) west of Fort Smith.

The **Peace-Athabasca Delta** is in a re-mote part of this remote park and is rarely visited. Getting to the delta requires some planning because no roads access the area. The most popular visitor destination on the delta is **Sweetgrass Station,** located 12 kilo-meters (7.5 mi) south of the Peace River. The site is on the edge of a vast meadow that ex-tends around the north and west shore of Lake Claire, providing a summer range for most of the park's bison. A cabin with bunks and a woodstove is available for visitors to the area at no charge, although reservations at the park information center are required. The cabin is an excellent base for exploring the meadows around Lake Claire and viewing the abundant wildlife. From Fort Smith, **Northwestern Air** (867/872-2216, www.nwal.ca) charges $420 each way to fly two people and their gear to Sweetgrass Station.

Practicalities

The **Park Information Centre** (126 McDou-gal Rd., Fort Smith, 867/872-7900, Mon.–Fri. 8:30 A.M.–5 P.M. plus summer weekends 10 A.M.–5 P.M.) offers trail information, a short slideshow, and an exhibit room. Another park office (780/697-3662, Mon.–Fri. 8:30 A.M.–5 P.M.) is in Fort Chipewyan. It has an inter-esting exhibit on the Peace River.

Within the park itself, the only developed facilities are at **Pine Lake,** 60 kilometers (37 mi) south of Fort Smith. The lake has a campground ($14 per night) with pit toilets, covered kitchen shelters, and firewood ($7). On a spit of land jutting into the lake beyond the campground is a picnic area with bug-proof shelters. The park staff presents a sum-mer interpretive program at various locations; check the schedule at the park information center or on the campground notice board.

North-Central Alberta

The area immediately north of Edmonton is a varied region that extends north out of the provincial capital's suburbs through rich agricultural land and into the wilderness of the boreal forest. The **Athabasca River** flows southwest to northeast through the region. It is linked to Edmonton by Highway 2, which follows the historic Athabasca Landing Trail—a supply route used by early explorers and traders for travel between the North Saskatchewan and Athabasca River Systems. From Athabasca, Highway 2 heads northwest to the city of Slave Lake, on the southeast shore of Lesser Slave Lake. From there, it continues along the lake's southern shore to High Prairie and into the Peace River Valley. Other major roads in the region include Highway 18, which runs east–west through the southern portion of the region and through the farming and oil towns of Westlock and Barrhead; Highway 33, which climbs into the Swan Hills, home to a subspecies of the now-extinct plains grizzly bear; and Highway 43, the main thoroughfare northwest from Edmonton to Grande Prairie. Adventurous souls driving to the Northwest Territories will want to travel the Bicentennial Highway (Highway 88) at least one-way. This gravel road opens up a remote part of the province that is otherwise accessible only by floatplane.

EDMONTON TO ATHABASCA

From downtown Edmonton, Highway 2 (called the St. Albert Trail in the vicinity of Edmonton) heads north into a once-forested land that is now heavily developed as farm and ranch country. The first town north of the city limits is **Morinville,** a farming community founded by French and German settlers more than 100 years ago. **St. Jean Baptiste Church,** built by the town's founders, is an imposing structure that has been declared a Provincial Historical Site.

Athabasca Landing Trail

The Athabasca Landing Trail was an historic trade route plied first by indigenous people and later used by the Hudson's Bay Company to carry goods between Fort Saskatchewan and Athabasca. Bits and pieces of the original trail can still be seen today, interspersed among the small towns and hamlets east of Highway 2.

At one time, the trail passed through **Gibbons,** a small town of 2,800 on the banks of the Sturgeon River. Sites of interest here include **Gibbons Anglican Church,** whose unique interior is shaped like a ship (you can wander through the church anytime) and **Sturgeon River Historical Museum** (Oliver Park, 780/923-2140, June–Aug. Wed.–Sun. 1:30–8:30 P.M., donation), which features a two-story log house and an old fire hall. Four kilometers (2.5 mi) north of Gibbons is one of Northern Alberta's finest courses, **Goose Hummock Golf Resort** (780/921-2444, $46), which is dominated by water hazards that come into play on all but three holes.

Old St. Mary's Ukrainian Catholic Church is 1.5 kilometers (0.9 mi) west of the hamlet of **Waugh.** It was the first church of its denomination to be built north of Edmonton and is adjacent to the original trail. The trail disappears north of Highway 18, but historic markers and buildings are accessible by following gravel roads east through **Tawatinaw** and **Rochester** (look for historic markers and log buildings on the roadside approaching the crest of the first ridge east of these towns).

ATHABASCA AND VICINITY

On the banks of the Athabasca River, 147 kilometers (91 mi) north of Edmonton, this town of 2,300 was probably the most famous of the many communities that formed vital links to the north. Athabasca (Where There are Reeds, in the language of the Cree) is on a gently sloping hill on the river's south bank, with the steep-sided Muskeg Creek Valley on one side and the Tawatinaw River on the other. Many historic buildings still stand in town, and the surrounding area is pristine wilderness, excellent for fishing, boating, and camping.

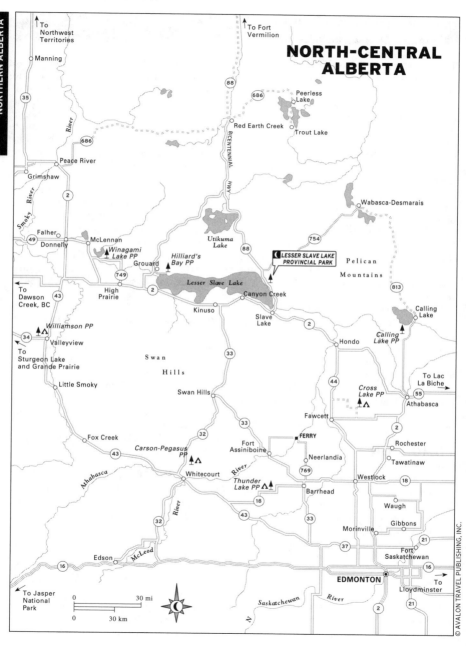

NORTHERN ALBERTA

↑To
Northwest
Territories

○ Manning

↑To Fort
Vermilion

NORTH-CENTRAL ALBERTA

35

River

88

686 ○ Peerless
Lake

○ 686

○ Peace River

Red Earth Creek

Trout Lake

○ Grimshaw

Smoky River

2

BICENTENNIAL HWY

○ Wabasca-Desmarais

Falher ○
49 ○ Donnelly

McLennan

*Winagami
Lake PP*

*Utikuma
Lake*

754

*Hilliard's
Bay PP*

Grouard

88

◖ **LESSER SLAVE LAKE
PROVINCIAL PARK**

P e l i c a n

749

To
Dawson
Creek, BC

43

High
Prairie

2

Lesser Slave Lake

M o u n t a i n s

813

Kinuso

Canyon Creek

Calling
Lake

Slave
Lake

2

Williamson PP

34

○ Valleyview

To
Sturgeon Lake
and Grande Prairie

S w a n

33

Hondo

*Calling
Lake PP*

55

To Lac
La Biche →

○ Little Smoky

H i l l s

Swan Hills

44

*Cross
Lake PP*

Athabasca

○ Fox Creek

43

32

Fawcett

2

○ Rochester

*Carson-Pegasus
PP*

33

Fort
Assiniboine

■ **FERRY**

○ Neerlandia

○ Tawatinaw

Athabasca

Whitecourt

River

769

Westlock

18

*Thunder
Lake PP*

Barrhead

○ Waugh

18

Gibbons

32

43

33

○ Morinville

21

River

McLeod

Edson

16

37

Fort
Saskatchewan

16

To Jasper
National
Park

0   30 mi

0   30 km

EDMONTON ●

N

Saskatchewan River

2

To
Lloydminster

21

© AVALON TRAVEL PUBLISHING, INC.

History

Athabasca Landing was founded by the Hudson's Bay Company in 1874 on the southernmost bend of the Athabasca River. Goods from the east were shipped to Fort Saskatchewan and transported north along the Athabasca Landing Trail, from where they were distributed throughout northern Canada. A thriving boat-building business began at the landing. Once the paddle wheelers and scows reached their destination along the river system, many were broken up and used for housing; others were loaded with furs for the return journey. Passengers who boarded the paddle wheelers from the landing were from all walks of life—traders, trappers, land speculators, settlers, North West Mounted Police (NWMP), geologists, missionaries, and anyone looking for a new life and adventure in Canada's great northern wilderness. Robert Service, the renowned poet, lived at Athabasca Landing for a time; much of his early work was about trappers and the people of the Athabasca River.

Sights

Although the Hudson's Bay Company buildings have long since disappeared, many later buildings from the days of the paddle wheelers remain. Beside the riverfront information center is an old wooden scow used by early river travelers. Further along is a railway station, circa 1912, while behind this building is a 1915 steam engine. Up the hill on 48th Street is an old brick schoolhouse, also built in 1913. Next door is the library (780/675-2735, Tues. and Thurs. noon–4 P.M.), which houses the **Athabasca Archives,** a comprehensive collection of photographs and newspapers.

Muskeg Creek Park, on the west side of town, offers hiking trails and good fishing during spring. The creek flows through a heavily forested ravine into a floodplain, then drains

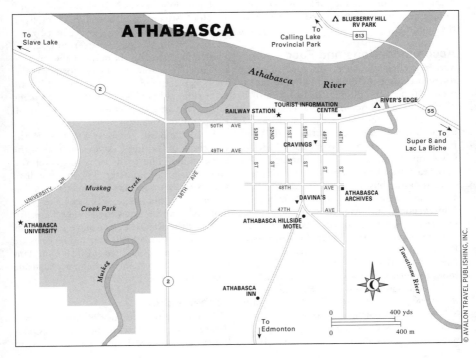

ATHABASCA

To Slave Lake

To Calling Lake Provincial Park

BLUEBERRY HILL RV PARK

813

Athabasca River

TOURIST INFORMATION CENTRE

RAILWAY STATION

RIVER'S EDGE

55

50TH AVE

49TH AVE

53RD ST 52ND ST 51ST ST 50TH ST 49TH ST 48TH ST

CRAVINGS

To Super 8 and Lac La Biche

48TH AVE

47TH AVE

DAVINA'S

ATHABASCA ARCHIVES

ATHABASCA HILLSIDE MOTEL

Muskeg Creek

Creek Park

UNIVERSITY DR

38TH AVE

ATHABASCA UNIVERSITY

Muskeg

ATHABASCA INN

To Edmonton

Tawatinaw River

0   400 yds

0   400 m

© AVALON TRAVEL PUBLISHING, INC.

into the Athabasca River. Wildlife abounds, berry picking is good in late summer, and cross-country skiing trails are laid in winter. Access to the park is from the elementary school on 48th Avenue.

On the west side of town, **Athabasca University** (780/675-6111, www.athabascau .ca) has a 12,000-square-meter (130,000-square-ft) facility on a 180-hectare (450-acre) site. It has a fulltime staff of 900, a choice of 500 programs at all levels including Masters, a library with 100,000 books, an extensive art collection, a fitness facility, and an annual budget exceeding $30 million—but there's not a single student in sight. That's because it's a correspondence university, one of the largest in North America and open to students regardless of their geographical location or previous academic levels. The 32,000 enrolled students work from home, communicating with their tutors via email, phone, fax, and snail mail. The campus is open to the public and has some unique artworks commissioned especially for the building.

Accommodations and Food

Several motels are on Highway 2 south of town, including **Athabasca Hillside Motel** (4804 46th Ave., 780/675-5111 or 888/675-8900, www.athabascahillsidemotel.com, $59 s or d), with kitchenettes in each of the 17 rooms. Much nicer is the **Super 8** (4820 Wood Heights Rd., 780/675-8888 or 800/800-8000, www.super8.com, $109 s or d), through town to the east. It's a larger, modern hotel with spacious rooms, a business center, free breakfast, and an adjacent A&W restaurant. **River's Edge Campground** (50th Ave., May–mid-Oct., unserviced sites $10, powered sites $15) sits on the edge of downtown where the Tawatinaw River drains into the much wider Athabasca River. Amenities are limited to a small bathroom complex with coin showers. Most RVers head north across the river to **Blueberry Hill RV Park** (Hwy. 813, 780/675-3733 or 800/859-9452, www.blueberryhillrvpark.ca, May–Oct., tenting $16, hookups $27), which has pull-through sites, modern washrooms, a laun-

dry, a playground, and free firewood. It's also adjacent to an excellent golf course.

Davina's (4807 50th St., 780/675-3304, Tues.–Fri. 7:30 a.m.–4 p.m., Sat. 9 a.m.–4 p.m.) is an English-style tearoom with a shaded verandah. One block over, **Cravings** (4911 49th St., 780/675-5576, Mon.–Fri. 9 a.m.–9 p.m.) is a friendly little place where you can get fresh muffins and coffee for the price of coffee only in the city, as well as more substantial mains such as teriyaki chicken stir fry ($12).

Information

The tourist information center (50th Ave., 780/675-2055, late May–early Sept. daily 10 a.m.–8 p.m.) is in an orange CN caboose along the riverfront.

Calling Lake Provincial Park

Lying along the south shore of one of Alberta's larger lakes, this 741-hectare (1,830-acre) park is on Highway 813, 55 kilometers (34 mi) north of Athabasca. A boreal forest of aspen surrounds the lake, giving way to a marshy area nearer the shore. Look for deer, moose, and black bears, as well as the occasional white pelican and blue heron. Fishing for northern pike, walleye, perch, and whitefish is the park's main attraction, although swimming and canoeing on the lake are also possible. Sites in the small campground are $20.

From the park, Highway 813 follows the east shore of Calling Lake to a hamlet of the same name. The road turns to gravel and continues 130 kilometers (81 mi) north to **Wabasca-Desmarais,** a native settlement between South and North Wabasca Lakes, then loops back and follows the Willow River for much of the way to Lesser Slave Lake. This is a remote region of Alberta, and services are few and far between, but wildlife is abundant and fishing is excellent in the many roadside lakes and rivers.

Amber Valley

This small hamlet just east of Athabasca was first settled in 1910 by 200 blacks from Oklahoma. They moved from their homeland to

escape racial persecution, led north by 22-year-old Jefferson Davis Edwards. The prejudice continued in Alberta, with locals suggesting they should head south because the climate wouldn't suit them. Despite the hard times, the community thrived and remained virtually all black. Since World War II, the population has declined, and today only a few black families remain.

ATHABASCA TO SLAVE LAKE

From Athabasca, Highway 2 heads northwest to Slave Lake, passing many summer communities along the shores of **Baptiste** and **Island Lakes,** both of which have good fishing for northern pike; their campgrounds are inexpensive. This section of the highway is known as the **Northern Woods and Water Route.** Just before **Hondo,** the route intersects Highway 44, which heads south 106 kilometers (66 mi) to Westlock and Highway 18. At Hondo, 72 kilometers (45 mi) from Athabasca, Highway 2A leads to **Fawcett Lake,** known for its good walleye fishing. At the lake are two campgrounds, cabins, and boat rentals.

SLAVE LAKE

The town of Slave Lake (pop. 6,500) is located on the southeastern shore of **Lesser Slave Lake,** 250 kilometers (155 mi) northwest of Edmonton. It began as an important staging point for steamboat freight and passengers heading for the Peace River Country and Yukon goldfields. The arrival of a rail line in 1914 meant a boom time for the fledgling community and the beginning of a lumber industry that continues today. In 1935, disastrous floods destroyed many of the buildings on the main street. Following that debacle, the town was relocated 3.5 kilometers (2.1 mi) to the south. Only a few foundations remain of the original settlement. Today the town has little to interest visitors, but Lesser Slave Lake has some of the best fishing in the province, with northern pike to nine kilograms, walleye to four kilograms, whitefish to 2.5 kilograms (5.5 lbs), and yellow perch to one kilogram (2.2 lbs)—enough to make any self-respect-

ing fisherman quit his job, pack the rod and reel, and head north.

But Isn't Slave Lake in the Arctic?

Well, no, but an explanation is in order. Lesser Slave Lake is one of *two* Slave Lakes in northwestern Canada. Both lakes are at the same longitude, but they're about 600 kilometers (370 mi) apart as the crow flies. The bigger one—the one that many people *think* is in the Arctic—is north of Alberta in the Northwest Territories (but still south of the Arctic Circle). The smaller, more southerly of the two is here in northern Alberta. Both are named after the Slavey Indians who traveled south up the Athabasca River from the big Slave Lake to the smaller Slave Lake on hunting and fishing expeditions. In early writings, and on maps, both lakes were denoted as Slave Lake. This led to confusion, especially because both were in what was then the Northwest Territories. To remedy the problem, the larger, northern body of water was renamed Great Slave Lake, and its Albertan counterpart, Lesser Slave Lake. Lesser Slave Lake is the third-largest lake in Alberta (only lakes Athabasca and Claire are larger) and the largest accessible by road. It is 90 kilometers (56 mi) long, 20 kilometers (12.5 mi) wide, has an area of 1,150 square kilometers (440 square mi), and is relatively shallow, especially along the south shore, where deltas have formed from the many northward-flowing Swan Hills watersheds.

And Why Are So Many Things Named "Sawridge"?

The original settlement on Lesser Slave Lake was named Sawridge, for the jagged range of hills to the north. Many prominent residents didn't like the name, so in 1922, they changed it to Slave Lake, but the original name lives on. Today it's the name of the local Indian band and a creek flowing through town, and many local businesses use the name as well.

◀ Lesser Slave Lake Provincial Park

At this 7,290-hectare (18,000-acre) park north of town, you'll find a campground, long sandy

beaches, unique sand dunes, and wetland and boreal forest habitats supporting diverse wildlife. Offshore is **Dog Island,** the lake's only island, home to a pair of bald eagles, pelicans, and other shorebirds. North of the Lesser Slave River are many access roads leading to **Devonshire Beach,** a seven-kilometer (4.3-mi) stretch of sandy beach popular for sunbaking and swimming. The sunsets from this beach are spectacular (at the north end is a viewing platform). The **North Shore,** to the north of Devonshire Beach, has a picnic area and provides access to the 23-kilometer (14.2-mi) **Freighter Lakeshore Trail,** which runs the entire length of the park. North Shore beaches are nonexistent, but a gravel road heading back toward Devonshire leads to a quiet one. At the north end of the park, a steep eight-kilometer (five-mi) road leads through a dense forest of lodgepole pine to the plateau-like summit of 1,030-meter (3,380-ft) Marten Mountain. The views are spectacular from this vantage point 500 meters (1,640 ft) above the lake. A 2.8-kilometer (1.7-mi) trail from the summit winds through an old-growth forest of balsam fir that has escaped major fires. The trail ends up at **Lily Lake,** a small, secluded lake (stocked with rainbow trout) from where Lily Creek flows into Lesser Slave Lake.

Fishing

Although fishing from the lake's edge and in nearby rivers can be productive, the big ones are hooked out on the lake, where pike grow to nine kilograms and walleye to four kilograms. Ask at the information center for fishing guides and rental outlets. For a small motorboat, expect to pay $20 per hour, $50 half day, or $100 full day.

Pilots at **Slave Air** (780/849-5353), based at the airport in town, will fly you to their favorite fishing lakes. Orloff Lake is a half hour to the east and has a campsite (flight is $325 for up to five people), and God's Lake is one hour north (flight is $575). If the pilot knows that the fishing is good, he won't charge you for the time spent on the ground between landing and takeoff (ground time).

Accommodations and Camping

The **Highway Motor Inn,** on Highway 2 by the tourist information center (600 14th Ave. SW, 780/849-2400 or 888/848-2400), has 75 basic rooms for $65 s, $75 d. The **Sawridge Inn and Conference Centre** (1200 Main St. S, 780/849-4101 or 800/661-6657, www.sawridge.com, 104 s, $114 d) is set on a large chunk of land at the entrance to town. It attracts a mix of business and highway travelers with the amenities of a full-service hotel and in-house dining options that include an English-style pub. The Business Class rooms are decidedly bigger than the standard rooms and come with Internet access and bathrobes for just $10 extra.

Lesser Slave Lake Provincial Park's **Marten River Campground** (6 km/3.7 mi north of town, 780/849-7100, May–Oct., unserviced sites $20, powered sites $25) has coin-operated showers, a beach, and a summer interpretive program. Immediately north, outside the park boundary, is **◖ Diamond Willow Family Resort** (780/849-2292, www.diamondwillowfr.com, unserviced sites $18, powered sites $20), a private campground with a sandy beach, a pitch-and-putt golf course, a nature trail, coin showers, a grocery store, and a café.

Food

The **Hearthstone Grill** in the Sawridge Inn (1200 Main St. S, 780/849-4101) is a casual dining room with bright decor and a relaxed atmosphere. It offers a good breakfast buffet with a wide selection of dishes ($10.95). The **Sawridge Truckstop** (on the corner of Hwy. 88 and Caribou Trail NE, 780/849-4030) is just that—a truck stop with vinyl seats, hearty meals, inexpensive prices, and very busy waitresses. It's open 24 hours.

Information

The tourist information center (off Hwy. 2, west of Main St., 780/849-4611, www.slavelake.com) is open May–August daily 10 A.M.–7 P.M.

Bicentennial Highway

This 430-kilometer (270-mi) road (also

known as Hwy. 88) connects Slave Lake with Fort Vermilion to the north and is an excellent alternative to the Mackenzie Highway for those traveling in that direction. It was renamed and renumbered to commemorate the bicentenary of Fort Vermilion in 1988. Services (gas, rooms, and restaurant) are available at the only community along the road, **Red Earth Creek**—a semipermanent oilfields town 130 kilometers (81 mi) north of Slave Lake. From there, Highway 686 heads east to **Peerless** and **Trout Lakes,** named for the excellent fishing, and west to the town of Peace River.

At Red Earth Creek, the Bicentennial Highway becomes a gravel road and parallels the Loon and Wabasca Rivers, following the eastern flanks of the **Buffalo Head Hills.** Seventy kilometers (43 mi) from Fort Vermilion, a turnoff to the west leads to **Wadlin Lake,** home to one of Alberta's four colonies of white pelicans. They nest on an island during summer, migrating south to the Gulf of Mexico each winter. The island is a Prohibited Access Wildlife Area, and the birds should not be disturbed during the breeding season because they are prone to abandoning their nests if approached. The lake has good fishing for northern pike and whitefish, and a primitive campground with sites for $12 a night.

(For Fort Vermilion, see the *Peace River Valley* section later in this chapter.)

TO THE PEACE RIVER

From Slave Lake, Highway 2 westbound follows the southern shore of Lesser Slave Lake to High Prairie. At **Kinuso** a small museum (780/775-3774, May–Aug. Mon.–Fri. 10 A.M.– 4 P.M., donation) centers around a stuffed grizzly bear that stands over 2.5 meters (eight ft) tall. A little farther along the highway, a nine-kilometer (5.6-mi) gravel road leads north to Lesser Slave Lake and 《 **Spruce Point Park** (780/775-2117, May to mid-Sept., $18–25), which bustles with families and fisherman throughout summer. From the main camping area, a wide grassed area leads down to a lakefront beach and a marina with boat and canoe

rentals and a fish-cleaning shed. Other park amenities include a general store (stocked with lots of fishing tackle), horseshoe pits, hiking trails, and showers.

Grouard and Vicinity

A town of 400 on Buffalo Bay near the west end of Lesser Slave Lake, Grouard grew up around the St. Bernard Mission, founded in 1884 by Father Emile Grouard. The town was destined to become the center of the north. It had a few thousand people and a rail line on the way, when, because of an unfortunate set of circumstances, everything changed. A sample of water from a nearby lake was sent to the railway headquarters to ensure that it was fit for the steam engines. Along the way it was either dropped, lost, or emptied and replaced by a sample of water from muskeg wetland. The new sample was tested and found to be of poor quality. The proposed route for the railway changed, and the once-thriving town collapsed.

On the grounds of Northern Lakes College, **Grouard Native Cultural Arts Museum** (780/751-3306, May–Sept. Tues.–Fri. 10 A.M.– 4 P.M., Sat. 10 A.M.–6 P.M., donation) is dedicated to promoting a better understanding of North American native cultures through exhibition of native arts and crafts as well as the outdoor re-creation of a native village.

Hilliard's Bay Provincial Park is 13 kilometers (eight mi) east of Grouard on the northwest shore of Lesser Slave Lake. It is a 2,330-hectare (5,800-acre) park with mixed woods, two sandy beaches, and a one-kilometer (0.6-mi) spit framed by a stand of gnarled paper birches. The **Boreal Forest Interpretive Trail** meanders through a forest habitat, where many species of mammals are present—look for tracks along the top of the ridges at the east end of the park. The park campground (780/849-7124, May–early October, unserviced sites $20, powered sites $25) has showers, kitchen shelters, and firewood.

Like Spruce Point Park near Kinuso, **Shaw's Point Lakeside Resort** (780/751-3900, www.shawspointresort.com, Apr.–Oct., $27–30) is a full-service campground catering

mostly to families and fishing enthusiasts. Facilities include two marinas, pontoon boat rentals (from $25 per hour), a par-3 golf course, a restaurant (daily 8 A.M.–10 P.M.), a general store, showers, and a laundry room. Access is from the road leading into Hillard's Bay Provincial Park. On the second weekend of August, Shaw's Point hosts the **Golden Walleye Classic,** North America's richest catch-and-release walleye tournament with over $60,000 in cash up for grabs. Walleye fishing is not the world's most exciting spectator sport, but amateur anglers are welcome to enter.

High Prairie

This town of 2,900 near the west end of Lesser Slave Lake has its long history catalogued at the **High Prairie and District Museum** (in the library on 53rd Ave., 780/523-2601, June–Sept. Tues.–Sat. 10 A.M.–5 P.M.), which also has a small exhibit on the missionaries at Grouard.

High Prairie Elk's Campground (east end of town, May–Sept., unserviced sites $15, powered sites $20) is a quiet place with showers and a laundry.

Winagami Lake Provincial Park

Winagami Lake, north of High Prairie on Highway 749, is ringed by a mix of paper birch, aspen, balsam fir, and poplar trees. The park is on the lake's eastern shore and is an excellent place for bird-watching; two platforms have been built for this purpose (the best time of year is May–June). The day-use area has been planted with ornamental shrubs, and a short hiking trail leads along the lakeshore. The campground (780/523-0041, May–Sept., unserviced sites $17, powered sites $20) has pit toilets, firewood, and kitchen shelters.

Winagami Wildland Provincial Park, along the northeastern arm of the lake (turn off nine km/5.6 mi south of McLennan), is also good for bird-watching. It's undeveloped except for a few short trails.

McLennan

Known as the Bird Capital of Canada, this town of 1,000 is on **Kimiwan Lake** at the con-

fluence of three major bird migration paths— the Mississippi, Pacific, and Central. An estimated 27,000 shorebirds and 250,000 waterfowl reside or pass through here; more than 200 different species are sighted annually. An excellent interpretive center (780/324-2004, summer daily 10 A.M.–7 P.M.) overlooking the lake has a display on migration patterns, computers loaded with information on local species, checklists, and binoculars for loan. From the center, a boardwalk leads through a wetland area to a gazebo and a bird blind. Panels along the boardwalk provide pictures and descriptions of commonly sighted species.

Continuing West

The small hamlet of **Donnelly,** 14 kilometers (8.7 mi) west of McLennan, is best known for the annual **Smoky River Agricultural Fair** (780/925-3889) held on the second weekend of August. The fair features home cooking, a parade, a petting zoo, demonstrations of country skills, a country-style beauty contest (the best-looking tractor wins), and the highlight of the weekend—the Antique Tractor Pull.

From west of Donnelly, Highway 2 heads north 63 kilometers (39 mi) to the town of Peace River. Highway 49 continues west to Spirit River and the turnoff to Grande Prairie. The first town along this route is **Falher,** known as the Honey Capital of Canada. One million bees in 48,000 hives produce 4.5 million kilograms (10 million lbs) of honey annually. Naturally, this industry has created a need for the town to construct the world's largest honeybee, which towers above a small park on Third Avenue (the main drag through town). At the east end of town are two strange-smelling alfalfa-processing plants. The alfalfa is dehydrated and pressed into pellets—more than 50,000 tons annually. You can watch all the action from the highway.

HIGHWAY 18 WEST

Seventy-three kilometers (45 mi) north of Edmonton on Highway 2, Highway 18 heads west through some of Canada's most productive mixed farming land. Major crops include

wheat, barley, oats, canola, and hay. Livestock operations include cattle, hogs, poultry, dairy cows, and sheep; the area is home to several large feedlots and Alberta's two largest livestock auctions. At the junction of Highways 2 and 18, a gravel road leads north to **Nilsson Bros. Inc.** (780/348-5893, www.nbinc.com), Canada's largest cattle auction market. Live auctions are held in summer every Tuesday morning. Buyers come from throughout North America, but anyone is welcome to attend. The auctioneer is lightning fast—Alberta's best beef cattle are sold hundreds at a time by gross weight. The facility is open every day; ask to have a look around. The staff restaurant, open for an hour at lunchtime, serves hearty meat-and-potato meals for a reasonable price. Just don't ask for lamb.

Highway 44 North

Highway 44 spurs north from Highway 18 at **Westlock,** an agricultural service center 11 kilometers (6.8 mi) west of Highway 2. It has the small **District Museum** (10216 100th St., 780/349-2887, Fri.–Sun. 1–5 P.M., free) filled with pioneer artifacts.

From Westlock, it is 106 kilometers (66 mi) north along Highway 44 to Hondo, halfway between Athabasca and Slave Lake. Along the way are two worthwhile detours. **Long Island Lake Municipal Park** (go 22 km/13.6 mi north from Westlock, then turn right at Dapp Corner and follow the signs) is a recreation area with fishing, swimming, canoeing, and camping (May–Sept., $15). Farther north, near the hamlet of Fawcett, is a turnoff to 2,068-hectare (5,150-acre) **Cross Lake Provincial Park.** Deer and moose are common here, and in late summer black bears often feed among the berry patches. A number of trails crisscross the park, some leading to the lake edge. The shallow lake is good for swimming, canoeing, and fishing for northern pike. The campground (780/675-8213, May–mid-Oct., unserviced sites are $18, powered sites $23) has pit toilets, firewood, kitchen shelters, coin-operated showers, and a concession.

Barrhead and Vicinity

Continuing west on Highway 18 takes you to Barrhead, an agriculture and lumber town of 4,200 located 1.5 hours northwest of Edmonton. **Barrhead Centennial Museum** (along Hwy. 33 at 57th Ave., 780/674-5203, mid-May–Aug. Mon.–Sat. 10 A.M.–5 P.M., Sun. 1–5 P.M., adults $1), with displays depicting the town's agricultural past, is north of downtown. The town's symbol is the great blue heron; you can see a model of one at the top end of 50th Street, or head out to Thunder Lake Provincial Park for the chance to see a real one. The biggest event of the year is the **Wildrose Rodeo Association Finals** on the third weekend of September.

An interesting loop drive from Barrhead is to take Highway 769 north to **Neerlandia** (settled by the Dutch in 1912 and named after their homeland), the small hamlet of **Vega,** and the Athabasca River. The river crossing is on the **Klondike Ferry,** one of the province's few remaining ferries. The next community along this route is **Fort Assiniboine,** which was a vital link in the Hudson's Bay Company chain of fur-trading posts. The original fort was built in 1824, making it one of the oldest settlements in Alberta. Although furs were traded at the fort, its main role was as a transportation link across the then-uncharted wilderness. The original is long gone, but a reconstruction is in the center of town (summer daily noon–5 P.M.). From Fort Assiniboine, it is 38 kilometers (24 mi) southeast back to Barrhead, completing the loop, or 62 kilometers (38 mi) northwest to Swan Hills.

Thunder Lake Provincial Park

Colonies of great blue herons reside at this 208-hectare (514-acre) park 21 kilometers (13 mi) west of Barrhead on Highway 18. The park is on the northeast shore of shallow Thunder Lake, set among stands of aspen and balsam fir. Bird-watching, especially for waterfowl, is excellent; look for herons on the islands in the quiet northwest corner of the lake. Grebes and black terns are also common. The lake's water level is artificially controlled to prevent flooding of cottages and beaches. This control results in poor

fishing, although the lake is stocked annually with northern pike and perch. Three short hiking trails begin from the day-use area, including one along the lakeshore that links to three other trails originating from the campground. The campground is beside the beach and is open year-round. It has pit toilets, coin-operated showers, a concession, firewood, kitchen shelters, and canoe rentals; unserviced sites are $20 and powered sites, found on Loop A, are $25.

SWAN HILLS

The town of Swan Hills (pop. 2,000) is in the hills of the same name 100 kilometers (62 mi) northwest of Barrhead. The hills were named, according to Indian legend, for giant swans that nested in a nearby river estuary. It's in the center of a region rich in oil and gas, but is best known economically for the **Swan Hills Treatment Centre,** the world's most modern special-waste treatment plant, which treats material that cannot be disposed of in a landfill, incinerator, or sewage system. Corrosive, combustible, and environmentally unfriendly materials such as lead, mercury, and pesticides are broken down into nontoxic compounds using a process of thermal oxidization and then either burned off or safely stored. Up to 45,000 tons of waste are treated annually.

The surrounding hills are wetter than the Canadian Rockies foothills, creating a unique environment of rainforest, boreal, and subarctic zones. The best place to observe this blend is at **Goose Mountain Ecological Reserve,** 24 kilometers (15 mi) west of town. Hiking and fishing are popular activities throughout the hills; the easiest area to access is **Krause Lake Recreation Area,** south of town. Old logging roads crisscross the entire region, making exploration easy with a full tank of gas and a map from the local information center. The hills provide refuge for the **Swan Hills grizzly bear,** a subspecies of the now-extinct plains grizzly and the only grizzly east of the Rocky Mountains.

The **Grizzly Trail** (Highway 33), linking Barrhead and Swan Hills, offers two interesting stops along its route. **Trapper Lea's Cabin** is 30 kilometers (19 mi) southeast of Swan Hills. It consists of two buildings constructed on the trapline of the "Wolf King of Alberta," the man who trapped the most wolves in the province during the early 1940s. Five kilometers (3.1 mi) farther south is a highway rest area from where a three-kilometer (1.9-mi) trail leads to the **geographic center of Alberta.** Follow the brown and yellow signs along an old seismic road to the center, indicated by an orange marker.

Practicalities

Swan Hills has several roadside motels, but each is usually full with work crews. Try the **Derrick Motor Inn** (in the plaza, 780/333-4405), where ordinary rooms are $55 s, $60 d. Instead of staying at the unappealing campground in town, head 30 kilometers (19 mi) southeast to Trapper Lea's Cabin (May–mid-Sept., $10) or 16 kilometers (10 mi) south to Freeman River (mid-May–mid-Sept., $10).

The tourist information center (Hwy. 33, opposite the Grizzly Motel, 780/333-2224) is open mid-May to August daily 10 A.M.–8 P.M.

Carson-Pegasus Provincial Park

This 1,178-hectare (2,900-acre) park is on the southern edge of the Swan Hills, 49 kilometers (30 mi) south of the town of Swan Hills and 30 kilometers (19 mi) north of Whitecourt. Because of its location in a transition zone, it contains forest typical of both the foothills (lodgepole pine and spruce) and the boreal forest (aspen, poplar, birch, and fir). More than 40 species of mammals have been recorded here, including deer, moose, and black bear. The epicenter of the park is McLeod Lake, where the fishing is excellent for rainbow trout (stocked annually) and the day-use area offers canoe, rowboat, and motorboat rentals ($7, $8, and $14 per hour, respectively) and a sandy beach. Northern pike, perch, and whitefish are caught in Little McLeod Lake. The general store (summer daily 9 A.M.–9 P.M.) sells groceries, fishing tackle, bait, and hot food, and has a laundry room. The campground has flush toilets, showers, kitchen shelters, and an interpretive theater. Rates of $24 for tenting and $27 for powered sites include a bundle of firewood.

WHITECOURT

Whitecourt (pop. 8,100) sits at the confluence of the Athabasca, McLeod, and Sakwatamau Rivers on Highway 43, 177 kilometers (110 mi) northwest of Edmonton and 341 kilometers (212 mi) southeast of Grande Prairie. Highway 32 also passes through town; Swan Hills is 74 kilometers (46 mi) north, and the Yellowhead Highway is 72 kilometers (45 mi) south. If you're coming in from the southeast, you'll pass a strip of motels and restaurants before descending to the Athabasca River and the older part of town, off to the right. Many of Whitecourt's earliest settlers were Yukon-bound in search of gold when they reached this lushly forested region and decided to settle here instead. To them, the area held plenty of opportunities that wouldn't require an arduous trek to the Klondike. When the railroad arrived, so did many more homesteaders. They took to cutting down trees to sell for firewood and railroad ties. Thus began Whitecourt's lumber industry; today the town is the Forest Centre of Alberta.

Sights

The two-story **Forest Interpretive Centre** (on the south side of town, 780/778-2214, July–Aug. daily 9 A.M.–6 P.M., the rest of the year Mon.–Fri. 9 A.M.–6 P.M., free) is dedicated to Alberta's forest industry. Displays re-create a forest environment and a logging camp, and a series of hands-on, interactive exhibits describe every aspect of the industry. The center also holds the town's information center (780/778-5363). Industrial tours are run by the interpretive center Monday–Friday in summer. Each of the four tours is to a forestry-related industry—a pulp mill, a newsprint plant, a sawmill, and a medium-density fiberboard plant. The **E. S. Huestis Demonstration Forest,** five kilometers (3.1 mi) north of Highway 43 on Highway 32, contains several stages of forest development. A seven-kilometer (4.3-mi) road leads through various ecosystems, including an old-growth coniferous forest and a deciduous forest, and past aspen and spruce cut blocks, a beaver dam, and an exotic plantation.

Accommodations and Camping

Most of Whitecourt's dozen motels are on Highway 43 as it enters town from the southeast. The best of these is the **Green Gables Inn** (3527 Caxton St., 780/778-4537 or 888/779-4537, www.greengablesinn.ca, $89–99 s or d), at the top end of the scale, has large, surprisingly nice rooms and a restaurant.

The **Lions Club Campground** (mid-Apr.–mid-Oct., tent sites $14, RVs $17–19), at the south end of the service strip, is set in a heavily forested area and has a laundry and showers. On the opposite side of town, one kilometer (0.6 mi) along Highway 43, is the full-service **Sagitawah Tourist Park** (780/778-3734, Apr.–Oct., $22–29). A better option still is the campground at **Carson-Pegasus Provincial Park,** 30 kilometers (19 mi) north of town on Highway 32 (see *Carson-Pegasus Provincial Park* earlier in this chapter).

HIGHWAY 43 WEST

From Whitecourt, Highway 43 continues northeast to **Fox Creek,** a small town surrounded by a wilderness where wildlife is abundant and the fishing legendary. If you don't believe the local fishing stories, head to the Home Hardware Store to see a 12-kilogram (26-lb) northern pike caught in a nearby lake. **Smoke** and **Iosegun Lakes** are two of the most accessible and offer excellent fishing for northern pike, walleye, perch, and whitefish. Both lakes have primitive camping.

Moose are abundant between Fox Creek and **Little Smoky,** 47 kilometers (26 mi) northwest, from where gravel roads lead to small lakes. This area is not noted for fossils, but a few years back a mammoth tusk was found in Waskahigan River, west of Little Smoky.

Valleyview

Valleyview (pop. 2,000) is an agricultural and oil-and-gas center that also serves travelers who pass through heading north to the Northwest Territories and west to Alaska. It is also one of the largest towns in Alberta without a pioneer museum.

The town's four motels fill up each night

with road-weary travelers. The **Horizon Motel** (780/524-3904 or 888/909-3908) has large rooms in an older wing ($69 s, $79 d), but make sure to request those in the newer wing. Spend the night with Alaska-bound campers at **Sherk's RV Park** (south side of town, 780/524-4949, May–Sept.), a full-service campground where all sites are $23.

Valleyview Tourist Information Centre (three km/1.9 mi south of town, 780/524-2410) is open mid-May to September daily 8 A.M.–8 P.M.

Sturgeon Lake

Sturgeon Lake, west of Valleyview, is known for its excellent northern pike, perch, and walleye fishing and two interesting provincial parks. **Williamson Provincial Park** may be only 17

hectares (42 acres), but it has a sandy beach, good swimming, and a campground (780/538-5350, May–mid-Sept., unserviced sites $20, powered sites $25). Protecting a much larger chunk of forested lakeshore is 3,100-hectare (7,660-acre) **Young's Point Provincial Park.** Here you'll find good bird-watching for forest birds and waterfowl, and productive fishing among the dense aquatic growth close to the shore. Much of the park is forested with a blend of aspen, white spruce, and lodgepole pine. Porcupines, deer, and coyotes wander the woods here, and if you're lucky, you might see red foxes, lynx, and black bears. Hiking trails begin at the day-use area and lead along the lake and to an active beaver pond. The campground (780/538-5350, unserviced sites $20, powered sites $25) has flush toilets and showers and is near a sandy beach.

West of Edmonton

From the provincial capital, the Yellowhead Highway (Hwy. 16) heads west through a region of aspen parkland and scattered lakes to the Canadian Rockies foothills and the border of Jasper National Park. The region's other main thoroughfare, Highway 40, spurs north off the Yellowhead Highway to Grande Cache and Willmore Wilderness Park. An area of frenzied oil activity during the early 1970s, the region west of Edmonton is the center for a large petroleum industry, as well as for farming, coal mining, forestry, and the production of electricity. The major towns are Edson and Hinton, both on the Yellowhead Highway.

FROM EDMONTON TOWARD HINTON

Long after leaving Edmonton's city limits, the Yellowhead Highway is lined with motels, industrial parks, and housing estates. The towns of Spruce Grove and Stony Plain flash by, and farming begins to dominate the landscape.

Wabamun and Nearby Lakes

Wabamun is the name of a town, lake, and provincial park 32 kilometers (20 mi) west of Stony Plain. The skyline around Wabamun Lake is dominated by high-voltage power lines coming from the three coal-fired generating plants that supply more than two-thirds of Alberta's electrical requirements. Fuel for the plants is supplied by nearby mining operations—the largest coal extraction sites in Canada.

Wabamun Lake Provincial Park is on sparkling blue Moonlight Bay at the lake's eastern end. The fishing is good for northern pike (especially in fall), a manmade beach is the perfect spot for a swim, and the hiking trail is a good spot for wildlife-viewing. Two geothermal outlets create a perfect environment for waterfowl in winter; expect to see up to 40 species at each site. The easiest outlet to get to is at the end of the wharf. The park campground (780/892-2702, mid-May–Sept., unserviced sites $20, powered sites $25) has almost 300 sites, but because of its proximity to Edmonton is very busy on weekends. Facilities include

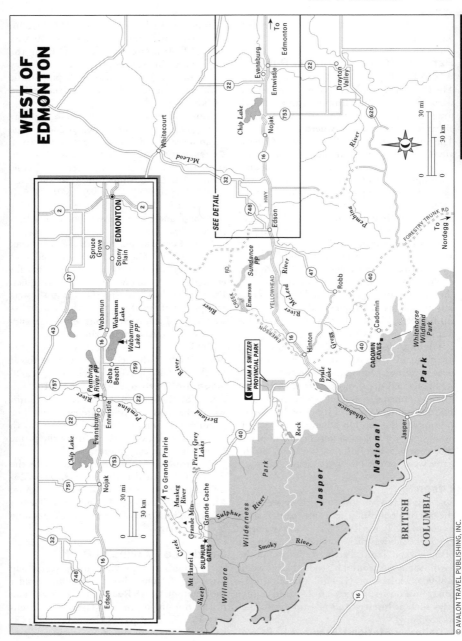

WEST OF EDMONTON

© AVALON TRAVEL PUBLISHING, INC.

coin-operated showers, firewood, kitchen shelters, and a concession.

Pembina River Provincial Park and Vicinity

The Pembina River Valley is the first true wilderness area west of Edmonton. The small towns of Entwistle and Evansburg straddle either side of the valley where the park lies. The only structures you'll see in this 167-hectare (413-acre) park are an old single-lane road bridge and the concrete foundations of what once was a railroad trestle. White spruce and aspen blanket the park and provide a habitat for many mammals, including beavers, mule deer, white-tailed deer, and moose. Fishing in the river is particularly good for northern pike and walleye, and those who don't fish might appreciate the deep swimming hole behind a weir, or the hiking trails in the northern part of the park. On the eastern side of the river, the campground (780/727-3643, May–Oct., unserviced sites $20, powered sites $25) has flush toilets, kitchen shelters, showers, an interpretive program, and firewood.

Highway 16 bypasses **Entwistle,** but the town's main street is worth a look for its historic buildings. Out on the highway are all the services you'll need: motels (from $60 s, $70 d), restaurants, gas, and, of course, mini-golf.

Continuing west on Highway 16 toward Edson, you'll pass **Chip Lake,** interesting primarily for the scatological story behind its name. It used to be called Buffalo Chip Lake, but the name was shortened for aesthetic reasons.

Edson

The site of today's town of Edson was once the starting point of a trail early settlers used to access the Peace River Valley to the north. Later, the site was picked as a divisional point of the Grand Trunk Pacific Railway, and the town sprang up around it. Today this town of 7,800, 199 kilometers (124 mi) west of Edmonton, relies on natural resource–based industries such as forestry and oil-and-gas to fuel its economy.

Galloway Station Museum is in RCMP Centennial Park (3rd Ave., 780/723-5696, mid-May–early Sept. daily 10 A.M.–4:30 P.M., adult $2). It houses artifacts reflecting the importance of transportation and industry to the town's growth. Also on display in the park are a restored 1917 caboose and a 1964 Lockheed jet.

Most motels are along the main highway through town—locally known as 2nd Avenue (heading east) and 4th Avenue (heading west). **Odyssey Inn** (5601 2nd Ave., 780/723-5505, from $69–79 s, $79–89 d) offers acceptable rooms. The **Sundowner Inn** (5150 2nd Ave., 780/723-5591 or 877/723-5591, $89 s, $99 d) has the basics and a few bonuses too—an indoor pool and a recreation room with a fireplace and pool table.

Lions Park Campground (east end of town, 780/723-3169, May–Sept., unserviced sites $15, powered sites $18) has 52 treed sites far enough from the highway to be relatively quiet. Facilities include extra-hot (and fast) showers and plenty of free firewood, which is just as well because you need a bonfire to cook anything on the oversized fire rings.

Ernie O's (4340 2nd Ave., 780/723-3600) is one of the best places in town to eat breakfast ($4–7). Nightly specials are $10. **Mountain Pizza & Steakhouse** (5102 4th Ave., 780/723-3900) is a classy pizza joint where the food and prices are excellent. The Mountain Extra Special Pizza ($18) is worth the extra bucks, or if it's Saturday the prime rib special is an easy choice.

The tourist information center is in the RCMP Centennial Park (3rd Ave., 780/723-4918, www.townofedson.ca, mid-May–Aug. Mon.–Fri. 8 A.M.–8 P.M., Sat.–Sun. 9 A.M.–8 P.M., and the rest of the year weekdays only 8 A.M.–4 P.M.).

Sundance Provincial Park

As an alternative to continuing west along Highway 16 from Edson to Hinton, consider the **Emerson Creek Road,** which links the two towns, running north of and parallel to Highway 16. The road passes through the 3,712-hectare (9,170-acre) Sundance Provincial Park,

protecting a variety of interesting geological features and the picturesque Emerson Lakes. (Emerson Creek Road is maintained primarily as a logging road, so drive with care and yield to trucks—yellow signs along the road are not kilometer markers.) From Edson, take 51st Street north from Highway 16 for 32 kilometers (20 mi), turning left (to the west) at the Silver Summit ski area sign; this is Emerson Creek Road, and from this point it's 83 kilometers (52 mi) to Hinton.

The two picturesque Emerson Lakes, between signs 53 and 52, were formed as the sheet of ice from the last ice age receded. A 5.7-kilometer (3.5-mi) trail winds around the lakes to an old trapper's cabin and past some active beaver dams; allow 90 minutes to complete the entire loop. The lakes are stocked with brook trout and Sundance Creek with rainbow and brown trout. A small campground (May–Sept., $9) at the lakes has sites with no facilities but free firewood. In the west of the park, between signs 18 and 19, a short trail follows **Canyon Creek** to a point where it cascades dramatically into a series of canyons.

If you're traveling west to east, the access point in Hinton is a little more difficult to find: take Switzer Drive south from Highway 16 and loop back under Highway 16, then continue for four kilometers (2.5 mi). Turn left (north) at Weldwood Bridge Road. Continue down to a bridge over the Athabasca River and follow this road until Emerson Creek Road is signed to the right.

HINTON

On the south bank of the Athabasca River and surrounded in total wilderness, this town of 9,500, 287 kilometers (178 mi) west of Edmonton, makes an ideal base for a couple of days' exploration. It's also only 75 kilometers (47 mi) from Jasper, but before speeding off to the famous mountain parks, take time out to explore Hinton's immediate vicinity. To the south are well-maintained roads leading into the historic Coal Branch; to the north are lakes, streams, canyons, hoodoos, and sand dunes. The town has some interesting sights, and the motels and

restaurants have prices you'll appreciate after spending time in Jasper.

Hinton began as a coal-mining and forestry town. These industries still play a major role in the town's economy, although the town now also benefits from being an important service stop along the Yellowhead Highway.

Don't be put off by the unappealing location of the **Natural Resource Interpretive Park,** behind the Canadian Tire store on the west side of town—much of the park is out of sight in the valley below. Up top are a lookout, a 154-ton dump truck, and panels describing local industry, while a trail leads down to a small arboretum and through an area of wetlands. On the campus of the **Hinton Training Centre** (1176 Switzer Dr., 780/865-8200, Mon.–Fri. 8:30 A.M.–4:30 P.M.) you'll find a small museum dedicated to the history of forestry, including a display on wildfire management. Adjacent is a 1922 ranger cabin. The museum is also the starting point for the **Interpretive Nature Trail**—a 1.6-kilometer (one-mi) path

dump truck at Hinton's Natural Resource Interpretive Park

that winds around the perimeter of the school, passing various forest environments, Edna the erratic (a huge boulder carried far from its source during the last ice age), and a viewpoint with magnificent views of the Athabasca River Valley and Canadian Rockies.

Accommodations

The strip of motels, hotels, restaurants, fast-food places, and gas stations along Highway 16 reflects the importance of Hinton as a service center, but I recommend giving the regular motels a miss and staying out of town at one of the following two accommodations.

Halfway between Hinton and Jasper, **◖ Overlander Mountain Lodge** (780/866-2330 or 877/866-2330, www.overlandermountainlodge.com, $174–425 s or d) has an inviting wilderness setting and energetic hosts with plenty of suggestions to keep you busy through the day. Choose from regular guest rooms in various styles (the Miette Rooms have a particularly appealing decor), cozy cabins, or a large three-bedroom log chalet. Mountain charm continues through to the dining room, where Canadian specialties anchor a seasonal menu.

The **◖ Black Cat Guest Ranch** (780/865-3084 or 800/859-6840, www.blackcatguestranch.ca) is another nearby mountain retreat. All of the rooms have private baths and mountain views. Horseback riding is available during the day, and in the evening, guests can relax in the large living room or hot tub. Three meals are included in the rates of $151 s, $192 d. To get to the ranch, take Highway 40 north for six kilometers (3.7 mi), turn left to Brûlé and continue for 11 kilometers (6.8 mi), then turn right and follow the signs.

If it's just a bed for the night you're after, it's hard to go past the **Best Canadian Motor Inn** (386 Smith St., 780/865-5099 or 888/700-2264, www.bestcdn.com, $99 s or d), along the main commercial strip. It offers 40 clean, medium-size rooms decorated in an unfussy alpine style. Amenities in each include compact cooking facilities, in-room coffee, and Internet access. A light breakfast is included in the very reasonable rates. **Holiday Inn Hinton** (393 Gregg Ave., 780/865-3321 or 888/465-4329, www.holidayinn.com, from $99 s, $109 d) has everything you'd expect from a Holiday Inn—reliable rooms, a restaurant, a fitness room, and kid-friendly extras like PlayStation.

The best nearby camping is in William A. Switzer Provincial Park toward Grande Cache (see *William A. Switzer Provincial Park* later in this chapter).

Food

Apart from the fast-food restaurants that line the highway from one end of town to the other, Hinton has little to offer the hungry traveler. The **Husky Restaurant,** as usual, serves filling meals at good prices; open 24 hours. If gas-station dining isn't your style, try the **Greentree Restaurant** in the Holiday Inn. A continental breakfast is $5.50; the lumberjack breakfast of steak, bacon, eggs, and hotcakes is $11. Lunch is $8–11 and dinner mains start at $14. **Tokyo Sushi** (Black Bear Inn, 571 Gregg Ave., 780/865-2120) has a modern family restaurant–style atmosphere and good-value Japanese food. Don't expect anything too adventurous—just tasty, inexpensive favorites like chicken teriyaki ($10) as well as filling sushi combos (from $12). A cooked breakfast here is just $8.

Information and Services

The **tourist information center** (Gregg Ave., 780/865-2777, summer daily 8 A.M.–7 P.M., the rest of the year Mon.–Fri. 9 A.M.–4:15 P.M.) is on the south side of the highway surrounded by gardens in the middle of the commercial strip. It's impossible to miss. Most of the best this region has to offer lies outside of Hinton, and in this regard, the staff does a wonderful job of supplying information on hiking, fishing, and canoeing opportunities that would otherwise be easy to miss.

The post office is on Parks Street. The **Koin Spin and Dry Laundromat** is at 220 Pembina Avenue.

Getting There and Around

The **Greyhound** bus depot (128 North St., 780/865-2367, www.greyhound.ca) is served

daily by buses from Edmonton and Jasper. **National** car rental has an office in the Holiday Inn (780/817-2662). For **Mountain Taxis,** call 780/865-1889.

THE COAL BRANCH

An area of heavily forested foothills south of Hinton has been the scene of feverish coal-mining activity for 90 years. Most of the mines, along with the towns of Mountain Park, Luscar, Leyland, Coal Spur, and Mercoal, have been abandoned. Two mines still operate, and two towns have survived, although the populations of **Cadomin** and **Robb** have dwindled to approximately 100 residents apiece. This area, so rich in history, is also a wilderness offering hiking, fishing, and spectacular views of the Canadian Rockies. The best way to access the region, known as the Coal Branch, is via Highway 40. The active mines are Cardinal River Coal's pit-mining operation and another at Gregg River. A viewpoint overlooks one of the largest pits. Look for bighorn sheep, oblivious to the rumbling trucks below, at natural salt deposits on the cliff above the viewpoint. If you're interested in touring the mines, contact the information center in Hinton, 780/865-2777. The tours are free, and take up most of the day, departing by bus from Hinton on Tuesday, Thursday, and Friday. A packed lunch is included.

From the junction beyond the mines, a spur branches south to Cadomin and Whitehorse Wildland Park; on your return trip, you can take Highway 40 northeast to Highway 47, passing through the coal-mining hamlet of Robb and rejoining Highway 16 just west of Edson. This 250-kilometer (155-mi) loop through the Coal Branch takes at least one day.

Cadomin

This remote little hamlet—once a town of 2,500—is best known as the gateway to Alberta's best known and most accessible caverns, **Cadomin Caves,** which can be seen in the mountain face west of town. Access is along a trail that begins two kilometers (1.2 mi) south of Cadomin, climbing 350 vertical

meters (1,150 ft) in three kilometers (1.9 mi) to the mouth of the cave. The caves are closed September–April as they are a hibernaculum for bats. Serious spelunkers can find out more and get a map of the cave system from the information center in Hinton.

Whitehorse Wildland Park

This 17,500-hectare (43,250-acre) area of wilderness lies south and west of Cadomin, adjacent to Jasper National Park. Highway 40 south from Cadomin enters the park after three kilometers (1.9 mi) and crosses Whitehorse Creek after another two kilometers (1.2 mi). At this bridge is a small campground ($11) nestled below a sheer rock wall. The campground is also the starting point for an overnight backcountry trail over Whitehorse Pass to Miette Hot Springs in Jasper National Park, a total of 40 kilometers (25 mi) one-way. A good turnaround point for a full-day hike is **Whitehorse Falls,** 10 kilometers (6.2 mi) from the trailhead.

Continuing south through the park, Highway 40 climbs above the tree line and passes what's left of **Mountain Park,** once a thriving community of 1,000 connected by rail to Coal Spur to the east. The mine at Mountain Park closed in 1950, and residents dismantled their houses and moved to new locations. Today all that remains is a cemetery, some foundations, and remnants of the narrow-gauge railway.

From here, the road continues climbing to the Cardinal Divide (the division between the Athabasca River System, which flows north, and the North Saskatchewan River System, which flows east), more than 2,000 meters (6,600 ft) above sea level. This magnificent ridge extends as far as the eye can see to the east and west. No trails are marked in this remote corner of the park, but walking through the treeless alpine landscape is possible in either direction.

HIGHWAY 40 TO GRANDE CACHE

Take divided Highway 16 west out of Hinton and, before you know it, Highway 40 spurs

north, passing the following sights and reaching Grande Cache after 142 kilometers (88 mi).

William A. Switzer Provincial Park

This 2,688-hectare (6,640-acre) park, in the foothills 26 kilometers (16 mi) northwest of Hinton on Highway 40, encompasses a series of shallow lakes linked by Jarvis Creek. Most of the park is heavily forested with lodgepole pine, spruce, and aspen. The northern section, however, is more wide open, and elk, moose, and deer can often be seen grazing there. An ill-fated attempt at beaver ranching was made in the 1940s (cement lodges built for the purpose can be seen near Beaver Ranch Campground). Soon after, Entrance Provincial Park was established and renamed Switzer in 1958. The lakes are excellent for canoeing, birdwatching, and wildlife-viewing, but fishing is considered average. Highway 40 divides the park roughly in two, with many access points. From the south, the first road loops around the west side of Jarvis Lake, passing a pleasant picnic area and camping before rejoining Highway 40. At the north end of Jarvis Lake is Kelley's Bathtub day-use area, where a short trail leads to a bird blind. The roads leading into the northern section of the park lead past various hiking trails, three more day-use areas, and three campgrounds.

The main campground is on **Gregg Lake.** It offers 164 sites, coin-operated showers, kitchen shelters, an interpretive theater, and winter camping; unserviced sites $20, powered sites $25. In the same vicinity are **Graveyard/ Halfway** and **Cache Campgrounds,** where sites range $14–17 per night. In the south of the park is **Jarvis Lake Campground** ($17). For more information on the park, call 780/865-5600; for campsite reservations, call 780/865-5152.

Roughly in the middle of the park is **The Lodge@Switzer** (780/865-4741 or 877/865-4741, www.venturescape.ca, from $119 s or

d), comprising chalets and cabins in a forested setting and adjacent to Blue Lake. The emphasis is on activities, with canoes, kayaks, mountain bikes, and fishing tackle for rent as well as nearby hiking trails, a spa and sauna, and a game room. Meal and accommodation packages run $90–110 per person per day, discounted October–April.

On to Grande Cache

From William A. Switzer Provincial Park, it is 118 kilometers (73 mi) to Grande Cache. A 32-kilometer (20-mi) gravel spur to **Rock Lake-Solomon Creek Wildland Provincial Park,** 15 kilometers (9.3 mi) north of Switzer park, makes a tempting detour. Although the park extends from Willmore Wilderness Park in the north to Brûlé Lake in the south, most is a remote, untracked wilderness. The only facilities are at Rock Lake itself. Ever since a Hudson's Bay Company post was established at the lake, the area has drawn hikers and anglers, attracted by mountain scenery, the chance of viewing abundant big game, excellent fishing for huge lake trout, and the remote location. Hiking trails lead around the lake and three kilometers (1.9 mi) to the remote northern reaches of Jasper National Park. Fortunately, you don't have to travel far to appreciate the rugged beauty of the lake and surrounding mountainscapes. The large campground has kitchen shelters, firewood, and pit toilets; sites are $20 per night.

From Rock Lake Road, Highway 40 continues to climb steadily, crossing Pinto Creek and Berland River (small campground), then following Muskeg River for a short while. Continuing north, the road then passes **Pierre Grey Lakes,** a string of five lakes protected as a provincial recreation area. The lakes lie in a beautiful spot, with birdlife prolific and the waters stocked annually with rainbow trout. From the boat launch, a rough trail leads 1.6 kilometers (one mi) along the lakeshore to the site of a trading post. Camping is $17 per night.

Grande Cache

Grande Cache is a remote town of 3,800, 450 kilometers (280 mi) west of Edmonton and 182 kilometers (113 mi) south of Grande Prairie. The surrounding wilderness is totally undeveloped, offering endless opportunities for hiking, canoeing, kayaking, fishing, and horseback riding.

The first Europeans to explore the area were fur trappers and traders, who cached furs near the site of the present town before taking them to major trading posts. At one point there was a small trading post on a lake south of town on Pierre Gray Lakes; its remains are still visible. Grande Cache is a planned town. Construction started in 1969 in response to a need for services and housing for miners and their families working at the Grande Cache Coal Corporation mine. The town was developed 20 kilometers (12.4 mi) south of the mine to maintain a scenic environment.

GRANDE CACHE TOURISM AND INTERPRETIVE CENTRE

This center (780/827-3300 or 888/827-3790, summer daily 9 A.M.–6 P.M., the rest of the year Mon.–Fri. 8:30 A.M.–4:30 P.M.) is outstanding, not just considering the size of the town that it represents, but for the wealth of information contained within it. It's easy to spend at least one hour in the two-story complex, with displays that include information about the human history of the region, the local industry, taxidermy, tree identification, and Willmore Wilderness Park. Other features include an information desk, a gift shop, and a large deck from where views extend across the Smoky River Valley to the highest peaks of the Canadian Rockies. Beside it are a 1942 ranger cabin and a few picnic tables.

RECREATION

Most of the serious hiking and horseback riding takes place in adjacent Willmore Wilderness Park (see next listing), but a variety of other recreational opportunities exist outside the park.

For great views of the surrounding area, consider climbing **Grande Mountain.** It's a steep trail, gaining 730 meters (2,400 ft) of elevation in 3.5 kilometers (2.1 mi), but from the summit the view across the Smoky River Valley to the Rocky Mountains is spectacular. The trail follows a power line the entire way to the peak and is easy to follow. To get to the trailhead, head northwest of town one kilometer (0.6 mi) and turn right at the cemetery gate. Park, walk along the road to the power line, veer right, and start the long slog to the summit. **Grande Cache Lake,** five kilometers (3.1 mi) south of town, has good swimming, canoeing, and fishing for rainbow trout. Many of the forestry roads are suitable for mountain biking; **Grande Cache Adventure Sports** (780/827-3764) rents bikes. Longtime local Terry Deamer operates **Taste of Wilderness Tours** (780/827-4250, www.tasteofwilderness.ab.ca), with guided hiking, canoeing, and rafting day trips. **Grande Cache Golf and Country Club** (780/827-5151, $28) is only nine holes, but you'll want to go around twice, however badly you're playing, because the scenery is distracting to say the least.

In recent years, Grande Cache has placed itself on the calendar of extreme ultra-marathoners the world over as host of the early-August **Canadian Death Race** (www.canadiandeath race.com). The foot race takes place along a super-demanding 125-kilometer (78-mi) course, which summits three peaks.

ACCOMMODATIONS AND CAMPING

Room rates in this mountain hideaway are surprisingly inexpensive, but because fewer than 250 rooms are available in the whole town, reservations should be made in advance. On the highway through town, the **Big Horn Motor Inn** (780/827-3744 or 888/880-2444, www.bighorninn.com, $55 s, $65 d) is the best value. Each of 37 rooms has a small fridge, some have kitchenettes, and a laundry room and a restaurant are on the

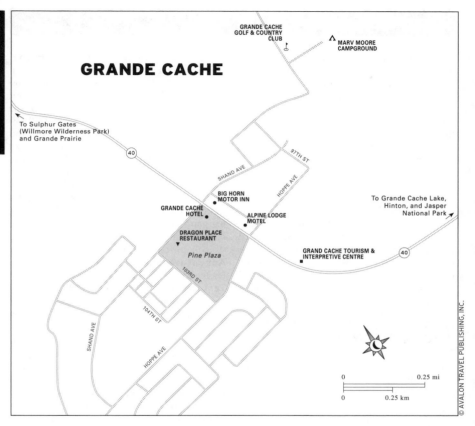

GRANDE CACHE

GRANDE CACHE
GOLF & COUNTRY
CLUB

MARV MOORE
CAMPGROUND

To Sulphur Gates
(Willmore Wilderness Park)
and Grande Prairie

40

97TH ST

SHAND AVE

HOPPE AVE

BIG HORN
MOTOR INN

GRANDE CACHE
HOTEL

ALPINE LODGE
MOTEL

DRAGON PLACE
RESTAURANT

Pine Plaza

To Grande Cache Lake,
Hinton, and Jasper
National Park

GRAND CACHE TOURISM &
INTERPRETIVE CENTRE

40

103RD ST

104TH ST

SHAND AVE

HOPPE AVE

0   0.25 mi

0   0.25 km

premises. Also along the highway is the similarly priced **Alpine Lodge Motel** (780/827-2450). If you're looking for something a little different, consider a stay at **Sheep Creek Back Country Lodge & Cabins** (780/831-1087 or 877/945-3786, www.sheepcreek.net, mid-June–mid-Sept., $50 s, $85 d), which is accessed by a short walking trail and a suspension bridge from 24 kilometers (15 mi) north of town. It attracts an eclectic array of guests—anglers, hunters, mountain bikers—but everyone is welcome. Each rustic cabin has a simple kitchen, bedroom, deck, chemical toilet, and gravity-fed shower. A communal fridge/freezer is located in the main building. Guests bring their own food and towels.

Camping

The only camping right in town is at **Marv Moore Campground** (780/827-2404, May–late Sept.), which has semiprivate, well-shaded sites and showers, kitchen shelters, a laundry, and firewood. Sites in the tenting area are $20; powered sites are $22. It's at the north end of town on Shand Avenue beside the golf course. Four forestry campgrounds at regular intervals along Highway 40 are managed by North of 40 Wilderness Campgrounds (780/827-6521). Of special note is the one at the south end of

© ANDREW HEMPSTEAD

Pleasant stretches of beach line the shore of Grande Cache Lake.

Sulphur Gates Provincial Recreation Area (west off Hwy. 40 north of town, May–Oct., $11), which makes a good base for exploring adjacent Willmore Wilderness Park. It has just 10 sites.

FOOD

On a clear day, the view from the **Family Restaurant** (Grande Cache Hotel, 780/827-3377, daily for breakfast, lunch, and dinner) is worth at least the price of a coffee. Soup-and-sandwich lunch specials are approximately $6, and pizza and pasta dishes start at $8. At the back of the hotel is **Rockies Bar and Grill,** with a regular bar menu and occasional live music. Across the plaza is **Dragon Place Restaurant** (780/827-3898, daily 11 A.M.–10 P.M.). This is your quintessential small-town Chinese restaurant, with big portions of all the usual westernized Chinese favorites. All mains except the seafood dishes are under $10. Up on the highway, the **Big Horn Motor Inn** (780/827-3744) has a restaurant that opens daily at 5:30 A.M.

INFORMATION AND SERVICES

The excellent **Grande Cache Tourism and Interpretive Centre** (780/827-3300 or 888/827-3790, www.visitgrandecache.com, summer daily 9 A.M.–7 P.M., the rest of the year Mon.–Fri. 9 A.M.–5 P.M.) is a great source of park information.

The post office is in the plaza, as is a laundry (beside IGA). **Home Hardware,** in the Pine Plaza, stocks camping and fishing gear.

WILLMORE WILDERNESS PARK

Willmore Wilderness Park is a northern extension of Jasper National Park. It lies south and west of Grande Cache, a small town on Highway 40 between Hinton and Grande Prairie. The 460,000-hectare (1,137,000-acre) wilderness is divided roughly in half by the Smoky River. The area west of the river is reached from Sulphur Gates. The east side is far less traveled—the terrain is rougher and wetter. The park is accessible only on foot, horseback, or, in winter, on skis. It is totally undeveloped—the trails that do exist are not maintained and in most cases are those once used by trappers.

The park is made up of long green ridges above the tree line and, farther west, wide passes and expansive basins along the Continental Divide. Lower elevations are covered in lodgepole pine and spruce, while at higher elevations the cover changes to fir. The diverse wildlife is one of the park's main attractions; white-tailed and mule deer, mountain goats, bighorn sheep, moose, elk, caribou, and black bears are all common. The park is also home to wolves, cougars, and grizzly bears.

Park Access and Travel

The easiest way to access the park is from Sulphur Gates Provincial Recreation Area, six kilometers (3.7 mi) north of Grande Cache on Highway 40 and then a similar distance along a gravel road to the west. Those not planning a trip into the park can still enjoy the cliffs at **Sulphur Gates** (formerly known as Hell's Gate), which is only a short walk from the end of the road. These 70-meter (230-ft) cliffs are

at the confluence of the Sulphur and Smoky Rivers. The color difference between the glacial-fed Smoky River and spring-fed Sulphur River is apparent as they merge.

One of the most popular overnight trips from Sulphur Gates is to **Clarke's Cache,** an easy 16-kilometer (10-mi) hike to the remains of a cabin where trappers once stored furs before taking them to trading posts farther afield. A good option for a day trip for fit hikers is to the 2,013-meter (6,600-ft) summit of **Mount Stearn** from a trailhead 3.5 kilometers (2.2 mi) along the access road to Sulphur Gates. The trail begins by climbing alongside a stream through montane, then subalpine forest, and then through open meadows before reentering the forest and forking and rejoining. The official trail then climbs steeply and continuously to Lightning Ridge (10 km/6.2 mi one-way), but an easier summit is reached by heading up through the grassed slopes to a summit knob, 6.5 kilometers (four mi) and 1,000 vertical meters (3,280 vertical

ft) from the road; allow 6–6.5 hours for the round trip.

Practicalities

Anyone planning an extended trip into the park should be aware that no services are available, most trails are unmarked, and certain areas are heavily used by horse-packers. **High Country Vacations** (780/827-3246 or 877/487-2457, www.packtrails.com) offers pack trips into the park; expect to pay around $200 per person per day, all-inclusive.

More information is available by contacting the Department of Sustainable Resource Development (www.srd.gov.ab.ca).

TO GRANDE PRAIRIE

From Grande Cache, a 181-kilometer (112-mi) gravel road follows the Smoky River out of the foothills and into the wide valley in which Grande Prairie lies. Along the route are service campgrounds and good opportunities for wildlife-viewing.

Grande Prairie and Vicinity

Grande Prairie, a city of 43,000, is in a wide, gently rolling valley surrounded by large areas of natural grasslands. Edmonton is 460 kilometers (286 mi) to the southeast, while Dawson Creek (British Columbia) and Mile Zero of the Alaska Highway are 135 kilometers (84 mi) to the northwest. Grasslands are something of an anomaly at such a northern latitude. To the south and west are heavily forested mountains, and to the north and east are boreal forests and wetlands. But the grasslands here, *la grande prairie,* provided the stimulus for growth in the region. Although so many of Alberta's northern towns began and grew as trading posts beside rivers, Grande Prairie grew as a result of the land's agricultural potential.

In the late 1800s, when the first settlers began making the arduous journey north to Peace River Country, the area had no roads and no communication to the outside world. Fami-

lies had to be entirely self-sufficient. But that didn't deter the first immigrants from journeying through 300 kilometers (186 mi) of dense forests and boggy muskeg to the prairie, which was isolated from southern farmland but highly suited to agriculture. When the Grand Trunk Pacific Railway reached Edson, to the south, settlers arrived over the **Edson Trail.** When the railway arrived from Dunvegan in 1916, the settlement—then on the floodplains of Bear Creek—boomed. The population continued to climb slowly but steadily until 1976, when the discovery of Alberta's largest gas reserve nearby boosted it to more than 20,000. Now the largest city in northwestern Alberta, Grande Prairie is a service, cultural, and transportation center.

SIGHTS

Although malls, motels, restaurants, and other services are spread out along Highway 2 west

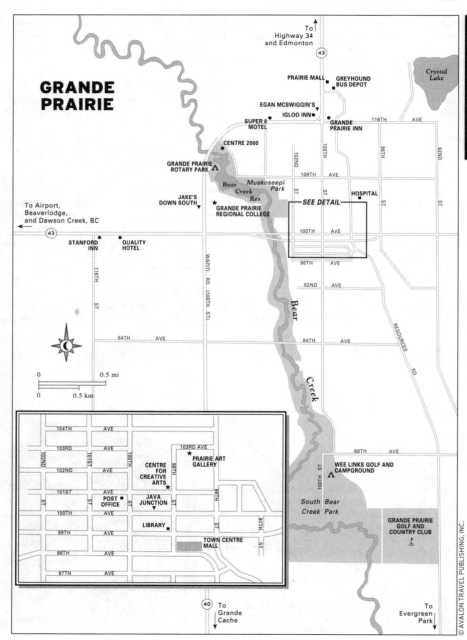

GRANDE PRAIRIE

To
Highway 34
and Edmonton

43

PRAIRIE MALL   GREYHOUND
BUS DEPOT

Crystal
Lake

EGAN MCSWIGGIN'S
IGLOO INN

SUPER 8
MOTEL

GRANDE
PRAIRIE INN

116TH   AVE

CENTRE 2000

102ND ST

100TH ST

96TH ST

92ND ST

GRANDE PRAIRIE
ROTARY PARK

108TH   AVE

Muskoseepi
Park

Bear
Creek
Res

JAKE'S
DOWN SOUTH

GRANDE PRAIRIE
REGIONAL COLLEGE

HOSPITAL

SEE DETAIL

To Airport,
Beaverlodge,
and Dawson Creek, BC

43

STANFORD
INN

QUALITY
HOTEL

100TH   AVE

96TH   AVE

116TH ST

WAPITI RD (108TH ST)

92ND   AVE

Bear

84TH   AVE

84TH   AVE

RESOURCES   RD

Creek

0   0.5 mi

0   0.5 km

104TH   AVE

103RD   AVE

103RD AVE

PRAIRIE ART
GALLERY

102ND ST

101ST ST

100TH ST

99TH ST

CENTRE
FOR
CREATIVE
ARTS

102ND   AVE

101ST   AVE

POST
OFFICE

JAVA
JUNCTION

100TH   AVE

99TH   AVE

LIBRARY

98TH   AVE

97TH   AVE

98TH ST

97TH ST

TOWN CENTRE
MALL

68TH   AVE

100TH ST

WEE LINKS GOLF AND
CAMPGROUND

South Bear
Creek Park

GRANDE PRAIRIE
GOLF AND
COUNTRY CLUB

40 To
Grande
Cache

To
Evergreen
Park

and north of town, the center of the city has managed to retain much of its original charm. A short walk west of downtown on 100th Avenue is **Bear Creek,** along which most of Grande Prairie's sights lie.

Muskoseepi Park

Muskoseepi (Bear Creek, in the Cree language) is a 405-hectare (1,000-acre) park that preserves a wide swathe of land through the heart of the city. At the north end of the park is **Bear Creek Reservoir,** the focal point of the park. Here you'll find an interpretive pavilion, a heated outdoor pool, tennis courts, mini-golf, and canoe rentals ($10 per hour). At the magnificent open-plan **Centre 2000,** Grande Prairie's main information center, a stairway leads up to the **Northern Lights Lookout.** From Centre 2000, 40 kilometers (25 mi) of hiking and biking trails follow both sides of Bear Creek to the city's outer edge.

Overlooking the reservoir (access from the Hwy. 2 bypass) is **Grande Prairie Regional College.** Designed by renowned architect Douglas Cardinal, the flowing curves of this brick building are the city's most distinctive landmark.

Grande Prairie Museum

Located in Muskoseepi Park and overlooking Bear Creek, this excellent museum (780/532-5482, summer daily 10 A.M.–6 P.M., the rest of the year Sun. 1–5 P.M., adult $3, child $2) is within easy walking distance (30 minutes) of Centre 2000 along Bear Creek. If you're driving, access is east along 102nd Avenue from downtown. Indoor displays include the Heritage Discovery Centre, which catalogs the area's early development through interactive exhibits, a natural history display, and dinosaur bones from a nearby dig site. Historic buildings outside include a church, a schoolhouse, a blacksmith shop, and a fire station.

Prairie Art Gallery

Housed in the 1929 Grande Prairie High School (10209 99th St., 780/532-8111, Mon.–

Grande Prairie Regional College

© ANDREW HEMPSTEAD

© ANDREW HEMPSTEAD

a typical example of the wooden churches that dotted the rural landscape of Alberta early in the 20th century

Fri. 10 A.M.–5 P.M., Sat.–Sun. 1–5 P.M.), but currently undergoing expansion slated for completion in 2008, this large facility has three main galleries displaying permanent and temporary exhibitions of work by artists from throughout Canada.

Kleskun Hill Natural Area

Kleskun Hill, 20 kilometers (12.5 mi) east of Grande Prairie along Highway 34, is the most northern badlands in North America. Approximately 70 million years ago, the land around these parts was a river delta, which today rises 100 meters (330 ft) above the surrounding prairie. Plant species normally associated with southern latitudes, such as prickly pear cactus, are found here. The only facility is a picnic area at the south end.

RECREATION AND EVENTS
Golf

Grande Prairie has several challenging and well-maintained golf courses. Greens fee ranges $28–50. My favorite is the 6,450-yard-long **The**

Dunes (780/538-4333 or 888/224-2252), on the Wapiti River seven kilometers (4.3 mi) south of the city. It features two distinct "nines," the first with tree-lined fairways, the second wide open in the style of a Scottish links course. Also south of the city are **Grande Prairie Golf and Country Club** (780/532-0340) and **Bear Creek Golf Club** (780/538-3393).

Theater

Two theaters offer performances September–April. **Grande Prairie Live Theatre,** based at the newly renovated Second Street Theatre (10130 98th Ave., 780/538-1616), is small, but all productions are popular. **Grande Prairie Regional College Theatre** (780/539-2911) hosts amateur dramas as well as touring performers and country-music stars.

Events

Evergreen Park, south of downtown, hosts many of the city's larger events, including a farmers market each Saturday during summer, horse racing, demolition derbies, and fall

harvest festivals. The weekend closest to May 31 is **Grande Prairie Stompede** (780/532-4646, www.gpstompede.com), a gathering of North America's best cowboys and chuck wagon drivers. The regional fair, with a livestock show, chuck wagon races, and a midway, is the last weekend of July. For further information on these events, call the park administration (780/532-3279). Muskoseepi Park hosts **National Aboriginal Day** on the fourth weekend of June.

Grande Prairie's climate is perfect for hot-air ballooning, and every couple of years the city plays host to a national or international competition.

ACCOMMODATIONS AND CAMPING

All motels are located west and north of downtown along Highway 2; the first two listed are to the west, whereas the others line the northern approach to the city.

Stanford Inn (11401 100th Ave., 780/539-5678 or 800/661-8160, www.stanfordinn.net, $90 s, $95 d) is a large 204-room complex, with mid-sized guest rooms, a fitness room, an outdoor hot tub, a restaurant, and a bar. The **Quality Hotel** (11201 100th Ave., 780/539-6000 or 800/661-7954, www.quality hotelgrandeprairie.com, $109–139 s or d) stands out not only for its sleek exterior, but inside for modern, well-designed rooms with all the amenities. A fitness center, business center, restaurant, and lounge are on-site. Rates include local calls, a light breakfast, and an airport shuttle. **Grande Prairie Inn** (11633 Clairmont Rd., 780/532-5221 or 800/661-6529, $96 s or d) is a full-service hotel right at the Highway 2 bypass. Facilities include an indoor pool, a restaurant, a lounge, and a nightclub. The **Super 8 Motel** (10050 116th Ave., 780/532-8288 or 800/800-8000, www.super8.com) is well priced at $95 s, $105 d. Don't expect any surprises here—just the usual high standard of reliable rooms, an indoor pool and water slide, a laundry facility, and a free continental breakfast.

Camping

Grande Prairie Rotary Park (along the Hwy. 2 bypass, 780/532-1137, May–Sept.) overlooks Bear Creek and is just across from Centre 2000. It has showers and a laundry room but few trees; tent sites down by the water are $17, RVs and trailers pay $23–27 (no reservations taken). At the south end of town, along 68th Avenue, is **Wee Links Golf & Campground** (9209 95th Ave., 780/538-4501, Apr.–Oct., $22) at a pitch-and-putt golf course and with powered sites.

FOOD

The dining scene in Grande Prairie is unremarkable at best. Downtown is **Java Junction** (9931 100th Ave., 780/539-5070, Mon.–Fri. 7:45 A.M.–4:30 P.M., Sat. 9 A.M.–4 P.M.), a small coffee shop with friendly staff; coffee and a muffin is $4, and soup, sandwich, and coffee is $7.50.

Jake's Down South (10702 108th St., 780/532-5667, daily 11 A.M.–10 P.M.) doesn't look like much from the outside, but the Southern-style food is as good as you're likely to come across in Grande Prairie. Think jambalaya ($17) and blackened catfish ($17). Across the road, the Grande Prairie Regional College has a cafeteria that bustles with students (and locals looking for a cheap meal) throughout the school year.

Egan McSwiggin's (upstairs at 11920 100th St., 780/402-7090) has a refined Irish-pub atmosphere with a cross-section of British fare on a long menu. The Grande Prairie Inn (11633 Clairmont Rd., 780/532-5221) holds the **Drake's Nest Café** (daily 7 A.M.–10 P.M.), offering a themed dinner buffet Wednesday–Sunday for $16.95 per person.

INFORMATION AND SERVICES

Overlooking Bear Creek Reservoir, **Centre 2000** (off the Hwy. 2 bypass at 11330 106th St., 780/513-0240, May–Sept.daily 8:30 A.M.–9 P.M., the rest of the year daily 8:30 A.M.–4:30 P.M.) houses the local tourist information center. One desk is staffed by Travel Alberta employees while an adjacent space is dedicated to supplying local infor-

mation. Another source of information is the website www.northernvisitor.com.

Grande Prairie Public Library (9910 99th Ave., 780/532-3580) is an excellent facility with wireless Internet access and regular modem-connected computers. It's open Monday–Thursday 10 A.M.–9 P.M., Friday–Saturday 10 A.M.–6 P.M., and Sunday 2–5 P.M.

The post office is at 10001 101st Avenue. **Towne Centre Laundry** is in the Towne Centre Mall at 99th Avenue and 100th Street. **Queen Elizabeth II Hospital** (780/538-7100) is at 10409 98th Street.

GETTING THERE AND AROUND

Grande Prairie Airport (two km/1.2 mi west of downtown, then north along Airport Rd.) is served by **Air Canada, WestJet,** and **Peace Air.** All three have daily flights to Calgary and Edmonton, with the latter also serving Peace River and Fort St. John.

The **Greyhound** bus depot (9918 121st Ave., 780/539-1111 or 800/661-8747, www.greyhound.ca) has a café and lockers. Buses leave four times daily to Edmonton, once daily to Peace River ($17.32), and twice daily to Dawson Creek (British Columbia).

For a taxi, call **Prairie Cabs** (780/532-1060) or **Swan Taxi** (780/539-4000).

VICINITY OF GRANDE PRAIRIE
Saskatoon Island Provincial Park

For thousands of years, natives have come to this area to collect, as the name suggests, Saskatoon berries. The "Island" part of the name dates to the 1920s, when much of what is now protected was an island; today the park is an isthmus between Little and Saskatoon Lakes. Sweet, purple-colored Saskatoon berries are still abundant and cover nearly one-third of the 102-hectare (250-acre) park. Late July and August are the best times for berry picking, although park rangers don't encourage the activity. **Little Lake,** with its abundant aquatic vegetation, provides an ideal habitat for trumpeter swans, North America's largest waterfowl. This park is one

of the few areas in Canada where the majestic bird can be viewed during the spring nesting season. Vegetation in the park is classified as northern aspen parkland, the only park in Alberta to represent this biome.

The campground (780/538-5350, May–Sept., unserviced sites $20, powered sites $25) has showers, groceries, a food concession, and mini-golf, and is beside a beach. Only 26 of the 96 sites have power, so arrive early in the day (especially on Friday) if you require hookups. The park is 20 kilometers (12.5 mi) west of Grande Prairie on Highway 2, then three kilometers (1.9 mi) north.

Beaverlodge and Vicinity

This small town, 40 kilometers (25 mi) west of Grande Prairie along Highway 2, is a northern agricultural center at the gateway to **Monkman Pass,** a pass through the Canadian Rockies found earlier in the 20th century. The only access to the pass is by four-wheel-drive vehicle. **Beaverlodge Hotel** houses a collection of more than 20,000 historical artifacts.

© ANDREW HEMPSTEAD

Sexsmith Blacksmith Shop

Two kilometers (1.2 mi) northwest from Beaverlodge, the **South Peace Centennial Museum** (780/354-8869, May–Sept. daily 10 A.M.–6 P.M., $3) started as a farmer's hobby and has grown into a working museum cataloging the agricultural history of Alberta, with displays housed in 15 buildings. Highlights include restored steam-powered farm equipment and a steam-driven sawmill. On **Pioneer Day,** the third Sunday of July, all of the farm machinery is started up and operated.

Sexsmith

North of Grande Prairie, the small town of Sexsmith—once known as the Grain Capital of the British Empire—has undergone extensive restoration. Its main street is now a pleas-ant place to stop, with most businesses fronted by early-1900s-style facades. One block off the main street is the **Sexsmith Blacksmith Shop** (780/568-3668, June–early Sept. Mon.–Fri. 9:30 A.M.–4:30 P.M., Sat.–Sun. 10 A.M.–4 P.M.), a working museum restored to its original 1916 condition. Inside the log structure are more than 10,000 artifacts, including caches of moonshine, which were hidden in the log walls to prevent detection by the North West Mounted Police (NWMP).

From Sexsmith, Highway 2 climbs slowly through a mixed-wood forest connecting the Saddle Hills, to the west, and the Birch Hills, to the northeast. After crossing a low, indistinguishable summit, the road begins descending into the Peace River Valley.

Peace River Valley

From its source in the interior of British Columbia, the Peace River has carved a majestic swath across the northwestern corner of Alberta's boreal forest. Explorers, trappers, settlers, and missionaries traveled upstream from Fort Chipewyan on Lake Athabasca and established trading posts along the fertile valley and surrounding plains. The posts at Fort Vermilion and Dunvegan have slipped into oblivion and are now designated as historical sites, but the town of Peace River has grown from a small post into an agriculture and distribution center that serves the entire Peace River region. The river—so named because on its banks peace was made between warring Cree and Beaver Indians—and the surrounding land are often referred to as Peace Country. This moniker is a throwback to the 1930s, when the government refused to build a rail link and many local residents favored seceding from Alberta and creating their own country.

UPPER PEACE VALLEY

The Upper Peace Valley extends 230 kilometers (143 mi) from the Alberta–British Colum-bia border to the town of Peace River. From Highway 49, on the south side of the river, and Highways 64 and 2 on the north side, roads lead down to the river and nine recreation and camping areas, initially developed for the bicentennial of Alexander Mackenzie's historical passage to the Pacific Ocean. The best way to start a visit to the region is to stop at **Rycroft,** at the junction of Highways 2 and 49. **Courtesy Corner** (780/765-3730, June–Aug. daily 9 A.M.–8 P.M.), an enormous red-and-white tepee situated right at the highway junction, houses an information center and sells local arts and crafts.

Moonshine Lake Provincial Park and Vicinity

More than 100 species of birds and, in winter, high concentrations of moose call Moonshine Lake Provincial Park home. Occupying 1,080 hectares (2,670 acres) 42 kilometers (26 mi) west of Rycroft, the park is best known for its rainbow trout fishing. Some people claim that the lake is named for the moon's reflection on its still water, although it more likely came from a fellow who sold moonshine to travelers en

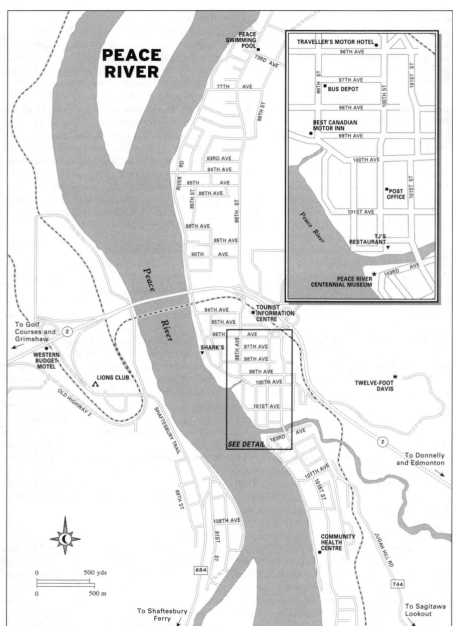

PEACE SWIMMING POOL

PEACE RIVER

73RD AVE

77TH AVE

99TH ST

83RD AVE

84TH AVE

RIVER RD

85TH AVE

85TH ST

86TH AVE

88TH AVE

98TH ST

89TH AVE

90TH AVE

TRAVELLER'S MOTOR HOTEL

96TH AVE

97TH AVE

98TH ST

100TH ST

101ST ST

BUS DEPOT

98TH AVE

BEST CANADIAN MOTOR INN

99TH AVE

100TH AVE

POST OFFICE

101ST ST

101ST AVE

TJ'S RESTAURANT

103RD AVE

PEACE RIVER CENTENNIAL MUSEUM

Peace River

To Golf Courses and Grimshaw

2

WESTERN BUDGET MOTEL

OLD HIGHWAY 2

LIONS CLUB

Peace River

94TH AVE

95TH AVE

96TH AVE

TOURIST INFORMATION CENTRE

SHARK'S

98TH AVE

97TH AVE

98TH AVE

99TH AVE

100TH AVE

101ST AVE

TWELVE-FOOT DAVIS

2

To Donnelly and Edmonton

SHAFTESBURY TRAIL

103RD AVE

SEE DETAIL

89TH ST

107TH AVE

101ST ST

JUDAH HILL RD

91ST ST

108TH AVE

COMMUNITY HEALTH CENTRE

744

0   500 yds

0   500 m

684

To Shaftesbury Ferry

To Sagitawa Lookout

route to Dawson Creek. Year-round campsites (unserviced sites $20, powered sites $25, no reservations taken) are scattered among stands of aspen, poplar, and white spruce. Amenities include showers, flush toilets, kitchen shelters, a concession, and firewood.

From south of the park, Highway 49 continues 54 kilometers (34 mi) to the Alberta–British Columbia border and another 19 kilometers (12 mi) to Dawson Creek at Mile Zero of the Alaska Highway. **Cotillion Park,** on the southern banks of the Peace River, is accessible along 35-kilometer (22-mi) Pillsworth Road (Hwy. 719), eight kilometers (five mi) from the border. Many large mammals frequent this secluded park, and sandstone cliffs here have been eroded into strange-looking pinnacles called hoodoos. Camping, with showers, is $18.

◖ Historic Dunvegan

As Highway 2 descends into the Peace River Valley from the south, it crosses Alberta's longest suspension bridge at Dunvegan—a point that was the site of many trading posts and a mission. On the north side of the river is the **Visitor Reception Centre** (780/835-7150, May–Sept. daily 10 A.M.–6 P.M.), featuring displays that tell the story of Dunvegan and its role in the early history of northern Alberta. On the riverbank are the restored church and rectory of the St. Charles Roman Catholic Mission, circa 1885 (look for the gnarled maple tree, planted by early missionaries, behind the mission site). A gravel road leads under the bridge to the site of the original settlement, **Fort Dunvegan,** which was built as a trading post for the North West Company in 1805, and in use until 1918. Nothing but depressions in the ground remain from the original settlement, but set back from the road is a white Hudson's Bay Company factor's house. Adjacent to these historic sites is **Dunvegan Provincial Park** (780/538-5350, April–Oct., unserviced sites $20, powered sites $25), a 67-site campground. Downstream from the fort is **Dunvegan Tea Room** (780/835-4585), in an old greenhouse—which, naturally, means it's a well-lit place and surrounded by plenty of greenery.

Highway 64

From **Fairview,** 26 kilometers (16 mi) northeast of Dunvegan, Highway 64 heads north then west, roughly following the Peace River into British Columbia. To the west, on the banks of the Peace River, are two campgrounds that form part of the Upper Peace Valley Recreation Area. **Pratt's Landing** ($14) is along Highway 682, and to the north, at the mouth of Montagneuse River, is **Carter Camp** ($14). Back on Highway 64 is the town of **Hines Creek** and its **End of Steel Museum and Heritage Park** (780/494-3991, June–mid-Sept. daily 10 A.M.–5 P.M.) featuring a caboose, a church, a trapper's cabin, and a Russian pioneer home. From Hines Creek, it is 98 kilometers (61 mi) to the British Columbia border.

PEACE RIVER

From all directions, the final approach into the town of Peace River is breathtaking. This town of 6,300 straddles the majestic Peace River below the confluence of the Smoky and Heart Rivers. Alexander Mackenzie was one of the earliest white men to visit the region. He established a post, named Fort Forks, on the south bank of the river, upstream of the present town. From here, after the winter of 1792–93, he completed his historic journey to the Pacific Ocean and became the first person to cross the North American continent north of Mexico. The first permanent settlers were missionaries who, apart from their zealous religious work, promoted the region for its agricultural potential and as a service center and distribution point for river transportation. When the rail link with Edmonton was completed in 1916, land was opened for homesteading, and settlers poured into town. The farming traditions they began continue on.

Sights

Many historic buildings line the main street (100th St.), and many have plaques with historical facts. The wide street is typical of early boomtowns in that its width allowed wagons to turn around. At the southern end of the street, across the mouth of the Heart River, is the **Peace River Centennial Museum** (10302 99th St., 780/624-

TWELVE-FOOT DAVIS

© ANDREW HEMPSTEAD

Pathfinder, pioneer, miner, trader. He was every man's friend and never locked his cabin door.

This fitting tribute adorns the headstone of Twelve-Foot Davis, one of the early pioneers of the Peace River Country.

Born Henry Fuller Davis in Vermont in 1820, Twelve-Foot was not a giant of a man. In fact, he was short. But he got his name from a claim he staked in the Cariboo goldfields in British Columbia. He noticed that two very successful claims had a 12-foot strip between them, so he staked the area and made a fortune. Although he was illiterate, Davis saw potential in selling supplies to the miners. He arrived in the Peace River Country in the 1870s, opening up trading posts as far apart as Hudson's Hope (British Columbia) and Fort Vermilion, but spending most of his later years running a post at Dunvegan. Davis was renowned for his hospitality, handing out sage advice to newcomers and baking pumpkin pies (a real treat in the north) for homesick Americans. He died at Grouard in 1900, and in accordance with his dying wishes, he now lies buried high above his beloved river (access from 100th Ave., and under Hwy. 2).

4261, daily 9 A.M.–5 P.M., adult $3), which has displays on native clothing, the fur trade, early explorers, and the development of the town, and an extensive photo collection and archives.

Two spots near downtown afford excellent views of the Peace River and the valley through which it flows. To access the closest, take 100th Avenue under Highway 2 and follow this winding road to its end, or, alternatively, take 101st Street south to 107th Avenue, which links up with Judah Hill Road. This road passes **Sagitawa Lookout,** from where you can see the town, the valley, and the confluence of the Peace and Smoky Rivers.

On the west side of the river is the site of **Shaftesbury,** a settlement that grew around an Anglican mission founded in 1887. From the site, Highway 684 follows the historic Shaftesbury Trail—used for hundreds of years by natives, explorers, traders, missionaries, and Klondikers—to Blakely's Landing, from which the free **Shaftesbury Ferry** now crosses the river all summer, daily 7 A.M.–midnight.

Tours

Peace Island Tours (780/624-4295, www.peace island.ab.ca) operates jet-boat trips, departing at 2 P.M., that head 60 kilometers (37 mi) down

Head to the restored railway station in Peace River for all your tourist information needs.

the Peace River to a 14-hectare (35-acre) island with log cabins. The seven-hour Supper Tour is $90 per person, whereas the overnight journey, including three meals, the boat ride, and lodging, is $170 per person.

Accommodations and Camping

The least expensive rooms in town are in an older wing of the **Best Canadian Motor Inn** (9810 98th St., 780/624-2586 or 888/700-2264, www.bestcdn.com). Pay $60 s, $68 d, or upgrade to newer rooms across the road for $90 s, $100 d. At the north end of downtown but still within walking distance of everything is the 138-room **Traveller's Motor Hotel** (9510 100th St., 780/624-3621 or 800/661-3227, $75–105 s or d), where you should avoid the least expensive rooms and instead request Business Class. This hotel has a sauna, restaurant, and lounge. The **Western Budget Motel** (7701 100th Ave., 780/624-3445, www.westernbudgetmotel.com, $69 s, $75 d) may be across the river from downtown, but the rooms are comfortable and there's an on-site restaurant.

Lions Club Park (on the west side of the river, 780/624-2120, April–Oct., unserviced sites $14, hookups $20–25) has well-shaded campsites, showers, and a laundry room.

Food

Restaurant choices are limited. Try busy **TJ's Restaurant** (10011 102nd Ave., 780/624-3427), where the Chinese dishes are better than the Canadian and there's generally a daily pasta special. Especially delicious is the Seafood Hotpot ($16). **Alexander's** (9510 100th St., 780/624-3621, daily 5:30 A.M.–10 P.M.), in the Traveller's Motor Hotel, offers a weekday lunchtime buffet, a seafood dinner buffet October–April on Friday, and a regular menu the rest of the week. In the same hotel is a café open from 5:30 A.M. Along River Road is **Shark's** (9606 94th St., 780/624-5007, daily for lunch and dinner), a pub with a nice patio.

Information

The **Mighty Peace Tourist Association** operates a tourist information center (780/338-2364

or 800/215-4535, www.mightypeace.com, June–Sept. daily 10 A.M.–6 P.M.) in the old Peace River railway station at the top end of 100th Street.

Getting There and Around

The airport, 13 kilometers (eight mi) west of town, is served by **Peace Air** (780/563-3060) from Edmonton. The **Greyhound** bus depot (9801 97th Ave., 780/624-2558, www.grey hound.ca) is downtown with daily services to Edmonton, Grande Prairie, and Hay River in the Northwest Territories. For a cab, call **Peace River Taxi** (780/624-3020).

MACKENZIE HIGHWAY

Named for 18th-century explorer Alexander Mackenzie, this route, also known as Highway 35, extends from Grimshaw, 24 kilometers (15 mi) west of Peace River, for 473 kilometers (294 mi) north to the Northwest Territories. It passes through a vast, empty land dominated by the Peace River and a seemingly endless forest of spruce, poplar, and jack pine. The main population centers are Manning and High Level. Along the way are many stump-filled fields, carved out of the boreal forest by farmers who, for the last 100 years, have eked out a living from some of the world's northernmost farmland. The only access to the Peace River is at Notikewin Provincial Park and at **Tompkin's Landing,** a ferry crossing east of Paddle Prairie.

When you're through exploring this wild northland, you have two alternatives to backtracking along Mackenzie Highway. One is to continue into the Northwest Territories and complete what is known as the **Deh Cho Connection,** which links the Mackenzie with the Liard and Alaska Highways—an 1,800-kilometer (1,200-mi) loop that finishes in Dawson Creek, British Columbia. The other option is to follow Highway 58 east from High Level and head south on the Bicentennial Highway 430 kilometers (267 mi) to Slave Lake.

Grimshaw

Best known as Mile Zero of the Mackenzie

Wide swathes of boreal forest along the Mackenzie Highway are regenerating after wildfires.

© ANDREW HEMPSTEAD

Highway, this town of 2,400 has grown around the railway as a farming center. For many years after the railway arrived, it was a jumping-off point for farmers, trappers, and homesteaders in Peace Valley Country. Make a point of stopping at the local information center (June–early Sept. 9 A.M.–5 P.M.), in a blue rail car at the main intersection. It's stocked with brochures for onward travel and staffed by friendly locals who seem genuinely interested in your travels. If it's open, they will recommend a visit to the **Antique Truck Museum** (780/332-2969, summer daily 10 A.M.–4 P.M., donation), right across the road. And so do I—it holds a large collection of lovingly restored vehicles and machinery collected from throughout the north.

Camp at nearby Queen Elizabeth Provincial Park (see listing in the following *Lac Cardinal* section) or continue 11 kilometers (6.8 mi) north to **The Creek Golf Course** (780/332-4949, May–Sept.), where camping with hookups and showers is $20 and a round of golf is $18.

AURORA BOREALIS

The aurora borealis, or northern lights, is an emotional experience for some, spiritual for others, and without exception is unforgettable – an exhibition of color that dances across the sky like a kaleidoscope.

Auroral light is created through a complex process – a spontaneous phenomenon with no pattern and no "season" – that occurs within the earth's atmosphere and starts with the sun. Essentially a huge atomic fusion reactor, the sun emits the heat and light that keep us alive, and also emits electronically charged ions that are thrust through space at high speeds. When these ions reach the earth's rarefied upper atmosphere – about 180 kilometers above the surface – they are captured by the earth's magnetic field and accelerated toward the poles. Along the way they collide with the atoms and molecules of the gases in the atmosphere, which in turn become temporarily charged or "ionized." This absorbed energy is then released by the ionized gases, often in the form of light. The color of the light varies from red to yellow to green, depending on the gas: Nitrogen atoms produce a violet and sometimes red color, oxygen a green and, at higher altitudes, an orange.

Because the magnetic field is more intense near the north and south magnetic poles, the lights are best seen at high latitudes. In northern Alberta the light show takes place up to 160 nights annually, with displays best north of Peace River. They generally start as a faint glow on the northeastern horizon after the sun has set, improving as the sky becomes darker.

Lac Cardinal

North of Grimshaw, on the eastern shore of Lac Cardinal, is **Queen Elizabeth Provincial Park.** The lake is very shallow, and no streams flow from it. This creates an ideal habitat for many species of waterfowl. Beavers, moose, and black bears are also present. The park campground (780/624-6486, mid-May–mid-Sept., unserviced sites $20, powered sites $25) has pit toilets, firewood, and kitchen shelters. Immediately south of the park is **Lac Cardinal Regional Pioneer Village** (780/332-2030, May–Sept. daily 11 A.M.–5 P.M., donation), featuring a large outdoor collection of memorabilia from the Peace River region.

To Manning

From Grimshaw, it is 40 kilometers (25 mi) north to the small hamlet of **Dixonville.** Here you'll find a trading post and the turnoff to Sulphur Lake (55 km/34 mi northwest along Hwy. 689), where camping is available.

A homestead built by a Latvian settler in 1918 is three kilometers (1.9 mi) south of **North Star,** on the old Highway 35. It has been declared a Provincial Historical Site, and although it's locked, you can look in the windows and see homemade wooden beds and a sauna, and appreciate the work that went into the hand-hewn log buildings.

Manning

As the highway descends into the picturesque Notikewin Valley, it passes through the relatively new town of Manning. Formerly called Aurora, this town of 1,200 is a service center for the region's agricultural and petroleum industries. At the south end of town, one kilometer (0.6 mi) east on Highway 691, is the excellent **Battle River Pioneer Museum** (780/836-2374, May–Sept. daily 1–6 P.M., in July and Aug. from 10 A.M., adult $3, child $1), which has a large collection of antique wrenches, taxidermy (including a rare albino moose), carriages and buggies, farm machinery, a birch necklace carved out of a single piece of wood, and a collection of prehistoric arrowheads—ask to see the one embedded in a whalebone.

Manning Motor Inn (780/836-2801, $81 s, $94 d) is at the south end of town and has a restaurant. **Town of Manning Campground** (May–Sept., $15) is immediately west of the

tourist information center in a shaded spot beside the Notikewin River. The campground is small (nine sites), but has some powered sites. It is also possible to camp at the golf course, north of town (780/836-2176, May–Sept., $15), which offers powered sites and a clubhouse restaurant. The **Old Hospital Museum** (780/836-3606, May–Sept. Mon.–Sat. 10 A.M.–5 P.M.) combines historic displays related to the building with an art gallery and the local information center.

Notikewin Provincial Park

Twenty-one kilometers (13 mi) north of Hotchkiss, Highway 692 turns east off Highway 35 and leads to Notikewin Provincial Park, a 970-hectare (2,400-acre) preserve at the confluence of the Notikewin and Peace Rivers. The 30-kilometer (19-mi) road to the park is partly paved and occasionally steep. In Notikewin (Battle, in the Cree language), a stand of 200-year-old spruce presides over Spruce Island, at the mouth of the Notikewin River. The island also supports an abundance of ostrich ferns growing to a height of two meters (six ft). Beavers, mule deer, moose, and the occasional black bear can be seen in the area. Bird species are diverse and include sandhill cranes, which rest at the mouth of the Notikewin River on their southern migration in September. The river offers good fishing for gold-eye, walleye, and northern pike. The campground (May–Oct., $17) has 19 sites but no hookups.

If you're looking for a spot to camp without detouring from Highway 35, continue 23 kilometers (14 mi) north to **Twin Lakes,** where camping is $15. Take time to walk the three-kilometer/1.9-mile (50-minute) circuit around the larger of the two lakes—it's a typical environment of boreal forest, and it has been unaffected by fire or deforestation for more than 80 years.

A Short Detour

The largest of eight Métis settlements established throughout the province during the 1930s is **Paddle Prairie,** 65 kilometers (40 mi) north of Twin Lakes. From 10 kilometers (6.2 mi) north of here, a gravel road

(Hwy. 697) leads east to the Peace River and Tomkin's Landing and one of only eight ferry crossings in the province (operates in summer, daily 24 hours). It then continues to La Crete and Fort Vermilion, crosses the Peace River, and intersects Highway 58, which heads west, rejoining the Mackenzie Highway at High Level.

La Crete (pop. 900) has grown into an agricultural center on the northern fringe of the continent's arable land. Most residents are Mennonites who moved to the region in the 1930s. They are from a traditional Protestant sect originating in Holland, whose members settled in remote regions throughout the world and established self-sufficient agricultural lifestyles, in hopes of being left to practice their faith in peace. On the streets and in the local restaurants, you'll hear their language, *Plattdeutsch* (Low German), which is spoken by Mennonites throughout the world.

To the southeast of this flat, prairielike area, the Buffalo Head Hills rise almost 700 meters (2,300 ft) above the surrounding land. The only way into the hills is along an 18-kilometer (11-mi) gravel road that spurs east from Highway 697 approximately 18 kilometers (11 mi) south of La Crete. To the west, an eight-kilometer (five-mi) road from town leads past a golf course to one of the Peace River's many natural sandbars, and to Etna's Landing, where there is good swimming.

Fort Vermilion

This town of 780, on the south bank of the Peace River, 40 kilometers (25 mi) north of La Crete and 77 kilometers (48 mi) east of High Level, vies with Fort Chipewyan as the oldest settlement in Alberta. It was named for the red clay deposits present in the banks of the river. The first trading post here was established a few kilometers downstream of present-day Fort Vermilion by the North West Company in 1788. Trade with the Beaver, Cree, and Dene was brisk, and by 1802 the Hudson's Bay Company had also established a post. In 1821, the companies merged, and in 1830 they moved operations to the town's present site. The area's

agricultural potential gained worldwide attention when locally grown wheat, transported along the river highway, won a gold medal at the 1876 World's Fair in Philadelphia. For 150 years, supplies arrived by riverboat or were hauled overland from the town of Peace River. When the Mackenzie Highway was completed, the river highway became obsolete. The last riverboat arrived in Fort Vermilion in 1952, but not until 1974, when a bridge was built across the Peace River, was the town linked to the outside world.

Many old buildings and cabins, in varying states of disrepair, still stand. Pick up a *Fort Vermilion Heritage Guide* from the **Fort Vermilion Heritage Centre** (780/927-4603, June–Aug. Mon.–Thurs. 9 A.M.–9 P.M., Fri.– Sat. 9 A.M.–5 P.M., Sun. 1–9 P.M.) to help identify the many historical sites in town. The **Mary Batt & Son General Store** was constructed from logs removed from the 1897 Hudson's Bay Company post.

Across from the river, the **Sheridan Lawrence Inn** (4901 River Rd., 780/927-4400, $79 s, $89 d) is the only place to stay in town. It offers 16 rooms and a small restaurant open daily from 7 A.M., with a Canadian and Chinese menu.

High Level

Named for its location on a divide between the Peace and Hay River watersheds, High Level (pop. 3,600), 279 kilometers (173 mi) north of Grimshaw, is the last town before the Alberta–Northwest Territories border. It is a major service center for a region rich in natural resources. The town expanded during the oil boom of the 1960s and has prospered ever since. The grain elevators, serving agricultural communities to the east, are the northernmost in the world. Forestry is also a major local industry; the town boasts one of the world's most productive logging and sawmill operations, turning out more than 250 million board-feet of lumber annually.

Fortunately, much of the surrounding forest is safe from loggers; the 75,000-square-kilometer (30,000-square-mi) **Footner Lake Forest** has poor drainage, forming major bogs

and permafrost that make timber harvest commercially unviable. The forest encompasses the entire northern part of the province west of Wood Buffalo National Park.

Northeast of High Level are the **Caribou Mountains,** which rise to a forested plateau 800 meters (2,600 ft) above the Peace River. At that altitude, and being so far north, the fragile environment is easily disturbed. The mountains are blanketed in white spruce, aspen, and pine, and two lakes—Margaret and Wentzel— offer excellent fly-fishing. Northwest of High Level are the Cameron Hills and **Bistcho Lake** (where Albertan fish hatcheries harvest walleye spawn). The most accessible part of the forest is **Hutch Lake,** 32 kilometers (20 mi) north of town. The lake is surrounded by aspen and poplar and is the source of the **Meander River.** The dominant feature here is **Watt Mountain** (780 m/2,600 ft), which you can see to the northwest of High Level. From Hutch Lake, a service road leads 10 kilometers (6.2 mi) to a lookout and 21 kilometers (13 mi) to a fire tower on the summit. The recreation area at the north end of the lake has a large picnic area, an interpretive trail, and camping. Maps are available at the tourist information center.

The only worthwhile sight in town is **Mackenzie Crossroads Museum** (at the south entrance to town, 780/926-2420, May–Sept. Mon.–Sat. 9 A.M.–7 P.M., the rest of the year Mon.–Fri. 9 A.M.–4 P.M., adult $2, student $1). Located in the tourist information center building, the museum is themed on a northern trading post, with interesting displays telling the human history of northern Alberta. In another room, the industries upon which High Level was built are described through photographs and interpretive boards. A three-dimensional map of northwestern Alberta gives a great perspective of this inaccessible part of the province.

Motel prices in High Level are just a warm-up for those over the border in the Northwest Territories, so don't be surprised at $80 rooms that you'd prefer to pay $40 for. The motels in town are usually full throughout the year with work crews. Least expensive is **Four Winds Hotel** (780/926-3736 or 888/449-4637, $58

s, $62 d). Each of the 75 air-conditioned rooms has a small fridge and a microwave, and guests have use of a laundry room. **Best Canadian Motor Inn** (780/926-2272, www.bestcdn.com, $68 s, $83 d) undergoes regular revamps and its medium-sized rooms are air-conditioned. A free municipal campground is immediately east of town on Highway 35 (but it's pretty grotty), and a primitive campground lies farther north at **Hutch Lake Recreation Area** (mid-May–Sept., $13).

The **Family Restaurant** (in front of the Family Motel, 780/926-3111) offers a Chinese buffet lunch ($10) and a regular dinner menu with main meals from $10. Another Chinese place is the **Canton Restaurant** (100th Ave., 780/926-3053); the combo dinners seem like a good deal, but portions are small, so stick to the main meals.

There is a large tourist information center (780/926-2470, June–Aug. Mon.–Fri. 9 A.M.–9 P.M., Sat.–Sun. 10 A.M.–8 P.M., the rest of the year Tues.–Fri. 9 A.M.–4:30 P.M., Sat. 1–4 P.M.).

The post office, banks, library, and several launderettes are located on 100th Street.

Rainbow Lake

Rainbow Lake is an oil field community of 1,100, 141 kilometers (88 mi) west of High Level along Highway 58. The town grew around oil-and-gas exploration during the 1960s, and today a pipeline links it to Edmonton. Vast reservoirs of these resources still lie underneath the ground, but with the recent surge in the price of oil there is much activity in and around the town. The town has a golf course, two motels, and two restaurants. A campground 24 kilometers (15 mi) southwest of town on the Buffalo River has a few primitive sites, which are free. The other option is **Rainbow Lake Recreation Area,** 48 kilometers (30 mi) south of town, where there's a beach with swimming, fishing, and campsites for $13.

Hay-Zama Lakes

This complex network of lakes, marshes, and streams is one of Canada's largest freshwater wetlands. It covers 800 square kilometers (310 square mi) and is home to more than 200 species of birds, including over 300,000 ducks and geese during fall migration. It's also the main source of the Hay River, which flows north to Great Slave Lake. This fragile ecosystem, 160 kilometers (100 mi) northwest of High Level, is relatively remote and would have remained that way except for the large reservoirs of oil that lie beneath its surface. Oil and birds do not mix, but drilling has gone ahead, with only a small section protected as a wildland provincial park. Strict environmental guidelines mean that most of the mining activity takes place during winter. Although no roads or camping areas are designated around the lakes, many gravel roads used by the natives and oil-exploration personnel lead through the area. The small community of **Zama City,** north of the lakes, has grown around the drilling project.

The Border or Bust

From High Level, it is 191 kilometers (119 mi) to the Alberta–Northwest Territories border. The road follows the Meander River to a town of the same name at the confluence of the Hay River, which then parallels the border. The settlement of **Meander River** is on a Dene Tha Indian Reserve and is noted for its many local artists. Watch for the local rabbit population living beside the road. North of the community, where the highway crosses the Hay River, a gravel road leads 63 kilometers (39 mi) to the oil town of Zama City. Campgrounds are located north of Meander River and just south of the small community of **Steen River,** a base for forest-fire-fighting planes. Alberta's northernmost community is **Indian Cabins,** 14 kilometers (8.7 mi) from the border. The cabins that gave the town its name are gone, but a traditional native cemetery with spirit houses covering the graves is just north of the gas station. In the trees is the scaffold burial site of a child whose body was placed in a hollowed-out log and hung between the limbs of two trees.

BACKGROUND

The Land

Alberta is the fourth-largest province in Canada. With an area of 661,185 square kilometers (255,000 square mi), it's larger than all U.S. states except Alaska and Texas. The province lies between the 49th and 60th parallels, bordered on the south by Montana, United States, and on the north by Canada's Northwest Territories. To the west is British Columbia, and to the east is Saskatchewan. Along its roughly rectangular outline, the only natural border is the Continental Divide in the southwest. Here, from the International Boundary to Jasper, the lofty peaks of the **Canadian Rockies** rise to heights of more than 3,000 meters (9,800 ft). The Canadian Rockies are only one small but exquisitely beautiful link in the Rocky Mountains chain, which forms the backbone of North America, extending from the jungles of central Mexico to the Arctic. Running parallel to the mountains along their eastern edge is a series of long, rolling ridges known as the **foothills.** This region is dominated by ranches in the south and undeveloped forests in the north. Finally, east of the foothills and across the rest of Alberta are **plains,** which cover almost three-quarters of the province. The plains provide practically all of Alberta's arable soil and natural resources. The term "plains" is very broad. Alberta's plains encompass three distinct vegetation zones: prairie,

© ANDREW HEMPSTEAD

parkland, and boreal forest (see the *Flora* section of this chapter).

GEOLOGY

The rocks of Alberta range in age from ancient to almost "brand-new," in geologic time. The 70-million-year-old Canadian Rockies, Alberta's most distinctive natural feature, are relatively young compared to the world's other major mountain ranges. By contrast, the Precambrian rock of the Canadian Shield, which is exposed in the province's northeast corner and underlying parts of the rest, was the progenitor of North America. It was the first land on the continent to remain permanently above sea level and is among the oldest rock on earth, formed more than 2.5 billion years ago.

Approximately 700 million years ago, in the Precambrian era, forces beneath the earth caused uplift, pushing the coastline of the Pacific Ocean—which then covered most of the province—westward. The ocean advanced and receded several times over the next half-billion years. Each time the ocean flooded eastward, it deposited layers of sediment on its bed, and the layers built up with each successive inundation. This sediment is now a layer of sedimentary rock covering most of Alberta, up to seven kilometers (4.3 mi) deep in the southwest.

Alberta's Oil

Oil pools are created when oil globules—converted from decayed organic matter by the forces of heat and pressure beneath the earth's surface—are trapped in porous rock capped by nonporous rock. During the Middle Devonian period, 375 million years ago, with the Pacific Ocean once again covering Alberta, coral reefs formed. Over time, this coral would be transformed into the porous rock that would hold the pools of oil. Also during this period, as well as in later years of the Paleozoic era, trillions of microscopic organisms in the sea died and sank to the bottom of the ocean, creating mass quantities of decaying organic matter in and around the coral. This organic matter would be transformed over time into the oil itself. Fi-

ALBERTA AND CALIFORNIA

0   100 mi

0   100 km

© AVALON TRAVEL PUBLISHING, INC.

nally, approximately 300 million years ago, in the Carboniferous period, the Pacific Ocean extended as far as the foothills, and many rivers flowed into it from the east, carrying with them sediment that covered the porous reefs in nonporous layers. All of the elements necessary to eventually create and contain reserves of oil were then in place. A few hundred million years of "cooking" later, the primordial goo that fuels our modern internal-combustion society is pumped nonstop from beneath Alberta. One other huge source of oil in Alberta isn't pumped, but *mined*. In the early Cretaceous period, 130 million years ago, the Arctic Ocean flooded Alberta from the north, laying down the **Athabasca Oil Sands** along the Arctic seaway. These sands hold 1.7 trillion barrels of heavy oil—more than all of the known reserves of conventional crude oil on the planet.

Birth of the Rockies

Also during the Cretaceous period, the Mackenzie Mountains began to rise, cutting off the Arctic seaway and forming an inland sea where

© ANDREW HEMPSTEAD

Erratics, huge boulders deposited far from their source during the last ice age, dot the foothills. These, the world's largest, are near Okotoks, south of Calgary.

marinelife such as ammonites, fish, and large marine reptiles flourished. Dinosaurs roamed the coastal areas, feeding on the lush vegetation as well as on each other.

Then, approximately 70 million years ago, two plates of the earth's crust collided. According to plate tectonics theory, the Pacific Plate butted into the North American Plate and was forced beneath it. The land at this subduction zone was crumpled and thrust upward, creating the Rocky Mountains. Layers of sediment laid down on the ocean floor over the course of hundreds of millions of years were folded, twisted, and squeezed; great slabs of rock broke away, and in some places, older strata were pushed on top of younger. By the beginning of the Tertiary period, approximately 65 million years ago, the present form of mountain contours was established and the geological framework of Alberta was in place. Then the forces of erosion went to work. The plains of the Late Tertiary period were at a higher altitude than those of today. The flat-topped

Caribou Mountains, Buffalo Head Hills, Cypress Hills, Clear Hills, and Porcupine Hills are remnants of those higher plains.

The Ice Ages

No one knows why, but approximately one million years ago the world's climate cooled and ice caps formed in Arctic regions, slowly moving south over North America and Eurasia. These advances, followed by retreats, occurred four times.

The final major glaciation began moving southward 35,000 years ago. A sheet of ice up to 2,000 meters (6,560 ft) deep covered all but the highest peaks of the Rocky Mountains and Cypress Hills. The ice scoured the terrain, destroying all vegetation as it crept slowly forward. In the mountains, these rivers of ice carved hollows, known as **cirques,** into the slopes of the higher peaks. They rounded off lower peaks and reamed out valleys from their preglacial "V" shape to a trademark postglacial U shape. The retreat of this ice sheet, be-

The Canadian Shield around Lake Athabasca is scarred from the retreat of glaciers during the last ice age.

ginning approximately 12,000 years ago, was just as destructive. Rock and debris that had been picked up by the ice on its march forward melted out during the retreat, creating high ridges known as **moraines.** Many of these moraines blocked natural drainages, resulting in thousands of lakes across the north. And meltwater drained into rivers and streams, incising deep channels into the sedimentary rock of the plains.

The only remnants of this ice age are the scattered ice fields along the Continental Divide—including the 325-square-kilometer (125-square- mile) **Columbia Icefield.** But wind and water erosion continues, uncovering dinosaur bones hidden among layers of sediment and carving an eerie landscape of badlands along the sides of many prairie river valleys.

Waterways

Alberta has three major watersheds draining 245 named rivers and 315 named creeks.

More than half of the province drains into the **Mackenzie River System,** which flows north into the Arctic Ocean. The **Peace River,** which originates in the interior of British Columbia and flows northeast through Alberta, and the **Athabasca River,** whose initial source is the Columbia Icefield, are the province's two major tributaries in this system. They eventually meet to form the Slave River, which flows into the Mackenzie at Great Slave Lake in the Northwest Territories.

Central Alberta is drained mainly by the **Saskatchewan River System,** which is the major source of water for Alberta's farmers. This river system, which eventually flows into Hudson Bay, has three main tributaries: the **North Saskatchewan River,** originating from the Columbia Icefield; the **Red Deer River,** originating in the heart of Banff National Park and flowing through Dinosaur Valley on its way east; and the **South Saskatchewan River.** The latter is fed largely by the **Bow River,** flowing down from Banff, and the **Oldman River,** which cascades out of the Rockies south of Kananaskis Country.

A small area in the south of the province is drained by the **Milk River,** which flows southeast into the Mississippi River System, ending up in the Gulf of Mexico.

The amount of water flowing into any one of Alberta's rivers depends on that particular river's source. Rivers originating from melt-out of the winter snowpack reach peak flow in midsummer and often run dry by late summer. Those that originate from glaciers run light in spring and reach a peak in midsummer but continue a light flow until winter. Those that rise in the foothills and higher areas of the plains have highly variable flows, depending entirely on precipitation.

CLIMATE

Alberta spans 11 degrees of latitude, and its varied topography includes elevations ranging from 170 meters (560 ft) above sea level in the extreme northeast to more than 3,700 meters (12,100 ft) above sea level along the Continental Divide. As a result, the climate of the

province varies widely from place to place. In addition, the Canadian Rockies create some of Alberta's unique climatic characteristics. As prevailing, moisture-laden westerlies blow in from British Columbia, the cold heights of the Rockies wring them dry. This cycle makes for clear, sunny skies in southern Alberta; Calgary gets up to 350 hours of sunshine in June alone, which is good news, unless you're a farmer. In winter, the dry winds blasting down the eastern slopes of the Rockies can raise temperatures on the prairies by up to 40°C (72°F) in 24 hours. Called **chinooks,** these desiccating blows are a phenomenon unique to Alberta.

Another interesting phenomenon occurring in southern Alberta's Rocky Mountain regions is the **temperature inversion,** in which a layer of warm air sits on top of a cold air mass. During these inversions, high- and low-country roles are reversed: Prairie residents can be shivering and bundling up while their mountain fellows are sunning themselves in shirtsleeves.

The Seasons

Overall, Alberta features cold winters and short, hot summers. May to mid-September is ideal for touring, camping out, and seeing the sights; one month on either side of this peak period and the weather is cooler but still pleasant; the rest of the year the skiing and snowboarding are fantastic.

January is usually the coldest month, when Calgary's mean average temperature is -13°C (8.5°F) and Fort McMurray's is -20°C (-4°F). In winter, extended spells of -30°C (-22°F) are not uncommon anywhere in the province, and temperatures occasionally drop below -40°C (-40°F). Severe cold weather is often accompanied by sunshine; the cold is a dry cold, unlike the damp cold experienced in coastal regions. Cold temperatures and snow can continue until mid-March. Groundhog Day (February 2) is noted, but Albertans realize spring is still a long way off for them.

After the March 21 spring equinox, daylight exceeds nighttime, and the coldest days of winter become a distant memory. Although spring officially continues to late June, snow often falls in May, many mountain lakes may remain frozen until early June, and snow cover on higher mountain hiking trails may remain until late July. Late snowfalls, although not welcomed by golfers in Calgary, provide important moisture for crops.

Summer is officially June 21–September 21, the dates of the summer and fall solstice, respectively. Air temperatures lag behind solar intensity as the sun melts snow, heats land surfaces, and warms the water of lakes and rivers. July is the hottest month and provides the most uniform temperatures throughout the province. On hot days, the temperature hits 30°C (86°F)—usually every other summer day in the south—and occasionally climbs above 40°C (104°F). Again, because of the dry air, these high temperatures are more bearable here than in coastal regions experiencing the same temperatures. Alberta records around 40 tornados each summer. The deadliest on record killed 27 people in Edmonton on July 31, 1987, while a tornado that touched down in Pine Lake in 2000, killing 12, was the deadliest in North America that year.

The frost-free growing season is over by late September, when the air develops a distinct chill. October brings the highest temperature variations of the year, with the thermometer hitting 30°C (86°F) but also dipping as low as -20°C (-4°F). Mild weather can continue until early December, but the first snow generally falls in October, and by mid-November winter has set in.

ENVIRONMENTAL ISSUES

Humans have been exploiting Alberta's abundant natural resources for 10,000 years. Indigenous people hunting bison obviously had little effect on ecological integrity, but over time, the eradication of the species by white settlers and the clearing of land for agriculture did. Today, minimizing the effects of the fossil-fuel industry, global warming, and development within national parks are hot-button environmental issues in Alberta.

WIND FARMS

Canada's largest concentration of "wind farms" is concentrated, naturally, somewhere that the wind blows consistently – in the southwestern corner of Alberta. When driving through the region it is impossible not to be intrigued by the sight of row upon row of wind turbines lining high ridges in all directions. Up to 50 meters (160 ft) high, each tower is topped by massive blades that are perfectly balanced to allow for a very low start-up speed. The kinetic energy of the wind turns the blades, which are connected to a shaft that then twists through a magnetic field within a generator. The end result is electricity, which is channeled into the provincial power grid. The generators vary in capacity from turbine to turbine, but on average each one produces enough electricity to power 320 homes. Currently, Canada's wind farms generate a combined total of 1,000 mega watts of electricity, which is enough to power around 300,000 homes. Alberta supplies the biggest chunk of the total amount (280 mega watts). It is estimated that by 2010, 5 percent of Canada's electricity will be generated from the wind and the wind could provide 20 percent of the country's total energy needs.

No official tours of the farms are offered, but use the **VisionQuest** website (www.visionquestwind.com) to access an audio driving tour (download it onto an mp3 player or CD before leaving home) of their facilities through the region. To learn more about the world's fastest growing energy source in the world,

© ANDREW HEMPSTEAD

check out the websites of the **Canadian Wind Energy Association** (www.canwea.ca) or the **American Wind Energy Association** (www.awea.org). Both sites are loaded with interesting information. The Albertan Pembina Institute has a "green energy" website designed especially for children (www.re-ennergy.ca).

Oil-and-Gas Industry

The oil-and-gas industry is vital to Alberta's economy, but along with all the money comes a number of environmental issues, none more talked about than the reduction of greenhouse gas emissions, which are absorbed by the air, and as a result contribute to global warming. Government and industry within Alberta work together closely to reduce emissions, mostly through modern technologies. Traditional techniques such as using sulfur from sour gas wells to make fertilizer are being joined by radical new ideas. Of these, one of the most interesting is the capture of carbon dioxide at its industrial source, from where the emission is compressed and then injected under the ground into depleted oil-and-gas reservoirs.

The use of alternative, non-polluting "green power" is increasing within Alberta exponentially. Almost 90 percent of power used by government facilities comes from renewable sources such as the sun and wind, and interest-free loans are offered for municipalities to become energy efficient. On a smaller scale,

there are projects such as the one at Cochrane High School, which combines the use of sun and wind to power the buildings. As elsewhere in the world, it is usually only when the ecology of somewhere special is threatened that the public hears about it. Development of an open pit mine at northern Alberta's McClelland Lake Wetlands, once considered for UNESCO World Heritage Site classification, is one such issue.

National Parks

Environmental issues within Alberta's national parks are an ongoing hot topic. On the surface, the commercialism of mountain parks seems to work against the mandate for their existence, but because the parks have grown from what were originally money-making exercises, the situation is unique. It is also important to remember that 100 years ago the parks were home to logging and mining operations and that wardens were directed to "exterminate all those animals which prey upon others." It wasn't *that* long ago that park lakes were stocked with nonnative fish for the pleasure of anglers, and still today wildlife is "managed" to some degree—by relocating troublesome bears and moving elk away from population centers.

The town of Banff, the largest urban center in any national park in the world, is center of much debate about development within Canada's national park system. The town does have a good reason for its existence—serving the needs of up to 50,000 visitors daily. Along with obvious amenities such as accommodations and restaurants comes needs such as a sewage plant, municipal infrastructure, schools, a hospital, and all the businesses you would expect to find in a mid-sized town. But you can also park in a multistory car park, go to Starbucks, get a tattoo, buy a bearskin rug, and sleep in a chain motel (obviously I'm not recommending this as an itinerary)—all within a national park. Many visitors only see the commercialism along Banff Avenue, but balancing human-use issues with the protection of the mountain ecosystem is behind decisions such as capping future development, closing the Banff airstrip and buffalo paddock, and restricting the use of mountain bikes on some local trails. Farther afield, the need to protect wildlife has led to speed restrictions and closures on roads passing through critical habitat, access to some areas of the backcountry has been curtailed, ski resorts only offer limited summer activities, and in some cases, such as in Kootenay National Park, accommodations in wildlife corridors have been expropriated.

An interesting human element to the discussion is the "need to reside," especially since Alberta has four population centers within national parks (two in Banff National Park, and one each in Jasper and Waterton Lakes National Parks). Parks Canada, the federal agency responsible for park management, regulates who may live within a national park. To be eligible one must have their primary employment or operate a licensed business within the park, but there are many vagrancies. For example, writing a guidebook about the parks is not deemed a need to reside (but being married to someone whose primary employment is within a national park does give the author a need to reside).

Flora

Alberta can be divided into two major geographical areas: the mountain-and-foothill region along its southwestern border, and the plains covering the rest of the province. Within each of these two main areas are distinct vegetation zones, the boundaries of which are determined by factors such as precipitation, latitude, and altitude.

THE MOUNTAINS AND FOOTHILLS

In southwest Alberta, west of Highway 2 between the U.S. border and Edmonton, the land climbs through foothills to the high peaks of the Rockies. Along the way it gains more than 2,000 meters (6,600 ft) of elevation and passes through the montane, subalpine, and alpine vegetation zones. Although Banff and Jasper National Parks are the obvious places to view these mountain biomes, the changes in vegetation are more abrupt and just as spectacular in less-visited Waterton Lakes National Park.

Montane

The foothills, along with most major valleys below an elevation of approximately 1,500 meters (4,920 ft), are primarily cloaked in montane forest. Aspen, balsam poplar, and white spruce thrive here, and lodgepole pine dominates areas affected by fire. On dry, south-facing slopes, Douglas fir is the climax species. Where sunlight penetrates the forest, such as along riverbanks, flowers such as lady's slipper, Indian paintbrush, and saxifrage are common. Large tracts of fescue grassland are common at lower elevations.

The montane forest holds the greatest diversity of life of any vegetation zone in the province and is prime winter habitat for larger mammals. But much of this habitat has been given over to agriculture and development.

Subalpine

Subalpine forests occur where temperatures are lower and precipitation higher than the montane. Generally, this is 1,500–2,200 meters (4,920–7,200 ft) above sea level. The climax species in this zone are Engelmann spruce and subalpine fir, although extensive forests of lodgepole pine occur in areas that have been scorched by fire in the last 100 years. At higher elevations, stands of larch are seen. Larches are conifers, but unlike other evergreens, their needles turn a burnt-orange color each fall, producing a magnificent display for photographers.

Alpine

The alpine zone extends from the tree line to mountain summits. Vegetation at these high altitudes occurs only where soil has been deposited. Large areas of alpine meadows burst with color for a short period each summer as lupines,

VEGETATION ZONES

Boreal   Forest

Edmonton

Parkland

Foothills

Mountains

Calgary

Prairie

0   100 mi

0   100 km

mountain avens, alpine forget-me-nots, moss campion, and a variety of heathers bloom.

THE PLAINS

Like the mountain-and-foothill region, Alberta's plains also are made up of three different vegetation zones. Across Highway 2, east of the mountains and foothills, southeast Alberta is dominated by the prairie—a vast, dry region of grasslands. Just north of the prairie is the aspen parkland, a belt of forest that runs across central Alberta to the foothills and covers approximately 10 percent of the province. Finally, Alberta's largest ecological zone by far, covering more than half of the province, is the boreal forest. It is located north of the aspen parkland and extends into the Northwest Territories to the tree line, where the tundra begins.

Prairie

Prairie is the warmest and driest ecological zone, with an annual precipitation less than 750 millimeters (30 inches). This harsh climate can support trees only where water flows, so for the most part the prairie is flat or lightly undulating open grassland. Irrigation has made agriculture possible across much of the south, and the patches of native grasses such as rough fescue and grama are rapidly disappearing. Among the cultivated pastureland and seemingly desolate plains, flowers punctuate the otherwise ochre-colored landscape. Alberta's floral emblem, the prickly wild rose, grows here, as do pincushion cactus, buckbrush (or yellow rose), and sagebrush. In river valleys, aspen, willow, and cottonwood grow along the banks.

The stands of large cottonwoods in Dinosaur Provincial Park were part of the reason this park was designated a UNESCO World Heritage Site. (The park is a good example of prairie habitat.) The Cypress Hills, which rise above the driest part of the province, contain vegetation not generally associated with the prairies, including spruce, aspen, a variety of berries, and the calypso orchid.

Aspen Parkland

Unique to Canada, this area is a transition zone between the prairie grassland to the south and the boreal forest to the north. As the name suggests, trembling aspen (named for light, flattened leaves that "tremble" in even the slightest wind) is the climax species, but much of this zone has been given over to agriculture—its forests burned and its soil tilled. Scattered stands of aspen, interspersed with willow, balsam poplar, and white spruce, still occur, whereas areas cleared by early settlers now contain fescue grass. Flowering plants such as prairie crocus, snowberry, prickly wild rose, and lily of the valley decorate the shores of the many lakes and marshy areas found in this biome. Elk Island National Park, best known for its mammal populations, is an ideal example of this unique habitat.

Boreal Forest

Only a few species of trees are able to adapt to the harsh northern climate characteristic of this zone. The area is almost totally covered in forest, with only scattered areas of prairielike vegetation occurring in the driest areas. In the southern part of the boreal forest, the predominant species are aspen and balsam poplar. Farther north, conifers such as white spruce, lodgepole pine, and balsam fir are more common, with jack pine growing on dry ridges and tamarack also present. The entire forest is interspersed with lakes, bogs, and sloughs, where black spruce and larch are the dominant species. Like the trees, the ground cover also varies with latitude. To the south, and in the upland areas where aspen is the climax species, the undergrowth is lush with a variety of shrubs, including raspberries, saskatoons, and buffalo berries. To the north, where drainage is generally poor, the ground cover is made up of dense mats of peat.

Most areas of boreal forest accessible by road have been affected by fire or development, but some areas of old growth can still be found. Highway 63, which ends in Fort McMurray, runs through pristine northern boreal forest. Sir Winston Churchill Provincial Park, on an island in Lac La Biche, hasn't been burned for more than 300 years and supports stands of balsam fir up to 150 years old.

Fauna

For 10,000 years, hundreds of thousands of bison roamed Alberta's plains, and wolves and grizzly bears inhabited all parts of the province, but this all changed with the arrival of Europeans. Trappers and traders first devastated beaver and mink populations, then killed off all of the bison, wolves, and grizzlies on the prairies.

Today, because of the foresight of early conservationists, mammal populations have stabilized and Alberta's wilderness once again provides some of North America's best opportunities for viewing wildlife.

THE DEER FAMILY
Deer
Alberta's mule deer and white-tailed deer are similar in size and appearance. Their color varies with the season but is generally light brown in summer, turning dirty gray in winter. Both species are considerably smaller than elk. The **mule deer** has a white rump, a white tail with a dark tip, and large mulelike ears. It inhabits open forests bordering prairie. The **white-tailed deer's** tail is dark on top, but when the animal runs, it holds its tail erect, revealing an all-white underside. White-tails frequent thickets along the rivers and lakes of the foothills and aspen parkland.

Elk
The elk, or wapiti, is common throughout the Rockies and foothills. It has a tan body with a dark-brown neck and legs, and a white rump. This second-largest member of the deer family weighs 250–450 kilograms (550–1,480 lbs) and stands 1.5 meters (five ft) at the shoulder. Stags grow an impressive set of antlers, which they shed each spring. Rutting season takes place between August and October; listen for the shrill bugles of the stags serenading the females. During the rut, randy males will challenge anything with their antlers and can be dangerous. In spring, females protecting their young can be equally dangerous.

Moose
The giant of the deer family is the moose, an awkward-looking mammal that appears to have been designed by a cartoonist. It has the largest antlers of any animal in the world, stands up to 1.8 meters (six ft) at the shoulder, and weighs more than 450 kilograms (1,480 lbs). Its body is dark brown, and it has a prominent nose, long spindly legs, small eyes, big ears, and an odd flap of skin called a "bell" dangling beneath its chin. Apart from all that, it's good-looking. Each spring the bull begins to grow palm-shaped antlers that are fully grown by August. Moose are solitary animals that prefer marshy areas and weedy lakes. They forage in and around ponds on willows, aspen, birch, grasses, and all aquatic vegetation. Although they may appear docile, moose will attack humans if they feel threatened.

Caribou
Small populations of woodland caribou inhabit the alpine regions of the mountains and the boreal forests of northern Alberta. They are migratory but travel far shorter distances than the barren-ground caribou of the Arctic. There are approximately 5,000 caribou within the province; diminishing habitat and declining numbers have led to their placement on Alberta's Threatened Wildlife List. These caribou are smaller than elk and have a dark-brown coat with creamy patches on the neck and rump. Both sexes grow antlers, but those of the females are shorter and have fewer points. On average, males weigh 180 kilograms (400 lbs), females 115 kilograms (250 lbs).

BEARS
Alberta's two species of bears—black bears and grizzlies—can be differentiated by size and shape. Grizzlies are larger than black bears and have a flatter, dish-shaped face and a distinctive hump of muscle behind their necks. Color is not a reliable way to tell them apart. Black bears are not always black. They can be

DINOSAURS OF ALBERTA

Dinosaur bones found in the Red Deer River Valley play an important role in the understanding of our prehistoric past. The bones date from the late Cretaceous period, around 70 million years ago; for reasons that have mystified paleontologists for over a century, dinosaurs disappeared during this period, after having roamed the earth for 150 million years. A recent theory, put together largely through work done in Alberta, suggests that while larger species disappeared, some of the smaller ones evolved into birds.

The bones of 35 dinosaur species – around 10 percent of all those currently known – have been discovered in Alberta. Like today's living creatures, they are classified in orders, families, and species. Of the two orders of dinosaurs, both have been found in the Red Deer River Valley. The bird-hipped dinosaurs (order Ornithischia) were herbivores, while the lizard-hipped dinosaurs (order Saurischia) were omnivores and carnivores.

Apart from their sheer bulk, many herbivores lacked any real defenses. Others developed their own protection; the chasmosaurus had a bony frill around its neck, the pachycephalosaurus had a 25-centimeter-thick (10-inch-thick) dome-shaped skull cap fringed with spikes, and the ankylosaurus was an armored dinosaur whose back was covered in spiked plates.

Among the most common herbivores that have been found in the valley are members of the family of duck-billed hadrosaurs. Fossilized eggs of one hadrosaur, the hypacrosaurus, were unearthed still encasing intact embryos.

Another common herbivore in the valley was a member of the horned ceratops family; over 300 specimens of the centrosaurus have been discovered in one "graveyard."

Of the lizard-hipped dinosaurs, the tyrannosaurs were most feared by herbivores. The 15-meter (49-ft) *Tyrannosaurus rex* is most famous among *Homo sapiens*. But the smaller albertosaurus, a remarkably agile carnivore weighing many tons, is the most common tyrannosaur found in the valley.

brown or cinnamon, causing them to be confused with the brown grizzly.

Black Bears

If you spot a bear feeding beside the road, chances are it's a black bear. These mammals are widespread throughout all forested areas of the province (except Cypress Hills Provincial Park) and number approximately 40,000. Their weight varies considerably, but males average 150 kilograms (330 lbs) and females 100 kilograms (220 lbs). Their diet is omnivorous, consisting primarily of grasses and berries but supplemented by small mammals. In winter, they can sleep for up to one month at a time before changing position.

Grizzly Bears

Most of Alberta's grizzlies are spread throughout the Rockies in Banff and Jasper National Parks, Kananaskis Country, and Alberta's four designated wilderness areas. A small population inhabiting the Swan Hills is distinct from those found in the mountains and is probably related more closely to the grizzlies that once roamed the prairies.

Grizzlies are widespread but not abundant in the province, numbering approximately 800. The three mountain national parks hold an estimated 200 grizzlies; the remainder are found in the surrounding undeveloped wilderness. Most sightings occur in alpine and subalpine zones, although sightings at lower elevations are not unusual, especially when snow falls early or late. The bears' color ranges from light brown to almost black, with dark tan being the most common. On average, males weigh 200–250 kilograms (440–550 lbs). The bears eat small- and medium-sized mammals and supplement their diet with berries in fall. Like black bears, they sleep through most of the winter. When they emerge in early spring, the bears scavenge carcasses of animals that succumbed to the win-

ter until the new spring vegetation becomes sufficiently plentiful.

WILD DOGS AND CATS
Foxes

The smallest of the North American wild canids (around the size of a house cat) is the **swift fox,** which had been eradicated from the Canadian prairies by 1928. The species was reintroduced to the southeastern corner of Alberta in 1983, and in the time since, the population has tripled to around 600. Although thriving in this dry and desolate landscape, the species is still considered endangered. It has a gray body with a long black-tipped bushy tail, large ears, and smoky gray facial spots.

The more adaptable **red fox** is slightly larger than the swift fox and is common throughout Alberta.

Coyotes

The resilient coyotes have survived human attempts to eradicate them from the prairies; today their eerie concerts of yips and howls can be heard across much of Alberta. A mottled mix of brown and gray, with lighter-colored legs and belly, the coyote is a skillful and crafty hunter that preys mainly on rodents. Both foxes and coyotes have the remarkable ability to hear the movement of small mammals under the snow, allowing them to hunt these animals without actually seeing them.

Wolves

Now inhabiting only the mountains and boreal forests, the wolf was once the target of a relentless campaign to exterminate the species. Wolves are larger than coyotes, resembling a large husky or German shepherd in size and stature. Their color ranges from snow white to brown or black. They are complex and intriguing animals that adhere to a hierarchical social order and are capable of expressing happiness, humor, and loneliness.

Wild Cats

The elusive **lynx** is identifiable by its pointy black ear tufts and an oversized-tabby-cat ap-

WILDLIFE AND YOU

Alberta's abundance of wildlife is one of its biggest drawing cards. To help preserve this unique resource, use common sense.

- **Do not feed the animals.** Many animals may seem tame, but feeding them endangers yourself, the animal, and other visitors, as animals become aggressive when looking for handouts.

- **Store food safely.** When camping, keep food in your vehicle or out of reach of animals. Just leaving it in a cooler isn't good enough.

- **Keep your distance.** Although it's tempting to get close to animals for a better look or a photograph, it disturbs the animal and can be dangerous.

- **Drive carefully.** The most common cause of premature death for larger mammals is being hit by cars.

pearance. The animal has broad, padded paws that distribute its weight, allowing it to "float" on the surface of snow. It is uncommon but widespread through remote, forested regions of the province. **Bobcats** live in the coulees and caves of badlands such as in Writing-on-Stone and Dinosaur Provincial Parks.

Solitary and secretive, **cougars** (also called mountain lions) can grow to a length of 1.5 meters (five ft) and can weigh 75 kilograms (165 lbs). These versatile hunters inhabit the mountain and foothill regions, numbering around 1,000 in the province.

OTHER LARGE MAMMALS
Mountain Goats

The remarkable rock-climbing ability of these nimble-footed creatures allows them to live on rocky ledges or near-vertical slopes, safe from predators. They also frequent the alpine meadows and open forests of the Rockies, where

they congregate around natural salt licks. The goats stand one meter at the shoulder and weigh 80–130 kilograms (175–290 lbs). Both sexes possess black horns and a peculiar beard, or rather, goatee.

Bighorn Sheep

Bighorn sheep are found on grassy mountain slopes throughout the mountains. The males have impressive horns that curve backward up to 360 degrees. The color of their coat varies with the season; in summer it is brownish-gray (with a cream-colored belly and rump), turning grayer in winter.

Pronghorn

Found roaming the prairie grasslands of southeastern Alberta, the pronghorn, often called pronghorn antelope, is one of the fastest animals in the New World, capable of sustained speeds up to 80 kilometers (50 mi) per hour. Other remarkable attributes also ensure its survival, including incredible hearing and eyesight, and the ability to go without water for long periods.

Bison

Conservative estimates put the population of bison at approximately 60 million before the coming of Europeans. Within Alberta, these shaggy beasts are found in Elk Island and Wood Buffalo National Parks and in several privately owned herds throughout the province. Two subspecies of bison inhabit Alberta, but they have mostly interbred. Wood bison are darker in color, larger (an average bull weighs 840 kg/1,850 lbs), and have long, straight hair covering the forehead. Plains bison are smaller, have shorter legs, a larger head, and frizzy hair. In summer they grow distinctive capes of woolly hair that cover their front legs, head, and shoulders.

RODENTS AND OTHER SMALL MAMMALS
Squirrels

Several species of squirrels are common in Alberta. The golden-mantled ground squirrel,

found in rocky outcrops of subalpine and alpine regions, has black stripes along its sides and looks like an oversized chipmunk. The Columbian ground squirrel has reddish legs, face, and underside, and a flecked, grayish back. The bushy-tailed red squirrel, a bold chatterbox of the forest, leaves telltale shelled cones at the bases of conifers. The lightly colored Richardson's ground squirrel, which chirps and flicks its thin tail when it senses danger, is found across much of Alberta; on the prairie, it is often misidentified as a gopher. Another species, the nocturnal northern flying fox, glides through the montane forests of mountain valleys, but is rarely seen.

Other Rodents

One of the animal kingdom's most industrious mammals is the **beaver.** Tipping the scales at approximately 20 kilograms (44 lbs), it has a flat, rudderlike tail and webbed back feet that enable it to swim at speeds up to 10 kilometers (6.2 mi) per hour. Beavers build their dam walls and lodges out of twigs, branches, sticks from felled trees, and mud. They eat the bark and smaller twigs of deciduous plants and store branches underwater, near the lodge, as a winter food supply. **Muskrats** also inhabit Alberta's waterways and wetlands. They are agile swimmers and are able to stay submerged for up to 12 minutes.

Closely related to muskrats are **voles,** which are often mistaken for mice. They inhabit the prairies and lower elevations of forested areas. **Kangaroo rats** live on the shortgrass prairie within the Palliser Triangle. They propel themselves with leaps of up to two meters (6.6 ft). The furry **shrew** has a sharp-pointed snout and is closely related to the mole. It must eat almost constantly because it is susceptible to starvation within only a few hours of its last meal. The **pygmy shrew,** widespread throughout Alberta, is the world's smallest mammal.

High in the mountains, **hoary marmots** are often seen sunning themselves in rocky areas at or above the tree line. When danger approaches, these large rodents emit a shrill whistle to warn their colony. **Porcupines** are

golden-mantled ground squirrel

common and widespread throughout all forested areas of the province.

Alberta has been rat-free since the 1950s.

Hares and Pikas

Hares and pikas are technically lagomorphs, distinguished from rodents by a double set of incisors in the upper jaw. Alberta's **varying hares** are commonly referred to as snowshoe hares because their thickly furred, wide-set hind feet mimic snowshoes. Unlike rabbits, which maintain a brown coat year-round, snowshoe hares turn white in winter, providing camouflage in the snowy climes they inhabit. One of their Albertan cousins, the **white-tailed prairie hare,** has been clocked at speeds of 60 kilometers (37 mi) per hour. Finally, the small, gray-colored pika, or rock rabbit, lives among the rubble and boulders of scree slopes above the tree line.

Weasels

The weasel family is composed of dozens of species of small, carnivorous mammals, many of which can be found in Alberta. Widely considered pests by farmers, they are highly prized for their furs. The smallest weasel, and the world's smallest carnivore, is the **least weasel,** widespread through lightly grassed areas and open meadows; it weighs just 70 grams. At the other end of the scale is the **wolverine,** largest of the weasels, weighing up to 16 kilograms (35 lbs). This solitary, cunning, and cautious creature inhabits northern forests and subalpine and lower alpine regions. Inhabiting the same environment are **fishers,** quick, agile hunters that feed at night. Also frequenting subalpine and lower alpine regions is the **marten,** which preys on birds, squirrels, mice, and voles as it moves through the trees. The **badger,** a larger member of the weasel family, inhabits the prairies and parklands, and although widespread, is rare and very secretive. It is endowed with large claws and strong forelegs, making it an impressive digger. Two other related species divide their time between land and water. **River otters** have round heads, short, thick necks, webbed feet, long facial whiskers, and grow

larger than one meter in length. These playful characters are active both day and night, and prey on beavers and muskrats. They are widespread but not common throughout the northern half of Alberta. **Mink,** at home in or out of water, are smaller than otters and feed on muskrats, mice, voles, and fish. Mink are especially sought-after for their pelts; they are raised in captivity for this purpose at mink farms throughout the province.

REPTILES AND AMPHIBIANS

Two species of **snakes,** the wandering garter snake and the red-sided garter snake (North America's northernmost reptile), are found as far north as the boreal forest. The other six species of snakes in the province, of which the plains garter snake is the most common, are restricted to the southern grasslands. Rattlesnakes are rarely encountered; their range is restricted to the badlands.

Three species of **frogs** and one species of **salamander** are present in Alberta.

FISH
Trout

Alberta's waters hold eight species of trout, all of which are classed as "cold-water" species—that is, they inhabit waters where the temperature ranges 4–18°C (39–64°F). The predominant species, the **rainbow trout,** is not native to the region; it was introduced from more-northern Canadian watersheds as a sport fish and is now common throughout lower-elevation lakes and rivers. It has an olive-green back and a red strip running along the center of its body. For over 50 years, the **bull trout,** Alberta's provincial fish, was perceived as a predator of more favored introduced species, and mostly removed. Today, what was once the most widespread trout east of the Continental Divide is confined to the headwaters of the Canadian Rockies' river systems, and is classed as a threatened species. While the bull trout has adapted to the harsh conditions of its reduced habitat, its continuing struggle for survival can be attributed to many factors, including a scarcity of food and a slow repro-

ductive cycle. Bull trout grow to 70 centimeters (27 inches) in length and weigh up to 10 kilograms (22 lbs). The **lake trout,** which grows to 20 kilograms (44 lbs), is native to large, deep lakes throughout the mountains and foothills. Identified by a silvery-gray body and irregular white splotches along its back, this species grows slowly, taking up to eight years to reach maturity and living up to 25 years. Named for a bright-red dash of color that runs from below the mouth almost to the gills, the **cutthroat trout** is native to southern Alberta's mountain streams, but has been introduced to high-elevation lakes and streams on both sides of the Canadian Rockies. **Brown trout,** introduced from Europe in 1924, are found in the Bow and Red Deer Rivers. Its body is a golden-brown color, and it is the only trout with both black and red spots. The **brook trout** is a colorful fish identified by a dark-green back with pale-colored splotches and purple-sheened sides. It is native to eastern Canada, but was introduced to the mountains as early as 1903 and is now widespread throughout lakes and streams on the Alberta side of the Continental Divide. **Golden trout** were introduced to a few mountain lakes around 1960 as a sport fish. They are a smallish fish, similar in color to rainbow trout.

Other Species

The **mountain whitefish** (commonly, but incorrectly, called arctic grayling by Albertan anglers) is a light-gray-colored fish that is native to most lower elevation lakes and rivers of the Canadian Rockies. Also inhabiting the region's waters are **arctic grayling** and **Dolly Varden** (named for a colorful character in a Charles Dickens story). Other fish inhabiting Alberta's waters include two species of **whitefish, sturgeon** (largest of the freshwater fish), **burbot, northern pike,** and **walleye.**

BIRDS

Bird-watching is popular in Alberta, thanks to the 340 species of birds recorded in the province and the millions of migratory birds that follow the Central Flyway each year. All

AMMONITE OR AMMOLITE?

Ammonites are fossilized molluscs that lived up to 400 million years ago but that became extinct 65 million years ago. The only living creature in the same cephalopod family is the nautilus, which has the same distinctive coiled shell.

Ammonite fossils are relatively common around the world, but those in Alberta are unique: Through a freak occurrence in nature, an ancient chemical reaction opalized the molluscs in a small area of southern Alberta, forming gem-quality *ammolite*. This extremely rare gemstone has an intriguing beauty that spans all colors of the rainbow. Mining is restricted to two commercial operations. One is operated by Richard Morgan, who quarries ammonite for only a couple of months a year then spends the rest of his time at a small Canmore factory (102 Bow Meadows Cres., 403/678-1786), sorting through the raw material and creating a variety of gems. Visitors are more than welcome to watch Richard at work. Out front is a small sales area with a huge ammonite fossil on display, along with loose gemstones and finished pieces for sale.

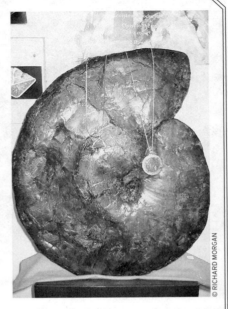

© RICHARD MORGAN

---

it takes is a pair of binoculars, a good book detailing species, and patience.

Shorebirds and Waterfowl

Alberta is home to 40 species of shorebirds, among them plovers, sandpipers, dowitchers, turnstones, gulls, terns, and herons. Of Alberta's ducks, **mallards** are present everywhere except the mountains, and **pintails** can often be seen feeding on grain in farmers' fields. The **wood duck** is much less common; identified by a distinctive crest, it can be spied around wetlands. Other widespread waterfowl species include **loons, grebes,** three species of **teal, geese,** and the threatened **trumpeter swan.**

Raptors

Raptors can be divided into two groups: those that hunt during day and those that hunt at night. Alberta's provincial bird, the **great** **horned owl,** is one of the latter. It is identified by its prominent "horns," which are actually tufts of feathers. Other nocturnal raptors in Alberta include the **pygmy owl, snowy owl,** and **great gray owl.**

Like owls, raptors that hunt during the day have adapted to specific environments—falcons to the prairies and hawks to forested areas. Falcons are easily distinguished among raptors for their long, pointed wings and narrow tails, allowing them to reach great speeds when in pursuit of prey. Most widespread of Alberta's falcons is the **prairie falcon,** whose territory extends from the prairies to the foothills. Other falcons present in Alberta include the **American kestrel,** which is commonly seen perched on fence posts and power poles throughout the prairies; the **merlin,** which tends to nest close to populated areas; and the rare **peregrine falcon,** which has been

© ANDREW HEMPSTEAD

osprey

clocked at speeds of up to 290 kilometers (180 mi) per hour when diving for prey. Hawks have adapted to hunting in wooded areas by developing short, rounded wings and long tails. The rust-colored **ferruginous hawk,** the largest hawk in North America, inhabits the treed areas of the prairies. The **marsh hawk** is widespread through the prairies and parklands and, as the name suggests, lives around areas of wetland. Farther north, the **red-tailed hawk** resides in the aspen parkland and the southern extent of boreal forest. Two species of eagles are also present in Alberta. **Bald eagles** soar over the northern half of the province, the foothills, and mountains. **Golden eagles** rest in open and sparsely vegetated areas of grasslands and mountains. Both species are migratory. **Ospreys** are uncommon; look for them around mountain and parkland lakes and rivers. They migrate to Alberta for the summer nesting sea-

son, always returning to the same nest, which they build high up in tall dead trees, on telephone poles, or on rocky outcrops, but always overlooking water. They feed on fish, hovering up to 50 meters (160 ft) above water, watching for movement, then diving into the water, thrusting their legs forward and collecting prey in their talons.

Others

Bird-watchers will be enthralled with the diversity of eastern and western bird species in Alberta. **Magpies, sparrows, starlings, grouse, ravens,** and **crows** are all widespread in the region. **Blackbirds, finches, thrushes, hummingbirds, woodpeckers, flycatchers,** and 28 species of **warblers** are common in forested areas. The popular campground visitor, the cheeky **gray jay,** is similar in appearance to that of the curious **Clark's nutcracker.**

History

THE EARLIEST INHABITANTS

The first *Homo sapiens* probably arrived in North America approximately 15,000 years ago—migrating from northeastern Asia across a land bridge spanning the Bering Strait. At the time, most of what is now western Canada was covered by an ice cap, so these first immigrants headed south along the coast and into the lower, ice-free latitudes of North America (to what is now the United States). Other waves of similar migrations followed, and eventually these ancestors of today's Native American fanned out across North and South America.

Thousands of years later, the receding polar ice cap began to uncover the land north of the 49th parallel. Native hunters probably first ventured into what is now Canada approximately 11,000 years ago, in pursuit of large mammals at the edge of the melting ice mass. The people who ended up in what would become Alberta came from the south, and in much later waves from the east, and formed several broad groups, within which many tribes formed, each with a distinct culture and language.

Most of the natives who inhabited what is now Alberta relied on bison (misnamed buffalo by early Europeans) for almost all of their needs. They ate the meat, both fresh and dried, then pounded into a powder form known as pemmican; made clothing, blankets, and tepee covers from the hides; fashioned bones into tools and ornaments; and used the dung as a source of fuel. One of their most successful ways of killing the huge beasts was by stampeding a whole herd over a cliff, at places known today as "buffalo jumps." (The best example of such a site is Head-Smashed-In Buffalo Jump, northwest of Fort Macleod.) They lived in tepees, which are conical-shaped tents comprising a frame of poles covered in buffalo hides. All cooking was done inside the tepee, with weapons, clothing, and food hung on the inside. During large gatherings, such as a buffalo hunt or the midsummer Sun Dance religious ceremony, thousands of tepees dotted the landscape.

Blackfoot

The Blackfoot Confederacy was a group of traditional prairie-dwellers and was the most warlike and feared of all native groups in Canada. Linguistically linked to the Algonkians, they were the "classic" Indian, depicted in story and film bedecked in costumes and headdresses and mounted on horses. (This perception is somewhat skewed, however, because the horse was a relatively modern addition to the plains, having been first introduced to North America by the Spanish in the mid-1600s and appearing north of the 49th parallel in the mid-1700s.) Before the arrival of Europeans, the Blackfoot Confederacy ruled the southern half of the province and comprised three allied bands, which hunted and camped together, intermarried, shared customs, and spoke dialects of the Algonkian language. They were the **Blackfoot** (best known today as **Siksika**), who lived along the North Saskatchewan River; the **Blood,** along the Red Deer River; and the **Peigan,** along the Bow River. As the Cree and Assiniboine to the north became armed with guns through their close links to the fur trade, the Blackfoot were pushed south, culminating in the last great intertribal battle in North America, which was fought against the Cree in 1870 within what is now Lethbridge city limits. By this time, the northernmost band of the once-powerful confederacy were the Siksika, who had been restricted to the land along the Bow River, while the Blood and Peigan lived to the south, with the Peigan territory extending well into Montana.

The **Sarcee** are also considered part of the Blackfoot nation but are of Athapaskan linguistic stock. This small tribe divided from the subarctic Beaver in the mid-1800s and integrated themselves with the Blackfoot in customs, lifestyle, and marriage but retained their original tongue.

Assiniboine

Circa 1650, the mighty Sioux nation, centered on the Great Lakes, began splintering, with

© ANDREW HEMPSTEAD

The history of the First Nations is brought to life throughout the province.

many thousands of its members moving north into present-day Canada, obtaining guns and metal objects from Europeans. These people became known as the Assiniboine, meaning "people who cook with stones." (Stones would be heated in a fire and then placed in a rawhide or birchbark basket with water; meat and vegetables were added, cooking as the water heated.) Slowly, generation after generation, smaller groups pushed westward along the Saskatchewan River System, allying themselves with the Cree but keeping their own identity and pushing through Blackfoot territory of the plains to reach the foothills approximately 200 years ago. They split into bands, moving north and south along the foothills and penetrating the wide valleys where hunting was productive. A lifestyle very different to that of the plains Indians evolved. Moving with the seasons, they lived in small familylike groups, diversifying their skills, becoming excellent hunters of mountain animals and gathering berries in fall, and becoming less dependent on buffalo. They were a steadfast yet friendly people,

and as Alexander Henry the Younger reported in 1811, "although [they are] the most arrant horse thieves in the world, they are at the same time the most hospitable to strangers who arrived in their camps." They knew themselves as the Nakoda, meaning "people." To the white man they were the Stoney, a shortening of the "Stone People," which in turn was an English interpretation of Assiniboine.

As the great buffalo herds were decimated, the Stoney were impacted less than the plains Indians because their reliance on the buffalo was almost nonexistent. But the effect of white man's intrusion on their lifestyle was still apparent. The missionaries of the day found that their teachings had more effect on the mountain people than those of the plains, so they intensified their efforts at converting the Stoney. Reverend John McDougall was particularly trusted, and in 1873 he built a small mission church by the Bow River at Morleyville. When the Stoney were presented with Treaty 7 in 1877, they chose to locate their reserve around the mission church at Morleyville. Abandoning

their nomadic lifestyle, they quickly learned farming. Unlike the plains Indians, they were almost self-sufficient on the reserve, not needing government rations, which the Blackfoot tribes survived on. Approximately 7,000 Stoney live on the Morley reserve today.

Cree

Before the arrival of Europeans, the Cree had inhabited most of eastern Canada for thousands of years. As the European fur traders pushed westward from Hudson Bay, the Cree followed, displacing enemies and adapting to new environments. By 1800, the Cree had moved as far west as the Peace River and to the northern slopes of the Rocky Mountains. They lived mostly in the forests fringing the prairies, acting as a middleman between Europeans and local natives, searching out furs and trading buffalo hides obtained from plains natives for European goods. Although not related, the Cree and Assiniboine mixed freely, camping, hunting, and fighting as a group.

Athapaskan

Athapaskan (often spelled Athabascan) is the mostly widely spread of all North American linguistic groups, extending from the Rio Grande to Alaska. It is believed that Athapaskan-speaking people moved into what is now Alberta approximately 7,000 years ago, following the receding ice cap and settling in forested areas throughout the subarctic. Athapaskans led a simple, nomadic life and were generally friendly toward each other and neighboring tribes. Although culturally diverse, the nature of this tribe's lifestyle left few archaeological remains; therefore, they are the least known of the natives who once lived within the boundaries of modern-day Alberta.

The southernmost Athapaskan group inhabiting Alberta was the **Beaver,** who were forced westward, up the Peace River watershed, by the warlike Cree in the late 1700s (the name Peace River originated after the two groups eventually made peace). Traditionally, the Beaver hunted caribou and bison that wandered north from the plains, but they were strongly influ-

enced by the fur trade. Another distinct band of Athapaskans settled along the Mackenzie River watershed and are known today as the Dene (DEN-ay), meaning "the people." The Dene lived a simple life, depending on fish, birds, and game such as caribou and moose, and traveling in birchbark canoes. Further divisions within the Dene nation relate more to the area in which they lived rather than to distinct language or lifestyles. These groups include the **Slave** (known as the Slavey in the Northwest Territories) and the **Chipewyan,** both of whose traditional home was the upper watershed of the Mackenzie River.

Métis

The exact definition of Métis varies across Canada, but the term originated in the 1700s to describe those born of a mixed racial heritage as the result of relationships between French traders and native Cree women. The Métis played an invaluable role in the fur trade because they were able to perform traditional tasks and were bilingual. By the early 1800s, a distinct Métis culture developed, mostly along major trading routes. As the fur trade ended, and the great buffalo herds disappeared, many Métis found themselves drawn toward the familiarity of their own people and settled along Central Canada's Red River. Government threats to take their land along the Red River led to the 1869 Riel Rebellion and the 1885 North West Rebellion, after which the displaced Métis drifted back westward to the boreal forests, eking out food by hunting, trapping, and fishing. They were a people stuck between two cultures; they were excluded from treaties signed by full-blooded natives but were not a part of mainstream Canadian society.

EXPLORATION AND THE FUR TRADE

In 1670, the British government granted the Hudson's Bay Company the right to govern Rupert's Land, a vast area of western Canada that included all of present-day Manitoba, Saskatchewan, Alberta, and the Northwest Territories. The land was rich in fur-bearing

© ANDREW HEMPSTEAD

This church at Dunvegan is one of many buildings that dates to the fur trade era.

Alberta—Buckingham House—right beside the North West Company's Fort George on the North Saskatchewan River. This practice of moving in right next to the competition—engaged in by both companies—produced a rivalry between the two that continued unabated until they merged in 1821.

Trading posts were scattered over the entire west. Most were made of solid log construction and were located beside rivers, the main routes for transportation. Furs were the only reason white men came west for more than a century. Traders lived by their own rules and were opposed to settlement, which would have changed their lifestyle. But change was in the wind. In 1857, the British government sent Captain John Palliser west to Rupert's Land to determine whether the land was fit for agriculture. The Palliser Report, which he prepared upon his return to England, was unfavorable regarding an area in what is now southern Alberta (known as "Palliser Triangle"), but it encouraged settlement to the north.

The Dominion of Canada

By 1867, some of the eastern provinces were tiring of British rule, and a movement was abuzz to push for Canadian independence. The British government, wary of losing Canada as it had lost the United States, passed legislation establishing the Dominion of Canada. It created a central government with certain powers and delegated other powers to the provinces.

At that time, the North-West Territories, as Rupert's Land had become known, was a foreign land to those in eastern Canada: life was primitive with no laws, and no post had more than a couple dozen residents. But in an effort to solidify the Dominion, the government bought the North-West Territories from the Hudson's Bay Company in 1869, even as beaver stock was being depleted and the whiskey trade was having disastrous effects on the native population.

THE END OF AN ERA

Long before Europeans entered what is now Alberta, native populations felt their influ-

mammals, which both the British and the French sought to exploit for profit. The Hudson's Bay Company first built forts around Hudson Bay and encouraged Indians to bring furs to the posts. Soon, however, French fur traders based in Montreal began traveling west to secure furs, forcing their British rivals to do the same.

In June 1754, Anthony Henday embarked on a journey up the North Saskatchewan River from York Factory on Hudson Bay, becoming the first white man to enter what is now Alberta on September 11, 1754. He returned to the east the following spring, bringing canoes loaded with furs and providing reports of snowcapped peaks.

In 1787, traders from Montreal formed the North West Company, whose men were known as Norwesters. One year later, Norwester Peter Pond built Fort Chipewyan on Lake Athabasca, which was the first fur-trading post in what is now Alberta. The Hudson's Bay Company built *its* first post in present-day

ence initially through the horse, which was a relatively modern addition to the plains, having been first introduced to North America by the Spanish in the mid-1600s and appearing north of the 49th parallel in the mid-1700s. Horses were followed by Europeans themselves, with their guns, alcohol, and diseases. From this time on, native lifestyle and the boundaries of the various tribes changed dramatically. For centuries, the buffalo population of the prairies had remained relatively constant. The Indians slaughtered many buffalo, but not enough to make a significant impact on total numbers. As beaver populations dwindled, however, traders turned to buffalo hides. Within 10 years, the once-prolific herds were practically eradicated. Without their traditional food source, the Indians of the plains were weakened and left susceptible to European-borne diseases such as smallpox and scarlet fever. The whiskey trade also took its toll on native populations. Living conditions among the Indians were pitiful, and frequent uprisings took place.

On June 6, 1874, a band of North West Mounted Police left Toronto under the command of Colonel James F. Macleod. Their task was to curb the whiskey trade and restore peace on the western prairies. They built a post on the Oldman River, and within one year three other posts had been established in what is now southern Alberta.

Facing starvation, the chiefs had no choice but to sign treaties, relegating the tribes to reserves, which consisted of land set aside by the government for specific native bands, and changing their nomadic lifestyles forever. The chief of all chiefs, Crowfoot, of the powerful Blackfoot Confederacy, signed the first major treaty on September 22, 1877, followed by the chiefs of the Peigans, Stoneys, Sarcees, and Bloods. Their self-sufficiency taken away, the tribes were forced to accept what they were given. They were no longer free, they no longer hunted or fought, their medicine men could do nothing to stop the spread of the white man's diseases, and they slowly lost their pride.

EUROPEAN SETTLEMENT

An essential ingredient to the success of settling the West was the construction of a rail line across the continent, replacing canoe and cart routes. This idea was met with scorn by those in the east, who saw it as unnecessary and uneconomical. In 1879, a line reached Winnipeg. After much debate was waged about creating a route through the Canadian Rockies, the Canadian Pacific Railway line reached Fort Calgary and what is now Banff in 1883. Workers pushed on across the mountains, and on November 7, 1885, the final spike was laid, linking the fledgling province of British Columbia to the rest of the country. A northern route, through Edmonton and Jasper, was completed by the Grand Trunk Railway in 1914.

With two expensive rail lines in place, the government set about putting them to use by settling the land and encouraging tourists to visit the thriving resort towns of Banff and Jasper. The prairies were surveyed and homesteads were offered at $10 per quarter section (160 acres). People from diverse ethnic backgrounds flooded the western prairies, tending to settle in communities of their own people. Life was hard for the early settlers; those in the south found the land dry, whereas those in the north had to clear land.

The first to take advantage of the extensive grasslands that had once supported millions of bison was Senator Matthew Cochrane, who in 1881 secured a grazing lease on 189,000 acres west of Calgary. This homestead was the first of many ranches to be claimed in the foothills, and many herds of cattle were driven to their new homes by American cowboys.

Entering the Confederation

British Columbia had gained provincial status in 1871, four years after the Dominion of Canada was established, but the North-West Territories remained under federal control. This region had been divided into districts, of which Alberta—named after Princess Louise Caroline Alberta, the fourth daughter of Queen Victoria—was one. On September 1, 1905, Alberta and Saskatchewan were admitted as provinces

PALLISER TRIANGLE

On July 4, 1857, Captain John Palliser set out west from Winnipeg on an assignment from the British government to make a comprehensive assessment of the agricultural potential, mineral reserves, soil quality, and timber resources of the prairies. Under his command were 20 men, two wagons, six Red River carts, and 29 horses. The expedition traveled the length and breadth of the prairies before eventually submitting their findings in 1862. Palliser's report favored a band of territory stretching from Manitoba to the Peace River in northern Alberta. On the other hand, to the south he reported a vast land of short-grass prairie that he called "an extension of the Great American Desert." He considered it unfit for agriculture, saying it "is desert or semi-desert in character... [and] can never be expected to become occupied by settlers." This region – extending along the U.S. border and as far north as Red Deer – soon became known as the Palliser Triangle. Although the report wasn't favorable to the southern part of the province, it changed people's perception of the West. His report led to the settlement of southern Alberta, but it didn't happen overnight. Eventually the CPR rail line was built across the prairies, and irrigation opened up arid parts of the land previously thought unsuitable for settlement.

of the Canadian Confederation, and Edmonton was named Alberta's capital.

For the years preceding World War I, the new province of Alberta led the way in Canadian agricultural export, but strict controls on wheat prices left many farmers in debt. After the war, the Canadian Wheat Board, later to become the Alberta Wheat Pool, was established to give farmers a fairer price and an incentive to stay on the land. The early 1930s were a time of terrible drought and worldwide depression, both of which hit especially hard in a province that depended almost entirely on agriculture. For the second time in 30 years, however, war bolstered the economy and agricultural production increased. For 50 years, agriculture was Alberta's primary industry and the main attraction for settlers, but this situation was to change dramatically.

THE DISCOVERY OF "BLACK GOLD"

Arguably the most important date in Canada's industrial history was February 13, 1947. Until that date, small discoveries of oil and gas beneath Alberta had been made, and the modest reserves under Turner Valley constituted the British Empire's largest oil field. But when Leduc Oil Well No. 1 belched black rings of smoke on that cold February morning, Alberta had hit the jackpot. A new economy for Alberta and all of Canada had begun.

American capitalists poured billions of dollars into Alberta as every valley, hill, and flat was surveyed. Seismic cut lines (lines cut through the forests by seismologists charting new oil fields) across northern Alberta are testimony to this frantic period. Early in 1948, a major field at Redwater was tapped, and farmers' fields throughout the province were soon littered with beam pumps bobbing up and down. Calgary became the financial and administrative headquarters of the industry, while Edmonton—at the center of many of the fields—became the technological, service, and supply center.

By 1954, the eight major fields had been proven to contain eight billion barrels of recoverable crude oil; the Leduc-Woodbend field alone had 1,278 wells, and Pembina had 1,700. But nothing came close to the staggering resources of the Athabasca Oil Sands in northern Alberta, where one trillion barrels of oil lay—more than all the proven reserves of conventional oil on earth. By 1967, Alberta was producing 67 percent of Canada's crude oil and 87 percent of its natural gas.

Each of the major fields needed services,

and towns such as Drayton Valley, Swan Hills, High Level, and Rainbow Lake sprang up in otherwise unsettled areas. In less than a decade, the province's population doubled to more than one million.

The 1970s

In the early 1970s, despite abundant resources and frenzied activity in Alberta, the eastern Canadian provinces were importing oil from overseas, taking advantage of low prices obtained, most notably, from the oil-exporting countries of the Middle East. But then the Arab oil ministers got smart, banding together to form the Organization of Petroleum Exporting Countries (OPEC). OPEC began demanding $6 a barrel—up from less than $2—and the price of oil quadrupled within three months. Suddenly, cheap, foreign oil was a thing of the past, and Alberta—after decades of feeling snubbed by the eastern provinces—held a trump card. With enormous reserves of oil and constitutional control over all of it, Alberta braced itself for the coming boom. The value of the province's petroleum resources tripled almost overnight; within another four years, it quadrupled again.

A change in government roughly coinciding with the oil boom also contributed to Alberta's success. For 36 years, the agricultural-based Social Credit party had controlled Alberta. But in 1971, the Conservative Party—led by Peter Lougheed—came to power. Lougheed was an uncompromising leader who cared little about what the powers in the eastern provinces thought of his policies. Described by many as an Albertan sheik, he tripled oil-royalty rates for the province, requiring Alberta's producers to pay the province 65 cents out of every dollar earned from the oil. The federal government refused to allow the oil companies to deduct those royalties on their federal income tax returns, and many major oil companies pulled out of Alberta. But not for long. Alberta had the goods, and with incentives from the government, the companies returned. This incident was only a slight hiccup in Lougheed's vision of a new and powerful west.

Revenues were flowing into the provincial coffers at $6,000 per minute; more millionaires were created than at any other time in Canadian history; and Calgary and Edmonton became two of North America's greatest boomtowns and the center of world oil technology. Calgary became the fastest-growing city in the country—a city of dreams, where no expense was spared and to where the power and wealth of eastern provinces moved.

After the Boom

The latter part of the 20th century was a quiet time. World oil prices steadied in the late 1970s, and international oil companies spent money elsewhere. But the boom's impact on the province continued to be positive. The Heritage Savings Trust Fund—a legacy of Lougheed's days—amassed fortunes in oil royalties to be spent on facilities for the people of Alberta. Kananaskis Country was the most grandiose creation of the fund, while other facilities, including interpretive centers, urban park systems, and museums, continue to preserve the province's natural and human history.

Self-made millionaires, who often came from humble beginnings, poured their enormous wealth back into the province that had made them rich. The philanthropies of oilman Eric Harvie, including the Glenbow Foundation, Banff Centre for the Arts, and Calgary Zoo, totaled at least $100 million. In 1978, Edmonton hosted the Commonwealth Games, and in 1988, Calgary hosted the Winter Olympic Games, both events providing boosts to Alberta's economy.

THE NEW MILLENNIUM

Calgary and Edmonton have embraced the information technology boom, diversifying a resource-based economy and helping keep Alberta's economic growth well above the national average. Nonrenewable resources are still the backbone of the economy, however, which was never more evident than in 2006, when oil prices rose over $70 a barrel. Once again, Alberta experienced a surge in energy investments. Although royalties from the petroleum

industry continue to pour into government coffers, impressive financial management is helping Alberta thrive economically. In turn, this growth is encouraging capital investment in resources, company relocation, and migration from eastern provinces. Albertans enjoy the benefits of the strong economy most directly because they pay a low rate of personal income tax and no provincial sales tax.

Alberta's annual population growth is currently 2 percent (more than double Canada's average), with the current population of 3.2 million up from 1.6 million in 1971. This growth has been greatest in the largest cities of Calgary (which welcomed its one millionth resident in 2006) and Edmonton (up 150 percent since 1996) as well as smaller centers such as the resort town of Canmore, whose population has increased over 300 percent in just 25 years, and oil-rich Fort McMurray, whose population has more than quadrupled in the last 20 years.

With a growing, relatively young, and well-educated population, a strong economy, low taxes, high oil prices, and staggering resources still available in the ground, the future remains bright for this Western frontier made good that just celebrated its 100th birthday in 2005.

Economy and Government

ECONOMY

In 2003, Alberta's Gross Domestic Product (GDP) was $150 billion, higher per capita than all other provinces. The province's fiscal fortunes have traditionally been closely tied to the land—based first on the fur trade, then agriculture, and for the final 30 years of the 1900s on abundant reserves of three fossil fuels—coal, oil, and natural gas. The province's location away from main trade routes had always hindered economic diversity and fostered a boom-or-bust dependence on natural resources and agriculture, which account for 14 percent of total GDP (against 2.6 percent elsewhere in Canada). And although Alberta's industrial and commercial sectors would collapse without these resources, the province is at the forefront of the information technology tidal wave, making its economy less susceptible to ever-changing commodity prices.

Oil

Alberta lies above a vast basin of porous rock containing abundant deposits of oil, natural gas, and coal. These were formed hundreds of millions of years ago in the Carboniferous period (hence "fossil fuels"), which gets its name from carbon, the main element in coal. An estimated 200 million barrels of recoverable oil occurs in three forms. Conventional **crude oil** is recovered through normal drilling methods. More than 5,000 pools holding a total of 1.6 billion barrels have been discovered, but half the oil production comes from just 25 of the pools. In total, 600,000 barrels are extracted daily, much of this amount from pumpjacks (known in the United States as nodding donkeys) you'll see in rural areas across the province. Most of this oil is refined for use as gasoline in cars, diesel for trucks, and heating fuel for homes. **Heavy oil** is more difficult to extract, and its uses are limited. In the future, however, as technology improves, recovery will become economically viable. **Oil sands** consist of a tarlike mixture of sand and bitumen that is mined then refined into synthetic crude for use in fuel products. The Athabasca Oil Sands, near Fort McMurray, are the world's largest such deposit, with 175 billion barrels recoverable using today's technology from a total reserve of 1.6 trillion barrels. Currently, 1.1 million barrels are extracted daily, with conservative estimates putting the rate at 11 million per day by 2035. As conventional crude diminishes, Alberta's heavy oil and oil sands are playing an increasingly important role in meeting world energy demands. Alberta is already the world's largest producer of synthetic crude, and it is estimated that 60

© ANDREW HEMPSTEAD

Ranching is a big part of Alberta's economy.

percent of the province's oil production will be of this form in the coming years. Currently, the province is contributing over 50 percent of Canada's total energy production. The Department of Energy promotes effective management of the province's oil resources and collects royalties for the government.

Natural Gas

Natural gas was first discovered near Medicine Hat in 1883, but it wasn't seen as a viable source of energy until 1900. The price of gas tends to mirror that of oil, and when prices peaked in 2001, drilling increased. Proven reserves stand at two trillion cubic feet, with five billion cubic feet extracted annually from 10,000 wells. Canada is the world's third-largest natural gas producer, with Alberta supplying over 80 percent of the country's total output. The province has always had more gas than it can use. After impurities are removed at gas plants, 75 percent of it is exported, via pipelines to other provinces and the United States. Gas is mostly used for home heating but

is also a source material for the petrochemical industry. Gas that contains more than 1 percent hydrogen sulphide is known as **sour gas.** It requires special processing to extract the hydrogen sulphide (which is used in fertilizers).

Coal

Coal is North America's most common fossil fuel. Alberta contains 60 percent of Canada's known coal resources, much of it low in sulphur, meaning it burns cleanly and efficiently. Large deposits were mined early on in Crowsnest Pass, Drumheller, and the foothills, and by the 1920s coal mining had developed into a major industry. Coal was first used to heat homes and provide fuel for steam locomotives, but oil took over those duties in the early 1950s. The industry was revived in 1962 when a coal-fired electric power plant opened at Wabamun, west of Edmonton. This market has since broadened, and seven Albertan mines supply 50 percent of Canada's coal, 70 percent of which is used for meeting 90 percent of Alberta's power needs.

Minerals

Industrial, nonmetallic minerals such as limestone, shale, and salt are mined for consumption within Alberta. Limestone mined on the edge of Banff National Park and in the Crowsnest Pass is processed to produce cement and chemical lime. Sulphur, which is extracted as a coproduct of natural gas, is exported to the large agricultural markets of the United States, Europe, and Africa for use in fertilizer. Metallic minerals such as copper, silver, and gold have all been mined at some stage, but compared to other areas of Canada, the province has been poorly explored. Four brining operations produce over one million tons of salt annually. Diamond exploration in the north of the province has led to a few finds, but not in amounts to make extraction viable.

Canada is the world's largest producer of uranium, the feedstock for nuclear reactors (15 percent of Canada's electricity comes from nuclear power). With demand continuing to outpace supply, exploratory drilling that led to a staking rush in southern Alberta in 2005 may have particular importance in the future.

Petrochemicals

Alberta produces 3.9 billion kilograms (8.6 billion lbs) of petrochemical products annually in four main plants, including the world's largest. Manufactured from crude oil and natural gas, the latter is used as a "feedstock" to produce ethylene, which is used in the production of consumer products such as plastic and nylon.

Agriculture

Although oil and gas form the backbone of Alberta's economy, 53,000 farms and ranches dominate the landscape. More than 20 million hectares are used for agriculture, more than half of them cultivated—a backbreaking job that was started when the first homesteaders moved west. Approximately 75 percent of this land is irrigated, thanks to massive projects such as the Oldman River Dam, and the remainder is dryland farmed. Alberta produces about 23 percent of Canada's total agricultural output, directly employing 50,000

people in the process. The largest portion of the province's $5 billion annual farm income comes from **beef** ($1.6 billion). Alberta has five million head of beef cattle—just under half of Canada's total—as well as 140,000 dairy cows. **Pork** comes in as the second-most important agri-food export. This industry is worth over $500 million to the local economy, with **poultry** eggs generating over $300 million annually.

Crops combined are worth over $2 billion. The most important crops, which combine for 70 percent of total revenue, are grains and oil seeds. These are **wheat,** used mainly for bread and pasta; **barley,** used for feeding livestock and making beer; and **canola** (recognizable by the bright yellow fields). Other crops include oats, rye, and flax. The largest areas of vegetable production are east of Lethbridge, where the corn and sugar-beet industries thrive.

Forestry

Although 60 percent of Alberta is forested, the forestry industry constitutes only 0.1 percent of the province's gross domestic product; current annual harvest is five million cubic meters. The main reason for such a small yield is the slow regrowth rate of the northern forests. The province has 300 sawmills, primarily producing dressed lumber. The forests are managed by the Department of Sustainable Resource Development.

Tourism

Worth $5.1 billion annually, tourism is the second-most important industry to Alberta's economy, lagging only slightly behind the petroleum industry in revenues and employing twice as many people. The province welcomes 20 million visitors annually. Of this total, 17 million are from Canada. One million are from the United States, and visitors from the United Kingdom, Japan, Germany, and Australia make up the bulk of the remainder. Banff National Park and West Edmonton Mall are Alberta's two most popular tourist attractions, although obviously they offer very different experiences. The **Travel Alberta** branch of the

government's Department of Economic Development markets the province worldwide as a tourist destination. The government has helped in other ways, too, investing millions of dollars of royalties from the oil-and-gas industry into improving facilities, building interpretive centers, and developing recreational playgrounds such as Kananaskis Country.

GOVERNMENT

Canada is part of the British Commonwealth, but the monarchy and the elected government of Great Britain have no control over Canada's political affairs. The British monarchy is represented in Canada by a governor general. The country's constitution is based on five important acts of British Parliament, the most recent being the Canada Act of 1982. That act gave Canada the power to amend its constitution, provided for recognition of the nation's multicultural heritage, and, most important for Alberta, strengthened provincial ownership of natural resources.

The Canadian government operates through three main agencies: the Parliament (made up of the Senate and the House of Commons), which makes the laws; the Executive (Cabinet), which applies the laws; and the Judiciary, which interprets the laws. Elections are held every five years, and the leader of whichever political party is voted into power by Canadian citizens becomes the head of government, known as the prime minister. The prime minister chooses a cabinet of ministers from members of his or her party. Each of the ministers is responsible for the administration of a department.

In Alberta, like in the other nine provinces, the monarchy is represented by a lieutenant governor. Like the governor general, the position is mainly ceremonial. The members of the Alberta Legislature are elected on a party system for a maximum of five years. The Progressive Conservative Party is currently in power. The other parties of consequence are the New Democratic Party, the Liberal Party,

© ANDREW HEMPSTEAD

The Alberta Legislature Building in Edmonton has been providing a home for provincial politicians since 1912.

and Alberta Alliance. The leader of the party in power is known as a premier, who oversees the running of 18 departments. With so much control over the province's natural resources and, in turn, Alberta's future, many premiers have enjoyed a particularly high profile. One such premier, Peter Lougheed, initiated the Heritage Savings Trust Fund, which collects billions of dollars in oil royalties for the people of Alberta. Initiated in 1976, the fund changed direction in the mid-1990s, steering toward long-term financial returns as opposed to specific projects. More recently, in 2006, a Prosperity Bonus of $400 was paid to each Albertan by the provincial government. Currently, the General Reserve Fund holds monies for programs and services, but most of the fund's $12 billion is invested.

For more information on Alberta's government, visit www.gov.ab.ca.

The People

For thousands of years before the arrival of Europeans to Alberta, several distinct indigenous peoples had lived off the land's abundant natural resources. With the coming of the Europeans, however, the native groups were overrun and reduced in numbers, today constituting only approximately 2.5 percent of Alberta's population. The Europeans came in droves—first drawn by game and arable land, and later by the oil-and-gas boom. People of many diverse cultures moved west, forming a melting pot of traditions. A census as early as 1921 noted 30 different languages in the province, in addition to the many distinct languages of the natives. Today, Alberta's population of three million is the fourth largest among the Canadian provinces and approximately 10 percent of the country's total. Alberta is Canada's fastest-growing province, with an annual population growth of 2 percent—double the national average.

First Nations

As indigenous peoples signed treaties, giving up traditional lands and settling on reserves (known as reservations in the United States), their lifestyles changed forever. They were no longer free to settle where they chose, they no longer hunted or fought, and their medicine men could do nothing to stop the spread of the white man's diseases. The first Indian Act, drafted in 1876, attempted to prepare natives for "European" society, but it ended up only isolating them further.

Those who are registered as members of a band are known as "status" Indians; that is, they have the right to use designated reserve lands and have access to federal funding. Originally, the Indian Act sought to assimilate natives by removing their "status" when they were considered ready to assimilate, such as when they earned a university degree, or in the case of native women, when they married a nonnative man. The Indian Act has been rewritten many times, including as recently as 1985, when many antiquated sections were repealed. The most important recent change freed natives from having to surrender their status to become a Canadian citizen and, therefore, to vote and own property. As a direct result of these changes, many natives who had lost their status, or in fact never had it, have been reclaiming it over the last 15 years. Therefore, the population of status Indians has grown considerably in recent years. Today, 87,000 status Indians live in Alberta, approximately 55,000 of them on reserves. Alberta has 93 reserves covering 6,600 square kilometers (2,550 square mi). The largest is a Blood reserve near Fort Macleod that covers 136,760 hectares (338,000 acres). Other major reserves include the Stoney reserve at Morley, the Sarcee (known officially as the Tsuu T'ina) reserve near Calgary, the Blackfoot reserve at Gleichen, and the Peigan reserve at Brocket. The reserves are administered by Indian and Northern Affairs Canada. The Congress of

FAMOUS ALBERTANS

Kurt Browning, multiple-time World Figure Skating champion, and the first person to compete a quadruple jump in competition, grew up on a ranch outside of Caroline.

Canada's unofficial national drink is the Caesar, which was first poured by Calgarian bartender **Walter Chell** in 1969.

Michael J. Fox was born in Edmonton, but had moved to Vancouver by age five.

In 1912 – just a few years after the telephone was invented – Edmontonian **Roman Gonsett** patented the world's first answering machine.

James Gosling, of Calgary, developed Java, a universal programming language that is now used as the link between software platforms.

Bret "Hitman" Hart is part of one of wrestling's best-known families. This former world champion was trained in the Calgary basement of his famous father, Stu, whose Stampede Wrestling show spawned some of the world's biggest stars.

Although she grew up in Fort McMurray, **Natasha Henstridge** was strutting the catwalks of Paris by age 15 before turning to acting and movies such as the *Species* trilogy.

One of the world's preeminent bear experts, **Stephen Herrero** calls Alberta home. In addition to authoring many books on the subject, he helped develop bear-proof trash bins.

Singer **k. d. lang** was born and raised in rural Consort, a far cry from the international stage.

After growing up in Fort Saskatchewan, **Evangeline Lilly** spent time as a missionary in the Philippines before snagging the role of Kate Austen on the TV drama *Lost*.

Singer-songwriter **Joni Mitchell** was born in Fort MacLeod in 1943. She moved to neighboring Saskatchewan as a young girl and by the mid-1960s was leading the folk music scene in New York City.

The first person in the world to climb the "Seven Summits" (the highest peak on each continent) was **Pat Morrow** of Canmore.

Fay Wray, born and raised in Cardston, had a date with an ape in the 1933 classic *King Kong*.

Aboriginal Peoples represents nonstatus Indians and status Indians living off reserves.

The First Nations are slowly but surely moving toward self-government, and in the process finding ways to have more involvement in decisions that affect their future. Some bands have already achieved self-government, along with a transfer of land ownership. Many reserves generate revenue from natural resources, and some bands have become wealthy by owning factories, housing developments, and, in the case of the Sarcee near Bragg Creek, a golf course. A monthly magazine, *Sweetgrass,* focuses on native issues in the province. For online articles and subscription information, go to the Aboriginal Multi-media Society website (www.ammsa.com).

Various names are used to describe aboriginal Canadians, and all can be correct in context. The government still uses the term "Indian," regardless of its links to Christopher Columbus's misconception that he had landed in India. "Native" is generally considered acceptable only when used in conjunction with "people," "communities," or "leaders." "Indigenous" or "aboriginal" can have insulting connotations when used in certain contexts. The First Nations people most often refer to themselves and others by none of the above, preferring to use band names.

Alberta's Métis population established a form of self-government in 1990, with the signing of the Métis Settlement Accord. This accord gave them ownership of more than 1.2 million acres, which included eight existing settlements, while still receiving federal government funding. The Métis Settlements General Council represents these people on a provincial level, while the Canadian Métis Council represents all "mixed-blood, nonstatus Aboriginals" nationally.

Nonnatives

In the last 100 years, Alberta has seen a great influx of people from around the world. The

Dominion census of 1881 recorded only 18,072 nonnatives in the province; Calgary had a population of only 75. The French, predominantly fur traders and missionaries, were the first permanent settlers and today constitute the fourth-largest ethnic group in the province. The first Asians to settle in the province were Chinese who came seeking gold in the 1860s and later settled, took up trades, and opened businesses.

One of the largest migrant influxes occurred between 1901 and 1906, when the Canadian government was selling tracts of land to homesteaders for $10. During this time, the population increased from 73,000 to 185,400; in another five years it doubled again. A large percentage of settlers during this period were British, and this group now constitutes Alberta's largest ethnic group. Germans also migrated to Alberta for various reasons and now constitute the province's second-largest ethnic group. Many people were lured by cheap land. Others, such as Hutterites, were persecuted in their homeland for refusing to fulfill military service. Sharing ancestry with the Amish (the main difference between the two is that Hutterites work and live as a cooperative). Around half of the world's 40,000 Hutterites call Alberta home. They have become the most successful of all ethnic groups at working the land, overseeing huge pork and poultry operations. They live a self-sufficient lifestyle in 180 tight-knit "colonies" throughout southern and central Alberta. Ukrainians make up the third-largest ethnic group. They were also attracted by the province's agricultural potential, and today more than 130,000 residents of Ukrainian descent live mostly in Edmonton and to the east.

The oil-and-gas boom brought a population explosion similar to that of 1901–1906, but this time, with one exception, the immigrants came from eastern provinces rather than from other countries. The exception was a wave of Americans, whose oil-business acumen and technological know-how were vital to the burgeoning industry. In Fort McMurray, there are enough Newfoundlanders to justify direct flights from St. John's and "Newfie nights" at local restaurants.

CULTURE
Religion
While the importance of religion in Alberta's history is undeniable, Albertans are less religious today than they were 50 or even 30 years ago. Also skewing the numbers somewhat is the fact that, as elsewhere in western society, many Albertans identify themselves with a specific religion, but do not attend services.

Christianity is the dominant faith in Alberta, with 70 percent of the population identifying themselves with this faith. Around 25 percent are not aligned with any specific religion, while the remaining five percent are mostly identified with Eastern faiths such as Islam. Roman Catholicism is the Christian denomination of choice for almost one in four Albertans. The other major Christian denominations represented in the province are Anglican and the United Church of Canada, with numbers of Presbyterian, Lutheran, and Baptist present but slowly declining. The Church of Jesus Christ of Latter-Day Saints is well represented in southwestern Alberta, especially in Cardston, which was settled by Mormons from Utah in 1887. Today, Mormonism is the religion of choice for around 75 percent of this town's population. Mirroring the rest of Canada, the number of Albertans considering themselves evangelicals—in organizations like the Pentecostal Assemblies, but also within existing denominations—is on the rise. Those that adhere to non-Christian religions such as Islam, Hinduism, and Buddhism are concentrated in Calgary and Edmonton, but pockets do exist outside of the big cities, with rural Brooks home to hundreds of Sudanese of Buddhist and Muslim faith.

Language
English is Alberta's official language and the first language of the vast majority of its residents. On a national level, Canada has two official languages—English and French. All communication from the federal government is in both languages, which becomes most apparent in national parks, where by law all signage and literature must be in both languages,

© ANDREW HEMPSTEAD

Cardston, in southern Alberta, is home to the first Mormon temple built outside of the United States.

and you will be greeted by parks' staff with "Hello, Bonjour." The Official Languages Act has many other components you will experience in everyday travel, including the requirement that Air Canada provide bilingual service and that most consumer goods sold within Canada have labeling in both English and French (exceptions include such things as books and items like jars of jam sold at fruit stands). French speakers (around 25 percent of the population) are concentrated in Quebec, but you'll experience pockets of Francophone culture in towns established by French fur traders, including at St. Paul and La Crete (both in northern Alberta). Most indigenous peoples speak English, although some elders hold their native tongue as a first language, including Nakoda, as spoken by the Stoney west of Calgary.

Country Music

For over a century, singers and songwriters have found inspiration in the ranching

WESTERN WEAR

You don't have to be able to ride a horse to dress like a cowboy – just ask the thousands of city folk who dress the part for the Calgary Stampede. Major department stores are the best places to find the basic Western accessories, whereas specialty shops are the places to go for gear that the real cowboys wear. Most of the latter sell handmade jewelry, authentic Stetsons, belt buckles big enough to fry an egg on, and hundreds of pairs of boots in every style imaginable. Calgary-based **Alberta Boot Company** is western Canada's only Western-boot manufacturer. With its longtime Albertan roots, **Lammle's** has grown to become one of North America's largest Western-wear retailers. It has 22 stores scattered around the province.

FESTIVALS AND EVENTS

Although a wide selection of Alberta's annual events are listed in the destination chapters, dozens of local and regional events take place around the province every month. To find additional events, check the Travel Alberta website (www.travelalberta.com) or visit local information centers. Below are some seasonal highlights.

SPRING

The year's first major event for cowboys is the **Rodeo Royal** held at Calgary's Saddledome in late March, followed the next weekend by the **Spring Outdoor Rodeo** in Medicine Hat and in April by the **Makin' 8 Silver Buckle Rodeo** in Red Deer. The annual spring migration of birds through the province is celebrated during the Tofield **Snow Goose Festival** through April. Calgary hosts an **International Children's Festival** in late May, with a wide variety of events for the younger generation. Alberta's winter resorts usually have snow on the ground until late spring, and many hold fun events at season's end, such as the **Slush Cup** at Sunshine Village.

SUMMER

Summer is the biggest event season in Alberta. Edmonton hosts a major festival just about every weekend, and something is almost always going on in the rest of the province as well.

The Gathering comes to Pincher Creek in mid-June. Hear cowpokes read poems by the light of the, uh, stars? Stars of another type come to perform at the **Calgary International Jazz Festival,** which takes place the last two weeks of June. The festival draws famous jazz musicians from around the world.

Canada Day, July 1, is a national holiday celebrated in many towns with various events, often including a rodeo (Ponoka hosts the largest of the week's rodeos). Vegreville celebrates its multicultural past on this weekend with the **Ukrainian Pysanka Festival.**

The best known of Alberta's events is the **Calgary Stampede,** the world's richest rodeo, with 10 days of action and a winner-take-all format. This Western extravaganza is a not-to-

© ANDREW HEMPSTEAD

The World Championship Miniature Chuckwagon Races are held at Cardston each summer.

lifestyle and mountain scenery of Alberta. In the 1930s, **Wilf Carter,** a cowboy by trade, began singing on Calgary radio. Within three years he had become a star in the United States as "Montana Slim," the yodeling cowboy. More recently, Albertans **Terri Clark, Paul Brandt, Carolyn Dawn Johnson,** and **Adam Gregory** have hit the big time south of the border. They followed the path carved by **k. d. lang,** of tiny Consort, who has more recently tended toward a mainstream dance/pop style of music, but who in the late 1980s became a country superstar with Grammy-winning albums pushing the boundaries of country music toward pop. Less known outside of Canada, **George Fox** and **Ian Tyson** have also made their mark on Canadian country music.

Large outdoor concerts that span over several days are popular venues for country music in

be-missed event that takes place over 10 days beginning the second Friday in July.

Equestrian events of a very different kind take place throughout summer just down the road from Stampede Park at **Spruce Meadows,** one of the world's finest international riding centers. The first event on the calendar, in early June, is the **National,** a show-jumping competition attracting thousands of enthusiasts.

In early July, the **International Street Performers Festival** offers more than 1,000 free performances at outdoor venues throughout Edmonton, while later in the month, Edmonton hosts the music and fun-filled **Capital Ex** and the **Edmonton Heritage Festival,** a celebration of Edmonton's history. In southern Alberta, the **Medicine Hat Exhibition and Stampede,** held annually since 1887, and **Rum Runner Days** in the Crowsnest Pass, are in mid-July. The third Saturday in July is **Parks Day,** which is celebrated by pancake breakfasts, guided hikes, and interpretive events in national and provincial parks throughout Alberta. **Jazz Festival Calgary** takes place in late June, and in July the city hosts a **folk music festival.** July ends on a high note with the **Red Deer International Air Show** on the last weekend, featuring performances by some of the world's best stunt pilots.

In early August is Canmore's popular **folk music festival.** The **Edmonton Folk Music Festival** picks and strums its way into town in early August, and **The Fringe,** held in Edmonton mid-August, is North America's largest alternative-theater festival. Calgary's cultural festivals are low-profile affairs compared to those in the capital, but the city does offer **Af-**

rikadey! in mid-August. The middle weekend of August is busy in southern Alberta, with rodeos in Pincher Creek and Bar U Ranch, while the Cardston Carriage Museum hosts the **World Championship Miniature Chuckwagon Races.** Also down south, the following weekend is Lethbridge's **Whoop-Up Days,** celebrating that city's colorful past.

FALL

Just when all of the summer festivals are winding down, the action at Spruce Meadows equestrian center, outside Calgary, is heating up. Held the first weekend of September, **Spruce Meadows Masters** is the world's richest show-jumping event and the finale to a packed season. At the same time, in the north of the province, the air over Grande Prairie is also alive with color with the **Canadian Hot Air Balloon Championships.** Jointly hosted by Calgary and Banff, the mid-October **Wordfest** is a popular literary gathering. The first weekend of November is **Banff Mountain Film Festival,** a gathering of the world's greatest adventure-film makers.

WINTER

Most Albertan towns and cities have **winter carnivals** featuring weird and wonderful events that only people affected by the long winter could dream up. The largest ones, each lasting two weeks in January, are in Calgary, Banff, Jasper, and Edmonton. The one in Canmore, in late January, is held in conjunction with the **International Dog Sled Race. First Night** is an alcohol-free celebration of the New Year that takes place in downtown Calgary and Edmonton.

Alberta. The biggest of these is the **Big Valley Jamboree,** at Camrose during the first weekend of August.

Although most cities have dance clubs and rock 'n' roll discos, Alberta's heritage lives on through the night in the country-music bars. Those like the **Ranchman's** in Calgary; **Cook County Saloon** in Edmonton; and dozens of small-town bars across the province keep the Western image alive. Many Western-style ven-

ues attract a more mainstream crowd by offering a wider variety of music, such as **Wild Bill's** in Banff, or a party atmosphere complete with scantily clad shooter girls, such as **Cowboys** in Edmonton.

Arts and Crafts

The arts and crafts of Canada's indigenous people are available throughout the province. Jewelry, beaded moccasins, baskets,

and leatherwork such as headdresses are favorite souvenirs. The stylistic art of the native people is also popular, but prints of the most recognizable works run into the thousands of dollars. Two of the best outlets are the **Indian Trading Post** in Banff and the **Craft Gallery Shop** in Edmonton. The **Alberta Craft Council** (780/488-6611, www.albertacraft.ab.ca) represents craft shops throughout Alberta and lists exhibitions on its website.

ESSENTIALS

Getting There

BY AIR

Calgary and Edmonton have international airports served by major airlines from throughout the world. Many flights from south of the border are routed through Calgary before continuing to Edmonton, giving you a choice of final destinations for little or no price difference.

Air Canada

Canada's national airline, Air Canada (514/ 393-3333 or 888/247-2262, www.aircanada.com) is one of the world's largest airlines. It offers direct flights to Calgary from all major Canadian cities, as well as from Los Angeles; San Francisco; Las Vegas; Denver; Phoenix; Houston; Chicago; Washington, D.C.; Dallas/Fort Worth; New York; and Orlando. Direct flights to Edmonton originate in all major Canadian cities west of Montreal, while flights from the U.S. cities noted above are routed through Calgary.

From Europe, Air Canada flies directly from London and Frankfurt to Calgary, and from other major European cities via Toronto. From the South Pacific, Air Canada operates flights via Honolulu from Sydney and in alliance with Air New Zealand from Auckland and other South Pacific islands to Honolulu and Los Angeles, where passengers change to an Air Canada plane

© ANDREW HEMPSTEAD

Alberta's most remote community, Fort Chipewyan, is linked to the outside world by Air Mikisew.

for the flight to Calgary. Asian cities served by direct Air Canada flights to Vancouver include Beijing, Nagoya, Osaka, Seoul, Shanghai, Taipei, and Tokyo. Air Canada's flights originating in the South American cities of Buenos Aires, Sao Paulo, Lima, and Bogota are routed through Toronto, where you'll need to change planes for either Calgary or Edmonton.

WestJet

Similar in concept to Southwest Airlines in the United States, WestJet (604/606-5525 or 800/538-5696, www.westjet.com) has daily flights to its Calgary hub, as well as to Edmonton from the following Canadian cities: Victoria, Vancouver, Regina, Saskatoon, Winnipeg, Thunder Bay, Hamilton, Toronto, Ottawa, Montreal, Halifax, and as far east as St. John's, Newfoundland.

U.S. Airlines

Air Canada offers flights into Alberta from the United States, but either Calgary or Edmonton

or both of the cities are also served by the following U.S. carriers: **Alaska Airlines** (800/252-7522, www.alaskaair.com) from Anchorage and Los Angeles; **American Airlines** (800/433-7300, www.aa.com) from Chicago and Dallas; **Continental Airlines** (800/231-0856, www.continental.com) from its Houston hub and New York (Newark); **Delta** (800/221-1212, www.delta.com) with summer-only flights from Atlanta and Salt Lake City; **Frontier Airlines** (800/432-1359, www.frontierairlines.com) from Denver; **Harmony Airways** (866/868-6789, www.harmonyairways.com) from Honolulu, Kauai, and Los Angeles; **Horizon Air** (800/547-9308, www.horizonair.com) from nearby Seattle; **Northwest Airlines** (800/225-2525, www.nwa.com) from Detroit, Memphis, and Minneapolis; **Skywest** (800/221-1212, www.skywest.com) from Salt Lake City; and finally **United Airlines** (800/241-6522, www.united.com) from Chicago, Denver, San Francisco, and Seattle.

AIR TAXES

Where do I start? The advertised airfare that looks so tempting is just a base fare, devoid of a raft of fees and taxes collected by numerous government agencies. On domestic flights within Canada, expect to pay around $80-100. This includes an **Air Travellers Security Tax** ($6 each sector for domestic flights, $17 for international flights), an insurance surcharge of $3 each way, and a fee of $9-20 each way that goes to **NAV Canada** for the operation of the federal navigation system. Advertised domestic fares are inclusive of **fuel surcharges,** but on international flights expect to pay up to $200 extra. All major Canadian airports charge an **Airport Improvement Fee** to all departing passengers, with Calgary charging $15 per passenger. You'll also need to pay this fee from your original departure point, and if connecting through Toronto another $8 is collected. And, of course, the above taxes are taxable, with the Canadian government collecting the 6 percent goods and services tax. There is a bright side to paying these extras: It is made easy for consumers, with airlines lumping all the charges together and into the ticket price.

International Airlines

Aside from the direct London and Frankfurt flights, Air Canada flights between continental Europe and Calgary are routed through Toronto. For all flights from the South Pacific, connections must be made in Los Angeles or Vancouver to either Calgary or Edmonton. Use your travel agent or the websites given in this section to find the best fares and connections. **Qantas** (800/227-4500, www.qantas.com.au) flies to Vancouver via Honolulu from Sydney, Melbourne, and Brisbane. **Air New Zealand** (800/663-5494, www.nzair.com) operates in alliance with Air Canada for flights to Calgary, with a variety of interesting options including stops in South Pacific destinations like Nandi (Fiji).

BY RAIL

This form of transportation, which opened up the West to settlers and the Canadian Rockies to tourists, began to fade with the advent of efficient air services. Scheduled services along the original transcontinental line through Calgary and Banff ended in 1991, but continue along a northern route that passes through Edmonton and Jasper.

VIA Rail

The *Canadian* runs between Toronto and Vancouver via Edmonton and Jasper three days a week in either direction and provides two classes of travel: Economy, which features lots of leg room, reclining seats, reading lights, pillows and blankets, and a Skyline Car complete with bar service; and Silver and Blue, which is more luxurious, featuring a variety of sleeping-room configurations, daytime seating, a domed lounge and dining car reserved exclusively for passengers in this class, shower kits for all passengers, and all meals.

If you're traveling to Alberta from the eastern provinces, the least expensive way to travel is on a **Canrailpass,** which allows unlimited travel anywhere on the VIA Rail system for 12 days within any given 30-day period. During high season (June 1–Oct. 15) the pass is adult $813, senior (over 60) and child $732, with extra days (up to three are allowed) $69 and $63, respectively. The rest of the year the fare is adult $508, senior and child $457, with extra days $43 and $38, respectively. VIA Rail has cooperated with Amtrak (800/872-7245) to offer the North America Rail Pass, with all the same seasonal dates and discounts as the Canrailpass. The cost for unlimited travel over 30 days is adult $1,149, senior and child $1,034; $815 and $734 respectively through the low season.

On regular fares, discounts of 25–40 percent apply to travel in all classes October–June.

CUTTING FLIGHT COSTS

Ticket structuring for air travel has traditionally been so complex that finding the best deal required some time and patience (or a good travel agent), but the process has gotten a lot easier in recent years. Air Canada leads the way, with streamlined ticketing options that are easy to understand.

The first step when planning your trip to Alberta is to contact the airlines that fly to Calgary or Edmonton and search out the best price they have for the time of year you wish to travel. While the Internet has changed the way many people shop for tickets, even if you use this invaluable tool for preliminary research, having a travel agent that you are comfortable dealing with – who takes the time to call around, does some research to get you the best fare, and helps you take advantage of any available special offers or promotional deals – is an invaluable asset in starting your travels off on the right foot.

In addition to your local agent, **Travel Cuts** (866/246-9762, www.travelcuts.com) and **Flight Centre** (877/967-5302, www.flight centre.ca), both with offices in all major cities, consistently offer the lowest airfares available, with the latter guaranteeing the lowest. Flight Centre offers a similar guarantee from its U.S. offices (866/967-5351, www.flightcentre.us), as well as those in Great Britain (tel. 0870/499-0040, www.flightcentre.co.uk), Australia (tel. 13-31-33, www.flightcentre.com.au), New Zealand (tel. 0800/24-35-44, www.flightcentre .co.nz), and South Africa (tel. 0860/400-727,

www.flightcentre.co.za). All Flight Centre toll-free numbers will put you through to the closest office from where you are calling. In London, **Trailfinders** (215 Kensington High St., Kensington, tel. 020/7938-3939, www.trailfinders .com) always has good deals to Canada and other North American destinations. Or use the services of an Internet-only company such as **Travelocity** (www.travelocity.com) or **Expedia** (www.expedia.com). The Dream Maps function on the Travelocity site (click on Dream Maps from the site map) is a fun and functional way to search for the best fares from your own home city. Also look in the travel sections of major newspapers – particularly in weekend editions – where budget fares and package deals are frequently advertised.

Many cheaper tickets have strict restrictions regarding changes of flight dates, lengths of stay, and cancellations. A general rule: The cheaper the ticket, the more restrictions. Most travelers today fly on APEX (advance-purchase excursion) fares. These are usually the best value, though some (and, occasionally, many) restrictions apply. These might include minimum and maximum stays and nonchangeable itineraries (or hefty penalties for changes); tickets may also be nonrefundable once purchased.

Edward Hasbrouck's *The Practical Nomad Guide to the Online Travel Marketplace* (Avalon Travel Publishing, 2001) is an excellent resource for working through the maze of online travel-planning possibilities.

Those over 60 and under 18, as well as students under 25, receive an additional 10 percent discount that can be combined with other seasonal fares. Check for advance-purchase restrictions on all discount tickets.

Rocky Mountaineer

Rocky Mountaineer Vacations (604/606-7245 or 877/460-3200, www.rockymountaineer .com) runs a luxurious rail trip between Vancouver and Banff or Jasper, through the spectacular interior mountain ranges of British

Columbia. Travel is during daylight hours only so you don't miss anything. Trains depart in either direction in the morning (every second or third day), overnighting at Kamloops. One-way travel in RedLeaf Service, which includes light meals, nonalcoholic drinks, and Kamloops accommodations, costs $749 per person d, $829 s from Vancouver to either Banff or Jasper and $819 and $899 respectively from Vancouver to Calgary. GoldLeaf Service is the ultimate in luxury. Passengers ride in a two-story glass-domed car, eat in a separate dining

area, and stay in Kamloops's most luxurious accommodations. GoldLeaf costs $1,499 per person d, $1,579 s from Vancouver to Banff or Jasper and $1,619 and $1,699 respectively to Calgary. Similarly priced is the Fraser Discovery Route, which links Whistler to Jasper via the Cariboo region of central British Columbia. Outside of high season (mid-April to May and the first two weeks of October), all fares are reduced around $150 per person in RedLeaf and $200 per person in GoldLeaf.

BY BUS

Greyhound (403/260-0877 or 800/661-8747, www.greyhound.ca) serves areas throughout Canada. From Vancouver, the main routes are along the TransCanada Highway to Banff and Calgary, and a more northern route through to Jasper and Edmonton. From the east, buses depart Toronto daily for Calgary and Edmonton along two different routes. If you're traveling to Alberta from the United States, get yourself to Great Falls, Montana, from where regular services continue north to the Coutts-Sweetgrass port of entry. There you change to a Canadian Greyhound bus. Calgary buses depart from the port of entry daily at 12:10 P.M.

Travel by Greyhound is simple—just roll up at the depot and buy a ticket. No reservations are necessary. Greyhound bus depots in all major Albertan cities are close to inexpensive accommodations and public transportation.

When calling for ticket information, ask about any special deals—including the **Go Anywhere Fare,** on which you can travel between any two points in North America for one low fare; $129 one way and $199 round-trip if bought 14 days in advance. Other discounts apply to regular-fare tickets bought 7 and 14 days in advance, travelers 65 and over, and two people traveling together. Greyhound's **Discovery Pass,** valid for unlimited travel throughout North America, is sold in periods of seven days ($283), 10 days ($415), 30 days ($522), and 60 days ($645). Passes can be bought 14 or more days in advance online, seven or more days in advance from any Canadian bus depot, or up to the day of departure from U.S. depots.

BY CAR OR RV

Most visitors to Alberta travel in their own vehicle or rent one upon arrival. Driver's licenses from all countries are valid in the province for up to three months. You should also obtain a one-year **International Driving Permit** before leaving home (U.S. licensed drivers do not require an IDP to drive in Canada). Inexpensive and available from most motoring organizations, they allow you to drive in Alberta (in conjunction with your regular license), without taking a test, for up to three months. You should also carry car registration papers or rental contracts. Proof of insurance must also be carried, and you must wear seat belts. All highway signs in Alberta give distances in **kilometers** and speeds in **kilometers per hour** (kph). The speed limit on major highways is 100 kph (62 mph).

Insurance

If entering Canada from the United States in

Mile Zero of the Mackenzie Highway in northern Alberta is the start of the only highway in Alberta to go all the way to the top of the province.

your own vehicle, check that your insurance covers travel in Canada. U.S. motorists are advised to obtain a Canadian Non-resident Interprovincial Motor Vehicle Liability Insurance Card, available through U.S. insurance companies, which is accepted as evidence of financial responsibility in Canada.

When renting a vehicle in Canada you have the option of purchasing a Loss Damage Waiver, along with other types of insurance, such as for your personal effects. Before leaving home, find out if you're already covered. Many people are—through gold credit cards, higher levels of motoring association membership, or home insurance (in the case of personal effects)—and additional coverage may be unnecessary.

Crossing into Canada by Land

Ports of Entry (border crossings) are spread at regular intervals along the entire U.S.-Canada border. The main port of entry into Alberta, and the only one open year-round 24 hours daily, is **Coutts-Sweetgrass,** north of Great Falls, Montana, along Highway 14. Beyond the border is a Travel Alberta Visitor Information Centre, from where it's 100 kilometers (62 mi) to Lethbridge and 310 kilometers (193 mi) to Calgary. If you're entering Alberta after visiting Montana's Glacier National Park, two ports of entry provide access—**Carway-Piegan** (year-round daily 7 A.M.–11 P.M.) and to the west **Chief Mountain** (mid-May–Sept. daily 9 A.M.–6 P.M. with extended hours June–Aug. 7 A.M.–10 P.M.). North of Havre, Montana, is the **Wild Horse** port of entry (mid-May–Sept. 8 A.M.–9 P.M. and Oct.–mid-May 8 A.M.–5 P.M.). Highway 41 north from Wild Horse leads 80 kilometers (50 mi) to Cypress Hills Provincial Park and a further 60 kilometers (37 mi) to Medicine Hat.

See *Visas and Officialdom* later in this chapter for more information on foreign entry to Canada. Also check the Citizenship and Immigration Canada website (www.cic.gc.ca) for the latest regulations.

Getting Around

BY AIR

Air Canada (514/393-3333 or 888/247-2262, www.aircanada.com) and its connectors offer scheduled flights to the two main cities and many larger towns within the province, including Calgary, Lethbridge, Medicine Hat, Edmonton, Grande Prairie, Fort McMurray, and High Level. **Peace Air** (780/624-3060 or 800/563-3060, www.peaceair.com) links Calgary and Edmonton to the northern town of Peace River. **Central Mountain Air** (888/865-8585, www.flycma.com) flies between Calgary and Edmonton, as well as farther afield to British Columbian centers.

BY RAIL

The only scheduled rail service within the province is between Jasper and Edmonton. This thrice-weekly service is part of the transcontinental route. For further information on VIA Rail services, see the *Getting There* section of this chapter.

BY BUS

Greyhound (403/265-9111 or 800/661-8747, www.greyhound.ca) bus routes radiate from Calgary and Edmonton to points throughout the province. Service is regular, fast, and efficient. The only downside is that in larger centers, bus depots are often located in seedy parts of town. Many depots have cafeterias, some have lockers, but none of them remain open all night.

Red Arrow (780/424-3339 or 800/232-1958, www.redarrow.pwt.ca) operates a more luxurious service that connects Calgary and Edmonton five to seven times daily, continuing twice daily to the oil-sands city of Fort McMurray. All Red Arrow buses are equipped with fold-down tables, a row of single seats on

one side of the bus, laptop plug-ins, and a range of complimentary refreshments.

Brewster (403/221-8242, www.brewster.ca) provides coach service between Calgary and Banff and Jasper National Parks. Brewster's advantage over Greyhound is that its service departs from Calgary International Airport and major Calgary hotels. One-way fare to Banff is $50, to Lake Louise $58, and to Jasper $94.

CAR AND RV RENTAL

All major car-rental agencies have outlets at Calgary and Edmonton International Airports as well as multiple city locations throughout the province. To ensure that a vehicle is available for you when you arrive, book in advance, especially through the busy June–September period.

In summer, expect to pay around $60 per day for an "economy" or "compact" car, $75 for an "intermediate," $85–100 for a "full-size," and over $100 for an SUV. Between late September and mid-June all vehicles are heavily discounted, with smaller vehicles available from $30 per day and $200 per week. All major agencies now offer unlimited mileage, but not for rentals originating in Banff or Jasper National Parks. Check to confirm this policy. In all cases, insurance costs from $20 per day and is compulsory unless covered by a personal policy or on your credit card. Charges apply if you need to drop off the car at an agency other than the rental location. All agencies provide free pickup and drop-off at major city hotels.

Vehicles can be booked through parent companies in the United States or elsewhere using the Web or toll-free numbers. **Discount** (403/299-1202 or 800/263-2355, www.discount car.com) is a Canadian company with 200 rental outlets across the country. Their vehicles are kept in service a little longer than the other majors, but they provide excellent rates, especially if booked in advance and even through summer. Other companies include **Alamo** (800/462-5266, www.alamo.com), **Avis** (800/974-0808, www.avis.ca), **Budget** (800/268-8900, www.budget.com), **Dollar** (800/800-4000, www.dollar.com), **Enterprise** (800/325-8007, www.enterprise.com), **Hertz** (800/263-0600,

www.hertz.ca), **National** (800/227-7368, www.nationalcar.com), **Rent-a-wreck** (800/327-0116, www.rentawreck.ca), and **Thrifty** (800/847-4389, www.thrifty.com).

RV Rental

Campervans and RVs (recreation vehicles) are a great way to get around Alberta without having to worry about accommodations each night. The downside is cost. The smallest vans, capable of sleeping two people, start at $100 per day with 100 free kilometers per day. Extra charges include insurance, a preparation fee (usually around $50 per rental), a linen/cutlery charge (around $60 per person per trip), and taxes. Major agencies, with rental outlets in Calgary, include **Cruise Canada** (403/291-4963 or 800/327-7799, or, in the U.S., 800/327-7778, www.cruisecanada.com), **Canadream** (403/291-1000 or 800/461-7368, www.canadream.com), and **Go West** (403/240-1814 or 800/661-8813, www.go-west.com). In most cases, a drop-off fee of $400 applies to drop-offs made in Vancouver from rentals originating in Calgary, or vice versa. At the end of the summer season (early September), look for some great online bargains.

TOURS

Day tours are offered in Calgary, Banff, and Jasper. These tours are a great way to orient yourself to the region and are relatively inexpensive. The main tour operator is **Brewster** (403/762-6700 or 877/791-5500, www.brewster.ca), which also offers tours to various parts of the province, as well as car rental and accommodation packages, overnight packages in Calgary and Edmonton, Calgary Stampede packages, golfing adventures, and round-trips to Alberta from Vancouver, British Columbia. Rocky Mountaineer Vacations (see *Getting There*) offer a wide variety of longer tours in conjunction with rail travel between Vancouver and Banff or Jasper.

Backpacker Bus

For young travelers on a budget, the **Moose Travel Network** (604/777-9905 or 888/244-6673, www.moosenetwork.com) is an excellent

way to travel to and around Alberta, with most of the focus on the Canadian Rockies. It runs along a number of different routes, including an 11-day loop originating in Vancouver and traveling to Jasper and Banff via Whistler ($520 per person), a five-day trip between Vancouver and Banff via the Okanagan Valley ($305), a two-day Banff–Jasper–Banff trip ($120), and a two-day Banff–Vancouver shuttle ($120). On any of these trips, you can get on and off wherever you please (and jump aboard the next bus as it passes through) or bond with the crowd and stay on the fixed itinerary. Nights are spent at hostels en route. This cost isn't included in the tour, but your reservation is (so you don't need to worry about trying to find an empty bed at each stop). Food is also extra, but often all travelers pitch in a token amount to purchase dinner at a grocery store along the way. Buses run 3–7 times a week through a May to mid-October season.

Visas and Officialdom

ENTERING CANADA
U.S. Citizens
Traditionally, U.S. citizens and permanent residents have needed only to present some form of identification that proves citizenship and/or residency to enter Canada. But as of January 23, 2007, the United States began requiring its citizens traveling by air to present a passport for reentry to the United States in accordance with the Western Hemisphere Travel Initiative. From January 1, 2008 the program will expand to include U.S. citizens reentering the United States by land and sea, who will also be required to present a passport. Therefore, it is imperative to carry a passport, even though one is not technically required for entry to Canada. For the latest, check out the travel section of the U.S. Department of State website (http://travel.state.gov). A good resource for passport information is www.getpassportnow.com.

Other Foreign Visitors
All other foreign visitors entering Canada must have a valid passport and may need a visitor permit or Temporary Resident Visa depending on their country of residence and the vagaries of international politics. At present, visas are not required for citizens of the United States, British Commonwealth, or Western Europe. The standard entry permit is for six months, and you may be asked to show onward tickets or proof of sufficient funds to last you through your intended stay. Extensions are available from the Citizenship and Immigration Canada office in Calgary. This department's website (www.cic.gc.ca) is the best source of the latest entry requirements.

CUSTOMS
You can take the following into Canada duty-free: reasonable quantities of clothes and personal effects, 50 cigars and 200 cigarettes, 200 grams of tobacco, 1.14 liters of spirits or wine, food for personal use, and gas (normal tank capacity). Pets from the United States can generally be brought into Canada, with certain caveats. Dogs and cats must be more than three months old and have a rabies certificate showing date of vaccination. Birds can be brought in only if they have not been mixing with other birds, and parrots need an export permit because they're on the endangered species list.

Handguns, automatic and semiautomatic weapons, and sawn-off rifles and shotguns are not allowed into Canada. Visitors with firearms must declare them at the border; restricted weapons will be held by Customs and can be picked up on exit from the country. Those not declared will be seized and charges may be laid. It is illegal to possess any firearm in a national park unless it is dismantled or carried in an enclosed case. Up to 5,000 rounds of ammunition may be imported but should be declared on entry.

On reentering the United States, if you've been in Canada more than 48 hours you can bring back up to US$400 worth of household and personal items, excluding alcohol and tobacco, duty-free. If you've been in Canada fewer than 48 hours, you may bring in only up to US$200 worth of such items duty-free.

For further information on all customs regulations contact **Canada Border Services Agency** (204/983-3500 or 800/461-9999, www.cbsa-asfc.gc.ca).

Recreation

The great outdoors is one of Alberta's prime attractions, and a diverse array of activities is available to those who seek them out. The mountains are the center of most activity. Raft and canoe tours operate on many mountain rivers, and the vast wilderness provides virtually limitless opportunities for camping, photography, and wildlife-viewing. The national parks are a major draw for hikers and climbers in summer, and downhill and cross-country skiers in winter. Fishing is good in almost all lakes and rivers in the province, and golfers can enjoy more than 230 courses. A comprehensive listing of all outfitters and tour operators is available from **Travel Alberta** (P.O. Box 2500, Edmonton, Alberta T5J 2Z1, 780/427-4321 or 800/252-3782, www.travelalberta.com).

HIKING

Hiking is, not surprisingly, the most popular outdoor activity in Alberta because it's free, anyone can participate, and the mountains offer some of the world's most spectacular scenery. **Banff National Park** holds the greatest variety of trails in the province. Here you can find anything from short interpretive trails with little elevation gain to strenuous slogs up high alpine passes. Trailheads for most of the best hikes are accessible by public transportation or on foot from the town of Banff. Trails farther north begin at higher elevations, from which access to the high country is less painful. The trails in **Jasper National Park** are oriented more toward the experienced backpacker, offering plentiful routes for long backcountry trips. Other areas popular for hiking are **Kananaskis Country,** where crowds are minimal; **Waterton Lakes National Park,** where many trails lead to beautiful subalpine lakes; and the province's four wilderness areas, which are located in remote mountain regions accessible only on foot.

Heli-hiking is an out-of-the-ordinary way to experience the high alpine without making the elevation gain on foot. The day starts with a helicopter ride into the alpine, where short guided hikes are offered and a picnic lunch is served. For details, contact **Alpine Helicopters** (403/678-4802). Another option is hiking into backcountry lodges. The **Alpine Club of Canada** (403/678-3200, www.alpine clubofcanada.ca) maintains a series of huts, each generally a full-day hike from the nearest road. Banff and Jasper National Parks have several privately owned backcountry lodges—great bases for day hiking—where on-site hosts provide hot meals; rates start at $180 per person per day including meals. Hikers must register at park information centers for all overnight hikes in national parks.

CYCLING AND MOUNTAIN BIKING

Alberta is perfect for both road biking and mountain biking. On-road cyclists appreciate the wide shoulders on all main highways, whereas those on mountain bikes enjoy the many designated trails in the mountain national parks. One of the most challenging and scenic on-road routes is the **Icefields Parkway** between Lake Louise and Jasper, which has several well-placed hostels along its length. Bike rentals are available in all cities and resort towns. Expect to pay $5–7 per hour and

PARKS AND PROTECTED AREAS

Alberta has five **national parks,** 68 **provincial parks,** 32 **wildland parks,** 16 **ecological reserves,** four **wilderness areas,** 150 **natural areas,** 248 **provincial recreation areas,** and one **forest reserve.** Combined, they encompass all of the province's most spectacular natural features, are home to many of Alberta's mammals, provide safe nesting areas for millions of birds, and protect areas that would otherwise be given over to agriculture or other resource-based industry.

NATIONAL PARKS

Created in 1885, **Banff National Park** was the first member of Canada's grand national park system. As well as being home to the jewel of the Canadian national parks system, Alberta holds four other equally unique parks. **Waterton Lakes,** to the south of Banff, and **Jasper,** to the north, are similarly beautiful mountain parks. The others are **Elk Island National Park,** where mammal densities are similar to those on the Serengeti Plain, and **Wood Buffalo National Park,** the second-largest national park in the world, which is accessible by road only through the Northwest Territories.

Parks Canada manages Canada's national park system, which consists of 39 parks spread across every province and territory, combining to represent all of the country's natural landscapes. Each of Alberta's five national parks has a year-round information center, or check out the Parks Canada website (www.pc.gc.ca).

PROVINCIAL PARKS

Provincial parks, numbering 70 throughout Alberta, protect areas of natural, historical, and cultural importance while providing ample recreational opportunities. All of the parks offer day-use facilities, and many more have campgrounds and summer interpretive programs. Those not to miss are **Glenbow Ranch Provincial Park,** along the Bow River on Calgary's western outskirts; **Writing-on-Stone Provincial Park,** so named for the abundant native rock art; **Dinosaur Provincial Park,** a UNESCO World Heritage Site with one of the world's highest concentrations of dinosaur bones; and **Cypress Hills Provincial Park,** a forested oasis that rises from the prairies. Provincial parks are managed by the Parks and Protected Areas division of

---

$22–28 per day for a regular town bike and up to $20 per hour and $60 per day for a full-suspension mountain bike.

The **Alberta Bicycle Association** (780/427-6352, www.albertabicycle.ab.ca) represents all racing and touring clubs in the province and can provide further information.

Cycle Tours

The three companies detailed below all concentrate on touring through the mountainous portion of the province. **Backroads** (510/527-1555 or 800/462-2848, www.backroads.com) has trips designed to suit all levels of fitness and all budgets. An average of six hours is spent cycling each day, but there's also always the option of riding in the support van. You can choose to stay in mid-priced accommodations (US$2,200 for six days) or stay in grand

mountain lodges (US$2,900 for six days). **VBT** (800/245-3868, www.vbt.com) offers a seven-day ride through the four contiguous national parks with midrange lodging and all meals included in the price of US$1,700. Affiliated with Trek bikes, it's upscale all the way with **Trek Travel** (920/478-4672 or 866/464-8735, www.trektravel.com, US$2,100–2,800 per person).

HORSEBACK RIDING

Horses are a traditional means of transportation in the Canadian West; many of the roads began as horse trails. Through the foothills, ranches still dominate the landscape, and at places like **Griffin Valley Ranch,** near Cochrane (403/932-7433, www.griffinvalley ranch.ca), unguided riding is permitted. Within the national parks, horse travel is re-

RECREATION   **497**

the Department of Community Development. If you're in the capital, it's worth visiting the department-run **Alberta Natural Heritage Information Centre** (2nd Floor, Oxbridge Place, 9820 106th St., Edmonton, 780/427-3582, www.cd.gov.ab.ca).

OTHER PARKS AND PROTECTED AREAS

Alberta's Provincial Parks Act of 1930 has evolved into the Recreation and Protected Areas Network, which incorporates all of the following designations:

Wilderness areas and **wildland parks** are just that – totally wild and total wilderness. These remote locations have no road access, making them perfect for wilderness trips for those with backcountry experience.

Also offering a high level of protection are **ecological reserves.** These are generally remote tracts of land and, although open to the public, they have been established under the Ecological Reserves Program primarily for scientific research.

Pockets of land that represent the diversity of Alberta's natural habitats are protected in **natural areas.** Certain forms of recreation are permitted, but natural areas are generally left in their natural state, with no facilities.

Finally, dotted throughout the province are provincial recreation areas, typically roadside stops in scenic locations or staging areas beside rivers, but always very accessible. Picnic facilities are provided, and some offer basic camping facilities.

All of these areas are managed by the **Department of Sustainable Resource Development** (Great West Life Building, 9920 108th St., Edmonton, 780/944-0313, www.srd.gov.ab.ca).

FOREST RESERVES

The Department of Sustainable Resource Development also manages forested lands and associated waterways. Most of these lands are scattered throughout the foothills and northern Alberta. Basic recreational facilities such as day-use areas and rustic campgrounds are provided free of charge. The Forestry Trunk Road, extending 1,000 kilometers (620 mi) between the Crowsnest Pass and Grande Prairie, traverses much of the province's forest-service land.

---

stricted to certain areas, but trail riding is a popular way to enjoy the scenery.

If you really want to get a feeling for Western life, consider taking an overnight horseback pack-trip. In the mountains, many of these guides have been operating since before the parks were established. Outside the parks, riding is available at many ranches and outfitting operations in the foothills and at Grande Cache. On an overnight trip, expect to ride for up to six hours per day, with nights spent at a remote mountain lodge or a tent camp, usually in a scenic location where you can hike, fish, or ride further. Rates range $150–200 per person per day, which includes the riding, accommodations, and food. These trips are offered near Canmore by **Brewster Mountain Pack Trains** (403/762-5454 or 800/691-5085, www.brewsteradventures

.com); in Banff National Park by **Warner Guiding and Outfitting** (403/762-4551 or 800/661-8352, www.horseback.com); and in Jasper National Park by **Skyline Trail Rides** (780/852-4215 or 888/852-7787) or **Tonquin Valley Adventures** (780/852-1188, www.tonquinadventures.com).

Guest ranches, where accommodations and meals are included in nightly packages, include **Brewster's Kananaskis Guest Ranch,** east of Canmore (403/673-3737 or 800/691-5085, www.brewsteradventures.com); **Boundary Ranch,** in Kananaskis Country (403/591-7171, www.boundaryranch.com); and **Black Cat Guest Ranch,** on the eastern outskirts of Jasper National Park (780/865-3084 or 800/859-6840, www.blackcatguestranch.ca). Expect to pay $140–180 per person per day for accommodations, meals, and trail riding.

NATIONAL PARK PASSES

Passes are required for entry into four of Alberta's five national parks (the exception is Wood Buffalo). The cost of a **National Parks Day Pass** is adult $6.50-9, senior $5.50-7.75, and child $3.50-4.50, depending on the park. There is a maximum per-vehicle entry fee of double the adult (or senior for vehicles carrying only seniors) rate. Passes are interchangeable between parks and are valid until 4 P.M. the day following purchase. An annual **National Parks of Canada Pass,** good for entry into all Canadian national parks for one year from the date of purchase, is adult $63, senior $54, to a maximum of $125 per vehicle. The annual **Discovery Package** includes entry into all parks as well as Parks Canada-managed National Historic Sites for adult $78, senior $67, child $39, to a maximum of $157 per vehicle.

Passes can be purchased at park gates, at all park information centers, and at campground fee stations. For more information, check the Parks Canada website (www.pc.gc.ca).

FISHING

Of 63 fish species present in Albertan waters, 18 are regarded as sport fish. Fishing is productive in almost all of Alberta's lakes, rivers, and streams. Over 300 lakes are stocked at least once annually. Although fishing is good throughout the province, dedicated anglers gravitate to the Bow and Crowsnest rivers, where fly-fishing is world-renowned, and to northern Alberta for trophy-sized lake trout and northern pike.

Rainbow trout are to western Canada what bass are to the eastern United States—a great fighting fish. They are found in lakes and rivers throughout Alberta and are the most common of the stocked fish because they are easy to raise and adapt to varying conditions. You can catch them on artificial flies, small spin-

ners, or spoons. The largest species of trout is the lake trout. The largest "lakies" generally come from northern lakes, including **Cold Lake,** where the 52-kilogram (115-lb) provincial record dates back to 1929. These fish live in the deep waters of the large lakes, so a motorboat is needed. In Banff National Park, **Lake Minnewanka** is an easily accessible lake-trout fishing center, with boats and tackle for rent and guides offering their services. Cutthroat trout inhabit the cold and clear waters of the highest mountain lakes, which generally involves hiking in to reach them. Fishing for cutthroat requires using the lightest of tackle because the water is generally very clear; fly-casting is most productive on the still water of lakes, whereas spinning is the preferred river-fishing method. Brook trout aren't native to Alberta, but they are found in rivers and lakes throughout the foothills and mountains. They are difficult to catch but grow to a decent size (two kg/4.4 lb is not uncommon). Brown trout, introduced from Europe, are found in some streams in the foothills of Kananaskis Country as well as in the Bow River. They are most often caught on dry flies, but they are difficult to hook onto. Golden trout, introduced from California, have been stocked in lakes west of Pincher Creek.

Walleye (also called pickerel) grow to 4.5 kilograms (10 lb) and are common in sandy-bottomed areas of lakes throughout the prairies. They are a popular catch with anglers, mostly because they taste so good. They feed only at night or in muddy waters, so catching them is more of a challenge than trout. They are most often caught using minnows or by jigging. Another species that prefers muddy waters, notably in the Red Deer River, is the goldeye. The monster fish of Alberta is the northern pike (also known as jackfish), whose length can exceed one meter; the provincial record is 17 kilograms (38 lb), caught in Keho Lake. The largest specimens inhabit northern lakes and rivers, and fish from this area tend to be better tasting because they eat a different diet. Jigging with a large lure around the weedy extremes of large lakes gives the angler the best chance of

© ANDREW HEMPSTEAD

Some hiking trails are short interpretive walks, while others are steep climbs to spectacular lookouts, such as the Bear's Hump Trail (pictured) in Waterton Lakes National Park.

hooking one of these monsters. Perch, at the other end of the size scale to pike but inhabiting the same shallow waters, are a fun, easy-to-catch fish—if you see kids fishing off a pier, chances are they're after perch. Arctic grayling, easily identified by a large dorsal fin, are common in cool clear lakes and streams throughout the far north of Alberta. These delicious fish are most often taken on dry flies, but their soft mouths make keeping them hooked somewhat of a challenge.

Each spring, approximately 300 lakes throughout the province are stocked with a variety of trout. "Stock stations" at Caroline and in the Crowsnest Pass maintain adult breeding stocks, which provide eggs to be hatched at Calgary's Sam Livingston Hatchery. These hatchlings are released each spring at lakes throughout the province (the fish's reproductive cycle is artificially reversed—they spawn in spring and the hatchlings are raised over winter—so that the released fish are of a decent size for a spring release). Rainbow trout, a

hardy fish that tolerate wide-ranging habitats, constitute the largest percentage of stocked fish, with more than three million released in 2003, for example. Bull trout, an endangered species, have been incorporated into the stocking program and were released in Chain Lakes in 2000 and in Upper Kananaskis Lake in early 2001. Many other trout species are stocked, including brook, brown, cutthroat, and lake, bringing the total number of fish stocked annually to approximately 6.5 million.

Fishing Licenses and Regulations

Alberta has an automated licensing system, with licenses sold in sporting stores, hardware stores, and gas stations. To use the system, a **Wildlife Identification Number** (WIN) card is needed. These cards are sold by all license vendors and cost $8 (valid for five years). Your card is then swiped through a vending machine, your name and number come up, and you're ready to purchase a license. An annual license for Canadian residents aged 16

and older is $22.50 (no license is required for those younger than 16 or for Albertans older than 64). Nonresidents aged 16 and older pay $61.50 for an annual license, $41.50 for a five-day license, or $23.50 for a single day.

The *Alberta Guide to Sportfishing Regulations,* which outlines all of the open seasons and bag limits, is available from outlets selling licenses, as well as from the Fish and Wildlife Division, Sustainable Resource Development (780/944-0313, www.srd.gov.ab.ca/fw). The department's website is a useful resource as it includes stock reports and fish identification charts.

Fishing in national parks requires a separate license, which is available from park offices and some sport shops; $10 for a seven-day license, $35 for an annual license.

CANOEING AND RAFTING

Canoeing, like horseback riding, has long been a form of transportation in the province, going back to the days of the voyageurs. Paddling provides an unparalleled opportunity for viewing wildlife around lakes that would otherwise be inaccessible. Canoes can be rented at all of the famous mountain lakes, but you can expect to pay for the experience—up to $35 per hour in the case of Lake Louise. Most provincial parks with lake systems also offer canoe rentals; expect to pay $8–12 per hour. **Paddle Canada** (613/269-2910 or 888/252-6292, www.paddlingcanada.com) is a national organization representing qualified guides.

Qualified guides operate commercial white-water rafting trips on mountain rivers such as the **Sunwapta River** in Jasper National Park and the **Kananaskis River** west of Calgary. Another popular river with those looking for whitewater thrills and spills is the **Kicking Horse River,** on the British Columbia side of the Rockies. Guides also operate on larger, quieter rivers such as **Milk River,** through Writing-On-Stone Provincial Park; **Red Deer River,** through the foothills and badlands; **Athabasca River,** in Jasper National Park; and **Bow River,** in Banff National Park. Extended nonguided trips are

possible along the Peace and Athabasca Rivers in the northern part of the province, but these trips should be attempted only by those with relevant experience.

SCUBA DIVING

Being landlocked, Alberta is not renowned for scuba diving. A few interesting opportunities do exist, however, and rentals are available in Lethbridge, Calgary, and Edmonton. The old townsite of **Minnewanka Landing,** in Banff National Park, has been flooded, and although a relatively deep dive, the site is interesting. **Patricia Lake,** in Jasper National Park, has a sunken barge developed as a prototype for mid-Atlantic plane refueling in World War II. Another sunken boat is found at the bottom of Emerald Bay in Waterton National Park. Nearby are some wagons that fell through ice many winters ago. For a list of dive operators and sites, contact **Alberta Underwater Council** (780/427-9125 or 888/307-8566, www.albertaunderwatercouncil.com).

Scuba diving is one of the lesser-known activities in Alberta.

© ANDREW HEMPSTEAD

GOLF

With beautiful scenery, long sunny days, more than 230 courses, and a golfing season that extends from April to October, Alberta is a golfer's hole-in-one. Rates range from $4 payable on an honor system at Rochon Sands (Central Alberta) to $200 on the famous resort courses in Banff and Jasper.

The best courses (in no particular order) are **Kananaskis Country Golf Course,** a 36-hole, Robert Trent Jones–designed course built in the 1980s at a cost of $1 million per hole; **Silvertip** and **Stewart Creek,** two challenging resort-style golf courses at Canmore; Banff's **Stanley Thompson Classic,** one of the world's most scenic and host of the 2006 Telus Skins; **Jasper Park Lodge Golf Course,** a challenging par-73 course surrounded by spectacular mountain scenery; **Wolf Creek Golf Resort,** a links-style oasis on the prairies between Calgary and Edmonton; and links-style **Redtail Landing** near Edmonton International Airport, which opened to much adulation in 2003.

Due to their popularity, the courses mentioned above require advance reservations. Getting a game on city courses can also be difficult at short notice, especially on weekends. Use the contact numbers in the destination chapters of this book to make your reservations. The website of the **Alberta Golf Association,** www.golfaga.org, has lots of good information on the courses.

SKIING AND SNOWBOARDING

Five world-class alpine resorts are perched among the high peaks of Alberta's Rockies. The largest in Alberta, and second-largest in all of Canada, is **Lake Louise,** overlooking the lake of the same name in Banff National Park. The area boasts 1,500 hectares (3,700 acres) of skiing and boarding on four distinct faces, with wide-open bowls and runs for all ability levels. Banff's other two resorts are **Sunshine Village,** sitting on the Continental Divide and accessible only by the world's fastest gondola, and **Ski Norquay,** a resort with heart-pounding

© ANDREW HEMPSTEAD

Silvertip Golf Course at Canmore is not only famed for its mountain setting, it's also rated as Canada's most difficult course.

Alberta turns into a white wonderland in winter, but most of the action is in the mountains, where world-class resorts lift skiers and boarders to the highest peaks.

runs overlooking the town of Banff. Just outside Banff in Kananaskis Country is **Nakiska,** developed especially for the downhill events of the 1988 Winter Olympic Games. **Marmot Basin,** in Jasper National Park, has minimal crowds with a maximum variety of terrain.

Nearly 50 other ski hills are scattered throughout the province, most with less than a 150-meter (500-ft) vertical drop. One area unique for its proximity to the city center is the **Edmonton Ski Club** in the North Saskatchewan River Valley, overlooking downtown Edmonton. **Canada Olympic Park,** within the Calgary city limits, was built for the 1988 Winter Olympic Games and maintains some of the world's finest ski-jumping facilities. Most major resorts begin opening in early December and close in May or, in the case of Sunshine Village, early June.

Other Winter Activities

Many hiking trails provide ideal routes for cross-country skiing, and many are groomed for that purpose. The largest concentration of groomed trails is in Kananaskis Country. Other areas are Banff, Jasper, and Waterton National Parks; the urban parks of Calgary and Edmonton; and the many provincial parks scattered throughout the province. Anywhere you can cross-country ski, you can also **snowshoe,** a traditional form of winter transportation that is making a comeback. **Ice fishing** for whitefish, lake trout, and burbot is good in all major rivers and those lakes large enough not to freeze to the bottom. **Sleigh rides** are offered in Banff, Lake Louise, and Jasper.

Winter travel brings its own set of potential hazards such as hypothermia, avalanches, frostbite, and sunburn. Precautions should be taken. All park information centers can provide information on hazards and advice on current weather conditions.

SPECTATOR SPORTS

Lacrosse is officially the national sport of Canada, but for most Albertans either **rodeo** or **hockey** (no need to call it "ice hockey" in Canada) is number one. Rodeo has its roots in the working lifestyle of cowboys. What began as friendly banter among cowboys as to who could ride the wildest horse and rope the fastest steer formed the basis of Wild West Shows that have evolved into a streamlined professional sport in which cowboys and cowgirls compete for millions of dollars. Alberta's most famous rodeo, and one of the world's best known, is the **Calgary Stampede** (www.calgarystampede.com), held every year in the second week of July. The **Canadian Professional Rodeo Association** (403/250-7440, www.rodeocanada.com) controls more than 60 annual events throughout Canada (most in Alberta) from Calgary's Rodeo Royal in March to the national finals held in Edmonton in early November. Smaller rodeos are sanctioned by regional associations, and these can be the most fun, with minimal admission charges, wild wipeouts, and fun riding events for local children; these are also included on the CPRA schedule.

The hockey season may be only eight months long, but to fans of the Edmonton Oilers and Calgary Flames—Alberta's National Hockey League (NHL) teams—it's a year-round obsession. The best seats are taken by die-hard season-ticket holders, but for $45–150 you can usually score tickets through Ticketmaster a few days in advance. Both cities also have professional Canadian Football League (CFL) teams that play June–October.

Accommodations and Food

ACCOMMODATIONS

Alberta has a wide range of accommodations to suit all budgets. The very best options are detailed in the destination chapters, while this section broadly describes various accommodation types and provides some hints to save money along the way.

For listings of most hotels, motels, lodges, and bed-and-breakfasts in Alberta, refer to the *Alberta Accommodation Guide,* produced annually (usually available by March) by the Alberta Hotel & Lodging Association. It lists their facilities and room rates but gives no ratings. The guide is available at all tourist information centers and online at www.explore alberta.com. For an advance copy contact Travel Alberta (780/427-4321 or 800/252-3782, www.travelalberta.com).

Hotels and Motels

Hotels and motels of some sort exist in just about every Albertan town. They range from substandard road motels advertising "Color TV" to sublime resorts, such as the Fairmont Banff Springs, high in the Canadian Rockies. The only time you'll have a problem finding a room is in Calgary during Stampede Week and in the national parks in July and August. In both cases, plan ahead or be prepared to camp. Accommodation prices in Banff and Jasper National Parks are slashed by as much as 70 percent outside summer. In cities, always ask for the best rate available and check local tourist literature for discount coupons. Rates are usually lower on weekends. All rates quoted in this handbook are for the cheapest category of rooms during the most expensive time period (summer). To all rates quoted you must add the 6 percent goods and services tax (GST) and 4 percent tourism tax. The former is refundable to nonresidents of Canada (keep receipts).

In some towns, you'll find older-style hotels (pubs) where bathrooms are shared, the phone is in the lobby, and check-in is at the bar. Rooms are generally sparsely furnished, and what furniture there is dates to the 1960s. Expect to pay from $30 single, $40 double for a shared bathroom, and a few bucks more for a private bathroom.

Park-at-your-door, single-story road motels are located in all towns and on the outskirts of all major cities. In most cases rooms are fine, but check before paying, just to make sure. Most motels have a few rooms with kitchenettes, but these fill fast. In the smaller towns, expect to pay $35–70 s, $45–80 d.

Most major towns and all cities have larger hotels, which typically have a restaurant, café, lounge, and pool. At these establishments, expect to pay from $60 s, $70 d for a basic room. Downtown hotels in Calgary and Edmonton begin at $100 s or d. Suites or executive suites, with kitchenettes and one or two bedrooms, can be good deals for little more money than a regular room.

Finding inexpensive lodging in the mountain national parks is difficult in summer. By late afternoon the only rooms left are in the more expensive categories, and by nightfall all of these rooms are booked, too. Hotel rooms in Banff and Jasper begin around $160.

Bed-and-Breakfasts

The bed-and-breakfast phenomenon is well entrenched in Alberta. Hosts are generally well-informed local people, and rooms are

Fairmont Banff Springs

immaculately tended. The establishments are often moneymaking ventures, so don't expect the bargains of European bed-and-breakfasts. The least expensive bed-and-breakfasts charge $50 s, $60 d, and while only a small percentage are over $150 per night, prices do go all the way up to $300.

The best way to find out about individual lodgings is from local tourist information centers or listings in the back of the *Alberta Accommodation Guide*. The **Alberta Bed and Breakfast Association** (www.bbalberta.com) inspects and approves 200 accommodations throughout the province. This association doesn't take bookings; for these, click on the links provided on their website, or contact the properties directly.

Backcountry Huts and Lodges

Scattered throughout the backcountry are 18 huts maintained by the Alpine Club of Canada. The huts are rustic—typically bunk beds, a woodstove, a wooden dining table, and an outhouse. Rates are $14–25 per person per night. Reserve in advance by contacting the Alpine Club of Canada (403/678-3200, www.alpineclubofcanada.ca).

Banff National Park has two privately operated backcountry lodges: **Shadow Lake Lodge,** northwest of Banff, and **Skoki Lodge,** east of Lake Louise. Jasper National Park is home to two backcountry lodges. All four require some degree of effort to reach—either by hiking or on horseback in summer, or by cross-country skiing in winter. The lodges are more than 10 kilometers (6.2 mi) from the nearest road. Rates begin at $120 per person including three meals. None have television, but all have running water and a congenial atmosphere.

Hostels

In addition to two private hostels (in Banff and Edmonton), **Hostelling International** operates 16 hostels in the province. They are located in Calgary, Edmonton, the town of Banff, Lake Louise, Canmore, all along the Icefields Parkway (which runs through Banff and Jasper National Parks), the town of Jasper, Waterton Lakes National Park, Kananaskis Country, and the town of Nordegg. During busy periods, males and females have separate dormitories. A sheet or sleeping bag is required, although these can usually be rented. All hostels are equipped with a kitchen and lounge room, and some have

laundries. Those in Banff and Lake Louise are world-class, with hundreds of beds as well as libraries and cafés. The five rustic hostels along the Icefields Parkway are evenly spaced, perfect for a bike trip along one of the world's great mountain highways. High-season rates for members are $15–34 per night, nonmembers $20–38. Hostels are an especially good bargain for skiers and snowboarders; for example a Lake Louise package including accommodations and lift pass costs $80. Whenever you can, make reservations in advance, especially in summer. The easiest way to do this from outside Canada is through Hostelling International's main website (www.hihostels.com).

If you plan to travel extensively using hostels, join Hostelling International before you leave home (otherwise it's $4 extra per night). In Canada, an annual membership for **HI-Canada** (613/237-7884, www.hihostels.ca) is $35.

In the United States, membership of **HI-USA** (301/495-1240, www.hiayh.org) is US$28. Other contact addresses include: **YHA England and Wales** (tel. 0870/770-8868, www.yha.org.uk), **YHA Australia** (tel. 02/9261-1111, www.yha.com), and **YHA New Zealand** (tel. 03/379-9970 or 0800/278-299, www .yha.co.nz). For other countries, click through the links provided at www.hihostels.com.

The **YMCA** and **YWCA** are other inexpensive lodging alternatives, often with prime locations. Calgary has a YWCA for women only; Banff has a YWCA open to both sexes with some family rooms (the Banff Y Mountain Lodge); Edmonton has one of each. Rates begin at $18 per night, with reasonable weekly rates available.

CAMPING AND RV PARKS

Those intending to camp or travel by RV are well catered to in Alberta. Calgary has a half-dozen campgrounds spread around its outskirts, Edmonton has one near downtown, and almost every town, no matter its size, has a municipal campground. These facilities range in price from free to $20 for a tent site and up to $38 with hookups, depending on facilities and location. Often campgrounds in smaller towns

are a bargain—it's not uncommon to pay $10 for a site with hookups and hot showers. Except in major cities, reservations aren't necessary—just roll up and pay the campground host or use the honor box.

Each of Alberta's national parks has excellent campgrounds. At least one campground in each park has hot showers and full hookups. Prices are $15–37. A percentage of sites in the most popular national park campgrounds can be reserved through the **Parks Canada Campground Reservation Service** (905/426-4648 or 877/737-3783, www.pccamping.ca) for a nonrefundable $11 reservation fee. If you're traveling in the height of summer and require electrical hookups, this booking system is highly recommended. The remaining campsites in the national parks operate on a first-come, first-served basis and often fill by midday in July and August. Banff, Jasper, and Waterton Lakes have winter camping but with limited facilities. Most provincial parks have a campground; prices are $15–30 depending on facilities available. Some have hookups,

BEAT THE CAMPING CROWD

Albertans love camping. Every weekend through summer, thousands of folks flee the cities for the great outdoors. National and provincial parks are the most popular destinations. With the vast majority of campsites offered on a first-come, first-served basis, campgrounds fill fast. This isn't usually a problem during the week, but by lunchtime Friday, keen campers are busy setting up camp for the weekend, and by late afternoon all sites will be filled. The official checkout time in both national and provincial parks is 11 A.M., but plan on arriving earlier than this to secure a site. When campgrounds in Banff and Jasper National Parks as well as Kananaskis Country are full, you'll be directed to overflow camping areas. These are little more than glorified parking lots, but, hey, it beats working.

showers, boat rentals, and occasionally laundry facilities. In national and provincial parks, firewood is supplied, but at a cost. In the national parks, a nightly fire permit costs $8, which includes as much wood as you need. Throughout the foothills, campgrounds managed by the Department of Sustainable Resource Development have pit toilets, picnic tables, and a supply of firewood. Most are accessed along the Forestry Trunk Road. These cost $12–15 per night.

Campground Terms

Campground operators use a variety of terms to describe the services offered and in this book I have tried to be as consistent as possible. Beginning with an easy one, an **RV** is any type of recreational vehicle, including a fifth-wheeler, motorcoach, campervan, camping trailer, or tent trailer. A **serviced site** is a campsite that offers the individual unit access to power, water, sewer, cable TV, the Internet, or a combination of any of these five services. A site with one or more of these services is known as a **hookup.** Sites with a combination of power, water, and sewer are known as **full hookups.** In this book, if a campground offers power as the only service, the sites are referred to as **powered.** The difference between a **tent site** and an **unserviced site** (one with no hookups) is that RVs are permitted on the latter. "Unserviced" does not mean the campground itself lacks facilities such as bathrooms. The term **dry camping** is sometimes used to describe a campsite with no hookups. **Boondocking** can also mean camping without hookups, but more often means simply camping for free in an undesignated area. Finally, a **pull-through** campsite means you can pull right though, with no need to back in or out.

Also, many of the more popular campgrounds, including all provincial parks, charge a **reservation fee** of up to $8 per reservation. This is *not* a deposit, but rather an additional charge.

Backcountry Camping

Backcountry camping in the national parks

and Kananaskis Country is $10 per person per night, while a season pass ($70) is valid for unlimited national park backcountry travel and camping for 12 months from its purchase date. Before heading out, you must register at the respective park information center (regardless of whether you have an annual pass) and pick up a Backcountry Permit (for those without an annual pass, this costs the nightly camping fee multiplied by the number of nights you'll be in the backcountry). Many popular backcountry campgrounds take reservations up to three months in advance. The reservation fee is $10 per party per trip. Most campgrounds in the backcountry have pit toilets, and some have bear bins for secure food storage. Fires are discouraged, so bring a stove.

FOOD AND DRINK

If you're RVing it or camping, eating cheap in Alberta is easy. The two largest supermarkets, Safeway and Sobeys, generally have the least expensive groceries, but prices are still higher than in the United States. In most of these big chain stores you'll find an excellent bakery. If you're barbecuing, know that most urban campgrounds discourage open fires, and provincial and national parks charge up to $8 for firewood.

For a three-course meal in a family-style restaurant, including a steak dish, expect to pay $30–40 per person—double that in the better eateries. Edmonton, Calgary, and Banff have an astonishing array of ethnic restaurants (Banff, a town of 8,000, has more than 100 restaurants). Inexpensive options are Husky restaurants, located in gas stations of the same name along all major routes; Boston Pizza, a chain of Canadian family-style restaurants; and Tim Hortons, best known for donuts but with other light meals offered.

Alberta Beef

Alberta beef—the staple of the province—is delicious and served in most restaurants. Most is exported, with prime middle cuts distributed throughout the province. Alberta beef is renowned for its flavor and tenderness, achieved

Everyone does!

through a combination of nutrient-rich prairie grasses and being finished on homegrown barley at feedlots. It is graded by Agriculture Canada, with Canada AAA and Canada Prime—marbled with thin streaks of fat that melt through the meat during cooking—the finest. The Alberta Beef Producers website (www.albertabeef.org) is a great source of information on the industry, and even includes recipes (although lightly seasoned with Hy's seasoning salt then grilled on an open barbecue is good enough for me). Bison meat, farmed throughout Alberta, is also popular but more expensive than beef. It's extremely lean, low-fat meat that can be bought in most forms, including hamburger, jerky, and regular cuts such as T-bones.

Local Produce

Since I wrote the first edition of this book a little over 15 years ago, the emphasis on homegrown produce has changed dramatically, and I am continually amazed at the ever-increasing number of restaurants promoting the cause. A good website for learning about the usage of local produce in regional cuisine is www.dinealberta.ca.

Fall is a wonderful time to pick up local produce straight from the farm. One of the local favorites is sweet-tasting Taber corn, which is sold from pickups and "farm gate" stalls through September. Through central and southern Alberta, be tempted by signs directing travelers to pick-your-own farms, where raspberries, Saskatoon berries, chokecherries, strawberries, black currants, and rhubarb are highlights. Click through to Alberta at www.pickyourown.org for locations. Another way to purchase fresh produce is at a **farmers market.** These take place throughout Alberta (often on Saturday mornings) and are denoted by a distinctive sign depicting a farmer with a hoe standing beside a pumpkin. By provincial law, sellers must have grown at least 80 percent of what they are selling (or their merchandise must be comprised of at least 80 percent ingredients they've grown). This means you're guaranteed fresh and local produce. One of the

best-known markets is held at the Millarville racetrack, west of Calgary, each summer Saturday morning. Get a complete list by contacting the **Alberta Farmers' Market Association** (780/644-5377, www.albertamarkets.com). The website www.growingalberta.com is another helpful resource.

Beer

Calgary and Edmonton each have specialty brewers that brew boutique beers for sale in the immediate area. Alberta's largest home-grown brewery is **Big Rock** in Calgary. Using one of North America's most modern breweries, Big Rock is unique in that it uses all natural ingredients and doesn't pasteurize the finished product; this shortens the shelf life, but retains a great deal more of the natural flavor. The two major Canadian brewers are Labbatt and Molson, who in addition to their national brands brew Kokanee and Pilsner, respectively, in western Canada. They also brew U.S. beers such as Budweiser under license for the Canadian market.

Conduct and Customs

Thanks to an abundance of natural resources and a fiscally conservative government, the province is debt-free—and got that way without raising taxes. In fact, the provincial coffers were so full of money that in 2006, each and every Albertan received a $400 check simply for living in Alberta. And in general, that makes Alberta a good place to live, work, and visit. Although Alberta has been led by a conservative government for seemingly forever, lifestyles in the main urban areas and resort towns are more liberal leaning.

Liquor Laws

Liquor laws in Canada are enacted on a provincial level, with Alberta having the most relaxed version. The minimum age for alcohol consumption in Alberta is 18 (it's 19 in most other provinces). Additionally, the liquor industry in Alberta is privatized. This means that there are a lot more liquor stores with less restrictions (open seven days, can sell cold beer, and more).

Like the rest of North America, driving in Alberta under the influence of alcohol or drugs is a criminal offence. Those convicted of driving with a blood-alcohol concentration above 0.8 face big fines and an automatic one-year license suspension. Second convictions (even if the first was out of province) lead to a three-year suspension. Note that in Alberta drivers below the limit can be charged with impaired driving. Alberta operates a Checkstop program, which gives the RCMP the power to stop drivers at random and test for alcohol. It is also illegal to have open containers of alcohol in a vehicle or in public places.

Smoking

Smoking is banned in virtually all public places across Canada. Most provinces have enacted province-wide bans on smoking in public places; Alberta is an exception. Instead, bylaws are enacted on a municipal level. While generally public places are smoke-free (Calgary is the major holdout, with proposal for bylaw enactment in 2008), Alberta is a hodgepodge of differing municipal bylaws. In Banff, for example, smoking is only permitted on restaurant/bar patios with no food or beverage service while down the road in Canmore, smoking is permitted on all patios. In Canmore, smoking is banned in all hotel rooms, yet in Banff there is no such official bylaw (although most rooms are designated nonsmoking).

Tipping

Gratuities are not usually added to the bill. In restaurants and bars, around 15 percent of the total amount is expected. But you should tip according to how good (or bad) the service was, as low as 10 percent or up to and over 20

percent for exceptional service. The exception to this rule is groups of eight or more, when it is standard for restaurants to add 15 to 20 percent to the bill as a gratuity. Tips are some-times added to tour packages, so check this in advance, but you can also tip guides on stand-alone tours. Tips are also given to bartenders, taxi drivers, bellmen, and hairdressers.

Tips for Travelers

EMPLOYMENT AND STUDY

The resort town of Banff is especially popular with young workers from across Canada and beyond. Aside from Help Wanted ads in local papers, a good place to start looking for work is the **Job Resource Centre** (314 Marten St., Banff, 403/760-3311, www.jobresourcecentre .com). The website www.bannflife.com also has a good selection of job listings.

International visitors wishing to work or study in Canada must obtain authorization *before* entering the country. Authorization to work will only be granted if no qualified Canadians are available for the work in question. Applications for work and study are available from all Canadian embassies and must be submitted with a nonrefundable processing fee. The Canadian government has a reciprocal agreement with Australia for a limited number of **holiday work visas** to be issued each year. Australian citizens aged 30 and under are eligible; contact your nearest Canadian embassy or consulate. For general information on immigrating to Canada contact **Citizenship and Immigration Canada** (www.cic.gc.ca).

VISITORS WITH DISABILITIES

A lack of mobility should not deter you from traveling to Alberta, but you should definitely do some research before leaving home.

If you haven't traveled extensively, start by doing some research at the website of the **Access-Able Travel Source** (www.access-able.com), where you will find databases of specialist travel agencies and lodgings in western Canada that cater to travelers with disabilities. **Flying Wheels Travel** (507/451-5005, www .flyingwheelstravel.com) caters solely to the needs of travelers with disabilities. The **Society** for **Accessible Travel and Hospitality** (212/447-7284, www.sath.org) supplies information on tour operators, vehicle rentals, specific destinations, and companion services. For frequent travelers, the annual membership fee (adult US$45, senior US$30) is well worthwhile. **Emerging Horizons** (www.emerging horizons.com) is a U.S. quarterly magazine dedicated to travelers with special needs.

Access to Travel (800/465-7735, www .accesstotravel.gc.ca) is an initiative of the Canadian government that includes information on travel within and between Canadian cities, including Calgary and Edmonton. The website also has a lot of general travel information for those with disabilities. The **Canadian National Institute for the Blind** (800/563-2642, www.cnib.ca) offers a wide range of services from its regional office in Edmonton (780/488-4871). Finally, the **Canadian Paraplegic Association** (613/723-1033, www.canparaplegic.org), with a chapter office in Calgary (403/228-3001), is another good source of information.

TRAVELING WITH CHILDREN

The natural wonders of Alberta make it a marvelous place to bring children on a vacation, and luckily for you many of the best things to do—walking, watching wildlife, and more—don't cost a cent.

Admission and tour prices for children are included throughout the destination chapters of this book. As a general rule, these reduced prices are for children aged 6–16 years. For two adults and two or more children, always ask about family tickets. Children under six nearly always get in free. Most hotels and motels will happily accommodate children, but always try

to reserve your room in advance and let the reservations desk know the ages of your kids. Often, children stay free in major hotels, and in the case of some major chains—such as Holiday Inn—eat free also. Generally, bed-and-breakfasts aren't suitable for children and in some cases don't accept kids at all. Ask ahead.

As a general rule, when it comes to traveling with children it's a good idea to let them help you plan the trip, looking at websites and reading up on the province together. To make your vacation more enjoyable if you'll be spending a lot of time on the road, rent a minivan (all major rental agencies have a supply). Don't forget to bring along favorite toys and games from home—whatever you think will keep your kids entertained when the joys of sightseeing wear off.

The website of **Travel Alberta** (www.travel alberta.com) has a section devoted to children's activities within the province. A handy source of general information is the website **Traveling with Your Kids** (www.travelwith yourkids.com).

Health and Safety

Compared to other parts of the world, Canada is a relatively safe place to visit. Vaccinations are required only if coming from an endemic area. That said, wherever you are traveling, carry a medical kit that includes bandages, insect repellent, sunscreen, antiseptic, antibiotics, and water-purification tablets. Good first-aid kits are available at most camping shops. Health care in Canada is mostly dealt with at a provincial level. The **Alberta Health** website (www.health.gov.ab.ca) is loaded with information.

Taking out a travel-insurance policy is a sensible precaution because hospital and medical charges start at around $1,000 per day. Copies of prescriptions should be brought to Canada for any medicines already prescribed.

Giardia

Giardiasis, also known as beaver fever, is a real concern for those heading into the backcountry. It's caused by an intestinal parasite, *Giardia lamblia,* that lives in lakes, rivers, and streams. Once ingested, its effects, although not instantaneous, can be dramatic; severe diarrhea, cramps, and nausea are the most common symptoms. Preventive measures should always be taken, including boiling all water for at least 10 minutes, treating all water with iodine, or filtering all water using a filter with a small enough pore size to block the *Giardia* cysts.

Winter Travel

Travel throughout the province during winter months should not be undertaken lightly. The best way to dress for the cold is in layers, including a waterproof outer layer. Most important, wear headgear. Before setting out in a vehicle, check antifreeze levels, and always carry a spare tire and blankets or sleeping bags. **Frostbite** is a potential hazard, especially when cold temperatures are combined with high winds (a combination known as **windchill**). Most often, frostbite leaves a numbing, bruised sensation, and the skin turns white. Exposed areas of skin, especially the nose and ears, are most susceptible.

Hypothermia occurs when the body fails to produce heat as fast as it loses it. It can strike at any time of the year but is more common during cooler months. Cold weather, combined with hunger, fatigue, and dampness, creates a recipe for disaster. Symptoms are not always apparent to the victim. The early signs are numbness, shivering, slurring of words, dizzy spells, and, in extreme cases, violent behavior, unconsciousness, and even death. The best treatment is to get the victim out of the cold, replace wet clothing with dry, slowly give hot liquids and sugary foods, and place the victim in a sleeping bag. Warming too quickly can lead to heart attacks.

Information and Services

MONEY

As in the United States, Canadian currency is based on dollars and cents. Coins come in denominations of 1, 5, 10, and 25 cents, and one and two dollars. The one-dollar coin is the gold-colored "loonie," named for the bird featured on it. The unique two-dollar coin, introduced in 1996, is silver with a gold-colored insert. Notes come in $5, $10, $20, $50, and $100 denominations.

All prices quoted in this book are in Canadian dollars unless otherwise noted. American dollars are accepted at many tourist areas, but the exchange rate is more favorable at banks. Currency other than U.S. dollars can be exchanged at most banks, airport money-changing facilities, and foreign-exchange brokers in Calgary, Banff, Jasper, and Edmonton. Travelers checks are the safest way to carry money, but a fee is often charged to cash them if they're in a currency other than Canadian dollars. All major credit and charge cards are honored at Canadian banks, gas stations, and most commercial establishments. Automatic teller machines (ATMs) can be found in almost every town.

Banks are open Monday–Thursday 9:30 A.M.–3:30 P.M. and until 4:30 or 5 P.M. on Friday.

Costs

The cost of living is lower in Alberta than in other provinces but higher than in the United States. By planning ahead, having a tent or joining Hostelling International, and being prepared to cook your own meals, it is possible to get by on less than $100 per person per day. Gasoline is sold in liters (3.78 liters equals one U.S. gallon) and, like the rest of North America, its price spiraled skyward when the price of oil rose through 2006. As of the writing of this edition, gas costs from $1.10 per liter for regular unleaded. In remote areas, such as along the Icefields Parkway, the price is higher, up to $1.50 per liter.

Tips are not usually added to a bill, and in general 15 percent of the total amount is given to restaurant servers, taxi drivers, doormen, bellhops, and bar staff.

Taxes

Canada imposes a 6 percent **goods and services tax (GST)** on most consumer purchases. Nonresident visitors can get a rebate for the GST they pay on short-term accommodations and on most consumer goods bought in the country and taken home. Items not included in the GST rebate program include gifts left in Canada, meals and restaurant charges, campground fees, services such as dry cleaning and shoe repair, alcoholic beverages, tobacco, automotive fuel, groceries, agricultural and fish products, prescription drugs and medical devices, and used goods that tend to increase in value, such as paintings, jewelry, rare books, and coins. The rebate is

CURRENCY EXCHANGE

At press time, the Canadian dollar had been gaining value against the greenback since dipping to record lows in 2002, when it was trading at US$1 per CDN$1.65.

At press time, exchange rates (into CDN$) for major currencies are:

- US$1 = $1.10
- AUS$1 = $0.90
- €1 = $1.60
- HK$10 = $1.60
- NZ$1 = $0.80
- UK£1 = $2.30
- ¥100 = $1.20

On the Internet, check current exchange rates at www.xe.com/ucc.

All major currency can be exchanged at banks in Canmore, Banff, and Jasper, or at airports in the gateway cities of Calgary, Edmonton, and Vancouver. Many Canadian businesses will accept U.S. currency, but you will get a better exchange rate from the banks.

available on services and retail purchases that total at least $100 and were paid for within 60 days before your exit from the country. Rebates can be claimed any time within one year from the date of purchase. Most visitors apply for the rebate at duty-free shops (also called Visitor Rebate Centres) when exiting the country. The duty-free shops can rebate up to $500 on the spot. For rebates more than $500, you'll need to mail your completed GST rebate form directly to Revenue Canada. In either case, keep all receipts. If claiming outside of Canada, you must have receipts validated upon leaving Canada. Rebate checks from the government are issued in Canadian funds. For more info, contact the program directly (902/432-5608 or 800/668-4748, www.cra-arc.gc.ca/visitors).

Alberta is the only province that doesn't impose a **Provincial Sales Tax,** which ranges 5–12 percent throughout the country. Alberta does have a 4 percent nonrefundable tourism tax on any accommodation with four or more rooms.

MAPS AND TOURIST INFORMATION
Maps
Specialty map shops are the best source for accurate, high-quality maps; in Calgary and Edmonton, contact **Map Town** (Calgary: 400 5th Ave. SW, 403/266-2241; Edmonton: 10344 105th St., 780/429-2600). By request they can send out a catalog of maps designed specifically for hiking (topographical maps), camping (road/access maps), fishing (hydrographic charts of more than 100 lakes), and canoeing (river details such as gradients). They can also supply Alberta wall maps, Canada wall maps, thematic maps, historic maps, and aerial photography. These maps are also available over the counter at some sport and camping stores. **Gem Trek** (403/266-2241 or 877/921-6277, www.gem trek.com) is an Albertan company that produces some of the best and most useful maps you're ever likely to find. They specialize in the Canadian Rockies, and the maps are

available throughout the region. **MapArt** (905/436-2525, www.mapart.com) produces a variety of maps for Alberta, including an annual *Road Atlas of Alberta.*

Tourist Offices
The best source of up-to-date information on all accommodations, attractions, and events is **Travel Alberta** (P.O. Box 2500, Edmonton, Alberta T5J 2Z4, 780/427-4321 or 800/252-3782, www.travelalberta.com). All major routes into the province have a **Travel Alberta Information Centre,** which is generally open in summer only (you must pay for road maps). Each town has a **tourist information center,** each with its own hours, and usually open June–August. When these centers are closed, head to the chamber of commerce (year-round Mon.–Fri. only) for information.

Online Travel Planning
The Travel Alberta website (www.travel alberta.com) provides links to regional tourist associations and local information centers. Only websites managed by official tourism offices are listed in this book. **Found Locally** is an Internet-based company that provides Web surfers with a wealth of information on Alberta's two largest cities, Calgary and Edmonton. The websites cover all aspects of entertainment and recreation, such as attractions, sporting events, concerts, movies, and hundreds of accommodations and restaurants. The restaurant listings are particularly comprehensive, with cuisine, price range, and business hours listed. The site also features daily weather information, transportation routings, and even notification of where the police have set up their latest photo-radar speed traps. Access the sites at www.foundlocally.com/calgary and www.foundlocally.com/edmonton.

COMMUNICATIONS
Postal Services
All mail posted in Canada must have Canadian postage stamps attached. First-class letters and postcards are $.51 to destinations within Canada, $.89 to the United States, and $1.40

HEADING
FARTHER AFIELD

If your travels take you beyond Alberta, you may find the following resources helpful for pre-trip planning:

- **Tourism British Columbia:** 250/387-1642 or 800/435-5622, www.hellobc.com

- **Yukon Department of Tourism:** 867/667-5036 or 800/661-0494, www.touryukon.com

- **Alaska Division of Tourism:** www.travelalaska.com

- **NWT Tourism:** 867/873-7200 or 800/661-0788, www.nwttravel.nt.ca

- **Nunavut Tourism:** 867/979-6551 or 866/686-2888, www.nunavut tourism.com

- **Tourism Saskatchewan:** 306/787-9600 or 877/237-2273, www.sask tourism.com

- **Travel Manitoba:** 204/945-3777 or 800/665-0040, www.travel manitoba.com

to all other destinations. Post offices are open Monday–Friday only. If you would like mail sent to you while traveling, have it addressed to yourself, c/o General Delivery, Main Post Office, in the city or town you request, Alberta, Canada. The post office will hold all general delivery mail for 15 days before returning it to the sender. The website of **Canada Post** is www.canadapost.ca.

Telephone

Alberta has two area codes. All of Alberta south of Highway 16, including Calgary and Banff, is 403, whereas the northern half of the province, including Edmonton and Jasper, is 780. Except for local calls, all numbers must be dialed with this prefix, including long-distance calls made within the province. The country code for Canada is 1, the same as the

United States. Public phones accept 5-, 10-, and 25-cent coins. Local calls from payphones are usually $.35 and most long-distance calls cost at least $2.50 for the first minute from public phones. Prepaid phone cards, which are available from gas stations and drug and grocery stores, provide considerable savings for those using public phones. They come in $5–50 amounts.

Internet

Internet access is available across Alberta, including in all city and resort hotels, many motels, and even some bed-and-breakfasts. For public access, the most reliable places to get online are local libraries, where more often than not you only need to show some identification to use a computer. At the libraries in Calgary, Edmonton, Canmore, Banff, and Jasper reservations may be needed. Internet booths can also be found in airports and some shopping malls.

WEIGHTS AND MEASURES
The Metric System

Canada officially adopted the metric system back in 1975, though you still hear grocers talking in ounces and pounds, golfers talking in yards, and seamen talking in nautical miles. Metric is the primary unit used in this book, but we've added imperial conversions for readers from the United States, Liberia, and Myanmar, the only three countries that have not adopted the metric system. You can also refer to the metric conversion chart in the back of this book.

Time Zones

Alberta is in the **mountain time zone,** one hour later than pacific time, two hours earlier than eastern standard time. The mountain time zone extends west into southern British Columbia, which includes Yoho and Kootenay National Parks as well as the towns of Golden and Radium Hot Springs.

Daylight saving is in effect from the second Sunday of March to the first Sunday in November. This is in line with the United States (except Arizona) and all other Canadian provinces (except Saskatchewan).

RESOURCES
Suggested Reading

NATURAL HISTORY

The Atlas of Breeding Birds of Alberta. Edmonton: Federation of Alberta Naturalists, 1992. Comprehensive study of all birds that breed in Alberta, with easy-to-read distribution maps, details on nesting and other behavioral patterns, and color plates.

Foster, John E., Dick Harrison, and I. S. MacLaren, eds. *Buffalo.* Edmonton: University of Alberta Press, 1992. A series of essays by noted historians and experts in the field of the American bison, addressing their disappearance from the prairies, and buffalo jumps. One essay deals with Wood Buffalo National Park.

Gadd, Ben. *Handbook of the Canadian Rockies.* Jasper: Corax Press, 1999. This classic full-color field guide is bulky for backpackers, but is a must-read for anyone interested in the natural history of the Canadian Rockies.

Hare, F. K. and M. K. Thomas. *Climate Canada.* Toronto: John Wiley & Sons, 1974. One of the most extensive works on Canada's climate ever written. Includes a chapter on how the climate is changing.

Herrero, Stephen. *Bear Attacks: Their Causes and Avoidances.* New York: The Lyons Press, 2002. Through a series of gruesome stories, this book catalogs the stormy relationship between people and bruins, provides hints on avoiding attacks, and tells what to do in case you're attacked.

Jones, Karen. *Wolf Mountains.* Calgary: University of Calgary Press, 2002. Explores the history of wolves in the Canadian Rockies, with emphasis on the often-controversial relationship between man and wolf.

Nelson, Joseph S. *The Fishes of Alberta.* Calgary: University of Calgary Press, 1992. Describes 59 species of fish and provides maps of their distribution. Also looks at fish management and fishing in the province.

Patterson, W. S. *The Physics of Glaciers.* London: Butterworth-Heinemann, 1999. Originally published by the Pergamon Press in 1969, this tome is a highly technical look at all aspects of glaciation, why glaciers form, how they flow, and their effect on the environment.

Rezendes, Paul. *Tracking and the Art of Seeing.* Charlotte, Virginia: Camden House Publishing, 1992. This is one of the best of many books dedicated to tracking North American mammals. It begins with a short essay on the relationship of humans with nature.

Vacher, André. *Summer of the Grizzly.* Saskatoon: Western Producer Prairie Books, 1985. True story of a grizzly bear that went on a terrifying rampage near the town of Banff.

Whitaker, John. *National Audubon Society Field Guide to North American Mammals.* New York: Random House, 1997. One of a series of field guides produced by the National Audubon Society, this one details mammals

through color plates and in-depth descriptions of characteristics, habitat, and range.

Wilkinson, Kathleen. *Wildflowers of Alberta.* Edmonton: University of Alberta Press, 1999. Color plates of all flowers found in the mountain national parks and beyond. Color plates and line drawings are indispensable for identification.

HUMAN HISTORY

Chastko, Paul A. *Developing Alberta's Oil Sands.* Calgary: University of Alberta Press, 2005. This big book covers it all—early history, the intriguing politics, extraction methods, and what the future holds.

Ducey, Brant E. *The Rajah of Renfrew.* Edmonton: University of Alberta Press, 1998. Written by his son, this is a lot more than the biography of "Mr. Baseball," Edmonton's John E. Ducey; it tells the story of the sport in Alberta from its earliest days.

Engler, Bruno. *Bruno Engler Photography.* Calgary: Rocky Mountain Books, 2002. Swiss-born Engler spent 60 years exploring and photographing the Canadian Rockies. This impressive hardcover book showcases over 150 of his most timeless images.

Fryer, Harold. *Ghost Towns of Alberta.* Langley, British Columbia: Stagecoach Publishing, 1976. Alberta's ghost towns are unlike those in the western part of the United States. Many towns have slipped into oblivion, and this guide looks at more of these than you'd ever dreamed existed. This title is out of print so look for it at used bookstores.

Hewitt, Steve. *Riding to the Rescue.* Toronto: University of Toronto Press, 2006. This book examines the Royal Canadian Mounted Police from World War I to the late 1930s, when they morphed from iconic horsemen to a modern police force.

Huck, Barbara. *In Search of Ancient Alberta.*

Winnipeg: Heartland, 1998. If you're interesting in learning about the province's ancient history by visiting various sites, this book is necessary reading.

Jenness, Diamond. *The Indians of Canada.* Toronto: University of Toronto Press, 1977. Originally published in 1932, this is the classic study of natives in Canada, although Jenness's conclusion that they were facing certain extinction by the end of the 20th century is obviously outdated.

Jones, David. *Empire of Dust.* Edmonton: University of Alberta, 1987. A sorry story of drought and the destruction it brought to Alderston (west of Medicine Hat), I had trouble getting beyond the first chapter until visiting the site.

Lavallee, Omer. *Van Horne's Road.* Montreal: Railfare Enterprises, 1974. William Van Horne was instrumental in the construction of Canada's first transcontinental railway. This is the story of his dream, and the boomtowns that sprung up along the route. Lavallee devotes an entire chapter to telling the story of the railway's push over the Canadian Rockies.

Marty, Sid. *Switchbacks: True Stories from the Canadian Rockies.* Toronto: McClelland & Stewart, 1999. This book tells of Marty's experiences in the mountains and of people he came in contact with in his role as a park warden. Along the way he describes the way his experiences with both nature and fellow humans have shaped his views on conservation.

McMillan, Alan D. *Native Peoples and Cultures of Canada.* Vancouver: Douglas & McIntyre, 1995. A comprehensive look at the archaeology, anthropology, and ethnography of the native peoples of Canada. The last chapters delve into the problems facing these people today.

Newman, Peter C. *Company of Adventurers.* Markham, Ontario: Penguin Books Canada, 1985. The story of the Hudson's Bay Company and its impact on Canada.

Sandor, Steve. *The Battle of Alberta.* Vancouver: Heritage House, 2005. Sports fans will enjoy reading about the history of the hockey rivalry between Edmonton and Calgary, which goes back as far as 1895.

Schäffer, Mary T. S. *A Hunter of Peace.* Banff: Whyte Museum of the Canadian Rockies, 1980. This book was first published in 1911 by G. P. Putnam & Sons, New York, under the name *Old Indian Trails of the Canadian Rockies.* Tales recount the exploration of the Rockies during the turn of the century. Many of the author's photographs appear throughout.

Scott, Chic. *Pushing the Limits.* Calgary: Rocky Mountain Books, 2000. A chronological history of mountaineering in Canada, with special emphasis on many largely unknown climbers and their feats, as well as the story of Swiss guides in Canada and a short section on ice-climbing.

Twigger, Robert. *Voyageur: Across the Rocky Mountains in a Birchbark Canoe.* London: Weidenfeld, 2006. This is the rollicking tale of author Twigger's adventures building a canoe and crossing the Canadian Rockies on a diet of porridge, fish, and whisky—exactly as Alexander Mackenzie had 200 years previously.

van Herk, Aritha. *Mavericks History of Alberta.* Toronto: Penguin Group, 2002. Delves beyond the usual focus of history texts to include infamous politicians and homegrown events such as Stampede Wrestling.

Wood, David G. *The Lougheed Legacy.* Toronto: Key Porter Books, 1985. Tells the story of Peter Lougheed's 14-year reign as premier of Alberta.

PALEONTOLOGY

Grady, Wayne. *The Dinosaur Project.* Toronto: Macfarlane, Walter, & Ross, 1993. Tells the story of paleontological expeditions to China and the Albertan badlands, and how the work has enhanced our knowledge of dinosaurs and their movements between Asia and North America. Accounts of actual field trips are given, as well as easy-to-read backgrounds on each area.

Gross, Renie. *Dinosaur Country.* Wardlow: Badlands Books, 1998. Combines descriptions of the various dinosaurs that once roamed Alberta, with stories of their discovery and an in-depth look at dinosaur hunting today.

Murphy-Lamb, Lisa. *Dinosaur Hunters.* Canmore: Altitude Publishing, 2003. A small, inexpensive book comprising short stories of dinosaur hunting in Alberta, from the first recorded dinosaur find by George Dawson to the province's own Dr. Phil Currie, one of the world's preeminent paleontologists.

Russell, D. A. *An Odyssey in Time: The Dinosaurs of North America.* Toronto: University of Toronto Press, 1989. Complete details of all known dinosaurs on the North American continent.

Spalding, David A. E. *Dinosaur Hunters.* Toronto: Key Porter Books, 1993. Tells the story of the men and women who have devoted their lives to the study of dinosaurs.

RECREATION

Chavich, Cinda. *High Plains: The Joy of Alberta Cuisine.* Toronto: Fitzhenry & Whiteside, 2001. Authored by a local writer with impeccable credentials, this guide proves there's more to the province than beef and berries. Includes information on food sources, recipes, restaurants, and shopping tips.

Corbett, Bill. *Best of Alberta: Day Trips from Calgary.* Vancouver: Whitecap Books, 2006. Multiple books have been written about the things to do and see in Banff, which this book covers, along with dozens of ideas for day-tripping south and north of the famous park—all within a two-hour drive of Calgary.

Corbett, Bill. *The 11,000ers.* Calgary: Rocky Mountain Books, 2004. A reference to all 54 mountain peaks in the Canadian Rockies higher than 11,000 feet. The author discusses the human history of each, as well as access and popular routes.

Daffern, Gillean. *Kananaskis Country Trail Guide.* Calgary: Rocky Mountain Books, 1997. Two volumes cover all the official and unofficial trails in Kananaskis Country.

Eastcott, Doug. *Backcountry Biking in the Canadian Rockies.* Calgary: Rocky Mountain Books, 1999. Details over 220 bicycling routes using simple maps, road logs, and black-and-white photography.

Johnson, Leslie. *Basic Mountain Safety from A to Z.* Canmore: Altitude Books, 2000. Everything you need to know about safety in the mountains, including a large section on camping.

Jones, Jon and John Martin. *Sport Climbs in the Canadian Rockies.* Calgary: Rocky Mountain Books, 2006. Keen sport climbers will love the ease of using this compact guide covering 1,600 routes, including maps.

Kane, Alan. *Scrambles in the Canadian Rockies.* Calgary: Rocky Mountain Books, 1999. Routes detailed in this guide lead to summits without the use of ropes or mountaineering equipment.

Mitchell, Barry. *Alberta's Trout Highway.* Red Deer: Nomad Creek Books, 2001. "Alberta's Trout Highway" is the Forestry Trunk Road (Highway 40), which runs the length of Alberta's foothills. Entertaining and useful descriptions of Mitchell's favorite fishing holes are accompanied by maps and plenty of background information.

Patton, Brian and Bart Robinson. *Canadian Rockies Trail Guide.* Banff: Summerthought Publishing, 2007. Now in its eighth edition, this is the ultimate authority for hiking in the Canadian Rockies. It covers 230 trails and 3,400 kilometers (2,100 mi) in the mountain

national parks as well as in surrounding provincial parks. A full page is devoted to each trail, making it the most comprehensive hiking book available.

Potter, Mike. *Backcountry Banff.* Calgary: Luminous Compositions, 2001. This book's title is a little misleading, for included are many shorter trails that can be enjoyed by everyone. Includes logged distances and readable trail descriptions of over 100 hikes in Banff National Park.

OTHER GUIDEBOOKS AND MAPS

Andrews, D. Larraine. *The Cowboy Trail.* Edmonton: Blue Couch Books, 2006. This book explores the route north through the foothills from the U.S. border in the south to Highway 16 in the north. Includes detailed information on everything from ranch vacations to toponomy.

Backroad Mapbooks. Vancouver: Mussio Ventures. This atlas series is perfect for outdoor enthusiasts, with detailed maps and highlights such as campgrounds, fishing spots, and swimming holes; www.backroadmapbooks.com.

Gem Trek Publishing. Cochrane, Alberta. This company produces tearproof maps for all regions of the Canadian Rockies. Relief shading clearly and concisely shows elevation, and all hiking trails have been plotted using GPS. On the back of each map are descriptions of attractions and hikes, along with general practical and educational information; www.gemtrek.com.

Gilchrist, John. *My Favourite Restaurants in Calgary and Banff.* Calgary: Escurial Incorporated, 2006. Every city has a food critic that everyone knows by name. In Calgary, it's John Gilchrist, and, as the name suggests, these are his favorite restaurants.

Larmour, Judy and Henry Saley. *Stop the Car!* Edmonton: Blue Couch Books, 2004. A detailed guide to everything there is to see and

do within central Alberta; includes lots of human and natural history.

MapArt. Driving maps for all of Canada, including provinces and cities. Maps are published as old-fashioned foldout versions, as well as laminated versions and in atlas form; www.mapart.com.

The Milepost. Bellevue, Washington: Vernon Publications. This annual publication is a must-have for those traveling through western Canada and Alaska. The maps and logged highway descriptions are incredibly detailed. Most Canadian bookstores stock *The Milepost,* or order by calling 800/726-4707 or visiting www.milepost.com.

PERIODICALS

The Canadian Alpine Journal. Canmore, Alberta. Annual magazine of the Alpine Club of Canada with articles from its members and climbers from around the world; www.alpineclubofcanada.ca.

Canadian Geographic. Ottawa: Royal Canadian Geographical Society. Bimonthly publication pertaining to Canada's natural and human histories and resources; www.canadiangeographic.ca.

Explore. Calgary. Bimonthly publication of adventure travel throughout Canada; www.explore-mag.com.

Nature Canada. Ottawa, Ontario. Quarterly magazine of the Canadian Nature Federation; www.cnf.ca.

Western Living. Vancouver, British Columbia. Lifestyle magazine for western Canada. Includes travel, history, homes, and cooking; www.westernliving.ca.

FREE CATALOGS

Alberta Accommodation Guide. Alberta Hotel & Lodging Association. Lists all hotels, motels,

and other lodging in the province. Available through Travel Alberta (780/427-4321 or 800/252-3782, www.travelalberta.com) or from local information centers. The online version is at www.explorealberta.com.

Alberta Campground Guide. Alberta Hotel & Lodging Association. Lists all campgrounds in the province. Available through Travel Alberta (780/427-4321 or 800/252-3782, www.travelalberta.com) or from local information centers. The online version is at www.explorealberta.com.

Tour Book: Western Canada and Alaska. Booklet available to members of the Canadian or American Automobile Association.

REFERENCE

Daffern, Tony. *Avalanche Safety for Skiers & Climbers.* Calgary: Rocky Mountain Books, 1992. Covers all aspects of avalanches, including their causes, practical information on how to avoid them, and a section on rescue techniques and first aid.

Guide to Manuscripts: The Fonds and Collections of the Archives, Whyte Museum of the Canadian Rockies. Banff: Whyte Museum of the Canadian Rockies, 1988. This book makes finding items in the Whyte Museum easy by providing alphabetical lists of all parts of the collection.

Johnson, Leslie. *Basic Mountain Safety from A to Z.* Canmore: Altitude Books, 2000. Everything you need to know about safety in the mountains, including a large section on camping.

Karamitsanis, Aphrodite, Tracey Harrison, and Merrily K. Aubrey, eds. *Place Names of Alberta.* Calgary: University of Alberta Press, 1991. An ongoing toponomy project. Volume 1 lists all geographic features of the mountains and foothills alphabetically, with explanations of each name's origin. Volume 2 does the same for southern Alberta's geographical features, while Volume 3 tackles northern Alberta.

Internet Resources

TRAVEL PLANNING

Canadian Tourism Commission
www.canadatourism.com
Official tourism website for all of Canada.

Tourism British Columbia
www.hellobc.com
Learn more about the province, plan your travels, and order tourism literature.

Travel Alberta
www.travelalberta.com
Learn more about the province, plan your travels, and order tourism literature. This official tourism site also has up-to-date event calendars, tips for traveling with children, and an extensive library of images.

Travel to Canada
www.westerncanadatravel.com
Website of this book's author, Andrew Hempstead. Includes general and up-to-date tips on travel to Canada.

PARKS

Parks Canada
www.pc.gc.ca
Official website of the agency that manages Canada's national parks and national historic sites. Website has information on each of Alberta's five national parks (fees, camping, and wildlife) and four national historic sites.

Parks Canada Campground Reservation Service
www.pccamping.ca
Online reservation service for national park campgrounds.

GOVERNMENT

Citizenship and Immigration Canada
www.cic.gc.ca
Check this government website for anything related to entry into Canada.

Environment Canada
www.weatheroffice.ec.gc.ca
Five-day forecasts from across Canada, including almost 100 locations through Alberta. Includes weather archives such as seasonal trends and snowfall history.

Government of Canada
www.gc.ca
The official website of the Canadian government.

Visitor Rebate Program
www.gc.ca
Go to this website to learn about how to get a refund of the six percent goods and services tax you paid on just about everything purchased in Canada.

ACCOMMODATIONS

Alberta Hotel & Lodging Association
www.explorealberta.com
Publishes Alberta's official accommodation and camping guides. You can use the website to check for accommodations or order a free hard copy.

Canadian Rocky Mountain Resorts
www.crmr.com
Small chain of four upscale resorts.

Fairmont Hotels and Resorts
www.fairmont.com
Lodging chain that owns famous mountain resorts such as the Banff Springs, Chateau Lake Louise, and Jasper Park Lodge, as well as historic gems in Edmonton and Calgary.

Hostelling International-Canada
www.hihostels.ca

Canadian arm of the worldwide organization.

CONSERVATION

Biosphere Institute of the Bow Valley
www.biosphereinstitute.org

Canmore-based organization mandated to gather and circulate information on management of the Bow River watershed. Online references include studies, publications, and human-use guidelines for the region.

Bow Valley Wildsmart
www.bvwildsmart.ca

This nonprofit organization has put together a wealth of information on how to stay safe in the Bow Valley watershed, including reported wildlife sightings.

Canadian Parks and
Wilderness Society
www.cpaws.org

Nonprofit organization that is instrumental in highlighting conservation issues throughout Canada. The link to the Calgary chapter provides local information and a schedule of guided walks.

Yellowstone to Yukon
Conservation Initiative
www.y2y.net

Network of 800 groups working on conservation issues in the Canadian Rockies and beyond.

TRANSPORTATION
AND TOURS

Air Canada
www.aircanada.ca

Canada's national airline.

Brewster
www.brewster.ca

Banff-based operator offering day trips, airport shuttles, and package tours throughout the province.

Rocky Mountaineer Vacations
www.rockymountaineer.com

Luxurious rail service from Vancouver to Banff and Jasper.

VIA Rail
www.viarail.ca

Passenger rail service across Canada.

PUBLISHERS

Altitude Publishing
www.altitudepublishing.com

Publisher of calendars, coffee-table books, field guides, and history books. Also the Amazing Stories series, comprising easy-to-read books about specific stories and people.

Gem Trek
www.gemtrek.com

You can pick up basic park maps free from local information centers, but this company produces much more detailed maps covering all the most popular regions of the Canadian Rockies.

Lone Pine
www.lonepinepublishing.com

Respected for its field guides, this company has books on almost every natural-history subject pertinent to Alberta.

Rocky Mountain Books
www.rmbooks.com

Check out the catalog of this Calgary publisher and you'll surely be impressed by the list of outdoor recreation guides.

Summerthought Publishing
www.summerthought.com

If you plan on doing lots of hiking, you'll want a copy of the authoritative *Canadian Rockies Trail Guide* by this Banff publisher.

Index

MUSEUMS

www.moon.com

For helpful advice on planning a trip, visit www.moon.com for the **TRAVEL PLANNER** and get access to useful travel strategies and valuable information about great places to visit. When you travel with Moon, expect an experience that is uncommon and truly unique.

HANDBOOKS | METRO | OUTDOORS | LIVING ABROAD

MOON ALBERTA

Avalon Travel Publishing
An Imprint of
Avalon Publishing Group, Inc.

AVALON
publishing group incorporated

1400 65th Street, Suite 250
Emeryville, CA 94608, USA
www.moon.com

Editor: Cinnamon Hearst
Series Manager: Kathryn Ettinger
Acquisitions Manager: Rebecca K. Browning
Copy Editor: Amy Scott
Graphics Coordinator: Nicole Schultz
Production Coordinators: Darren Alessi, Amber Pirker
Cover Designer: Nicole Schultz
Map Editor: Albert Angulo
Cartographers: Kat Bennett, Mike Morgenfeld,
  Aaron Darden
Cartography Director: Mike Morgenfeld
Indexer: Judy Hunt

ISBN-10: 1-56691-835-9
ISBN-13: 978-1-56691-835-0
ISSN: 1547-2930

Printing History
1st Edition – 1995
6th Edition – April 2007
5 4 3 2 1

KEEPING CURRENT

If you have a favorite gem you'd like to see included in the next edition, or see anything
that needs updating, clarification, or correction, please drop us a line. Send your
comments via email to feedback@moon.com, or use the address above.

MAP SYMBOLS

Symbol	Name		Symbol	Name
≡≡≡	Expressway	◖	Highlight	✗
───	Primary Road	○	City/Town	✗
───	Secondary Road	◉	State Capital	▲ Mountain
- - -	Unpaved Road	⊛	National Capital	✦ Unique Natural Feature
- - - -	Trail	★	Point of Interest	
··········	Ferry	•	Accommodation	⌇ Waterfall
·—·—·	Railroad	▼	Restaurant/Bar	▲ Park
▨▨▨	Pedestrian Walkway	■	Other Location	❶ Trailhead
▥▥▥	Stairs	Λ	Campground	⛷ Skiing Area

Mountain, Unique Natural Feature, Waterfall, Park, Trailhead, Skiing Area, Archaeological Site, Church, Gas Station, Glacier, Mangrove, Reef, Swamp

CONVERSION TABLES

$$°C = (°F - 32) / 1.8$$
$$°F = (°C \times 1.8) + 32$$

1 inch = 2.54 centimeters (cm)
1 foot = 0.304 meters (m)
1 yard = 0.914 meters
1 mile = 1.6093 kilometers (km)
1 km = 0.6214 miles
1 fathom = 1.8288 m
1 chain = 20.1168 m
1 furlong = 201.168 m
1 acre = 0.4047 hectares
1 sq km = 100 hectares
1 sq mile = 2.59 square km
1 ounce = 28.35 grams
1 pound = 0.4536 kilograms
1 short ton = 0.90718 metric ton
1 short ton = 2,000 pounds
1 long ton = 1.016 metric tons
1 long ton = 2,240 pounds
1 metric ton = 1,000 kilograms
1 quart = 0.94635 liters
1 US gallon = 3.7854 liters
1 Imperial gallon = 4.5459 liters
1 nautical mile = 1.852 km

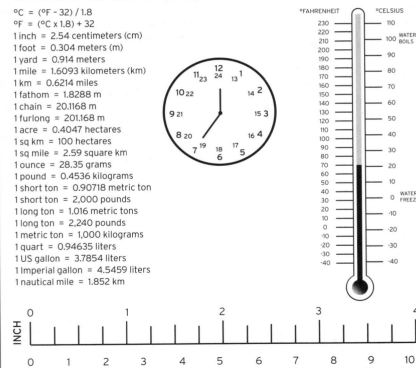